# NEW ENGLAND
# HIKING

# NEW ENGLAND HIKING

The Complete Guide to More Than 380 Hikes

Fourth Edition

Michael Lanza

**AVALON
TRAVEL**

**FOGHORN OUTDOORS NEW ENGLAND HIKING**
**The Complete Guide to More Than 380 Hikes**

**Fourth Edition**

**Michael Lanza**

Printing History
1st edition—1997
4th edition—February 2005
5  4  3  2  1

Avalon Travel Publishing
An Imprint of
Avalon Publishing Group, Inc.

AVALON
publishing group incorporated

ISBN: 1-56691-589-9
ISSN: 1093-2720

Editor: Ellie Behrstock
Series Manager: Grace Fujimoto
Acquisitions Editor: Rebecca Browning
Copy Editor: Donna Leverenz
Graphics Coordinator: Deb Dutcher
Production Coordinator: Jacob Goolkasian
Cover and Interior Designer: Darren Alessi
Map Editors: Olivia Solís, Naomi Adler Dancis
Cartographers: Kat Kalamaras, Mike Morgenfeld
Indexer: Ellie Behrstock

Front cover photo: Mt. Kearsarge, New Hampshire, © David Brownell

Printed in the United States of America by Worzalla

# About the Author

© MICHAEL LANZA

Freelance writer and photographer Michael Lanza is Northwest Editor of *Backpacker* magazine and writes a monthly column and other articles for *AMC Outdoors;* his work has also appeared in *National Geographic Adventure, Outside,* and numerous other publications, and he is the author of three other guidebooks. An avid backpacker, climber, cyclist, and skier, he has hiked extensively in the western United States as well as New England, where he first began hiking. He formerly syndicated a weekly column about New England outdoor activities in about 20 daily newspapers throughout the region and co-hosted a call-in show about the outdoors on New Hampshire Public Radio. A native of Leominster, Massachusetts, Lanza has a B.S. in photojournalism from Syracuse University and spent 10 years as a reporter and editor at Massachusetts and New Hampshire newspapers. He now lives in Boise, Idaho, with his wife, Penny Beach, and their son Nate and daughter Alex, and frequently visits New England to hike.

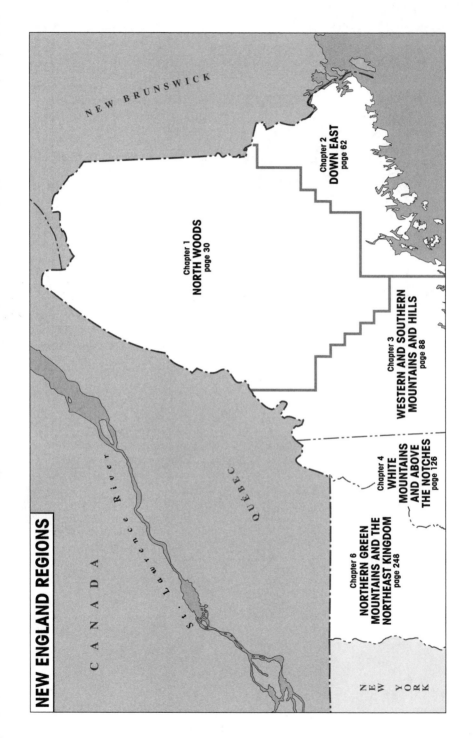

NEW ENGLAND REGIONS

CANADA

St. Lawrence River

NEW BRUNSWICK

QUEBEC

NEW YORK

Chapter 1
NORTH WOODS
page 30

Chapter 2
DOWN EAST
page 62

Chapter 3
WESTERN AND SOUTHERN
MOUNTAINS AND HILLS
page 88

Chapter 4
WHITE
MOUNTAINS
AND ABOVE
THE NOTCHES
page 126

Chapter 6
NORTHERN GREEN
MOUNTAINS AND THE
NORTHEAST KINGDOM
page 248

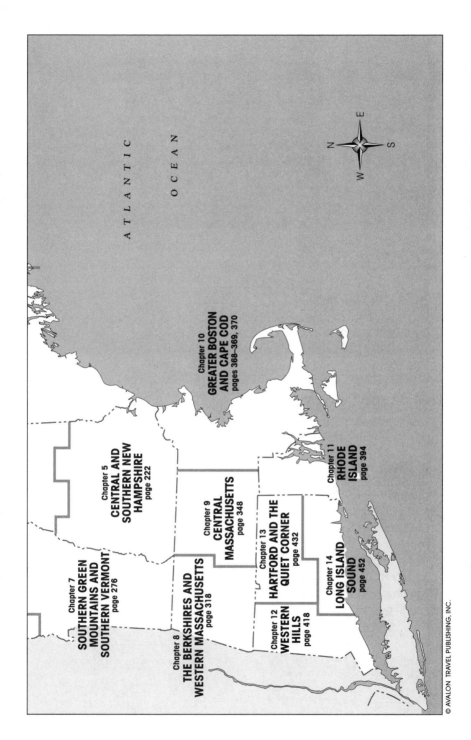

ATLANTIC OCEAN

Chapter 10
GREATER BOSTON
AND CAPE COD
pages 368–369, 370

Chapter 5
CENTRAL AND
SOUTHERN NEW
HAMPSHIRE
page 222

Chapter 7
SOUTHERN GREEN
MOUNTAINS AND
SOUTHERN VERMONT
page 276

Chapter 9
CENTRAL
MASSACHUSETTS
page 348

Chapter 11
RHODE
ISLAND
page 394

Chapter 8
THE BERKSHIRES AND
WESTERN MASSACHUSETTS
page 318

Chapter 13
HARTFORD AND THE
QUIET CORNER
page 432

Chapter 12
WESTERN
HILLS
page 418

Chapter 14
LONG ISLAND
SOUND
page 452

© AVALON TRAVEL PUBLISHING, INC.

© MICHAEL LANZA

# Contents

# Our Commitment

We are committed to making *Foghorn Outdoors New England Hiking* the most accurate, thorough, and enjoyable guide to the region. With this fourth edition you can rest assured that every hiking trail in this book has been carefully reviewed and that the most up-to-date information is included. Be aware that with the passing of time some of the fees listed herein may have changed, and trails may have closed unexpectedly. If you have a specific need or concern, it's best to call the location ahead of time.

If you would like to comment on the book, whether it's to suggest a hike we overlooked, or to let us know about any noteworthy experience—good or bad—that occurred while using *Foghorn Outdoors New England Hiking* as your guide, we would appreciate hearing from you. Please address correspondence to:

*Foghorn Outdoors New England Hiking,* fourth edition
Avalon Travel Publishing
1400 65th Street, Suite 250
Emeryville, CA 94608

email: atpfeedback@avalonpub.com
If you send us an email, please put "New England Hiking" in the subject line.

# How to Use This Book

*New England Hiking* is divided into 14 chapters, based on major regions in each of the six New England states. Regional maps in each chapter show the location of all the hikes in that chapter.

**For Maine trails:** see pages 25–119

**For New Hampshire trails:** see pages 121–241

**For Vermont trails:** see pages 243–312

**For Massachusetts trails:** see pages 313–392

**For Rhode Island trails:** see pages 393–412

**For Connecticut trails:** see pages 413–460

There are two ways to search for the perfect hike:

1. If you know the name of the specific trail you want to hike, or the name of the surrounding geographical area or nearby feature (town, national or state park, or forest, mountain, lake, river, etc.), look it up in the index and turn to the corresponding page.

2. If you want to find out about hiking possibilities in a particular part of a state, turn to the map at the beginning of that chapter. You can then determine the area where you would like to hike and identify which hikes are available; then turn to the corresponding numbers for those hikes in the chapter.

## What the Ratings Mean

Every hike in this book has been rated on a scale of 1 to 10 for its overall quality and on a scale of 1 to 10 for difficulty.

The quality rating is based largely on scenic qualities, although it also takes into account how crowded a trail is and whether or not you see or hear civilization.

The difficulty rating is calculated based on the following scale:

**10** The hike entails all of the following qualities: climbs 3,000 feet or more in elevation, covers at least seven miles, and has rugged and steep terrain with some exposure.

**9** The hike entails at least two of the following qualities: climbs 2,500 feet or more in elevation, covers at least seven miles, and/or has rugged and steep terrain with some exposure.

**8** The hike entails one or more of the following qualities: climbs 2,000 feet or more in elevation, covers at least seven miles, or has rugged and steep terrain with possible exposure.

**7** The hike entails at least two of the following qualities: climbs 1,500 feet or more in elevation, covers at least five miles, and/or has steep and rugged sections.

**6** The hike entails one of the following qualities: climbs 1,500 feet or more in elevation, covers at least five miles, or has steep and rugged sections.

**5** The hike covers at least four miles and either climbs 1,000 feet or more in elevation or has steep, rugged sections.

**4** The hike entails one of the following qualities: climbs 1,000 feet or more in elevation, covers at least four miles, or has steep, rugged sections.

**3** The hike has some hills—though not more than 1,000 feet of elevation gain—and covers at least three miles.

**2** The hike either has some hills—though not more than 1,000 feet of elevation gain—or covers at least three miles.

**1** The trail is relatively flat and less than three miles.

## Trail Names, Distances, and Times

Each trail in this book has a number, name, mileage information, and estimated completion time. The trail's number allows you to find it easily on the corresponding chapter map. The name is either the actual trail name (as listed on signposts and maps) or a name I've given to a series of trails or a loop trail. In the latter cases, the name is taken from the major destination or focal point of the hike. Most mileage listings are precise, though a few are very good estimates. All mileages and approximate times refer to round-trip travel unless specifically noted as one-way. In the case of one-way hikes, a car or bike shuttle is advised. The estimated time is based on how long I feel an average adult in moderate physical condition would take to complete the hike. Actual times can vary widely, especially on longer hikes.

## Hike Descriptions

The description for each listing is intended to give you some idea of what kind of terrain to expect, what you might see, and how to follow the hike from beginning to end. I've sometimes added a special note about the hike or a suggestion on how to combine it with a nearby hike or expand upon your outing in some other way.

Some hike descriptions begin with the (F) icon. The (F) icon indicates that the hike appears on a Best Hikes list.

Also, there are a couple of terms used throughout the book that reflect the land usage history in New England. Although some New Englanders may be familiar with them, others may not. Forest roads are generally dirt or gravel roads maintained by the land manager and are typically not open to motor vehicles except those of the manager. Woods roads, or "old woods roads," are abandoned thoroughfares—many were formerly public routes between colonial communities—now heavily overgrown, but recognizable as a wide path. Their condition can vary greatly.

## User Groups

I have designated a list of user groups permitted on each trail, including hikers, bicyclists, dogs, horses, hunters, cross-country skiers, snowshoers, and wheelchair users. While this book is intended primarily as a hiking guide, it includes some trails that are mediocre hikes yet excellent mountain biking or cross-country skiing routes. The snowshoe reference is intended as a guide for beginners; experienced snowshoers know that many of New England's bigger mountains can be climbed on snowshoes in winter, but this book indicates when snowshoeing a trail may require advanced winter hiking skills. As always, the individual must make the final judgment regarding safety issues in winter.

Wheelchair accessibility is indicated when stated by the land or facility manager, but concerned persons should call to find out if their specific needs will be met. The hunting reference is included to remind hikers to be aware of the hunting season when hiking, and that they may be sharing a trail with hunters, in which case they should take the necessary precautions (wearing a bright color, preferably fluorescent orange) to avoid an accident in the woods. Hunting is a popular sport throughout New England; the season varies from state to state, but generally extends from fall into early winter. Call the state departments of fish and game or parks and forests offices to find out actual dates.

# Maps

Information on how to obtain maps for a trail and environs is provided for each hike listing. When several maps are mentioned, you might want to ask the seller about a map's detail, weatherproofness, range, and scale when deciding which one to obtain. Consider also which maps will cover other hikes that interest you. Prices are usually indicative of quality and detail. I've also listed the appropriate USGS (United States Geologic Survey) map or maps covering that area. Be advised that many USGS maps do not show trails or forest roads, and that trail locations may not be accurate if the map has not been updated recently. All of New England is covered by the standard 7.5-minute series maps (scale 1:24,000) except Massachusetts, which is covered by 7.5-by-15-minute series (1:25,000). Three index maps cover New England, showing the 7.5-minute and 15-minute maps: Maine, New Hampshire/Vermont, Massachusetts/Connecticut/Rhode Island.

See the Resource Guide in this book for map sources. To order individual USGS maps or the New England index maps, write to USGS Map Sales, Federal Center, Box 25286, Denver, CO 80225.

# Contact

Most of the hikes in this book list at least one contact agency, trail club, or organization for additional information. Many hikes will give you a sample of something bigger—a long-distance trail or public land. Use the contact info to explore beyond what is found in these pages. And remember to support the organizations listed here that maintain the trails you hike.

© MICHAEL LANZA

# Introduction

Dear fellow hiker,

I have a single black-and-white photograph from what was probably my first hike up a New England mountain. It shows two friends and me standing on a rocky summit. In the distance, clouds blot out much of the sky. The wind lifts our hair and fills our shirts; it appears to be a cool day in early autumn.

I no longer recall what peak we hiked, only that it was in New Hampshire and that the hike had been the idea of one of my friends; I was tagging along on an outing that seemed like something I might enjoy. In fact, my recollection of the entire day amounts to little more than a lingering sense of the emotions it generated for me—kind of an artifact of memory, like an arrowhead dug up somewhere.

I was perhaps 18 or 20 years old, and standing on top of that little mountain struck me as quite possibly the most intense and wonderful thing I'd ever done.

Of course, at that age most people have limited experience with things intense and wonderful. But I found that as my fascination with high places grew, so did the inspiration that began on that first summit.

I have since done much hiking all over New England and taken my thirst for that feeling to bigger mountains out West—hiking, backpacking, and climbing in the Sierra Nevada, the Cascades and Olympics, the Tetons and Wind River Range, the Rockies from Colorado to Alberta, and Alaska. My work allows me to spend many days and nights every year in wild country.

When asked to write this book, I realized I would spend a summer at home for a change, hiking those New England trails I had not yet visited but which belong in a guide this comprehensive. Although I expected to sorely miss the West, instead I found myself enjoying a reunion of sorts with my hiking roots. I finally got to many places throughout New England that had been on my checklist for some time. And, to my surprise, the hikes I relished most were those I had known the least about, those scattered trails that for various reasons attract relatively few hikers.

With this fourth edition of *New England Hiking,* I've updated all the hike descriptions, including the addition of new, Web-based information, the sections providing tips on hiking in New England, and the listing of regional resources. This book is the product of many days on the trail and a reflection of many personal memories. As you use it to explore New England's backcountry, I urge you to walk lightly, to do your part to help preserve these fragile places, and to venture beyond the popular, well-beaten paths to lesser-known destinations.

I also invite you to help let me know about any inaccuracies by writing to my publisher, Avalon Travel Publishing, at the following address: New England Hiking, Avalon Travel Publishing, 1400 65th Street, Suite 250, Emeryville, CA 94608.

I hope this book helps you find the same kind of experiences I have enjoyed in these mountains and forests—to discover your own arrowhead.

—*Michael Lanza*

# New England Overview

Few regions of the country offer the wealth and variety of hiking or the great trail access that's available in New England. You can walk some of the nation's finest Seacoast trails and tramp amid the most rugged peaks in the East—all in the same weekend. Four distinct seasons mean hikers can walk through springtime forests exploding in greenery and autumn woods vibrant with world-famous foliage color, view rare alpine wildflowers, enjoy warm summer days in shady woods or cool fall afternoons on craggy summits, and experience challenging winter mountaineering. New England boasts two major national forests, one of the country's most popular national parks, a national seashore, the nation's first long trail (Vermont's aptly named Long Trail), and 734 miles—more than one-third—of the 2,174-mile Appalachian National Scenic Trail, in addition to countless state parks, forests, and private preserves.

New England's tradition of recreational woods, mountain exploring, and trail-building dates back at least to Darby Field's historic first ascent of Mount Washington in 1642. Thanks to the efforts of many people and clubs beginning in the 19th century and continuing strongly today, the region boasts literally thousands of miles of trails, more than the most prolific hiker could cover in a lengthy lifetime. What's more, in recent years the growing popularity of hiking has led to the expansion of hiking clubs, the resurrection of old, forgotten trails, like the Monadnock-Sunapee Greenway, Wapack Trail, Midstate Trail, Metacomet-Monadnock Trail, and Metacomet Trail, and the creation of new footpaths, like the Cohos Trail. Beyond the hiking trails, old abandoned roads and carriageways lacing the forests are perfect for easy hikes, snowshoeing, cross-country skiing, and mountain biking.

## State Profiles

Each New England state has its own character and presents diverse hiking opportunities. Hikers of any age, ability, or experience can find a suitable trail in any region of these six states.

### Maine

Sprawling over more than 33,000 square miles—roughly the area of the other five New England states combined—Maine offers a variety of hiking experiences probably unmatched in New England. Maine's most prominent mountains comprise the northernmost reaches of the Appalachian chain, stretching from the White Mountain National Forest in western Maine to Baxter State Park in the far north. The Appalachian Trail, extending 281 miles through Maine alone, forms the backbone of the trail network through this region of vast wilderness lakes and rugged peaks. Acadia National Park offers world-famous Seacoast hiking in rugged mountains.

### New Hampshire

New Hampshire is home to probably the most popular destination in New England among serious hikers: the White Mountain National Forest. It covers nearly 800,000 acres and pushes numerous summits and ridges far above tree line, with 48 summits higher than 4,000 feet. The Appalachian Trail extends for 161 miles through New Hampshire, from the Connecticut River in Hanover to the Mahoosuc Range on the Maine border. The state also manages 206 state parks and forests from the coast to the remote and wild North Country. Two long-distance trails in southern New Hampshire—the 21-mile Wapack Trail and the 50-mile Monadnock-Sunapee Greenway—offer scenic hiking over hills that see far fewer boots than the popular corners of the

Whites. And the smaller mountains and hills scattered around the state reward hikers with sweeping views that demand less driving and hiking time than the big peaks up north.

## Vermont

Like no other state in New England, Vermont is defined by its mountains. The Green Mountains run the length of the state, rolling up from round, forested hills in the south to the taller, sometimes craggy peaks in the state's midsection and on to the rambling hills and peaks of the north country. The Green Mountains are the locus of much of the state's hiking—the 350,000-acre Green Mountain National Forest has 500 miles of hiking trails. Running for about 270 miles along the Green Mountains' spine, from the edge of Massachusetts to the Canadian border, the Long Trail (LT) is the nation's first long-distance hiking trail. Although an estimated 60 to 80 people through-hike the Long Trail every year, countless day hikers access parts of the trail. But there are also many hikes beyond the Green Mountains, many of them easy to moderately difficult.

## Massachusetts

Massachusetts offers a great diversity of trails, from the rolling green hills of the Berkshires to the wonderful coastal hikes in the Cape Cod National Seashore. The Bay State also boasts one of the largest state park and forest systems in the country, with nearly 100 properties covering more than 270,000 acres—most of them crisscrossed by trails and old woods roads—and three long-distance trails bisecting the state north to south: 89 miles of the Appalachian Trail, the 117-mile Metacomet-Monadnock Trail, and the 92-mile Midstate Trail.

## Rhode Island

Similar to Connecticut, tiny Rhode Island offers quality hiking trails, many of them tucked away and little-used. Trail highlights include nature preserves where you can do some great bird-watching or just find a quiet patch of woods, and the sprawling Arcadia Management Area, with its miles of trails and woods roads for hiking, mountain biking, and horseback riding.

## Connecticut

While the bigger peaks of northern New England steal the show for spectacle and remoteness, don't overlook the extensive trail system in Connecticut. The so-called Blue Trails network comprises more than 700 miles of trail across the state, much of that on private land and maintained by volunteer members of the nonprofit Connecticut Forest and Park Association. The Appalachian Trail jogs for 52 miles through northwestern Connecticut's hills. Numerous private preserves have trails open to the public. And from Macedonia Brook State Park and People's State Forest in the west to Mashamoquet Brook State Park and Pachaug State Forest in the east, Connecticut is peppered with dozens of state lands ideal for activities from hiking and mountain biking to snowshoeing and cross-country skiing. The trails here are more civilized than elsewhere in New England; most are short hikes with little elevation gain and loss, and many offer bucolic views of a well-settled, pastoral landscape.

## Ⓕ Hiking Blazes

New England's forests abound with blazes—slashes of paint on trees used to mark trails. Sometimes the color of blazes seems random and unrelated to other trails in the same area, but most major trails and trail systems are blazed consistently. The Appalachian Trail (AT) bears white blazes for its entire length, including its 734 miles through five New England states. Most side trails connecting to the AT are blue blazed. Vermont's 270-mile Long Trail, which coincides with the AT for more than 100 miles, is also blazed in white. Connecticut's Blue Trails system of hiking paths scattered across the state is, as the name suggests, marked entirely with blue blazes.

Although not all trails are well blazed, popular and well-maintained trails usually are—you'll see a colored slash of paint at frequent intervals at about eye level on tree trunks. Double slashes are sometimes used to indicate a sharp turn in the trail. Trails are blazed in both directions, so whenever you suspect you may have lost the trail, turn around to see whether you can find a blaze facing in the opposite direction; if so, you'll know you're still on the trail.

Above tree line, trails may be marked either with blazes painted on rock or with cairns, which are piles of stones constructed at regular intervals. In the rocky terrain on the upper slopes of New England's highest peaks, care may be needed to discern artificially constructed cairns from the landscape surrounding them, but the cairns in rocky areas are usually built higher and are obviously man-made.

# The Appalachian Trail

Perhaps the most famous hiking trail in the world, the Appalachian Trail runs 2,174 miles from Springer Mountain in Georgia to Mount Katahdin in Maine, along the spine of the Appalachian Mountains in 14 states. About 734 miles—or more than one-third—of the AT's length passes through five New England states: Connecticut (52 miles), Massachusetts (90 miles), Vermont (150 miles), New Hampshire (161 miles) and Maine (281 miles). New England boasts some of the AT's most spectacular, best-known, and rugged stretches, including the White Mountains, the southern Green Mountains, the Riga Plateau of Massachusetts and Connecticut, and Maine's Mahoosuc, Saddleback, and Bigelow ranges, 100-mile Wilderness, and Katahdin. A few hundred people hike the entire trail end to end every year, but thousands more take shorter backpacking trips and dayhikes somewhere along the AT.

Maintained by hiking clubs that assume responsibility for different sections of the AT, the trail is well marked with signs and white blazes on trees and rocks above treeline. Shelters and campsites are spaced out along the AT so that backpackers have choices of where to spend each night, but those shelters can fill up during the busy season of summer and early fall, especially on weekends. The prime hiking season for the AT in New England depends on elevation and latitude, but generally, that season runs from May–October in southern New England and mid-June–early October at higher elevations in northern New England.

# Hiking Tips

## Climate

With New England's biggest peaks in the northern states and its smaller hills and flatlands in the southern states, as well as an ocean moderating the Seacoast climate, this region's fair-weather hikers can find a trail to explore virtually year-round. But the wildly varied character of hiking opportunities here also demands some basic knowledge of and preparation for hitting the trails.

The ocean generally keeps coastal areas a little warmer in winter and cooler in summer than inland areas. Otherwise, any time of year, average temperatures typically grow cooler as you gain elevation or move northward.

New England's prime hiking season stretches for several months from spring through fall, with the season's length depending on the region. In general, summer high temperatures range from 60°F to 90°F with lows from 50°F to around freezing at higher elevations. Days are often humid in the forests and lower elevations and windy on the mountaintops. July and August see occasional thunderstorms, but July through September are the driest months. August is usually the best month for finding ripe wild blueberries along many trails, especially in northern New England.

Black flies, or mayflies, emerge by late April or early May and pester hikers until late June or early July, while mosquitoes come out in late spring and dissipate (but do not disappear) by midsummer. No-see-ums (tiny biting flies that live up to their name) plague some wooded areas in summer. September is often the best month for hiking, with dry, comfortable days, cool nights, and few bugs. Fall foliage colors peak anywhere from mid-September or early October in northern New England to early or mid-October in the south; by choosing your destinations well and moving north to south, you can hike through vibrant foliage for three or four successive weekends. The period from mid-October into November offers cool days, cold nights, no bugs, few people, and often little snow.

In the higher peaks of Vermont's Green Mountains, New Hampshire's White Mountains, Maine's northern Appalachians, and along the Appalachian Trail in parts of western Massachusetts and Connecticut, high-elevation snow disappears and alpine wildflowers bloom in late spring; by late October, wintry winds start blowing and snow starts flying (though it can snow above 4,000 feet in any month of the year). Spring trails are muddy at low elevations—some are closed to hiking during the April/May "mud season"—and buried under deep, slushy snow up high, requiring snowshoes. Winter conditions set in by mid-November and can become very severe, even life threatening. Going above tree line in winter is considered a mountaineering experience by many (though these mountains lack glacier travel and high altitude), so be prepared for harsh cold and strong winds.

The strongest wind gust ever recorded on Earth was measured on April 12, 1934, at the weather observatory on the summit of New Hampshire's Mount Washington. The gust was clocked at 231 mph. The summit of Mount Washington remains in clouds 60 percent of the time. Its average temperature year-round is 26.5°F; winds average 35 mph and exceed hurricane force (75 mph) on average 104 days a year.

In the smaller hills and flatlands of central and southern New England, the snow-free hiking season often begins by early spring and lasts into late autumn. Some of these trails are even occasionally free of snow during the winter, or offer opportunities for snowshoeing or cross-country

# Ⓕ Cross-Country Skiing and Snowshoeing

Many hikes in this book are great for cross-country skiing or snowshoeing in winter. But added precaution is needed. Days are short and the temperature may start to plummet by midafternoon, so carry the right clothing and don't overestimate how far you can travel in winter. Depending on snow conditions and your own fitness level and experience with either snowshoes or skis, a winter outing can take much longer than anticipated—and certainly much longer than a trip of similar distance on groomed trails at a cross-country ski resort. Breaking your own trail through fresh snow can also be very exhausting—take turns leading, and conserve energy by following the leader's tracks, which also serve as a good return trail.

The proper clothing becomes essential in winter, especially the farther you wander from roads. Wear a base layer that wicks moisture from your skin and dries quickly, middle layers that insulate and do not retain moisture, and a windproof shell that breathes well and is waterproof or water-resistant (the latter type of garment usually breathes much better than something that's completely waterproof). Size boots to fit over a thin, synthetic liner sock and a thicker, heavyweight synthetic-blend sock. For your hands, often the most versatile system consists of gloves and/or mittens that also can be layered, with an outer layer that's water- and windproof and preferably also breathable.

Most importantly, don't overdress: Remove layers if you're getting too hot. Avoid becoming wet with perspiration, which can lead to too much cooling. Drink plenty of fluids and eat snacks frequently to maintain your energy level; feeling tired or cold on a winter outing may be an indication of dehydration or hunger.

As long as you're safe, cautious, and aware, winter is a great time to explore New England's trails. Have fun out there.

skiing in woods protected from strong winds, with warmer temperatures than you'll find on the bigger peaks up north. Many Seacoast trails, even in Maine, rarely get snow, though they can get occasional heavy snowfall and be icy. For more information about weather-related trail conditions, refer to the individual hike listings.

## Basic Hiking Safety

Few of us would consider hiking a high-risk activity. But like any physical activity, it does pose certain risks, and it's up to us to minimize them. For starters, make sure your physical condition is adequate for your objective—the quickest route to injury is overextending either your skills or your physical abilities. You wouldn't presume that you could rock climb a 1,000-foot cliff if you've never climbed before; don't assume you're ready for one of New England's hardest hikes if you've never—or not very recently—done anything nearly as difficult.

Build up your fitness level by gradually increasing your workouts and the length of your hikes. Beyond strengthening muscles, you must strengthen the soft connective tissue in joints like knees and ankles that are too easily strained and take weeks or months to heal from injury. Staying active in a variety of activities—hiking, running, bicycling, Nordic skiing, etc.—helps develop good overall fitness and decreases the likelihood of an overuse injury. Most importantly, stretch muscles before and after a workout to reduce the chance of injury.

**First-Aid Checklist**

Although you're probably at greater risk of injury while driving to the trailhead than you are on the trail, it's wise to carry a compact and lightweight first-aid kit for emergencies in the backcountry, where an ambulance and hospital are often hours, rather than minutes, away.

Prepare any first-aid kit with attention to the type of trip, the destination, and the needs of people hiking (for example, children or persons with medical conditions). Pack everything into a thick, clear plastic resealable bag. And remember, merely carrying a first-aid kit does not make you safe; knowing how to use what's in it does.

A basic first-aid kit consists of:
- two large cravats
- two large gauze pads
- four four-inch-by-four-inch gauze pads
- several one-inch adhesive bandages
- one roll of one-inch athletic tape
- safety pins
- one six-inch Ace bandage
- several alcohol wipes
- tube of povidone iodine ointment (for wound care)
- moleskin or Spenco Second Skin (for blisters)
- knife or scissors
- paper and pencil
- aspirin or an anti-inflammatory
- SAM splint (a versatile and lightweight splinting device available at many drug stores)
- blank SOAP note form

New England's most rugged trails—and even parts of its more moderate paths—can be very rocky and steep. Uneven terrain is often a major contributor to falls resulting in serious, acute injury. Most of us have a fairly reliable self-preservation instinct—and you should trust it. If something strikes you as dangerous or beyond your abilities, don't try it, or simply wait until you think you're ready for it.

An injury far from a road also means it may be hours before the victim reaches a hospital. Basic training in wilderness first aid is beneficial to anyone who frequents the mountains, even recreational hikers. New England happens to have two highly respected sources for such training, and the basic course requires just one weekend. Contact SOLO (Conway, NH, 603/447-6711, website: www.soloschools.com) or Wilderness Medical Associates (Bryant Pond, Maine, 888/945-3633, website: www.wildmed.com) for information.

In parts of New England, ticks transmit Lyme disease. Wear long pants tucked into socks. Check one another's skin and clothing for ticks, bearing in mind that some are very small. Remove a tick right away, pulling it off gently with tweezers or your fingers. Don't crush it.

# Clothing and Gear

Much could be written about how to outfit oneself for hiking in a region like New England, with its significant range of elevations and latitudes, alpine zones, huge seasonal temperature swings, and fairly wet climate. But in the simplest of terms, you should select your clothing and equipment based on:

- the season and the immediate weather forecast
- the amount of time you plan to be out (a couple of hours, a full day, more than one day)
- the distance you'll be wandering from major roads
- the elevation you will hike to
- the abilities of your hiking companions

At lower elevations amid the protection of trees or on a warm day, you may elect to bring no extra clothing for an hour-long outing, or no more than a light jacket for a few hours or more. The exception to this is in the Seacoast region, where hikes are more exposed to cool wind. But higher elevations, especially above tree line, get much colder than the valleys—about three degrees Fahrenheit per thousand feet—and winds can grow much stronger. Many a White Mountains hiker has departed from a valley basking in summerlike weather and reached a summit wracked by wintry winds and lying under a carpet of fresh snow, even during the summer months. Insulative layers, a jacket that protects against wind and precipitation, a warm hat, and gloves are always a good idea when climbing New England's highest peaks. When you're not sure, take an extra layer of clothing, just in case.

The most important piece of gear may be well-fitting, comfortable, supportive shoes or boots. Finding the right footwear requires trying on various models and walking around in them in the store before deciding. Everyone's feet are different, and shoes or boots that feel great on your friend won't necessarily fit you well. Deciding how heavy your footwear should be depends on variables like how often you hike, whether you easily injure feet or ankles, and how much weight you'll carry. Generally, I recommend hiking in the most lightweight footwear that you find comfortable and adequately supportive.

Trekking poles relieve your feet and legs of tens of thousands of pounds of pressure over the course of an all-day hike. They are particularly useful in helping prevent knee and back pain from rigorous hiking.

When hiking with a small child in a child-carrier pack, keep a small mirror in your pocket so you can frequently check on your passenger without having to stop and remove the pack.

Above all, use good judgment and proceed with caution.

# Foot Care

At an Appalachian Mountain Club seminar on winter backpacking that I attended years ago, one instructor told us that, besides the brain, "Your feet are the most important part of your body." Hurt any other body part and we might conceivably still make it home under our own power. Hurt our feet, and we're in trouble.

Take care of your feet. Wear clean socks that wick moisture from your skin while staying dry. Make sure your shoes or boots fit properly, are laced properly, and are broken in if they require it. Wear the appropriate footwear for the type of hiking you plan to do. If you anticipate your socks getting wet from perspiration or water, bring extra socks; on a multiday trip, have dry socks for each day, or at least change socks every other day. On hot days, roll your socks down over your boot tops to create what shoe manufacturers call "the chimney effect," cooling your feet by forcing air into your boots as you walk.

## Ⓕ SOAP Note

The SOAP note is a standardized form used in wilderness first aid to evaluate injuries in the backcountry and formulate a plan for getting the victim to safety. Here's an explanation of the acronym, which doubles as a set of guidelines for managing an injury sustained in the backcountry:

**S**ubjective analysis (patient's name, age, sex)

**O**bjective analysis (vital signs, results of patient exam, time)

**A**ssessment (diagnosis of potential problems)

**P**lan (how you intend to deal with the patient's problems, and your long-term plan—e.g., getting the patient to help, or waiting for help to arrive)

Avid hikers especially should be educated on first aid and safety, and a 16-hour basic wilderness first-aid course would be a perfect start. Such a course will cover many topics, among them, the SOAP note.

Whenever I stop for a short rest on the trail—even if only for five or 10 minutes—I sit down, pull off my boots and socks, and let them and my feet dry out. When backpacking, wash your feet at the end of the day. If you feel any hot spots developing, intervene before they progress into blisters. A slightly red or tender hot spot can be protected from developing into a blister with an adhesive bandage, tape, or a square of moleskin.

If a blister has formed, clean the area around it thoroughly to avoid infection. Sterilize a needle or knife in a flame, then pop and drain the blister to promote faster healing. Put an antiseptic ointment on the blister. Cut a piece of moleskin or Second Skin (both of which have a soft side and a sticky side with a peel-off backing) large enough to overlap the blistered area. Cut a hole as large as the blister out of the center of the moleskin, then place the moleskin over the blister so that the blister is visible through the hole. If done properly, you should be able to walk without aggravating the blister.

## Water and Food

Streams and brooks run everywhere in New England. If you're out for more than a day in the backcountry, finding water is rarely a problem (except on ridge tops and summits). But protozoans and bacteria are common in backcountry water sources, and campers do not always maintain an appropriate distance between their messes and the stream. Assume you should always treat water from backcountry sources, whether by using a filter or iodine tablets, boiling, or another proven method. Day hikers will usually find it more convenient to simply carry enough water from home for the hike.

Most of us require about two liters of water per day when we're not active. Like any physical activity, hiking increases your body's fluid needs by a factor of two or more. On a hot, sticky summer day in New England, or even on a cold, dry winter day (when the air draws moisture from your body even though you may not be perspiring), you'll need even more water than you would on a cool autumn afternoon. A hot drink on the trail in winter doesn't warm you any more than a cold drink, but it sure does feel better. Carry an insulated water bottle with tea, hot chocolate, or another favorite hot drink.

A good rule of thumb for an all-day hike is two liters of water per person, but even that could leave you mildly dehydrated, so carry a third liter if you can. Dehydration can lead to other, more serious problems, like heat exhaustion, hypothermia, frostbite, and injury. If you're well hydrated, you will urinate frequently and your urine will be clear. The darker your urine, the greater your level of dehydration. If you feel thirsty, dehydration has already commenced. In short: Drink a lot.

Similarly, your body consumes a phenomenal amount of calories walking up and down a mountain. Feed it frequently. Carbohydrates like bread, chocolate, dried fruit, fig bars, snack bars, fresh vegetables, and energy bars provide a source of quick energy. Fats contain about twice the calories per pound than carbs or protein, and provide the slow-burning fuel that keeps you going all day and warm through the night if you're sleeping outside; sate your need for fats by eating cheese, chocolate, canned meats or fish, pepperoni, sausage, or nuts.

On hot days, "refrigerate" your water and perishables like cheese and chocolate: Fill a water bottle (the collapsible kind works best) with very cold water, and ice cubes if possible. Wrap it and your perishables in a thick, insulating fleece and bury it inside your pack. Or the night before, fill a solid bottle (like a Nalgene) halfway and freeze it, then fill the remainder with water in the morning before you leave for the hike.

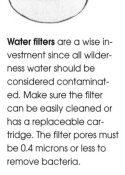

**Water filters** are a wise investment since all wilderness water should be considered contaminated. Make sure the filter can be easily cleaned or has a replaceable cartridge. The filter pores must be 0.4 microns or less to remove bacteria.

# Animals

The remarkable recovery of New England's mountains and forests during the past century from the abuses of the logging industry has spawned a boom in the populations of many wild animals, from increased numbers of black bears and moose to the triumphant return of the bald eagle. For the most part, you don't have to worry about your safety in the backcountry. In years of hiking, I've seen two bears in New England—and both were running across the gravel Perimeter Road in Maine's Baxter State Park as I drove it. I've never encountered a bear on the trail, though I've seen scat and other signs of their presence.

Still, a few sensible precautions are in order. If you're camping in the backcountry, know how to hang or store your food properly to keep it from bears and smaller animals like mice, which are more likely to be a problem. You certainly should never approach our region's two large mammals: moose, which you may see in northern New England, or bear, which you may never see. These creatures are wild and unpredictable, and a moose can weigh several hundred pounds and put the hurt on a much smaller human. The greatest danger posed by moose is that of hitting one while driving on dark back roads at night; hundreds of collisions occur in Maine and New Hampshire every year, often wrecking vehicles and injuring people. At night, drive more slowly than you would during daylight.

## Low-Impact Practices

Many of New England's trails receive heavy use, making it imperative that we all understand how to minimize our physical impact on the land. The nonprofit organization Leave No Trace (LNT) advocates a set of principles for low-impact backcountry use that are summarized in these basic guidelines:

- Plan ahead and prepare
- Travel and camp on durable surfaces
- Dispose of waste properly
- Leave what you find
- Minimize campfire impact
- Respect wildlife
- Be considerate of other visitors

Below are more recommendations that apply to many backcountry areas in New England:

- Choose a campsite at least 200 feet from trails and water sources, unless you're using a designated site. Make sure your site bears no evidence of your stay when you leave.
- Avoid building campfires; cook with a backpacking stove.
- Carry out everything you carry in.
- Do not leave any food behind, even buried, as animals will dig it up. Learn how to hang food appropriately to keep it from bears. Black bears have spread their range over much of New England in recent years, and problems have arisen in isolated backcountry areas where human use is heavy.
- Bury human waste beneath six inches of soil at least 200 feet from any water source. Burn and bury, or carry out, used toilet paper.
- Even biodegradable soap is harmful to the environment, so simply wash your cooking gear with water away from any streams or ponds.
- Avoid trails that are very muddy in spring; that's when they are most susceptible to erosion.
- And last but not least, know and follow any regulations for the area you will be visiting.

LNT offers more in-depth guidelines for low-impact camping and hiking on its website: www.lnt.org. You can also contact them by mail or phone: Leave No Trace Inc., P.O. Box 997, Boulder, CO 80306, 303/442-8222 or 800/332-4100.

## Trail Etiquette

One of the great things about hiking—at least for as long as I've been hiking—has always been the quality of the people you meet on the trail. Hikers generally do not need an explanation of the value of courtesy, and I hope that will always ring true.

Personally, I yield the trail to others whether I'm going uphill or down. All trail users should yield to horses by stepping aside for the safety of everyone present. Likewise, horseback riders should, whenever possible, avoid situations where their animals are forced to push past hikers on very narrow trails. Mountain bikers should yield to hikers, announce their approach, and pass nonbikers slowly. During hunting season, nonhunters should wear blaze orange, or an equally bright, conspicuous color. Most of the hunters I meet are responsible and friendly and deserve like treatment.

Many of us enjoy the woods and mountains for the quiet, and we should keep that in mind on the trail, at summits, or backcountry campsites. Many of us share the belief that things like cell phones, radios, CD players, and hand-held personal computers do not belong in the mountains; if you must use them, use discretion.

New England has seen some conflict between hikers and mountain bikers, but it's important to remember that solutions to those issues are never reached through hostility and rudeness. Much more is accomplished when we begin from a foundation of mutual respect and courtesy. After all, we're all interested in preserving and enjoying our trails.

Large groups have a disproportionate impact on backcountry campsites and on the experience of other people. Be aware of and respect any restrictions on group size. Even where no regulation exists, keep your group size to no more than 10 people.

Dogs can create unnecessary friction in the backcountry. Dog owners should respect any regulations and not presume that strangers are eager to meet their pet. Keep your pet under physical control whenever other people are approaching.

# Best Hikes

Can't decide where to hike this weekend? Here are my picks for the best hikes in New England in 16 categories:

##  Top 10 Trails for Fall Foliage Viewing

**Tumbledown Mountain via any trail,** Western and Southern Mountains and Hills, page 102. From the top of this Maine peak, you'll have a blanket of colors spread out before you as far as New Hampshire's Mount Washington.

**Welch and Dickey,** White Mountains and Above the Notches, page 210. This relatively easy hike offers plenty of rest stops and viewpoints to take in the sights.

**Mount Chocorua via any trail,** White Mountains and Above the Notches, page 214. Hikers who complete this steep ascent are rewarded with superb forest views, including a gorgeous array of fiery colors in the autumn.

**Squam Mountains,** Central and Southern New Hampshire, page 225. This popular hike features year-round lake views and a great seasonal show.

**Mount Monadnock via any trail,** Central and Southern New Hampshire, page 236. Bring kids on this trek for crisp autumn air and a colorful view.

**Mount Hunger,** Northern Green Mountains and the Northeast Kingdom, page 258. Try this trail in the fall for a dazzling display, or in winter for views of snow-capped peaks.

**Camel's Hump via any trail,** Northern Green Mountains and the Northeast Kingdom, page 260. Spectacular foliage is the payoff for those who tackle this difficult climb in the autumn.

**Stratton Mountain and Stratton Pond,** Southern Green Mountains and Southern Vermont, page 307. Not for the faint of heart, the observation tower at the top of Stratton Mountain provides expansive views and a place to catch your breath.

**Monument Mountain,** The Berkshires and Western Massachusetts, page 333. This is an easy trek, with blooming mountain laurel in the summer and glorious foliage in autumn.

**Lion's Head,** Western Hills, page 419. Views on this Connecticut stretch of the Appalachian Trail impress even through-hikers near the end of their journey.

##  Top 10 Coastline or Island Hikes

**Ocean Lookout,** Down East, page 64. Short and sweet, this hike offers easy access to expansive views of the islands of Maine's Penobscot Bay.

**Isle au Haut: Western Head Loop,** Down East, page 66. Lucky hikers will spot seals and other marine life in the scenic coves visible from this loop trail.

**Acadia Traverse,** Down East, page 80. By traversing Mount Desert Island's east side, ambitious hikers can hit the six major peaks of Maine's Acadia National Park.

**Great Head,** Down East, page 83. This short cliff-top walk provides superb views of the Maine coastline from Frenchman Bay to Otter Cliffs.

**Ocean Path,** Down East, page 84. When you hear the thunderous surf pound the craggy shoreline, you'll know why this is a favorite among Acadia National Park visitors.

**Bar Head Drumlin/Plum Island,** Greater Boston and Cape Cod, page 372. Combining sandy beach, rocky shores, and terrain shaped by a receding glacier some 10,000 years ago, this easy hike offers far more than your usual coastal stroll.

**Great Island Trail,** Greater Boston and Cape Cod, page 388. Classic Cape Cod, this six-mile trail features sandy dunes and expansive bay views.

**Aquinnah,** Greater Boston and Cape Cod, page 392. This easy beach stroll out at the western point of Martha's Vineyard leads to colorful cliffs perfect for sunset watching.

**Newport Cliff Walk,** Rhode Island, page 406. Although it offers ocean views, most walk this famous trail to gawk at spectacular mansions of Gatsby-esque proportions.

**Block Island: Mohegan Bluffs,** Rhode Island, page 411. It's not hard to see why the Nature Conservancy dubbed Block Island one of the Western Hemisphere's Last Great Places—step off the ferry and you'll discover an abundance of natural wonders and historical features.

#  Top 10 Hikes to Waterfalls

**Katahdin Stream Falls,** North Woods, page 41. You'll cross Katahdin Stream on a wooden bridge as you make the easy walk to this 50-foot cascade.

**Step Falls,** Western and Southern Mountains and Hills, page 107. Maine hikers can take a leisurely stroll to this spectacular set of falls, just half a mile from the parking lot.

**Mount Caribou,** Western and Southern Mountains and Hills, page 113. The Caribou Trail–Mud Brook Trail, a 7.3-mile loop, is dotted with several lovely waterfalls.

**Glen Ellis Falls,** White Mountains and Above the Notches, page 161. Visit in springtime, when heavy water flows make this 70-foot cascade even more spectacular.

**Ethan Pond/Thoreau Falls,** White Mountains and Above the Notches, page 171. This 10.4-mile trek has two spur trails, leading to the double pleasures of Ripley Falls and Thoreau Falls.

**Mounts Lincoln and Lafayette,** White Mountains and Above the Notches, page 187. You'll pass several cascades and brooks on this 8.8-mile hike, including the dramatic Cloudland Falls.

**Arethusa Falls and Frankenstein Cliff,** White Mountains and Above the Notches, page 196. You'll pass several cascades and pools on this moderate hike, including the tallest falls in the state.

**Ripley Falls,** White Mountains and Above the Notches, page 197. An easy, one-mile walk is the typical route to this 100-foot cascade.

**Bash Bish Falls,** The Berkshires and Western Massachusetts, page 340. Though worth a trip year-round, spring snowmelt enhances this dramatic, boulder-strewn cascade.

**Wadsworth Falls State Park,** Hartford and the Quiet Corner, page 447. Little Falls and Big Falls provide an abundance of tumbling water on this easy, wooded trail.

# Top 10 Hikes to Lakes and Swimming Holes

**Sandy Stream Pond/Whidden Ponds Loop,** North Woods, page 35. Dogs aren't permitted on this loop trail, but hikers will pass by two ponds that are frequented by moose.

**100-Mile Wilderness,** North Woods, page 49. An expedition along this remote and lengthy Maine route passes by scores of alpine ponds and cold mountain streams.

**Gulf Hagas,** North Woods, page 55. You'll find plenty of cool, calm pools on a hike through this spot, known as Maine's Little Grand Canyon.

**Jordan Pond Loop,** Down East, page 75. This easy trail around Jordan Pond affords great views of wooded slopes.

**Emerald Pool,** White Mountains and Above the Notches, page 178. The name says it all—a beautiful spot reached by an easy walk.

**Skylight Pond,** Southern Green Mountains and Southern Vermont, page 281. The 4.8-mile round-trip hike is an easy day trip, but many take advantage of the nearby lodge to stretch this into an overnighter.

**Lime Rock Preserve,** Rhode Island, Page 398. A nice walk in the woods culminating in a loop around a pond.

**Long And Ell Ponds,** Rhode Island, page 405. Short, but scenic, with pond views from atop ledges and cliffs.

**Breakneck Pond,** Hartford and the Quiet Corner, page 436. If you're in the mood for a long walk in the woods, try walking around this undeveloped pond for a bit of solitude and beauty.

**West Hartford Reservoir,** Hartford and the Quiet Corner, page 437. This mixed-use trail around a reservoir is a favorite of both hikers and bikers from nearby Hartford.

##  Top 10 Hikes Under Five Miles

**The Bubbles/Eagle Lake Loop,** Down East, page 74. This Maine loop trail provides unforgettable views of Jordan Pond from a collection of exposed ledges.

**Dorr and Cadillac Mountains,** Down East, page 79. You'll hit two great Mount Desert Island peaks in this three-mile hike.

**Mount Willard,** White Mountains and Above the Notches, page 172. It doesn't take much effort to reach the superb viewpoints from the cliffs of this mount—the trail rises less than 1,000 feet in about three miles.

**Welch and Dickey,** White Mountains and Above the Notches, page 210. With its relatively gentle grade, this hike is a good choice for those seeking summit-top views without putting in a long day's work.

**Mount Cardigan: West Side Loop,** Central and Southern New Hampshire, page 227. Beloved by many, Mount Cardigan is easily ascended via this steady climb.

**Mount Monadnock via any trail,** Central and Southern New Hampshire, page 236. This popular mount, designated a National Natural Landmark, can be ascended via either of two trails, each topping out at about 4.5 miles.

**Mount Mansfield: the Long Trail,** Northern Green Mountains and the Northeast Kingdom, page 257. The Long Trail is only 4.6 miles in length, but the elevation gain makes this a challenging climb.

**Mount Hunger,** Northern Green Mountains and the Northeast Kingdom, page 258. Expect great valley views and splendid fall foliage on this ascent.

**Monument Mountain,** The Berkshires and Western Massachusetts, page 338. Topping out at just over 1.5 miles, the Hickey Trail will take you to the 1,640-foot summit of Squaw Peak.

**Lion's Head,** Western Hills, page 419. Far less crowded than nearby Bear Mountain, this 4.6-mile trek also offers delightful views of the Connecticut countryside.

##  Top 10 Easy Backpacking Hikes

**Russell Pond/Davis Pond loop,** North Woods, page 33. This is a relatively easy trail looping through a remote portion of Maine's Baxter State Park, with several ponds along the way.

**Half a 100-Mile Wilderness (northern half),** North Woods, page 53. This trek offers a multiday hike through remote and rugged territory.

**Kilkenny Loop,** White Mountains and Above the Notches, page 131. One of the least-traveled portions of the White Mountains, this hike makes a good overnight trip for those seeking peace and quiet.

**Mahoosuc Range: Gentian Pond,** White Mountains and Above the Notches, page 135. With great views at dusk, the shelter at Gentian Pond is a fine place to rest your feet for the night.

**Big Branch Wilderness,** Southern Green Mountains and Southern Vermont, page 299. A 14-mile trek with good fishing opportunities en route.

**Stratton Mountain and Stratton Pond,** Southern Green Mountains and Southern Vermont, page 307. Overnight hikers can choose to camp at the North Shore tenting area or stay the night at the Stratton shelter.

**Glastenbury Mountain,** Southern Green Mountains and Southern Vermont, page 310. A good two-day trip punctuated with an overnight stay at the roomy Goddard shelter.

**The Long Trail: Massachusetts Line to Route 9,** Southern Green Mountains and Southern Vermont, page 311. Although this hike is over 14 miles long, the flat terrain makes it a good choice for novice backpackers.

**The Riga Plateau,** The Berkshires and Western Massachusetts, page 339. This hike covers a lovely stretch of the Appalachian Trail with easy, ridge-top terrain.

**Bear Mountain,** Western Hills, page 419. At 2,316-foot, Connecticut's Bear Mountain is a good choice for beginner backpackers.

 ## Top 10 Difficult Backpacking Hikes

**100-Mile Wilderness,** North Woods, page 49. The longest stretch of roadless trail in New England, the southern half is harder than the northern.

**Bigelow Range,** Western and Southern Mountains and Hills, page 89. Don't underestimate this steep climb, but the payoff is big views of the Maine mountains and as far off as Mount Washington.

**Saddleback Range,** Western and Southern Mountains and Hills, page 97. Up and down, up and down, up and down . . . bring the trekking poles for this hike.

**The Mahoosuc Range,** Western and Southern Mountains and Hills, page 110. Maine's Mahoosuc Notch is called "the hardest mile on the Appalachian Trail," but the rest of this range is no walk in the park.

**Presidential Range Traverse,** White Mountains and Above the Notches, page 145. You'll experience the biggest hills in New England, carpeted with boulders, wildflowers blooming in summer, and the best views in the region.

**The Carter-Moriah Range,** White Mountains and Above the Notches, page 147. A challenging traverse, but good training for harder ranges like the Presidentials.

**Twins-Bonds Traverse,** White Mountains and Above the Notches, page 193. One of the most remote backpacking trips in New England, a favorite of the author's.

**The Long Trail: Route 17, Appalachian Gap, to the Winooski River,** Northern Green Mountains and the Northeast Kingdom, page 267. Camel's Hump is the prize, but the rest of this hike is filled with wonderful surprises.

**The Monroe Skyline,** Northern Green Mountains and the Northeast Kingdom, page 269. Professor Will Monroe knew what he was doing when he was the catalyst for relocating the Long Trail onto this scenic ridge crest—now the trail's finest stretch.

**The Long Trail: Route 103 to U.S. 4,** Southern Green Mountains and Southern Vermont, page 293. For northbound hikers, here's where the LT gets rough, culminating at the rocky crown of Killington Peak.

 ## Top 10 Summit Hikes

**North Traveler Mountain,** North Woods, page 31. Don't get discouraged by several false summits on the way to the peak of Traveler Mountain—the views only improve as you ascend up the ridge.

**The Owl,** North Woods, page 42. You'll experience a little-visited part of Baxter State Park, with imposing views of Katahdin to the east.

**Bigelow Mountain,** Western and Southern Mountains and Hills, page 91. A great choice for fit hikers, with the option of adding a second summit on day two.

**Mount Abraham,** Western and Southern Mountains and Hills, page 96. Like Vermont's Mount Abraham, Maine's peak by the same name also rises above the tree line and provides expansive views.

**Saddleback Mountain and The Horn,** Western and Southern Mountains and Hills, page 100. On a clear day, hikers who undertake this challenging ascent are rewarded with views of Katahdin to the north and Mount Washington to the southwest.

**Mount Adams via any trail,** White Mountains and Above the Notches, page 138. With top marks for both scenic beauty and trail difficulty, Mount Adams' lofty summit tops out at a whopping 5,799 feet.

**Mount Madison via any trail,** White Mountains and Above the Notches, page 141. Some of the most strenuous hikes in the region, the trails up Mount Madison rise up 4,000 feet of elevation.

**Mount Chocorua via any trail,** White Mountains and Above the Notches, page 214. Diminutive compared to other peaks in the White Mountains, the views from this 3,500-foot summit are still striking.

**Camel's Hump: Long Trail/Bamforth Ridge,** Northern Green Mountains and the Northeast Kingdom, page 262. An arduous 11.8 mile hike to 4,083-foot peak, with views of the Adirondacks, Lake Champlain, the Green Mountains, and the Whites.

**Mount Abraham,** Southern Green Mountains and Southern Vermont, page 277. At 4,006 feet, Mount Abraham is one of just four Vermont summits to thrust a rocky crown above tree line.

# Ⓕ Top 10 Hikes for Solitude and Remoteness

**North Traveler Mountain,** North Woods, page 31. You're likely to have this trail to yourself as you take in sweeping ridge-top views.

**Peak of the Ridges,** North Woods, page 32. A challenging and isolated ridgeline hike with a 2,500-foot elevation gain.

**100-Mile Wilderness,** North Woods, page 49. For nearly 100 miles, this multiday trek weaves along a remote, northern section of the Appalachian Trail.

**White Cap Mountain,** North Woods, page 54. This 3,654-foot summit can be reached via a two- or three-day tromp through a remote, roadless area.

**Old Blue Mountain,** Western and Southern Mountains and Hills, page 102. This hike offers a challenging day hike to a 3,600-foot summit on a remote stretch of the Appalachian Trail.

**Diamond Peaks,** White Mountains and Above the Notches, page 127. Up in a little-traveled portion of New Hampshire, this mixed-use trail is rarely busy.

**Sugarloaf Mountain,** White Mountains and Above the Notches, page 128. A mid-sized peak in one of the least-crowded parts of New Hampshire, this 3.5-mile hike has some steeply inclined sections.

**North Percy Peak,** White Mountains and Above the Notches, page 129. This hike is more accessible than Sugarloaf Mountain, yet still a good choice for those seeking peace and quiet.

**Pemigewasset Wilderness Traverse,** White Mountains and Above the Notches, page 194. A relatively easy route through valleys and flat areas, this traverse cuts through a federally designated wilderness area.

**Breakneck Pond,** Hartford and the Quiet Corner, page 436. A top pick in Connecticut for its relative sense of serenity and isolation.

# ⑤ Top 10 Easy and Scenic Walks

**Kidney Pond Loop,** North Woods, page 46. A relaxed ramble on this lovely Maine loop trail will lead you to Kidney Pond and several other small bodies of water.

**Screw Auger Falls,** Western and Southern Mountains and Hills, page 106. Minutes from the parking lot, this is a favorite swimming spot for families with small children.

**Sabbaday Falls,** White Mountains and Above the Notches, page 208. A gravel trail, just under a mile long, follows a babbling brook to this lovely cascade.

**Smuggler's Notch,** Northern Green Mountains and the Northeast Kingdom, page 252. Long a route for illegal trade, today this notch is a pleasant spot for a stroll among massive boulders and steep cliffs.

**Mount Greylock: Rounds Rock,** The Berkshires and Western Massachusetts, page 325. Good for small kids, this short trail leads to several lookout points facing Mount Greylock.

**Maudslay State Park,** Greater Boston and Cape Cod, page 371. Visitors here can take in the park's lovely gardens and mountain laurels, or sit in on park-sponsored educational events.

**World's End,** Greater Boston and Cape Cod, page 385. A bevy of interconnecting carriage paths, designed in the late 1800s by famed landscape architect Frederick Law Olmsted, today provides views of Boston's skyline.

**Nauset Marsh,** Greater Boston and Cape Cod, page 390. Just over a mile long, this loop trail is well marked and features interpretive signs about the marsh and its varied plant life.

**Norman Bird Sanctuary,** Rhode Island, page 403. A two-mile walk on a rocky ridgeline, the Hanging Rock Trail is contained within a private sanctuary.

**Mount Tom State Park Tower,** Western Hills, page 425. Follow the yellow blazes up to this stone tower for a lovely view of the Connecticut hills.

# ⑤ Top 10 Hikes for Children

**The Beehive,** Down East, page 81. Older children will be thrilled by the vertical scramble up this rocky Maine trail.

**Sabattus Mountain,** Western and Southern Mountains and Hills, page 115. Keep energetic kids in sight along the wide path of this short ascent.

**Sabbaday Falls,** White Mountains and Above the Notches, page 208. Less than a mile from the parking lot, the cascading falls here drop through a narrow gorge to the delight of young and old alike.

**Welch and Dickey,** White Mountains and Above the Notches, page 210. Young leaf-collectors will enjoy this hike during the peak of foliage season.

**Mount Chocorua via any trail,** White Mountains and Above the Notches, page 214. Young adventurers will be challenged and thrilled by this difficult hike—and reaching the summit is an accomplishment for hikers of any age.

**Mount Cardigan: East Side Loop,** Central and Southern New Hampshire, page 228. With expansive views and steep sections of trail, this is a popular pick for older children looking for the next level of adventure.

**Mount Monadnock via any trail,** Central and Southern New Hampshire, page 236. Designated a National Natural Landmark, this is a regional favorite—and a great choice for older kids looking to for a chance to top a summit.

**Stowe Pinnacle,** Northern Green Mountains and the Northeast Kingdom, page 258. Let your kids forge the trail by spotting the blue blazes that mark this relatively easy hike.

**Crow Hills,** Central Massachusetts, page 352. This gentle loop crams a lot into 0.7 miles—the varied scenery includes cliffs, forests, and ponds.

**Block Island: Clay Head Trail and the Maze,** Rhode Island, page 408. An easy trail with great sea views, this trail is a great pick for kids of any age who'll go wild over a game of hike-and-seek in the Maze.

## Ⓕ Top 10 Hikes to Mountain Ridges

**Mount Katahdin: Knife Edge Loop,** North Woods, page 37. A tough trail on rugged terrain, but one of the best ways for ambitious hikers to take in the mother of all Maine mountains.

**Doubletop Mountain,** North Woods, page 46. A challenging hike with expansive views on the alpine portion of the trail.

**Cadillac Mountain: South Ridge Trail,** Down East, page 78. Explore the highest peak on Maine's Mount Desert Island by way of this spectacular seven-mile hike.

**Mount Jefferson: the Castellated Ridge,** White Mountains and Above the Notches, page 142. The shortest route from trailhead to 5,000-foot peak in the region, this 6.6-mile trek incorporates the dramatic Castellated Ridge.

**Presidential Range Traverse,** White Mountains and Above the Notches, page 145. A multiday trek with 15 continuous ridge-top miles above the tree line.

**The Baldies Loop,** White Mountains and Above the Notches, page 177. On this grueling 10-mile trek, four miles are on open ridge that afford spectacular views.

**Mounts Lincoln and Lafayette,** White Mountains and Above the Notches, page 187. Hikers flock here in summertime to enjoy the ridgeline views on this 8.8-mile hike.

**Mount Mansfield: Sunset Ridge and Laura Cowles Trails,** Northern Green Mountains and the Northeast Kingdom, page 253. Ascend Vermont's tallest peak via the thrillingly exposed Sunset Ridge, but be prepared for gusty winds.

**Mount Tom,** The Berkshires and Western Massachusetts, page 336. A relatively easy way to experience the magnificence of ridgeline hiking, this hike ascends less than 500 feet.

**Ragged Mountain Preserve Trail,** Hartford and the Quiet Corner, page 443. This loop trail, partially set atop high cliffs, affords broad views in all directions.

## Ⓕ Top 10 Hikes for Rugged Mountain Terrain

**Katahdin Traverse,** North Woods, page 38. This hike is best as an overnighter with a scramble up Cathedral Trail to Katahdin's summit on Day 2.

**Mount Katahdin: the Abol Trail,** North Woods, page 39. Perhaps the oldest existing trail up Katahdin, this route climbs a whopping 4,000 feet in 7.6 miles.

**Mount O-J-I,** North Woods, page 45. Aside from Katahdin, this is one of the most grueling treks in Baxter State Park, but you'll be rewarded with several fine viewpoints just below the summit.

**Tumbledown Mountain Loop Trail,** Western and Southern Mountains and Hills, page 103. Although this trail tops out at just over four miles, a steeply graded trail strewn with boulders makes the terrain tough to navigate.

**Mount Adams: King Ravine,** White Mountains and Above the Notches, page 138. A brutal but sensational hike up New England's second-highest peak.

**Mount Madison: Madison Gulf and Webster Trails,** White Mountains and Above the Notches, page 141. Gaining 4,000 feet in elevation over 11.5 miles, this trail will test even the most experienced hikers.

**Mount Washington: Huntington Ravine and the Alpine Garden,** White Mountains and Above the Notches, page 149 Another super-tough White Mountains trail, this one should only be attempted in summer and early fall due to the possibility of slippery ice formations in the colder months.

**Mount Washington: Tuckerman Ravine,** White Mountains and Above the Notches, page 151. For those hardy souls looking to top New England's tallest mountain, this is the standard route.

**Mount Tripyramid,** White Mountains and Above the Notches, page 209. A chance for experienced trekkers to hit three summits in one long day.

**Mount Mansfield: Hell Brook Trail,** Northern Green Mountains and the Northeast Kingdom, page 255. Not all the tough trails are found in the White Mountains—this Vermont ascent covers some of the region's most rugged terrain.

##  Top 10 Hikes to Watch the Sunrise

**Mount Katahdin: the Abol Trail,** North Woods, page 39. You'll want to start your day early when tackling this 4,000 foot elevation gain.

**Cadillac Mountain via any trail,** Down East, page 77. Start your day with a view of the sun rising up out of the Atlantic and casting its light down on a collection of nearby islands.

**The Mahoosuc Range,** Western and Southern Mountains and Hills, page 110. Break up this multiday hike by catching a glorious sunrise from the summit of Fulling Mill Mountain.

**Twins-Bonds Traverse,** White Mountains and Above the Notches, page 193. Take your pick—the five summits on this trek allow you numerous chances to catch a stellar sunrise.

**Skylight Pond,** Southern Green Mountains and Southern Vermont, page 281. Ease into the morning here after slumbering in comfort at the Skyline Lodge.

**Mount Everett,** The Berkshires and Western Massachusetts, page 338. Watch the day dawn over rolling hills and gentle valleys.

**Bar Head Drumlin/Plum Island,** Greater Boston and Cape Cod, page 372. Begin your day with cormorants, herons, and kingfishers at the nearby Parker River National Wildlife Refuge.

**Halibut Point,** Greater Boston and Cape Cod, page 374. Ease into your day with a relaxing amble around this rocky shore.

**Bear Mountain,** Western Hills, page 419. Enjoy this popular Connecticut loop without the usual weekend crowds by hitting the trail early in the day.

**Mount Tom State Park Tower,** Western Hills, page 425. Instead of a morning of Saturday cartoons, bring the kids here for great views of the Connecticut countryside.

##  Top 10 Hikes to Watch the Sunset

**Isle au Haut: Eben's Head,** Down East, page 65. Usher in the evening from this rocky, surf-pounded bluff on Maine's Isle au Haut.

**Presidential Range Traverse,** White Mountains and Above the Notches, page 145. You'll have your choice of nine prime peaks for sunset viewing as you traverse this deservedly acclaimed route.

**The Carter-Moriah Range,** White Mountains and Above the Notches, page 147. Before turning in for the night at the Imp Mountain campsite, watch the setting sun from a ledge just below the shelter.

**Great Bay National Estuarine Reserve: Sandy Point Trail,** Central and Southern New Hampshire, page 234. This easy boardwalk trail is a great pick for abundant bird life and can't-fail sunsets.

**Mount Philo,** Northern Green Mountains and the Northeast Kingdom, page 260. The westward panorama from these cliffs includes sprawling views of Lake Champlain and the Adirondacks.

**Falls of Lana and Rattlesnake Cliffs,** Southern Green Mountains and Southern Vermont, page 284. Along with a bevy of pools and cascades, this moderate hike allows long-ranging views of the Adirondacks to the west.

**Mount Tom,** The Berkshires and Western Massachusetts, page 336. Imposing basalt cliffs and wide-open views of the Berkshires are part of this popular hike's appeal.

**Great Island Trail,** Greater Boston and Cape Cod, page 388. A favorite for watching the sun set into Cape Cod Bay.

**Aquinnah,** Greater Boston and Cape Cod, page 392. Bring a picnic and enjoy the sunset on this easy beach walk.

**Peak Mountain,** Hartford and the Quiet Corner, page 435. An abundance of cozy, westward-facing ledges makes this a romantic choice for sunset lovers.

# Ⓕ Top 10 Trails for Bird-Watching

**Great Bay National Estuarine Reserve: Sandy Point Trail,** Central and Southern New Hampshire, page 234. A tidal estuary of nearly 5,000 acres, this reserve is home to bald eagles, osprey, grey blue herons, and other birds.

**Wachusett Meadow to Wachusett Mountain,** Central Massachusetts, page 359. Expansive views with long sight lines provide ample opportunity to spot birds in flight.

**Great Meadows National Wildlife Refuge,** Greater Boston and Cape Cod, page 375. One of the best birding regions in Massachusetts, over 200 species of birds have been spotted in this 3,000-acre refuge.

**Caratunk Wildlife Refuge,** Greater Boston and Cape Cod, page 386. Another favorite for migratory birds, this wildlife refuge features a loop trail through wetlands.

**Powder Mill Ledges,** Rhode Island, page 399. Birders on these three loop trails update the visitor center information board with records of recent sightings—see if you can add to the list!

**Norman Bird Sanctuary,** Rhode Island, page 403. A private sanctuary since 1949, this is a good spot to see a variety of winged creatures.

**Kimball Wildlife Sanctuary,** Rhode Island, Page 407. Three loop trails provide ample bird-watching opportunities on this refuge owned by the state's Audubon Society.

**Ninigret National Wildlife Refuge,** Rhode Island, Page 408. A former naval training area, this Charleston site has been a refuge to migrating and wintering birds since 1971.

**Block Island via any trail,** Rhode Island, page 408. The spring and fall migrations bring hundreds of thousands of birds to this island off the coast of Rhode Island.

**Westwoods Preserve,** Long Island Sound, page 460. Passing several marshes and the small Lost Pond, this trail offers numerous opportunities to spot birds and other wildlife.

# Maine

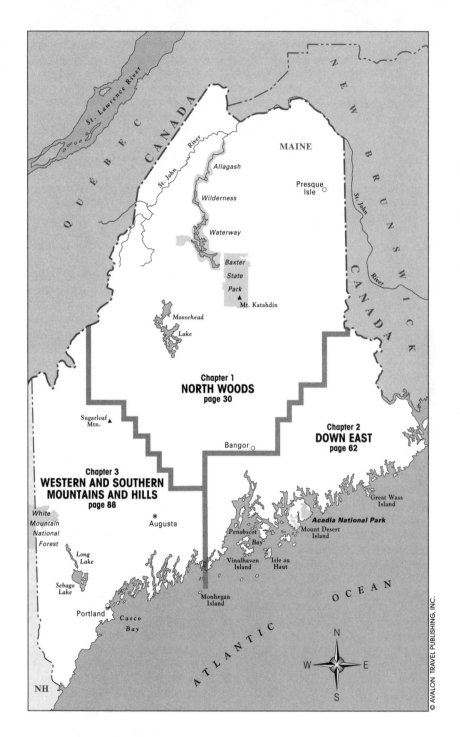

## Chapter 1

© MICHAEL LANZA

# North Woods

# North Woods

The 26 hikes described in this section all lie on public land and fall within two of Maine's greatest hiking areas: Baxter State Park, and the 100-Mile Wilderness stretch of the Appalachian Trail. This chapter covers that part of Maine east of U.S. 201 and north of Routes 2 and 9.

With 204,733 acres remaining as close to true wilderness as managed lands come, Baxter is Maine's flagship state park. It provides a hiking experience that's rare in New England: remote and untamed. Maine's highest peak, 5,267-foot Katahdin, dominates the park's south end and attracts the bulk of hiker traffic. But Baxter Park boasts more than 47 other peaks, many of them with trails to overlooked summits as nice as anything east of the Rockies. I've hiked peaks like the Brothers, Coe, Doubletop, and Traveler on a sunny Labor Day weekend and seen few other people. You'll never grow tired of hiking Katahdin, but don't miss out on Baxter's other gems.

At busy times in summer, some parking lots at popular trailheads—usually Katahdin trails—fill up, and the park will not allow any more vehicles in those lots on that day, effectively forcing visitors who come later to choose other trailheads and hikes. There are no overflow parking areas, but trailhead parking north of Katahdin rarely fills, so you can always find someplace to hike. The park's Tote Road is not open to vehicles in winter, when access is by ski or snowshoe and reaching anyplace within the park requires a multiday trip. Millinocket Road is maintained in winter as far as Abol Bridge Campground. The road to the park's Matagamon Gate entrance is maintained only as far as a private campground about four miles east of the gate.

There are no public water sources in Baxter Park; treat your water or bring an adequate supply with you.

Advance reservations for campground sites and backcountry campsites are recommended, and in winter a permit is required for staying overnight; in addition, park authorities require that visitors show that they have winter backcountry experience.

The 100-Mile Wilderness stretch of the Appalachian Trail is neither officially designated federal wilderness nor true wilderness as found in the American West or Alaska—you may hear the distant thrum of logging machinery while hiking here. But the Wilderness does offer some of the most remote hiking in New England, and the big lakes here are home to loons and many other birds and a favorite haunt of moose. The 100-Mile Wilderness stretch is also the longest hike you can do on trail in the region without crossing a paved or public road (it crosses several logging roads). It has seen a tremendous growth in popularity since the 1990s. The busiest month is August, when you're likely to encounter lots of other backpackers, though still not as many as on Bigelow Mountain or on popular White Mountains trails. The hiking season begins with the disappearance of snow in late spring—though the black flies, no-see-ums, and mosquitoes also emerge—and extends into October, when the first snow may start flying. The peaks along the Appalachian Trail are not as tall as elsewhere in New England, but they are rugged.

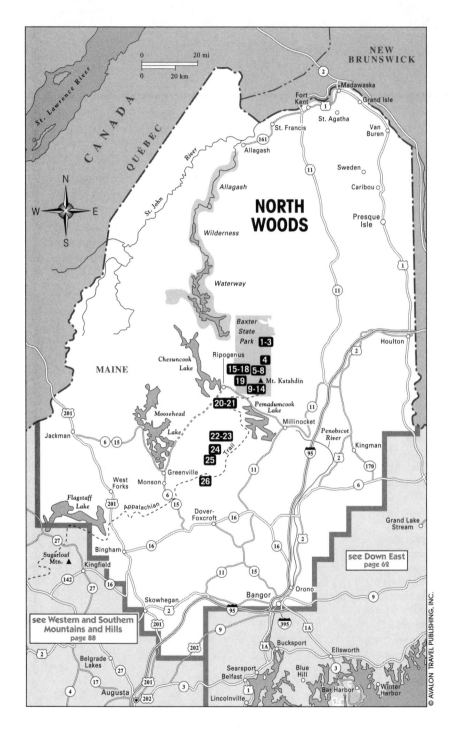

# 1 SOUTH BRANCH FALLS
## 1 mi/1 hr

**in northern Baxter State Park**

This stretch of South Branch Ponds Brook might more aptly be called South Branch Gorge, since the biggest vertical drop the stream makes is only about four feet. But the stream cuts a narrow channel through rock in a scenic gorge about a quarter mile long. From the parking area, follow the trail for 0.5 mile, descending gently at first, then somewhat steeply for the last 0.1 mile to the stream. Take one of the short side paths that lead to views of the gorge before heading back the way you came.

**User groups:** Hikers only. No wheelchair facilities. Bikes, dogs, and hunting are prohibited.

**Access, fees:** Baxter Park is open from May 15–November 1 (no camping in the park after October 15) and from December 1–March 31. An entrance fee of $12 per vehicle is charged at the gatehouse, but vehicles bearing Maine registration can enter at no charge. During the summer season, the park's Togue Pond Gate opens at 6 A.M. and closes at 10 P.M.—though it may open at 5 A.M. some summer days— and the Matagamon Gate opens at 6 A.M. and closes at 10 P.M. The road is not maintained to the trailhead in winter, but it can be skied.

**Maps:** For a park trails map, get the *Baxter State Park and Katahdin* map for $7.95 from the DeLorme Publishing Company, 800/642-0970, website: www.DeLorme.com; or the *Rangeley-Stratton/Baxter State Park-Katahdin* map, $7.95 in waterproof Tyvek, from the Appalachian Mountain Club, 800/262-4455, website: www.outdoors.org. For topographic area maps, request Wassataquoik Lake and the Traveler from USGS Map Sales, Federal Center, Box 25286, Denver, CO 80225, 888/ASK-USGS (888/275-8747), website: http://mapping.usgs.gov.

**Directions:** Take I-95 in Maine to Exit 56 for Medway/Millinocket. Drive west on Route 157 through East Millinocket to Millinocket. Follow signs for Baxter State Park; the park's Togue Pond gatehouse is 18 miles from Millinocket. Just beyond the gatehouse, take the gravel Tote Road's left fork and drive 34.8 miles. Turn right at a sign for South Branch Pond Campground. Drive 1.3 miles to a turnout on the right. Or from the junction of Routes 11 and 159 in Patten, drive west on Route 159 to Shin Pond and follow the access road to Baxter State Park's Matagamon gatehouse, which is 24 miles from Patten. From the gatehouse, drive about 7.3 miles and turn left at the sign for South Branch Pond Campground. Drive 1.3 miles to a turnout on the right.

**Contact:** Baxter State Park, 64 Balsam Drive, Millinocket, ME 04462-2190, 207/723-5140, website: www.baxterstateparkauthority.com.

# 2 NORTH TRAVELER MOUNTAIN
## 5 mi/3.5 hrs
**in northern Baxter State Park**

Traveler Mountain feels less like New England than any other mountain in the region. With much of its sprawling upper ridges denuded by fires decades ago and kept bare by a harsh climate, I half expect to see mountain goats grazing and hear the whistling of marmots up here. What you hear, however, is next to nothing. You can enjoy blissful solitude for several hours on Traveler. The North Traveler Trail climbs more than 2,000 feet in elevation up a ridge to the 3,144-foot north peak, with almost continuous sweeping views.

From the parking area, walk the road into the campground, toward the northernmost South Branch Pond. (Traveler Mountain defines the skyline to the left, or east, above the pond.) Bear left through the campground, passing several sites, and turn right (south) onto the Pogy Notch Trail, which parallels the pond. In 0.1 mile, turn left onto the blue-blazed North Traveler Trail, immediately ascending the fairly steep, rocky ridge. Just 0.3 mile from the pond, you emerge onto open ledges with your first views of the two South Branch Ponds, across to the South Branch Mountains, and south toward Katahdin. The views only improve as you continue up the ridge, where loose stones can make footing difficult and false summits can make the hike seem longer than its five miles. The trail passes through a little birch grove with fresh blueberries in late summer (I ate my share on an early September hike). Follow the blazes and cairns to the open summit, where there are views in every direction, including north to the wilderness. Due south is the 3,541-foot summit of the Traveler, connected to North Traveler by a trailless, three-mile ridge. Descend the way you came.

**User groups:** Hikers only. No wheelchair facilities. This trail should not be attempted in winter except by hikers experienced in mountaineering and prepared for severe winter weather, and is not suitable for skis. Bikes, dogs, horses, and hunting are prohibited.

**Access, fees:** Baxter Park is open from May 15–November 1 (no camping in the park after October 15) and from December 1–March 31. An entrance fee of $12 per vehicle is charged at the gatehouse, but vehicles bearing Maine registration can enter at no charge. During the summer season, the park's Togue Pond Gate opens at 6 A.M. and closes at 10 P.M.—though it may open at 5 A.M. some summer days—and the Matagamon Gate opens at 6 A.M. and closes at 10 P.M. The road is not maintained to the trailhead in winter, but it can be skied.

**Maps:** For a park trail map, get the *Baxter State Park and Katahdin* map for $7.95 from the DeLorme Publishing Company, 800/642-0970, website: www.DeLorme.com; or the *Rangeley-Stratton/Baxter State Park-Katahdin* map, $7.95 in waterproof Tyvek, from the Appalachian Mountain Club, 800/262-4455, website: www.outdoors.org. For topographic area maps, request Wassataquoik Lake and the Traveler from USGS Map Sales, Federal Center, Box 25286, Denver, CO 80225, 888/ASK-USGS (888/275-8747), website: http://mapping.usgs.gov.

**Directions:** Take I-95 in Maine to Exit 56 for Medway/Millinocket. Drive on Route 157 west through East Millinocket to Millinocket. Follow signs for Baxter State Park; the park's Togue Pond gatehouse is 18 miles from Millinocket. Just beyond the gatehouse, take the gravel Tote Road's left fork and drive 34.8 miles. Turn right at a sign for South Branch Pond Campground. Drive 2.1 miles to a parking area on the left, before the campground. Or from the junction of Routes 11 and 159 in Patten, drive west on Route 159 to Shin Pond and follow the access road to Baxter State Park's Matagamon gatehouse, which is 24 miles from Patten. From the gatehouse, continue about 7.3 miles and turn left at the sign for South Branch Pond Campground.

**Contact:** Baxter State Park, 64 Balsam Drive, Millinocket, ME 04462-2190, 207/723-5140, website: www.baxterstateparkauthority.com.

## ❸ PEAK OF THE RIDGES
**7.2 mi/6 hrs**
**in northern Baxter State Park**

Like the North Traveler hike, this 7.2-mile round-trip trek to Traveler Mountain's Peak of the Ridges follows a long, open ridge, but is longer and more arduous, making it even more remote and challenging than the North Traveler hike. It ascends about 2,500 feet in elevation.

From the parking area, walk the road into the campground, toward the northernmost South Branch Pond. Bear left through the campground, passing several sites, and turn right (south) onto the Pogy Notch Trail, which parallels the pond. In a mile, the trail passes a junction with the Howe Brook Trail and then crosses an often-dry streambed; follow the blue blazes to the left, eventually turning away from the streambed. Within another 0.4 mile, the trail turns left and ascends steeply 0.1 mile to another junction. Turn left onto the Center Ridge Trail, which climbs relentlessly and at times steeply. But you don't have to go far to enjoy your first views of the two South Branch Ponds, across to the South Branch Mountains and south toward Katahdin. After crossing an extensive talus field—where following the trail can be difficult, so watch carefully for blazes and cairns—the trail terminates at the Peak of the Ridges, a high point about a mile west of the 3,541-foot summit of the Traveler, and connected to it by a trailless ridge. Follow the same route back to your car.

**User groups:** Hikers only. No wheelchair facilities. This trail should not be attempted in winter except by hikers experienced in mountaineering and prepared for severe winter weather. It is not suitable for skis. Bikes, dogs, horses, and hunting are prohibited.

**Access, fees:** Baxter Park is open from May 15–November 1 (no camping in the park after October 15) and from December 1–March 31. An entrance fee of $12 per vehicle is charged at the gatehouse, but vehicles bearing Maine registration can enter at no charge. During the summer season, the park's Togue Pond Gate opens at 6 A.M. and closes at 10 P.M.—though it may open at 5 A.M. some summer days—and the Matagamon Gate opens at 6 A.M. and closes at 10 P.M. The road is not maintained to the trailhead in winter, but it can be skied.

**Maps:** For a park trails map, get the *Baxter State Park and Katahdin* map for $7.95 from the DeLorme Publishing Company, 800/642-0970, website: www.DeLorme.com; or the *Rangeley-Stratton/Baxter State Park–Katahdin* map, $7.95 in waterproof Tyvek, from the Appalachian Mountain Club, 800/262-4455, website: www.outdoors.org. For topographic area maps, request Wassataquoik Lake and the Traveler from USGS Map Sales, Federal Center, Box 25286, Denver, CO 80225, 888/ASK-USGS (888/275-8747), website: http://mapping.usgs.gov. **Directions:** Take I-95 in Maine to Exit 56 for Medway/Millinocket. Drive on Route 157 west through East Millinocket to Millinocket. Follow signs for Baxter State Park; the park's Togue Pond gatehouse is 18 miles from Millinocket. Just beyond the gatehouse, take the gravel Tote Road's left fork and drive 34.8 miles. Turn right at a sign for South Branch Pond Campground. Drive 2.1 miles to a parking area on the left, before the campground. Or from the junction of Routes 11 and 159 in Patten, drive west on Route 159 to Shin Pond and follow the access road to Baxter State

Park's Matagamon gatehouse, which is 24 miles from Patten. From the gatehouse, drive about 7.3 miles and turn left at the sign for South Branch Pond Campground.

**Contact:** Baxter State Park, 64 Balsam Drive, Millinocket, ME 04462-2190, 207/723-5140, website: www.baxterstateparkauthority.com.

## ▲ RUSSELL POND/ DAVIS POND LOOP

**19 mi/3 days**
**in central Baxter State Park**

Ever since I backpacked this Baxter Park loop with two friends several years ago, I've longed to get back and repeat it. Visitors to this magnificent park who hike only Katahdin—especially on a busy weekend like Labor Day—may not get a sense of remoteness. But Baxter is far enough removed from the rest of the world that if you wander away from the big mountain, you're in some real wilderness. And that's what this loop is all about. On a recent trip, my friends and I saw only a handful of other backpackers at Russell Pond and hikers on the popular Chimney Pond Trail, and one day we saw more moose (two) than people (none). The only steep stretches of this hike are the climbs to Davis Pond in the Northwest Basin and above Davis Pond to the Northwest Plateau, and the descent off Hamlin Peak. Much of this loop is easy hiking that fit backpackers can accomplish in a few hours of hiking per day. The loop hike is spread out over three days to take advantage of two excellent backcountry camping areas at Russell and Davis Ponds. At the latter, you have the lean-to and pristine hanging valley to yourself.

From Roaring Brook Campground, follow the Russell Pond Trail north a relatively flat seven miles to Russell Pond Campground, where a ranger is posted and canoes can be rented for a small fee. The hiking has small ups and downs, but is easy. Listen for early morning or evening splashes in the pond—it's probably a moose grazing. On day two, head southwest on the Northwest Basin Trail, which climbs gradually alongside a rock-strewn stream, passing small pools that invite a very chilly swim. It's a bit more than five miles and about 1,700 feet uphill to the Davis Pond lean-to.

The final day takes you up the Northwest Basin Trail onto the rocky, alpine Northwest Plateau area. At 2.2 miles past, and about 1,600 feet above Davis Pond, turn left onto the Hamlin Ridge Trail, soon passing over Hamlin Peak (4,751 feet), one of Maine's 14 4,000-footers. The trail descends the open, rocky Hamlin Ridge, with constant views down into the cliff-ringed North Basin to your left (north) and toward Katahdin on the right (south). About two miles from Hamlin Peak, you reach the North Basin Trail. To the right, it's less than a mile downhill to Chimney Pond (via the Chimney Pond Trail for the final 0.3 mile); this hike, however, turns left, following the North Basin Trail a short distance to the North Basin Cutoff, where you turn right. (For a view into the North Basin, continue straight ahead on the North Basin Trail for 0.3 mile to Blueberry Knoll; once you enjoy the vista, double back to the cutoff.) Follow the cutoff for a bit more than a half mile to the Chimney Pond Trail, turn left, and it's another 2.3 miles to Roaring Brook Campground.

**User groups:** Hikers only. No wheelchair facilities. This trail should not be attempted in winter except by experienced skiers or snowshoers prepared for severe winter weather. The trail can be skied as far as Russell Pond, but it grows very steep on the climb to Davis Pond. Bikes, dogs, horses, and hunting are prohibited.

**Access, fees:** Baxter Park is open from May 15–November 1 (no camping in the park after October 15) and from December 1–March 31. An entrance fee of $12 per vehicle is charged at the gatehouse, but vehicles bearing Maine registration can enter at no charge. During the summer season, the park's Togue Pond Gate opens at 6 A.M. and closes at 10 P.M.–though it may open at 5 A.M. some summer days. The road is not maintained to the trailhead in winter, but it can be skied. A fee of $9 per person

per night is charged for lean-to shelters ($12 in winter) and tent sites (minimum $18 per night per shelter), and $10 per person per night for a bunkhouse ($18 in winter). Advance reservations for backcountry campsites are recommended. On this hike, Russell Pond has a bunkhouse (capacity 13), four tent sites, and four lean-tos (capacity four to eight); Davis Pond has one lean-to (capacity six).

**Maps:** For a park trails map, get the *Baxter State Park and Katahdin* map for $7.95 from the DeLorme Publishing Company, 800/642-0970, website: www.DeLorme.com; or the *Rangeley-Stratton/Baxter State Park-Katahdin* map, $7.95 in waterproof Tyvek, from the Appalachian Mountain Club, 800/262-4455, website: www.outdoors.org. For topographic area maps, request Mount Katahdin and Katahdin Lake from USGS Map Sales, Federal Center, Box 25286, Denver, CO 80225, 888/ASK-USGS (888/275-8747), website: http://mapping.usgs.gov.
**Directions:** Take I-95 in Maine to Exit 56 for Medway/Millinocket. Drive on Route 157 west through East Millinocket to Millinocket. Follow signs for Baxter State Park; the park's Togue Pond gatehouse is 18 miles from Millinocket. Just beyond the gatehouse, take the gravel Tote Road's right fork and drive 8.1 miles to Roaring Brook Campground. The Russell Pond Trail begins beside the ranger station (where there is a hiker register).
**Contact:** Baxter State Park, 64 Balsam Drive, Millinocket, ME 04462-2190, 207/723-5140, website: www.baxterstateparkauthority.com.

## 5 SOUTH TURNER MOUNTAIN
**4 mi/3 hrs**

**in southern Baxter State Park**
Though just 3,122 feet in elevation, South Turner's craggy summit gives a rare view of the entire Katahdin massif from the east side. It's so overshadowed by the big mountain that many hikers don't even know about it—enhancing your chances of summiting in solitude. Sandy Stream Pond is a good place for moose viewing in the early morning or at dusk. You could

combine this four-mile hike with the Sandy Stream Pond/Whidden Ponds Loop.

From the ranger station, follow the Russell Pond Trail a quarter mile and then turn right onto the South Turner Mountain Trail/Sandy Stream Pond Trail. You soon reach Sandy Stream Pond's southeast shore, which the trail follows. As you come around the pond's far end, the South Turner Mountain Trail turns right (the Whidden Pond Trail leads left) and soon begins the steep, 1,600-foot ascent of South Turner; much of the trail cuts through dense forest. The final stretch breaks out of the trees to wide views. Descend the same way you came.

**User groups:** Hikers only. No wheelchair facilities. This trail may be difficult to snowshoe because of its steepness and severe winter weather, and is not suitable for skis. Bikes, dogs, horses, and hunting are prohibited.

**Access, fees:** Baxter Park is open from May 15–November 1 (no camping in the park after October 15) and from December 1–March 31. An entrance fee of $12 per vehicle is charged at the gatehouse, but vehicles bearing Maine registration can enter at no charge. During the summer season, the park's Togue Pond Gate opens at 6 A.M. and closes at 10 P.M.—though it may open at 5 A.M. some summer days. The road is not maintained to the trailhead in winter, but it can be skied.

**Maps:** For a park trails map, get the *Baxter State Park and Katahdin* map for $7.95 from the DeLorme Publishing Company, 800/642-0970, website: www.DeLorme.com; or the *Rangeley-Stratton/Baxter State Park-Katahdin* map, $7.95 in waterproof Tyvek, from the Appalachian Mountain Club, 800/262-4455, website: www.outdoors.org. For topographic area maps, request Mount Katahdin and Katahdin Lake from USGS Map Sales, Federal Center, Box 25286, Denver, CO 80225, 888/ASK-USGS (888/275-8747), website: http://mapping.usgs.gov.

**Directions:** Take I-95 in Maine to Exit 56 for Medway/Millinocket. Drive on Route 157 west through East Millinocket to Millinocket. Follow signs for Baxter State Park; the park's Togue Pond gatehouse is 18 miles from Millinocket. Just beyond the gatehouse, take the gravel Tote Road's right fork and drive 8.1 miles to Roaring Brook Campground. The Russell Pond Trail begins beside the ranger station (where there is a hiker register).

**Contact:** Baxter State Park, 64 Balsam Drive, Millinocket, ME 04462-2190, 207/723-5140, website: www.baxterstateparkauthority.com.

## 6 SANDY STREAM POND/ WHIDDEN PONDS LOOP

**1.5 mi/1 hr**

**in southern Baxter State Park**

This relatively flat, easy loop hits two ponds where moose are often seen, especially early in the morning or around dusk. I sat with friends on rocks on the Sandy Stream Pond shore one morning and watched a huge bull moose casually grazing on underwater plants. And the view across the southernmost of the Whidden Ponds toward the North Basin of Hamlin and Howe Peaks is terrific. Start this hike early enough, and you could catch the sunrise hitting the North Basin and moose at Sandy Stream Pond. You might also want to combine it with a jaunt up South Turner Mountain.

From the ranger station, follow the Russell Pond Trail a quarter mile, then turn right onto the South Turner Mountain Trail/Sandy Stream Pond Trail. You soon reach the southeast shore of Sandy Stream Pond, which the trail follows. As you come around the far end of the pond, the South Turner Mountain Trail leads right; this hike turns left onto the Whidden Pond Trail, following it for a mile to the first of the Whidden Ponds (also the largest and the only one directly accessed by a trail). You might turn right onto the Russell Pond Trail and walk along the pond's shore for a bit. Eventually, turn back (south) on the Russell Pond Trail for the easy hike of a bit more than a mile back to Roaring Brook Campground.

**User groups:** Hikers only. No wheelchair facilities. Bikes, dogs, horses, and hunting are prohibited. This trail should not be attempted in winter except by experienced skiers or snowshoers prepared for severe winter weather.

**Access, fees:** Baxter Park is open from May 15–November 1 (no camping in the park after October 15) and from December 1–March 31. An entrance fee of $12 per vehicle is charged at the gatehouse, but vehicles bearing Maine registration can enter at no charge. During the summer season, the park's Togue Pond Gate opens at 6 A.M. and closes at 10 P.M.—though it may open at 5 A.M. some summer days. The road is not maintained to the trailhead in winter, but it can be skied.

**Maps:** For a park trails map, get the *Baxter State Park and Katahdin* map for $7.95 from the DeLorme Publishing Company, 800/642-0970, website: www.DeLorme.com; or the *Rangeley-Stratton/Baxter State Park-Katahdin* map, $7.95 in waterproof Tyvek, from the Appalachian Mountain Club, 800/262-4455, website: www.outdoors.org. For topographic area maps, request Mount Katahdin and Katahdin Lake from USGS Map Sales, Federal Center, Box 25286, Denver, CO 80225, 888/ASK-USGS (888/275-8747), website: http://mapping.usgs.gov.

**Directions:** Take I-95 in Maine to Exit 56 for Medway/Millinocket. Drive on Route 157 west through East Millinocket to Millinocket. Follow signs for Baxter State Park; the park's Togue Pond gatehouse is 18 miles from Millinocket. Just beyond the gatehouse, take the gravel Tote Road's right fork and drive 8.1 miles to Roaring Brook Campground. The Russell Pond Trail begins beside the ranger station (where there is a hiker register).

**Contact:** Baxter State Park, 64 Balsam Drive, Millinocket, ME 04462-2190, 207/723-5140, website: www.baxterstateparkauthority.com.

## 7 HAMLIN PEAK
### 9.5 mi/6 hrs

**in southern Baxter State Park**

Hamlin Peak, at 4,751 feet, is Maine's second highest peak and one of 14 4,000-footers in the state, though it's also considered part of the Katahdin massif. Swarms of hikers climb Katahdin on summer weekends, but far fewer venture up onto Hamlin—and they are missing a lot. The constant views along the Hamlin Ridge, both into the North Basin and back toward the South Basin and Katahdin, are among the most magnificent in Maine. This 9.5-mile round-trip hike climbs about 3,200 feet in elevation and is fairly strenuous.

From Roaring Brook Campground, follow the Chimney Pond Trail an easy 2.3 miles to just beyond the Basin Ponds. Don't bypass the short side path leading right to the southernmost of the Basin Ponds, where there's a great view of your destination, Hamlin Ridge, and the North Basin. Turn right onto the North Basin Cutoff, which soon meets up with the North Basin Trail. To the right a short distance is Blueberry Knoll and views into the North Basin and South Basin. Experienced hikers will see that it's possible to bushwhack down to the pair of tiny ponds on the North Basin floor and explore that rugged glacial cirque. This hike turns left (southwest) onto the North Basin Trail, and soon takes a right and begins ascending the Hamlin Ridge Trail. Two miles farther you reach Hamlin Peak, a mound of rocks slightly higher than the vast surrounding tableland, or plateau. Descend the way you came.

Special note: For visitors making this peak part of an extended stay at Baxter State Park, another enjoyable way of hiking Hamlin is from Chimney Pond Campground, which is 3.3 miles from Roaring Brook Campground via the Chimney Pond Trail. Backpack in to Chimney Pond (be sure to make your camping reservations months in advance), and hike Hamlin Peak via the Chimney Pond, North Basin, and Hamlin Ridge trails (four miles, 2.5 hours). Chimney Pond is a good staging point for hikes of Katahdin, or even for beginning the Russell Pond/Davis Pond backpacking loop in the reverse direction.

**User groups:** Hikers only. No wheelchair facilities. This trail should not be attempted in winter except by hikers experienced in mountaineering and prepared for severe winter weather. Bikes, dogs, horses, and hunting are prohibited.

**Access, fees:** Baxter Park is open from May 15–November 1 (no camping in the park after October 15) and from December 1–March 31. An entrance fee of $12 per vehicle is charged at the gatehouse, but vehicles bearing Maine registration can enter at no charge. During the summer season, the park's Togue Pond Gate opens at 6 A.M. and closes at 10 P.M.–though it may open at 5 A.M. some summer days. The road is not maintained to the trailhead in winter, but it can be skied.

**Maps:** For a park trails map, get the *Baxter State Park and Katahdin* map for $7.95 from the DeLorme Publishing Company, 800/642-0970, website: www.DeLorme.com; or the *Rangeley-Stratton/Baxter State Park-Katahdin* map, $7.95 in waterproof Tyvek, from the Appalachian Mountain Club, 800/262-4455, website: www.outdoors.org. For topographic area maps, request Mount Katahdin and Katahdin Lake from USGS Map Sales, Federal Center, Box 25286, Denver, CO 80225, 888/ASK-USGS (888/275-8747), website: http://mapping.usgs.gov.

**Directions:** Take I-95 in Maine to Exit 56 for Medway/Millinocket. Drive on Route 157 west through East Millinocket to Millinocket. Follow signs for Baxter State Park; the park's Togue Pond gatehouse is 18 miles from Millinocket. Just beyond the gatehouse, take the gravel Tote Road's right fork and drive 8.1 miles to Roaring Brook Campground. The Chimney Pond Trail begins beside the ranger station (where there is a hiker register).

**Contact:** Baxter State Park, 64 Balsam Drive, Millinocket, ME 04462-2190, 207/723-5140, website: www.baxterstateparkauthority.com.

## 8 KATAHDIN: KNIFE EDGE LOOP

**9.3 mi/9 hrs**

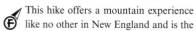

**in southern Baxter State Park**

This hike offers a mountain experience like no other in New England and is the best way to take in as much of Maine's greatest mountain as possible in a day. The hike encompasses Chimney Pond (set deep in the vast glacial cirque known as the South Basin), a challenging scramble up the Cathedral Trail, Katahdin's four peaks, the infamous Knife Edge, and the open Keep Ridge. Don't underestimate its length, difficulty, or dangers: Two of my several visits to the 5,267-foot Katahdin have come on the heels of hiker deaths on the Knife Edge (one fell, two were struck by lightning). This 9.3-mile loop gains 3,800 feet in elevation and covers some of New England's most rugged terrain—fit, experienced hikers often take eight hours or more. Once you're on the Knife Edge, there's no alternate descent route.

Follow the fairly easy Chimney Pond Trail 3.3 miles to the pond camping area (many visitors make this hike and go no farther, because the views from Chimney Pond are so beautiful). Behind the Chimney Pond ranger station, pick up the Cathedral Trail, which climbs steeply up a rockslide and the right flank of Katahdin's sweeping head wall, passing the three prominent stone buttresses known as the Cathedrals. You can scramble off trail onto each of the Cathedrals for great South Basin views.

At 1.4 miles from Chimney Pond, bear left where the trail forks, soon reaching the Saddle Trail and more level ground. Turn left (southeast) and walk 0.2 mile to the main summit, Baxter Peak, where a large sign marks the Appalachian Trail's northern terminus. Continue straight over the summit (southeast) on the Knife Edge Trail, following an increasingly narrow, rocky ridge that runs 1.1 miles to Katahdin's Pamola Peak. The trail hooks left at South Peak, and the stretch from here to Pamola becomes precipitous. At times, the footpath is barely two feet wide, with sharp drops to either side. At Chimney Peak, you scramble down the vertical wall of a ridge cleft, a spot known to intimidate more than a few hikers. Then you scramble up the other side (not as difficult) onto Pamola Peak. From here, turn right (east) on the Helon Taylor Trail, which descends the Keep Ridge, much of it open, for 3.1 miles to the Chimney Pond Trail. Turn right and walk 0.1 mile to Roaring Brook Campground.

**User groups:** Hikers only. No wheelchair facilities. This trail should not be attempted in winter except by hikers experienced in mountaineering and prepared for severe winter weather, and is only suitable for skis as far as Chimney Pond. Bikes, dogs, horses, and hunting are prohibited.

**Access, fees:** Baxter Park is open from May 15–November 1 (no camping in the park after October 15) and from December 1–March 31. An entrance fee of $12 per vehicle is charged at the gatehouse, but vehicles bearing Maine registration can enter at no charge. During the summer season, the park's Togue Pond Gate opens at 6 A.M. and closes at 10 P.M.—though it may open at 5 A.M. some summer days. The road is not maintained to the trailhead in winter, but it can be skied.

**Maps:** For a park trails map, get the *Baxter State Park and Katahdin* map for $7.95 from the DeLorme Publishing Company, 800/642-0970, website: www.DeLorme.com; or the *Rangeley-Stratton/Baxter State Park-Katahdin* map, $7.95 in waterproof Tyvek, from the Appalachian Mountain Club, 800/262-4455, website: www.outdoors.org. For topographic area maps, request Mount Katahdin and Katahdin Lake from USGS Map Sales, Federal Center, Box 25286, Denver, CO 80225, 888/ASK-USGS (888/275-8747), website: http://mapping.usgs.gov.

**Directions:** Take I-95 in Maine to Exit 56 for Medway/Millinocket. Drive on Route 157 west through East Millinocket to Millinocket. Follow signs for Baxter State Park; the park's Togue Pond gatehouse is 18 miles from Millinocket. Just beyond the gatehouse, take the gravel Tote Road's right fork and drive 8.1 miles to Roaring Brook Campground. The Chimney Pond Trail begins beside the ranger station (where there is a hiker register).

**Contact:** Baxter State Park, 64 Balsam Drive, Millinocket, ME 04462-2190, 207/723-5140, website: www.baxterstateparkauthority.com.

## 9 KATAHDIN TRAVERSE
### 10.9 mi one-way/
### 10 hrs or 1–2 days

**in southern Baxter State Park**

If my one lament about hiking the Katahdin Knife Edge Loop is that you miss the Hunt Trail, this traverse of Katahdin remedies that dilemma. Although this 10.9-mile hike, which ascends more than 4,100 feet, could be accomplished in a very long day (its length is compounded by the necessity of shuttling vehicles between Katahdin Stream and Roaring Brook Campgrounds), you can also spread it out over two days, with an overnight at Chimney Pond Campground. On the second day, you may have time to make an early morning scramble up the Cathedral Trail (Katahdin: Knife Edge Loop hike) to catch Katahdin's summit free of the afternoon crowds, or to hike up onto the spectacular Hamlin Ridge (Hamlin Peak hike).

From Katahdin Stream Campground, follow the white-blazed Hunt Trail for 5.2 miles to Katahdin's main summit, 5,267-foot Baxter Peak. (See the Katahdin: Hunt Trail hike for a more detailed description.) Turn right (east) on the Knife Edge Trail, which continues for a mile over South Peak and Knife Edge's narrow crest to Chimney Peak, drops very steeply into a notch, and climbs a few hundred feet up onto Pamola Peak (Katahdin: Knife Edge Loop hike). From here, the Dudley Trail drops steeply 1.3 miles to Chimney Pond. On day two, the 3.3-mile hike out to Roaring Brook Campground is an easy couple of hours.

**User groups:** Hikers only. No wheelchair facilities. This trail should not be attempted in winter except by hikers experienced in mountaineering and prepared for severe winter weather, and is not suitable for skis. Bikes, dogs, horses, and hunting are prohibited.

**Access, fees:** Baxter Park is open from May 15–November 1 (no camping in the park after

October 15) and from December 1–March 31. An entrance fee of $12 per vehicle is charged at the gatehouse, but vehicles bearing Maine registration can enter at no charge. During the summer season, the park's Togue Pond Gate opens at 6 A.M. and closes at 10 P.M.—though it may open at 5 A.M. some summer days. The road is not maintained to the trailhead in winter, but it can be skied.

**Maps:** For a park trails map, get the *Baxter State Park and Katahdin* map for $7.95 from the DeLorme Publishing Company, 800/642-0970, website: www.DeLorme.com; or the *Rangeley-Stratton/Baxter State Park-Katahdin* map, $7.95 in waterproof Tyvek, from the Appalachian Mountain Club, 800/262-4455, website: www.outdoors.org. For topographic area maps, request Mount Katahdin and Katahdin Lake from USGS Map Sales, Federal Center, Box 25286, Denver, CO 80225, 888/ASK-USGS (888/275-8747), website: http://mapping.usgs.gov.

**Directions:** Take I-95 in Maine to Exit 56 for Medway/Millinocket. Drive on Route 157 west through East Millinocket to Millinocket. Follow signs for Baxter State Park; the park's Togue Pond gatehouse is 18 miles from Millinocket. Just beyond the gatehouse, take the gravel Tote Road's right fork and drive 8.1 miles to Roaring Brook Campground, and leave a vehicle in the parking lot. The Chimney Pond Trail—where you will end this hike—begins beside the ranger station. Drive a second vehicle back to the fork in the Tote Road, turn right, and drive eight miles to Katahdin Stream Campground. Turn right onto the campground road and continue 0.1 mile to the day-use parking area. The Hunt Trail begins here.

**Contact:** Baxter State Park, 64 Balsam Drive, Millinocket, ME 04462-2190, 207/723-5140, website: www.baxterstateparkauthority.com.

## 10 KATAHDIN: ABOL TRAIL
**7.6 mi/7 hrs**
**in southern Baxter State Park**

 This trail follows the path of the 1816 Abol landslide, and may be the oldest existing route up the 5,267-foot Katahdin. It's the shortest way to Katahdin's main summit, Baxter Peak, but by no means easy: It climbs 4,000 feet, and the slide's steepness and loose rock make for an arduous ascent, complicated by the possibility of falling rock. And descending this trail is harder than going up, though not impossible (but believe me, it's rough on the knees).

From the day-use parking area on the Tote Road, walk to the back of the campground loop and pick up the Abol Trail. The trail leads through woods for more than a mile to the broad slide base. Pick your way carefully up the slide; watch for rockfall caused by hikers above, and take care not to kick anything down onto hikers below. At 2.6 miles, the trail reaches the level ground of the Tableland, a beautiful, sprawling alpine area, and 0.2 mile farther it connects with the Hunt Trail near Thoreau Spring. Turn right on the Hunt Trail for the final mile to Katahdin's summit, Baxter Peak, which is also the Appalachian Trail's northern terminus. By shuttling vehicles between Abol and Katahdin Stream Campgrounds, you can ascend the Abol and descend the Hunt Trail, a nine-mile hike if you go to Baxter Peak.

**User groups:** Hikers only. No wheelchair facilities. This trail should not be attempted in winter except by hikers experienced in mountaineering and prepared for severe winter weather, and is not suitable for skis. Bikes, dogs, horses, and hunting are prohibited.

**Access, fees:** Baxter Park is open from May 15–November 1 (no camping in the park after October 15) and from December 1–March 31. An entrance fee of $12 per vehicle is charged at the gatehouse, but vehicles bearing Maine registration can enter at no charge. During the summer season, the park's Togue Pond Gate opens at 6 A.M. and closes at 10 P.M.—though it may open at 5 A.M. some summer days. The road is not maintained to the trailhead in winter, but it can be skied.

**Maps:** For a park trails map, get the *Baxter State Park and Katahdin* map for $7.95 from the DeLorme Publishing Company, 800/642-0970, website: www.DeLorme.com; or the *Rangeley-Stratton/Baxter State Park-Katahdin* map, $7.95 in waterproof Tyvek, from the Appalachian Mountain Club, 800/262-4455, website: www.outdoors.org. For topographic area maps, request Mount Katahdin and Katahdin Lake from USGS Map Sales, Federal Center, Box 25286, Denver, CO 80225, 888/ASK-USGS (888/275-8747), website: http://mapping.usgs.gov.

**Directions:** Take I-95 in Maine to Exit 56 for Medway/Millinocket. Drive on Route 157 west through East Millinocket to Millinocket. Follow signs for Baxter State Park; the park's Togue Pond gatehouse is 18 miles from Millinocket. Just beyond the gatehouse, take the gravel Tote Road's left fork and drive 5.7 miles to Abol Campground and day-use parking on the left, opposite the campground entrance.

**Contact:** Baxter State Park, 64 Balsam Drive, Millinocket, ME 04462-2190, 207/723-5140, website: www.baxterstateparkauthority.com.

## 🔟 LITTLE ABOL FALLS
**1.6 mi/1 hr**

**in southern Baxter State Park**

This easy walk along a path of packed dirt and gravel ascends gently for 0.8 mile to where one of the Abol Stream branches drops over 12-foot falls into a pleasant little pool. This can be a popular hike, so if you want some solitude, go in the early morning or late in the day. From the parking area, walk up the campground road. The Little Abol Falls Trail begins at the rear of the campground, just to the right of the Abol Trail.

**User groups:** Hikers only. No wheelchair facilities. This trail should not be attempted in winter except by experienced skiers or snowshoers prepared for severe winter weather. Bikes, dogs, horses, and hunting are prohibited.

**Access, fees:** Baxter Park is open from May 15–November 1 (no camping in the park after October 15) and from December 1–March 31. An entrance fee of $12 per vehicle is charged at the gatehouse, but vehicles bearing Maine

registration can enter at no charge. During the summer season, the park's Togue Pond Gate opens at 6 A.M. and closes at 10 P.M.—though it may open at 5 A.M. some summer days. The road is not maintained to the trailhead in winter, but it can be skied.

**Maps:** For a park trails map, get the *Baxter State Park and Katahdin* map for $7.95 from the DeLorme Publishing Company, 800/642-0970, website: www.DeLorme.com; or the *Rangeley-Stratton/Baxter State Park-Katahdin* map, $7.95 in waterproof Tyvek, from the Appalachian Mountain Club, 800/262-4455, website: www.outdoors.org. For topographic area maps, request Doubletop Mountain and Mount Katahdin from USGS Map Sales, Federal Center, Box 25286, Denver, CO 80225, 888/ASK-USGS (888/275-8747), website: http://mapping.usgs.gov.

**Directions:** Take I-95 in Maine to Exit 56 for Medway/Millinocket. Drive on Route 157 west through East Millinocket to Millinocket. Follow signs for Baxter State Park; the park's Togue Pond gatehouse is 18 miles from Millinocket. Just beyond the gatehouse, take the gravel Tote Road's left fork and drive 5.7 miles to the day-use parking area on the left, opposite the entrance to Abol Campground.

**Contact:** Baxter State Park, 64 Balsam Drive, Millinocket, ME 04462-2190, 207/723-5140, website: www.baxterstateparkauthority.com.

## 🔢 KATAHDIN: HUNT TRAIL
**10 mi/8 hrs**

**in southern Baxter State Park**

This is the trail I followed on my first hike of the 5,267-foot Katahdin, when I fell in love with this magnificent mountain. Were it not for the Knife Edge, I'd describe the Hunt Trail as the most interesting route up the mountain. The trail is rugged, gains 4,100 feet in elevation, and traverses a substantial area above timberline; it's not uncommon for people to spend a very long day on this hike.

From the campground, follow the white-blazed Hunt Trail (it's the Appalachian Trail's final stretch, so in the fall you may see some through-hikers finishing their 2,174-mile journey). Just over a mile from the campground, a side trail leads left to roaring Katahdin Stream Falls. The trail continues upward through the woods, with occasional views. It abruptly breaks out above the trees, where you use iron rungs drilled into the stone to scale a short but vertical rock face.

The trail ascends the rocky, open ridge crest to the Tableland, a mile-wide plateau at about 4,500 feet, a tundra littered with rocks. The trail passes Thoreau Spring near the Abol Trail junction before ascending the summit cone to the main summit, Baxter Peak, where on a clear day you enjoy one of the finest mountain views in New England. A large sign marks the Appalachian Trail's northern terminus. Some 2,000 feet below is the blue dot of Chimney Pond. To the right (east) is the serrated crest of the Knife Edge, and to the north lie Hamlin Peak, the Howe Peaks, and the vast Baxter Park wilderness. Descend the same way you came up.

**User groups:** Hikers only. No wheelchair facilities. This trail should not be attempted in winter except by hikers experienced in mountaineering and prepared for severe winter weather, and is not suitable for skis. Bikes, dogs, horses, and hunting are prohibited.

**Access, fees:** Baxter Park is open from May 15–November 1 (no camping in the park after October 15) and from December 1–March 31. An entrance fee of $12 per vehicle is charged at the gatehouse, but vehicles bearing Maine registration can enter at no charge. During the summer season, the park's Togue Pond Gate opens at 6 A.M. and closes at 10 P.M.—though it may open at 5 A.M. some summer days. The road is not maintained to the trailhead in winter, but it can be skied.

**Maps:** For a park trails map, get the *Baxter State Park and Katahdin* map for $7.95 from the DeLorme Publishing Company, 800/642-0970, website: www.DeLorme.com; or the *Rangeley-Stratton/Baxter State Park-Katahdin*

map, $7.95 in waterproof Tyvek, from the Appalachian Mountain Club, 800/262-4455, website: www.outdoors.org. For topographic area maps, request Mount Katahdin and Katahdin Lake from USGS Map Sales, Federal Center, Box 25286, Denver, CO 80225, 888/ASK-USGS (888/275-8747), website: http://mapping.usgs.gov.

**Directions:** Take I-95 in Maine to Exit 56 for Medway/Millinocket. Drive on Route 157 west through East Millinocket to Millinocket. Follow signs for Baxter State Park; the park's Togue Pond gatehouse is 18 miles from Millinocket. Just beyond the gatehouse, take the left fork of the gravel Tote Road and drive eight miles to Katahdin Stream Campground. Turn right onto the campground road and continue 0.1 mile to the day-use parking area, where the Hunt Trail begins.

**Contact:** Baxter State Park, 64 Balsam Drive, Millinocket, ME 04462-2190, 207/723-5140, website: www.baxterstateparkauthority.com.

## 🔢 KATAHDIN STREAM FALLS
**2.4 mi/1.5 hrs**
**in southern Baxter State Park**

Katahdin Stream Falls tumbles about 50 feet and is visible from the trail after an easy walk of just over a mile. From the parking area, follow the white blazes of the Hunt Trail, which is the Appalachian Trail's final stretch. It ascends easily through the woods. After passing the Owl Trail one mile out, continue 0.1 mile on the Hunt Trail and cross Katahdin Stream on a wooden bridge. Just 0.1 mile farther, side paths lead to the waterfall. After enjoying the falls, head back the way you came.

**User groups:** Hikers only. No wheelchair facilities. This trail should not be attempted in winter except by experienced skiers or snowshoers prepared for severe winter weather. Bikes, dogs, horses, and hunting are prohibited.

**Access, fees:** Baxter Park is open from May 15–November 1 (no camping in the park after October 15) and from December 1–March 31. An entrance fee of $12 per vehicle is charged at the gatehouse, but vehicles bearing Maine registration can enter at no charge. During the summer season, the park's Togue Pond Gate opens at 6 A.M. and closes at 10 P.M.—though it may open at 5 A.M. some summer days. The road is not maintained to the trailhead in winter, but it can be skied.

**Maps:** For a park trails map, get the *Baxter State Park and Katahdin* map for $7.95 from the DeLorme Publishing Company, 800/642-0970, website: www.DeLorme.com; or the *Rangeley-Stratton/Baxter State Park-Katahdin* map, $7.95 in waterproof Tyvek, from the Appalachian Mountain Club, 800/262-4455, website: www.outdoors.org. For topographic area maps, request Doubletop Mountain and Mount Katahdin from USGS Map Sales, Federal Center, Box 25286, Denver, CO 80225, 888/ASK-USGS (888/275-8747), website: http://mapping.usgs.gov.

**Directions:** Take I-95 in Maine to Exit 56 for Medway/Millinocket. Drive on Route 157 west through East Millinocket to Millinocket. Follow signs for Baxter State Park; the park's Togue Pond gatehouse is 18 miles from Millinocket. Just beyond the gatehouse, take the gravel Tote Road's left fork and drive eight miles. Turn right into the Katahdin Stream Campground and continue 0.1 mile to the day-use parking area.

**Contact:** Baxter State Park, 64 Balsam Drive, Millinocket, ME 04462-2190, 207/723-5140, website: www.baxterstateparkauthority.com.

## 🔢 THE OWL
**6 mi/6 hrs**
**in southern Baxter State Park**

One of the most arduous hikes in Baxter State Park and one of its best-kept secrets, this six-mile round-tripper climbs some 2,600 feet to the 3,736-foot summit of the Owl, which is visible from the Hunt Trail/Appalachian Trail ridge on neighboring Katahdin. On the Thursday of a busy Labor Day weekend that saw hundreds of hikers on Katahdin, I encountered just seven other people on the Owl and spent a half hour at the summit completely alone.

From the parking area, follow the white blazes of the Hunt Trail, which is the Appalachian Trail's final stretch, ascending easily through the woods. After one mile, turn left at the sign for the Owl Trail, which you find lined with ripe blueberries in late August and early September. Within a mile from the Hunt Trail, you pass huge boulders. About 0.2 mile below the summit, you emerge onto an open ledge with a great view down into the Katahdin Stream ravine and across it to Katahdin. Some hikers may want to turn around from here, because the trail grows increasingly difficult and exposed.

If you decide to persevere, scramble up rocks to a second ledge, where a boulder perches at the brink of a precipice. After another short scramble, you reach the level shoulder of the Owl. The trail follows the crest of that narrow ridge, ducking briefly through a subalpine forest and ascending slightly to the bare ledges at the summit, where there are sweeping views in every direction. An example of Baxter's famed striped forest is visible to the west. Katahdin dominates the skyline to the east; the Northwest Plateau lies to the northeast; the Brothers, Coe, and O-J-I to the west; and the wilderness lakes along the Appalachian Trail to the south. Descend along the same route.

**User groups:** Hikers only. No wheelchair facilities. This trail should not be attempted in winter except by hikers experienced in mountaineering and prepared for severe winter weather, and is not suitable for skis. Bikes, dogs, horses, and hunting are prohibited.

**Access, fees:** Baxter Park is open from May 15–November 1 (no camping in the park after October 15) and from December 1–March 31. An entrance fee of $12 per vehicle is charged at the gatehouse, but vehicles bearing Maine registration can enter at no charge. During the summer season, the park's Togue Pond Gate opens at 6 A.M. and closes at 10 P.M.—though it may open at 5 A.M. some summer days. The road is not maintained to the trailhead in winter, but it can be skied.

**Maps:** For a park trails map, get the *Baxter State Park and Katahdin* map for $7.95 from the DeLorme Publishing Company, 800/642-0970, website: www.DeLorme.com; or the *Rangeley-Stratton/Baxter State Park-Katahdin* map, $7.95 in waterproof Tyvek, from the Appalachian Mountain Club, 800/262-4455, website: www.outdoors.org. For topographic area maps, request Doubletop Mountain and Mount Katahdin from USGS Map Sales, Federal Center, Box 25286, Denver, CO 80225, 888/ASK-USGS (888/275-8747), website: http://mapping.usgs.gov.

**Directions:** Take I-95 in Maine to Exit 56 for Medway/Millinocket. Drive on Route 157 west through East Millinocket to Millinocket. Follow signs for Baxter State Park; the park's Togue Pond gatehouse is 18 miles from Millinocket. Just beyond the gatehouse, take the gravel Tote Road's left fork and drive eight miles. Turn right into the Katahdin Stream Campground and continue 0.1 mile to the day-use parking area.

**Contact:** Baxter State Park, 64 Balsam Drive, Millinocket, ME 04462-2190, 207/723-5140, website: www.baxterstateparkauthority.com.

## 🔢 NORTH BROTHER
### 8.5 mi/6 hrs

**in southern Baxter State Park**

At 4,143 feet, Maine's seventh-highest mountain has a fairly extensive area above tree line around its summit, and the excellent views from the peak encompass Katahdin to the southeast, the remote Northwest Plateau and Basin to the east, Fort and Traveler mountains to the north, Doubletop to the west, and the wild, trailless area known as the Klondike to the immediate south. The hike gains about 2,900 feet in elevation.

From the parking lot, pick up the Marston Trail. At 1.2 miles, the Mount Coe Trail branches right; bear left with the Marston Trail. At two miles the trail passes a small pond, and at 3.4 miles it reaches a second junction with the Mount Coe Trail. To reach

the open summit of South Brother (3,930 feet), which has views comparable to North Brother for somewhat less effort, turn right at this junction and follow the Mount Coe Trail over fairly flat terrain for 0.7 mile to a side path leading left 0.3 mile to the top of South Brother. (South Brother adds two miles and more than 400 feet of climbing to this hike.) A good example of Baxter's famous striped forest is visible between South and North Brother. From the South Brother summit trail junction, turn left and climb 0.8 mile to North Brother's summit. Return the same way you hiked up.

Special note: You can combine this hike with the hike up Mount Coe, and bag South Brother as well, in a loop of 9.4 miles. The best route is to ascend the Mount Coe slide, hitting Coe first, then continuing on the Mount Coe Trail to South Brother, and finally bagging North Brother, then descending the Marston Trail. See the Mount Coe hike description for more information.

**User groups:** Hikers only. No wheelchair facilities. This trail should not be attempted in winter except by hikers experienced in mountaineering and prepared for severe winter weather, and is not suitable for skis. Bikes, dogs, horses, and hunting are prohibited.

**Access, fees:** Baxter Park is open from May 15–November 1 (no camping in the park after October 15) and from December 1–March 31. An entrance fee of $12 per vehicle is charged at the gatehouse, but vehicles bearing Maine registration can enter at no charge. During the summer season, the park's Togue Pond Gate opens at 6 A.M. and closes at 10 P.M.—though it may open at 5 A.M. some summer days. The road is not maintained to the trailhead in winter, but it can be skied.

**Maps:** For a park trails map, get the *Baxter State Park and Katahdin* map for $7.95 from the DeLorme Publishing Company, 800/642-0970, website: www.DeLorme.com; or the *Rangeley-Stratton/Baxter State Park-Katahdin* map, $7.95 in waterproof Tyvek, from the

Appalachian Mountain Club, 800/262-4455, website: www.outdoors.org. For topographic area maps, request Doubletop Mountain and Mount Katahdin from USGS Map Sales, Federal Center, Box 25286, Denver, CO 80225, 888/ASK-USGS (888/275-8747), website: http://mapping.usgs.gov.

**Directions:** Take I-95 in Maine to Exit 56 for Medway/Millinocket. Drive on Route 157 west through East Millinocket to Millinocket. Follow signs for Baxter State Park; the park's Togue Pond gatehouse is 18 miles from Millinocket. Just beyond the gatehouse, take the gravel Tote Road's left fork and drive 13.5 miles to a parking area on the right for the Marston Trail.

**Contact:** Baxter State Park, 64 Balsam Drive, Millinocket, ME 04462-2190, 207/723-5140, website: www.baxterstateparkauthority.com.

# 16 MOUNT COE
## 6.6 mi/6 hrs

**in southern Baxter State Park**

Mount Coe's 3,764-foot summit has a sweeping view of the southern end of Baxter State Park, including east over the Klondike and toward Katahdin and the Northwest Plateau. This 6.6-mile out-and-back hike ascends about 2,500 feet. From the parking area, follow the Marston Trail for 1.2 miles and then bear right onto the Mount Coe Trail. It ascends easily at first, reaching the foot of the Mount Coe rockslide, still in the forest, within a quarter of a mile. The trail emerges about a mile farther onto the open, broad scar of the slide, and for the next half mile climbs the slide's steep slabs and loose stone; this section becomes treacherous when wet, with the potential for injurious falls. Watch closely for the blazes and rock cairns, because the trail zigzags several times across the slide.

Near the top of the slide, a side trail—easy to overlook—branches right, leading 0.7 mile to the Mount O-J-I summit. This hike continues straight up the slide, enters the scrub forest, and reaches the Mount Coe summit 3.3

miles from the trailhead. It's possible to continue over Coe toward the Brothers (see the North Brother hike). This hike descends the same way you came.

**User groups:** Hikers only. No wheelchair facilities. This trail should not be attempted in winter except by hikers experienced in mountaineering and prepared for severe winter weather, and is not suitable for skis. Bikes, dogs, horses, and hunting are prohibited.

**Access, fees:** Baxter Park is open from May 15–November 1 (no camping in the park after October 15) and from December 1–March 31. An entrance fee of $12 per vehicle is charged at the gatehouse, but vehicles bearing Maine registration can enter at no charge. During the summer season, the park's Togue Pond Gate opens at 6 A.M. and closes at 10 P.M.—though it may open at 5 A.M. some summer days. The road is not maintained to the trailhead in winter, but it can be skied.

**Maps:** For a park trails map, get the *Baxter State Park and Katahdin* map for $7.95 from the DeLorme Publishing Company, 800/642-0970, website: www.DeLorme.com; or the *Rangeley-Stratton/Baxter State Park-Katahdin* map, $7.95 in waterproof Tyvek, from the Appalachian Mountain Club, 800/262-4455, website: www.outdoors.org. For topographic area maps, request Doubletop Mountain and Mount Katahdin from USGS Map Sales, Federal Center, Box 25286, Denver, CO 80225, 888/ASK-USGS (888/275-8747), website: http://mapping.usgs.gov.

**Directions:** Take I-95 in Maine to Exit 56 for Medway/Millinocket. Drive on Route 157 west through East Millinocket to Millinocket. Follow signs for Baxter State Park; the park's Togue Pond gatehouse is 18 miles from Millinocket. Just beyond the gatehouse, take the gravel Tote Road's left fork and drive 13.5 miles to a parking area on the right for the Marston Trail.

**Contact:** Baxter State Park, 64 Balsam Drive, Millinocket, ME 04462-2190, 207/723-5140, website: www.baxterstateparkauthority.com.

## 17 MOUNT O-J-I
**6.2 mi/6 hrs**
**in southern Baxter State Park**

This 6.2-mile loop up 3,410-foot Mount O-J-I is one of the most arduous hikes in Baxter State Park, excluding Katahdin. It climbs about 2,300 feet, but more significantly, involves fairly serious scrambling. Traditionally, this hike ascended the mountain's north rockslide—the logical ascent route, being the more difficult of the two slides—and descended the south slide. But Baxter Park officials decided after the summer of 2000 to no longer maintain the north slide as a trail, though hikers may continue to use it as a bushwhacking route. The maintained trail up O-J-I ascends and descends the south slide. Both slides are steep, with lots of loose rock and slabs that are hazardous when wet. Hiking time can vary greatly depending upon your comfort level on exposed rock. But you enjoy extensive views from the slides to the west and south, and excellent views from points near the summit. By the way, O-J-I takes its name from the shapes of three slides when seen from the southwest, although the slides have expanded and the letters have become obscured in recent decades.

From the parking area, walk the road toward Foster Field for about 50 feet, and turn right onto the O-J-I Trail. For the first 0.4 mile, the terrain is flat, crossing wet areas. The junction where the former North Slide Trail and the South Slide Trail diverge is no longer marked as such, so you'll have to watch for the path of the former North Slide Trail if you want to take it. Otherwise, go up the South Slide. The North Slide Trail reaches an often-dry streambed at 1.1 miles; turn left and follow it upward for 0.1 mile to the base of the north slide. Follow the trail's cairns and blazes, snaking up the slide for about a mile. The trail then reenters the woods; at 2.5 miles, turn left onto the Old Jay Eye Rock Trail, which leads 0.4 mile down a ridge to Old Jay Eye Rock, a boulder perched on the crest of the open ridge where there are long views in every direction. (Skipping this side trail cuts 0.8 mile from this hike's distance.) Double back to the main trail and follow it another 0.2 mile to the largely wooded summit, where you get a view toward Mount Coe. Continuing over the summit, the ridge opens up more, with sweeping views of Coe, Katahdin, Doubletop Mountain, and the wilderness lakes to the south. Turn right and descend the south slide, which reenters the forest within a mile and reaches the junction with the North Slide Trail 2.5 miles below O-J-I's summit. Turn left for the flat walk of 0.4 mile back to the road.

**User groups:** Hikers only. No wheelchair facilities. This trail should not be attempted in winter except by hikers experienced in mountaineering and prepared for severe winter weather, and is not suitable for skis. Bikes, dogs, horses, and hunting are prohibited.

**Access, fees:** Baxter Park is open from May 15–November 1 (no camping in the park after October 15) and from December 1–March 31. An entrance fee of $12 per vehicle is charged at the gatehouse, but vehicles bearing Maine registration can enter at no charge. During the summer season, the park's Togue Pond Gate opens at 6 A.M. and closes at 10 P.M.—though it may open at 5 A.M. some summer days. The road is not maintained to the trailhead in winter, but it can be skied.

**Maps:** For a park trails map, get the *Baxter State Park and Katahdin* map for $7.95 from the DeLorme Publishing Company, 800/642-0970, website: www.DeLorme.com; or the *Rangeley-Stratton/Baxter State Park–Katahdin* map, $7.95 in waterproof Tyvek, from the Appalachian Mountain Club, 800/262-4455, website: www.outdoors.org. For topographic area maps, request Doubletop Mountain and Mount Katahdin from USGS Map Sales, Federal Center, Box 25286, Denver, CO 80225, 888/ASK-USGS (888/275-8747), website: http://mapping.usgs.gov.

**Directions:** Take I-95 in Maine to Exit 56 for Medway/Millinocket. Drive on Route 157 west through East Millinocket to Millinocket. Follow signs for Baxter State Park; the park's Togue Pond gatehouse is 18 miles from Millinocket. Just beyond the gatehouse, take the gravel Tote Road's left fork and drive 10.5 miles to a parking area on the right for the Mount O-J-I Loop, just before Foster Field.

**Contact:** Baxter State Park, 64 Balsam Drive, Millinocket, ME 04462-2190, 207/723-5140, website: www.baxterstateparkauthority.com.

## 18 DOUBLETOP MOUNTAIN
### 6 mi/5.5 hrs
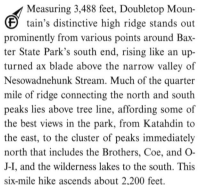

**in southern Baxter State Park**

Measuring 3,488 feet, Doubletop Mountain's distinctive high ridge stands out prominently from various points around Baxter State Park's south end, rising like an upturned ax blade above the narrow valley of Nesowadnehunk Stream. Much of the quarter mile of ridge connecting the north and south peaks lies above tree line, affording some of the best views in the park, from Katahdin to the east, to the cluster of peaks immediately north that includes the Brothers, Coe, and O-J-I, and the wilderness lakes to the south. This six-mile hike ascends about 2,200 feet.

From the parking area, cross the road onto the campground road and follow it past campsites. At half a mile, the campground road ends at the start of the Doubletop Trail. The trail begins relatively flat, until crossing a stream at 1.2 miles, where it begins a very steep climb. It levels out briefly on the mountain's north shoulder and then ascends again. After climbing a short iron ladder, you emerge above the forest a few steps from the North Peak of Doubletop, which is marked by a sign, at 3.1 miles. The trail drops off that summit to the west, then turns south and follows the ridge for 0.2 mile to the South Peak. Return the same way you hiked up.

**User groups:** Hikers only. No wheelchair facilities. This trail should not be attempted in winter except by hikers experienced in mountaineering and prepared for severe winter weather, and is not suitable for skis. Bikes, dogs, horses, and hunting are prohibited.

**Access, fees:** Baxter Park is open from May 15–November 1 (no camping in the park after October 15) and from December 1–March 31. An entrance fee of $12 per vehicle is charged at the gatehouse, but vehicles bearing Maine registration can enter at no charge. During the summer season, the park's Togue Pond Gate opens at 6 A.M. and closes at 10 P.M.—though it may open at 5 A.M. some summer days. The road is not maintained to the trailhead in winter, but it can be skied.

**Maps:** For a park trails map, get the *Baxter State Park and Katahdin* map for $7.95 from the DeLorme Publishing Company, 800/642-0970, website: www.DeLorme.com; or the *Rangeley-Stratton/Baxter State Park-Katahdin* map, $7.95 in waterproof Tyvek, from the Appalachian Mountain Club, 800/262-4455, website: www.outdoors.org. For a topographic area map, request Doubletop Mountain from USGS Map Sales, Federal Center, Box 25286, Denver, CO 80225, 888/ASK-USGS (888/275-8747), website: http://mapping.usgs.gov.

**Directions:** Take I-95 in Maine to Exit 56 for Medway/Millinocket. Drive on Route 157 west through East Millinocket to Millinocket. Follow signs for Baxter State Park; the park's Togue Pond gatehouse is 18 miles from Millinocket. Just beyond the gatehouse, take the gravel Tote Road's left fork and drive 16.9 miles, then turn left into the Nesowadnehunk Field Campground. Drive 0.3 mile to the parking area on the right.

**Contact:** Baxter State Park, 64 Balsam Drive, Millinocket, ME 04462-2190, 207/723-5140, website: www.baxterstateparkauthority.com.

## 19 KIDNEY POND LOOP
### 3.1 mi/1.5 hrs

**in southern Baxter State Park**

This easy 3.1-mile loop around lovely Kidney Pond offers a chance at seeing moose or other wildlife, and good views across the pond toward Katahdin, Doubletop, and O-J-I. Side paths lead to such scenic lakeshore spots as Colt's Point, a peninsula jutting into the pond. Paths radiate outward from the loop trail like spokes from a wheel's hub, leading to Rocky Pond and other nearby ponds. You could spend hours exploring the various little water bodies in this corner of Baxter State Park.

This hike follows the loop trail around the pond. From the rear of the parking area, pick up the trail at a sign for the Kidney Pond Loop. The trail follows the pond's shore at first, then skirts wide of it into the woods at its southern end. Where a trail bears right toward Daicey Pond about halfway through the hike, go left, passing through woods, following and crossing a stream, and eventually reaching the campground road. Turn left on the road and walk the quarter mile back to the parking area.

**User groups:** Hikers only. No wheelchair facilities. This trail should not be attempted in winter except by experienced skiers or snowshoers prepared for severe winter weather. Bikes, dogs, horses, and hunting are prohibited.

**Access, fees:** Baxter Park is open from May 15–November 1 (no camping in the park after October 15) and from December 1–March 31. An entrance fee of $12 per vehicle is charged at the gatehouse, but vehicles bearing Maine registration can enter at no charge. During the summer season, the park's Togue Pond Gate opens at 6 A.M. and closes at 10 P.M.—though it may open at 5 A.M. some summer days. The road is not maintained to the trailhead in winter, but it can be skied.

**Maps:** For a park trails map, get the *Baxter State Park and Katahdin* map for $7.95 from the DeLorme Publishing Company, 800/642-0970, website: www.DeLorme.com; or the *Rangeley-Stratton/Baxter State Park-Katahdin* map, $7.95 in waterproof Tyvek, from the Appalachian Mountain Club, 800/262-4455, website: www.outdoors.org. For a topographic area map, request Doubletop Mountain from USGS Map Sales, Federal Center, Box 25286, Denver, CO 80225.

**Directions:** Take I-95 in Maine to Exit 56 for Medway/Millinocket. Drive on Route 157 west through East Millinocket to Millinocket. Fol-

low signs for Baxter State Park; the park's Togue Pond gatehouse is 18 miles from Millinocket. Just beyond the gatehouse, take the dirt perimeter road's left fork and drive 10.6 miles, then turn left at a sign for Kidney Pond Camps. Drive 1.1 miles to the parking area.

**Contact:** Baxter State Park, 64 Balsam Drive, Millinocket, ME 04462-2190, 207/723-5140, website: www.baxterstateparkauthority.com.

## 20 POLLYWOG GORGE
**3.8 mi/2.5 hrs**
**southwest of Baxter State Park**

This hike makes a 3.8-mile loop mostly along the Appalachian Trail through scenic Pollywog Gorge, finishing on a 1.2-mile stretch of logging road. From a small ledge high above the stream, you peer down a precipitous cliff into the gorge. Day hikers could easily combine this with the Nesuntabunt Mountain hike (see next listing). Immediately before the bridge over Pollywog Stream, turn left (southbound) on the AT and follow it one mile to a side path leading about 150 feet to the gorge overlook. Continue south on the AT through woods and around Crescent Pond to the logging road, 2.6 miles from the hike's start. Turn left and follow the road 1.2 miles back to the bridge.

**User groups:** Hikers only. No wheelchair facilities. Dogs are discouraged along the Appalachian Trail in Maine. This trail should not be attempted in winter except by hikers prepared for severe winter weather, and is not suitable for skis. Bikes, horses, and hunting are prohibited.

**Access, fees:** A toll is charged on private Jo-Mary Road, which isn't passable at certain times of year due to snow or muddy conditions. The Rainbow Stream lean-to is located 2.4 miles north on the AT from the Pollywog Stream bridge (not along this hike). It's legal to camp anywhere along the AT in the 100-Mile Wilderness; low-impact camping is encouraged.

**Maps:** For a trail map, refer to map 1 in the

*Map and Guide to the Appalachian Trail in Maine,* a set of seven maps and a guidebook for $24.95 from the Maine Appalachian Trail Club or the Appalachian Trail Conference (see addresses below). For a topographic area map, request Rainbow Lake West from USGS Map Sales, Federal Center, Box 25286, Denver, CO 80225.

**Directions:** From Route 11, 15.5 miles south of the junction of Routes 11 and 157 in Millinocket and near where Route 11 crosses over Bear Brook, turn west onto private, gravel Jo-Mary Road. In 0.2 mile, pass through a gate and pay a vehicle toll. Continue six miles from the gate and bear right at a sign for the Appalachian Trail. Follow that road another 20.2 miles (ignoring unimproved roads diverging from it) to where the AT crosses Pollywog Stream on a bridge, and park at the roadside.

**Contact:** Maine Appalachian Trail Club, P.O. Box 283, Augusta, ME 04332-0283, website: www.matc.org. Appalachian Trail Conference, 799 Washington St., P.O. Box 807, Harpers Ferry, WV 25425-0807, 304/535-6331, website: www.appalachiantrail.org.

## 21 NESUNTABUNT MOUNTAIN
### 2.4 mi/1.5 hrs
**southwest of Baxter State Park**

At barely more than 1,500 feet, tiny Nesuntabunt Mountain merits notice only because the surrounding terrain is relatively flat and low here among the wilderness lakes along the Appalachian Trail's northern reaches. From an open ledge, down a short side path off the AT at Nesuntabunt's summit, hikers get a sweeping view of vast Nahmakanta Lake and Mount Katahdin, when clouds aren't smothering Maine's highest peak. You can turn this 2.4-mile hike into an overnight trip by pushing 1.9 miles beyond Nesuntabunt to the Wadleigh Stream lean-to and continuing south along Nahmakanta's isolated shore. (From Wadleigh Stream, it's 2.6 miles south along the AT to the lake's southern tip.) Or you might want to combine this hike with nearby Pollywog Gorge.

From the logging road, walk southbound (to the right) along the white-blazed AT for 1.2 miles, climbing about 500 feet to Nesuntabunt's summit. Turn left onto a side path to the open ledge. Retrace your steps to the hike's beginning.

**User groups:** Hikers only. No wheelchair facilities. Dogs are discouraged along the Appalachian Trail in Maine. This trail should not be attempted in winter except by hikers experienced in mountaineering and prepared for severe winter weather, and is not suitable for skis. Bikes, horses, and hunting are prohibited.

**Access, fees:** A toll is charged on private Jo-Mary Road, which isn't passable at certain times of year due to snow or muddy conditions. The Wadleigh Stream lean-to is located 3.1 miles south on the AT from the access road and 1.9 miles south of the Nesuntabunt Mountain summit. It's legal to camp anywhere along the AT in the 100-Mile Wilderness; low-impact camping is encouraged.

**Maps:** For a trail map, refer to map 1 in the *Map and Guide to the Appalachian Trail in Maine,* a set of seven maps and a guidebook for $24.95 from the Maine Appalachian Trail Club or the Appalachian Trail Conference (see addresses below). For a topographic area map, request Rainbow Lake West from USGS Map Sales, Federal Center, Box 25286, Denver, CO 80225.

**Directions:** From Route 11, 15.5 miles south of the junction of Routes 11 and 157 in Millinocket and near where Route 11 crosses over Bear Brook, turn west onto the private, gravel Jo-Mary Road. In 0.2 mile, pass through a gate and pay a vehicle toll. Continue six miles from the gate and bear right at a sign for the Appalachian Trail. Follow that road another 19 miles (ignoring unimproved roads diverging from it) to the AT crossing, and park at the roadside.

**Contact:** Maine Appalachian Trail Club, P.O. Box 283, Augusta, ME 04332-0283, website: www.matc.org. Appalachian Trail Conference,

799 Washington St., P.O. Box 807, Harpers Ferry, WV 25425-0807, 304/535-6331, website: www.appalachiantrail.org.

## 22 100-MILE WILDERNESS
### 99.4 mi one-way/9–10 days 8  10
**between Monson and Baxter State Park**

The 100-Mile Wilderness is a stretch of the Appalachian Trail in northern Maine that runs for 99.4 miles without crossing a paved or public road. It starts just north of Monson on Route 15 and ends at the West Branch of the Penobscot River at Abol Bridge on the Golden Road, a private logging road just outside the Baxter State Park southern boundary. The trail, however, does cross a few logging roads that provide vehicle access to the AT in the 100-Mile Wilderness. Although it has grown more popular in recent years, the 100-Mile Wilderness still constitutes one of the most remote backpacking experiences possible in New England. On an August trip, my companions and I spent evenings by ourselves on the shores of vast wilderness lakes, listening to the hysterical song of loons, and enjoying wonderful sunsets and sunrises. We swam in chilly streams and walked hours at a time some days without encountering another hiker.

This stretch of trail is busiest in August and early September, when the weather is warm and drier, the mosquitoes have dissipated somewhat (though certainly not disappeared), and AT through-hikers are passing through on their way to Katahdin. This far north, the prime hiking season is short, usually commencing once the ground has dried out in July and lasting to early October, when the cooler temperatures start to feel like winter. The number of days spent on this trail can vary greatly. Generally, the southern half, below Crawford Pond, is more mountainous and rugged; and from Crawford north the trail covers easier, flatter terrain around several vast wilderness lakes. The trail is well marked with the white blazes of the AT, and there are signs at many junctions.

Because this is such a long hike, descrip-

tions in mileage distances beginning at Route 15 and finishing at Abol Bridge are as follows:

From Route 15 (mile 0), the AT enters the woods at a trail sign; there is ample parking at a turnout. Traversing relatively easy terrain, the trail passes a series of ponds: the east shore of Spectacle Pond (mile 0.1), the south shore of Bell Pond (1.2), and then a short side path leading right to the west shore of Lily Pond (1.9). With relatively easy hiking from the highway, you reach the Leeman Brook lean-to (3.0), which sleeps six and sits above a small gorge and falls with reliable water. Continuing north, the trail crosses a gravel road (4.2) and then passes the west and north shores of Mud Pond (5.2). It crosses a gravel road (6.5) and then reaches the top of 60-foot Little Wilson Falls (6.6), one of the highest waterfalls along the AT. The trail turns sharply right, following the rim of the long, deep gorge below the falls, then descends steeply, eventually fording Little Wilson Stream (6.8) with a good view upstream into the gorge. Turn left onto a gravel road (7.2) and follow it for 100 yards, and then turn right into the woods. At mile 7.4, the trail reaches a half-mile-long ridge of exposed slate with good views to the east. At the Big Wilson logging road (9.1), turn left, follow it for 0.6 mile; then turn right off the road (9.7) and ford Big Wilson Stream, which can be difficult in high water. A bridge across the stream is 1.5 miles downstream. At mile 10, cross the Canadian Pacific Railroad line.

Less than a half mile from the railroad right-of-way, a short side path leads right to the Wilson Valley lean-to (10.4), which sleeps six; there is water at a nearby spring. At mile 11.6, cross open ledges with views of Barren Mountain. The trail fords Wilbur Brook (13.6) and Vaughn Stream (13.7) above a spectacular 20-foot waterfall that drops into a broad pool. At a logging road (14.2), turn right for 100 yards and then left again into the woods. (That road continues another 1.6 miles southwest to the old Bodfish Farm site, from which it's nearly 12 miles to Monson on Elliotsville Road.) Ford Long Pond

Stream (14.3), walk alongside narrow pools and flumes of smooth rock, and then reach a short side path at 15 miles that leads left to Slugundy Gorge, a scenic gorge and falls. Just beyond, another side path leads left 150 yards to the Long Pond Stream lean-to, which sleeps eight; get water from the nearby brook.

Beyond the shelter, the AT begins the steep climb of Barren Mountain. At mile 16.2, a side path leads to the right about 250 feet to the top of the Barren Slide, from which there are excellent views south of Lake Onawa and Boarstone Mountain. Following the ridge, the trail reaches the 2,670-foot summit of Barren Mountain (18.2), which offers sweeping views, particularly south and west; also here is an abandoned fire tower, no longer open. Dropping back into the woods, you pass a side trail (19.1) leading right 0.3 mile to the beautiful tarn called Cloud Pond and the nearby lean-to, which sleeps six; water can be obtained from a spring or the pond.

Continuing along the Barren-Chairback Ridge, the trail bounces like a yo-yo over rugged terrain, passing over the wooded 2,383-foot summit of Fourth Mountain (21.2), cliffs on Third Mountain that offer some views (23.7), and a side path leading right 0.2 mile to West Chairback Pond (24.3). Just beyond that path, the AT crosses a good stream where you may want to load up on water if you're planning to stay at the Chairback Gap lean-to, where the spring may run dry in late summer. The trail climbs steeply over Columbus Mountain, then drops into Chairback Gap, passing in front of the lean-to there, which sleeps six; the spring is about 200 yards downhill along the trail. The trail then ascends to the top of 2,219-foot Chairback Mountain (26.5), traversing its long, open crest with excellent views west and north. At the end of the ridge, the trail descends a very steep slope (26.6) of loose talus, trending left near its bottom. It passes over open ledges (26.9) with views back to Chairback Mountain, then a side path (28.7)—the sign for which is easily overlooked—leading left 0.2 mile to

East Chairback Pond. At mile 29.9, cross a wide logging road; half a mile to the right (east) is a parking area heavily used by day visitors to Gulf Hagas. The road continues east for 7.1 miles to the Katahdin Iron Works Museum.

Crossing the road, the AT passes through woods to the West Branch of the Pleasant River (30.4), a wide channel that was knee-deep during our August trip, but could be dangerous at high water. (Before fording the river, you will notice a blue-blazed trail leading back to the parking area on the logging road.) After crossing the river, the AT follows easy ground through a forest of tall white pines; a short side path (30.7) leads right to the Hermitage, a stand of white pines up to 130 feet tall. At mile 32, the AT hooks right, and a blue-blazed trail leads straight ahead to the 5.2-mile loop through Gulf Hagas, one of the most scenic areas along the AT corridor through Maine and a very worthwhile (and packless!) detour if you have the time (see the Gulf Hagas hike description). The AT ascends steadily northward for 4.2 miles, through dense forest where campsites are difficult to find, following Gulf Hagas Brook to the Carl A. Newhall lean-to and tent sites; the lean-to, accessed by a short side path off the AT (35.9), sleeps six, and water is available from the brook. Climbing steeply, the trail passes over the 2,683-foot summit of Gulf Hagas Mountain (36.8), where there are limited views to the west from just north of the true summit, and then descends to the Sidney Tappen campsite (37.7) for tents only; a nearby spring provides water. It continues north along the arduous ridge, over 3,178-foot West Peak (38.4), with limited views, and the wooded summit of 3,244-foot Hay Mountain (40.0).

At mile 40.6, the White Brook Trail departs to the right (east), descending 1.9 miles to logging roads that eventually link with the road to Katahdin Iron Works. The AT then climbs to the highest point on the ridge and one of the finest views along the 100-Mile Wilderness, the 3,654-foot summit of White Cap Mountain (41.7), where you get your first view on this hike of Mount Katahdin to the north. White Cap is the last big peak in the 100-Mile Wilderness. Descending north off White Cap and passing an open ledge with another good view toward Katahdin (42.5), the trail reaches the Logan Brook lean-to (43.1), which sleeps six and has marginal tent sites and a good stream nearby. Cross a gravel road (44.7) and then reach a lean-to (46.8), which opened in 1996 and sleeps at least six. The trail fords the East Branch of the Pleasant River (47.0), which could be difficult at high water, and then climbs over 2,017-foot Little Boardman Mountain (50.2); just 0.1 mile south of the summit are good views from open ledges.

Descending easily, the AT crosses the dirt Kokadjo-B Pond Road (51.6); to reach Route 11, you would turn right (east), continue 8.4 miles to Jo-Mary Road, then bear right, and continue another 6.2 miles to Route 11. The AT crosses Kokadjo-B Pond Road, enters the woods, and soon reaches the east shore of Crawford Pond (51.7). Then a side path (51.9), marked by a sign, leads left about 200 feet to Sand Beach, a beautiful little beach of crushed pebbles. Descending very slightly northward along an old woods road, the AT reaches a side path (54.8) leading 150 feet to the right to the Cooper Brook Falls lean-to and the spectacular cascades along Cooper Brook. Continuing along that flat woods road, the trail crosses the dirt Jo-Mary Road (58.5) beside a bridge over Cooper Brook. To reach Route 11, turn right (east) and follow Jo-Mary Road for 12 miles. To keep on the AT, cross the road and reenter the woods. The trail passes a side path (59.8) leading right 0.2 mile to the shore of Cooper Pond.

Continuing north on flat, easy terrain, the AT crosses a gravel road (61.4), fords several streams in succession (61.5), crosses another old logging road (62.0), and reaches a short side path (62.7), veering right to the Antlers campsite, a tenting area set amid red pines on a land point jutting into vast Lower Jo-Mary Lake. From that junction, the AT hooks left

and swings around the lake's west shore to a junction with the Potaywadjo Ridge Trail (64.2), which leads left and ascends steadily for one mile to broad, open ledges on Potaywadjo Ridge, with sweeping views of the lakes and mountains to the south and east. This is one of the finest viewpoints in the northern half of the 100-Mile Wilderness and a great place for picking blueberries in late August. From that junction, the AT ascends the wooded end of the ridge and then drops to the Potaywadjo Spring lean-to (66.2), which sleeps six; nearby is a large, reliable spring. Following easy terrain again, the AT crosses Twitchell Brook (66.7) and passes a junction with a side path (66.8) leading a short distance to the right to the shore of Pemadumcook Lake, where you get an excellent view across the water to Katahdin. Cross Deer Brook (68.0), an old logging road (68.8) that leads 0.2 mile to the right to a cove on Pemadumcook, and then ford a tributary of Nahmakanta Stream (68.9). A high-water bypass trail 0.2 mile long diverges from the AT (69.3) and then rejoins it (69.4). At mile 70, you ford Tumbledown Dick Stream.

The AT parallels Nahmakanta Stream, where footing grows difficult over many rocks and roots, and then crosses a gravel road (73.4); to reach Route 11, you would turn left (southwest) and continue 24 miles on this gravel road to the Jo-Mary Road. The AT crosses the gravel road and reenters the woods. At mile 73.8, the AT reaches the south shore of Nahmakanta Lake near a short side path leading to a gravel beach. It follows the lakeshore, skirting into the woods and out onto the rocky shore to a short side path (76.0) leading right to a sandy beach; the path emerges at one end of the beach, near a small spring. From here, the AT crosses Wadleigh Stream (76.3) and then reaches the Wadleigh Stream lean-to (76.4), which sleeps six; the nearby stream provides water. The trail then makes a steep ascent up Nesuntabunt Mountain; from its north summit (78.3), a short side path leads to an open ledge with an excellent view from high above Nahmakanta Lake toward Katahdin. Descending somewhat more moderately off Nesuntabunt, the AT crosses a logging road (79.5); to the right (north), it's 1.2 miles to Pollywog Bridge, and to the left (south) it's 25.2 miles to Route 11. This hike crosses the logging road and reenters the woods.

After circling Crescent Pond (80.1), the AT passes a short side path (81.1) leading left to a rather exposed ledge high above Pollywog Gorge. It then parallels Pollywog Stream to a logging road (82.1); to reach Route 11, you would turn south and follow the road 26.4 miles. The AT turns left and crosses the stream on a bridge. Walk past a dirt road branching right and reenter the woods to the right. The trail follows a picturesque gorge along Rainbow Stream for about two miles and then reaches the Rainbow Stream lean-to (84.5), which sleeps six; water is available from the stream. After crossing the stream, the trail follows the Rainbow Deadwaters for 1.6 miles to the west end of Rainbow Lake (86.5). From here, easy terrain leads to a small clearing (89.8); to the right, a short path leads to tent sites at the Rainbow Spring Campsite, and to the left, it's just a short walk to the spring and the lakeshore. Continuing along the big lake's shore, the AT reaches the Rainbow Mountain Trail at mile 90, which bears right and climbs a fairly easy 1.1 miles to the bare summit of Rainbow Mountain and excellent views, especially toward Katahdin.

The AT continues to the east end of Rainbow Lake (91.7), passes a side path (91.8) leading right 0.1 mile to Little Beaver Pond and 0.4 mile to Big Beaver Pond, and then ascends to Rainbow Ledges (93.5); from various points along the ledges you get long views south and northeast to Katahdin. Descending easily, the AT fords Hurd Brook (96.0), which can be difficult when the water is high, and reaches the Hurd Brook lean-to on the other side of the brook; it sleeps six, and water is available from the brook. From here, the trail rolls through fairly easy terrain to Golden Road (99.3). Turn right and follow the road to Abol Bridge (99.4), the terminus of this memorable trek.

**User groups:** Hikers only. No wheelchair facilities. Dogs are discouraged along the Appalachian Trail in Maine. This trail should not be attempted in winter except by hikers prepared for severe winter weather, and is not suitable for skis. Bikes, horses, and hunting are prohibited.

**Access, fees:** A fee is charged for access to privately owned Golden Road; it has been $8 per vehicle in the past, but could change. There are numerous shelters along the Appalachian Trail, and it's legal to camp anywhere along the AT in the 100-Mile Wilderness; low-impact camping is encouraged. A fee-based shuttle to road crossings along the Appalachian Trail, as well as other hiker services, is offered by Shaw's Lodging, 17 Pleasant St., P.O. Box 157, Monson, ME 04464, 207/997-3597, website: www.shawslodging.com. A hiker shuttle, free Kennebec River ferry service, and other hiker services along the Appalachian Trail in Maine are also provided by Steve Longley, P.O. Box 90, Route 201, The Forks, ME 04985, 207/663-4441 or (in Maine only) 888/FLOAT-ME, website: www.riversandtrails.com.

**Maps:** For a trail map, refer to maps 1, 2, and 3 in the *Map and Guide to the Appalachian Trail in Maine,* a set of seven maps and a guidebook for $24.95 from the Maine Appalachian Trail Club or the Appalachian Trail Conference (see addresses below). For topographic area maps, request Rainbow Lake East, Rainbow Lake West, Wadleigh Mountain, Nahmakanta Stream, Pemadumcook Lake, Jo-Mary Mountain, Big Shanty Mountain, Silver Lake, Barren Mountain East, Barren Mountain West, Monson East, and Monson West from USGS Map Sales, Federal Center, Box 25286, Denver, CO 80225.

**Directions:** You need to shuttle two vehicles for this trip. Take I-95 in Maine to Exit 56 for Medway/Millinocket. Drive on Route 157 west through East Millinocket to Millinocket. Follow signs for Baxter State Park. About a mile beyond the North Woods Trading Post (before the park entrance), bear left onto Golden Road, a private logging road where you pass through a gate and pay a toll. Continue about seven miles to the private campground at Abol Bridge. Drive over the bridge and park in the dirt lot on the left, about 0.1 mile east of where the Appalachian Trail emerges at the road. Drive a second vehicle to Monson, and pick up Route 15 north for 3.5 miles to a large turnout on the right and the trailhead for the Appalachian Trail.

**Contact:** Maine Appalachian Trail Club, P.O. Box 283, Augusta, ME 04332-0283; website: www.matc.org. Appalachian Trail Conference, 799 Washington St., P.O. Box 807, Harpers Ferry, WV 25425-0807, 304/535-6331; website: www.appalachiantrail.org.

## 23 HALF A 100-MILE WILDERNESS
### 47.8 or 51.6 mi one-way/
### 4–6 days
**between Monson and Baxter State Park**

Backpackers seeking one of the most remote experiences possible in New England, but who don't have the time to hike the entire 100-Mile Wilderness—the stretch of the Appalachian Trail in northern Maine that crosses no paved or public road for 99.4 miles—can instead backpack "half a wilderness." The AT crosses the dirt Kokadjo-B Pond Road, identified on some maps as Johnson Pond Road, a logical place to begin or conclude a trek of either the northern or southern half of the 100-Mile Wilderness. The 51.6 trail miles from this logging road south to Route 15 are characterized by rugged hiking over a landscape dominated by low mountains boasting sporadic but long views of a forest expanse with few signs of civilization. The 47.8 miles of trail north to Golden Road at Abol Bridge have an entirely different personality, traversing mostly flat, low terrain around sprawling wilderness lakes. The southern portion can take five days or more; the northern is easier and can be done in four days by fit hikers. See the trail notes

on the 100-Mile Wilderness hike for a detailed description of both options.

**User groups:** Hikers only. No wheelchair facilities. Dogs are discouraged along the Appalachian Trail in Maine. This trail should not be attempted in winter except by hikers experienced in mountaineering and prepared for severe winter weather, and is not suitable for skis. Bikes, horses, and hunting are prohibited.

**Access, fees:** A vehicle toll (most recently $8) is charged for access to privately owned Golden Road and Jo-Mary Road, which aren't passable at certain times of year due to snow or muddy conditions. There are numerous shelters along the Appalachian Trail, and it's legal to camp anywhere along the AT in the 100-Mile Wilderness; low-impact camping is encouraged. A fee-based shuttle to road crossings along the Appalachian Trail, as well as other hiker services, is offered by Shaw's Lodging, 17 Pleasant St., P.O. Box 157, Monson, ME 04464, 207/997-3597; website: www.shawslodging.com. A hiker shuttle, free Kennebec River ferry service, and other hiker services along the Appalachian Trail in Maine are also provided by Steve Longley, P.O. Box 90, Route 201, The Forks, ME 04985, 207/663-4441 or (in Maine only) 888/FLOAT-ME; website: www.riversandtrails.com.

**Maps:** For a trail map, refer to maps 1, 2, and 3 in the *Map and Guide to the Appalachian Trail in Maine*, a set of seven maps and a guidebook for $24.95 from the Maine Appalachian Trail Club or the Appalachian Trail Conference (see addresses below). For topographic area maps, request Rainbow Lake East, Rainbow Lake West, Wadleigh Mountain, Nahmakanta Stream, Pemadumcook Lake, Jo-Mary Mountain, Big Shanty Mountain, Silver Lake, Barren Mountain East, Barren Mountain West, Monson East, and Monson West from USGS Map Sales, Federal Center, Box 25286, Denver, CO 80225.

**Directions:** You need to shuttle two vehicles for this trip. To backpack the northern half of the 100-Mile Wilderness, take I-95 in Maine to Exit

56 for Medway/Millinocket. Drive on Route 157 west through East Millinocket to Millinocket. Follow signs for Baxter State Park. About a mile beyond the North Woods Trading Post (before the park entrance), bear left onto Golden Road, a private logging road where you pass through a gate and pay a toll. Continue about seven miles to the private campground at the Abol Bridge over the West Branch of the Penobscot River. Drive over the bridge and park in the dirt lot on the left, about 0.1 mile east of where the Appalachian Trail emerges at the road. Drive a second vehicle back to Millinocket. From the junction of Routes 11 and 157, go south on Route 11 for 15.5 miles and turn right (west) onto gravel Jo-Mary Road. Continue 0.2 mile and pass through a gate where a vehicle toll is collected. Proceed another six miles and bear left at a fork, following the sign for Gauntlet Falls/B-Pond (ignore the sign for the Appalachian Trail, which is also reached via the right fork). Continuing another 2.6 miles, bear right where the B-Pond Road branches left. At 14.6 miles from Route 11, the AT crosses the road 0.1 mile south of Crawford Pond; park off the road.

To backpack the southern half of the 100-Mile Wilderness, leave one car at the AT crossing of the above-mentioned logging road near Crawford Pond, then return to Route 11 and drive south to Monson. Pick up Route 15 north for 3.5 miles to a large turnout on the right and the trailhead for the Appalachian Trail at the 100-Mile Wilderness's southern end.
**Contact:** Maine Appalachian Trail Club, P.O. Box 283, Augusta, ME 04332-0283, website: www.matc.org. Appalachian Trail Conference, 799 Washington St., P.O. Box 807, Harpers Ferry, WV 25425-0807, 304/535-6331, website: www.appalachiantrail.org.

## 24 WHITE CAP MOUNTAIN
**23 mi/2–3 days**
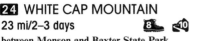
**between Monson and Baxter State Park**

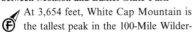 At 3,654 feet, White Cap Mountain is the tallest peak in the 100-Mile Wilderness, the 99.4-mile stretch of the Appalachian Trail through northern Maine that isn't crossed by a paved or public road. White Cap is also the last big peak in the Wilderness for northbound hikers and offers excellent views, especially toward Katahdin. A remote summit, White Cap can be reached on a two- or three-day trek via the logging road that accesses the AT near Gulf Hagas.

From the parking area, follow the blue-blazed trail 0.2 mile to the white-blazed Appalachian Trail at the West Branch of the Pleasant River, a normally knee-deep channel about 80 feet across, which you must ford (bring a pair of sandals or old sneakers for this stony crossing). Continue along the wide, flat AT, past a side trail 0.2 mile from the river, which leads to campsites at Hay Brook. At 0.3 mile, another side path leads about 200 feet into the Hermitage, a grove of ancient white pine trees, some as tall as 130 feet. The AT continues over easy ground among other giant pines to the junction with the Gulf Hagas Trail, 1.3 miles from the river (a worthwhile detour from this hike; see the Gulf Hagas hike description). The AT turns sharply right and ascends steadily northward for 4.2 miles, following Gulf Hagas Brook through dense forest to the Carl A. Newhall lean-to and tent sites, reached by a short side path off the AT; the lean-to sleeps six, and water is available from the brook.

Climbing steeply, the trail passes over the 2,683-foot summit of Gulf Hagas Mountain 6.6 miles from the road, where there are limited views to the west from just north of the true summit. After descending to the Sidney Tappen campsite, the AT yo-yos north along the arduous ridge, over 3,178-foot West Peak (8.2 miles), with limited views, and the wooded summit of 3,244-foot Hay Mountain (9.8 miles). The trail dips again, passing a junction at 10.4 miles with the White Brook Trail (which descends east 1.9 miles to logging roads that eventually link with the road to Katahdin Iron Works). The AT then climbs to the White Cap summit. Return the way you came.

**User groups:** Hikers only. No wheelchair facilities. Dogs are discouraged along the Appalachian Trail in Maine. This trail should not be attempted in winter except by hikers experienced in mountaineering and prepared for severe winter weather, and is not suitable for skis. Bikes, horses, and hunting are prohibited.

**Access, fees:** This section of the Appalachian Trail is reached via a private logging road, and a nominal per-person toll is collected; children under 15 enter free. The access road isn't passable at certain times of year due to snow or muddy conditions. The Carl A. Newhall lean-to, with tent sites, is located 5.7 miles north on the AT from the parking area, and the Sidney Tappen campsite, for tents only, lies 1.8 miles farther north. It's legal to camp anywhere along the AT in the 100-Mile Wilderness; low-impact camping is encouraged.

**Maps:** For a trail map, refer to map 2 in the *Map and Guide to the Appalachian Trail in Maine,* a set of seven maps and a guidebook for $24.95 available from the Maine Appalachian Trail Club or the Appalachian Trail Conference (see addresses below). For topographic area maps, request Hay Mountain, Big Shanty Mountain, Barren Mountain East, and Silver Lake from USGS Map Sales, Federal Center, Box 25286, Denver, CO 80225.

**Directions:** From Route 11, 5.5 miles north of Brownville Junction and 25.6 miles south of Millinocket, turn west onto a gravel road at a sign for Katahdin Iron Works. Follow it nearly seven miles to a gate where an entrance fee is collected. Beyond the gate, cross the bridge and turn right. Drive three miles, bear left at a fork, and then continue another 3.7 miles to a parking area (half a mile before the road's crossing of the Appalachian Trail).

**Contact:** Maine Appalachian Trail Club, P.O. Box 283, Augusta, ME 04332-0283, website: www.matc.org. Appalachian Trail Conference, 799 Washington St., P.O. Box 807, Harpers Ferry, WV 25425-0807, 304/535-6331, website: www.appalachiantrail.org.

## 25 GULF HAGAS
**8 mi/5.5 hrs**
**between Monson and Baxter State Park**

Known as Maine's Little Grand Canyon, Gulf Hagas is a deep, narrow canyon along the West Branch of the Pleasant River that inspired a friend and me to ooh and aah nonstop throughout our hike along its rim. At every turn we'd think we had seen a view without comparison in New England, then we'd reach another lookout that completely blew us away again. Admiring its sheer walls that drop right into a boulder-choked, impassable river, it's easy to understand why the Abenaki gave it the name "hagas," their word for "evil place." The blue-blazed loop trail through the gulf is a 5.2-mile detour off the Appalachian Trail in the 100-mile Wilderness, but the round-trip hike from the parking area is eight miles. This trail goes through very little elevation gain or loss, but runs constantly up and down over rugged, rocky terrain; your hike could easily take more than the estimated 5.5 hours, especially when you start hanging out at the many waterfalls and clifftop viewpoints. Be forewarned: This is a very popular hike in summer, so expect crowds.

From the parking area, follow the blue-blazed trail 0.2 mile to the white-blazed Appalachian Trail at the West Branch of the Pleasant River, a normally knee-deep channel about 80 feet across, which you must ford (bringing a pair of sandals or old sneakers for this stony crossing makes it much easier on the feet). Continuing along the wide, flat AT, pass a side trail 0.2 mile from the river that leads to campsites at Hay Brook. At 0.3 mile, another side path leads about 200 feet into the Hermitage, a grove of ancient white pine trees, some as tall as 130 feet. The AT continues over easy ground among other giant pines to the junction with the Gulf Hagas Trail, 1.3 miles from the river. The AT turns sharply right, but continue straight onto the blue-blazed trail, immediately crossing Gulf Hagas Brook. Bear left onto the loop trail. At 0.1 mile, a side path leads left to beautiful Screw Auger Falls on Gulf Hagas Brook. At 0.2 mile, another side path leads to the bottom of Screw Auger. (The brook continues down through a series of cascades and pools, including some spots ideal for swimming.)

The Gulf Hagas Trail continues down to the canyon rim, weaving in and out of the forest to views from the canyon rim and dropping down to the riverbank in places. Significant features along the rim include Hammond Street Pitch, a view high above the river, reached on a short path at 0.7 mile; the Jaws Cascades (seen from side paths or views at 1.2, 1.4, and 1.5 miles); Buttermilk Falls at 1.8 miles; Stair Falls at 1.9 miles; Billings Falls at 2.7 miles; and a view down the gulf from its head at 2.9 miles. Three miles into the loop, turn right onto the Pleasant River Road, an old logging road that is at first a footpath but widens over the 2.2 miles back to the start of this loop. The logging road provides much easier walking and a faster return route than doubling back along the gulf rim.

**User groups:** Hikers only. No wheelchair facilities. Dogs are discouraged along the Appalachian Trail in Maine. Portions of this trail are difficult to ski or snowshoe. Bikes, horses, and hunting are prohibited.

**Access, fees:** Gulf Hagas is reached via a private logging road, and a nominal per-person toll is collected; children under 15 enter free. The access roads are not passable at certain times of year due to snow or muddy conditions.

**Maps:** For a trail map, refer to map 2 in the *Map and Guide to the Appalachian Trail in Maine,* a set of seven maps and a guidebook for $24.95 available from the Maine Appalachian Trail Club or the Appalachian Trail Conference (see addresses below). For topographic area maps, request Barren Mountain East and Silver Lake from USGS Map Sales, Federal Center, Box 25286, Denver, CO 80225.

**Directions:** From Route 11, 5.5 miles north of Brownville Junction and 25.6 miles south of Millinocket, turn west onto a gravel road at a sign for Katahdin Iron Works. Follow it nearly seven miles to a gate where an entrance fee is collected. Beyond the gate, cross the bridge and turn right. Drive three miles, bear left at a fork, and then continue another 3.7 miles to a parking area (half a mile before the road crosses the Appalachian Trail).

**Contact:** Maine Appalachian Trail Club, P.O. Box 283, Augusta, ME 04332-0283, website: www.matc.org. Appalachian Trail Conference, 799 Washington St., P.O. Box 807, Harpers Ferry, WV 25425-0807, 304/535-6331, website: www.appalachiantrail.org.

## 26 BARREN MOUNTAIN AND SLUGUNDY GORGE
**8 mi/6 hrs**
**northeast of Monson**

By employing dirt logging roads to access this stretch of the Appalachian Trail, you can make a one-day or an overnight hike into this picturesque and varied area of the 100-Mile Wilderness (see the hike by that name). The round-trip hike to the summit of Barren Mountain entails eight demanding miles round-trip and 2,000 feet of climbing, but it's just 1.6 miles round-trip to Slugundy Gorge. Barren and Slugundy are reached by walking north on the AT, but just half a mile south on the trail lies a broad, 20-foot-high waterfall along Vaughn Stream (an easy detour not figured into this hike's distance). The one caveat about this hike is that Long Pond Stream can be very difficult to cross, so it's best to go in late summer or early fall, when water levels are down.

From the dirt road, turn right (north) onto the AT. Within 0.1 mile, ford Long Pond Stream. The trail parallels pools and flumes in the stream for more than half a mile; after it turns uphill, a short side path leads left to Slugundy Gorge, a scenic gorge and falls. Just beyond, another side path leads left 150 yards to the Long Pond Stream lean-to. Beyond the shelter, the AT begins the steep Barren Mountain climb. At two miles, a side path leads right about 250 feet to the top of the Barren Slide, from which there are excellent views south of Lake Onawa and Boarstone Mountain. Following the ridge, the trail reaches the aptly named, 2,670-foot summit of Barren Mountain two miles beyond the slide, where there are sweeping views, particularly south and west; an abandoned fire tower stands at the summit. Continuing north on the AT for 0.9 mile brings you to a side trail leading right 0.3 mile to the beautiful tarn called Cloud Pond and the nearby lean-to, but to finish this hike, turn around and hike back the way you came.

**User groups:** Hikers only. No wheelchair facilities. Dogs are discouraged along the Appalachian Trail in Maine. Portions of this trail are difficult to ski or snowshoe. Bikes, horses, and hunting are prohibited.

**Access, fees:** Parking and access are free. The dirt roads from Monson aren't passable at certain times of year due to snow or muddy conditions. The Long Pond Stream lean-to is along the Appalachian Trail 0.9 mile into this hike, and the Cloud Pond lean-to lies 1.2 miles beyond the summit of Barren Mountain. It's legal to camp anywhere along the AT in the 100-Mile Wilderness; low-impact camping is encouraged.

**Maps:** For a trail map, refer to map 3 in the *Map and Guide to the Appalachian Trail in Maine,* a set of seven maps and a guidebook for $24.95 from the Maine Appalachian Trail Club or the Appalachian Trail Conference (see addresses below). For topographic area maps, request Monson East, Barren Mountain West, and Barren Mountain East from USGS Map Sales, Federal Center, Box 25286, Denver, CO 80225.

**Directions:** From the center of Monson, drive half a mile north on Route 15 and turn right onto Elliottsville Road. Continue 7.8 miles to Big Wilson Stream, cross the bridge, and then turn left onto a dirt road. Drive another 2.8 miles to the Bodfish Farm, bear left at a fork and go 2.9 miles farther to where the white-blazed Appalachian Trail crosses the dirt road, known as the Bodfish Farm–Long Pond Tote Road; park at the roadside.

**Contact:** Maine Appalachian Trail Club, P.O. Box 283, Augusta, ME 04332-0283, website: www.matc.org. Appalachian Trail Conference, 799 Washington St., P.O. Box 807, Harpers Ferry, WV 25425-0807, 304/535-6331, website: www.appalachiantrail.org.

## Chapter 2

© MICHAEL LANZA

# Down East

**D**own East Maine harbors some of the best coastal hiking you'll find anywhere. This chapter's 26 hikes are all within Acadia National Park and Camden Hills State Park. Occupying 47,633 acres of granite-domed mountains, woodlands, lakes, ponds, and ocean shoreline, mostly on Mount Desert Island, Acadia is one of the country's smallest, yet most popular, national parks. Glaciers carved a unique landscape here of mountains rising as high as 1,500 feet virtually out of the ocean—most of them thrusting bare summits into the sky—and innumerable islands, bays, and coves that collaborate to create a hiking environment unlike any other in New England.

Acadia boasts more than 120 miles of hiking trails and 45 miles of carriage roads ideal for hiking, running, mountain biking, snowshoeing, or cross-country skiing. Many of the hikes described in this chapter are relatively short but lead to spectacular views of mountains, ocean, and islands. Although some trails are steep and rugged, most of these hikes are suitable for young children.

July and August are crowded months on Mount Desert Island. May, June, September, and October are much less crowded; spring tends to be cool and sometimes rainy, while fall is drier, with its share of both warm and cool days. Snowfall is rare in winter.

From May 1–October 31, the park entrance fee is $20 per vehicle—or $5 for walkers, bicyclists, or motorcyclists—for a seven-day pass. A one-year vehicle pass costs $40. From late June–mid-October, the Island Explorer shuttle bus provides free transportation from local lodges and campgrounds to points within the park and across Mount Desert Island; contact Downeast Transportation, 207/667-5796, website: www.exploreacadia.com/index.html. Camping reservations can be made by calling 800/365-CAMP or through the park's website. There are two campgrounds in Acadia: Blackwoods Campground, off Route 3 just south of Cadillac Mountain and east of Seal Harbor, is open year-round; Seawall Campground, off Route 102A east of Bass Harbor, opens in late June and closes after Labor Day.

Isle au Haut, the outermost island in Penobscot Bay, harbors a remote outpost of Acadia National Park. Reached by a mail boat/ferry from Stonington (contact the Isle au Haut Boat Company, 207/367-5193, website: www.isleauhaut.com), Isle au Haut (pronounced "eyel a ho" locally) has 18 miles of hiking trails on rocky coastline and low hills, a couple of dirt roads, and a campground with five lean-to shelters and a water pump less than a quarter of a mile from the boat landing at Duck Harbor. Isle au Haut can be visited on a day trip or for overnight stays.

Isle au Haut's lean-to shelters can be reserved from May 15–October 15 by contacting the park; reservations are required. Reservations requests cannot be postmarked or made in person at park headquarters before April 1. Camping reservations cost $25 per site, regardless of the number of nights. Camping is limited to three nights from mid-June–mid-September, and five nights the rest of the year. You can pitch a tent inside the lean-to only (which is advised in early summer, when the mosquitoes are vicious). Park rangers discourage bikes because of the limited roads, and bikes are prohibited from hiking trails. No wheelchair facilities are available.

Across the 5,500 acres of Camden Hills State Park, 25 miles of hiking trails follow the coast and weave through the Megunticook Mountain range above the town of Camden, where the hills rise from near sea level to 1,380 feet. The trails offer a variety of hiking experiences, from coastal walks to quiet, forested heights and dramatic cliff-top views. Because these hikes are nearby and similar in character to the hikes in Acadia, hikers planning a trip to Acadia or Camden should consider linking up the two places. The park also has a campground and picnic area.

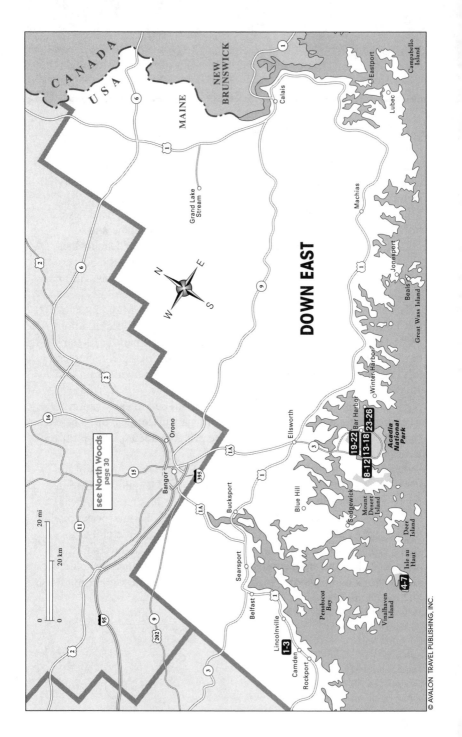

© AVALON TRAVEL PUBLISHING, INC.

# ◼ MAIDEN CLIFF
## 2 mi/1.5 hrs

**in Camden Hills State Park**

This is my favorite hike in Camden Hills State Park. The Scenic Trail follows the open cliff tops high above sprawling Megunticook Lake, with extensive views of the hills to the west. It is a great hike for late in the day, when the sun is sinking toward those hills and sparkling off the lake.

From the parking lot, follow the wide Maiden Cliff Trail, which ascends steadily through the woods for a half mile. Bear right on the Ridge Trail, reaching an open area and the junction with the Scenic Trail in 0.3 mile. Turn left (northwest) on the Scenic Trail, following the cliff tops with outstanding views for a quarter mile and then descending into the woods again to reach the junction with the Maiden Cliff Trail (marked by a sign) a half mile from the Ridge Trail. Before descending the Maiden Cliff Trail back to your car, continue ahead 100 feet to the Maiden Cliff; here a large wooden cross marks the spot where a young girl named Elenora French fell to her death in 1864. The cliffs seem to drop almost straight down into the lake. Double back and descend the Maiden Cliff Trail for nearly a mile to the parking lot.

**User groups:** Hikers, snowshoers, and dogs. Dogs must be leashed. No wheelchair facilities. This trail is not suitable for skis. Bikes and horses are prohibited. Hunting is allowed in season.

**Access, fees:** Parking and access are free at the Maiden Cliff Trailhead. A fee of $2 per person (age 12 and over) is charged at the state park entrance. It's 50 cents for children age 5–12, and children under 5 and adults over 65 are free. The park season is May 15–October 15, although this trail is accessible year-round. No staff is on duty and no fee is collected off-season.

**Maps:** A basic trail system map is available at the state park entrance on U.S. 1, two miles north of the Route 52 junction in Camden. Or get the *Camden-Pleasant-Weld/Mahoosuc-Evans map*, $7.95 in waterproof Tyvek, from the Appalachian Mountain Club, 800/262-4455, website: www.outdoors.org. For topographic area maps, request Camden and Lincolnville from USGS Map Sales, Federal Center, Box 25286, Denver, CO 80225, 888/ASK-USGS (888/275-8747), website: http://mapping.usgs.gov.

**Directions:** From the junction of Route 52 and U.S. 1 in Camden, drive west on Route 52 for three miles to a parking area on the right (just before Megunticook Lake). The Maiden Cliff Trail begins at the back of the lot.

**Contact:** Camden Hills State Park, 280 Belfast Rd., Camden, ME 04843, 207/236-3109 in season, 207/236-0849 off-season. Maine Department of Conservation, Bureau of Parks and Lands, 286 Water St., Key Bank Plaza, 3rd and 5th floors, Augusta, ME 04333-0022, 207/287-3821, website: www.state.me.us/doc/parks/.

# ◼ MOUNT MEGUNTICOOK TRAVERSE
## 5.3 mi one-way/3 hrs

**in Camden Hills State Park**

This fairly easy traverse of the highest mountain in Camden Hills State Park combines the good views of the Maiden Cliff (see previous listing) and Ocean Lookout (see following listing) hikes with a pleasant walk along the mostly wooded ridge—though this ridge has its own views as well.

From the parking area on Mount Battie Road, follow the Mount Megunticook Trail for a mile to Ocean Lookout, where you get terrific views south and east of the Camden area and the Penobscot Bay islands. Continue northwest on the Ridge Trail, passing over the wooded 1,380-foot summit of Megunticook, a half mile beyond Ocean Lookout. A mile past the summit, stay left on the Ridge Trail where Zeke's Trail branches right; then a half mile farther, stay right where the Jack Williams Trail enters from the left. Two miles past the summit, walk straight onto the Scenic Trail, following the open cliff tops with views of

Megunticook Lake and the hills to the west. Descending into the woods again, you reach the Maiden Cliff Trail (marked by a sign) a half mile from the Ridge Trail. Before heading down, though, continue ahead 100 feet to the Maiden Cliff; here a large wooden cross marks the spot where a young girl named Elenora French fell to her death in 1864. The cliffs seem to drop almost straight down into the lake. Double back and descend the Maiden Cliff Trail for nearly a mile to the parking lot on Route 52.

**User groups:** Hikers, snowshoers, and dogs. Dogs must be leashed. No wheelchair facilities. This trail is not suitable for skis. Bikes and horses are prohibited. Hunting is allowed in season.

**Access, fees:** Parking and access are free at the Maiden Cliff Trailhead. A fee of $2 per person (age 12 and over) is charged at the state park entrance. It's 50 cents for children age 5–12, and children under 5 and adults over 65 are free. The park season is May 15–October 15, although this trail is accessible year-round. No staff is on duty and no fee is collected off-season.

**Maps:** A basic trail system map is available at the state park entrance. Or get the *Camden-Pleasant-Weld/Mahoosuc-Evans map,* $7.95 in waterproof Tyvek, from the Appalachian Mountain Club, 800/262-4455, website: www.outdoors.org. For topographic area maps, request Camden and Lincolnville from USGS Map Sales, Federal Center, Box 25286, Denver, CO 80225, 888/ASK-USGS (888/275-8747), website: http://mapping.usgs.gov.

**Directions:** Two vehicles must be shuttled at either end of this hike. From the junction of Route 52 and U.S. 1 in Camden, drive west on Route 52 for three miles to a parking area on the right (just before Megunticook Lake). The Maiden Cliff Trail begins at the back of the lot. Leave one vehicle there. Drive back to Camden and head north on U.S. 1 for two miles to the state park entrance on the left. Past the entrance gate, turn left on the Mount

Battie Road and then right into a parking lot marked with a sign reading "Hikers Parking." The Mount Megunticook Trail begins at the back of the lot.

**Contact:** Camden Hills State Park, 280 Belfast Rd., Camden, ME 04843, 207/236-3109 in season, 207/236-0849 off-season. Maine Department of Conservation, Bureau of Parks and Lands, 286 Water St., Key Bank Plaza, 3rd and 5th floors, Augusta, ME 04333-0022, 207/287-3821, website: www.state.me.us/doc/parks/.

## 3 OCEAN LOOKOUT
**2 mi/1.5 hrs**
**in Camden Hills State Park**

This relatively easy hike to the best viewpoint on Mount Megunticook—which is the biggest hill in Camden Hills State Park— is very popular because it offers a wide view of the Camden area and the Penobscot Bay islands. My wife and I hiked up here on a weekday afternoon and had the view to ourselves for a little while: Mount Battie was visible below us, and a cloud bank rolling in off the ocean crested like a wave over Camden.

Follow the Mount Megunticook Trail for one mile to Ocean Lookout, 1,300 feet above the sea. The wooded summit of 1,380-foot Mount Megunticook lies a half mile farther north on the Ridge Trail (see the previous descriptions of the Mount Megunticook Traverse hike), but this hike ends at the lookout. After you've looked out, return the same way you came.

**User groups:** Hikers, snowshoers, and dogs. Dogs must be leashed. No wheelchair facilities. This trail is not suitable for skis. Bikes and horses are prohibited. Hunting is allowed in season.

**Access, fees:** A fee of $2 per person (age 12 and over) is charged at the state park entrance; it's 50 cents for children age 5–12, and children under 5 and adults over 65 are free. The park season is May 15–October 15. No staff is on duty and no fee is collected off-season.

**Maps:** A basic trail system map is available at

the state park entrance. Or get the *Camden-Pleasant-Weld/Mahoosuc-Evans map,* $7.95 in waterproof Tyvek, from the Appalachian Mountain Club, 800/262-4455, website: www.outdoors.org. For topographic area maps, request Camden and Lincolnville from USGS Map Sales, Federal Center, Box 25286, Denver, CO 80225, 888/ASK-USGS (888/275-8747), website: http://mapping.usgs.gov.

**Directions:** The entrance to Camden Hills State Park is along U.S. 1, two miles north of the Route 52 junction in Camden. After passing through the entrance gate, turn left on Mount Battie Road and then right into a parking lot marked with a sign reading "Hikers Parking." The Mount Megunticook Trail begins at the back of the lot.

**Contact:** Camden Hills State Park, 280 Belfast Rd., Camden, ME 04843, 207/236-3109 in season, 207/236-0849 off-season. Maine Department of Conservation, Bureau of Parks and Lands, 286 Water St., Key Bank Plaza, 3rd and 5th floors, Augusta, ME 04333-0022, 207/287-3821, website: www.state.me.us/doc/parks/.

# 4 ISLE AU HAUT: EBEN'S HEAD
## 1 mi/0.75 hr

**in Acadia National Park on Isle au Haut**

Eben's Head is the rocky bluff jutting into the ocean at the mouth of Duck Harbor opposite the boat landing. I watched the sunset behind Eben's Head two nights straight before getting up early one morning and walking the trail out onto the head. There, I stood atop cliffs above the pounding surf, watching morning fog slowly lift off the ocean. I also spent some time exploring the cove on the other side of Eben's Head before returning the same way I hiked in. I highly recommend the short walk out here to catch the sunset or sunrise—or on any foggy morning or evening.

From the boat landing at Duck Harbor, turn left on the trail toward the water pump. Pass the trail branching right for the campground and continue straight onto Western Head Road.

Follow it past the water pump and out to the main road. Turn left and follow the dirt main road around Duck Harbor. About 0.1 mile after the main road turns inland, you'll pass the Duck Harbor Trail on the right; then turn left onto the Eben's Head Trail, which leads through woods out to that rocky bluff visible from the boat landing.

**User groups:** Hikers and dogs. Dogs must be leashed in the park and are prohibited in the campground. No wheelchair facilities. The island rarely gets enough snow for winter activities. Bikes, horses, and hunting are prohibited.

**Access, fees:** Isle au Haut is reached by mail boat/ferry from Stonington, Maine, to Duck Harbor, the starting point for the four Isle au Haut hikes described in this chapter. The round-trip cost in 2004 was $32 for adults and $16 for children under age 12. For information, contact the Isle au Haut Boat Company, P.O. Box 709, Sea Breeze Ave., Stonington, ME 04651, 207/367-5193, website: www.isleauhaut .com. The ferry is a small boat and does not transport motor vehicles. The Duck Harbor Campground has five lean-to shelters that can sleep up to six people each, and each lean-to site has a fire ring and picnic table. The lean-to shelters can be reserved from May 15–October 15 by contacting the park (see contact information below); reservations are required. Reservations requests cannot be postmarked or made in person at park headquarters before April 1. Camping reservations cost $25 per site, regardless of the number of nights.

**Maps:** A basic map of island trails and roads is issued free to visitors arriving on the ferry or to those with camping reservations. The park website has a map of Isle au Haut. Good trail maps of the area are the waterproof *Acadia National Park* (map 212) for $9.95 from Trails Illustrated, 800/962-1643, website: http://maps.nationalgeographic.com/trails/; and the *Hiking and Biking Map to Acadia National Park and Mount Desert Island,* $7.95 in waterproof Tyvek, from the Appalachian Mountain Club, 800/262-4455, website:

www.outdoors.org. For topographic island maps, request Isle au Haut West and Isle au Haut East from USGS Map Sales, Federal Center, Box 25286, Denver, CO 80225, 888/ASK-USGS (888/275-8747), website: http://mapping.usgs.gov.

**Directions:** To reach the dock where the ferry departs for Isle au Haut, take Route 15 to Main Street in Stonington and turn left at Bartlett's Market; the ferry landing is past the firehouse, at the end of the pier.

**Contact:** Acadia National Park, P.O. Box 177, Eagle Lake Rd., Bar Harbor, ME 04609-0177, 207/288-3338, website: www.nps.gov/acad. Friends of Acadia, P.O. Box 45, 43 Cottage St., Bar Harbor, ME 04609, 207/288-3340 or 800/625-0321, website: www.friendsofacadia.org.

## 5 ISLE AU HAUT: WESTERN HEAD LOOP

**5 mi/3 hrs**

**in Acadia National Park on Isle au Haut**

If you have time for just one hike on Isle au Haut, this is the one to take. It follows the stunning rocky coast around Western Head, offers the opportunity at low tide to wander onto the tiny island known as Western Ear, and climbs over 314-foot Duck Harbor Mountain, which boasts the most sweeping views on the island. Although much of the hike is relatively flat, the trail is fairly rugged in places. My companions on this hike ranged in age from 11 to 71, and we all equally enjoyed exploring the shore and woods—as well as receiving a surprise visit from a seal.

From the boat landing at Duck Harbor, follow the trail leading left toward the water pump. Pass the trail branching right for the campground and continue straight until reaching Western Head Road. Bearing left along the road, it's about 200 yards to the water pump (if you need water). For this hike, take the grassy road to the right and follow it for less than a mile. Turn right onto the Western Head Trail, which reaches the coast within about a half mile. The trail turns left (south)

and follows the rugged coast out to the point at Western Head, where that trail ends and the Cliff Trail begins. (At low tide, you can walk across the narrow channel out to Western Ear. Be careful not to get trapped out there, or you'll have to wait hours for the tide to go out again.)

The Cliff Trail heads northward into the woods, alternately following more rugged coastline and turning back into the forest to skirt steep cliffs. It reaches the end of Western Head Road in less than a mile. Turn left and follow the road about a quarter mile. When you see a cove on your right, turn right (watch for the trail sign, which is somewhat hidden) onto the Goat Trail. (The Western Head Road leads directly back to the Duck Harbor landing, a hike of less than two miles, and is a good option for hikers who want to avoid the steep rock scrambling on Duck Harbor Mountain.) Follow the Goat Trail along the coast for less than a half mile. At scenic Squeaker Cove, turn left onto the Duck Harbor Mountain Trail; from here it's a bit more than a mile back to the Duck Harbor landing. The trail grows steep, involving somewhat exposed scrambling up rock slabs, and traverses several open ledges on Duck Harbor Mountain, with terrific long views of Isle au Haut Bay to the west (including Vinalhaven Island, the nearest piece of land across Isle au Haut Bay) and the Penobscot Bay islands and peninsulas to the north. The trail then descends to Western Head Road; turn right for Duck Harbor.

**User groups:** Hikers and dogs. Dogs must be leashed in the park and are prohibited from the campground. No wheelchair facilities. The island rarely gets enough snow for winter activities. Bikes, horses, and hunting are prohibited.

**Access, fees:** Isle au Haut is reached by mail boat/ferry from Stonington, Maine, to Duck Harbor, the starting point for the four Isle au Haut hikes described in this chapter. The round-trip cost in 2004 was $32 for adults and $16 for children under age 12. For information, contact the Isle au Haut Boat Company, P.O. Box 709, Sea Breeze Ave., Stonington, ME 04651, 207/367-5193, website: www.isleauhaut.com. The ferry is a small boat and does not transport motor vehicles. The Duck Harbor Campground has five lean-to shelters that can sleep up to six people each, and each lean-to site has a fire ring and picnic table. The lean-to shelters can be reserved from May 15–October 15 by contacting the park (see contact information below); reservations are required. Reservations requests cannot be postmarked or made in person at park headquarters before April 1. Camping reservations cost $25 per site, regardless of the number of nights.

**Maps:** A basic map of island trails and roads is issued free to visitors arriving on the ferry or to those with camping reservations. The park website has a map of Isle au Haut. Good trail maps of the area are the waterproof *Acadia National Park* (map 212) for $9.95 from Trails Illustrated, 800/962-1643, website: http://maps.nationalgeographic.com/trails/; and the *Hiking and Biking Map to Acadia National Park and Mount Desert Island,* $7.95 in waterproof Tyvek, from the Appalachian Mountain Club, 800/262-4455, website: www.outdoors.org. For topographic island maps, request Isle au Haut West and Isle au Haut East from USGS Map Sales, Federal Center, Box 25286, Denver, CO 80225, 888/ASK-USGS (888/275-8747), website: http://mapping.usgs.gov.

**Directions:** To reach the dock where the ferry departs for Isle au Haut, drive Route 15 to Main Street in Stonington and turn left at Bartlett's Market; the ferry landing is past the firehouse, at the end of the pier.

**Contact:** Acadia National Park, P.O. Box 177, Eagle Lake Rd., Bar Harbor, ME 04609-0177, 207/288-3338, website: www.nps.gov/acad. Friends of Acadia, P.O. Box 45, 43 Cottage St., Bar Harbor, ME 04609, 207/288-3340 or 800/625-0321, website: www.friendsofacadia.org.

## 6 ISLE AU HAUT: DUCK HARBOR MOUNTAIN/MERCHANT POINT LOOP

**4.5 mi/2.5 hrs**

**in Acadia National Park on Isle au Haut**

This loop offers another way of hiking Duck Harbor Mountain and takes you out to rugged coastline, scenic coves, and Merchant Point. My companions and I saw few other people on these trails one June day—but we did see a seal, ducks, and cormorants, and we explored a wonderful cove strewn with smooth stones. This hike traverses the mountain in the opposite direction from the Western Head Loop (see previous listing). It's easier going up the mountain from this side, so hikers squeamish about the rock scrambling on the other side can hike up this way for the views, then just double back to Duck Harbor.

From the boat landing at Duck Harbor, turn left on the trail toward the water pump. Pass the trail branching right for the campground, and continue straight until you reach Western Head Road. Bearing left along the road, it's about 200 yards to the water pump (if you need water). For this hike, take the grassy road to the right and follow it about a quarter mile, then turn left onto the Duck Harbor Mountain Trail. Follow it a little more than a mile over several open ledges with commanding views of the Isle au Haut's southern end. Reaching the trail's terminus at Squeaker Cove, turn left onto the Goat Trail, which moves in and out between woods and the coast. In less than a mile you reach a trail junction; left leads back to the dirt main road (where you would turn left for Duck Harbor), but bear right on a trail out to the rocky protrusion of Merchant Point (a great lunch spot). From the point, the trail turns back into the forest, crosses a marshy area, and reaches the main road. Turn left and follow the road a bit more than a mile to the head of Duck Harbor. Turn left onto Western Head Road, passing the water pump on the way back to the landing.

**User groups:** Hikers and dogs. Dogs must be

leashed in the park and are prohibited from the campground. No wheelchair facilities. The island rarely gets enough snow for winter activities. Bikes, horses, and hunting are prohibited.

**Access, fees:** Isle au Haut is reached by mail boat/ferry from Stonington, Maine, to Duck Harbor, the starting point for the four Isle au Haut hikes described in this chapter. The round-trip cost in 2004 was $32 for adults and $16 for children under age 12. For information, contact the Isle au Haut Boat Company, P.O. Box 709, Sea Breeze Ave., Stonington, ME 04651, 207/367-5193, website: www.isleauhaut.com. The ferry is a small boat and does not transport motor vehicles. The Duck Harbor Campground has five lean-to shelters that can sleep up to six people each, and each lean-to site has a fire ring and picnic table. The lean-to shelters can be reserved from May 15–October 15 by contacting the park (see contact information below); reservations are required. Reservations requests cannot be postmarked or made in person at park headquarters before April 1. Camping reservations cost $25 per site, regardless of the number of nights.

**Maps:** A basic map of island trails and roads is issued free to visitors arriving on the ferry or to those with camping reservations. The park website has a map of Isle au Haut. Good trail maps of the area are the waterproof *Acadia National Park* (map 212) for $9.95 from Trails Illustrated, 800/962-1643, website: http://maps.nationalgeographic.com/trails/; and the *Hiking and Biking Map to Acadia National Park and Mount Desert Island,* $7.95 in waterproof Tyvek, from the Appalachian Mountain Club, 800/262-4455, website: www.outdoors.org. For topographic island maps, request Isle au Haut West and Isle au Haut East from USGS Map Sales, Federal Center, Box 25286, Denver, CO 80225, 888/ASK-USGS (888/275-8747), website: http://mapping.usgs.gov.

**Directions:** To reach the dock where the ferry departs for Isle au Haut, take Route 15 to Main Street in Stonington and turn left at Bartlett's

Market; the ferry landing is past the firehouse, at the end of the pier.

**Contact:** Acadia National Park, P.O. Box 177, Eagle Lake Rd., Bar Harbor, ME 04609-0177, 207/288-3338, website: www.nps.gov/acad. Friends of Acadia, P.O. Box 45, 43 Cottage St., Bar Harbor, ME 04609, 207/288-3340 or 800/625-0321, website: www.friendsofacadia.org.

## 7 ISLE AU HAUT: EASTERN HEAD
**6.5 mi/3.5 hrs**

**in Acadia National Park on Isle au Haut**

The Eastern Head of Isle au Haut attracts few hikers, probably for a variety of reasons, none of which reflect how nice a spot this is. It is not connected to the rest of the national parkland on the island, it is fairly distant from Duck Harbor, and the trail out to Eastern Head is not marked or easy to find—all of which help explain why my wife and I had this stretch of battered shoreline to ourselves for an entire afternoon. The trail to Eastern Head, however, was virtually obliterated by a December 2000 storm, but the trail has since reopened.

The best way to take this hike is to combine it with the Duck Harbor Mountain/Merchant Point Loop, but what follows is the most direct route to Eastern Head. This hike is fairly flat. From the boat landing at Duck Harbor, turn left on the trail toward the water pump. Upon reaching Western Head Road, continue straight, passing the water pump, out to the main road. Turn right and follow the dirt main road for more than two miles (passing the trail coming from Merchant Point on the right) to a cove on Head Harbor where there are several small homes. Respect the fact that this is private land along the town road. The road bends to the left and becomes pavement. Less than 0.1 mile after the pavement begins, turn right onto an unmarked dirt road; a yellow house lies a short distance down this road on the left. Follow the road for about a half mile to its end, where it becomes a little-used, grassy lane and terminates at a red house. An old car sits in the yard, as a ranger described it to me, "melting into the ground." The unmarked but obvious trail begins here and continues nearly a mile out to the coast at Thunder Gulch, a deep chop reaching about 100 feet back into the oceanside cliffs. You can wander around the cliff tops here and enjoy a view of the ocean and a tiny island called Eastern Ear (which cannot be reached on foot). Return the way you came.

**User groups:** Hikers and dogs. Dogs must be leashed in the park and are prohibited in the campground. No wheelchair facilities. The island rarely gets enough snow for winter activities. Bikes, horses, and hunting are prohibited.

**Access, fees:** Isle au Haut is reached by mail boat/ferry from Stonington, Maine, to Duck Harbor, the starting point for the four Isle au Haut hikes described in this chapter. The round-trip cost in 2004 was $32 for adults and $16 for children under age 12. For information, contact the Isle au Haut Boat Company, P.O. Box 709, Sea Breeze Ave., Stonington, ME 04651, 207/367-5193, website: www.isleauhaut .com. The ferry is a small boat and does not transport motor vehicles. The Duck Harbor Campground has five lean-to shelters that can sleep up to six people each, and each lean-to site has a fire ring and picnic table. The lean-to shelters can be reserved from May 15–October 15 by contacting the park (see contact information below); reservations are required. Reservations requests cannot be postmarked or made in person at park headquarters before April 1. Camping reservations cost $25 per site, regardless of the number of nights.

**Maps:** A basic map of island trails and roads is issued free to visitors arriving on the ferry or to those with camping reservations. The park website has a map of Isle au Haut. Good trail maps of the area are the waterproof *Acadia National Park* (map 212) for $9.95 from Trails Illustrated, 800/962-1643, website: http://maps.nationalgeographic.com/trails/; and the *Hiking and Biking Map to Acadia National Park and Mount Desert Island,* $7.95 in waterproof Tyvek, from the Appalachian Moun-

tain Club, 800/262-4455, website: www.out-doors.org. For topographic island maps, request Isle au Haut West and Isle au Haut East from USGS Map Sales, Federal Center, Box 25286, Denver, CO 80225, 888/ASK-USGS (888/275-8747), website: http://mapping.usgs.gov.

**Directions:** To reach the dock where the ferry departs for Isle au Haut, drive on Route 15 to Main Street in Stonington and turn left at Bartlett's Market; the ferry landing is past the firehouse, at the end of the pier.

**Contact:** Acadia National Park, P.O. Box 177, Eagle Lake Rd., Bar Harbor, ME 04609-0177, 207/288-3338, website: www.nps.gov/acad. Friends of Acadia, P.O. Box 45, 43 Cottage St., Bar Harbor, ME 04609, 207/288-3340 or 800/625-0321, website: www.friendsofacadia.org.

## 8 BERNARD AND MANSELL MOUNTAINS
**3.7 mi/2.5 hrs**
**in Acadia National Park**

While Bernard (1,071 feet) and Mansell (949 feet) are the two highest mountains on Mount Desert Island's west side, their summits are wooded, so these trails lack the spectacular views of other peaks in Acadia National Park. Still, this loop offers a scenic walk through the woods, is fairly challenging, and does take you past a few good views of the bays and Long Pond. The cumulative elevation gain on this 3.7-mile hike is about 1,200 feet.

From the parking area, hike west on the Long Pond Trail, soon bearing left onto the Cold Brook Trail. In less than a half mile, cross Gilley Field and follow a road a short distance to the Sluiceway Trail on the right. It climbs fairly steeply to the South Face Trail, where you turn left for the Bernard Mountain summit, a few minutes' walk away. Backtrack and follow the trail down into Great Notch and straight ahead to the summit of Mansell Mountain. Continue over the summit, picking up the Perpendicular Trail, which descends the rugged east face of Mansell, often passing below low cliffs, to the Long Pond Trail. Turn right for the parking area.

**User groups:** Hikers, snowshoers, and dogs. Dogs must be leashed. No wheelchair facilities. This trail is not suitable for skis. Bikes, horses, and hunting are prohibited.

**Access, fees:** Parking and access are free.

**Maps:** A basic park map is available at the visitor center, and the park website (see contact information below) has maps showing roads, trails, and carriage roads. Good trail maps of the area are the waterproof *Acadia National Park* (map 212) for $9.95 from Trails Illustrated, 800/962-1643, website: http://maps.nationalgeographic.com/trails/ and the *Hiking and Biking Map to Acadia National Park and Mount Desert Island,* $7.95 in waterproof Tyvek, from the Appalachian Mountain Club, 800/262-4455, website: www.outdoors.org. For a topographic area map, request Southwest Harbor from USGS Map Sales, Federal Center, Box 25286, Denver, CO 80225, 888/ASK-USGS (888/275-8747), website: http://mapping.usgs.gov.

**Directions:** From Route 102 in Southwest Harbor, turn west onto Seal Cove Road. Take a right onto Long Pond Road and follow it to the parking area at the south end of Long Pond (and a great view of the pond). The park visitor center is located north of Bar Harbor at the junction of Route 3 and the start of the Park Loop Road.

**Contact:** Acadia National Park, P.O. Box 177, Eagle Lake Rd., Bar Harbor, ME 04609-0177, 207/288-3338, website: www.nps.gov/acad. Friends of Acadia, P.O. Box 45, 43 Cottage St., Bar Harbor, ME 04609, 207/288-3340 or 800/625-0321, website: www.friendsofacadia.org.

## 9 BEECH MOUNTAIN
### 1.2 mi/1 hr

**in Acadia National Park**

Want a scenic hike with long views that avoids the crowds common on the east side of Acadia? This is the one, and it entails just a bit more than a mile of hiking and a few hundred feet of elevation gain. Soon after leaving the parking lot, the trail forks; the loop can be hiked in either direction, but I recommend bearing left. You soon emerge onto an open ledge with a terrific view east and north: from the islands south of Mount Desert to Acadia, Sargent, and Penobscot mountains and the myriad waterways to the north. A short distance farther up the trail is the summit, where trees block any view, but you can climb one flight of stairs on the closed fire tower for a 360-degree view. Beyond the summit, bear right onto the descent trail, which offers magnificent views over Long Pond and all the way to Camden Hills.

**User groups:** Hikers, snowshoers, and dogs. Dogs must be leashed. No wheelchair facilities. This trail is not suitable for skis. Bikes, horses, and hunting are prohibited.

**Access, fees:** Parking and access are free.

**Maps:** A basic park map is available at the visitor center, and the park website (see contact information below) has maps showing roads, trails, and carriage roads. Good trail maps of the area are the waterproof *Acadia National Park* (map 212) for $9.95 from Trails Illustrated, 800/962-1643, website: http://maps.nationalgeographic.com/trails/ and the *Hiking and Biking Map to Acadia National Park and Mount Desert Island,* $7.95 in waterproof Tyvek, from the Appalachian Mountain Club, 800/262-4455, website: www.outdoors.org. For a topographic area map, request Southwest Harbor from USGS Map Sales, Federal Center, Box 25286, Denver, CO 80225, 888/ASK-USGS (888/275-8747), website: http://mapping.usgs.gov.

**Directions:** From the junction of Routes 198 and 102 in Somesville, drive south on Route 102 for 0.8 mile and turn right onto Pretty Marsh Road at the sign for Beech Mountain and the Beech Cliffs. Drive 0.2 mile, turn left onto Beech Hill Road, and then drive 3.1 miles to the parking lot at the end of the road. The trailhead is on the right as you enter. The park visitor center is located north of Bar Harbor at the junction of Route 3 and the start of the Park Loop Road.

**Contact:** Acadia National Park, P.O. Box 177, Eagle Lake Rd., Bar Harbor, ME 04609-0177,

207/288-3338, website: www.nps.gov/acad. Friends of Acadia, P.O. Box 45, 43 Cottage St., Bar Harbor, ME 04609, 207/288-3340 or 800/625-0321, website: www.friendsofacadia.org.

## 10 BEECH AND CANADA CLIFFS

**0.7 mi/0.75 hr**

**in Acadia National Park**

From the parking lot, this almost flat, short hike leads to the crest of cliffs high above Echo Lake. A quarter mile up the trail you reach a junction: to the right is the trail to the Canada Cliffs, to the left the trail to the Beech Cliffs. Both entail a short walk to worthwhile views, but the Beech Cliffs may be closed in late spring and early summer to protect nesting peregrine falcons. The Canada Cliffs should be open all year.

**User groups:** Hikers, snowshoers, and dogs. Dogs must be leashed. No wheelchair facilities. This trail is not suitable for skis. Bikes, horses, and hunting are prohibited.

**Access, fees:** Parking and access are free.

**Maps:** A basic park map is available at the visitor center, and the park website (see contact information below) has maps showing roads, trails, and carriage roads. Good trail maps of the area are the waterproof *Acadia National Park* (map 212) for $9.95 from Trails Illustrated, 800/962-1643, website: http://maps.nationalgeographic.com/trails/ and the *Hiking and Biking Map to Acadia National Park and Mount Desert Island,* $7.95 in waterproof Tyvek, from the Appalachian Mountain Club, 800/262-4455, website: www.outdoors.org. For a topographic area map, request Southwest Harbor from USGS Map Sales, Federal Center, Box 25286, Denver, CO 80225, 888/ASK-USGS (888/275-8747), website: http://mapping.usgs.gov.

**Directions:** From the junction of Routes 198 and 102 in Somesville, drive south on Route 102 for 0.8 mile and turn right onto Pretty Marsh Road at the sign for Beech Mountain and the Beech Cliffs. Continue 0.2 mile, turn left onto Beech Hill Road, and then drive 3.1

miles to the parking lot at the end of the road; the trailhead is on the left as you enter. The park visitor center is located north of Bar Harbor at the junction of Route 3 and the start of the Park Loop Road.

**Contact:** Acadia National Park, P.O. Box 177, Eagle Lake Rd., Bar Harbor, ME 04609-0177, 207/288-3338, website: www.nps.gov/acad. Friends of Acadia, P.O. Box 45, 43 Cottage St., Bar Harbor, ME 04609, 207/288-3340 or 800/625-0321, website: www.friendsofacadia.org.

## 11 ACADIA MOUNTAIN

**2.5 mi/1.5 hrs**

**in Acadia National Park**

At 681 feet, Acadia Mountain is the biggest hill on the west side of Somes Sound—the only true fjord in the eastern United States—and offers excellent views of the sound, the towns of Northeast Harbor and Southwest Harbor, and the islands south of Mount Desert. Although you scramble a little up rocks on the way up, climbing about 500 feet, this easy hike is a good one for young children.

From the turnout, cross the highway to the trail. It soon branches; stay left, cross a fire road (your route of descent), and proceed to the open ledges at the summit. The trail continues past the summit to even better views from ledges atop the mountain's east face. The trail then turns right, descending steep ledges with good views, and reaches a junction with the fire road (which resembles a trail here). Turn right, and the road soon widens. Just before reaching the highway, turn left onto the Acadia Mountain Trail, which leads back to the start.

**User groups:** Hikers, snowshoers, and dogs. Dogs must be leashed. No wheelchair facilities. This trail is not suitable for skis. Bikes, horses, and hunting are prohibited.

**Access, fees:** Parking and access are free.

**Maps:** A basic park map is available at the visitor center, and the park website (see contact information below) has maps showing roads, trails, and carriage roads. Good trail maps of

the area are the waterproof *Acadia National Park* (map 212) for $9.95 from Trails Illustrated, 800/962-1643, website: http://maps.nationalgeographic.com/trails/ and the *Hiking and Biking Map to Acadia National Park and Mount Desert Island,* $7.95 in waterproof Tyvek, from the Appalachian Mountain Club, 800/262-4455, website: www.outdoors.org. For a topographic area map, request Southwest Harbor from USGS Map Sales, Federal Center, Box 25286, Denver, CO 80225, 888/ASK-USGS (888/275-8747), website: http://mapping.usgs.gov. **Directions:** From the junction of Routes 198 and 102 in Somesville, drive south on Route 102 for 3.4 miles to a turnout on the right (there is a sign) at the trailhead for Acadia Mountain. The park visitor center is located north of Bar Harbor at the junction of Route 3 and the start of the Park Loop Road.
**Contact:** Acadia National Park, P.O. Box 177, Eagle Lake Rd., Bar Harbor, ME 04609-0177, 207/288-3338, website: www.nps.gov/acad. Friends of Acadia, P.O. Box 45, 43 Cottage St., Bar Harbor, ME 04609, 207/288-3340 or 800/625-0321, website: www.friendsofacadia.org.

##  FLYING MOUNTAIN
**0.6 mi/0.5 hr**
**in Acadia National Park**

This is a short hike up a hill that rises just 284 feet above Somes Sound, but that offers views of the fjord from open ledges. The trail begins at the parking area and ascends steadily; the last stretch is a bit steep. Once on the ledges, be sure to continue over them to the true summit, marked by a signpost, where the views are even better than those you see when you first reach the ledges.
**User groups:** Hikers, snowshoers, and dogs. Dogs must be leashed. No wheelchair facilities. This trail is not suitable for skis. Bikes, horses, and hunting are prohibited.
**Access, fees:** Parking and access are free.
**Maps:** A basic park map is available at the visitor center, and the park website (see contact information below) has maps showing roads,

trails, and carriage roads. Good trail maps of the area are the waterproof *Acadia National Park* (map 212) for $9.95 from Trails Illustrated, 800/962-1643, website: http://maps.nationalgeographic.com/trails/ and the *Hiking and Biking Map to Acadia National Park and Mount Desert Island,* $7.95 in waterproof Tyvek, from the Appalachian Mountain Club, 800/262-4455, website: www.outdoors.org. For a topographic area map, request Southwest Harbor from USGS Map Sales, Federal Center, Box 25286, Denver, CO 80225, 888/ASK-USGS (888/275-8747), website: http://mapping.usgs.gov. **Directions:** From the junction of Routes 198 and 102 in Somesville, go south on Route 102 for 5.4 miles and turn left on Fernald Point Road. Drive one mile to parking on the left at Valley Road. The park visitor center is north of Bar Harbor, at the junction of Route 3 and Park Loop Road.
**Contact:** Acadia National Park, P.O. Box 177, Eagle Lake Rd., Bar Harbor, ME 04609-0177, 207/288-3338, website: www.nps.gov/acad. Friends of Acadia, P.O. Box 45, 43 Cottage St., Bar Harbor, ME 04609, 207/288-3340 or 800/625-0321, website: www.friendsofacadia.org.

## 13 PENOBSCOT AND SARGENT MOUNTAINS
**4.5 mi/3 hrs**
**in Acadia National Park**

While nearly everyone who comes to Acadia National Park knows of Cadillac Mountain, few have heard of—and even fewer will actually hike—Penobscot and Sargent Mountains, which rise abruptly to the west of Jordan Pond. Yet the elevations of Sargent at 1,373 feet and Penobscot at 1,194 feet rank them as the second- and fifth-highest peaks on Mount Desert Island. And the ridge connecting them pushes nearly as much area above the trees as Cadillac's scenic South Ridge. For much of this 4.5-mile hike, which climbs more than 1,200 feet in elevation, you enjoy long views east to the Pemetic and Cadillac Mountains, south to the many offshore islands, and west across Somes Sound and Penobscot Bay to the Camden Hills.

From the parking area, head down the dirt access road toward Jordan Pond and turn left onto a trail leading to the Jordan Pond House. The Penobscot Mountain Trail begins behind the Jordan Pond House, soon ascending steep ledges that require some scrambling. Up on the ridge the hiking gets much easier. Beyond Penobscot's summit, the trail dips into a small saddle between the mountains. Turn left onto the Sargent Pond Trail, passing the small pond in the woods. Turn right onto the Sargent Mountain South Ridge Trail, ascending the long slope to the summit, marked by a pile of rocks. Just beyond the summit, turn right onto the Jordan Cliffs Trail, which traverses above the cliffs visible from Jordan Pond. Cross a carriage road and turn left onto the Penobscot Mountain Trail to return.

**User groups:** Hikers, snowshoers, and dogs. Dogs must be leashed. No wheelchair facilities. This trail is not suitable for skis. Bikes, horses, and hunting are prohibited.

**Access, fees:** Parking and access are free.

**Maps:** A basic park map is available at the visitor center, and the park website (see contact information below) has maps showing roads, trails, and carriage roads. Good trail maps of the area are the waterproof *Acadia National Park* (map 212) for $9.95 from Trails Illustrated, 800/962-1643, website: http://maps.nationalgeographic.com/trails/ and the *Hiking and Biking Map to Acadia National Park and Mount Desert Island,* $7.95 in waterproof Tyvek, from the Appalachian Mountain Club, 800/262-4455, website: www.outdoors.org. For a topographic area map, request Southwest Harbor from USGS Map Sales, Federal Center, Box 25286, Denver, CO 80225, 888/ASK-USGS (888/275-8747), website: http://mapping.usgs.gov.

**Directions:** Take Route 3 south from Bar Harbor to Seal Harbor. Turn right at the Acadia National Park entrance and left on the Park Loop Road, following it to the Jordan Pond parking area. Or from the park visitor center, follow the Park Loop Road south. Where it splits, turn right and continue to the Jordan Pond parking area. The park visitor center is located north of Bar Harbor, at the junction of Route 3 and the start of the Park Loop Road.

**Contact:** Acadia National Park, P.O. Box 177, Eagle Lake Rd., Bar Harbor, ME 04609-0177, 207/288-3338, website: www.nps.gov/acad. Friends of Acadia, P.O. Box 45, 43 Cottage St., Bar Harbor, ME 04609, 207/288-3340 or 800/625-0321, website: www.friendsofacadia.org.

## 14 JORDAN POND/SARGENT MOUNTAIN CARRIAGE ROAD LOOP

**16 mi/8 hrs**

**in Acadia National Park**

While the Jordan Pond area is popular with bicyclists, the farther you wander from the pond, the fewer people you see on the carriage roads. This moderately hilly loop makes for a pleasant ride over the gravel roadways traveled by the country's upper crust decades ago. As with the Jordan Pond/Eagle Lake/Bubble Pond Carriage Road Loop (see listing in this chapter), I recommend doing this on a bike or skis rather than hiking; on a bike, it will take about three hours.

From the Jordan Pond parking area, go south on the Park Loop Road a short distance and turn right onto a carriage road. Stay right, soon ascending a gradual slope above Jordan Pond. Turn right, then left, and follow the northwest shoreline of Eagle Lake. At the lake's northwest corner, turn left. After passing Aunt Betty Pond—where there's a view across the pond toward Sargent Mountain—turn right and contour around Sargent. After passing Upper Hadlock Pond on the right, the carriage road makes a U-turn; take the first right after that. Stay left all the way back to Jordan Pond.

**User groups:** Hikers, bikers, dogs, horses, skiers, and snowshoers. Dogs must be leashed. No wheelchair facilities. Hunting is prohibited.

**Access, fees:** Parking and access are free.

**Maps:** A basic park map is available at the visitor center, and the park website (see contact information below) has maps showing roads, trails, and carriage roads. A map of the carriage roads, showing the intersection signpost numbers—which other maps do not show—is available at the park website. Good trail maps of the area are the waterproof *Acadia National Park* (map 212) for $9.95 from Trails Illustrated, 800/962-1643, website: http://maps.nationalgeographic.com/trails/ and the *Hiking and Biking Map to Acadia National Park and Mount Desert Island,* $7.95 in waterproof Tyvek, from the Appalachian Mountain Club, 800/262-4455, website: www.outdoors.org. For topographic area maps, request Seal Harbor and Southwest Harbor from USGS Map Sales, Federal Center, Box 25286, Denver, CO 80225, 888/ASK-USGS (888/275-8747), website: http://mapping.usgs.gov.

**Directions:** Drive Route 3 south from Bar Harbor to Seal Harbor. Turn right at the Acadia National Park entrance and left on the Park Loop Road, following it to the Jordan Pond parking area. You can bike to the start from Blackwoods Campground, adding about seven miles round-trip: Bike Route 3 toward Seal Harbor, and where the highway crosses a bridge over the Park Loop Road, carry your bike down a footpath to the Loop Road; then follow it north and turn left onto a carriage path just before the Jordan Pond House. The park visitor center is located north of Bar Harbor at the junction of Route 3 and the start of the Park Loop Road.

**Contact:** Acadia National Park, P.O. Box 177, Eagle Lake Rd., Bar Harbor, ME 04609-0177, 207/288-3338, website: www.nps.gov/acad. Friends of Acadia, P.O. Box 45, 43 Cottage St., Bar Harbor, ME 04609, 207/288-3340 or 800/625-0321, website: www.friendsofacadia.org.

## 15 THE BUBBLES/ EAGLE LAKE LOOP

**4.2 mi/2 hrs**

**in Acadia National Park**

If the view of the Bubbles from the south end of Jordan Pond is one of Acadia's most famous, then the views of Jordan Pond and the steep hills enclosing it from the open ledges atop North and South Bubble rival any in the national park. Best of all, they are reached with little effort, ascending just a few hundred feet.

This loop takes in Conners Nubble—a commanding overlook of Eagle Lake—and finishes with a walk along the rocky shore of Eagle Lake. For a shorter walk, the round-trip hike to the summit of North Bubble alone is 1.2 miles. From the Bubble Rock parking area, the Bubble-Pemetic Trail heads west, then northwest through the woods, then turns sharply left, and climbs to the saddle between

The Bubbles, above Jordan Pond, Acadia National Park

North and South Bubble. Turn left to reach the summit of South Bubble. Backtrack and ascend the North Bubble Trail to that summit, which is higher than the South Bubble summit. Continue over North Bubble, crossing a carriage road, to Conners Nubble. Descend and turn right onto the Eagle Lake Trail, right again on the Jordan Pond Carry Trail, and left on the Bubble-Pemetic Trail to return to the parking area.

**User groups:** Hikers, dogs, skiers, and snowshoers. Dogs must be leashed. No wheelchair facilities. Bikes, horses, and hunting are prohibited.

**Access, fees:** Parking and access are free.

**Maps:** A basic park map is available at the visitor center, and the park website (see contact information below) has maps showing roads, trails, and carriage roads. Good trail maps of the area are the waterproof *Acadia National Park* (map 212) for $9.95 from Trails Illustrated, 800/962-1643, website: http://maps.nationalgeographic.com/trails/ and the *Hiking and Biking Map to Acadia National Park and Mount Desert Island,* $7.95 in waterproof Tyvek, from the Appalachian Mountain Club, 800/262-4455, website: www.outdoors.org. For topographic area maps, request Seal Harbor and Southwest Harbor from USGS Map Sales, Federal Center, Box 25286, Denver, CO 80225, 888/ASK-USGS (888/275-8747), website: http://mapping.usgs.gov.

**Directions:** Drive on Route 3 south from Bar Harbor to Seal Harbor. Turn right at the Acadia National Park entrance and left on the Park Loop Road, following it to the Bubble Rock parking area, 1.6 miles past the Jordan Pond parking area. Or from the park visitor center, follow the Park Loop Road south. Where it splits, turn right for the Bubble Rock parking area. The park visitor center is located north of Bar Harbor, at the junction of Route 3 and the start of the Park Loop Road.

**Contact:** Acadia National Park, P.O. Box 177, Eagle Lake Road, Bar Harbor, ME 04609-0177, 207/288-3338, website: www.nps.gov/acad.

Friends of Acadia, P.O. Box 45, 43 Cottage St., Bar Harbor, ME 04609, 207/288-3340 or 800/625-0321, website: www.friendsofacadia.org.

## 16 JORDAN POND LOOP
### 3.3 mi/1.5 hrs
**in Acadia National Park**

This fairly easy, flat trail loops around scenic Jordan Pond. You're constantly gazing across the water to the steep mountainsides surrounding it—from the cliffs and rounded humps of the Bubbles to the wooded slopes of Penobscot and Pemetic Mountains. The easiest walking is along the pond's east shore; on the northeast and especially the northwest shores, the trail crosses areas of boulders that require some scrambling and rock-hopping. Although these patches are not too difficult to navigate, you can avoid them altogether by hiking in a counterclockwise direction and turning back upon reaching these sections.

From the Jordan Pond parking area, continue down the dirt road to the shore and turn right onto the wide gravel path of the Jordan Pond Shore Trail. At the pond's southwest corner, the trail reaches a carriage road; turn left over a bridge, then immediately left onto the trail again, soon reaching the famous view of the Bubbles from the pond's south end. Just beyond that, the trail completes the loop at the dirt access road. Turn right for the parking lot.

**User groups:** Hikers, dogs, skiers, and snowshoers. Dogs must be leashed. No wheelchair facilities. Bikes, horses, and hunting are prohibited.

**Access, fees:** Parking and access are free.

**Maps:** A basic park map is available at the visitor center, and the park website (see contact information below) has maps showing roads, trails, and carriage roads. Good trail maps of the area are the waterproof *Acadia National Park* (map 212) for $9.95 from Trails Illustrated, 800/962-1643, website: http://maps.nationalgeographic.com/trails/ and the *Hiking*

*and Biking Map to Acadia National Park and Mount Desert Island,* $7.95 in waterproof Tyvek, from the Appalachian Mountain Club, 800/262-4455, website: www.outdoors.org. For topographic area maps, request Seal Harbor and Southwest Harbor from USGS Map Sales, Federal Center, Box 25286, Denver, CO 80225, 888/ASK-USGS (888/275-8747), website: http://mapping.usgs.gov.

**Directions:** Take Route 3 south from Bar Harbor to Seal Harbor. Turn right at the Acadia National Park entrance and left on the Park Loop Road, following it to the Jordan Pond parking area. Or from the park visitor center, follow the Park Loop Road south. Where it splits, turn right for the Jordan Pond parking area. The park visitor center is located north of Bar Harbor at the junction of Route 3 and the start of the Park Loop Road.

**Contact:** Acadia National Park, P.O. Box 177, Eagle Lake Rd., Bar Harbor, ME 04609-0177, 207/288-3338, website: www.nps.gov/acad. Friends of Acadia, P.O. Box 45, 43 Cottage St., Bar Harbor, ME 04609, 207/288-3340 or 800/625-0321, website: www.friendsofacadia.org.

## 17 JORDAN POND/EAGLE LAKE/BUBBLE POND CARRIAGE ROAD LOOP

**11.5 mi/6 hrs**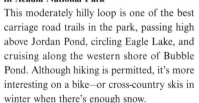

**in Acadia National Park**

This moderately hilly loop is one of the best carriage road trails in the park, passing high above Jordan Pond, circling Eagle Lake, and cruising along the western shore of Bubble Pond. Although hiking is permitted, it's more interesting on a bike—or cross-country skis in winter when there's enough snow.

From the Bubble Pond parking area, follow the carriage road north along Eagle Lake. At the lake's northwest corner, turn left and follow the carriage road along the lake's western shore. After angling away from the lake (around Conners Nubble), turn right, then left, soon passing above Jordan Pond. At the pond's south end, turn left and cross the Park Loop

Road. Follow this carriage road all the way back to Bubble Pond. Along the way, you pass a carriage road leading to the right across a bridge over the Loop Road; the loop beginning across the bridge climbs Day Mountain, a fun if challenging ride up and a fast ride down for mountain bikers who have the time and energy to add a few miles to this trail's distance.

**User groups:** Hikers, bikers, dogs, skiers, and snowshoers. Dogs must be leashed. No wheelchair facilities. Horses and hunting are prohibited.

**Access, fees:** Parking and access are free.

**Maps:** A basic park map is available at the visitor center, and the park website (see contact information below) has maps showing roads, trails, and carriage roads. A map of the carriage roads, showing the intersection signpost numbers—which other maps do not show—is available at the park website. Good trail maps of the area are the waterproof *Acadia National Park* (map 212) for $9.95 from Trails Illustrated, 800/962-1643, website: http://maps.nationalgeographic.com/trails/ and the *Hiking and Biking Map to Acadia National Park and Mount Desert Island,* $7.95 in waterproof Tyvek, from the Appalachian Mountain Club, 800/262-4455, website: www.outdoors.org. For a topographic area map, request Seal Harbor and Southwest Harbor from USGS Map Sales, Federal Center, Box 25286, Denver, CO 80225, 888/ASK-USGS (888/275-8747), website: http://mapping.usgs.gov.

**Directions:** Take Route 3 south from Bar Harbor to Seal Harbor. Turn right at the Acadia National Park entrance and left on the Park Loop Road, following it 2.6 miles past the Jordan Pond parking area to the Bubble Pond parking area. From the park visitor center, follow the Park Loop Road south. Where it splits, turn right for the Bubble Pond parking area. You can bike to the start from Blackwoods Campground, adding about seven miles roundtrip: Bike Route 3 toward Seal Harbor and where the highway crosses a bridge over the

Park Loop Road, carry your bike down a footpath to the Loop Road and follow it north. Just before the Jordan Pond House, turn right onto this carriage road loop. The park visitor center is north of Bar Harbor at the junction of Route 3 and Park Loop Road.

**Contact:** Acadia National Park, P.O. Box 177, Eagle Lake Rd., Bar Harbor, ME 04609-0177, 207/288-3338, website: www.nps.gov/acad. Friends of Acadia, P.O. Box 45, 43 Cottage St., Bar Harbor, ME 04609, 207/288-3340 or 800/625-0321, website: www.friendsofacadia.org.

## 18 PEMETIC MOUNTAIN
### 3.3 mi/2.5 hrs
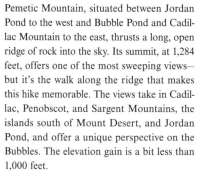
**in Acadia National Park**

Pemetic Mountain, situated between Jordan Pond to the west and Bubble Pond and Cadillac Mountain to the east, thrusts a long, open ridge of rock into the sky. Its summit, at 1,284 feet, offers one of the most sweeping views— but it's the walk along the ridge that makes this hike memorable. The views take in Cadillac, Penobscot, and Sargent Mountains, the islands south of Mount Desert, and Jordan Pond, and offer a unique perspective on the Bubbles. The elevation gain is a bit less than 1,000 feet.

From the Jordan Pond parking area, follow the dirt access road to the southeast shore of Jordan Pond. Turn left, follow the Jordan Pond Shore Trail a short distance, and then turn left onto the Pond Trail. Cross the Park Loop Road and in less than a half mile, turn left onto the Pemetic Mountain West Cliff Trail, ascending the ridge. At the junction with the Pemetic Mountain Trail, turn left (north) and proceed to the summit. Double back and follow the Pemetic Mountain Trail all the way to the Pond Trail, then turn right to go back the way you came.

**User groups:** Hikers, dogs, skiers, and snowshoers. Dogs must be leashed. No wheelchair facilities. Bikes, horses, and hunting are prohibited.

**Access, fees:** Parking and access are free.

**Maps:** A basic park map is available at the visitor center, and the park website (see contact information below) has maps showing roads, trails, and carriage roads. Good trail maps of the area are the waterproof *Acadia National Park* (map 212) for $9.95 from Trails Illustrated, 800/962-1643, website: http://maps.nationalgeographic.com/trails/ and the *Hiking and Biking Map to Acadia National Park and Mount Desert Island,* $7.95 in waterproof Tyvek, from the Appalachian Mountain Club, 800/262-4455, website: www.outdoors.org. For topographic area maps, request Seal Harbor and Southwest Harbor from USGS Map Sales, Federal Center, Box 25286, Denver, CO 80225, 888/ASK-USGS (888/275-8747), website: http://mapping.usgs.gov.

**Directions:** Take Route 3 south from Bar Harbor to Seal Harbor. Turn right at the Acadia National Park entrance and left on the Park Loop Road, following it to the Jordan Pond parking area. Or from the park visitor center, follow the Park Loop Road south. Where it splits, turn right and continue to the Jordan Pond parking area. The park visitor center is located north of Bar Harbor at the junction of Route 3 and the start of the Park Loop Road.

**Contact:** Acadia National Park, P.O. Box 177, Eagle Lake Rd., Bar Harbor, ME 04609-0177, 207/288-3338, website: www.nps.gov/acad. Friends of Acadia, P.O. Box 45, 43 Cottage St., Bar Harbor, ME 04609, 207/288-3340 or 800/625-0321, website: www.friendsofacadia.org.

## 19 CADILLAC MOUNTAIN: WEST FACE TRAIL
### 2.8 mi/2.5 hrs
**in Acadia National Park**

This trail offers the most direct and difficult route up Mount Desert Island's highest peak, 1,530-foot Cadillac Mountain. It involves a great deal of scrambling over steep slabs of open rock, relentlessly strenuous hiking, and about 1,200 feet of elevation gain. Descending may be more difficult than ascending. Much of the trail lies in the woods, but the occasional views—which become more frequent as you climb higher—down to Bubble Pond and of the deep cleft separating Cadillac and Pemetic Mountains are spectacular. I like this trail for its challenge and relatively light hiker traffic.

From the parking area, cross the carriage road and pick up the Cadillac Mountain West Face Trail at the north end of Bubble Pond. In just under a mile of steep climbing, you top out on the mountain's South Ridge. Turn left onto the Cadillac Mountain South Ridge Trail and follow it to the summit. Head back along the same route.

**User groups:** Hikers and dogs. Dogs must be leashed. No wheelchair facilities. This trail is not suitable for skis or snowshoes. Bikes, horses, and hunting are prohibited.

**Access, fees:** Parking and access are free.

**Maps:** A basic park map is available at the visitor center, and the park website (see contact information below) has maps showing roads, trails, and carriage roads. Good trail maps of the area are the waterproof *Acadia National Park* (map 212) for $9.95 from Trails Illustrated, 800/962-1643, website: http://maps.nationalgeographic.com/trails/ and the *Hiking and Biking Map to Acadia National Park and Mount Desert Island,* $7.95 in waterproof Tyvek, from the Appalachian Mountain Club, 800/262-4455, website: www.outdoors.org. For topographic area maps, request Seal Harbor and Southwest Harbor from USGS Map Sales, Federal Center, Box 25286, Denver, CO 80225, 888/ASK-USGS (888/275-8747), website: http://mapping.usgs.gov.

**Directions:** Take Route 3 south from Bar Harbor to Seal Harbor. Turn right at the Acadia National Park entrance and left on the Park Loop Road, following it 2.6 miles past the Jordan Pond parking area to the Bubble Pond parking area. Or from the park visitor center, follow the Park Loop Road south. Where it splits, turn right for the Bubble Pond parking area. The park visitor center is located north of Bar Harbor at the junction of Route 3 and Park Loop Road.

**Contact:** Acadia National Park, P.O. Box 177, Eagle Lake Rd., Bar Harbor, ME 04609-0177, 207/288-3338, website: www.nps.gov/acad. Friends of Acadia, P.O. Box 45, 43 Cottage St., Bar Harbor, ME 04609, 207/288-3340 or 800/625-0321, website: www.friendsofacadia.org.

## 20 CADILLAC MOUNTAIN: SOUTH RIDGE TRAIL
**7 mi/4 hrs**
**in Acadia National Park**

The long, spectacular, wide-open South Ridge of the highest peak on Mount Desert Island—1,530-foot Cadillac Mountain—affords one of the longest and most scenic hikes in Acadia National Park. How many mountain ridges offer views not only of surrounding hills, but also of the ocean and a profusion of islands? This seven-mile round-tripper climbs about 1,300 feet, making it one of the most challenging outings in the park.

One of my first hikes ever in Acadia, it remains one of my favorites. A relatively short and somewhat steep hike through the woods brings you onto the broad ridge; then you have an easy walk and sweeping views all the way to the summit. About a mile from Route 3, take the loop trail out to Eagle Crag, which offers views to the east; the loop trail rejoins the South Ridge Trail in 0.2 mile. Continuing up the South Ridge, you break out above the trees to views west to Pemetic and Sargent Mountains, and east and south to Frenchman Bay and numerous islands. At three miles, the trail passes a junction with the Cadillac Mountain West Face Trail (which descends left, or west), reaches a switchback in the paved summit road, and veers right, winding another half mile to the summit. Return the same way you came.

**User groups:** Hikers, snowshoers, and dogs. Dogs must be leashed. No wheelchair facilities. This trail is not suitable for skis. Bikes, horses, and hunting are prohibited.

**Access, fees:** Parking and access are free.

**Maps:** A basic park map is available at the visitor center, and the park website (see contact information below) has maps showing roads, trails, and carriage roads. Good trail maps of the area are the waterproof *Acadia National Park* (map 212) for $9.95 from Trails Illustrated, 800/962-1643, website: http://maps.nationalgeographic.com/trails/ and the *Hiking and Biking Map to Acadia National Park and Mount Desert Island,* $7.95 in waterproof Tyvek, from the Appalachian Mountain Club, 800/262-4455, website: www.outdoors.org. For a topographic area map, request Seal Harbor from USGS Map Sales, Federal Center, Box 25286, Denver, CO 80225, 888/ASK-USGS (888/275-8747), website: http://mapping.usgs.gov.

**Directions:** Drive Route 3 south from Bar Harbor to the Blackwoods Campground entrance. The Cadillac Mountain South Ridge Trail enters the woods on the right about 50 yards past the campground entrance road; there is parking at the roadside. Campers in Blackwoods can pick up the trail at the west end of the campground's south loop (adding 1.4 miles to the hike's round-trip distance). The park visitor center is located north of Bar Harbor, at the junction of Route 3 and the start of the Park Loop Road.

**Contact:** Acadia National Park, P.O. Box 177, Eagle Lake Rd., Bar Harbor, ME 04609-0177, 207/288-3338, website: www.nps.gov/acad. Friends of Acadia, P.O. Box 45, 43 Cottage St., Bar Harbor, ME 04609, 207/288-3340 or 800/625-0321, website: www.friendsofacadia.org.

## 21 DORR AND CADILLAC MOUNTAINS

**3 mi/2 hrs**

**in Acadia National Park**

This moderate hike combines the highest peak on Mount Desert Island, 1,530-foot Cadillac Mountain, with its neighbor to the east, 1,270-foot Dorr, a mountain just as scenic and far less crowded. For much of this hike, you enjoy continuous views that take in Champlain Mountain, the islands of Frenchman Bay, and the rugged terrain atop Dorr and Cadillac. While just three miles long, this hike's cumulative elevation gain exceeds 1,500 feet.

From the parking area, turn left onto the Jessup Path and right onto the Dorr Mountain East Face Trail, which ascends numerous switchbacks up the steep flank of the mountain. Turn left onto the Dorr Mountain Trail; the trail actually passes just north of Dorr's true summit, which is reached by walking a nearly flat 0.1 mile south on the Dorr Mountain South Ridge Trail. Double back and turn left (west) onto the Dorr Mountain Notch Trail, which drops into the rugged—though not very deep—notch between Dorr and Cadillac. (This distinctive notch is visible from Route 3 south of the Tarn.) Follow the trail up the open east slope of Cadillac to the summit. Descend the way you came, but instead of turning right onto the Dorr Mountain East Face Trail, continue straight on the somewhat more forgiving Dorr Mountain Trail and then turn right onto the Jessup Path for the parking area.

**User groups:** Hikers and dogs. Dogs must be leashed. No wheelchair facilities. The trail would be very difficult to snowshoe and is not suitable for skis. Bikes, horses, and hunting are prohibited.

**Access, fees:** Parking and access are free.

**Maps:** A basic park map is available at the visitor center, and the park website (see contact information below) has maps showing roads, trails, and carriage roads. Good trail maps of the area are the waterproof *Acadia National Park* (map 212) for $9.95 from Trails Illustrated, 800/962-1643, website: http://maps.nationalgeographic.com/trails/ and the *Hiking and Biking Map to Acadia National Park and Mount Desert Island,* $7.95 in waterproof Tyvek, from the Appalachian Mountain Club, 800/262-4455, website: www.outdoors.org. For a topographic area map, request Seal Harbor from USGS Map Sales, Federal Center, Box 25286, Denver, CO 80225, 888/ASK-USGS (888/275-8747), website: http://mapping.usgs.gov.

**Directions:** Take Route 3 south from Bar Harbor or north from Blackwoods Campground, and turn into the parking area at the Tarn, just south of the Sieur de Monts entrance to the Park Loop Road. The park visitor center is located north of Bar Harbor, at the junction of Route 3 and the start of the Park Loop Road. **Contact:** Acadia National Park, P.O. Box 177, Eagle Lake Rd., Bar Harbor, ME 04609-0177, 207/288-3338, website: www.nps.gov/acad. Friends of Acadia, P.O. Box 45, 43 Cottage St., Bar Harbor, ME 04609, 207/288-3340 or 800/625-0321, website: www.friendsofacadia.org.

## 22 ACADIA TRAVERSE
### 13.5 mi one-way/10 hrs
### in Acadia National Park

While poring over my maps of Acadia National Park one evening (my idea of a wild night), I noticed that I could link trails and create a traverse of Mount Desert Island's east side—hitting the park's six major peaks and using no roads (though crossing a few). At roughly 13 miles, the traverse would be an ambitious but feasible day hike. So I recruited five guinea pigs—um, fellow intrepid adventurers—including my wife's 13-year-old nephew, Brendan, and we embarked on a hike that far exceeded our expectations.

On this Acadia Traverse, you hit the national park's tallest hills and spend much of the day above the trees, with sweeping views from a succession of long, open ridges. And it's a long day: Including time spent on short rest stops (but not including time spent shuttling vehicles), we were out for 10 hours, finishing just before sunset. The cumulative elevation gain is about 4,700 feet—more than hiking up Mount Washington. And many of these trails—particularly the Beechcroft, the Cadillac Mountain West Face, and a section of the Penobscot Mountain Trail—are very steep. There are water sources on top of Cadillac Mountain and at the Jordan Pond House for refilling bottles. An exciting alternative start would be on the Precipice Trail of Champlain Mountain (which is often closed in late spring and early summer to protect nesting peregrine falcons).

Follow the Bear Brook Trail south to the summit of Champlain Mountain; within minutes of setting out, you enjoy views of the Frenchman Bay islands. Turn right (west) and descend the Beechcroft Trail 0.8 mile to the small pond called the Tarn (crossing Route 3). Ascend the Dorr Mountain East Face Trail, then turn left (south) onto the Dorr Mountain Trail, and take it to the top of Dorr Mountain, one mile from the Tarn. (To reach the true summit, turn left, or south, on the Dorr Mountain South Ridge Trail for a flat 0.1 mile, then double back.) The Dorr Mountain Notch Trail dips 0.4 mile into the shallow but spectacular notch between Dorr and Cadillac, and then climbs the open slope for half a mile to the Cadillac Mountain summit.

Descend the Cadillac Mountain South Ridge Trail for half a mile to the Cadillac Mountain West Face Trail, which drops very steeply for nearly a mile to a parking lot at the north end of Bubble Pond. Follow the carriage road south roughly 0.1 mile; then turn right onto the Pemetic Mountain Trail and take it over Pemetic's summit, 1.3 miles from Bubble Pond. Continue south over the long, rocky ridge for just over half a mile and then bear right onto the Pemetic West Cliff Trail. That trail descends 0.6 mile to the Pond Trail; turn right, and descend easily another 0.4 mile to the Park Loop Road. Cross the road, enter the woods, and turn left on a trail to the Jordan Pond House. The Penobscot Mountain Trail begins behind the Jordan Pond House and leads 1.5 miles to the summit of Penobscot, at one point going straight up steep, rocky terrain. Pick up the Sargent Pond Trail north and west—passing the tiny alpine pond nestled in conifers—then turn right (north) onto the Sargent Mountain South Ridge Trail, gradually climbing the long ridge to the 1,373-foot summit, a mile beyond Penobscot's, for the final panoramic view of this hike.

Descend west on the Grandgent Trail (be careful not to confuse it with the Sargent Mountain North Ridge Trail, which will add mileage to your hike at a time when you don't want it) for just over a mile to the top of little Parkman Mountain. Turn left onto the Parkman Mountain Trail, descending southward. You cross two carriage roads; at the second crossing, turn right and follow that carriage road a short distance to a connector leading left to the parking area on Route 198, a mile from the Parkman summit. Then take off your boots and vigorously massage your feet.

**User groups:** Hikers and dogs. Dogs must be leashed. No wheelchair facilities. The trail would be very difficult to snowshoe or ski. Bikes, horses, and hunting are prohibited.

**Access, fees:** From May 1–October 31, the park charges an entrance fee of $20 per vehicle for a seven-day pass or $5 for walkers, bicyclists, or motorcycles for a seven-day pass, at an entrance station beyond the Sieur de Monts entrance on the one-way Park Loop Road, through which you must pass after this hike. A one-year vehicle pass costs $40.

**Maps:** A basic park map is available at the visitor center, and the park website (see contact information below) has maps showing roads, trails, and carriage roads. Good trail maps of the area are the waterproof *Acadia National Park* (map 212) for $9.95 from Trails Illustrated, 800/962-1643, website: http://maps.nationalgeographic.com/trails/ and the *Hiking and Biking Map to Acadia National Park and Mount Desert Island,* $7.95 in waterproof Tyvek, from the Appalachian Mountain Club, 800/262-4455, website: www.outdoors.org. For a topographic area map, request Seal Harbor from USGS Map Sales, Federal Center, Box 25286, Denver, CO 80225, 888/ASK-USGS (888/275-8747), website: http://mapping.usgs.gov.

**Directions:** Two vehicles are needed for this traverse. Leave one vehicle at the northernmost of the two parking areas north of Upper Hadlock Pond along Route 198 in Northeast Harbor. Then drive to the hike's start, a turnout on the Park Loop Road at the Bear Brook

Trail, 0.2 mile past a picnic area. If you're traveling with a group of friends, you might leave a third vehicle roughly halfway through the hike, at either the Bubble Pond or Jordan Pond parking areas, in case you can't finish the hike. The park visitor center is located north of Bar Harbor at the junction of Route 3 and the start of the Park Loop Road.

**Contact:** Acadia National Park, P.O. Box 177, Eagle Lake Rd., Bar Harbor, ME 04609-0177, 207/288-3338, website: www.nps.gov/acad. Friends of Acadia, P.O. Box 45, 43 Cottage St., Bar Harbor, ME 04609, 207/288-3340 or 800/625-0321, website: www.friendsofacadia.org.

## 23 THE BEEHIVE
### 1.3 mi/1.5 hrs
**in Acadia National Park**

The climb up the cliffs on the Beehive's east face looks as if it's strictly for technical rock climbers when you stare up at it from the Sand Beach parking lot. The trail zigs and zags up ledges on the nearly vertical face, requiring hand-and-foot scrambling and the use of iron ladder rungs drilled into the rock. Though it's a fairly short climb, and just a half-mile walk some 400 feet uphill, this trail is not for anyone in poor physical condition or uncomfortable with exposure and heights. On the other hand, it's a wonderful trail for hikers looking for a little adventure—and for children old enough to know not to wander off a precipice. All the way up, you're treated to unimpeded views over Frenchman Bay and the coast, from Sand Beach and Great Head south to Otter Cliffs. On the summit, you look north to Champlain Mountain and northwest to Dorr and Cadillac Mountains.

From the parking area, cross the Loop Road and walk a few steps to the right, to the Bowl Trail. You will soon turn onto the Beehive Trail and follow it to the summit. Continuing over the summit, turn left onto the Bowl Trail and make the easy descent back to the Loop Road. A very scenic and popular 3.7-mile loop links this with the Gorham Mountain Trail

hikers ascending The Beehive, Acadia National Park

information below) has maps showing roads, trails, and carriage roads. Good trail maps of the area are the waterproof *Acadia National Park* (map 212) for $9.95 from Trails Illustrated, 800/962-1643, website: http://maps.nationalgeographic.com/trails/ and the *Hiking and Biking Map to Acadia National Park and Mount Desert Island,* $7.95 in waterproof Tyvek, from the Appalachian Mountain Club, 800/262-4455, website: www.outdoors.org. For a topographic area map, request Seal Harbor from USGS Map Sales, Federal Center, Box 25286, Denver, CO 80225, 888/ASK-USGS (888/275-8747), website: http://mapping.usgs.gov.

**Directions:** Drive the Park Loop Road to the east side of Mount Desert Island and the large parking area at Sand Beach, half a mile south of the entrance station. The park visitor center is located north of Bar Harbor, at the junction of Route 3 and the start of the Park Loop Road.

**Contact:** Acadia National Park, P.O. Box 177, Eagle Lake Rd., Bar Harbor, ME 04609-0177, 207/288-3338, website: www.nps.gov/acad. Friends of Acadia, P.O. Box 45, 43 Cottage St., Bar Harbor, ME 04609, 207/288-3340 or 800/625-0321, website: www.friendsofacadia.org.

(see next listing) and Ocean Path (see listing in this chapter).

**User groups:** Hikers and dogs. Dogs must be leashed. No wheelchair facilities. The trail would be very difficult to snowshoe and is not suitable for skis. Bikes, horses, and hunting are prohibited.

**Access, fees:** From May 1–October 31, the park charges an entrance fee of $20 per vehicle for a seven-day pass or $5 for walkers, bicyclists, or motorcycles for a seven-day pass, at an entrance station beyond the Sieur de Monts entrance on the one-way Park Loop Road, through which you must pass after this hike. A one-year vehicle pass costs $40.

**Maps:** A basic park map is available at the visitor center, and the park website (see contact

## 24 GORHAM MOUNTAIN/ CADILLAC CLIFFS

**2 mi/1.5 hrs**

**in Acadia National Park**

I hiked over Gorham Mountain after making the climb of the Beehive and thinking nothing could match that experience. But I had to change my mind after walking along Gorham's long, open ridge, enjoying views of Acadia's coast and countless islands. At just 525 feet high, Gorham's rocky crown is easily reached. Only the Cadillac Cliffs Trail requires some scrambling, and that can be avoided. From the parking area, follow the Gorham Mountain Trail, then turn right onto the Cadillac Cliffs Trail, which passes below the cliffs and rejoins the Gorham Mountain Trail just below the summit. Descend the Gorham Mountain Trail. A 3.7-mile loop links this with the Beehive (see prior listing) and Ocean Path (see listing in this chapter) trails.

**User groups:** Hikers, dogs, skiers, and snowshoers. Dogs must be leashed. No wheelchair facilities. Bikes, horses, and hunting are prohibited.

**Access, fees:** From May 1–October 31, the park charges an entrance fee of $20 per vehicle for a seven-day pass or $5 for walkers, bicyclists, or motorcycles for a seven-day pass, at an entrance station beyond the Sieur de Monts entrance on the one-way Park Loop Road, through which you must pass after this hike. A one-year vehicle pass costs $40.

**Maps:** A basic park map is available at the visitor center, and the park website (see contact information below) has maps showing roads, trails, and carriage roads. Good trail maps of the area are the waterproof *Acadia National Park* (map 212) for $9.95 from Trails Illustrated, 800/962-1643, website: http://maps.nationalgeographic.com/trails/ and the *Hiking and Biking Map to Acadia National Park and Mount Desert Island,* $7.95 in waterproof Tyvek, from the Appalachian Mountain Club, 800/262-4455, website: www.outdoors.org. For a topographic area map, request Seal Harbor from USGS Map Sales, Federal Center, Box 25286, Denver, CO 80225, 888/ASK-USGS (888/275-8747), website: http://mapping.usgs.gov.

**Directions:** Take the Park Loop Road to the east side of Mount Desert Island and the parking area at the Gorham Mountain Trail and Monument Cove, south of Sand Beach and north of Otter Cliffs. The park visitor center is located north of Bar Harbor at the junction of Route 3 and the start of the Park Loop Road.

**Contact:** Acadia National Park, P.O. Box 177, Eagle Lake Rd., Bar Harbor, ME 04609-0177, 207/288-3338, website: www.nps.gov/acad. Friends of Acadia, P.O. Box 45, 43 Cottage St., Bar Harbor, ME 04609, 207/288-3340 or 800/625-0321, website: www.friendsofacadia.org.

## 25 GREAT HEAD
**1.6 mi/1 hr**
**in Acadia National Park**

This short, easy walk leads out to the top of tall cliffs rising virtually out of the ocean, offering spectacular views that stretch from the islands of Frenchman Bay to Otter Cliffs. It's a popular hike, but like many popular hikes, it tends to attract most folks during the day. Two friends and I found solitude out here one sunny late afternoon in early June.

From the parking area, follow the wide gravel path into the woods, soon reaching a trail entering from the left—the way this loop returns. Continue straight ahead, passing above Sand Beach (a trail leads down to the beach) and then ascending slightly. Where the trail forks, be sure to stay to the right (the left fork cuts off the walk along the cliffs), soon emerging at the cliffs. To return, follow the blue blazes north back to the gravel path and then turn right to head back to the parking area.

**User groups:** Hikers, dogs, skiers, and snowshoers. Dogs must be leashed. No wheelchair facilities. Bikes, horses, and hunting are prohibited.

**Access, fees:** From May 1–October 31, the park charges an entrance fee of $20 per vehicle for a seven-day pass or $5 for walkers, bicyclists, or motorcycles for a seven-day pass, at an entrance station beyond the Sieur de Monts entrance on the one-way Park Loop Road, through which you must pass after this hike. A one-year vehicle pass costs $40.

**Maps:** A basic park map is available at the visitor center, and the park website (see contact information below) has maps showing roads, trails, and carriage roads. Good trail maps of the area are the waterproof *Acadia National Park* (map 212) for $9.95 from Trails Illustrated, 800/962-1643, website: http://maps.nationalgeographic.com/trails/ and the *Hiking and Biking Map to Acadia National Park and*

*Mount Desert Island,* $7.95 in waterproof Tyvek, from the Appalachian Mountain Club, 800/262-4455, website: www.outdoors.org. For a topographic area map, request Seal Harbor from USGS Map Sales, Federal Center, Box 25286, Denver, CO 80225, 888/ASK-USGS (888/275-8747), website: http://mapping.usgs.gov.

**Directions:** Drive on the Park Loop Road to the east side of Mount Desert Island, past the Precipice parking area. Immediately before the Loop Road entrance station (fee charged), turn left onto an unmarked road. Drive 0.2 mile, turn right, drive another 0.4 mile, and pull into a parking area on the left. The park visitor center is located north of Bar Harbor at the junction of Route 3 and the start of Park Loop Road.

**Contact:** Acadia National Park, P.O. Box 177, Eagle Lake Rd., Bar Harbor, ME 04609-0177, 207/288-3338, website: www.nps.gov/acad. Friends of Acadia, P.O. Box 45, 43 Cottage St., Bar Harbor, ME 04609, 207/288-3340 or 800/625-0321, website: www.friendsofacadia.org.

## 26 OCEAN PATH
**3.6 mi/2 hrs**

**in Acadia National Park**

This is one of the most popular hikes in the national park—and for good reason. The Ocean Path follows the rugged shoreline from Sand Beach to Otter Point, passing over the top of Otter Cliffs—the island's tallest cliffs, popular with rock climbers. About midway along this trail is the famous Thunder Hole, where incoming waves crash into a channel-like pocket in the rocks, trapping air to create a loud and deep popping noise; it's most impressive around high tide.

From the parking area, the trail veers right. The shore here is mostly rocky, but constantly changes character over the course of this trail—some beaches are covered exclusively with small, round stones, others only with large rocks. As it approaches Otter Cliffs, the trail enters a small woods (across the road from another parking lot) and emerges atop Otter

Cliffs. The trail continues beyond the cliffs to Otter Point, where it was extended a short distance in recent years to include a particularly scenic section right along the shore at Otter Point. Hike back along the same route.

**User groups:** Hikers and dogs. Dogs must be leashed. No wheelchair facilities. This trail rarely receives enough snow for skis or snowshoes. Bikes, horses, and hunting are prohibited.

**Access, fees:** From May 1–October 31, the park charges an entrance fee of $20 per vehicle for a seven-day pass or $5 for walkers, bicyclists, or motorcycles for a seven-day pass, at an entrance station beyond the Sieur de Monts entrance on the one-way Park Loop Road, through which you must pass after this hike. A one-year vehicle pass costs $40.

**Maps:** A basic park map is available at the visitor center, and the park website (see contact information below) has maps showing roads, trails, and carriage roads. Good trail maps of the area are the waterproof *Acadia National Park* (map 212) for $9.95 from Trails Illustrated, 800/962-1643, website: http://maps.nationalgeographic.com/trails/ and the *Hiking and Biking Map to Acadia National Park and Mount Desert Island,* $7.95 in waterproof Tyvek, from the Appalachian Mountain Club, 800/262-4455, website: www.outdoors.org. For a topographic area map, request Seal Harbor from USGS Map Sales, Federal Center, Box 25286, Denver, CO 80225, 888/ASK-USGS (888/275-8747), website: http://mapping.usgs.gov.

**Directions:** Drive on the Park Loop Road to Mount Desert Island's east side and the large parking area at Sand Beach, half a mile south of the entrance station. The park visitor center is located north of Bar Harbor at the junction of Route 3 and the start of the Park Loop Road.

**Contact:** Acadia National Park, P.O. Box 177, Eagle Lake Rd., Bar Harbor, ME 04609-0177, 207/288-3338, website: www.nps.gov/acad. Friends of Acadia, P.O. Box 45, 43 Cottage St., Bar Harbor, ME 04609, 207/288-3340 or 800/625-0321, website: www.friendsofacadia.org.

## Chapter 3

© MICHAEL LANZA

# Western and Southern Mountains and Hills

# Western and Southern Mountains and Hills

The 32 hikes in this chapter include some of the state's biggest and most popular hiking destinations, like Bigelow Mountain and the Saddleback Range; some of New England's most rugged backcountry in the Mahoosuc Range; some of the finest small-mountain hiking in New England, such as Tumbledown Mountain and Pleasant Mountain; and some of the region's most wonderfully obscure trails, like the hikes of Evans Notch.

Fifteen of this chapter's hikes lie on or very near the Appalachian Trail, and several lead to beautiful cascades and waterfalls, like Screw Auger Falls and Step Falls in Grafton Notch. Although the neighboring White Mountains draw all the limelight, this part of Maine remains quietly spectacular.

Winter access gets trickier on many of these hikes. Some roads, such as Route 113 through Evans Notch, are not maintained in winter, and others simply are often covered with ice and snow. Many of the trails in this chapter see little or no visitors in winter, meaning you'll probably be breaking trail through snow, without the security of knowing other people might come along to help you out in case of an emergency. That can be exciting, but it's certainly riskier.

A few hikes are on private land left open to public use in keeping with a long-standing tradition in Maine—a state where more than 90 percent of the total land area is privately held. Consequently, some hikes' descriptions do not list any contact agency for additional information; in other words, you explore these places with the understanding that you alone are responsible for yourself. Bear in mind that while most of these private-land trails have been open to public use for many years, access can be restricted or denied at any time. Respect private property when on it, obey "No Trespassing" signs, and assume that hunting is allowed in season unless posted otherwise.

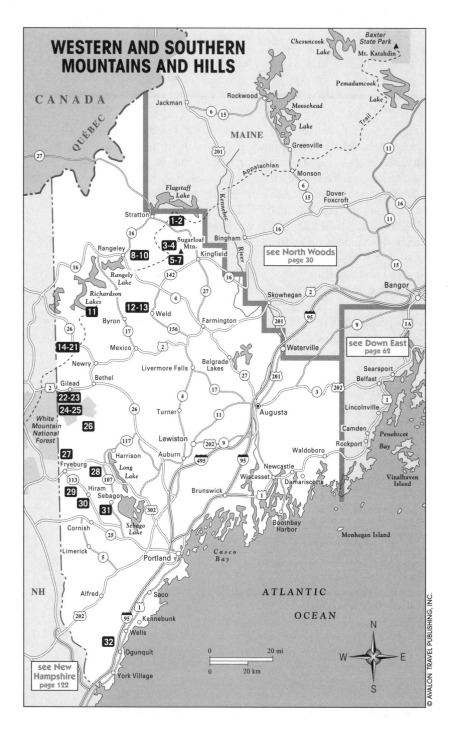

# 1 BIGELOW RANGE

**16.7 mi one-way/2 days**

**east of Stratton**

A darling of Maine hikers, Bigelow Mountain is unquestionably one of the two or three most spectacular peaks in the state; only Katahdin and Bigelow's neighbor to the south, the Saddleback Range, warrant comparison. Reflecting the state's affection for this range, Maine voters supported a grassroots movement and in 1976 created the Bigelow Preserve, a 35,000-acre park encompassing the entire Bigelow Range—including about 17 miles of the Appalachian Trail—and 21 miles of shoreline on sprawling Flagstaff Lake. Both of Bigelow's summits rise well above tree line, affording long views in every direction. Perhaps the best view is north to Flagstaff Lake and the vast wilderness of Maine's North Woods (though a few logging clear-cuts tarnish that view). On rare clear days, you can

Bigelow Mountain

see north to Katahdin and southwest to Mount Washington.

This 16.7-mile, two-day backpacking trip traverses the entire Bigelow Mountain range along the Appalachian Trail. The distance is moderate for two days, but don't underestimate the trail's ruggedness. From East Flagstaff Road, follow the white blazes of the AT southbound, passing a blue-blazed side trail at 1.4 miles that leads 0.1 mile to the Little Bigelow lean-to, where there is a good spring and tent space. From there, the AT climbs steadily until cresting the eastern end of the long, low ridge of Little Bigelow Mountain three miles from the road. There are excellent views from open ledges west toward Bigelow Mountain and the ski area at Sugarloaf Mountain, across the Carrabassett Valley. The trail follows the relatively flat, wooded ridge top, passing another open ledge with a view of Bigelow and Flagstaff Lake at 4.5 miles. It then descends about 1,000 feet over less than two miles into Safford Notch, where the forested floor is littered with giant boulders, some of them stacked dramatically atop one another.

At 6.3 miles from East Flagstaff Road, a side trail leads left (southwest) 0.3 mile to tent platforms at the Safford Notch campsite. Just 0.1 mile farther down the AT, the Safford Brook Trail exits right (north), leading 2.2 miles to East Flagstaff Road (and 2.5 miles to Flagstaff Lake). The AT climbs steeply out of Safford Notch, over and around boulders, gaining about 2,000 feet in elevation over two miles to Bigelow's east summit, 4,088-foot Avery Peak. On the way up Avery, the trail passes a side path at 7.5 miles that leads 0.1 mile to an excellent view east and north from atop the cliff called the "Old Man's Head." Beyond that side path, the AT ascends the crest of a narrow, wooded ridge, breaking out of the trees for the final 0.1 mile up Avery

Peak. Passing over Avery, the trail descends into the wooded col between the summits, reaching the Avery tenting area at 8.7 miles, where I once found the lone water source, a spring, dried up in early September.

The ascent grows fairly steep up West Peak, the true summit at 4,145 feet, 0.7 mile from Avery Peak. The AT descends to and follows the up-and-down ridge connecting Bigelow to the 3,805-foot summit of South Horn, where you get a good view to the west from directly above Horns Pond. Just 0.1 mile farther, a side trail leads 0.2 mile to the summit of North Horn (3,792 feet). Continue steeply downhill on the AT, reaching the Horns Pond lean-tos and tent sites at 11.6 miles from East Flagstaff Road and half a mile from South Horn. Horns Pond is a scenic tarn nestled in a tiny bowl at about 3,200 feet on Bigelow's west slope. From here, the AT climbs slightly out of the bowl, passing the junction with the Horns Pond Trail 0.2 mile south of Horns Pond and a short side path to a pond overlook at 0.3 mile. The trail then descends steadily, swinging south and passing the Bigelow Range Trail junction nearly two miles from Horns Pond, to the Cranberry Stream campsite at 14.8 miles (3.2 miles south of Horns Pond and 1.9 miles north of Route 27/16). At 15.8 miles, the AT crosses Stratton Brook on a bridge before reaching Route 27/16 at mile 16.7 of this trip, 5.1 miles from Horns Pond.

Special note: The traverse of this range ranks among the most popular backpacking treks in New England. Especially during the warmer months, the campsites and shelters fill quickly, even during the week. Bringing a tent is recommended. Also take care to walk only on the trail above tree line, where fragile alpine vegetation is easily trampled.

**User groups:** Hikers only. No wheelchair facilities. Dogs are discouraged along the Appalachian Trail in Maine. Bikes and horses are prohibited. Hunting is allowed in season in the Bigelow Preserve, but not on or near trails. This trail should not be attempted in winter except by hikers experienced in mountaineering and prepared for severe winter weather, and is not suitable for skis.

**Access, fees:** Parking and access are free. Camp at existing camping areas and shelters: Little Bigelow lean-to at 1.4 miles south of East Flagstaff Road, Safford Notch campsite at 6.3 miles, Avery tenting area at 8.7 miles, Horns Pond lean-tos and tent sites at 11.6 miles, and the Cranberry Stream campsite at 14.8 miles. Stephen Martelli of Stratton runs a fee-based hiker shuttle service to road crossings along the Appalachian Trail between Grafton Notch and Monson; call 207/246-4642. For information about a hiker shuttle, free Kennebec River ferry service, and other hiker services along the Appalachian Trail in Maine, contact Steve Longley, P.O. Box 90, Route 201, The Forks, ME 04985, 207/663-4441 or 888/FLOAT-ME (in Maine only), website: www.riversandtrails.com.

**Maps:** A free contour map of trails in the Bigelow Preserve is available at some trailheads and from the Maine Bureau of Public Lands (see address below). For a trail map, refer to map 5 in the *Map and Guide to the Appalachian Trail in Maine,* a set of seven maps and a guidebook for $24.95 from the Maine Appalachian Trail Club or the Appalachian Trail Conference (see addresses below). Also available is the *Rangeley-Stratton/Baxter State Park-Katahdin* map, $7.95 in waterproof Tyvek, which is available in many stores and from the Appalachian Mountain Club, 800/262-4455, website: www.outdoors.org. For topographic area maps, request Little Bigelow Mountain, the Horns, Sugarloaf Mountain, and Poplar Mountain from USGS Map Sales, Federal Center, Box 25286, Denver, CO 80225, 888/ASK-USGS (888/275-8747), website: http://mapping.usgs.gov.

**Directions:** You need to shuttle two vehicles for this trip. To do the hike from north to south, as described here, leave one vehicle at the junction of the Appalachian Trail and Routes 27 and 16, 5.3 miles south of where Routes 27 and 16 split in Stratton and 16 miles north of where Routes 27 and 16 split in Kingfield. Then drive on Route 16 east to North New Portland. Turn left (north) in front of the country store onto Long Falls Dam Road and follow it for 17.4 miles. Bear left onto the dirt Bog Brook Road. Drive 0.7 mile, bear left onto the dirt East Flagstaff Road, and drive 0.1 mile. Park either in the gravel pit on the right, or at the roadside where the Appalachian Trail crosses the road just beyond the pit.

**Contact:** Maine Department of Conservation, Bureau of Parks and Lands, 286 Water St., Key Bank Plaza, 3rd and 5th floors, Augusta, ME 04333-0022, 207/287-3821, website: www.state.me.us/doc/parks/. Maine Appalachian Trail Club, P.O. Box 283, Augusta, ME 04332-0283, website: www.matc.org. Appalachian Trail Conference, 799 Washington St., P.O. Box 807, Harpers Ferry, WV 25425-0807, 304/535-6331, website: www.appalachiantrail.org.

## ❷ BIGELOW MOUNTAIN
**13.8 mi/10.5 hrs or 1–2 days**
**east of Stratton**

Ⓕ This hike up one of Maine's most spectacular and popular mountains, Bigelow, can be accomplished in a single long day by fit hikers getting an early start. But there are two camping areas along the trail that offer the option of a two-day trip, leaving your heavy pack behind for the day hike to Bigelow's summits. The cumulative elevation gained by hitting both of Bigelow's summits is nearly 4,000 feet. (To make a loop hike of about 12.5 miles instead of this route over Bigelow's two summits, go up the Fire Warden's Trail, which begins a little more than a half mile beyond the AT crossing of Stratton Brook Pond Road. Climb the Fire Warden's Trail for 3.5 miles to Avery col, turn right, or northbound, on the AT for 0.4 mile to Avery Peak, then turn around and descend the AT southbound for nearly eight miles to Stratton Brook Road. Turn left and walk the road for 0.5 mile to complete the loop. The upper half mile of the Fire Warden's Trail is very steep and severely eroded.)

For the Bigelow summit hike, begin at Stratton Brook Pond Road and follow the white blazes of the Appalachian Trail northbound into the woods. Within a quarter mile you will cross a logging road and Stratton Brook on a bridge. The AT ascends steadily, passing the Cranberry Stream campsite at 1.1 miles and a junction with the Bigelow Range Trail at 2.4 miles. Stay on the AT, which swings east and climbs past a short side trail out to ledges above Horns Pond at four miles, and then passes the Horns Pond Trail junction 0.1 mile farther. The trail drops slightly into the bowl, home to the tiny mountain tarn called Horns Pond and a camping area with two lean-tos and tent sites, at 4.3 miles.

The AT climbs steeply for the next half mile, passing a side trail leading 0.2 mile to North Horn (3,792 feet) at 4.7 miles and reaching the 3,805-foot South Horn summit at 4.8 miles, with a good view over Horns Pond and north to Flagstaff Lake. Descending steeply off South Horn, you follow an up-and-down ridge for more than a mile, then climb steeply to West Peak, Bigelow's true summit at 4,145 feet, 6.9 miles in. The rocky, open summit affords views in every direction: north over Flagstaff Lake and the wilderness of the North Woods, all the way to Katahdin on a clear day, and southwest to Washington when conditions are right. For this hike, turn around and descend the same way you came. To reach 4,088-foot Avery Peak, continue northbound on the AT, dropping into the saddle between Bigelow's two summits, passing the Avery tenting area at 7.2 miles, and then climbing to the open summit of Avery Peak. Hiking to Avery and back adds 1.4 miles and an hour (possibly more) to this hike's distance.

Special note: Bigelow Mountain ranks among the most popular peaks in New England. Especially during the warmer months, the campsites and shelters fill quickly, even during the week. Bringing a tent is recommended. Also take care to walk only on the trail above tree line, where fragile alpine vegetation is easily trampled.

**User groups:** Hikers only. No wheelchair facilities. Dogs are discouraged along the Appalachian Trail in Maine. This trail should not be attempted in winter except by hikers experienced in mountaineering and prepared for severe winter weather, and is not suitable for skis. Bikes and horses are prohibited. Hunting is allowed in season in the Bigelow Preserve, but not on or near trails.

**Access, fees:** Parking and access are free. Camp at existing camping areas and shelters, which along this route include the Cranberry Stream campsite 1.1 miles from Stratton Brook Pond Road, the Horns Pond lean-tos and tent sites at 4.3 miles, and the Avery tenting area at 7.2 miles.

**Maps:** A free contour map of trails in the Bigelow Preserve is available at some trailheads and from the Maine Bureau of Public Lands (see address below). For a trail map, refer to map 5 in the *Map and Guide to the Appalachian Trail in Maine,* a set of seven maps and a guidebook for $24.95 from the Maine Appalachian Trail Club or the Appalachian Trail Conference (see addresses below). Also available is the *Rangeley-Stratton/Baxter State Park-Katahdin* map, $7.95 in waterproof Tyvek, which is available in many stores and from the Appalachian Mountain Club, 800/262-4455, website: www.outdoors.org. For topographic area maps, request Horns and Sugarloaf Mountain from USGS Map Sales, Federal Center, Box 25286, Denver, CO 80225, 888/ASK-USGS (888/275-8747), website: http://mapping.usgs.gov.

**Directions:** From Route 27/16, turn north onto Stratton Brook Pond Road, five miles east of where Routes 27 and 16 split in Stratton and about 16.3 miles west of where Routes 27 and 16 split in Kingfield (and about 0.3 mile west of where the Appalachian Trail crosses Route 27/16). Drive 1.4 miles to where the AT crosses the dirt road and park at the roadside.

**Contact:** Maine Department of Conservation, Bureau of Parks and Lands, 286 Water St., Key Bank Plaza, 3rd and 5th floors, Augusta, ME 04333-0022, 207/287-3821, website: www.state.me.us/doc/parks/. Maine Appalachian Trail Club, P.O. Box 283, Augusta, ME 04332-0283, website: www.matc.org. Appalachian Trail Conference, 799 Washington St., P.O. Box 807, Harpers Ferry, WV 25425-0807, 304/535-6331, website: www.appalachiantrail.org.

## 🖸 NORTH CROCKER MOUNTAIN
**10.4 mi/7 hrs**

**south of Stratton**

Despite North Crocker Mountain's 4,168-foot elevation, Maine's fifth-highest summit does little to distinguish itself in the area of visual spectacle. The low spruce trees that grow right to the top of the peak obscure the views; I tried standing on the summit cairn to see over the trees, but it didn't help much. There is actually a decent view toward Sugarloaf Mountain and Mount Abraham just beyond the summit, heading south on the AT. But for someone looking to tick off a 4,000-footer or for a quiet and moderate hike up a wooded ridge, this 10.4-mile trip is a fine day's outing. In winter, with a snowpack at the summit, you might actually be able to see over the trees; but bear in mind that this could be a very long hike if you have to break trail in snowshoes all the way. The North and South Crocker Mountain hike (see next listing) provides a shorter route over both Crocker peaks.

From Route 16/27, follow the white blazes of the AT southbound. It rises gently at first and never grows more than moderately steep before reaching the wooded North Crocker summit, 5.2 miles and 2,700 vertical feet from the highway. Continuing south on the AT to the South Crocker summit (4,010 feet) adds two miles round-trip to this hike's distance. Retrace your steps to return to your car.

**User groups:** Hikers and snowshoers. No wheelchair facilities. Dogs are discouraged along the Appalachian Trail in Maine. This trail is not suitable for skis. Bikes, horses, and hunting are prohibited.

**Access, fees:** Parking and access are free.

**Maps:** For a trail map, refer to map 6 in the *Map and Guide to the Appalachian Trail in Maine,* a set of seven maps and a guidebook for $24.95 available from the Maine Appalachian Trail Club or the Appalachian Trail Conference (see addresses below). Also available is the *Rangeley-Stratton/Baxter State Park-Katahdin* map, $7.95 in waterproof Tyvek, which is available in many stores and from the Appalachian Mountain Club, 800/262-4455, website: www.outdoors.org. For topographic area maps, request Sugarloaf Mountain and Black Nubble from USGS Map Sales, Federal Center, Box 25286, Denver, CO 80225, 888/ASK-USGS (888/275-8747), website: http://mapping.usgs.gov.

**Directions:** Park where the Appalachian Trail crosses Route 27/16, 5.3 miles south of where Routes 27 and 16 split in Stratton and 16 miles north of where Routes 27 and 16 split in Kingfield.

**Contact:** Maine Appalachian Trail Club, P.O. Box 283, Augusta, ME 04332-0283, website: www.matc.org. Appalachian Trail Conference, 799 Washington St., P.O. Box 807, Harpers Ferry, WV 25425-0807, 304/535-6331, website: www.appalachiantrail.org.

## ■ NORTH AND SOUTH CROCKER MOUNTAIN

**6.2 mi/4.5 hrs**

**south of Stratton**

This 6.2-mile hike offers the most direct route up Maine's 5th- and 12th-highest peaks, the 4,000-footers North and South Crocker. Their wooded summits, unfortunately, offer only very limited views. South Crocker has the better view of the two, toward Sugarloaf Mountain and Mount Abraham from a small ledge. The best view on North Crocker is from the trail just shy of the actual summit, but it essentially mirrors the perspective from the south summit. The hike up South Crocker, however, does cross open slopes with nice views to the north and east. The cumulative

elevation gained by hitting both summits is about 2,800 feet.

From Caribou Valley Road, turn right onto the Appalachian Trail northbound. It climbs steadily, and in one mile reaches a side path leading 0.1 mile to the Crocker Cirque campsite. Above the campsite, the AT heads straight up a very steep and loose slope of broken slate, which can be treacherous when wet and very difficult to descend even when dry; there are views from here of Crocker Cirque. The trail enters the woods again, then traverses an old rock slide, with views out toward the Bigelow Range. Climbing steadily from there, the Appalachian Trail reaches a side path 2.1 miles from Caribou Valley Road that leads about 150 feet to the South Crocker summit ledge. Continuing north, the AT drops down into the saddle between the two summits and then climbs to the higher of the two mountains, North Crocker, 3.1 miles from the road. Head back the same way you hiked up.

**User groups:** Hikers only. No wheelchair facilities. Dogs are discouraged along the Appalachian Trail in Maine. Access to this trail by car during the winter may be limited since Caribou Valley Road may not be plowed; however, it could be skied as far as the AT crossing. Winter attempts on North and South Crocker Mountain should be made only by people experienced in mountaineering and prepared for severe weather. Bikes, horses, and hunting are prohibited.

**Access, fees:** Parking and access are free. The dirt Caribou Valley Road was improved in recent years all the way to the AT crossing and is now usually passable for cars during the warm months. The Crocker Cirque campsite, with three tent platforms, lies 0.1 mile down a side path off the AT, one mile north of Caribou Valley Road.

**Maps:** For a trail map, refer to map 6 in the *Map and Guide to the Appalachian Trail in Maine,* a set of seven maps and a guidebook for $24.95 from the Maine Appalachian Trail Club or the Appalachian Trail Conference (see addresses below). Also available is the *Rangeley-Stratton/Baxter State Park-Katahdin* map, $7.95 in waterproof Tyvek, which is available in many stores and from the Appalachian Mountain Club, 800/262-4455, website: www.outdoors.org. For a topographic area map, request Sugarloaf Mountain from USGS Map Sales, Federal Center, Box 25286, Denver, CO 80225, 888/ASK-USGS (888/275-8747), website: http://mapping.usgs.gov.

**Directions:** From Route 27/16, about a mile west of the entrance to the Sugarloaf USA ski resort in Carrabassett, turn south onto the dirt Caribou Valley Road. Drive 4.3 miles to the Appalachian Trail crossing and park at the roadside.

**Contact:** Maine Appalachian Trail Club, P.O. Box 283, Augusta, ME 04332-0283, website: www.matc.org. Appalachian Trail Conference, 799 Washington St., P.O. Box 807, Harpers Ferry, WV 25425-0807, 304/535-6331, website: www.appalachiantrail.org.

## 5 SUGARLOAF MOUNTAIN
### 5.8 mi/4.5 hrs
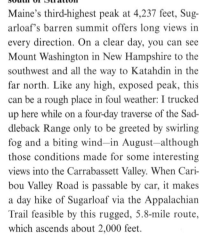
#### south of Stratton

Maine's third-highest peak at 4,237 feet, Sugarloaf's barren summit offers long views in every direction. On a clear day, you can see Mount Washington in New Hampshire to the southwest and all the way to Katahdin in the far north. Like any high, exposed peak, this can be a rough place in foul weather: I trucked up here while on a four-day traverse of the Saddleback Range only to be greeted by swirling fog and a biting wind—in August—although those conditions made for some interesting views into the Carrabassett Valley. When Caribou Valley Road is passable by car, it makes a day hike of Sugarloaf via the Appalachian Trail feasible by this rugged, 5.8-mile route, which ascends about 2,000 feet.

From Caribou Valley Road, follow the white-blazed AT to the left (south), immediately crossing the South Branch of the Carrabassett River, which can be dangerous at times of high water.

The AT then climbs very steeply up Sugarloaf Mountain, involving short stretches of tricky scrambling up a heavily eroded trail. The trail emerges from the woods high on the north slope of Sugarloaf, with views to South and North Crocker across the valley. It reenters the woods and then reaches a junction with the Sugarloaf Mountain Trail 2.3 miles from Caribou Valley Road. Turn left onto that trail and follow its rocky path steeply uphill for 0.6 mile to the exposed Sugarloaf summit, where there are ski area buildings and long views in every direction. Descend the same route back to the road.

Special note: Sugarloaf can be linked with Spaulding Mountain by continuing on the AT southbound, a 10.2-mile round-trip from Caribou Valley Road. An ambitious hiker can continue on to Mount Abraham, making a 17.4-mile day hike or two-day backpacking trip. See the listings for those hikes for more details.

**User groups:** Hikers only. No wheelchair facilities. Dogs are discouraged along the Appalachian Trail in Maine. Access to this trail by car during the winter may be limited since Caribou Valley Road may not be plowed; however, it could be skied as far as the AT crossing. Winter attempts on Sugarloaf should be made only by people experienced in mountaineering and prepared for severe weather. Bikes, horses, and hunting are prohibited.

**Access, fees:** Parking and access are free. The dirt Caribou Valley Road was improved in recent years all the way to the AT crossing and is now usually passable for cars during the warm months.

**Maps:** For a trail map, refer to map 6 in the *Map and Guide to the Appalachian Trail in Maine,* a set of seven maps and a guidebook for $24.95 from the Maine Appalachian Trail Club or the Appalachian Trail Conference (see addresses below). Also available is the *Rangeley-Stratton/Baxter State Park-Katahdin* map, $7.95 in waterproof Tyvek, which is available in many stores and from the Appalachian Mountain Club, 800/262-4455, website: www.outdoors.org. For a topographic area map, request Sugarloaf Mountain from USGS Map Sales, Federal Center, Box 25286, Denver, CO 80225, 888/ASK-USGS (888/275-8747), website: http://mapping.usgs.gov.

**Directions:** From Route 27/16, about a mile west of the entrance to the Sugarloaf USA ski resort in Carrabassett, turn south onto the dirt Caribou Valley Road. Drive 4.3 miles to the Appalachian Trail crossing and park at the roadside.

**Contact:** Maine Appalachian Trail Club, P.O. Box 283, Augusta, ME 04332-0283, website: www.matc.org. Appalachian Trail Conference, 799 Washington St., P.O. Box 807, Harpers Ferry, WV 25425-0807, 304/535-6331, website: www.appalachiantrail.org.

## 6 SPAULDING MOUNTAIN
**9 mi/7 hrs**

**south of Stratton**

Earlier editions of this guide described Spaulding at "just 12 feet short of 4,000 feet high," but since a recent measure of its height put it at 4,010 feet, Spaulding is sure to enjoy a slight boost in popularity—at least among peak-baggers. (At the same time, Mount Redington, immediately west of Spaulding, saw its height adjusted from 3,984 feet to 4,010 feet, tying it with Spaulding and increasing Maine's tally of 4,000-footers from 12 to 14.) It offers better—if not spectacular—views than a pair of 4,000-footers to the north, the Crockers. Just a 0.2-mile detour off the Appalachian Trail, its summit has three short side paths that lead to views toward Sugarloaf Mountain and Mount Abraham. The total elevation gained by hiking Spaulding alone is about 2,000 feet. One of the features I enjoy most about this hike is walking the fairly flat ridge from Sugarloaf to Spaulding, a quiet stretch of trail through a lush forest of hemlock, ferns, and moss. Keep quiet and watch for wildlife—prolific hiker Ed Hawkins, of New Hampshire, tells me he ran into a bull moose with a 26-point rack on Spaulding's summit in the fall of 1999. He and

his companions estimated the antlers spanned nearly six feet.

From Caribou Valley Road, turn left (south) on the AT, immediately crossing the South Branch of the Carrabassett River, which can be dangerous at times of high water. The trail climbs very steeply up Sugarloaf Mountain, involving short stretches of tricky scrambling on a heavily eroded trail. It breaks out of the woods high on the Sugarloaf north slope, with views to South and North Crocker across the valley. It reenters the woods and then reaches a junction with the Sugarloaf Mountain Trail, 2.3 miles from Caribou Valley Road (see the special note below). From the Sugarloaf Mountain Trail junction, follow the AT along the fairly flat ridge from Sugarloaf to Spaulding. About 0.1 mile south of the Sugarloaf Mountain Trail junction, a side path leads about 40 feet to a good view. The AT continues along the wooded ridge to a junction with the Spaulding Mountain Trail, 4.4 miles from Caribou Valley Road. That trail leads 0.1 mile uphill to Spaulding's summit. Return the way you came.

Special note: Spaulding can be linked with Sugarloaf Mountain—Maine's third-highest peak, with views in every direction—for a 10.2-mile round-trip from Caribou Valley Road. An ambitious hiker can continue on to Mount Abraham—making a 17.4-mile day hike or two-day backpacking trip. See the listings for those hikes for more details.

**User groups:** Hikers only. No wheelchair facilities. Dogs are discouraged along the Appalachian Trail in Maine. This trail may be difficult to snowshoe and is not suitable for skis. Bikes, horses, and hunting are prohibited.

**Access, fees:** Parking and access are free. The dirt Caribou Valley Road was improved in recent years all the way to the AT crossing. The Spaulding Mountain lean-to is located down a short side path off the AT, 5.2 miles south of Caribou Valley Road and 0.8 mile south of the Spaulding Mountain Trail/Appalachian Trail junction.

**Maps:** For a trail map, refer to map 6 in the

Map and Guide to the Appalachian Trail in *Maine,* a set of seven maps and a guidebook for $24.95 from the Maine Appalachian Trail Club or the Appalachian Trail Conference (below). Also available is the *Rangeley–Stratton/Baxter State Park–Katahdin* map, $7.95 in waterproof Tyvek, which is available in many stores and from the Appalachian Mountain Club, 800/262-4455, website: www.outdoors.org. For a topographic area map, request Sugarloaf Mountain from USGS Map Sales, Federal Center, Box 25286, Denver, CO 80225, 888/ASK-USGS (888/275-8747), website: http://mapping.usgs.gov.

**Directions:** From Route 27/16, about a mile west of the entrance to the Sugarloaf USA ski resort in Carrabassett, turn south onto the dirt Caribou Valley Road. Drive 4.3 miles to the Appalachian Trail crossing and park at the roadside.

**Contact:** Maine Appalachian Trail Club, P.O. Box 283, Augusta, ME 04332-0283, website: www.matc.org. Appalachian Trail Conference, 799 Washington St., P.O. Box 807, Harpers Ferry, WV 25425-0807, 304/535-6331, website: www.appalachiantrail.org.

## ⑦ MOUNT ABRAHAM
### 16 mi/12 hrs or 1–2 days
**south of Stratton**

Ⓕ Mount Abraham boasts one of the largest alpine areas in Maine, with more than four miles of ridge above tree line featuring excellent panoramic views. But because Appalachian Trail hikers have to make a 3.4-mile detour to climb Abraham, it attracts fewer visitors than some peaks in western Maine, such as neighboring Saddleback Mountain. I actually stood alone on this rocky summit one August morning on a trip where I saw at least several other hikers every day. This 16-mile hike to bag one of Maine's 14 4,000-footers is difficult and long—a conceivable one-day goal for fit hikers getting an early start at a time of year that affords lots of daylight, but it also makes for a satisfying two-day trip. The

cumulative elevation gain on the round-trip is about 3,200 feet.

From Caribou Valley Road, turn left (southbound) on the AT, immediately crossing the South Branch of the Carrabassett River, which can be dangerous at times of high water. The trail then climbs very steeply up Sugarloaf Mountain, involving short stretches of tricky scrambling up a heavily eroded trail. The trail emerges from the woods high on the north slope of Sugarloaf, with views to South and North Crocker across the valley. It reenters the woods and then reaches a junction with the Sugarloaf Mountain Trail 2.3 miles from Caribou Valley Road. (For a scenic 1.2-mile detour off this hike, follow that rocky trail steeply uphill to the exposed 4,237-foot Sugarloaf summit, Maine's third-highest peak, where there are ski area buildings and long views in every direction.) From the Sugarloaf Mountain Trail junction, follow the AT along the fairly flat ridge connecting Sugarloaf to Spaulding Mountain—a quiet stretch through a lush forest of hemlock, ferns, and moss. About 0.1 mile south of the Sugarloaf Mountain Trail junction, a side path leads some 40 feet to a good view. The AT continues along the wooded ridge to a junction with the Spaulding Mountain Trail, 4.4 miles from Caribou Valley Road. (That trail, which is not included in this hike's distance, leads 0.1 mile uphill to Spaulding's 4,010-foot summit, where three short side paths lead to limited views toward Sugarloaf and Abraham—see the previous listing for the Spaulding Mountain hike.) From the Spaulding Mountain Trail junction, the AT descends 0.8 mile to a side path leading 150 feet to the Spaulding Mountain lean-to, where there is space for tents.

The AT follows moderate terrain southward, reaching the Mount Abraham Trail 1.1 miles from the Spaulding lean-to. On this blue-blazed trail, it's 1.7 miles one-way to Abraham's 4,043-foot summit. Although it's relatively flat for the first half mile, after emerging from the woods the trail climbs over three bumps on a ridge, crossing rough talus slopes. From the summit, marked by the rusting remains of an old fire tower, the Horn and Saddleback Mountain are visible to the southwest, and the Bigelow Range can be seen to the north. About 30 feet from the tower, along the Fire Warden's Trail, there is a primitive stone shelter with a shingled roof and enough space under its very low ceiling for a few people to crawl inside (not a place I'd want to spend a night). About 100 feet beyond the summit stand several tall cairns. For this hike, return to Caribou Valley Road via the same route you took up.

Special note: Abraham can be linked with Sugarloaf and Spaulding Mountains on a marathon 17.4-mile day hike or a more moderate two-day backpacking trip, adding just 1.4 miles to this hike.

**User groups:** Hikers only. No wheelchair facilities. Dogs are discouraged along the Appalachian Trail in Maine. The Caribou Valley Road may not be plowed in winter to provide access to this trail, though it could be skied as far as the AT crossing. Winter attempts on Abraham should be made only by people experienced in mountaineering and prepared for severe weather. Bikes, horses, and hunting are prohibited.

**Access, fees:** Parking and access are free. The dirt Caribou Valley Road was improved in recent years all the way to the AT crossing and is now usually passable for cars during the warm months. The Spaulding Mountain lean-to is located down a short side path off the AT, 5.2 miles south of Caribou Valley Road.

**Maps:** For a trail map, refer to map 6 in the *Map and Guide to the Appalachian Trail in Maine,* a set of seven maps and a guidebook for $24.95 from the Maine Appalachian Trail Club or the Appalachian Trail Conference (see addresses below). Also available is the *Rangeley-Stratton/Baxter State Park-Katahdin* map, $7.95 in waterproof Tyvek, which is available in many stores and from the Appalachian Mountain Club, 800/262-4455, website: www.outdoors.org. For topographic area maps, request

Sugarloaf Mountain and Mount Abraham from USGS Map Sales, Federal Center, Box 25286, Denver, CO 80225, 888/ASK-USGS (888/275-8747), website: http://mapping.usgs.gov.

**Directions:** From Route 27/16, about a mile west of the entrance to the Sugarloaf USA ski resort in Carrabassett, turn south onto the dirt Caribou Valley Road. Drive 4.3 miles to the Appalachian Trail crossing and park at the roadside.

**Contact:** Maine Appalachian Trail Club, P.O. Box 283, Augusta, ME 04332-0283, website: www.matc.org. Appalachian Trail Conference, 799 Washington St., P.O. Box 807, Harpers Ferry, WV 25425-0807, 304/535-6331, website: www.appalachiantrail.org.

## 8 SADDLEBACK RANGE
**32.2 mi one-way/3–4 days**
**east of Rangeley**

The Saddleback Range stands out as one of the three premier mountain ranges in Maine—the other two being the greater Katahdin region and the Bigelow Range—and a multiday traverse of its peaks is as rugged, varied, and scenic a mountain experience as can be had anywhere in New England. Seven of the eight summits rise above 4,000 feet, and four of them thrust extensive areas above tree line, offering long, panoramic views. Three miles of ridge above the trees extend from Saddleback Mountain to the Horn. Wintry storms with dangerously high winds occur year-round, so avoid this exposed ground if bad weather threatens. (On my own traverse of this range, I had overcast weather until my final day, hiking over Saddleback Junior, the Horn, and Saddleback.) This traverse could be accomplished in three days but I took four, allowing time to make the side trips to Sugarloaf Mountain and Mount Abraham at a moderate pace. Both side trips add to this hike's 32.2-mile distance.

From Route 16/27, follow the white blazes of the Appalachian Trail southbound. It rises gently at first and never grows more than moderately steep before reaching the wooded North

Crocker Mountain summit (4,168 feet), 5.2 miles from the highway. There are limited views over the tops of low spruce trees. A better view is along the AT just south of the summit, looking toward Sugarloaf Mountain and Mount Abraham. Continuing south on the AT, you drop into the shallow col between the two summits of Crocker, then climb to the top of South Crocker (4,010 feet), a mile away from North Crocker. The actual summit is reached via a 100-foot side path off the AT. An open ledge there affords a limited view toward Sugarloaf and Abraham.

Descending south, the AT crosses an open slope of loose, broken rocks with views north and east toward the Bigelow Range. Footing becomes difficult descending the steep and very loose final half mile to Crocker Cirque campsite, just over a mile from South Crocker's summit and 7.3 miles from Route 27/16. One mile farther south, the AT crosses the dirt Caribou Valley Road (which was improved in recent years all the way to the AT crossing, providing another access to the AT; Route 27/16 is 4.3 miles down Caribou Valley Road). From the road, the AT immediately crosses the South Branch of the Carrabassett River—which can be dangerous at times of high water—then climbs very steeply up Sugarloaf Mountain, involving short stretches of tricky scrambling. The trail emerges from the woods high on Sugarloaf's north slope, with views of the Crockers across the valley. It reenters the woods and then reaches a junction with the Sugarloaf Mountain Trail 3.3 miles south of Crocker Cirque campsite (and 2.3 miles from Caribou Valley Road); this rocky trail leads steeply uphill 0.6 mile to the exposed 4,237-foot Sugarloaf summit, Maine's third-highest peak, where there are ski area buildings and long views in every direction. From the Sugarloaf Mountain Trail junction, the AT follows the fairly flat ridge connecting Sugarloaf to Spaulding Mountain—a quiet trail stretch through a lush forest of hemlock, ferns, and moss. About 0.1 mile south of the Sugarloaf Mountain Trail junction, a side path leads

about 40 feet to a good view. The AT continues along the wooded ridge to a junction with the Spaulding Mountain Trail, 5.4 miles from Crocker Cirque campsite; this trail leads 0.1 mile uphill to Spaulding's 4,010-foot summit, where three short side paths lead to limited views toward Sugarloaf and Abraham.

From the Spaulding Mountain Trail junction, the AT descends 0.8 mile to a side path leading 150 feet to the Spaulding Mountain lean-to, where there is also space for tents. The AT follows moderate terrain south, reaching the Mount Abraham Trail 1.1 miles from the Spaulding lean-to. On this blue-blazed trail, it's 1.7 miles one-way to the 4,043-foot Abraham summit. Although it's relatively flat for the first half mile, after emerging from the woods, the trail climbs over three bumps on a ridge, crossing talus slopes reminiscent of bigger mountains like Washington or Katahdin. But the views from Abraham are among the best in the range. From the Mount Abraham Trail junction, the AT southbound passes a view toward Abraham within 0.2 mile, and then over the wooded top of Lone Mountain in a mile.

Descending, the trail follows and then crosses beautiful Perham Stream (immediately after crossing a logging road), its narrow current choked with moss-covered rocks. The AT crosses a second logging road and, 1.2 miles from Perham Stream, crosses another gem, Sluice Brook, which parallels the trail for 0.7 mile before pouring through a narrow flume. The trail crosses a gravel road and descends very steeply to Orbeton Stream, 5.3 miles from the Spaulding lean-to. I crossed the wide stream on stones in August, but fording it could be difficult in high water. From Orbeton, the AT makes one of its steepest and most arduous ascents in this range, more than two miles to the open ledges of Poplar Ridge, where there are views to the south and east. A half mile beyond the ledges is the Poplar Ridge lean-to (a small brook provides water, but I found it barely trickling in August).

From the shelter, the AT climbs steadily 1.4 miles to the open summit of Saddleback Junior (3,655 feet), with excellent views in all directions. I reached this summit at 7 A.M., early enough to see a cloud tail wave like a flag from the Saddleback summit while fog still sat low in the valleys to the north. Follow white blazes and cairns across the Saddleback Junior top, descend about 500 feet, and then climb steeply 1,000 feet to the open, 4,041-foot summit of the Horn, two miles from Saddleback Junior. Again the views are spectacular, encompassing the Rangeley Lake area and Saddleback Mountain to the west, and extending north to Katahdin and southwest to Washington on a clear day.

Descend south on the AT, crossing mostly open ground with nonstop views, and then ascend Saddleback's ledges to the lower of its two summits. Walk the easy ridge to the true summit, at 4,120 feet, 1.6 miles from the Horn's summit. Continuing south, the AT drops back into the woods a mile below the summit and then crosses a logging road nearly a mile below tree line. The trail crosses a good stream 0.2 mile beyond the logging road and crosses Saddleback Stream 0.6 mile farther. At 3.7 miles from Saddleback's summit, a side path leads a short distance to the Caves, actually passageways through giant boulders that have cleaved from the cliff above over the eons. Just 0.2 mile past the Caves, the trail reaches the Piazza Rock lean-to area, a popular backcountry campsite less than two miles from Route 4. There are tent sites and a large shelter, but this place fills quickly on weekends. A side path off the AT leads about 200 yards uphill to Piazza Rock, an enormous horizontal slab protruding improbably from the cliff. You can follow the trail up onto the slab with a little scrambling. From the lean-to area, the AT descends south for 1.8 miles to Route 4, this hike's terminus.

**User groups:** Hikers only. No wheelchair facilities. Dogs are discouraged along the Appalachian Trail in Maine. This trail should not be attempted in winter except by hikers experienced in mountaineering and prepared for severe winter weather, and is not suitable for skis. Bikes, horses, and hunting are prohibited.

**Access, fees:** Parking and access are free. There are three lean-to shelters and one campsite along this section of the Appalachian Trail: the Crocker Cirque campsite, with three tent platforms, lies 0.1 mile down a side path off the AT, 7.3 miles south of Route 27/16; the Spaulding Mountain lean-to is located down a short side path off the AT, 6.2 miles south of the Crocker Cirque campsite; the Poplar Ridge lean-to sits along the AT, eight miles south of the Spaulding Mountain lean-to; and the Piazza Rock lean-to lies on a short side path off the AT, 8.9 miles south of the Poplar Ridge lean-to. For information about a hiker shuttle, free Kennebec River ferry service, and other hiker services along the Appalachian Trail in Maine, contact Steve Longley, P.O. Box 90, Route 201, The Forks, ME 04985, 207/663-4441 or 888/FLOAT-ME (in Maine only), website: www.riversandtrails.com. Stephen Martelli of Stratton also runs a hiker shuttle service to road crossings along the Appalachian Trail between Grafton Notch and Monson; call 207/246-4642.

**Maps:** For a trail map, refer to map 6 in the *Map and Guide to the Appalachian Trail in Maine,* a set of seven maps and a guidebook for $24.95 from the Maine Appalachian Trail Club or the Appalachian Trail Conference (see addresses below). Also available is the *Rangeley-Stratton/Baxter State Park-Katahdin* map, $7.95 in waterproof Tyvek, which is available in many stores and from the Appalachian Mountain Club, 800/262-4455, website: www.outdoors.org. For topographic area maps, request Sugarloaf Mountain, Black Nubble, Mount Abraham, Redington, and Saddleback Mountain from USGS Map Sales, Federal Center, Box 25286, Denver, CO 80225, 888/ASK-USGS (888/275-8747), website: http://mapping.usgs.gov. **Directions:** You need to shuttle two vehicles for this backpacking trip. To do the hike from north to south, as described here, leave one vehicle where the Appalachian Trail crosses Route 4, about 12 miles north of the junction of Routes 4 and 142 in Phillips and 10.1 miles south of the junction of Routes 4 and 16. Then drive to the hike's start, where the AT crosses Route 27/16, 5.3 miles south of where Routes 27 and 16 split in Stratton and 16 miles north of where Routes 27 and 16 split in Kingfield. **Contact:** Maine Appalachian Trail Club, P.O. Box 283, Augusta, ME 04332-0283, website: www.matc.org. Appalachian Trail Conference, 799 Washington St., P.O. Box 807, Harpers Ferry, WV 25425-0807, 304/535-6331, website: www.appalachiantrail.org.

## 9 SADDLEBACK MOUNTAIN AND THE HORN

**13.4 mi/8.5 hrs**

**southeast of Rangeley**

Saddleback Mountain rises to 4,120 feet, offering some of the best views in the state from its summit and the open, three-mile ridge linking it and its neighboring 4,000-footer, the Horn. A round-trip hike on the Appalachian Trail from Route 4 to the true Saddleback summit—the first of its two summits reached from this direction—is a strenuous 10.2-mile day hike. Continuing to the Horn makes the round-trip distance a very challenging 13.4 miles, with a cumulative 3,800 feet of uphill. Although these are among the most sought-after Maine summits, avoid this exposed ridge in inclement weather. Also carry plenty of water, as there is no water source above the outlet to Moose and Deer Pond.

From Route 4, follow the white blazes of the AT northbound. Within 0.1 mile, the trail crosses a bridge over Sandy River and then climbs steadily to the Piazza Rock lean-to and camping area, 1.8 miles from the road (a very popular destination among weekend backpackers). A side path off the AT leads about 200 yards uphill to Piazza Rock, an enormous horizontal slab protruding improbably from the cliff. You can follow the trail up onto the slab with a little scrambling. Following the AT 0.2 mile north of the camping area, pass another side path leading a short distance to the Caves, actually passageways through giant boulders that have cleaved from the cliff above over the eons. Just over a mile beyond the Caves side path, the AT crosses Saddleback Stream, and 0.6 mile farther it crosses the Moose and Deer Pond outlet, the last water source on this hike. At 4.7 miles from Route 4, the trail emerges above tree line on Saddleback and ascends the open ridge another mile to the summit. Views here are spectacular, encompassing the Rangeley Lake area to the west, the Horn to the northeast, and extending north to Katahdin and southwest to Washington on a clear day. The AT continues down into the slight saddle that gives the mountain its name, over Saddleback's second summit, then drops more steeply over ledges for several hundred feet into the col between Saddleback and the Horn. It turns upward again, climbing gently to the 4,041-foot summit of the Horn, 1.6 miles from Saddleback's summit, where again the views are long in every direction. The AT continues north, but this hike returns via the same route you came.

**User groups:** Hikers only. No wheelchair facilities. Dogs are discouraged along the Appalachian Trail in Maine. This trail should not be attempted in winter except by hikers experienced in mountaineering and prepared for severe winter weather, and is not suitable for skis. Bikes, horses, and hunting are prohibited.

**Access, fees:** Parking and access are free. The Piazza Rock lean-to and camping area is reached via a short side path off the Appalachian Trail, 1.8 miles north of Route 4.

**Maps:** For a trail map, refer to map 6 in the *Map and Guide to the Appalachian Trail in Maine,* a set of seven maps and a guidebook for $24.95 from the Maine Appalachian Trail Club or the Appalachian Trail Conference (see addresses below). Also available is the *Rangeley-Stratton/*

*Baxter State Park-Katahdin* map, $7.95 in waterproof Tyvek, which is available in many stores and from the Appalachian Mountain Club, 800/262-4455, website: www.outdoors.org. For topographic area maps, request Redington and Saddleback Mountain from USGS Map Sales, Federal Center, Box 25286, Denver, CO 80225, 888/ASK-USGS (888/275-8747), website: http://mapping.usgs.gov.

**Directions:** Park in the roadside turnout where the AT crosses Route 4, about 12 miles north of the junction of Routes 4 and 142 in Phillips and 10.1 miles south of the junction of Routes 4 and 16 in Rangeley.

**Contact:** Maine Appalachian Trail Club, P.O. Box 283, Augusta, ME 04332-0283, website: www.matc.org. Appalachian Trail Conference, 799 Washington St., P.O. Box 807, Harpers Ferry, WV 25425-0807, 304/535-6331, website: www.appalachiantrail.org.

## 🔟 PIAZZA ROCK AND THE CAVES

**4 mi/3 hrs**

**southeast of Rangeley**

Many Appalachian Trail hikers continue beyond Piazza Rock and the Caves on their way to bag Saddleback Mountain and the Horn. But these two interesting geological formations just a couple miles from the road offer a wonderful destination for a short hike that climbs little more than a few hundred feet—especially suited for children. Piazza Rock is an enormous horizontal slab protruding improbably from the cliff. The Caves are interesting passageways through giant boulders that have cleaved from the cliff above over the eons. The lean-to and camping area nearby provides the option of an overnight trip, though the area is very popular and fills quickly on summer and fall weekends.

From Route 4, follow the white blazes of the AT northbound. Within 0.1 mile, the trail crosses a bridge over Sandy River and then climbs steadily to the Piazza Rock lean-to and camping area, 1.8 miles from the highway. Turn

left on a side path that leads about 200 yards uphill to Piazza Rock. You can follow the trail up onto the slab with a little scrambling. Follow the AT 0.2 mile north of the camping area and turn onto another side path leading a short distance to the Caves. Hike back to your vehicle the same way you came.

**User groups:** Hikers and snowshoers. No wheelchair facilities. Dogs are discouraged along the Appalachian Trail in Maine. This trail is not suitable for skis. Bikes, horses, and hunting are prohibited.

**Access, fees:** Parking and access are free. The Piazza Rock lean-to and camping area is reached via a short side path off the Appalachian Trail, 1.8 miles north of Route 4.

**Maps:** For a trail map, refer to map 6 in the *Map and Guide to the Appalachian Trail in Maine,* a set of seven maps and a guidebook for $24.95 from the Maine Appalachian Trail Club or the Appalachian Trail Conference (see addresses below). Also available is the *Rangeley-Stratton/Baxter State Park-Katahdin* map, $7.95 in waterproof Tyvek, which is available in many stores and from the Appalachian Mountain Club, 800/262-4455, website: www.outdoors.org. For topographic area maps, request Redington and Saddleback Mountain from USGS Map Sales, Federal Center, Box 25286, Denver, CO 80225, 888/ASK-USGS (888/275-8747), website: http://mapping.usgs.gov.

**Directions:** Park in the roadside turnout where the AT crosses Route 4, about 12 miles north of the junction of Routes 4 and 142 in Phillips and 10.1 miles south of the junction of Routes 4 and 16 in Rangeley.

**Contact:** Maine Appalachian Trail Club, P.O. Box 283, Augusta, ME 04332-0283, website: www.matc.org. Appalachian Trail Conference, 799 Washington St., P.O. Box 807, Harpers Ferry, WV 25425-0807, 304/535-6331, website: www.appalachiantrail.org.

## ⓫ OLD BLUE MOUNTAIN
**5.6 mi/4 hrs**
**north of Andover**

From the first steps up this remote stretch of the Appalachian Trail to the 3,600-foot summit of Old Blue Mountain, this is a hike without a dull moment. I made this trek on the first weekend of spring—which retains a decidedly wintry feel in the northern mountains—and enjoyed a wilderness experience on a trail that had seen few, if any, hikers all winter. We broke trail through drifted snow deep enough at times to bury the blazes on trees, climbed around and over blown-down trees, and took four hours to hike less than three miles up. For a more moderate yet still fairly remote hiking experience, day hike Old Blue between July and early October—but be prepared for any type of weather. The elevation gain is about 2,200 feet.

The AT leaves South Arm Road (look for a sign a few steps in from the road) and climbs steeply above spectacular Black Brook Notch. Atop the cliffs, watch for an open ledge to the trail's right with an unobstructed view of the notch. The AT then meanders through dense woods, at one point offering a good view toward Old Blue's summit. The summit itself is a broad plateau covered with scrub trees and offering views in all directions. Visible to the south are the Mahoosucs and the slopes of the Sunday River Ski Area; to the northeast are the Saddleback Range and Bigelow Mountain. Descend the same way you came.

**User groups:** Hikers and snowshoers. No wheelchair facilities. Dogs are discouraged along the Appalachian Trail in Maine. This trail should not be attempted in winter except by hikers experienced in mountaineering and prepared for severe winter weather, and is not suitable for skis. Bikes, horses, and hunting are prohibited.

**Access, fees:** Parking and access are free.

**Maps:** For a trail map, refer to map 7 in the *Map and Guide to the Appalachian Trail in Maine,* a set of seven maps and a guidebook

for $24.95 from the Maine Appalachian Trail Club or the Appalachian Trail Conference (see addresses below). For topographic area maps, request Metallak Mountain and Andover from USGS Map Sales, Federal Center, Box 25286, Denver, CO 80225, 888/ASK-USGS (888/275-8747), website: http://mapping.usgs.gov.

**Directions:** From the junction of Routes 5 and 120 in Andover, head east on Route 120 for half a mile and then turn left onto South Arm Road. Drive another 7.7 miles into Black Brook Notch to where the AT crosses the road. Park at the roadside.

**Contact:** Maine Appalachian Trail Club, P.O. Box 283, Augusta, ME 04332-0283, website: www.matc.org. Appalachian Trail Conference, 799 Washington St., P.O. Box 807, Harpers Ferry, WV 25425-0807, 304/535-6331, website: www.appalachiantrail.org.

## ⓬ TUMBLEDOWN MOUNTAIN BROOK TRAIL
**3.8 mi/3 hrs**
**northwest of Weld**

Of the two hikes up spectacular Tumbledown Mountain that are described in this guide, this one is significantly easier and more appropriate for children and casual hikers, although it climbs a little more in elevation—about 1,900 feet. (See the following listing for Tumbledown Mountain Loop Trail for another option and more description of Tumbledown.) All trail junctions are marked with signs. The Brook Trail follows an old logging road for its first mile and then climbs more steeply for the next half mile to Tumbledown Pond, a scenic alpine tarn tucked amid Tumbledown's three summits. From the pond, turn left (west) on the Tumbledown Ridge Trail and hike up a moderately steep, open ridge of rock for 0.4 mile to East Peak, where there are sweeping mountain views to the east, south, and west, all the way to Mount Washington in New Hampshire.

This hike ends here and returns the way you came. But to reach West Peak—the true sum-

a hiker atop Tumbledown Mountain

mit at 3,068 feet—follow the Tumbledown Ridge Trail another 0.3 mile west; it drops down into the saddle between the peaks and then climbs the rocky ridge to West Peak (adding 0.6 mile to this hike's distance). See the special note in the Tumbledown Mountain Loop Trail listing for a third possible hike in this area.

**User groups:** Hikers and dogs. No wheelchair facilities. This trail may be difficult to snowshoe and is not suitable for bikes, horses, or skis. Hunting is allowed in season.

**Access, fees:** Parking and access are free.

**Maps:** For a contour map of trails, obtain the *Camden-Pleasant-Weld/Mahoosuc-Evans map*, $7.95 in waterproof Tyvek, from the Appalachian Mountain Club, 800/262-4455, website: www.outdoors.org. For a topographic area map, request Weld, Madrid, Roxbury, and Jackson Mountain from USGS Map Sales, Federal Center, Box 25286, Denver, CO 80225, 888/ASK-USGS (888/275-8747), website: http://mapping.usgs.gov.

**Directions:** From the junction of Routes 142 and 156 in Weld, drive 2.4 miles north on Route 142 to Weld Corner. Turn left onto West Side

Road at the Mount Blue State Park sign. Continue a half mile and bear right on a dirt road. Drive 2.3 miles on that road, passing the Mountain View Cemetery, and then bear right again on another dirt road, heading toward Byron Notch. From that intersection, it's 1.6 miles to the Brook Trail; park at the roadside.

**Contact:** There is no contact agency for this hike.

## 13 TUMBLEDOWN MOUNTAIN LOOP TRAIL

**4.2 mi/4 hrs**
**northwest of Weld**

With a 700-foot cliff on its south face, a pristine alpine pond, and more than a half mile of open, rocky ridge, Tumbledown Mountain seems far taller than 3,068 feet. The views from the ridge and the two peaks (East and West) take in a landscape of mountains and lakes offering few, if any, signs of human presence. As a pair of peregrine falcons circled overhead, I stood alone on the West Peak, enjoying a sunny July day and long views of mountains and lakes to the east, south, and west, all the way to Mount Washington and the White Mountains in New Hampshire (the tall ridge looming in the distance to the southwest). Of the two hikes up Tumbledown described in this guide, this 4.2-mile trek is far and away more difficult; some hikers will not feel comfortable climbing up through the wet, fallen boulders near the top of the Loop Trail. (See the previous listing, Tumbledown Mountain Brook Trail, for an easier route up Tumbledown.) All trail junctions are marked with signs. No trail exists to the north peak, which, along with Jackson Mountain, blocks views to the north. The hike climbs about 1,700 feet.

Begin on the Loop Trail, which enters the woods across from the dirt parking lot. The trail soon begins a very steep ascent of 1.3 miles to the Great Ledges, a flat, open shelf below the towering cliff of Tumbledown. The trail trends to the right along the ledges for nearly 0.2 mile and then turns steeply upward again. Just before reaching the saddle between the East and West peaks—1.9 miles from the trailhead—you have to scramble up through a passage between boulders that typically runs with water. In the saddle, turn left (west) on the Tumbledown Ridge Trail for the 0.1-mile, moderate climb to West Peak, the true summit at 3,068 feet. Double back to the saddle, then follow the Tumbledown Ridge Trail 0.2 mile to East Peak. From here, it's nearly a half mile down the Tumbledown Ridge Trail to Tumbledown Pond and the junction with the Brook Trail. Turn right (south) on the Brook Trail, which leads 1.5 miles to the road; it descends steeply at first, but the last mile follows an old logging road.

Special note: Ken Morgan, an avid hiker in Maine, recommends another loop hike up Tumbledown Mountain and Little Jackson Mountain via the Parker's Ridge Trail, Pond Link Trail, and Little Jackson Trail, saying the views from the upper parts of the first and last of those trails are fabulous.

**User groups:** Hikers only. No wheelchair facilities. A sign at the Loop Trail's start advises against bringing children or dogs on this trail because of its difficulty. This trail would be very difficult to snowshoe and is not suitable for bikes, dogs, horses, or skis. Hunting is allowed in season.

**Access, fees:** Parking and access are free.

**Maps:** For a contour map of trails, obtain the *Camden-Pleasant-Weld/Mahoosuc-Evans map,* $7.95 in waterproof Tyvek, from the Appalachian Mountain Club, 800/262-4455, website: www.outdoors.org. For topographic area maps, request Weld, Madrid, Roxbury, and Jackson Mountain from USGS Map Sales, Federal Center, Box 25286, Denver, CO 80225, 888/ASK-USGS (888/275-8747), website: http://mapping.usgs.gov.

**Directions:** From the junction of Routes 142 and 156 in Weld, drive 2.4 miles north on Route 142 to Weld Corner. Turn left onto West Side Road at the Mount Blue State Park sign. Continue a half mile and bear right on a dirt road. Drive 2.3 miles on that road, passing the Mountain View Cemetery, and then bear right again on another dirt road (there's no sign), heading toward Byron Notch. From that intersection, it's 1.6 miles to the Brook Trail (park at the roadside) and three miles to the Loop Trail (park in a dirt lot on the left). For this hike, you need to either leave vehicles at each trailhead, or park at the Loop Trail and walk the 1.4 miles on the dirt road between the two trailheads at the hike's end.

**Contact:** There is no contact agency for this hike.

## 14 TABLE ROCK, GRAFTON NOTCH

**2.5 mi/1.5 hrs**

**in Grafton Notch State Park**

Flanked to the south by Old Speck Mountain and to the north by Baldpate Mountain, Grafton Notch takes a deep bite out of this western Maine stretch of the Appalachians and marks the northern terminus of the Mahoosuc Range. Perched hundreds of feet up Baldpate Mountain, the broad, flat Table

Rock overlooks the notch. Visible from Route 26, it affords commanding views of the notch and Old Speck. This 2.5-mile loop over Table Rock employs the orange-blazed Table Rock Trail, which ascends very steeply and relentlessly for a mile. The difficult section can be avoided by hiking the more moderate Appalachian Trail and the upper part of the Table Rock Trail both ways, instead of just on the descent, as described here. But while it was physically demanding, I enjoyed the steep trail stretch, particularly when it emerged at the slab caves below Table Rock. The vertical ascent is nearly 1,000 feet.

From the parking lot, pick up the white-blazed Appalachian Trail heading north, crossing the highway. After reentering the woods, follow the AT for 0.1 mile and then turn right at the sign for Table Rock. The trail almost immediately grows steep, emerging a mile later at the so-called slab caves, which are actually intriguing cavities amid boulders rather than true caves. The trail turns right and circles around and up onto Table Rock. To descend, walk off the back of Table Rock, following the blue-blazed trail for a half mile to the left until reaching the AT. Turn left (south), and follow the AT nearly a mile back to Route 26. Cross the highway to the parking lot.

**User groups:** Hikers only. No wheelchair facilities. Dogs are discouraged along the Appalachian Trail in Maine. This trail would be difficult to snowshoe and is not suitable for skis. Bikes, horses, and hunting are prohibited.

**Access, fees:** Grafton Notch State Park is open from May 15–October 15, though the trails are accessible year-round. Visitors using the parking lot at this trailhead are asked to pay a self-service fee of $1 per adult and 50 cents per child. There is a box beside the parking lot.

**Maps:** A very basic map of Grafton Notch State Park trails is available from park rangers, who are usually on duty at high-traffic areas such as Screw Auger Falls; it can also be obtained through the park office or the Maine Bureau of Parks and Lands (see addresses below). For a contour map of trails, refer to map 7 in the *Map and Guide to the Appalachian Trail in Maine,* a set of seven maps and a guidebook for $24.95 from the Maine Appalachian Trail Club or the Appalachian Trail Conference (see addresses below). For a topograpic area map, request Old Speck Mountain from USGS Map Sales, Federal Center, Box 25286, Denver, CO 80225, 888/ASK-USGS (888/275-8747), website: http://mapping.usgs.gov.

**Directions:** This hike begins from a large parking lot (marked by a sign reading "Hiking Trail") where the Appalachian Trail crosses Route 26 in Grafton Notch State Park, 6.7 miles north of the sign at the state park's southern entrance and 1.8 miles south of the sign at the state park's northern entrance.

**Contact:** Grafton Notch State Park, 1941 Bear River Rd., Newry, ME 04261, 207/824-2912 or 207/624-6080 off-season. Maine Department of Conservation, Bureau of Parks and Lands, 286 Water St., Key Bank Plaza, 3rd and 5th floors, Augusta, ME 04333-0022, 207/287-3821, website: www.state.me.us/doc/parks/. Maine Appalachian Trail Club, P.O. Box 283, Augusta, ME 04332-0283, website: www.matc.org. Appalachian Trail Conference, 799 Washington St., P.O. Box 807, Harpers Ferry, WV 25425-0807, 304/535-6331, website: www.appalachiantrail.org.

## 15 MOTHER WALKER FALLS
### 0.2 mi/0.25 hr
**in Grafton Notch State Park**

This short walk on an easy, wide path leads to a couple of viewpoints above what is more of a gorge than a falls. From the turnout, walk down the stairs. A gravel path leads both to the right and to the left, and both directions lead a short distance to views into the narrow gorge, in which the stream drops through several short steps for 100 yards or more. To the right, the walkway ends at a fence. If you go left, you have greater liberty to explore the stream and gorge. It can be difficult to get a good view into the gorge because of the forest's density and terrain's rugged nature along the stream.

**User groups:** Hikers, snowshoers, and dogs. Dogs must be leashed. No wheelchair facilities. This trail is not suitable for bikes, horses, or skis. Hunting is allowed in season.

**Access, fees:** Parking and access are free.

**Maps:** Although no map is needed for this walk, a very basic map of Grafton Notch State Park trails is available from park rangers, who are usually on duty at Screw Auger Falls; it can also be obtained through the park office or the Maine Bureau of Parks and Lands (see addresses below). For a topographic area map, request Old Speck Mountain from USGS Map Sales, Federal Center, Box 25286, Denver, CO 80225, 888/ASK-USGS (888/275-8747), website: http://mapping.usgs.gov.

**Directions:** This hike begins from a roadside turnout marked by a sign for Mother Walker Falls, on Route 26 in Grafton Notch State Park, 2.2 miles north of the sign at the state park's southern entrance, and 6.3 miles south of the sign at the state park's northern entrance.

**Contact:** Grafton Notch State Park, 1941 Bear River Rd., Newry, ME 04261, 207/824-2912 or 207/624-6080 off-season. Maine Department of Conservation, Bureau of Parks and Lands, 286 Water St., Key Bank Plaza, 3rd and 5th floors, Augusta, ME 04333-0022, 207/287-3821, website: www.state.me.us/doc/parks/.

## 16 SCREW AUGER FALLS
**0.1 mi/0.25 hr**
**in Grafton Notch State Park**

A popular swimming hole for families and a scenic attraction for tourists, Screw Auger Falls lies just a few minutes' stroll down a flat walkway from the parking lot. The Bear River pours over smooth stone slabs, tumbling through the impressive waterfall and a tight gorge of water-sculpted rock reminiscent of Southwestern slot canyons (albeit on a smaller scale). While today it sits in the heart of 3,192-acre Grafton Notch State Park, the falls

once sported a water-powered log saw. Up until the early 20th century, the logging community of Grafton, with a population of more than 100, sprawled up through the notch. Interestingly, the town's children attended school during the summer because the notch road was often impassable in winter.

**User groups:** Hikers, dogs, and wheelchair users. Dogs must be leashed. This trail is not suitable for bikes, horses, or skis. Hunting is allowed in season.

**Access, fees:** Parking and access are free.

**Maps:** Although no map is needed for this walk, a very basic map of Grafton Notch State Park trails is available from park rangers, who are usually on duty at Screw Auger Falls; it can also be obtained through the park office or the state Bureau of Parks and Lands (see addresses below). For a topographic area map, request Old Speck Mountain from USGS Map Sales, Federal Center, Box 25286, Denver, CO 80225, 888/ASK-USGS (888/275-8747), website: http://mapping.usgs.gov.

**Directions:** This hike begins from a large parking lot marked by a sign for Screw Auger Falls, on Route 26 in Grafton Notch State Park, one mile north of the sign at the state park's southern entrance and 7.5 miles south of the sign at the state park's northern entrance.

**Contact:** Grafton Notch State Park, 1941 Bear River Rd., Newry, ME 04261, 207/824-2912 or 207/624-6080 off-season. Maine Department of Conservation, Bureau of Parks and Lands, 286 Water St., Key Bank Plaza, 3rd and 5th floors, Augusta, ME 04333-0022, 207/287-3821, website: www.state.me.us/doc/parks/.

## 17 EYEBROW TRAIL
**2.3 mi/1.5 hrs**
**in Grafton Notch State Park**

The Eyebrow Trail is a rugged side loop off the Appalachian Trail that offers a spectacular Grafton Notch view from the crest of Old Speck Mountain's towering cliffs, which are visible from the parking lot. Be forewarned: Parts of the trail are severely eroded and could be unpleasant, especially in wet weather. The elevation gain is about 1,000 feet.

From the parking lot, walk southbound on the white-blazed AT for about 100 yards and then bear right onto the Eyebrow Trail. The trail climbs very steeply over rugged terrain—at one point traversing an exposed slab of rock that could be dangerous when wet or icy. A bit more than a mile from the trailhead, the Eyebrow Trail passes over a series of four ledges. The view of Grafton Notch from the first ledge, a small overlook, is pretty good; the third ledge's view is largely obscured by trees. But from the second and fourth ledges you get an excellent, cliff-top view of Grafton Notch. The summit of Old Speck Mountain (see listing in this chapter) looms high to the right, Table Rock (see listing in this chapter) is distinguishable on the face of Baldpate Mountain directly across the notch, and Sunday River Whitecap rises prominently to the southeast. After enjoying the view, continue along the Eyebrow Trail 0.1 mile to its upper junction with the AT. Turn left and descend the AT for 1.1 miles back to the trailhead.

**User groups:** Hikers only. No wheelchair facilities. Dogs are discouraged along the Appalachian Trail in Maine. This trail should not be attempted in winter except by hikers experienced in mountaineering and prepared for severe winter weather, and is not suitable for skis. Bikes, horses, and hunting are prohibited.

**Access, fees:** Grafton Notch State Park is open from May 15–October 15, though the trails are accessible year-round. Visitors using the parking lot at this trailhead are asked to pay a self-service fee of $1 per adult and 50 cents per child. There is a box beside the parking lot. The Old Speck summit and northeast slopes are within Grafton Notch State Park in Maine.

**Maps:** Map 1 in the *Map and Guide to the Appalachian Trail in New Hampshire and Vermont,* an eight-map set and guidebook available for $18.95 ($12.95 for the maps alone) from the Appalachian Trail Conference (see address below), covers the entire Mahoosuc Range.

So does the *Camden-Pleasant-Weld/Mahoosuc-Evans map,* $7.95 in waterproof Tyvek, available in many stores and from the Appalachian Mountain Club, 800/262-4455, website: www.outdoors.org. Map 7 in the *Map and Guide to the Appalachian Trail in Maine,* a set of seven maps and a guidebook for $24.95 from the Appalachian Trail Conference, covers just the AT in Maine, including this hike. For a topographic area map, request Old Speck Mountain from USGS Map Sales, Federal Center, Box 25286, Denver, CO 80225, 888/ASK-USGS (888/275-8747), website: http://mapping.usgs.gov.

**Directions:** Park in the large parking lot located where the white-blazed Appalachian Trail crosses Route 26 (marked by a sign reading "Hiking Trail"), 6.7 miles north of the sign at the state park's southern entrance and 1.8 miles south of the sign at the state park's northern entrance.

**Contact:** Grafton Notch State Park, 1941 Bear River Rd., Newry, ME 04261, 207/824-2912 or 207/624-6080 off-season. Maine Department of Conservation, Bureau of Parks and Lands, 286 Water St., Key Bank Plaza, 3rd and 5th floors, Augusta, ME 04333-0022, 207/287-3821, website: www.state.me.us/doc/parks/. Appalachian Mountain Club Pinkham Notch Visitor Center, P.O. Box 298, Gorham, NH 03581, 603/466-2721, website: www.outdoors.org. Appalachian Trail Conference, 799 Washington St., P.O. Box 807, Harpers Ferry, WV 25425-0807, 304/535-6331, website: www.appalachiantrail.org.

## 18 STEP FALLS

**1 mi/0.5 hr**

**south of Grafton Notch State Park, in Newry**

On a typical, stiflingly hot and humid July day, I walked these cool hemlock woods to the lower part of Step Falls. Seeing it for the first time, I thought, "Nice." Then I rounded a bend in Wight Brook for my first glimpse of the upper falls and thought, "Wow!" I won't try to build up these falls with some verbose description—this is the sort of place you should discover without expectations.

From the parking lot, follow the obvious, white-blazed trail for a half mile to the falls. The trail is an easy, flat walk; take care not to wander off it onto false trails, because such roaming tramples vegetation. Return the same way.

**User groups:** Hikers and snowshoers. No wheelchair facilities. This trail is not suitable for bikes, dogs, horses, or skis. Hunting is prohibited.

**Access, fees:** Parking and access are free. The preserve is closed from dusk to dawn.

**Maps:** No map is needed for this easy walk. But for a topographic area map, request Old Speck Mountain from USGS Map Sales, Federal Center, Box 25286, Denver, CO 80225, 888/ASK-USGS (888/275-8747), website: http://mapping.usgs.gov.

**Directions:** This hike begins from a large dirt parking lot off Route 26, 0.6 mile south of the Grafton Notch State Park southern entrance. Watch for a dirt road, marked by a small sign, on the south side of a small bridge over Wight Brook; it leads 100 feet to the parking area.

**Contact:** The Nature Conservancy Maine Chapter, Fort Andross, 14 Maine St., Suite 401, Brunswick, ME 04011, 207/729-5181, email: naturemaine@tnc.org, website: http://nature.org.

# 19 OLD SPECK MOUNTAIN
## 7.6 mi/5 hrs

### in Grafton Notch State Park

This 7.6-mile round-trip hike brings you to the summit of Maine's fourth-highest peak and one of the state's 14 4,000-footers at 4,180 feet—a summit that lacked views until a fire tower was built there in 1999, replacing an old, unsafe tower. Now you can climb the tower for 360-degree views. Also, an area was cleared at the summit to land a helicopter carrying building supplies for the tower, opening up views north to the Baldpate Range. There are good views of the Mahoosuc Range from about a half mile south of the summit of Old Speck on the Mahoosuc Trail/AT; that distance is not calculated in this hike's total mileage. There

are also views along the Old Speck Trail, which coincides with the Appalachian Trail, from the shoulder of Old Speck out over the vast sweep of woodlands to the north. You can also turn onto the upper part of the Eyebrow Trail and hike just 0.1 mile to a ledge with a wonderful view of Grafton Notch. This hike's other attractions are the brook cascades, which the trail parallels lower on the mountain. The hike climbs about 2,700 feet in elevation.

From the parking lot in Grafton Notch, follow the white blazes of the AT/Old Speck Trail southbound. At 3.5 miles, the trail reaches a junction with the Mahoosuc Trail. Turn left for the easy, final 0.3-mile climb to Old Speck's summit. Head back along the same route.

**User groups:** Hikers only. No wheelchair facilities. Dogs are discouraged along the Appalachian Trail in Maine. This trail should not be attempted in winter except by hikers experienced in mountaineering and prepared for severe winter weather, and is not suitable for skis. Bikes, horses, and hunting are prohibited.

**Access, fees:** Grafton Notch State Park is open from May 15–October 15, though the trails are accessible year-round. Visitors using the parking lot at this trailhead are asked to pay a self-service fee of $1 per adult and 50 cents per child. There is a box beside the parking lot. The Old Speck summit and northeast slopes are within Grafton Notch State Park in Maine.

**Maps:** Map 1 in the *Map and Guide to the Appalachian Trail in New Hampshire and Vermont,* an eight-map set and guidebook available for $18.95 ($12.95 for the maps alone) from the Appalachian Trail Conference (see address below), covers the entire Mahoosuc Range. So does the *Camden-Pleasant-Weld/Mahoosuc-Evans map,* $7.95 in waterproof Tyvek, available in many stores and from the Appalachian Mountain Club, 800/262-4455, website: www.outdoors.org. Map 7 in the *Map and Guide to the Appalachian Trail in Maine,* a set of seven maps and a guidebook for $24.95 from the Appalachian Trail Conference, covers just the AT in Maine, including this hike.

For a topographic area map, request Old Speck Mountain from USGS Map Sales, Federal Center, Box 25286, Denver, CO 80225, 888/ASK-USGS (888/275-8747), website: http://mapping.usgs.gov.

**Directions:** Park in the large parking lot located where the white-blazed Appalachian Trail crosses Route 26 (marked by a sign reading "Hiking Trail"), 6.7 miles north of the sign at the state park's southern entrance and 1.8 miles south of the sign at the state park's northern entrance.

**Contact:** Grafton Notch State Park, 1941 Bear River Rd., Newry, ME 04261, 207/824-2912 or 207/624-6080 off-season. Maine Department of Conservation, Bureau of Parks and Lands, 286 Water St., Key Bank Plaza, 3rd and 5th floors, Augusta, ME 04333-0022, 207/287-3821, website: www.state.me.us/doc/parks/. Appalachian Mountain Club Pinkham Notch Visitor Center, P.O. Box 298, Gorham, NH 03581, 603/466-2721, website: www.outdoors.org. Appalachian Trail Conference, 799 Washington St., P.O. Box 807, Harpers Ferry, WV 25425-0807, 304/535-6331, website: www.appalachiantrail.org.

## 20 MAHOOSUC NOTCH
**6.5 mi/6 hrs**
**south of Grafton Notch State Park**

While backpacking the northern Mahoosuc Range with a friend a few years back, I was descending toward our introduction to Mahoosuc Notch—which bears a reputation as the hardest mile on the Appalachian Trail—when we encountered another backpacker. He had just come through the notch, so we curiously inquired about it. He smiled wickedly and said, "The notch was full of surprises this morning." Indeed. On a 70-degree Indian summer day, we dropped into the notch and immediately the temperature plummeted about 20 degrees. Giant boulders, which over the eons have toppled off the towering cliffs that embrace the notch, lay strewn about its floor, a maze of stone through which we picked our careful way,

crawling through cavelike passages, constantly scrambling over and around obstacles.

Mahoosuc Notch can be day hiked via the Notch Trail from Success Pond Road when the road is passable; it's 6.5 miles round-trip, climbs a cumulative 1,300 feet or so, and can easily take several hours. Follow the white blazes of the AT carefully through the notch. From Success Pond Road, the trail ascends gently eastward. At 2.2 miles, it reaches a junction with the Mahoosuc Trail, which coincides with the AT. Continue straight ahead (northbound) on the AT, soon entering the boulder realm of the notch. Upon reaching the opposite end—you will know when you're through it—turn around and return the way you came. For a two- or three-day loop that incorporates the notch and allows you to avoid backtracking, see the following listing for the Mahoosuc Range.

**User groups:** Hikers only. No wheelchair facilities. Dogs are discouraged along the Appalachian Trail in Maine. Bikes, horses, and hunting are prohibited.

**Access, fees:** Parking and access are free. Success Pond Road, a private logging road that parallels the Mahoosuc Range on its west side, isn't maintained in winter and may not be passable due to mud in spring; it may also be difficult to follow because side roads branch from it.

**Maps:** For a map of trails, see Map 1 in the *Map and Guide to the Appalachian Trail in New Hampshire and Vermont,* an eight-map set and guidebook available for $18.95 ($12.95 for the maps alone) from the Appalachian Trail Conference (see address below), covers the entire Mahoosuc Range. Or the *Camden-Pleasant-Weld/Mahoosuc-Evans map,* $7.95 in waterproof Tyvek, available in many stores and from the Appalachian Mountain Club, 800/262-4455, website: www.outdoors.org. For topographic area maps, request Success Pond and Old Speck Mountain from USGS Map Sales, Federal Center, Box 25286, Denver, CO 80225, 888/ASK-USGS (888/275-8747), website: http://mapping.usgs.gov.

**Directions:** The Mahoosuc Notch Trail begins on the dirt Success Pond Road, which runs south from Route 26, 2.8 miles north of where the white-blazed Appalachian Trail crosses the highway in Grafton Notch State Park. To access Success Pond Road from the south, drive north on Route 16 from its southern junction with U.S. 2 in Gorham for about 4.5 miles and turn east on the Cleveland Bridge across the Androscoggin River in Berlin. Bear left onto Unity Street; go through traffic lights 0.7 mile from Route 16, and then continue 0.1 mile and bear right onto Hutchins Street. Drive 0.8 mile farther and turn sharply left, passing the paper company mill yard. Just 0.3 mile farther, turn right onto Success Pond Road. From Hutchins Street, it's about 11 miles to the trailhead parking area on the right at the Notch Trail sign.

**Contact:** Appalachian Mountain Club Pinkham Notch Visitor Center, P.O. Box 298, Gorham, NH 03581, 603/466-2721, website: www.outdoors.org. Appalachian Trail Conference, 799 Washington St., P.O. Box 807, Harpers Ferry, WV 25425-0807, 304/535-6331, website: www.appalachiantrail.org.

## 21 THE MAHOOSUC RANGE
### 30.6 mi one-way/4–5 days 9. 10
**between Shelburne, New Hampshire, and Grafton Notch State Park**

Ⓕ I've considered the Mahoosucs one of my favorite New England mountain ranges since my first foray into this wild, remote string of rugged hills one March weekend several years ago. A friend and I spent three days here and saw no one else; and the hiker log in our shelter indicated no more than a half-dozen people had visited since November. On an autumn trip here, I enjoyed one of my finest sunrises ever from the open south summit of Fulling Mill Mountain. Among the trek's many highlights are the ridge walk over Goose Eye Mountain, and Mahoosuc Notch, a boulder-strewn cleft in the range, often referred to as the hardest mile on the Appalachian Trail. The Mahoosucs grow much busier from July through October than they are in March, of course, and their popularity has mushroomed in recent years.

Only one peak in the Mahoosucs—Old Speck—rises above 4,000 feet, but there's nary a flat piece of earth through the entire range. Read: Very tough hiking. This trek traverses the Mahoosucs on the Appalachian Trail from U.S. 2 in Shelburne, New Hampshire, to Grafton Notch, Maine, a 30.6-mile outing that can easily take five days. For a shorter trip, consider a two- or three-day hike from Grafton Notch to either the Mahoosuc Notch Trail (see previous listing for Mahoosuc Notch hike) or the Carlo Col Trail.

Beginning on an old woods road, the Centennial Trail ascends steadily, and steeply at times, to the Mount Hayes eastern summit at 2.8 miles, which offers good views of the Carter-Moriah Range and the northern Presidentials to the south and southwest. At 3.1 miles, turn right (north) on the Mahoosuc Trail, which coincides with the AT. (Just 0.2 mile to the left is a good view from the Mount Hayes summit.) At 4.9 miles, the AT passes over the open summit of Cascade Mountain, and at 6.1 miles a side path leads 0.2 mile to the Trident Col campsite. It skirts Page Pond at 7.1 miles, and at 7.7 miles a side path leads to views from Wocket Ledge. At 8.8 miles, the trail runs along the north shore of Dream Lake; at the lake's far end, the Peabody Brook Trail diverges right, leading 3.1 miles south to North Road. (The Dryad Falls Trail branches east from the Peabody Brook Trail 0.1 mile from the AT and leads 1.8 miles to the Austin Brook Trail.) At 11 miles, the AT descends to Gentian Pond and a lean-to near its shore.

Continuing northbound, the trail climbs steeply up Mount Success, reaching the summit at 13.8 miles. After the Success Trail diverges left (west) at 14.4 miles (leading 2.4 miles to Success Pond Road), the AT descends steeply and then climbs to the Carlo Col Trail junction at 16.2 miles. (That trail leads 0.2 mile to the Carlo Col shelter and 2.6 miles west to

Success Pond Road.) At 16.6 miles it passes over Mount Carlo's open summit, descends, and then climbs—very steeply near the top—to Goose Eye Mountain's high ridge at 18 miles. Walk the open ridge to the left a short distance for the terrific view from the west peak, where the Goose Eye Trail diverges left (west), leading 3.1 miles to Success Pond Road. Then turn north again on the AT, descend, and follow it as it skirts the 3,794-foot east peak, around which the AT was rerouted in the 1990s because of damage by hikers to fragile alpine vegetation on its summit. (The two Wright Trail branches reach the AT immediately south and north of the east peak, both leading east about four miles to the Sunday River Ski Area road in Ketchum.) Descend again, climb over the summit of North Peak at 19.6 miles, and reach the Full Goose shelter at 20.6 miles. The AT climbs steeply north from the shelter to the barren South Peak summit, with views in nearly every direction. It swings left and then descends steeply to the junction with the Mahoosuc Notch Trail at 22.1 miles (the trail leads 2.2 miles west to Success Pond Road).

The next trail mile traverses the floor of Mahoosuc Notch, flanked by tall cliffs that usually leave the notch in cool shadow. Follow the white blazes carefully through the jumbled terrain of boulders, where carrying a backpack can be very difficult. At the notch's far end, at 23.1 miles, the AT swings uphill for the sustained climb of Mahoosuc Arm, passes ledges with good views, and then drops downhill to beautiful Speck Pond—at 3,430 feet one of the highest ponds in Maine. There is a lean-to just above the pond's shore, at 25.7 miles; nearby, the Speck Pond Trail descends west 3.6 miles to Success Pond Road. From the shelter, the AT ascends north up Old Speck Mountain, traversing open ledges with excellent views to the south, then reentering the woods to reach a junction with the Old Speck Trail at 26.8 miles (where the Mahoosuc Trail ends). From that junction, the Old Speck Trail continues straight ahead 0.3 mile over easy ground to the wooded 4,180-foot summit of Old Speck, where an abandoned fire tower stands. The AT coincides with the Old Speck Trail for the circuitous, 3.5-mile descent to Grafton Notch, culminating at the parking lot.

**User groups:** Hikers only. No wheelchair facilities. Dogs are discouraged along the Appalachian Trail in Maine. This trail should not be attempted in winter except by hikers experienced in mountaineering and prepared for severe winter weather, and is not suitable for skis. Bikes, horses, and hunting are prohibited.

**Access, fees:** Parking and access are free. Camping is permitted only at the five backcountry campsites along the Appalachian Trail through the Mahoosuc Range; backpackers must stay in the shelters or use the tent platforms and pay a fee of $8 per person per night. The Old Speck summit and northeast slopes are within Grafton Notch State Park in Maine, but the rest of the Mahoosucs are on private property and not a part of the White Mountain National Forest.

**Maps:** Map 1 in the *Map and Guide to the Appalachian Trail in New Hampshire and Vermont,* an eight-map set and guidebook available for $18.95 ($12.95 for the maps alone) from the Appalachian Trail Conference (see address below), covers the entire Mahoosuc Range. So does the *Camden-Pleasant-Weld/Mahoosuc-Evans map,* $7.95 in waterproof Tyvek, available in many stores and from the Appalachian Mountain Club, 800/262-4455, website: www.outdoors.org. Map 7 in the *Map and Guide to the Appalachian Trail in Maine,* a set of seven maps and a guidebook for $24.95 from the ATC, covers just the AT in Maine (roughly the northern half of the Mahoosuc Range). For topographic area maps, request Berlin, Shelburne, Success Pond, Gilead, and Old Speck Mountain from USGS Map Sales, Federal Center, Box 25286, Denver, CO 80225, 888/ASK-USGS (888/275-8747), website: http://mapping.usgs.gov.

**Directions:** You need to shuttle two vehicles for this backpacking trip. To hike the range from south to north, as described here, leave one vehicle in the large parking lot located where the white-blazed Appalachian Trail crosses Route 26 in Grafton Notch State Park (marked by a sign reading "Hiking Trail"), 6.7 miles north of the sign at the state park's southern entrance and 1.8 miles south of the sign at the state park's northern entrance. To reach the start of this hike, turn north off U.S. 2 onto North Road in Shelburne, New Hampshire, about 3.2 miles east of the southern junction of U.S. 2 and Route 16 in Gorham. Cross the Androscoggin River, turn left onto Hogan Road, and continue 0.2 mile to a small parking area for the Centennial Trail.

**Contact:** Appalachian Mountain Club Pinkham Notch Visitor Center, P.O. Box 298, Gorham, NH 03581, 603/466-2721, website: www.outdoors.org. Appalachian Trail Conference, 799 Washington St., P.O. Box 807, Harpers Ferry, WV 25425-0807, 304/535-6331, website: www.appalachiantrail.org. Grafton Notch State Park, 1941 Bear River Rd., Newry, ME 04261, 207/824-2912 or 207/624-6080 off-season. Maine Department of Conservation, Bureau of Parks and Lands, 286 Water St., Key Bank Plaza, 3rd and 5th floors, Augusta, ME 04333-0022, 207/287-3821, website: www.state.me.us/doc/parks/.

## 22 THE ROOST

**1 mi/0.75 hr**

**White Mountain National Forest, south of Gilead**

From the turnout, walk south across the bridge and turn left (east) on the Roost Trail. Cross two small brooks within the first quarter mile and then walk an old woods road. Less than a half mile from the trailhead, turn left (where indicated by an arrow and yellow blazes). Cross a brook and climb steeply uphill for the final 0.2 mile to the rocky knob of a summit, where the views are largely obscured by trees. Follow the view sign and trail downhill for 0.1 mile to open ledges with a good view overlooking the Wild River Valley. Turn around and return the way you came. The elevation gain is about 500 feet.

**User groups:** Hikers, snowshoers, and dogs. No wheelchair facilities. This trail is not suitable for bikes, horses, or skis. Hunting is allowed in season.

**Access, fees:** Parking and access are free. Route 113 through Evans Notch is not maintained in winter, and gates are used to close off a 9.1-mile stretch of the highway. But you can drive to parking areas near the gates and ski or snowshoe the road beyond the gates to access this area. The northern gate on Route 113 is 1.6 miles south of the junction of U.S. 2 and Route 133 in Gilead. The southern gate sits on the Maine–New Hampshire line, 0.2 mile south of Brickett Place in North Chatham and immediately north of the White Mountain National Forest Basin Recreation Area entrance. The distance given for this hike is from the trailhead.

**Maps:** For a contour map of trails, get the *Map of Cold River Valley and Evans Notch* for $6 from Chatham Trails Association President Allen Cressy, P.O. Box 74, Bethel, ME 04217, 207/824-0508; the *Carter Range-Evans Notch/North Country-Mahoosuc* map, $7.95 in waterproof Tyvek, available in many stores and from the Appalachian Mountain Club, 800/262-4455, website: www.outdoors.org; or the *Trail Map and Guide to the White Mountain National Forest* for $4.95 from the DeLorme Publishing Company, 800/642-0970. For a topographic area map, request Speckled Mountain from USGS Map Sales, Federal Center, Box 25286, Denver, CO 80225, 888/ASK-USGS (888/275-8747), website: http://mapping.usgs.gov.

**Directions:** Drive to a turnout just north of the bridge over Evans Brook on Route 113, 3.7 miles south of the junction of Route 113 and U.S. 2 in Gilead and seven miles north of where Route 113 crosses the Maine–New Hampshire border.

**Contact:** White Mountain National Forest Supervisor, 719 North Main St., Laconia, NH 03246, 603/528-8721, TDD for the hearing impaired 603/528-8722, website: www.fs.fed.us/r9/white.

## 23 MOUNT CARIBOU
**7.3 mi/4.5 hrs**
**White Mountain National Forest,**
**south of Gilead**

I first attempted this hike on a winter backpacking trip, when a friend and I had to walk the road for three miles to the trailhead but never reached the summit because the trail became difficult to follow under a blanket of snow. Months later, in shorts and a T-shirt, I completed this scenic 7.3-mile loop over Mount Caribou, a hill with unusually excellent summit views for its 2,828-foot elevation. There are also beautiful cascades and falls along the Caribou Trail. Mount Caribou lies within the Caribou-Speckled Mountain Wilderness of the White Mountain National Forest. This loop gains more than 1,800 feet in elevation.

The Caribou Trail-Mud Brook Trail loop begins and ends at the parking area; this 7.3-mile hike follows it clockwise. Yellow blazes mark both trails only sporadically, though the paths are well used and obvious (except when covered with snow). Hike north (left from the parking area) on the Caribou Trail, crossing a wooden footbridge over a brook at 0.3 mile. About a half mile past the footbridge, the trail crosses Morrison Brook and trends in a more easterly direction—making several more stream crossings over the next two miles, some of which could be difficult at high water times. One stretch of about a half mile makes five crossings near several waterfalls and cascades, including 25-foot Kees Falls. Three miles from the trailhead, the Caribou Trail reaches a junction with the Mud Brook Trail, marked by a sign. Turn right (south) on the Mud Brook Trail and follow it a half mile, climbing steadily, to the open ledges of the summit. From various spots on the ledges you enjoy views of western Maine's low mountains and lakes in virtually every direction. Numerous false trails lead through the summit's scrub brush, so take care to follow cairns and faint yellow blazes over the summit, continuing on the Mud Brook Trail. A half mile below the summit, the trail

traverses a cliff top with a good view east. From the summit, it's nearly four miles back to the parking area. Along its lower two miles, the trail parallels and twice crosses Mud Brook.

**User groups:** Hikers, snowshoers, and dogs. No wheelchair facilities. This trail is not suitable for bikes, horses, or skis. Hunting is allowed in season.

**Access, fees:** Parking and access are free. Route 113 through Evans Notch is not maintained in winter, and gates are used to close off a 9.1-mile stretch of the highway. But you can drive to parking areas near the gates and ski or snowshoe the road beyond the gates to access this area. The northern gate on Route 113 is 1.6 miles south of the junction of U.S. 2 and Route 133 in Gilead. The southern gate sits on the Maine–New Hampshire line, 0.2 mile south of Brickett Place in North Chatham and immediately north of the White Mountain National Forest Basin Recreation Area entrance. The distance given for this hike is from the trailhead.

**Maps:** For a contour map of trails, get the *Map of Cold River Valley and Evans Notch* for $6 from Chatham Trails Association President Allen Cressy, P.O. Box 74, Bethel, ME 04217, 207/824-0508; the *Carter Range-Evans Notch/North Country-Mahoosuc* map, $7.95 in waterproof Tyvek, available in many stores and from the Appalachian Mountain Club, 800/262-4455, website: www.outdoors.org; or the *Trail Map and Guide to the White Mountain National Forest* for $4.95 from the DeLorme Publishing Company, 800/642-0970. For a topographic area map, request Speckled Mountain from USGS Map Sales, Federal Center, Box 25286, Denver, CO 80225, 888/ASK-USGS (888/275-8747), website: http://mapping.usgs.gov.

**Directions:** The hike begins from a parking lot on Route 113, 4.8 miles south of its junction with U.S. 2 in Gilead and 5.9 miles north of where Route 113 crosses the Maine–New Hampshire border.

**Contact:** White Mountain National Forest Supervisor, 719 North Main St., Laconia, NH 03246,

603/528-8721, TDD for the hearing impaired 603/528-8722, website: www.fs.fed.us/r9/white.

## 24 EAST ROYCE
**2.8 mi/2 hrs**
**White Mountain National Forest, south of Gilead**

From the parking lot, the trail immediately crosses a braided stream and begins a steep climb—both portents of what lies ahead on this short but rigorous 2.8-mile hike. The hike up East Royce makes several stream crossings, passing picturesque waterfalls and cascades, and ascends a relentlessly steep mountainside. I hustled up here one morning after a day of heavy downpours and found the streams swelled nearly to bursting. The summit proves worth the effort, with sweeping views that encompass the dramatic cliffs of West Royce, the peaks of South and North Baldface, and the lakes and lower hills of western Maine. The hike ascends about 1,700 feet.

From the parking lot, follow the East Royce Trail a mile to where the Royce Connector Trail enters from the left. Turn right with the East Royce Trail, reaching open ledges that involve somewhat exposed scrambling within a quarter mile, and the summit just 0.1 mile farther.

Special note: Across Route 113 from the parking area, the Spruce Hill Trail enters the woods beside a series of cascades worth checking out when the water is high.

**User groups:** Hikers, snowshoers, and dogs. No wheelchair facilities. This trail is not suitable for bikes, horses, or skis. Hunting is allowed in season.

**Access, fees:** Parking and access are free. Route 113 through Evans Notch is not maintained in winter, and gates are used to close off a 9.1-mile stretch of the highway. But you can drive to parking areas near the gates, and ski or snowshoe the road beyond the gates to access this area. The northern gate on Route 113 is 1.6 miles south of the junction of U.S. 2 and Route 133 in Gilead. The southern gate sits on the Maine–New Hampshire line, 0.2 mile

south of Brickett Place in North Chatham and immediately north of the White Mountain National Forest Basin Recreation Area entrance. The distance given for this hike is from the trailhead.

**Maps:** For a contour map of trails, get the *Map of Cold River Valley and Evans Notch* for $6 from Chatham Trails Association President Allen Cressy, P.O. Box 74, Bethel, ME 04217, 207/824-0508; the *Carter Range-Evans Notch/North Country-Mahoosuc* map, $7.95 in waterproof Tyvek, available in many stores and from the Appalachian Mountain Club, 800/262-4455, website: www.outdoors.org; or the *Trail Map and Guide to the White Mountain National Forest* for $4.95 from the DeLorme Publishing Company, 800/642-0970. For a topographic area map, request Speckled Mountain from USGS Map Sales, Federal Center, Box 25286, Denver, CO 80225, 888/ASK-USGS (888/275-8747), website: http://mapping.usgs.gov.

**Directions:** The East Royce Trail begins at a parking lot on the west side of Route 113, 7.6 miles south of the junction of U.S. 2 and Route 113 in Gilead and 3.1 miles north of where Route 113 crosses the Maine–New Hampshire border.

**Contact:** White Mountain National Forest Supervisor, 719 North Main St., Laconia, NH 03246, 603/528-8721, TDD for the hearing impaired 603/528-8722, website: www.fs.fed.us/r9/white.

## 25 SPECKLED AND BLUEBERRY MOUNTAINS
**7.9 mi/5 hrs**
**White Mountain National Forest, south of Gilead**

The views from the barren Speckled Mountain summit are among the best in the area. My wife and I had this summit and the cliffs of Blueberry Mountain to ourselves one summer afternoon when the wind blew hard enough to knock us around. This hike's cumulative elevation gain is about 2,400 feet.

From the parking area, pick up the Bickford Brook Trail. At 0.6 mile, turn right at the sign for the Blueberry Ridge Trail. Immediately the trail makes a stream crossing at a narrow gorge that definitely could be dangerous during high water. (If the stream is impassable or if you would prefer a less strenuous hike to the summit of Speckled Mountain, skip this trail and follow the Bickford Brook Trail all the way to the summit, an 8.6-mile round-trip. That option would be the easier route on snowshoes as well.) Continue up the Blueberry Ridge Trail for 0.7 mile to a junction with the Lookout Loop, a half-mile detour out to the Blueberry Mountain cliffs and a great panoramic view of lakes and hills to the south and east, including Pleasant Mountain (see listing later in this chapter). The Lookout Loop rejoins the Blueberry Ridge Trail; follow it to the right. (Hikers seeking a shorter day can turn left and descend the Blueberry Ridge and Bickford Brook Trails, a round-trip of 3.1 miles.) It ascends the two-mile ridge, much of it open, with wide views over your shoulder of the peaks across Evans Notch: East and West Royce, Meader, and North and South Baldface. At the upper junction with the Bickford Brook Trail, turn right (east) for the easy half-mile hike to the Speckled Mountain summit, a bald crown of rock with great views in almost every direction. Descend the same way, except stay on the Bickford Brook Trail all the way (4.3 miles) back to the parking area.

**User groups:** Hikers, snowshoers, and dogs. No wheelchair facilities. This trail is not suitable for bikes, horses, or skis. Hunting is allowed in season.

**Access, fees:** Parking and access are free. Route 113 through Evans Notch is not maintained in winter, and gates are used to close off a 9.1-mile stretch of the highway. But you can drive to parking areas near the gates, and ski or snowshoe the road beyond the gates to access this area. The northern gate on Route 113 is 1.6 miles south of the junction of U.S. 2 and Route 133 in Gilead. The southern gate sits on the Maine–New Hampshire line, 0.2 mile south of Brickett Place in North Chatham

and immediately north of the White Mountain National Forest Basin Recreation Area entrance. The distance given for this hike is from the trailhead.

**Maps:** For a contour map of trails, get the *Map of Cold River Valley and Evans Notch* for $6 from Chatham Trails Association President Allen Cressy, P.O. Box 74, Bethel, ME 04217, 207/824-0508; the *Carter Range-Evans Notch/North Country-Mahoosuc* map, $7.95 in waterproof Tyvek, available in many stores and from the Appalachian Mountain Club, 800/262-4455, website: www.outdoors.org; or the *Trail Map and Guide to the White Mountain National Forest* for $4.95 from the DeLorme Publishing Company, 800/642-0970. For a topographic area map, request Speckled Mountain from USGS Map Sales, Federal Center, Box 25286, Denver, CO 80225, 888/ASK-USGS (888/275-8747), website: http://mapping.usgs.gov.

**Directions:** This hike begins at Brickett Place, a parking area beside a brick building on Route 113 in North Chatham, 0.2 mile north of where Route 113 crosses the Maine–New Hampshire border and 10.5 miles south of the junction of Route 113 and U.S. 2 in Gilead.

**Contact:** White Mountain National Forest Supervisor, 719 North Main St., Laconia, NH 03246, 603/528-8721, TDD for the hearing impaired 603/528-8722, website: www.fs.fed.us/r9/white.

## 26 SABATTUS MOUNTAIN
### 1.5 mi/1 hr

**outside Center Lovell**

This short but popular local hike leads to the top of a sheer drop of hundreds of feet, providing wide views of nearly unbroken forest and mountains, including Pleasant Mountain (see listing later in this chapter) to the south and the White Mountains to the east. This is a great hike for young children and fall foliage lovers. Follow the wide trail, which ascends steadily—and at times steeply—for 0.75 mile to the summit. Walk the cliff top to the right for the best views of the Whites. Return the same way.

**User groups:** Hikers, snowshoers, and dogs. No wheelchair facilities. This trail is not suitable for bikes, horses, or skis. Hunting is allowed in season.

**Access, fees:** Parking and access are free.

**Maps:** No map is needed for this hike. The *Camden-Pleasant-Weld/Mahoosuc-Evans map* shows the location of Sabattus Mountain, but not its trail; the map costs $7.95 in waterproof Tyvek, from the Appalachian Mountain Club, 800/262-4455, website: www.outdoors.org. For a topographic area map, request Center Lovell from USGS Map Sales, Federal Center, Box 25286, Denver, CO 80225, 888/ASK-USGS (888/275-8747), website: http://mapping.usgs.gov.

**Directions:** From the Center Lovell Inn on Route 5 in Center Lovell, drive north for 0.2 mile on Route 5 and turn right on Sabattus Road. Continue for 1.5 miles and then bear right on the dirt Sabattus Mountain Road. Park in a small dirt lot or at the roadside 0.3 mile farther. The trail begins across the road from the lot.

**Contact:** There is no contact agency for this hike.

## 27 JOCKEY CAP
### 0.4 mi/0.5 hr
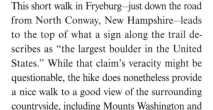
**east of Fryeburg**

This short walk in Fryeburg—just down the road from North Conway, New Hampshire—leads to the top of what a sign along the trail describes as "the largest boulder in the United States." While that claim's veracity might be questionable, the hike does nonetheless provide a nice walk to a good view of the surrounding countryside, including Mounts Washington and Chocorua in the White Mountains.

Follow the wide and obvious trail into the woods. As the cliffs on the face of Jockey Cap come into view through the trees, the trail circles to the left around the boulder and emerges from the woods at a spot where you can safely walk up onto the cap. Return the same way.

**User groups:** Hikers, snowshoers, and dogs. No wheelchair facilities. This trail is not suitable for bikes, horses, or skis. Hunting is prohibited.

**Access, fees:** Parking and access are free. The trail is open to the public year-round.

**Maps:** No map is needed for this short walk, but for a topographic area map, request Fryeburg from USGS Map Sales, Federal Center, Box 25286, Denver, CO 80225, 888/ASK-USGS (888/275-8747), website: http://mapping.usgs.gov.

**Directions:** From the junction of U.S. 302, Route 5, and Route 113 in Fryeburg, drive east on U.S. 302 for one mile and park at the Jockey Cap Country Store on the left. The Jockey Cap Trail begins at a gate between the store and the cabins to the right.

**Contact:** This trail crosses private land owned by the Jockey Cap Motel and Country Store, 207/935-2306, and land owned by the town of Fryeburg and managed by its recreation department, 207/935-3933.

## 28 PLEASANT MOUNTAIN
### 5.7 mi/3.5 hrs
**between Fryeburg, Denmark, and Bridgeton**

Rising barely more than 2,000 feet above sea level, Pleasant Mountain is probably one of the finest low-elevation ridge walks in New England. Walking the ridge brings you alternately through beautiful forest, over open ledges, and to several distinct summit humps with sweeping views. Big Bald Peak may be the nicest stretch of the ridge, though the views from the main summit are excellent also. The cumulative elevation gain is about 1,600 feet.

For a shorter hike, go to either the main summit via the Ledges Trail (3.6 miles, 2.5 hours round-trip) or to Big Bald Peak via the Bald Peak Trail (2.2 miles, 1.5 hours). For the full loop, begin on the Bald Peak Trail, ascending steadily beside a stream; watch for short waterfalls and a miniature flume. You'll pass the Sue's Way Trail and North Ridge Trail entering from the right, but stay left, climbing steeply to Big Bald Peak, then following the Bald Peak Trail southward along the ridge, with excellent views. The Bald Peak Trail eventually joins the wide Fire Warden's Trail. Turn left for the 2,006-foot summit of Pleasant Mountain. Continue over the summit to pick up the Ledges Trail, which descends along open ledges with terrific views to the south. The lower sections of this trail can be muddy and running with water. At the road, if you did not shuttle two vehicles, turn left and walk 1.5 miles to the Bald Peak Trailhead.

**User groups:** Hikers, snowshoers, and dogs. No wheelchair facilities. This trail is not suitable for bikes, horses, or skis. Hunting is allowed in season.

**Access, fees:** Parking and access are free.

**Maps:** See the *Camden-Pleasant-Weld/Mahoosuc-Evans map,* $7.95 in waterproof Tyvek, available in many stores and from the Appalachian Mountain Club, 800/262-4455, website: www.outdoors.org. For a topographic area map, request Pleasant Mountain from USGS Map Sales, Federal Center, Box 25286, Denver, CO 80225, 888/ASK-USGS (888/275-8747), website: http://mapping.usgs.gov.

**Directions:** From the junction of U.S. 302 and Route 93, west of Bridgeton, drive 4.5 miles west on 302 and turn left onto Mountain Road (heading toward the Shawnee Peak Ski Area). Drive another 1.8 miles to a turnout at the Bald Peak Trailhead (marked by a sign on the right). If you have two vehicles, leave one at the Ledges Trailhead (marked by a sign) 1.5 miles farther down the road. Otherwise, you walk that stretch of road to finish this loop.

**Contact:** There is no contact agency for this hike.

### 29 BURNT MEADOW MOUNTAIN
**2.4 mi/2 hrs**
**outside Brownfield**

A nice, short local hike, this hill near Brownfield has an open summit with views in almost every direction, from the White Mountains to the lakes of western Maine. When my wife and I hiked it one July afternoon, we found ripe blueberries to nibble on. This hike gains about 1,200 feet in elevation.

From the parking area, walk uphill to the old T-bar of a former ski area. Turn left and follow the T-bar and a worn footpath uphill. Ignore the sign with an arrow pointing to the right, which you encounter within the first half mile, and continue straight ahead under the T-bar. The trail grows quite steep, with lots of loose stones and dirt. Footing may become very tricky here in spring. Where the T-bar ends in a small clearing, turn left onto a trail marked by blue blazes, which leads at a more moderate angle to the summit. Watch for a good view from ledges on the left before reaching the summit. The broad top of Burnt Meadow Mountain offers views to the west, north, and south; continue over it and you get views to the south and east. Descend the way you came.

**User groups:** Hikers, snowshoers, and dogs. No wheelchair facilities. This trail is not suitable for bikes, horses, or skis. Hunting is allowed in season.

**Access, fees:** Parking and access are free.

**Maps:** For a topographic area map, request Brownfield from USGS Map Sales, Federal Center, Box 25286, Denver, CO 80225, 888/ASK-USGS (888/275-8747), website: http://mapping.usgs.gov.

**Directions:** From the junction of Route 5/113 and Route 160 in East Brownfield, turn west on Route 160 and continue 1.1 miles. Turn left, staying on Route 160, and continue another 0.3 mile. Turn right onto the paved Fire Lane 32. The parking area is 0.2 mile farther. The trailhead isn't marked, but there's an obvious parking area. The trail starts at the parking area's right side.

**Contact:** There is no contact agency for this hike.

### 30 MOUNT CUTLER
**2.6 mi/1.5 hrs**
**in Hiram**

Mount Cutler rises abruptly from the Saco River valley in Hiram and is really a nice hike up a relatively small hill. Cross the railroad tracks, turn left, and then enter the woods on the right at a wide trail. Soon you branch right onto a red-blazed trail. The blazes appear sporadically at times, and on rocks rather than on trees higher up the mountain, making the trail potentially difficult to follow (particularly in winter). The trail ascends steep ledges overlooking the town of Hiram and grows narrow; care is needed over the ledges. But once you gain the ridge, the walking grows much easier as you pass through forests with a mix of hardwoods and hemlocks, and traverse open areas with sweeping views. The east summit ledges, with views of the Saco Valley, are a good destination for a round-trip hike of about 1.5 miles. Continue on the trail along the ridge and into a saddle, where there's a birch tree grove. A faint footpath leads up the left side of the slope to the main summit, which is wooded. Just beyond it and to the right, however, is an open area with great views toward Pleasant Mountain and the White Mountains.

**User groups:** Hikers, snowshoers, and dogs. No wheelchair facilities. This trail is not suitable for bikes, horses, or skis. Hunting is allowed in season.

**Access, fees:** Parking and access are free.

**Maps:** For topographic area maps, request Hiram and Cornish from USGS Map Sales, Federal Center, Box 25286, Denver, CO 80225, 888/ASK-USGS (888/275-8747), website: http://mapping.usgs.gov.

**Directions:** From the junction of Route 117 and Route 5/113, drive over the concrete bridge; take an immediate left and then a right onto Mountain View Avenue. Drive about 0.1 mile and park at the roadside near the railroad tracks.

**Contact:** There is no contact agency for this hike.

## 31 DOUGLAS HILL
**1.2 mi/0.5 hr**

**south of Sebago**

This 169-acre preserve formerly owned by The

Nature Conservancy is now owned by the town of Sebago. A short walk to the hill's open summit and its stone tower gives you expansive views of Sebago Lake, Pleasant Mountain, and the mountains to the northwest as far as Mount Washington.

From the registration box, walk through the stone pillars, follow the yellow-blazed Woods Trail a short distance, and then bear left onto the Ledges Trail (also blazed yellow). This trail leads over interesting open ledges with good views, though they are slick when wet. At the summit, climb the stone tower's steps; on top is a diagram identifying the distant peaks. A nature trail, blazed orange, makes a 0.75-mile loop off the summit and returns to it. Descend back to the parking lot via the Woods Trail.

**User groups:** Hikers only. No wheelchair facilities. This trail is not suitable for bikes or horses and is not open in winter. Dogs are prohibited. Hunting is allowed in season.

**Access, fees:** Parking and access are free; just register at the trailhead. The preserve is open only during daylight hours.

**Maps:** A free guide and map to Douglas Hill may be available at the trailhead registration box. For topographic area maps, request Steep Falls and North Sebago from USGS Map Sales, Federal Center, Box 25286, Denver, CO 80225, 888/ASK-USGS (888/275-8747), website: http://mapping.usgs.gov.

**Directions:** From the junction of Routes 107 and 114 in East Sebago, drive a half mile north on Route 107 and turn left onto Douglas Mountain Road (which is one mile south of Sebago center). Drive 0.8 mile to a hilltop and take a sharp left. In another half mile, turn left into a small parking area.

**Contact:** Sebago Town Hall, 207/787-2457.

## 32 MOUNT AGAMENTICUS
**1 mi/0.75 hr**

**west of Ogunquit**

This one-mile hike up and down tiny Agamenticus is an easy walk to a summit with a fire tower that offers 360-degree views of the

Seacoast region and southern Maine and New Hampshire. From the parking area, follow the trail along an old woods road, soon climbing moderately. The trail ascends ledges, crosses the summit road, and emerges after half a mile at the summit. Return the way you came or descend the summit road.

**User groups:** Hikers, snowshoers, and dogs. No wheelchair facilities. This trail is not suitable for bikes, horses, or skis. Hunting is allowed in season.

**Access, fees:** Parking and access are free.

**Maps:** No map is needed for this hike. For topographic area maps, request York Harbor and North Berwick from USGS Map Sales, Federal Center, Box 25286, Denver, CO 80225, 888/ASK-USGS (888/275-8747), website: http://mapping.usgs.gov.

**Directions:** Take I-95 to Exit 4 in Ogunquit. At the end of the off-ramp, turn left, passing over the highway, and then immediately turn right onto Mountain Road. Follow it for about 2.7 miles to the base of the Agamenticus summit road and a dirt parking area.

**Contact:** The Nature Conservancy Maine Chapter, Fort Andross, 14 Maine St., Suite 401, Brunswick, Maine 04011, 207/729-5181, email: naturemaine@tnc.org, website: http://nature.org. The Nature Conservancy Southern Maine field office, 207/646-1788.

# New Hampshire

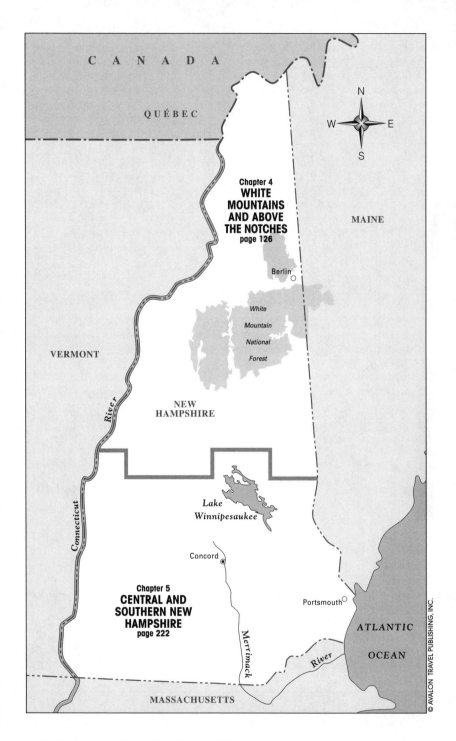

## Chapter 4

© MICHAEL LANZA

# White Mountains and Above the Notches

# White Mountains and Above the Notches

When hikers and backpackers think of New Hampshire, they usually think of the White Mountains. With numerous summits that reach above tree line within a national forest encompassing about 800,000 acres and 1,200 trail miles, the Whites are the most spectacular range east of the Rockies.

Besides encompassing the classic and popular Presidential Range—which has seven summits higher than 5,000 feet—this chapter's 82 hikes will take you to more obscure peaks throughout the White Mountains and in New Hampshire's sprawling, wild northern woods, "above the notches." Several hikes in this chapter lie along the new 162-mile Cohos Trail, which stretches from U.S. 302 to the Canadian border; full completion of the trail is anticipated in 2004 or 2005.

The southern Whites feature trails from the heights of Franconia Ridge and Mount Moosilauke to spectacular Zealand and Crawford Notches and the peaks around Waterville Valley, and from the largest federal wilderness in the Northeast (the Pemigewasset) to some of New England's most impressive waterfalls; this huge area of the White Mountains is a treasure trove of classic hiking. And I-93 makes much of the southern Whites more accessible to population centers than the northern Whites.

Some of these hikes (Mounts Lincoln and Lafayette, Mount Chocorua, Zealand Notch, Mount Moosilauke) are among the most popular in New England , and it's common to see crowds of hikers on them on nice weekends in summer and fall—and even in winter. Others (Mounts Flume and Liberty and Mount Tripyramid) are much less trampled. Some of the lower peaks (Welch and Dickey, The Moats, Cathedral Ledge, Mount Willard) in this chapter offer the best views per ounce of sweat that you'll find anywhere in New England, while other peaks (Flume and Tripyramid) rank among the region's most rugged and difficult.

Hikes to the bigger peaks of the Whites often entail more than 3,000 or even 4,000 feet of elevation gain, at least several miles round-trip, very rugged terrain, and the possibility of severe weather year-round. You should be well prepared any time of year, and don't go in winter without the right equipment and training.

Along the Appalachian Trail, dogs must be kept under control, and horses, bikes, hunting, and firearms are prohibited. Cross-country skiing and snowshoeing are allowed, though the trail is often too rugged for skiing.

Keep group sizes to no more than 10 people in any federal wilderness area in the White Mountain National Forest (a good guideline to follow in nonwilderness areas as well, because large groups disproportionately affect the land and the experience of other hikers); contact the White Mountain National Forest (see Resources appendix) for information on permits for larger groups.

In the White Mountain National Forest, fires are prohibited above timberline, and camping is prohibited within a quarter mile of any hut or shelter except at authorized tent sites. Camping is permitted above timberline only where there exists a base of at least two feet of snow. Timberline is defined as that elevation at which trees are less than eight feet tall, and is often indicated by trailside signs. Stay on the trail in the alpine zone (the area above timberline) to avoid damaging fragile alpine vegetation.

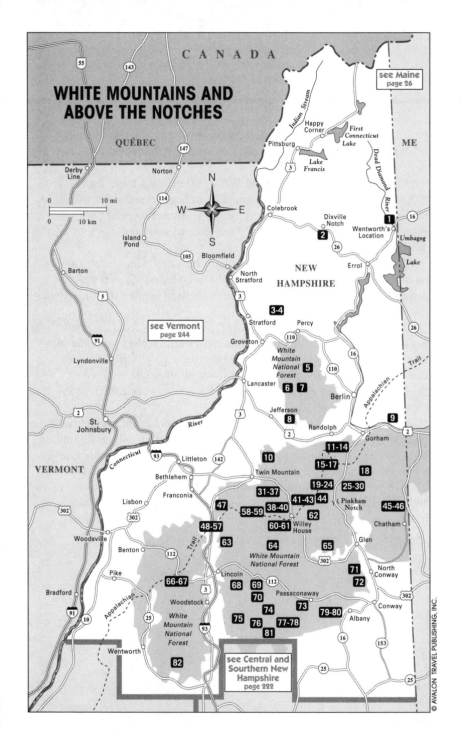

# 1 DIAMOND PEAKS

**7 mi/4.5 hrs**

**in the Second College Grant near Wentworth's Location**

Here's a wild, seven-mile hike in the North Country—way north of the White Mountains—that's too far from anything approaching civilization to ever become popular. You can mountain bike or cross-country ski the 2.5 miles of flat road to the trailhead to give this little adventure a mixed flavor. The hike up Diamond Peaks climbs about 600 feet.

About 0.2 mile past the Mount Dustan Store in the Wentworth's Location village center, turn left at a small cemetery onto Dead Diamond Road. Remember how far north you are—this road will be snow covered from mid-autumn well into spring and may be a mud bog until July. Follow it for 2.5 miles to the Management Center. The yellow-blazed trail up the Diamond Peaks begins at a sign on the right (east) side of the road, across from the Management Center. It rises gently through the woods at first (easy skiing, but bikes are prohibited), then makes a short but steep ascent up the rocky hillside. You pass a short spur trail on the left, marked by a sign, which leads to Alice Ledge, with a good view of the Dead Diamond River Valley. The grade becomes moderate again until the final push up to the first of the three Diamond Peaks. The trail ascends the ridge along the top of tall cliffs, with several good views of the valley below and the wooded hills across the valley. Just below the first peak's wooded summit is an open ledge overlooking the precipitous cliffs. The trail ends atop the tall cliffs of the second peak. Follow the same route back.

**User groups:** Hikers, snowshoers, and dogs. No wheelchair facilities. This trail may be difficult to ski and is not suitable for horses. Bikes are prohibited. Hunting is allowed in season.

**Access, fees:** The hike is on private land in the state's far north, within the Second College Grant, a township of nearly 27,000 acres owned

by Dartmouth College in Hanover. The college uses gates to control access. A permit from the Outdoor Programs Office at Dartmouth College is required to park within the grant and is available only to persons affiliated with the college or its Outing Club. However, day use by the public is allowed, provided you park outside the grant.

**Maps:** The Outdoor Programs Office at Dartmouth College (see address below) sells a waterproof contour trail map of the Second College Grant for $2. To obtain a topographic area map, request Wilsons Mills from USGS Map Sales, Federal Center, Box 25286, Denver, CO 80225, 888/ASK-USGS (888/275-8747), website: http://mapping.usgs.gov.

**Directions:** From the junction of Routes 16 and 26 in Errol, follow Route 16 north into Wentworth's Location. Stop and ask about parking at the Mount Dustan Store in the village center. Or park at the turnout along Route 16 about 0.2 mile past the store (about 75 yards beyond a small cemetery and Dead Diamond Road).

**Contact:** Dartmouth College Outdoor Programs Office, 119 Robinson Hall, Dartmouth College, Hanover, NH 03755, 603/646-2834, website: www.dartmouth.edu/~doc.

# 2 TABLE ROCK, DIXVILLE NOTCH

**0.7 mi/1.5 hrs**

**in Dixville Notch State Park**

Scrambling up the steep, rocky trail to Table Rock, I was stopped by an odd sound piercing the silence. Hearing it again, I realized the source—a bull moose. In late September, the bellowing of a moose in rut is not an unusual sound in the North Country. Vibrant fall foliage, however, is an unusual sight by this late in autumn: Winter arrives sooner here than in the White Mountains farther south. This hike is along the new, 162-mile Cohos Trail, which stretches from the southern Presidential Range to the Canadian border; full completion of the trail is anticipated in 2004 or 2005.

the view of Dixville Notch from Table Rock

dents in the North Country Trailmaster program. They reopened an old trail along the south side of the notch going eastbound all the way down to Huntington Falls and out to the picnic area near the Whittemore graveyard next to Route 26 east of the notch. This new trail makes it possible to swing over Route 26 to the Sanguinary Mountain Trail to a number of cliffs (very good views) on the north side of the notch and out to the perch high above the Balsams. Then the trail descends steeply down to the junction of Route 26 and The Balsams resort driveway."

**User groups:** Hikers only. No wheelchair facilities. This trail would be very difficult to snowshoe and is not suitable for bikes, dogs, horses, or skis. Hunting is allowed in season.

**Access, fees:** Parking and access are free.

**Maps:** For information, a guidebook, and maps to the Cohos Trail, contact the Cohos Trail Association (see address below). For a topographic area map, request Dixville Notch from USGS Map Sales, Federal Center, Box 25286, Denver, CO 80225, 888/ASK-USGS (888/275-8747), website: http://mapping.usgs.gov.

**Directions:** Park in the ample turnout along Route 26 in Dixville Notch, immediately west of the highest point of the road in the notch, where a sign marks the Dixville Notch Heritage Trail start (behind the state park sign).

**Contact:** New Hampshire Division of Parks and Recreation, P.O. Box 1856, Concord, NH 03302-1856, 603/271-3254. Cohos Trail Association, 252 Westmoreland Rd., Spofford, NH 03462, 603/363-8902, website: www.cohostrail.org.

From the road, the trail climbs very steeply over difficult, rocky ground for 0.3 mile to the cliff tops flanking the notch. Turn right, walk uphill another 40 feet or so, and then walk the long gangplank of Table Rock. This giant buttress of shattered rock thrusting far out from the main cliff face presents a rare perch hundreds of feet above the floor of one of New Hampshire's wildest notches. The precipitous drops off either side of the narrow walkway make it a rather unnerving adventure. With the notch so far from population centers, you may have this place to yourself, as I did. Although you can link other trails in the notch on a five-mile loop, this hike descends the way you came—arguably more difficult and dangerous than the ascent, because of the steepness and frequently wet rock.

There is now also a five-mile loop hike around Dixville Notch. Although I have not done it myself, Kim Nilsen of the Cohos Trail Association tells me it was "made possible by the completion of the Three Brothers Trail by stu-

## ❸ SUGARLOAF MOUNTAIN
### 3.5 mi/2.5 hrs
### in Nash Stream State Forest

The 39,601-acre Nash Stream Forest in New Hampshire's quiet North Country offers some of the most remote and lonely hiking in the Granite State—and on some sizable hills, no less. Were 3,701-foot Sugarloaf just a few hundred feet taller, peak-baggers would flock here. As it is, the state forest sees few visitors. I stood alone on this summit one afternoon in late September, enjoying a panorama of peaks stretching into Vermont, Maine, and Quebec. In fact, Sugarloaf fronts a large range of peaks that are virtually unknown to many hikers and that nearly rival in size the Pilot Range of the northern White Mountain National Forest to the south. This 3.5-mile hike ascends about 2,100 feet in elevation. This hike is along the new, 162-mile Cohos Trail, which stretches from the southern Presidential Range to the Canadian border; full completion of it is anticipated in 2004 or 2005.

From the parking area, follow the old jeep road past a cabin. Within 0.3 mile, a snowmobile trail diverges left, but continue straight ahead. The road ascends steeply without pause—a real calf-burner. But I felt I had no right to complain about its difficulty after seeing moose tracks following the same trail upward; he was carrying a lot more weight than I was. (I also found the angle perfect for letting my momentum carry me in a run on the descent.) The upper part of the trail eases somewhat, passing an excellent spring and skirting left around a major blowdown just before reaching the craggy summit, about 1.7 miles from the trailhead. Hike back the same way.

**User groups:** Hikers, snowshoers, and dogs. Dogs must be leashed. No wheelchair facilities. This trail is not suitable for bikes, horses, or skis. Hunting is allowed in season.

**Access, fees:** Parking and access are free. Nash Stream Road is typically open from Memorial Day to early November, depending on weather, and can be cross-country skied in winter.

**Maps:** An oversized locator map is posted along the entrance road. For information, a guidebook, and maps for the Cohos Trail, contact the Cohos Trail Association (see address

below). For topographic area maps, request Tinkerville, Blue Mountain, Stratford, and Percy Peaks from USGS Map Sales, Federal Center, Box 25286, Denver, CO 80225, 888/ASK-USGS (888/275-8747), website: http://mapping.usgs.gov.

**Directions:** From Route 110, 2.6 miles east of the junction of Route 110 and U.S. 3 in Groveton and 4.3 miles west of the Stark Union Church in Stark, turn north on Emerson Road. Drive 2.2 miles and turn left onto the dirt Nash Stream Road. Continue a half mile to an open area with an oversized locator map posted on a sign. From the map, follow Nash Stream Road another 4.6 miles, bear left, and continue 3.2 miles. Drive over a bridge and another 100 feet to a parking area on the left.

**Contact:** New Hampshire Division of Forests and Lands, P.O. Box 1856, Concord, NH 03302-1856, 603/271-3456. New Hampshire Division of Parks and Recreation, Bureau of Trails, P.O. Box 1856, Concord, NH 03302-1856, 603/271-3254. Cohos Trail Association, 252 Westmoreland Rd., Spofford, NH 03462, 603/363-8902, website: www.cohostrail.org.

## ◪ NORTH PERCY PEAK
**4 mi/3 hrs**
**in Nash Stream State Forest**

More accessible than Sugarloaf Mountain, which is also located in the sprawling, 39,601-acre Nash Stream State Forest, the 3,418-foot, scrub-covered summit of North Percy Peak offers long views in every direction. The orange-blazed Percy Peaks Trail climbs through hardwoods to the base of a partially overgrown path up a rockslide. The trail, once called the Slide Trail, used to run straight up the slide and exposed slabs. These were dangerously slick when wet and the trail was closed following the death of a hiker 30 years ago; this old trail has since been rerouted. The Percy Peaks Trail now angles southeast away from the slabs, rounds the peak to a col between North Percy and South Percy, and then runs at a steep angle up vast southern slabs near the summit. Remember where the trail reenters the woods at the tree line: The trail is only sporadically blazed and marked with cairns above tree line, and the landscape of scrub brush quickly becomes ubiquitous. Lose your way back to the trail and you'll be bushwhacking through viciously dense subalpine vegetation, or you'll find yourself at the brink of a cliff with nowhere to go but back. The vertical ascent is about 2,200 feet. This hike is along the new, 162-mile Cohos Trail, which stretches from the southern Presidential Range to the Canadian border; full completion of it is anticipated in 2004 or 2005.

North Percy can now be approached from two other trails that have been opened in the past two years as part of the long-distance Cohos Trail. A mile north of the Percy Peaks Trail trailhead at Long Mountain Brook begins the Percy Loop Trail. Follow yellow blazes that rise moderately up the northeast flank of North Percy, first on an ancient logging road and then on a new trail. The trail eventually rounds the peak to the col where it meets the Percy Peak Trail coming up from the other side of the mountain. These two trails now make it possible, with a one-mile walk on the dirt Nash Stream Road—which connects the Percy Loop and Percy Peaks Trails—to make a complete circuit around North Percy Peak.

North Percy may also be approached from the south on the newly rebuilt Old Summer Club Trail, which was originally marked nearly 100 years ago. To reach the trail, one must park at the state parking lot at Christine Lake in Percy hamlet. Walk out of the parking lot and turn left. Take the first right into the woods and pass the gate. Walk 0.4 mile and turn left onto an old logging road. Follow the road a mile easily uphill until it crosses the Jimmy Cole Brook Road—a gated, grassy road. The Old Summer Club Trail begins on the north side of the road, passes a massive boulder, and ascends gradually at first and then moderately steeply. In 0.25 mile it passes a side spur

trail that leads to the fine cliffs of Victor Head 20 minutes up the trail.

The Old Summer Club Trail, marked with yellow blazes, passes two branches of Jimmy Cole Brook and begins a moderate uphill pull to a granite rib that takes some hand- and footwork to scale. Walk the rib northwest into the col between North and South Percy Peaks. Turn right at the junction with the South Percy Trail and walk 300 feet north to the Percy Peaks Trail. Turn right and make your way to the summit of North Percy.

**User groups:** Hikers, snowshoers, and dogs. Dogs must be leashed. No wheelchair facilities. This trail is not suitable for bikes, horses, or skis. Hunting is allowed in season.

**Access, fees:** Parking and access are free. Nash Stream Road is typically open from Memorial Day to early November, depending on weather, and can be cross-country skied in winter.

**Maps:** An oversized locator map is posted along the entrance road. For information, a guidebook, and maps for the Cohos Trail, contact the Cohos Trail Association (see address below). For topographic area maps, request Tinkerville, Blue Mountain, Stratford, and Percy Peaks from USGS Map Sales, Federal Center, Box 25286, Denver, CO 80225, 888/ASK-USGS (888/275-8747), website: http://mapping.usgs.gov.

**Directions:** From Route 110, 2.6 miles east of the junction of Route 110 and U.S. 3 in Groveton, and 4.3 miles west of the Stark Union Church in Stark, turn north on Emerson Road. Drive 2.2 miles and turn left onto the dirt Nash Stream Road. Continue a half mile to an open area with an oversized locator map posted on a sign. From the map, follow the Nash Stream Road another 2.2 miles to a turnout on the right.

**Contact:** New Hampshire Division of Forests and Lands, P.O. Box 1856, Concord, NH 03302-1856, 603/271-3456. New Hampshire Division of Parks and Recreation, Bureau of Trails, P.O. Box 1856, Concord, NH 03302-1856, 603/271-3254. Cohos Trail Association, 252 Westmoreland Rd., Spofford, NH 03462, 603/363-8902, website: www.cohostrail.org.

## **5** ROGERS LEDGE
**10 mi/6 hrs**

**in the northern White Mountain National Forest east of Lancaster and west of Berlin**

This 10-mile, fairly easy hike passes through a relatively untrammeled area of the White Mountain National Forest before reaching Rogers Ledge and its beautiful mountain views. From the parking lot, follow the Mill Brook Trail 3.8 easy miles to the Kilkenny Ridge Trail. Turn right (north) and walk this easy stretch of the Kilkenny 0.6 mile to Rogers Ledge. At 2,945 feet, this high ledge overlooks the Presidentials to the south, the Pilot Range to the southwest, and Berlin and the Mahoosuc Range to the east. After enjoying the view, follow the same route back. The elevation gain from the trailhead to Rogers Ledge is about 1,500 feet.

**User groups:** Hikers, snowshoers, and dogs. No wheelchair facilities. This trail may be difficult to ski and is not suitable for bikes or horses. Hunting is allowed in season.

**Access, fees:** No backcountry permit is needed, but a permit is required for day use or overnight parking at any White Mountain National Forest trailhead, as indicated by signs posted at most trailheads. Permits are available at several area stores and from the national forest (see address below) at a cost of $5 for seven consecutive days or $20 per year. A $3 one-day permit can be purchased at self-service stations at national forest trailheads, but the permit is good only for the trailhead at which it's purchased. The entrance gate to the U.S. Fish Hatchery on York Pond Road is closed from 4 P.M.–8 A.M., but not locked; close and pin the gate again after passing through if it is closed when you arrive. There is a backcountry campsite with a pit toilet on the Kilkenny Ridge Trail, 0.1 mile north of the Mill Brook Trail junction.

**Maps:** For a contour map of hiking trails, get the *Carter Range-Evans Notch/North Country-Mahoosuc* map, $7.95 in waterproof Tyvek,

available in many stores and from the Appalachian Mountain Club, 800/262-4455, website: www.outdoors.org; or the *Trail Map and Guide to the White Mountain National Forest* for $7.95 from the DeLorme Publishing Company, 800/642-0970. For topographic area maps, request West Milan, Milan, Pliny Range, and Berlin from USGS Map Sales, Federal Center, Box 25286, Denver, CO 80225, 888/ASK-USGS (888/275-8747), website: http://mapping.usgs.gov.

**Directions:** From the junction of Routes 16 and 110 in Berlin, drive north on Route 110 for about seven miles and turn left onto York Pond Road at a sign for the U.S. Fish Hatchery. Follow the paved road to the hatchery and then follow the Mill Brook Trail signs to a small parking area at the end of a short dirt road behind the hatchery office.

**Contact:** White Mountain National Forest Supervisor, 719 North Main St., Laconia, NH 03246, 603/528-8721, TDD for hearing impaired 603/528-8722, website: www.fs.fed .us/r9/white. New Hampshire Division of Parks and Recreation, Bureau of Trails, P.O. Box 1856, Concord, NH 03302-1856, 603/271-3254.

## **6** KILKENNY LOOP
**18.5 mi one-way/2 days**

**in the northern White Mountain National Forest east of Lancaster and west of Berlin**

Imagine, in a national forest as heavily used as the White Mountains, hiking a trail of pine-needle duff and moss that actually gives softly like a cushion underfoot. Or taking a two-day backpacking trip during the height of the foliage season and seeing just a few other people. That was the experience two friends and I had on a traverse of the Pilot Range, much of it on the Kilkenny Ridge Trail. Located within the national forest's northernmost reaches, the Pilot Range is far removed from population centers and boasts no giant peaks to attract hikers. Instead, you revel in the solitude and quiet in a forest not yet loved to death, passing a mountain pond and impressive, if sporadic, views. This hike includes side trips to Rogers Ledge and the Horn, perhaps the two best views in the range.

In previous editions of this book, I described a Kilkenny Traverse beginning at the fish hatchery and ending at the Heath's Gate trailhead, but Heath's Gate is on private land and has since been closed to the public. The hike described here instead loops back to the York Pond Road about two miles from where you begin the hike; you can either shuttle vehicles or use one vehicle and just walk two miles of road. This hike's distance includes the two miles of walking down York Pond Road. The cumulative elevation gained on this two-day trip is about 4,000 feet.

Follow the gently rising Mill Brook Trail 3.8 miles to the Kilkenny Ridge Trail, passing through an extensive area of birch forest. Drop your packs and turn right (north) for the side trip of 1.2 miles to Rogers Ledge, an open ledge atop cliffs with sweeping views south to the Presidentials, southwest to the unfolding Pilot Range, and southeast to Berlin's smokestacks and the Mahoosuc Range beyond. Double back to your packs and hike southwest on the Kilkenny Ridge Trail for 2.1 miles, much of it an easy walk, with a moderate hill climb just before you reach Unknown Pond and the intersection with the Unknown Pond Trail. Turn right at the pond, walk the trail paralleling its shore for less than 0.1 mile, and then turn left with the Kilkenny Ridge Trail. It climbs fairly steeply, gaining several hundred feet in elevation over 1.7 miles to a side trail leading left (east) 0.3 mile to the craggy, 3,905-foot summit of the Horn, with expansive views in every direction. Reaching the very summit of the Horn requires a little hand and foot scrambling, but it's not difficult.

Back on the Kilkenny Ridge Trail, continue southwest over the wooded summit of the Bulge (3,920 feet) and on to the highest point on the ridge, 4,170-foot Mount Cabot, 2.8 miles from Unknown Pond. Cabot's summit is wooded, with no views, but a mile farther down the Kilkenny Ridge Trail lies Bunnell Rock, with a wide view to the south. From Cabot's summit, the Kilkenny Ridge Trail coincides with the Mount Cabot Trail for 1.4 miles; where they split, bear left (east) with the Kilkenny Ridge Trail and follow it for another 0.3 mile to the Bunnell Notch Trail. They coincide for 0.1 mile; where they split, stay left (east) on the Bunnell Notch Trail for another 2.6 miles. Turn left on the York Pond Trail and follow it 0.2 mile back to York Pond Road, which you can walk down about two miles to the fish hatchery and the Mill Brook trailhead.

**User groups:** Hikers, snowshoers, and dogs. No wheelchair facilities. This trail is not suitable for bikes, horses, or skis. Hunting is allowed in season.

**Access, fees:** No backcountry permit is needed, but a permit is required for day use or overnight parking at any White Mountain National Forest trailhead, as indicated by signs posted at most trailheads. Permits are available at several area stores and from the national forest (see address below) at a cost of $5 for seven consecutive days or $20 per year. A $3 one-day permit can be purchased at self-service stations at national forest trailheads, but the permit is good only for the trailhead at which it's purchased. The U.S. Fish Hatchery entrance gate on York Pond Road is closed from 4 P.M.–8 A.M., but not locked; close and pin the gate again after passing through if it is closed when you arrive. There are two backcountry campsites with pit toilets on the Kilkenny Ridge Trail, 0.1 mile north of the Mill Brook Trail junction, the other at Unknown Pond, and a cabin with bunks on the Kilkenny Trail 0.4 mile south of the Mount Cabot summit.

**Maps:** For a map of hiking trails, get the *Carter Range–Evans Notch/North Country–Mahoosuc* map, $7.95 in waterproof Tyvek, available in many stores and from the Appalachian Mountain Club, 800/262-4455, website: www.outdoors.org; or the *Trail Map and Guide to the White Mountain National Forest* for $7.95 from the DeLorme Publishing Company, 800/642-

0970. For topographic area maps, request West Milan, Milan, Pliny Range, and Berlin from USGS Map Sales, Federal Center, Box 25286, Denver, CO 80225, 888/ASK-USGS (888/275-8747), website: http://mapping.usgs.gov.

**Directions:** You can either shuttle vehicles to either end of this hike or use one vehicle and hike two miles of road at the end of the trip. From the junction of Routes 16 and 110 in Berlin, drive north on Route 110 for about seven miles and turn left onto York Pond Road at the U.S. Fish Hatchery sign. Follow the paved road to the hatchery and then follow signs for the Mill Brook Trail to a small parking area at the end of a short dirt road behind the hatchery office. The hike begins there and ends at the York Pond Trail, which begins two miles farther down York Pond Road.

**Contact:** White Mountain National Forest Supervisor, 719 North Main St., Laconia, NH 03246, 603/528-8721, TDD for the hearing impaired 603/528-8722, website: www.fs.fed.us/r9/white.

## ⑦ MOUNT CABOT
**11.5 mi/7 hrs**

**in the northern White Mountain National Forest east of Lancaster and west of Berlin**
Although Mount Cabot (4,170 feet) has a wooded summit with no views, it attracts hikers for its status as one of New Hampshire's 48 official 4,000-footers. Still, there are hardly the crowds up here that are found on peaks of comparable size to the south. And Bunnell Rock, an open ledge along this hike, offers a broad view of this corner of the Pilot Range. In previous editions of this book, the hike up Cabot was described from the Heath's Gate trailhead, but Heath's Gate is on private land and has since been closed to the public. The hike described here reaches the summits of Cabot and The Horn—which has the best view on this loop—and takes in Unknown Pond, making it actually a more scenic (though longer) hike than the one I'd described in earlier editions. This hike gains nearly 3,000 feet over its course.

Follow the York Pond Trail for 0.2 mile, then bear right onto the Bunnell Notch Trail and follow it for 2.6 miles, to where it meets the Kilkenny Ridge Trail (the Bunnell Notch Trail may not be blazed, making it challenging to follow in winter but not difficult when there's no snow). The Bunnell Notch Trail generally follows the north side of the stream all the way to the junction with the Kilkenny Ridge Trail at the height of land in the col. Bear right onto the two trails, which coincide for 0.1 mile. Where they split, stay to the right on the Kilkenny Ridge Trail for another 0.3 mile, to where it joins the Mount Cabot Trail. Turn right, and follow the Kilkenny Ridge/Mount Cabot Trail uphill—passing the great view from Bunnell Rock along the way—for 1.4 miles to the wooded summit of Mount Cabot. The Kilkenny Ridge Trail continues northward past Cabot's summit, bouncing up and down along a wooded ridge. It passes over the 3,920-foot summit of the Bulge, and, 1.1 miles from Cabot's summit, reaches a side path that leads 0.3 mile to the craggy, 3,905-foot summit of the Horn, which is reached by an easy scramble and offers great views of the Whites. Backtrack to the Kilkenny Ridge Trail, turn right (north), and descend, steeply at times, for 1.7 miles to Unknown Pond. Turn right (southeast), following the pond's shoreline briefly; where the Kilkenny Ridge Trail swings left (northeast), continue straight ahead on the Unknown Pond Trail, descending 3.3 miles to York Pond Road. Turn right and walk a short distance up the road to the York Pond Trail and your vehicle.

**User groups:** Hikers, snowshoers, and dogs. No wheelchair facilities. This trail is not suitable for bikes, horses, or skis. Hunting is allowed in season.

**Access, fees:** No backcountry permit is needed, but a permit is required for day use or overnight parking at any White Mountain National Forest trailhead, as indicated by signs posted at most trailheads. Permits are available at several area stores and from the national forest (see address below) at a cost of $5 for seven consecutive days or $20 per year. A $3 one-day permit can be purchased at self-service stations at national forest trailheads, but the permit is good only for the trailhead at which it's purchased. The U.S. Fish Hatchery entrance gate on York Pond Road is closed from 4 P.M.–8 A.M., but not locked; close and pin the gate again after passing through if it is closed when you arrive. The York Pond Road has been plowed all the way to its end in recent winters, but check first with the White Mountain National Forest (see contact information below). There is a cabin with bunks on the Kilkenny Ridge Trail 0.4 mile south of the Mount Cabot summit.

**Maps:** For a contour map of hiking trails, get the *Carter Range-Evans Notch/North Country-Mahoosuc* map, $7.95 in waterproof Tyvek, available in many stores and from the Appalachian Mountain Club, 800/262-4455, website: www.outdoors.org; or the *Trail Map and Guide to the White Mountain National Forest* for $7.95 from the DeLorme Publishing Company, 800/642-0970. For topographic area maps, request Pliny Range and Stark from USGS Map Sales, Federal Center, Box 25286, Denver, CO 80225, 888/ASK-USGS (888/275-8747), website: http://mapping.usgs.gov.

**Directions:** From the junction of Routes 16 and 110 in Berlin, drive north on Route 110 for about seven miles and turn left onto York Pond Road at the U.S. Fish Hatchery sign. Follow the paved road to the hatchery and then continue about two miles farther to a small parking area on the right, just before the end of York Pond Road. The York Pond Trail begins at the end of the road.

**Contact:** White Mountain National Forest Supervisor, 719 North Main St., Laconia, NH 03246, 603/528-8721, TDD for the hearing impaired 603/528-8722, website: www.fs.fed.us/r9/white.

# 8 MOUNTS STARR KING AND WAUMBEK

**7.2 mi/4.5 hrs**

**in the White Mountain National Forest near Jefferson**

Just a 20-minute drive from the popular peaks of the Presidential Range, this underappreciated hike sees much less foot traffic. A friend and I hiked the trail one winter day when the clouds were building up around the northern Presidentials just to the southeast, and we had clear weather on Starr King and Waumbek (elevation 4,006 feet). Plus, we saw no one else. While the trail has no terribly steep sections, the climb to Starr King gains about 2,400 feet in elevation, and continuing to Waumbek adds another 200 feet of ascent.

Ascending steadily but at a moderate grade, the trail leads 2.6 miles to the Starr King top and a sweeping view of the Whites, from the Presidential Range (southeast) to the Pemigewasset Wilderness peaks (south) and Franconia Ridge (southwest). Ed Hawkins, an avid hiker in New Hampshire, tells me he has counted more than 30 4,000-foot peaks visible from this outlook. The trail continues another mile on easy terrain to the summit of one of New Hampshire's least-visited 4,000-footers, Mount Waumbek. This route is a good introduction to winter hiking because the trail is almost completely in the woods and protected. Low trees obstruct the view from Waumbek for most of the year, but when there's snow on the ground, you get some views similar to those from Starr King. Watch for signs and arrows indicating turns in the trail early on. It's sporadically blazed but not too difficult to follow. At the edge of an open area on Starr King's summit sits a fireplace from a former shelter. On Waumbek's summit, the Kilkenny Ridge Trail leads east and north into the Pilot Range, toward Mount Cabot, Unknown Pond, and Rogers Ledge. This hike descends the same way you came.

**User groups:** Hikers, snowshoers, and dogs. No wheelchair facilities. This trail is not suitable for bikes, horses, or skis. Hunting is allowed in season.

**Access, fees:** No backcountry permit is needed, but a permit is required for day use or overnight parking at any White Mountain National Forest trailhead, as indicated by signs posted at most trailheads. Permits are available at several area stores and from the national forest (see address below) at a cost of $5 for seven consecutive days or $20 per year. A $3 one-day permit can be purchased at self-service stations at national forest trailheads, but the permit is good only for the trailhead at which it's purchased.

**Maps:** For a contour map of hiking trails, get the *Carter Range-Evans Notch/North Country-Mahoosuc* map, $7.95 in waterproof Tyvek, available in many stores and from the Appalachian Mountain Club, 800/262-4455, website: www.outdoors.org; or the *Randolph Valley and the Northern Peaks* map, available for $5 in waterproof Tyvek from the Randolph Mountain Club (see address below). For a topographic area map, request Pliny Range from USGS Map Sales, Federal Center, Box 25286, Denver, CO 80225, 888/ASK-USGS (888/275-8747), website: http://mapping.usgs.gov.

**Directions:** From the junction of Route 115A and U.S. 2 in Jefferson, follow U.S. 2 east for 0.2 mile. Turn left up a narrow road at a sign for the Starr King Trail. The road ends in about 0.1 mile at a small parking area at the trailhead. (The road is not maintained in winter; park at the Jefferson swimming pool on U.S. 2 near the town center, a short walk from the trailhead.)

**Contact:** White Mountain National Forest Supervisor, 719 North Main St., Laconia, NH 03246, 603/528-8721, TDD for the hearing impaired 603/528-8722, website: www.fs.fed .us/r9/white. Randolph Mountain Club, P.O. Box 279, Randolph, NH 03581, website: www.randolphmountainclub.org.

## 9 MAHOOSUC RANGE: GENTIAN POND

**7 mi/4 hrs**

**in Shelburne**

While Gentian Pond may seem an unlikely destination for a hike, it's actually a picturesque big puddle tucked into an evergreen woods amid the steep and rugged Mahoosucs. The thing to do is load up a backpack for two or three days and stay in the shelter at Gentian Pond—the dusk view southward to the Androscoggin Valley and the Carter-Moriah Range is fantastic. The shelter is a good base for exploring this end of the Mahoosucs. A friend and I once spent three days in March here and saw no one else—and the shelter's register showed only a handful of visitors all winter. Expect more hiker traffic during the warmer months, of course, but not the level you'd see on many of the popular White Mountains trails. Go in June to see hundreds of rare white and pink lady's slippers in bloom along the trail. The hike climbs about 800 feet uphill.

The Austin Brook Trail follows old logging roads for more than two miles. After narrowing to a hiking trail, it skirts the edge of a swampy area, and then gains much of its elevation in the last half-mile push up to the shelter, where it meets the Mahoosuc Trail, which is also the Appalachian Trail. To return to your vehicle, follow the Austin Brook Trail back out.

**User groups:** Hikers, snowshoers, and dogs. No wheelchair facilities. This trail could be skied easily for the first two miles along logging roads, but it grows more difficult where the trail narrows and would be very difficult for its steep final half mile. This trail is not suitable for bikes or horses. Hunting is allowed in season.

**Access, fees:** Parking and access are free. The Mahoosuc Range is on private property, not within the White Mountain National Forest. Camping is only allowed at shelters and designated camping areas.

**Maps:** For a contour map of hiking trails, get

the *Carter Range-Evans Notch/North Country-Mahoosuc* map, $7.95 in waterproof Tyvek, available in many stores and from the Appalachian Mountain Club, 800/262-4455, website: www.outdoors.org; or map 7 in the *Map and Guide to the Appalachian Trail in New Hampshire and Vermont*, an eight-map set and guidebook for $19.95 ($14.95 for the maps alone) from the Appalachian Trail Conference (see address below). For a topographic area map, request Shelburne from USGS Map Sales, Federal Center, Box 25286, Denver, CO 80225, 888/ASK-USGS (888/275-8747), website: http://mapping.usgs.gov.

**Directions:** In Shelburne Village, which lies between Gorham and Gilead, Maine, turn off U.S. 2 onto Meadow Road, crossing the Androscoggin River. At North Road, turn left. Immediately on the right you'll see an old logging road that leads to the Austin Brook Trail; there may be limited roadside parking here. The trail begins a half mile farther west on North Road, where there is some additional parking.

**Contact:** Appalachian Mountain Club Pinkham Notch Visitor Center, P.O. Box 298, Gorham, NH 03581, 603/466-2721, website: www.outdoors.org. Appalachian Trail Conference, P.O. Box 807, Harpers Ferry, WV 25425, 304/535-6331, website: www.appalachiantrail.org. New Hampshire Division of Parks and Recreation, Bureau of Trails, P.O. Box 1856, Concord, NH 03302-1856, 603/271-3254.

## 🔟 CHERRY MOUNTAIN: OWL'S HEAD TRAIL

**3.8 mi/3.5 hrs**

**in the White Mountain National Forest south of Jefferson**

On the broad, open ledges of the Owl's Head on Cherry Mountain, you get an expansive view of the Presidential Range—and maybe a little solitude to boot in this quiet corner of the White Mountains. I stood up here alone one cool, windy autumn day, not seeing another person until I passed two hikers on my way

back down again. The trail ascends less than 2,000 feet in elevation.

From the parking lot, the Owl's Head Trail enters a thin strip of woods, crosses a small brook, and emerges immediately into a cleared area. Head straight across the clearing to a post marker that reads "Path." Watch for orange blazes. Follow a wide double track for about 300 feet past the post, watching closely for where the trail enters the woods to the right (a spot I easily overlooked). The trail has been relocated a bit in this area in recent years, so keep an eye out for signs of recent trail work and brush clearing. The hiking is fairly easy at first, crossing some logged areas—watch for cairns and trail markers. It then begins climbing at a moderate grade. Thanks to work done by the Randolph Mountain Club, the trail no longer ascends the steep, loose, former rockslide path, so it's much easier. About 1.8 miles from the road, the trail crests the Cherry Mountain ridge; walk a relatively flat 0.1 mile to the ledges. To the south, the trail continues on to Mount Martha, 0.8 mile farther, where there is a good view. Return along the same route.

This hike is along the new, 162-mile Cohos Trail, which stretches from the southern Presidential Range to the Canadian border; full completion of the trail is anticipated in 2004 or 2005.

**User groups:** Hikers and dogs. No wheelchair facilities. This trail may be difficult to snowshoe and is not suitable for bikes, horses, or skis. Hunting is allowed in season.

**Access, fees:** No backcountry permit is needed, but a permit is required for day use or overnight parking at any White Mountain National Forest trailhead, as indicated by signs posted at most trailheads. Permits are available at several area stores and from the national forest (see address below) at a cost of $5 for seven consecutive days or $20 per year. A $3 one-day permit can be purchased at self-service stations at national forest trailheads, but the permit is good only for the trailhead at which it's purchased.

**Maps:** Maps covering this area's hiking trails include the *Franconia-Pemigewasset Range* map, for $7.95 in waterproof Tyvek, available in many stores and from the Appalachian Mountain Club, 800/262-4455, website: www.outdoors.org; the map *Randolph Valley and the Northern Peaks* map, available for $5 in waterproof Tyvek from the Randolph Mountain Club (see address below); and the *Trail Map and Guide to the White Mountain National Forest* for $7.95 from the DeLorme Publishing Company, 800/642-0970. For information, a guidebook, and maps to the Cohos Trail, contact the Cohos Trail Association (see address below). For topographic area maps, request Bethlehem and Mount Washington from USGS Map Sales, Federal Center, Box 25286, Denver, CO 80225, 888/ASK-USGS (888/275-8747), website: http://mapping.usgs.gov.

**Directions:** The trailhead parking area is on Route 115, 5.8 miles north of the junction of Route 115 and U.S. 3 and four miles south of the junction of Route 115 and U.S. 2.

**Contact:** White Mountain National Forest Supervisor, 719 North Main St., Laconia, NH 03246, 603/528-8721, TDD for the hearing impaired 603/528-8722, website: www.fs.fed.us/r9/white. Randolph Mountain Club, P.O. Box 279, Randolph, NH 03581, website: www.randolphmountainclub.org. Cohos Trail Association, 252 Westmoreland Rd., Spofford, NH 03462, 603/363-8902, website: www.cohostrail.org.

### 11 MOUNTS ADAMS AND MADISON: THE AIR LINE

**9.5 mi/8 hrs**

**in the White Mountain National Forest south of Randolph**

This is the most direct route to the second-highest peak summit in New England—5,799-foot Mount Adams—though not necessarily the fastest. It follows Adams's spectacular Durand Ridge, giving hikers extended views from atop high cliffs, down into King Ravine, southwest across the prominent ridges on the north-ern flanks of Mounts Adams and Jefferson, and north across the Randolph Valley to the Pilot Range peaks. Some scrambling is necessary, and you need to be comfortable with exposure—there's an interesting little foot ledge traverse that can get your heart pumping. This route allows a fit hiker blessed with good weather the option of hitting both Adams and Madison in a day. The vertical ascent to Adams is nearly 4,500 feet, and Madison adds about another 500 feet. If the weather turns bad, descend the Valley Way, which enters the woods more quickly than other trails. On this hike, the Appalachian Trail coincides with the Osgood Trail up Mount Madison and with the Gulfside Trail, which this hike crosses on Mount Adams.

From the parking lot at Appalachia, the Air Line makes a 4.3-mile beeline to Adams's summit, with the final 1.5 miles above the trees. Descend via the Air Line—or go for Madison's summit (5,366 feet). To reach Madison from Adams's summit, either backtrack 0.8 mile on the Air Line to the Air Line cutoff leading 0.2 mile toward the Madison hut, or take a somewhat more difficult but very scenic option: the less-traveled, mile-long Star Lake Trail, which descends southeast from Adams's summit, then swings northeast and traverses the steep northeast face of Adams. It passes beautiful Star Lake on the way to the hut. From the hut, follow the Osgood Trail a half mile to Madison's summit, then descend north via the Watson Path, Scar Trail, and the Valley Way back to Appalachia. If you descend the Valley Way, be sure to take the side paths that parallel it past Tama Fall and Gordon Fall, which are marked by signs not far from the trailhead and do not add any appreciable distance to this hike.

**User groups:** Hikers and dogs. No wheelchair facilities. This trail should not be attempted in winter except by hikers experienced in mountaineering and prepared for severe winter weather, and is not suitable for bikes, horses, or skis. Hunting is allowed in season.

**Access, fees:** Parking and access are free.

**Maps:** Several maps cover this area's hiking trails, including the *Presidential Range* map, for $7.95 in waterproof Tyvek, available in many stores and from the Appalachian Mountain Club, 800/262-4455, website: www.outdoors.org; the *Randolph Valley and the Northern Peaks* map, available for $5 in waterproof Tyvek from the Randolph Mountain Club (see address below); map 2 in the *Map and Guide to the Appalachian Trail in New Hampshire and Vermont,* an eight-map set and guidebook available for $19.95 ($14.95 for the maps alone) from the Appalachian Trail Conference (see address below); and the *Trail Map and Guide to the White Mountain National Forest* for $7.95 from the DeLorme Publishing Company, 800/642-0970. For a topographic area map, request Mount Washington from USGS Map Sales, Federal Center, Box 25286, Denver, CO 80225, 888/ASK-USGS (888/275-8747), website: http://mapping.usgs.gov.

**Directions:** Park in the large lot at the Appalachia Trailhead on U.S. 2 in Randolph, 2.1 miles west of the northern junction of U.S. 2 and Route 16 in Gorham, and 7.1 miles east of the junction of U.S. 2 and Route 115. The Air Line begins there.

**Contact:** White Mountain National Forest Supervisor, 719 North Main St., Laconia, NH 03246, 603/528-8721, TDD for the hearing impaired 603/528-8722, website: www.fs.fed .us/r9/white. Appalachian Trail Conference, 799 Washington St., P.O. Box 807, Harpers Ferry, WV 25425-0807, 304/535-6331, website: www.appalachiantrail.org. The Appalachian Mountain Club Pinkham Notch Visitor Center has up-to-date weather and trail information about the Whites; call 603/466-2725. Randolph Mountain Club, P.O. Box 279, Randolph, NH 03581, website: www.randolph mountainclub.org.

## 12 MOUNT ADAMS: KING RAVINE

**8.8 mi/8 hrs**

**in the White Mountain National Forest south of Randolph**

This route through King Ravine is one of the most difficult and spectacular hikes in the White Mountains, and an adventurous way up the second-highest peak in New England: 5,799-foot Mount Adams. Besides involving hard scrambling over boulders and up the talus of a very steep ravine headwall, you will gain nearly 4,400 feet in elevation from the trailhead to Adams's summit. I hiked this on a banner June day with my friend Larry from Seattle, who's climbed all over Washington's Cascades and Olympics and was making his first trip to New England. At one point, he turned to me and gushed, "Mike, I love trails like this."

From the Appalachia parking lot, pick up the Air Line trail and follow it for 0.8 mile, ascending steadily but at an easy grade through mixed deciduous forest, and then bear right on the Short Line. Follow that trail for 1.9 miles—it coincides for nearly a half mile with the Randolph Path—until it joins the King Ravine Trail. The Short Line parallels Cold Brook, which drops through numerous cascades, drawing near the brook in spots—though much of the trail is separated from the brook by forest too dense to bushwhack through. Immediately after you turn onto the King Ravine Trail, a sign marks Mossy Fall on the right, a five-foot-tall waterfall that drops into a shallow pool. The forest here is dense but low, and you start getting views of the ravine walls towering high overhead. Beyond Mossy Fall, the trail grows much steeper, weaving amid massive boulders that have tumbled off the ravine cliffs over the eons. Scrambling atop one of these boulders offers an unforgettable view of King Ravine; the cabin visible on the western wall is Crag Camp, managed by the Randolph Mountain Club.

Just past the junction with the Chemin des Dames at 2.1 miles—a trail that scales the steep ravine wall to the left, or east, to join the Air Line atop the ridge—the King Ravine Trail divides. To the left is an easier route known as the Elevated, which skirts most of the boulders that the route to the right passes through and offers more ravine views. To the right, the Subway will have you crawling through boulder caves, at times removing your pack to squeeze through narrow passages. The two trails rejoin within about 200 yards. The Great Gully Trail diverges right soon afterward, and then the King Ravine Trail offers another choice of options: to the left, the main trail; to the right, a side loop through the Ice Caves, where ice tends to linger year-round. Again, these two paths rejoin within a short distance, then the trail emerges completely from the trees and reaches the base of the King Ravine headwall, 0.7 mile past the Short Line trail junction. The King Ravine Trail grows its steepest up the headwall, basically following a talus slope. Over a half mile, the trail gains 1,100 feet in elevation, and footing is tricky on the sometimes loose rocks.

Atop the headwall, the trail passes between rocky crags at a spot called the Gateway. On the other side, 1.2 miles past the Short Line junction, turn right on the Air Line and follow it for 0.6 mile over treeless alpine terrain to the Adams summit. On the way down, you have the option of bagging the Mount Madison summit as well. (See Mounts Adams and Madison: the Air Line, and other Mount Adams hike descriptions in this chapter for more on the summit views.) Descend the Air Line; it's 4.3 miles back to the trailhead.

**User groups:** Hikers and dogs. No wheelchair facilities. This trail should not be attempted in winter except by hikers experienced in mountaineering and prepared for severe winter weather, and is not suitable for bikes, horses, or skis. Hunting is allowed in season.

**Access, fees:** Parking and access are free.

**Maps:** Several maps cover this area's hiking trails, including the *Presidential Range* map, for $7.95 in waterproof Tyvek, available in many stores and from the Appalachian Mountain Club, 800/262-4455, website: www.out-doors.org; the *Randolph Valley and the Northern Peaks* map, available for $5 in waterproof Tyvek from the Randolph Mountain Club (see address below); map 2 in the *Map and Guide to the Appalachian Trail in New Hampshire and Vermont,* an eight-map set and guidebook available for $19.95 ($14.95 for the maps alone) from the Appalachian Trail Conference (see address below); and the *Trail Map and Guide to the White Mountain National Forest* for $7.95 from the DeLorme Publishing Company, 800/642-0970. For a topographic area map, request Mount Washington from USGS Map Sales, Federal Center, Box 25286, Denver, CO 80225, 888/ASK-USGS (888/275-8747), website: http://mapping.usgs.gov.

**Directions:** Park in the large lot at the Appalachia trailhead on U.S. 2 in Randolph, 2.1 miles west of the northern junction of U.S. 2 and Route 16 in Gorham, and 7.1 miles east of the junction of U.S. 2 and Route 115. The Air Line begins there.

**Contact:** White Mountain National Forest Supervisor, 719 North Main St., Laconia, NH 03246, 603/528-8721, TDD for the hearing impaired 603/528-8722, website: www.fs.fed.us/r9/white. Appalachian Trail Conference, 799 Washington St., P.O. Box 807, Harpers Ferry, WV 25425-0807, 304/535-6331, website: www.appalachiantrail.org. The Appalachian Mountain Club Pinkham Notch Visitor Center has up-to-date weather and trail information about the Whites; call 603/466-2725. Randolph Mountain Club, P.O. Box 279, Randolph, NH 03581, website: www.randolphmountainclub.org.

## 13 MOUNT ADAMS: LOWE'S PATH

**9.5 mi/8 hrs**

**in the White Mountain National Forest south of Randolph**

This is the easiest route to the Mount Adams summit, which at 5,799 feet is the second-highest peak in New England and one of the most interesting. I've hiked it several times, in summer, fall, and winter, and have never gotten bored with this mountain. The trail has moderate grades and is well protected until timberline, but the last 1.5 miles are above the trees. It's also the oldest trail coming out of the Randolph Valley, cut in 1875–1876.

Lowe's Path ascends gently at first, making several crossings of brooks through an area often wet and muddy. After 2.5 miles you reach the Log Cabin, a Randolph Mountain Club shelter where a caretaker collects the $5 per person nightly fee. About 0.7 mile farther, at timberline, a trail branching left leads 0.1 mile to the RMC's Gray Knob cabin, which is winterized and costs $10 per night per person. This trail junction offers the first sweeping views, with the Mount Jefferson Castellated Ridge thrusting its craggy teeth skyward and much of the White Mountains visible on a clear day. From here, Lowe's Path cuts through some krummholz (the dense stands of stunted and twisted conifers that grow at timberline) and then ascends the barren talus, where it can be tricky to find the cairns. Nearly a mile from the Gray Knob Trail, you scramble over the rock mound known as Adams 4, then hike the final 0.7-mile stretch to the 5,799-foot summit to be rewarded with some of the best views in these mountains. To the south are Mounts Jefferson, Clay, and Washington, and to the north lies Madison. This crescent-shaped ridge nearly encloses the largest glacial cirque in the region, the Great Gulf.

**User groups:** Hikers and dogs. No wheelchair facilities. This trail should not be attempted in winter except by hikers experienced in mountaineering and prepared for severe winter weather, and is not suitable for bikes, horses, or skis. Hunting is allowed in season.

**Access, fees:** Access is free. There is a parking fee of $2 per day per vehicle at Lowe's Store parking lot.

**Maps:** Several maps cover this area's hiking trails, including the *Presidential Range* map, for $7.95 in waterproof Tyvek, available in many stores and from the Appalachian Mountain Club, 800/262-4455, website: www.outdoors.org; the *Randolph Valley and the Northern Peaks* map, available for $5 in waterproof Tyvek from the Randolph Mountain Club (see address below); map 2 in the *Map and Guide to the Appalachian Trail in New Hampshire and Vermont*, an eight-map set and guidebook available for $19.95 ($14.95 for the maps alone) from the Appalachian Trail Conference (see address below); and the *Trail Map and Guide to the White Mountain National Forest* for $7.95 from the DeLorme Publishing Company, 800/642-0970. For a topographic area map, request Mount Washington from USGS Map Sales, Federal Center, Box 25286, Denver, CO 80225, 888/ASK-USGS (888/275-8747), website: http://mapping.usgs.gov.

**Directions:** Park at Lowe's Store and gas station on U.S. 2, five miles east of the junction with Route 115 and 8.4 miles west of the north junction of U.S. 2 and Route 16 in Gorham. Cross U.S. 2, walking to the right (west), and turn up a dirt driveway that leads about 50 yards to Lowe's Path (on the right).

**Contact:** White Mountain National Forest Supervisor, 719 North Main St., Laconia, NH 03246, 603/528-8721, TDD for the hearing impaired 603/528-8722, website: www.fs.fed.us/r9/white. Appalachian Trail Conference, 799 Washington St., P.O. Box 807, Harpers Ferry, WV 25425-0807, 304/535-6331, website: www.appalachiantrail.org. The Appalachian Mountain Club Pinkham Notch Visitor Center has up-to-date weather and trail information about the Whites; call 603/466-2725. Randolph Mountain Club, P.O. Box 279, Randolph, NH 03581, website: www.randolphmountainclub.org.

## 14 MOUNT MADISON: MADISON GULF AND WEBSTER TRAILS

**11.5 mi/10 hrs**

**in the White Mountain National Forest south of Randolph**

The Madison headwall ascent on the Madison Gulf Trail is without question one of the most difficult hikes I have ever done in the White Mountains. At 11.5 miles and 4,000 feet of elevation gain, this hike also represents one of the most strenuous days you could spend in these parts. But it also rates as one of the wildest hikes in these mountains—and you may well see no other hikers on the trail. On this hike, the Appalachian Trail coincides with the Madison Gulf Trail south of the Osgood Trail junction, and with the Osgood Trail from Madison hut over the Madison summit to the Daniel Webster (scout) Trail.

From the parking area, follow the Great Gulf Link Trail a flat mile to the Great Gulf Trail. Turn right and continue about three easy miles (passing the Osgood Trail junction in less than two miles); soon after a jog left in the trail, turn right (north) onto the Madison Gulf Trail. You are in the Great Gulf, the enormous glacial cirque nearly enclosed by the high peaks of the northern Presidentials, which loom around you. The Madison Gulf Trail grows increasingly steep, following Parapet Brook through a dense forest for about two miles to the base of the formidable headwall. Moss-covered glacial-erratic boulders fill the streambed; one huge boulder has a tall tree growing atop it. You cross a lush, boggy area along a shelf at the headwall's base, then attack the main headwall, which involves scrambling over steep, exposed rock ledges that can be hazardous in wet weather.

After a strenuous mile, the trail reaches the flat saddle between Mounts Madison and Adams, where you find the AMC's Madison hut and Star Lake, a beautiful little tarn and one of the few true alpine ponds in the Whites. From the hut, turn right (east) on the Osgood

Trail leading to Madison's ridgelike summit (elevation 5,366 feet). Continue over the summit and down the open Osgood Ridge for a half mile. The Daniel Webster Trail branches left (northeast) at Osgood Junction, heading diagonally down a vast talus slope to the woods, leading another 3.5 miles to the campground road in Dolly Copp. Turn right and walk 0.2 mile down the road to your car.

**User groups:** Hikers and dogs. No wheelchair facilities. This trail should not be attempted in winter except by hikers experienced in mountaineering and prepared for severe winter weather, and is not suitable for bikes, horses, or skis. Hunting is allowed in season.

**Access, fees:** No backcountry permit is needed, but a permit is required for day use or overnight parking at any White Mountain National Forest trailhead, as indicated by signs posted at most trailheads. Permits are available at several area stores and from the national forest (see address below) at a cost of $5 for seven consecutive days or $20 per year. A $3 one-day permit can be purchased at self-service stations at national forest trailheads, but the permit is good only for the trailhead at which it's purchased.

**Maps:** Several maps cover this area's hiking trails, including the *Presidential Range* map, for $7.95 in waterproof Tyvek, available in many stores and from the Appalachian Mountain Club, 800/262-4455, website: www.outdoors.org; the *Randolph Valley and the Northern Peaks* map, available for $5 in waterproof Tyvek from the Randolph Mountain Club (see address below); map 2 in the *Map and Guide to the Appalachian Trail in New Hampshire and Vermont,* an eight-map set and guidebook available for $19.95 ($14.95 for the maps alone) from the Appalachian Trail Conference (see address below); and the *Trail Map and Guide to the White Mountain National Forest* for $7.95 from the DeLorme Publishing Company, 800/642-0970. For a topographic area map, request Mount Washington from USGS Map Sales, Federal Center, Box 25286, Denver, CO

80225, 888/ASK-USGS (888/275-8747), website: http://mapping.usgs.gov.

**Directions:** From Gorham, drive south on Route 16 to the U.S. Forest Service's Dolly Copp Campground (entrance on right), which is operated on a first-come, first-served basis. From Pinkham Notch, drive north on Route 16; the campground will be on your left. Drive to the end of the campground road and park in the dirt lot at the start of the Great Gulf Link Trail. About a quarter mile before the parking lot, you pass the start of the Daniel Webster (scout) Trail, which is where you will end this hike.

**Contact:** White Mountain National Forest Supervisor, 719 North Main St., Laconia, NH 03246, 603/528-8721, TDD for the hearing impaired 603/528-8722, website: www.fs.fed.us/r9/white. Appalachian Trail Conference, 799 Washington St., P.O. Box 807, Harpers Ferry, WV 25425-0807, 304/535-6331, website: www.appalachiantrail.org. The Appalachian Mountain Club Pinkham Notch Visitor Center has up-to-date weather and trail information about the Whites; call 603/466-2725. Randolph Mountain Club, P.O. Box 279, Randolph, NH 03581, website: www.randolphmountainclub.org.

## 15 MOUNT JEFFERSON: THE CASTELLATED RIDGE
**10 mi/9 hrs**

**in the White Mountain National Forest south of Bowman**

The stretch of the Castle Trail above timberline ranks among the most spectacular ridge walks in New England—but you work hard getting there, climbing some 4,200 feet on this 10-mile round-tripper. The Castellated Ridge narrows to a rocky spine jutting above the krummholz (the dense stands of stunted and twisted conifers that grow at timberline), with long, sharp drops off either side. The ridge acquired its name from the three castles, or towers, of barren rock you scramble over and around, which are visible from a distance. This can be a dangerous place in nasty weather. A friend and I once backpacked in early October as far as the first castle only to turn back in the face of ice, snow, and a looming whiteout—then returned a week later to hike the ridge in shorts and T-shirts. On a clear day, from Jefferson's summit (5,716 feet), you can see almost all of the Whites and all the way to Vermont's Green Mountains. I've even caught glimpses of New York's Adirondacks, beyond the Green Mountains, on super clear days. You also walk briefly on the Appalachian Trail where it coincides with the Gulfside Trail north of Jefferson's summit.

From the parking area, follow the dirt driveway to the right for about 150 yards until you reach a somewhat hidden marker on the right where the Castle Trail enters the woods. In the first half mile there's a bridgeless crossing of the Israel River, which can be difficult at high water. The hiking is fairly easy at first. Approximately one mile beyond the stream crossing, the trail passes the junction with the Israel Ridge Path on the left, on which you will return. The last certain water source is located at a brook a short distance up that path. The trail ascends the ridge, growing steep and passing through an interesting subalpine forest before reaching the junction with the Link at 3.5 miles out.

The Castle Trail requires scrambling from this point, reaching the first castle a quarter mile past the Link junction. Continue up the ridge to the vast talus field covering the upper flanks of Mount Jefferson, watching carefully for cairns. The trail follows a direct line to the summit, where twin rock mounds are separated by a short distance; the first you encounter, farther west, is the true summit, five miles from the trailhead.

Descend to the trail junction between the two summits, walk north on the Jefferson Loop Trail toward Mount Adams for 0.4 mile, and then continue on the Gulfside Trail for another 0.2 mile into Edmands Col. Bear left onto the Randolph Path, which leads to the right (northeast) around the Castle Ravine headwall

0.7 mile from Edmands Col to the Israel Ridge Path. The trails coincide briefly, then split; stay to the left on the Israel Ridge Path, continuing nearly a half mile to just beyond the Perch Path junction, where the Emerald Trail diverges left. If you have time, make the worthwhile 20-minute detour on the Emerald Trail out to Emerald Bluff, which offers a stunning view of Castle Ravine. The Israel Ridge Path continues down into the woods, eventually rejoining the Castle Trail 2.4 miles below the Perch Path junction. Turn right and continue to the trailhead parking area, 1.3 miles ahead.

**User groups:** Hikers and dogs. No wheelchair facilities. This trail should not be attempted in winter except by hikers experienced in mountaineering and prepared for severe winter weather, and is not suitable for bikes, horses, or skis. Hunting is allowed in season.

**Access, fees:** No backcountry permit is needed, but a permit is required for day use or overnight parking at any White Mountain National Forest trailhead, as indicated by signs posted at most trailheads. Permits are available at several area stores and from the national forest (see address below) at a cost of $5 for seven consecutive days or $20 per year. A $3 one-day permit can be purchased at self-service stations at national forest trailheads, but the permit is good only for the trailhead at which it's purchased.

**Maps:** Several maps cover this area's hiking trails, including the *Presidential Range* map, for $7.95 in waterproof Tyvek, available in many stores and from the Appalachian Mountain Club, 800/262-4455, website: www.out-doors.org; the *Randolph Valley and the Northern Peaks* map, available for $5 in waterproof Tyvek from the Randolph Mountain Club (see address below); map 2 in the *Map and Guide to the Appalachian Trail in New Hampshire and Vermont,* an eight-map set and guidebook available for $19.95 ($14.95 for the maps alone) from the Appalachian Trail Conference (see address below); and the *Trail Map and Guide to the White Mountain National Forest* for $7.95

from the DeLorme Publishing Company, 800/642-0970. For a topographic area map, request Mount Washington from USGS Map Sales, Federal Center, Box 25286, Denver, CO 80225, 888/ASK-USGS (888/275-8747), website: http://mapping.usgs.gov.

**Directions:** The parking area is on the south side of U.S. 2 in Randolph, 4.1 miles east of the junction of U.S. 2 and Route 115.

**Contact:** White Mountain National Forest Supervisor, 719 North Main St., Laconia, NH 03246, 603/528-8721, TDD for the hearing impaired 603/528-8722, website: www.fs.fed.us/r9/white. Appalachian Trail Conference, 799 Washington St., P.O. Box 807, Harpers Ferry, WV 25425-0807, 304/535-6331, website: www.appalachiantrail.org. The AMC's Pinkham Notch Visitor Center has up-to-date reports on weather in the Presidential Range; call 603/466-2721. Randolph Mountain Club, P.O. Box 279, Randolph, NH 03581, website: www.randolphmountainclub.org.

### **16** MOUNT JEFFERSON: RIDGE OF THE CAPS
**6.6 mi/5 hrs**
**in the White Mountain National Forest south of Jefferson**

Beginning at an elevation of 3,008 feet, the highest trailhead accessed by a public road in the White Mountains, the Caps Ridge Trail provides the shortest route from a trailhead to a 5,000-foot summit in these mountains: five miles round-trip if you go up and down the Caps Ridge Trail. This hike extends the distance to 6.6 miles to make a loop and incorporate the spectacular Castellated Ridge. Despite the relatively short distance compared to other Presidential Range hikes, all of this loop's trails are rugged. Though its 2,700 feet of elevation gain does not compare with most other routes up Presidential Range summits, this hike is fairly strenuous. See the next hike's trail notes for more information about the views from the Castellated Ridge and Mount Jefferson's summit.

Follow the Caps Ridge Trail, which rises steadily through conifer forest; at mile one, an open ledge offers sweeping views to the Ridge of the Caps above, the Castellated Ridge to the north, and the southern Presidentials to the south. You may also see the black smoke from the cog railway chugging up Mount Washington. The potholes in the granite on the ledge were left by glaciers in the last Ice Age. Continue up the Caps Ridge Trail, immediately passing the junction with the Link trail, on which this route returns. The Caps Ridge Trail soon emerges from the woods and zigzags up the craggy ridge, with excellent views of most of the Whites. When the ridge becomes less distinct in a sprawling talus slope, you are near Jefferson's summit, a pile of rocks rising to 5,716 feet above the ocean.

For a five-mile total hike, descend the way you came. To continue on this hike, descend the other side of Jefferson's summit cone, follow the summit loop trail northward just a few steps, and then turn left (northwest) onto the Castle Trail. Follow its cairns, descending at a moderate angle over the vast boulder fields of Jefferson, to the prominent Castellated Ridge. The trail follows close to the ridge crest, passing the three distinct stone castles along it. At 1.5 miles below the summit, turn left (south) on the Link, which wends a rugged— and in spots heavily eroded—path through dense forest for 1.6 miles back to the Caps Ridge Trail. Turn right (west) and descend a mile back to the trailhead.

**User groups:** Hikers and dogs. No wheelchair facilities. This trail is not accessible in winter and is not suitable for bikes or horses. Hunting is allowed in season.

**Access, fees:** No backcountry permit is needed, but a permit is required for day use or overnight parking at any White Mountain National Forest trailhead; signs indicating so are posted at most of them. Permits are available at several area stores and from the national forest (see address below) at a cost of $5 for seven consecutive days or $20 per year. A $3 one-day permit can be purchased at self-service stations at national forest trailheads, but the permit is good only for the trailhead at which it's purchased.

**Maps:** Several maps cover this area's hiking trails, including the *Presidential Range* map, for $7.95 in waterproof Tyvek, available in many stores and from the Appalachian Mountain Club, 800/262-4455, website: www.outdoors.org; the *Randolph Valley and the Northern Peaks* map, available for $5 in waterproof Tyvek from the Randolph Mountain Club (see address below); map 2 in the *Map and Guide to the Appalachian Trail in New Hampshire and Vermont,* an eight-map set and guidebook available for $19.95 ($14.95 for the maps alone) from the Appalachian Trail Conference (see address below); and the *Trail Map and Guide to the White Mountain National Forest* for $7.95 from the DeLorme Publishing Company, 800/642-0970. For a topographic area map, request Mount Washington from USGS Map Sales, Federal Center, Box 25286, Denver, CO 80225, 888/ASK-USGS (888/275-8747), website: http://mapping.usgs.gov.

**Directions:** The hike begins from the Caps Ridge Trail parking lot at the height of land in Jefferson Notch. From U.S. 2 in Jefferson, turn south onto Valley Road and follow it more than a mile. Then turn left onto the gravel Jefferson Notch Road and continue on it for about four miles to the trailhead. From U.S. 302 in Bretton Woods, turn onto the Base Road at a sign for the Mount Washington Cog Railway and drive 5.6 miles. Then turn left on Jefferson Notch Road and follow it to Jefferson Notch. Or from U.S. 302 in Crawford Notch, 0.2 mile north of the visitor information center, turn onto Mount Clinton Road. Follow it 3.7 miles, cross Base Road, and continue straight ahead onto Jefferson Notch Road.

**Contact:** White Mountain National Forest Supervisor, 719 North Main St., Laconia, NH 03246, 603/528-8721, TDD for the hearing impaired 603/528-8722, website: www.fs.fed.us/r9/white. Appalachian Trail Conference, 799

Washington St., P.O. Box 807, Harpers Ferry, WV 25425-0807, 304/535-6331, website: www.appalachiantrail.org. The AMC's Pinkham Notch Visitor Center has up-to-date reports on weather in the Presidential Range; call 603/466-2721. Randolph Mountain Club, P.O. Box 279, Randolph, NH 03581, website: www.randolphmountainclub.org.

## 17 PRESIDENTIAL RANGE TRAVERSE

**20 mi one-way/2.5 days**

**in the White Mountain National Forest between Gorham and Crawford Notch**

This is the premier backpacking trek in New England—in fact, nowhere else east of the Rockies can you hike a 15-mile ridge entirely above timberline. The route hits nine summits, seven of them higher than 5,000 feet—including New England's highest, 6,288-foot Mount Washington—and each with its own unique character. From the junction of the Osgood and Daniel Webster Trails to the junction of the Crawford Path and the Webster Cliffs Trail, this hike coincides with the Appalachian Trail. The route covers some very rugged terrain and is quite strenuous, with a cumulative vertical ascent of well more than 8,000 feet. The task is complicated by the fact that the odds of having three straight days of good weather in these peaks may be only slightly better than those of winning the lottery. Finding appropriate campsites can be difficult, too, because of the prohibition against camping above timberline (see detailed White Mountain National Forest regulations at the beginning of this chapter). Skipping the side paths to summits and staying on the Gulfside Trail, Westside Trail, and Crawford Path will reduce the distance slightly and the elevation gain significantly. Masochistic types have been known to attempt this traverse in a single day, a feat known in some circles as the Death March (two friends and I attempted it once, only to have to descend from Washington when gray clouds abruptly smothered the mountain, leaving us in a pea-soup fog). A winter traverse of the Presidentials is a mountaineering challenge considered by many to be good training for Alaskan peaks in summer.

My route here deviates a bit from the more common approach to this traverse—Lowe's Path (see Mount Adams: Lowe's Path in this chapter)—incorporating two scenic trails that see fewer hikers. The first, the Daniel Webster (scout) Trail, begins at the Dolly Copp Campground road and ascends moderately through the woods to a vast, open talus slope where the climbing grows steeper. Upon reaching Osgood Ridge, you're treated to a stunning view of the Great Gulf Wilderness and the peaks of the northern Presidentials. Follow the Osgood Trail to the top of Mount Madison, 4.1 miles from the trailhead, its 5,366-foot summit a narrow ridge of boulders. Continue over the summit on the Osgood Trail a half mile down to Madison hut and turn left for the Star Lake Trail, a less-traveled footpath that passes the beautiful little tarn named Star Lake and winds a mile up the steep east side of 5,799-foot Mount Adams, the second-highest peak in New England. Adams has five distinct summits, several ridges and ravines, and excellent views. Descend via Lowe's Path nearly a half mile over an expansive talus field to the giant cairn at Thunderstorm Junction, where several trails meet.

From here, you can descend the Spur Trail a mile to the Randolph Mountain Club's Crag Camp cabin, or follow Lowe's Path for 1.3 miles to the Gray Knob cabin. To continue on, turn left (southwest) onto the Gulfside Trail (which follows the ridge to Mount Washington while avoiding the summits). At 0.6 mile south of Thunderstorm Junction, you pass the Israel Ridge Path branching to the right toward the RMC's Perch camping area (one mile away via Israel Ridge, Randolph Path, and the Perch Path). From Edmands Col (the saddle 1.3 miles south of Thunderstorm Junction and 0.6 mile north of the Mount Jefferson summit), hike 0.2 mile southwest and bear right onto the Jefferson Loop Trail, climbing 0.4 mile to Mount Jefferson's top. Of its two summits, the westernmost (to your right from this direction) is the highest at 5,716 feet. The other summit is 11 feet lower.

Continue between the two summits on the loop trail and rejoin the Gulfside Trail. About a half mile farther, after dipping down through Sphinx Col, bear left onto the Mount Clay Loop Trail. On a day when you see two dozen hikers on Jefferson, you may have Clay to yourself. This is probably because Clay is considered a shoulder of Mount Washington rather than a distinct peak. Yet, on Clay's broad 5,533-foot summit, you can observe abundant alpine wildflowers (particularly in the second half of June) and peer down the sheer headwall of the Great Gulf. The Clay Loop rejoins the Gulfside in 1.2 miles, and then it's another mile to the roof of New England, Washington's 6,288-foot summit, finishing via the Crawford Path. The summit has a visitor center with a cafeteria and bathrooms—which many hikers consider as much of a blemish on the mountain as the cog railway, which belches black smoke carrying tourists up and down Washington's west slope.

From the summit, turn southwest onto the Crawford Path and follow it 1.4 miles down to Lakes of the Clouds, the location of another AMC hut. Just south of the hut, bear right off the Crawford onto the Mount Monroe Loop Trail for the steep half-mile climb to its 5,372-foot summit (a great place to catch the sunset if you're staying at the Lakes hut). The Monroe Loop rejoins the Crawford Path southbound 0.3 mile past the summit. The Crawford then traverses the bump on the ridge known as Mount Franklin (5,001 feet), also not considered a distinct summit. About two miles south of the Lakes hut, bear right for the loop over 4,760-foot Mount Eisenhower. A mile south of Eisenhower, follow the Webster Cliffs Trail 0.1 mile to the 4,312-foot summit of Mount Pierce, then double back and turn left on the Crawford Path, descending nearly three miles.

Just before reaching U.S. 302 in Crawford Notch, turn right onto the Crawford Connector path leading 0.2 mile to the parking area on the Mount Clinton Road.

**User groups:** Hikers and dogs. No wheelchair facilities. This hike should not be attempted in winter except by hikers experienced in mountaineering and prepared for severe winter weather, and is not suitable for skis. Bikes, horses, and hunting are prohibited.

**Access, fees:** No backcountry permit is needed, but a permit is required for day use or overnight parking at any White Mountain National Forest trailhead, as indicated by signs posted at most trailheads. Permits are available at several area stores and from the national forest (see address below) at a cost of $5 for seven consecutive days or $20 per year. A $3 one-day permit can be purchased at self-service stations at national forest trailheads, but the permit is good only for the trailhead at which it's purchased. The Appalachian Mountain Club (see contact information below) operates the Madison and Lakes of the Clouds huts, where a crew prepares meals and guests share bunkrooms and bathrooms. The Randolph Mountain Club operates two cabins on Mount Adams: Crag Camp (capacity 20) and the winterized Gray Knob (capacity 15), both of which cost $10 per person per night and are run on a first-come, first-served basis. The RMC also operates two open-sided shelters on Adams, the Perch (capacity eight, plus four tent platforms) and the Log Cabin (capacity 10), both of which cost $5 per night, with the fee collected by a caretaker. All shelters are open year-round.

**Maps:** Several maps cover this area's hiking trails, including the *Presidential Range* map, for $7.95 in waterproof Tyvek, available in many stores and from the Appalachian Mountain Club, 800/262-4455, website: www.outdoors.org; map 2 in the *Map and Guide to the Appalachian Trail in New Hampshire and Vermont,* an eight-map set and guidebook available for $19.95 ($14.95 for the maps alone) from the Appalachian Trail Conference (see address below); and the *Trail Map and Guide to the White Mountain National Forest* for $7.95 from the DeLorme Publishing Company, 800/642-0970. For a topographic area map, request Mount Washington from USGS Map Sales, Federal Center, Box 25286, Denver, CO 80225, 888/ASK-USGS (888/275-8747), website: http://mapping.usgs.gov.

**Directions:** From Gorham, drive south on Route 16 to the U.S. Forest Service's Dolly Copp Campground (entrance on right), which is operated on a first-come, first-served basis. Drive to the end of the campground road to a dirt parking lot at the Great Gulf Link Trailhead. About a quarter mile before the parking lot is the start of the Daniel Webster (scout) Trail, which is where you begin this hike. Leave a second vehicle at the other end of this traverse, just off U.S. 302 in Crawford Notch State Park. The Crawford Path Trailhead parking area is on Mount Clinton Road, opposite the Crawford House site and just north of Saco Lake.

**Contact:** White Mountain National Forest Supervisor, 719 North Main St., Laconia, NH 03246, 603/528-8721, TDD for the hearing impaired 603/528-8722, website: www.fs.fed .us/r9/white. Appalachian Trail Conference, 799 Washington St., P.O. Box 807, Harpers Ferry, WV 25425-0807, 304/535-6331, website: www .appalachiantrail.org. The Appalachian Mountain Club Pinkham Notch Visitor Center has up-to-date weather and trail information about the Whites; call 603/466-2725.

## 18 THE CARTER-MORIAH RANGE

**20 mi one-way/3 days**    4  9
**in the White Mountain National Forest between Pinkham Notch and Shelburne**

This section of the Appalachian Trail just might have you cursing one moment, uttering expressions of awe the next. This is a great three-day ridge walk on the AT, with excellent views of the Presidential Range to the

west and the Wild River Valley to the east. The cumulative elevation gained on this 20-mile hike is more than 6,700 feet.

From the Appalachian Mountain Club Visitor Center, follow the Lost Pond Trail to the Wildcat Ridge Trail; turn left (east), and you will soon begin the steep climb to the ridge, passing over open ledges with commanding views of Mount Washington—a good destination for a short day hike. The first of Wildcat's five summits that you'll encounter—Peak E, 4,041 feet high—is a 3.8-mile round-trip hike of about three hours. The trail traverses the roller coaster Wildcat Ridge, up and down five humped summits with few views. Just beyond the final peak is a short spur trail to a view atop cliffs overlooking Carter Notch and the Carter Range that will make you eat all your nasty comments about this trail. Descend north a steep mile—including a traverse of about 25 feet across a loose, very steep rockslide area—turning right (east) onto the Nineteen-Mile Brook Trail for the final 0.2 mile into the notch and circling around the larger of two ponds there. Tent sites can be found near the junction of the Wildcat Ridge and Nineteen-Mile Brook Trails, or ask a caretaker at the AMC hut in Carter Notch about nearby sites.

From the notch, hike north, climbing steeply on the Carter-Moriah Trail, passing one ledge with a view of the entire notch from high above it. You'll pass a side trail leading to a good spring. A bit more than a mile from the notch, the trail passes over the highest point on this ridge, Carter Dome, at 4,832 feet. Unfortunately, trees block any views. The trail continues nearly a mile to the rocky summit of Mount Hight (4,675 feet)—the nicest summit in the range, with 360-degree views of the Presidentials and far into Maine to the east. From Hight, the Carter-Moriah Trail turns sharply left (west) a short distance, drops north down a steep slope into the forest for a half mile to Zeta Pass, then continues north over the wooded summits of South Carter and Middle Carter (2.7 miles from Mount Hight). As the ridge ascends gradually again toward North Carter, you break into the alpine zone and some of the best views on this hike, particularly west to Mount Washington. From the viewless summit of North Carter, the trail drops several hundred feet over rock ledges that require scrambling, passes over the hump known as Imp Mountain, and reaches the spur trail to the Imp campsite in two miles. Check out the view at sunset from the ledge just below the shelter.

Continuing north on the Carter-Moriah Trail, you cross over some open ledges on Imp Mountain before the trail ascends steadily onto the open southern ledges of Mount Moriah two miles from the shelter. A short distance farther, the Carter-Moriah Trail peels off left toward the town of Gorham; this hike continues on the AT, which at this point coincides with the Kenduskeag Trail—but drop your pack and make the short detour on the Carter-Moriah for the rocky scramble up the spur trail to Moriah's summit. Backtrack to the Kenduskeag—an Abenaki word meaning "a pleasant walk"—and follow its often wet path 1.5 miles to the Rattle River Trail, where you'll turn left (north). The trail descends steeply at first, through a dense, damp forest, then levels out before reaching the Rattle River shelter in 2.5 miles. From there, it's less than two miles to a parking lot on U.S. 2 in Shelburne, the terminus of this traverse.

**User groups:** Hikers and dogs. No wheelchair facilities. This trail should not be attempted in winter except by hikers experienced in mountaineering and prepared for severe winter weather, and is not suitable for skis. Bikes, horses, and hunting are prohibited.

**Access, fees:** No backcountry permit is needed, but a permit is required for day use or overnight parking at any White Mountain National Forest trailhead, as indicated by signs posted at most trailheads. Permits are available at several area stores and from the national forest (see address below) at a cost of $5 for seven consecutive days or $20 per year. A $3 one-day permit can be purchased at self-service stations at national forest trailheads, but the permit is good only for the trailhead at which it's purchased. Backcountry campsites along this route are scarce and camping is prohibited along much of the high ridge. Carry cash for camping overnight at the Appalachian Mountain Club hut in Carter Notch ($25 per person per night) or the AMC's Imp campsite ($8 per person per night).

**Maps:** For a contour map of hiking trails, obtain the *Carter Range–Evans Notch/North Country–Mahoosuc* map, $7.95 in waterproof Tyvek, available in many stores and from the Appalachian Mountain Club, 800/262-4455, website: www.outdoors.org; the *Trail Map and Guide to the White Mountain National Forest* for $7.95 from the DeLorme Publishing Company, 800/642-0970, website: www.DeLorme.com; or map 2 in the *Map and Guide to the Appalachian Trail in New Hampshire and Vermont,* an eight-map set and guidebook for $19.95 ($14.95 for the maps alone) from the Appalachian Trail Conference (see address below). For a topographic area map, request Carter Dome from USGS Map Sales, Federal Center, Box 25286, Denver, CO 80225, 888/ASK-USGS (888/275-8747), website: http://mapping.usgs.gov.

**Directions:** You will need to shuttle two vehicles for this traverse. Leave one at the hike's terminus, a parking area where the Appalachian Trail crosses U.S. 2, 3.6 miles east of the southern junction of U.S. 2 and Route 16 in Shelburne. The hike begins at the Appalachian Mountain Club Visitor Center on Route 16 in Pinkham Notch at the base of Mount Washington, 12 miles south of the junction with U.S. 2 in Gorham and about eight miles north of Jackson.

**Contact:** White Mountain National Forest Supervisor, 719 North Main St., Laconia, NH 03246, 603/528-8721, TDD for the hearing impaired 603/528-8722, website: www.fs.fed.us/r9/white. Appalachian Trail Conference, 799 Washington St., P.O. Box 807, Harpers Ferry, WV

25425-0807, 304/535-6331, website: www.appalachiantrail.org.

## 19 MOUNT WASHINGTON: HUNTINGTON RAVINE AND THE ALPINE GARDEN

**8 mi/8 hrs**

**in the White Mountain National Forest in Pinkham Notch**

Discard all your preconceived notions of hard trails. Huntington Ravine has earned a reputation as the most difficult regular hiking trail in the White Mountains for good reason. The trail ascends the ravine headwall, involving very exposed scrambling up steep slabs of rock with significant fall potential. Inexperienced scramblers should shy away from this route, and persons carrying a heavy pack may want to consider another way up the mountain. The ravine is strictly a summer and early fall hike, and even in those seasons snow can fall, treacherous ice can form, or the steep rock slabs may be slick with water. I've hiked this trail in good August weather, but had to turn back from a technical rock climb up another section of Huntington's headwall when sleet fell in September. The headwall, the Alpine Garden, and the top of the Lion Head all lie above tree line and are exposed to the weather. From late fall through early spring, the headwall is draped with ice and snow, and is a prized destination for experienced ice climbers. For hikers comfortable with exposure and rugged scrambling, Huntington Ravine has few equals. And this eight-mile loop, which climbs about 3,400 feet in elevation, will lead you through a variety of mountain terrain found on few other peaks east of the Rockies. I've deliberately avoided Washington's crowded summit with this hike, because the alternative to going to the summit, walking across the Alpine Garden, is such a treat. But the description below details how to reach the summit if that's your goal.

From the Appalachian Mountain Club Visitor Center, follow the wide Tuckerman Ravine Trail. Less than 1.5 miles up, the Huntington Ravine Trail diverges right (north); watch closely for it, because the sign may be partly hidden by trees, and the path is narrow and easily overlooked. This trail climbs steeply in spots, and you get fleeting glimpses of the ravine headwall above. Within 1.5 miles from the Tuckerman Ravine Trail, you reach a flat, open area on the Huntington Ravine floor—and your first sweeping view of the massive headwall, riven by several ominous gullies separating tall cliffs. Novice hikers can reach this point without any trouble, and the view of the ravine is worth it. Nearby is a first-aid cache bearing a plaque memorializing Albert Dow, a climber and mountain rescue volunteer killed by an avalanche in Huntington Ravine during a 1982 search for a pair of missing ice climbers.

The trail leads through a maze of giant boulders to the headwall base and then heads diagonally up the talus. On the headwall proper, the well-blazed trail ascends rock slabs, which may be wet, and sections of blocky boulders. Two miles from the Tuckerman Ravine Trail, you reach the top of the ravine and the broad tableland known as the Alpine Garden, where colorful wildflowers bloom from mid-June (which is a little early to attempt the headwall, so hike up the Lion Head Trail) through August.

By following the Huntington Ravine Trail a quarter mile farther, you can pick up the Nelson Crag Trail for the final mile (or not quite a mile) to Washington's summit and then descend the Tuckerman Ravine and Lion Head Trails to rejoin this loop at the other side of the Alpine Garden—adding two miles and about 800 feet of ascent to this hike. But this hike takes a finer route—free from the tourists who flock to the summit via the auto road or cog railway—crossing the Alpine Garden to the Lion Head. Turn left (south) onto the Alpine Garden Trail, which traverses the mile-wide, tundralike plain. In a short distance, you see to your left the top of a prominent cliff known as the Pinnacle, which is part of the Huntington Ravine headwall; the view from atop the

Pinnacle merits the short detour, but take care to walk on rocks and not the fragile alpine vegetation. The sprawling boulder pile of the mountain's upper cone rises up on your right.

Once you're across the Alpine Garden, turn left (east) onto the Lion Head Trail. The flat trail follows the crest of a prominent buttress, above the cliffs that form the northern or right-hand wall of Tuckerman Ravine. There are numerous good views down into the ravine before the trail drops back into the woods again, descending steeply and eventually rejoining the Tuckerman Ravine Trail about two miles from the AMC Visitor Center. Turn left (east) and head down.

**User groups:** Hikers only. No wheelchair facilities. This trail is not suitable for bikes, dogs, horses, or skis, and should not be attempted in winter except by hikers experienced in mountaineering and prepared for severe winter weather. Hunting is prohibited.

**Access, fees:** No backcountry permit is needed, but a permit is required for day use or overnight parking at any White Mountain National Forest trailhead, as indicated by signs posted at most trailheads. Permits are available at several area stores and from the national forest (see address below) at a cost of $5 for seven consecutive days or $20 per year. A $3 one-day permit can be purchased at self-service stations at national forest trailheads, but the permit is good only for the trailhead at which it's purchased.

**Maps:** For a map of hiking trails, get the *Presidential Range* map for $7.95 in waterproof Tyvek, available in many stores and from the Appalachian Mountain Club, 800/262-4455, website: www.outdoors.org; map 2 in the *Map and Guide to the Appalachian Trail in New Hampshire and Vermont,* an eight-map set and guidebook available for $19.95 ($14.95 for the maps alone) from the Appalachian Trail Conference (see address below); or the *Trail Map and Guide to the White Mountain National Forest* for $7.95 from the DeLorme Publishing Company, 800/642-0970. For a topographic

area map, request Mount Washington from USGS Map Sales, Federal Center, Box 25286, Denver, CO 80225, 888/ASK-USGS (888/275-8747), website: http://mapping.usgs.gov.

**Directions:** The hike begins from the Appalachian Mountain Club Visitor Center on Route 16 in Pinkham Notch at the base of Mount Washington, 12 miles south of the junction of Route 16 and U.S. 2 in Gorham and about eight miles north of Jackson. The trailhead is behind the visitor center.

**Contact:** White Mountain National Forest Supervisor, 719 North Main St., Laconia, NH 03246, 603/528-8721, TDD for the hearing impaired 603/528-8722, website: www.fs.fed.us/r9/white. Appalachian Trail Conference, 799 Washington St., P.O. Box 807, Harpers Ferry, WV 25425-0807, 304/535-6331, website: www.appalachiantrail.org. The AMC's Pinkham Notch Visitor Center has up-to-date reports on weather in the Presidential Range; call 603/466-2721.

## 20 MOUNT WASHINGTON: THE LION HEAD

**8.2 mi/7 hrs**

**in the White Mountain National Forest in Pinkham Notch**

The preceding and following hikes both suggest the Lion Head Trail as a logical descent route off Mount Washington. But it's also a less-traveled route up New England's highest peak than the Tuckerman Ravine Trail in summer, and it's the standard route for a challenging winter ascent. The actual winter Lion Head Trail follows a different route than the summer trail to avoid avalanche hazard. Trail signs are posted in the appropriate places when each trail is opened or closed for the season. To check on the status of the changeover, call the AMC's Pinkham Notch Visitor Center (see address below). For more information about Mount Washington, see the trail notes for the preceding or following hikes.

From Pinkham Notch, pick up the wide Tuckerman Ravine Trail, follow it for 2.3 miles, and then turn right onto the Lion Head Trail.

It soon begins steep switchbacks up the face of the Lion Head ridge, breaking out of the forest within a half mile of the Tuckerman Ravine Trail junction for excellent views of Pinkham Notch and the Carter Range across the notch. Shortly after leaving the forest, the trail crests the Lion Head for much flatter walking across the Alpine Garden, a tundra-like plateau that's one of the best places in these mountains to view alpine wildflowers from late spring well into summer, depending on how long the snow lingers. To your left, the ridge drops away abruptly into Tuckerman Ravine; straight ahead lies Washington's summit, still more than 1,200 feet higher.

At 1.1 miles from the Tuckerman Ravine Trail, the Lion Head Trail crosses the Alpine Garden Trail, and soon afterward begins climbing Mount Washington's summit cone. A half mile farther, turn right onto the Tuckerman Ravine Trail and follow it another 0.4 mile to Washington's summit. Descend the way you came.

**User groups:** Hikers only. No wheelchair facilities. This trail is not suitable for bikes, dogs, horses, or skis, and should not be attempted in winter except by hikers experienced in mountaineering and prepared for severe winter weather. Hunting is prohibited.

**Access, fees:** No backcountry permit is needed, but a permit is required for day use or overnight parking at any White Mountain National Forest trailhead, as indicated by signs posted at most trailheads. Permits are available at several area stores and from the national forest (see address below) at a cost of $5 for seven consecutive days or $20 per year. A $3 one-day permit can be purchased at self-service stations at national forest trailheads, but the permit is good only for the trailhead at which it's purchased.

**Maps:** For a map of hiking trails, obtain the *Presidential Range* map for $7.95 in waterproof Tyvek, available in many stores and from the Appalachian Mountain Club, 800/262-4455, website: www.outdoors.org; map 2 in the *Map and Guide to the Appalachian Trail in New Hampshire and Vermont,* an eight-map set and guidebook available for $19.95 ($14.95 for the maps alone) from the Appalachian Trail Conference (see address below); or the *Trail Map and Guide to the White Mountain National Forest* for $7.95 from the DeLorme Publishing Company, 800/642-0970. For a topographic area map, request Mount Washington from USGS Map Sales, Federal Center, Box 25286, Denver, CO 80225, 888/ASK-USGS (888/275-8747), website: http://mapping.usgs.gov.

**Directions:** The hike begins from the Appalachian Mountain Club Visitor Center on Route 16 in Pinkham Notch at the base of Mount Washington, 12 miles south of the junction of Route 16 and U.S. 2 in Gorham and about eight miles north of Jackson. The trailhead is behind the visitor center.

**Contact:** White Mountain National Forest Supervisor, 719 North Main St., Laconia, NH 03246, 603/528-8721, TDD for the hearing impaired 603/528-8722, website: www.fs.fed.us/r9/white. Appalachian Trail Conference, 799 Washington St., P.O. Box 807, Harpers Ferry, WV 25425-0807, 304/535-6331, website: www.appalachiantrail.org. The AMC's Pinkham Notch Visitor Center has up-to-date reports on weather in the Presidential Range; call 603/466-2721.

## 21 MOUNT WASHINGTON: TUCKERMAN RAVINE

**8.4 mi/7 hrs**

**in the White Mountain National Forest in Pinkham Notch**

This trail is the standard route and most direct way up the 6,288-foot Mount Washington, the Northeast's highest peak, so it typically sees hundreds of hikers on nice weekends in summer and early autumn. It's also a busy place in spring, when skiers make the hike up into Tuckerman Ravine to ski its formidable headwall. Although the crowds can diminish the mountain experience, the ravine is spectacular, an ascent of the headwall is a serious challenge, and reaching Washington's summit is an accomplishment sought by many. This is the common route for first-time hikers of Washington. The trail on the ravine headwall is sometimes closed due to ice; check on weather and conditions at the visitor center. While hiking the headwall, watch out for rocks kicked loose by hikers above you and be careful not to dislodge any rocks yourself. When you pass over the Mount Washington summit, you'll be walking on the Appalachian Trail. The elevation gained on this hike is about 4,300 feet.

From behind the visitor center, the wide Tuckerman Ravine Trail ascends at a moderate grade, passing the short side path to Crystal Cascade within a half mile. As you continue up the Tuckerman Ravine Trail, you'll pass intersections with several trails. At 2.5 miles the trail reaches the floor of the ravine, a worthwhile destination in itself; to the right is the Lion Head, and to the left the cliffs of Boott Spur. (From the Hermit Lake shelter, which is along the Tuckerman Ravine Trail, walk to the right less than a quarter mile for a striking reflection of Boott Spur in Hermit Lake.) The trail then climbs the headwall, reaching its lip a mile from Hermit Lake, and follows rock cairns nearly another mile to the summit. Although many hikers descend Tuckerman's headwall, an easier way down is via the Lion Head Trail, which diverges left from the Tuckerman Ravine Trail just below the summit and then rejoins it 0.1 mile below Hermit Lake.

**User groups:** Hikers only. No wheelchair facilities. This trail is not suitable for bikes, dogs, horses, or skis, and should not be attempted in winter except by hikers experienced in mountaineering and prepared for severe winter weather. Hunting is prohibited.

**Access, fees:** No backcountry permit is needed, but a permit is required for day use or overnight parking at any White Mountain National Forest trailhead, as indicated by signs posted at most trailheads. Permits are available at several area stores and from the national forest (see address below) at a cost of $5 for seven consecutive days or $20 per year. A $3 one-day permit can be purchased at self-serv-

ice stations at national forest trailheads, but the permit is good only for the trailhead at which it's purchased.

**Maps:** Several maps cover this area's hiking trails, including the *Presidential Range* map for $7.95 in waterproof Tyvek, available in many stores and from the Appalachian Mountain Club, 800/262-4455, website: www.outdoors.org; map 2 in the *Map and Guide to the Appalachian Trail in New Hampshire and Vermont,* an eight-map set and guidebook available for $19.95 ($14.95 for the maps alone) from the Appalachian Trail Conference (see address below); and the *Trail Map and Guide to the White Mountain National Forest* for $7.95 from the DeLorme Publishing Company, 800/642-0970. For a topographic area map, request Mount Washington from USGS Map Sales, Federal Center, Box 25286, Denver, CO 80225, 888/ASK-USGS (888/275-8747), website: http://mapping.usgs.gov.

**Directions:** The hike begins from the Appalachian Mountain Club Visitor Center on Route 16 in Pinkham Notch, at the base of Mount Washington, 12 miles south of the junction of Route 16 and U.S. 2 in Gorham and about eight miles north of Jackson. The trailhead is behind the visitor center.

**Contact:** White Mountain National Forest Supervisor, 719 North Main St., Laconia, NH 03246, 603/528-8721, TDD for the hearing impaired 603/528-8722, website: www.fs.fed.us/r9/white. Appalachian Trail Conference, 799 Washington St., P.O. Box 807, Harpers Ferry, WV 25425-0807, 304/535-6331, website: www.appalachiantrail.org. The AMC's Pinkham Notch Visitor Center has up-to-date reports on weather in the Presidential Range; call 603/466-2721.

## 22 MOUNT WASHINGTON: AMMONOOSUC RAVINE/ JEWELL TRAIL

**9.6 mi/7.5 hrs**

**in the White Mountain National Forest north of Crawford Notch**

Like any route up the Northeast's biggest hill,

this hike offers great views and rough terrain. Like most others, it is also a popular loop. And like any other route to the 6,288-foot summit of Mount Washington, this one can run you into some nasty weather. One September day not long ago I left behind a sun-splashed valley and ventured up here, only to reach the Lakes of the Clouds hut and find fog engulfing the mountain and a bitterly cold wind raking across the alpine zone. Dressed warmly and waiting patiently, I watched the clouds slowly dissipate under a warm sun—and made my way to the summit. This hike traverses exposed ground from just below the Lakes hut until you have descended more than a half mile down the Jewell Trail. The Ammonoosuc Ravine Trail provides the most direct route— 3.1 miles—to the AMC's Lakes of the Clouds hut, in the saddle between Mounts Washington and Monroe. There are tricky stretches on the ravine's steep upper headwall, which can be slick with water, and several brook crossings, some of which would be impossible in times of high water. This hike climbs about 3,800 feet in elevation.

From the parking lot, follow the Ammonoosuc Ravine Trail, which climbs moderately, passing picturesque Gem Pool about two miles out. For the next half mile, the trail makes a steep ascent of the headwall, passing several cascades and pools and good views back into Ammonoosuc Ravine. At three miles, you leave the last scrub vegetation behind and enter the alpine zone; take care to walk on rocks and not the fragile plant life. From the Lakes hut (reached at 3.1 miles), the detour south to the 5,384-foot summit of Monroe adds a relatively easy one-mile round-trip and 360 feet of climbing to this hike. From the Lakes hut to the junction of the Jewell and Gulfside Trails, this hike follows the route of the Appalachian Trail.

To continue the hike, turn left (north) from the Lakes hut onto the Crawford Path, which passes by the two tiny tarns that give the hut its name and ascends more than 1,000 verti-cal feet over 1.4 miles to the top of Washington, where there is a visitor center, private weather observatory, and other buildings. Descend the Crawford Path from the summit for 0.2 mile and bear right onto the Gulfside Trail heading north. Follow it 1.4 miles, walking the crest of the exposed ridge, passing the loop trail up Mount Clay, to the Jewell Trail. (Making the loop hike over Mount Clay adds about two miles and a couple hundred feet of climbing to this hike, but you'll get great views from the top of Clay and a relatively secluded summit.) Turn left and descend the Jewell for 3.7 miles to the parking lot. It descends steep ground through several switchbacks at first, then proceeds at a more moderate grade.

**User groups:** Hikers and dogs. No wheelchair facilities. This trail should not be attempted in winter except by hikers experienced in mountaineering and prepared for severe winter weather, and is not suitable for skis. Bikes, horses, and hunting are prohibited.

**Access, fees:** No backcountry permit is needed, but a permit is required for day use or overnight parking at any White Mountain National Forest trailhead, as indicated by signs posted at most trailheads. Permits are available at several area stores and from the national forest (see address below) at a cost of $5 for seven consecutive days or $20 per year. A $3 one-day permit can be purchased at self-service stations at national forest trailheads, but the pass is good only for the trailhead at which it's purchased. Mount Clinton Road is not maintained in winter. The Appalachian Mountain Club operates the Lakes of the Clouds hut, where a crew prepares meals and guests share bunkrooms and bathrooms; call 603/466-2727 for reservation and rate information.

**Maps:** For a map of hiking trails, obtain the *Presidential Range* map for $7.95 in waterproof Tyvek, available in many stores and from the Appalachian Mountain Club, 800/262-4455, website: www.outdoors.org; map 2 in the *Map and Guide to the Appalachian Trail in New Hampshire and Vermont,* an eight-map set and guidebook available for $19.95 ($14.95 for the maps alone) from the Appalachian Trail Conference (see address below); or the *Trail Map and Guide to the White Mountain National Forest* for $7.95 from the DeLorme Publishing Company, 800/642-0970. For a topographic area map, request Mount Washington from USGS Map Sales, Federal Center, Box 25286, Denver, CO 80225, 888/ASK-USGS (888/275-8747), website: http://mapping.usgs.gov.

**Directions:** From the junction of U.S. 302 and U.S. 3 in Twin Mountain, drive east on U.S. 302 for 4.6 miles and turn left at signs for the Mount Washington Cog Railway. Continue 6.7 miles to a large parking lot on the right. Or from U.S. 302 in Crawford Notch, 0.2 mile north of the visitor information center, turn onto Mount Clinton Road (which is not maintained in winter). Follow it 3.7 miles and turn right. Continue 1.1 miles and turn right into the parking lot.

**Contact:** White Mountain National Forest Supervisor, 719 North Main St., Laconia, NH 03246, 603/528-8721, TDD for the hearing impaired 603/528-8722, website: www.fs.fed.us/r9/white. Appalachian Trail Conference, 799 Washington St., P.O. Box 807, Harpers Ferry, WV 25425-0807, 304/535-6331, website: www.appalachiantrail.org. The AMC's Pinkham Notch Visitor Center has up-to-date reports on weather in the Presidential Range; call 603/466-2721.

### 23 MOUNTS WASHINGTON AND MONROE: CRAWFORD PATH

**16.4 mi/11 hrs**

**in the White Mountain National Forest and Crawford Notch State Park**

This is a hike typically covered in two days, with a stay at the AMC's Lakes of the Clouds hut, but the gentle nature of the Crawford Path allows very fit hikers to do this in a day. The southern ridge of the Presidentials is far less rugged than the northern ridge, yet the views surpass those of most hikes in New England.

Another draw: the Lakes of the Clouds, which are among the few true alpine tarns in the White Mountains. The 5,372-foot Mount Monroe rolls like a wave south from the 6,288-foot Mount Washington—and if you do spend a night at the hut, make the short walk up onto Monroe to watch the sunset. Remember that weather changes quickly on these peaks and may even be radically different atop Washington than on the other summits. I once hiked up the Crawford Path in early September, leaving a valley enjoying 65-degree temperatures, to find fresh snow on Mount Pierce—and to hear that Washington's summit was being bombarded by 100 mph winds.

From the parking area, follow the Crawford Connector 0.2 mile to the Crawford Path, considered the oldest continuously maintained footpath in the country. (Nearby, a side path leads left for 0.4 mile over rough ground to Crawford Cliff, with a good view of Crawford Notch.) From the connector trail junction, the Crawford Path ascends steadily, passing a short side path in 0.4 mile that leads to Gibbs Falls. Less than three miles from U.S. 302, the trail emerges from the forest and meets the Webster Cliff Trail (turning right and walking about 150 yards south on that trail brings you to the 4,312-foot summit of Mount Pierce). From this point to Washington's summit, this hike follows the Appalachian Trail. Turn left, following the Crawford Path over more level ground, with views in all directions. A bit more than a mile from the Webster Cliffs Trail junction, the Mount Eisenhower loop trail diverges for the 0.4-mile climb to Eisenhower's 4,760-foot summit, then descends, steeply in spots, another 0.4 mile to rejoin the Crawford Path. Although bagging Eisenhower entails 300 feet of climbing and 0.2 mile more hiking than taking the Crawford Path around the summit, the view from its summit is worth the small effort. The Crawford Path continues to ascend at a very gentle grade until, six miles from U.S. 302, the Mount Monroe Loop branches left for its two summits (from this direction, the second, or northernmost, summit is the highest).

It's the same distance, 0.7 mile, via either the Crawford Path or the Monroe Loop to where the two trails meet again north of Monroe, but the Monroe Loop involves another 350 feet of elevation gain and is much more exposed. From the northern junction of the trails, the Crawford Path leads a flat 0.1 mile to the Lakes of the Clouds hut. From there, it's a steady climb for 1.4 miles over very rocky terrain up the barren summit cone of Washington to the roof of New England. Return via the same route.

**User groups:** Hikers and dogs. No wheelchair facilities. This trail should not be attempted in winter except by hikers experienced in mountaineering and prepared for severe winter weather, and is not suitable for skis. Bikes, horses, and hunting are prohibited.

**Access, fees:** No backcountry permit is needed, but a permit is required for day use or overnight parking at any White Mountain National Forest trailhead, as indicated by signs posted at most trailheads. Permits are available at several area stores and from the national forest (see address below) at a cost of $5 for seven consecutive days or $20 per year. A $3 one-day permit can be purchased at self-service stations at national forest trailheads, but the pass is good only for the trailhead at which it's purchased. The Appalachian Mountain Club operates the Lakes of the Clouds hut in the saddle between the summits of Washington and Monroe, where a crew prepares meals and guests share bunkrooms and bathrooms; call 603/466-2727 for reservation and rate information, or see the website: www.outdoors.org.

**Maps:** For a map of hiking trails, obtain the *Presidential Range* map for $7.95 in waterproof Tyvek, available in many stores and from the Appalachian Mountain Club, 800/262-4455, website: www.outdoors.org; map 2 in the *Map and Guide to the Appalachian Trail in New Hampshire and Vermont,* an eight-map set and guidebook available for $19.95 ($14.95 for the maps alone) from the Appalachian Trail Conference (see address below); or the *Trail Map and Guide to the White Mountain National Forest* for $7.95 from the DeLorme Publishing Company, 800/642-0970, website: www.DeLorme.com). For a topographic area map, request Mount Washington from USGS Map Sales, Federal Center, Box 25286, Denver, CO 80225, 888/ASK-USGS (888/275-8747), website: http://mapping.usgs.gov.

**Directions:** Drive on U.S. 302 into Crawford Notch. The trailhead parking area is 0.1 mile up Mount Clinton Road, which leaves U.S. 302 opposite the Crawford House site, just north of Saco Lake.

**Contact:** White Mountain National Forest Supervisor, 719 North Main St., Laconia, NH 03246, 603/528-8721, TDD for the hearing impaired 603/528-8722, website: www.fs.fed.us/r9/white. Appalachian Trail Conference, 799 Washington St., P.O. Box 807, Harpers Ferry, WV 25425-0807, 304/535-6331, website: www.appalachiantrail.org. The AMC's Pinkham Notch Visitor Center has up-to-date reports on weather in the Presidential Range; call 603/466-2721.

## 24 MOUNT WASHINGTON: BOOT SPUR/GULF OF SLIDES
**7.2 mi/5 hrs**
**in the White Mountain National Forest in Pinkham Notch**

The summit of 6,288-foot Mount Washington, with its commercial development and access by road and cog railway, is one of the least appealing features of this sprawling mountain—which is why I sometimes prefer a hike like this one, with its stiff climb onto a high shoulder of Washington and views down into two of its ravines. The ascent to the high point named Boott Spur is about 3,500 feet.

From the Appalachian Mountain Club Visitor Center, follow the Tuckerman Ravine Trail for nearly a half mile. Shortly after passing the side path to Crystal Cascade, turn left onto the Boott Spur Trail. In another 1.7 miles, a side path leads a short distance right to Ravine Outlook, high above Tuckerman Ravine. Return to the Boott Spur Trail, which emerges from the woods nearly two miles from the Tuckerman Ravine Trail and passes between the halves of Split Rock at 2.2 miles. It then ascends the open ridge known as Boott Spur, with excellent views down into Tuckerman Ravine. Although the grade is moderate, a few false summits along the steplike ridge deceive many hikers. Once atop the shoulder, three miles from the Tuckerman Ravine Trail, turn left (south) onto the Davis Path and follow it for a half mile. Then turn left again (southeast) onto the Glen Boulder Trail, which circles around the rim of the Gulf of Slides, a popular destination for backcountry skiers in winter and spring. Much of the Glen Boulder Trail is above tree line, with long views to the south and good views east toward Wildcat Mountain and the Carter Range. At 1.5 miles from the Davis Path, you'll pass the Glen Boulder, an enormous glacial erratic set precariously on the mountainside. A bit more than a mile past the boulder, back down in the woods, turn left onto the Direttissima, the trail heading back to the visitor center parking lot.

**User groups:** Hikers only. No wheelchair facilities. This trail should not be attempted in winter except by hikers experienced in mountaineering and prepared for severe winter weather, and is not for bikes, dogs, horses, or skis. Hunting is prohibited.

**Access, fees:** No backcountry permit is needed, but a permit is required for day use or overnight parking at any White Mountain National Forest trailhead, as indicated by signs posted at most trailheads. Permits are available at several area stores and from the national forest (see address below) at a cost of $5 for seven consecutive days or $20 per year. A $3 one-day permit can be purchased at self-service stations at national forest trailheads, but the pass is good only for the trailhead at which it's purchased.

**Maps:** For a map of hiking trails, obtain the *Presidential Range* map for $7.95 in waterproof Tyvek, available in many stores and from the Appalachian Mountain Club, 800/262-4455, website: www.outdoors.org; or the *Trail Map and Guide to the White Mountain National Forest* for $7.95 from the DeLorme Publishing Company, 800/642-0970. For a topographic area map, request Mount Washington from USGS Map Sales, Federal Center, Box 25286, Denver, CO 80225, 888/ASK-USGS (888/275-8747), website: http://mapping.usgs.gov.

**Directions:** The hike begins from the Appalachian Mountain Club Visitor Center on Route 16 in Pinkham Notch, at the base of Mount Washington, 12 miles south of the junction of Route 16 and U.S. 2 in Gorham and about eight miles north of Jackson. The trailhead is behind the visitor center.

**Contact:** White Mountain National Forest Supervisor, 719 North Main St., Laconia, NH 03246, 603/528-8721, TDD for the hearing impaired 603/528-8722, website: www.fs.fed.us/r9/white. The AMC's Pinkham Notch Visitor Center has up-to-date reports on weather in the Presidential Range; call 603/466-2721.

## 25 SQUARE LEDGE

1.2 mi/0.75 hr

**in the White Mountain National Forest in Pinkham Notch**

Square Ledge is the aptly named cliff that's obvious when you're standing in the parking lot at the Appalachian Mountain Club Visitor Center on Route 16 and looking due east across the road. The view from atop this cliff is one of the best you can get of Pinkham Notch, and it takes in the deep ravines on the east side of New England's highest peak, 6,288-foot Mount Washington. The hiking trail is 1.2 miles, but you can make a longer loop by getting onto the cross-country skiing trail. A fairly wide skiing trail of only moderate difficulty starts just north of the hiking trail on Route 16, directly across from the AMC Visitor Center; it is marked by diamond-shaped plastic markers. This hike is a great trip on snowshoes because the trees are bare, the forest more open, and you get almost continuous views of the east side of Mount Washington (see this chapter's six hikes up Mount Washington). I snowshoed up here on a gorgeous late March afternoon, as the sun was dropping behind Washington. In winter, there may be ice just below the cliffs of Square Ledge, or you may have to remove your snowshoes if there's no snow or ice and the rocks at the cliff's base are exposed. There is a bit of easy scrambling up six or eight feet of rock to get onto Square Ledge.

From the AMC Visitor Center, cross Route 16 and walk south about 100 feet to where the Lost Pond Trail, a part of the white-blazed Appalachian Trail, crosses a bog on a boardwalk and enters the woods. About 50 feet into the woods, turn left on the blue-blazed Square Ledge Trail. The trail almost immediately crosses the ski trail. It ascends gradually—you will only gain about 400 feet in elevation from the road to Square Ledge—through a mixed forest with lots of white birch trees, some of them pretty fat. Watch for the sporadic blazes marking the trail, especially in winter, when the pathway may be less obvious. At 0.1 mile from the road, turn left and follow a side path 100 feet to Ladies Lookout, where you'll get a decent view toward Washington. Back on the Square Ledge Trail, continue through the woods, skirt around Hangover Rock—easy to recognize—then turn right and climb more steeply uphill. As you reach the bottom of the gully on the right (south) side of the Square Ledge cliffs, turn and look to your right; you will see the ski trail about 20 feet through the trees. Remember this spot for your descent. Scramble up the gully to the right of the cliffs. At the top of the gully, scramble up the rocks to the top of the ledge.

After enjoying the view, backtrack down the gully to its base. From here, you can either return the same way you came, making a 1.2-mile round-trip, or turn left, cut through the woods, and extend your hike by less than a mile on the ski trail. Once on the ski trail, turn

left and follow it to the Loop Trail, which loops off and returns to the ski trail. At the far end of the Loop Trail, you'll get another view toward Washington. After completing the loop, descend on the ski trail to the point where it crosses the hiking trail. Turn left on the hiking trail, and you'll be back at Route 16 within minutes.

**User groups:** Hikers and snowshoers. There is a separate trail for cross-country skiers. No wheelchair access. Dogs must be under control at all times. Hunting is allowed in season.

**Access, fees:** No backcountry permit is needed, but a permit is required for day use or overnight parking at any White Mountain National Forest trailhead, as indicated by signs posted at most trailheads. Permits are available at several area stores and from the national forest (see address below) at a cost of $5 for seven consecutive days or $20 per year. A $3 one-day permit can be purchased at self-service stations at national forest trailheads, but the permit is good only for the trailhead at which it's purchased.

**Maps:** For a map of hiking trails in this area, obtain the *Presidential Range* map for $7.95 in waterproof Tyvek, available in many stores and from the Appalachian Mountain Club, 800/262-4455, website: www.outdoors.org; or the *Trail Map and Guide to the White Mountain National Forest* for $7.95 from the DeLorme Publishing Company, 800/642-0970. For a topographic area map, request Mount Washington from USGS Map Sales, Federal Center, Box 25286, Denver, CO 80225, 888/ASK-USGS (888/275-8747), website: http://mapping.usgs.gov.

**Directions:** The hike begins from the Appalachian Mountain Club Visitor Center on Route 16 in Pinkham Notch, at the base of Mount Washington, 12 miles south of the junction of Route 16 and U.S. 2 in Gorham and about eight miles north of Jackson. The trailhead is across the highway from the visitor center.

**Contact:** White Mountain National Forest Supervisor, 719 North Main St., Laconia, NH 03246, 603/528-8721, TDD for the hearing

impaired 603/528-8722, website: www.fs.fed
.us/r9/white. The AMC's Pinkham Notch Visitor Center has up-to-date reports on weather in the Presidential Range; call 603/466-2721.

## 26 MOUNT HIGHT/CARTER DOME/CARTER NOTCH

**10 mi/7.5 hrs**

**in the White Mountain National Forest north of Pinkham Notch**

This very scenic 10-mile loop takes you over the most rugged summit with the most expansive views in the Carter Range—craggy Mount Hight—onto the ninth-highest peak in the Granite State, 4,832-foot Carter Dome, and into a boulder-strewn mountain notch where towering cliffs flank a pair of tiny ponds. The total elevation gained is about 3,500 feet.

From the trailhead, hike the Nineteen-Mile Brook Trail for nearly two miles, and turn left (east) onto the Carter Dome Trail. In about two miles, at Zeta Pass, you might exercise the option of exploring 4,430-foot South Carter (adding 1.5 miles to this hike) by heading north (left) on the Carter-Moriah Trail; then double back to Zeta Pass. This hike heads south (right) on the Carter-Moriah Trail, which follows the Appalachian Trail from Zeta Pass to the junction of the Nineteen-Mile Brook and Wildcat Ridge Trails. The trail climbs steeply, requiring some scrambling over rocks, to the bare summit of 4,675-foot Mount Hight. There you have a 360-degree panorama of the Presidential Range dominating the skyline to the west, the Carters running north, and the lower hills of eastern New Hampshire and western Maine to the south and east. Continue south on the Carter-Moriah Trail, over the viewless summit of Carter Dome, and descend into Carter Notch. There's a great view of the notch from open ledges before you start the knee-pounding drop. At the larger of the two Carter Lakes in the notch, two miles past Mount Hight, turn right (northwest) onto the Nineteen-Mile Brook Trail for the nearly four-mile walk back to the parking area.

**User groups:** Hikers and dogs. No wheelchair facilities. This trail would be difficult to snowshoe in severe winter weather, and is not suitable for skis. Bikes, horses, and hunting are prohibited.

**Access, fees:** No backcountry permit is needed, but a permit is required for day use or overnight parking at any White Mountain National Forest trailhead, as indicated by signs posted at most trailheads. Permits are available at several area stores and from the national forest (see address below) at a cost of $5 for seven consecutive days or $20 per year. A $3 one-day permit can be purchased at self-service stations at national forest trailheads, but the pass is good only for the trailhead at which it's purchased.

**Maps:** For a map of hiking trails, obtain the *Carter Range-Evans Notch/North Country-Mahoosuc* map, $7.95 in waterproof Tyvek, available in many stores and from the Appalachian Mountain Club, 800/262-4455, website: www.outdoors.org; the *Trail Map and Guide to the White Mountain National Forest* for $7.95 from the DeLorme Publishing Company, 800/642-0970, website: www.DeLorme.com; or map 2 in the *Map and Guide to the Appalachian Trail in New Hampshire and Vermont,* an eight-map set and guidebook for $19.95 ($14.95 for the maps alone) from the Appalachian Trail Conference (see address below). For a topographic area map, request Carter Dome from USGS Map Sales, Federal Center, Box 25286, Denver, CO 80225, 888/ASK-USGS (888/275-8747), website: http://mapping.usgs.gov.

**Directions:** The Nineteen-Mile Brook Trail begins at a turnout on Route 16, a mile north of the Mount Washington Auto Road.

**Contact:** White Mountain National Forest Supervisor, 719 North Main St., Laconia, NH 03246, 603/528-8721, TDD for the hearing impaired 603/528-8722, website: www.fs.fed .us/r9/white. Appalachian Trail Conference, 799 Washington St., P.O. Box 807, Harpers Ferry, WV 25425-0807, 304/535-6331, website: www.appalachiantrail.org.

## 27 WILDCAT MOUNTAIN
8.5 mi/5.5 hrs

**in Pinkham Notch in the White Mountain National Forest**

The summit of this 4,000-foot peak is wooded and uninteresting, but the walk along Nineteen-Mile Brook and the view from the top of the cliffs overlooking Carter Notch and the Carter Range—reached via a short spur trail just below Wildcat Mountain's 4,422-foot summit—make this hike very worthwhile. Because this end of Wildcat Mountain does not tend to lure many hikers, you might have that viewpoint to yourself (as a friend and I once did at the tail end of a backpacking trip through the Carter Range). This hike climbs nearly 3,000 feet.

From Route 16, the Nineteen-Mile Brook Trail ascends very gently toward Carter Notch, paralleling the wide, rock-strewn streambed and crossing two tributaries. Just 0.2 mile before the trail drops down into the notch—and 3.5 miles from Route 16—turn right onto the Wildcat Ridge Trail, which is also part of the Appalachian Trail. It climbs the steep east face of Wildcat Mountain and crosses a rockslide path about 25 feet across that is steep and severely eroded, with loose footing in summer and often dangerous, icy conditions in winter. Upon reaching more level ground, shortly before topping the long ridge of Wildcat Mountain, watch for the spur trail branching left that leads about 30 feet to the top of the cliffs overlooking Carter Notch. Return to the parking area the way you came—and on the descent, I highly recommend the half-mile detour down into Carter Notch on the Nineteen-Mile Brook Trail.

**User groups:** Hikers, snowshoers, and dogs. No wheelchair facilities. This trail is not suitable for skis. Bikes, horses, and hunting are prohibited.

**Access, fees:** No backcountry permit is needed, but a permit is required for day use or overnight parking at any White Mountain National Forest trailhead, as indicated by signs posted at most trailheads. Permits are available at several area stores and from the national forest (see address below) at a cost of $5 for seven consecutive days or $20 per year. A $3 one-day permit can be purchased at self-service stations at national forest trailheads, but the pass is good only for the trailheads at which it's purchased.

**Maps:** For a map of hiking trails, obtain the *Presidential Range* map or the *Carter Range-Evans Notch/North Country-Mahoosuc* map, $7.95 each in waterproof Tyvek, available in many stores and from the Appalachian Mountain Club, 800/262-4455, website: www.outdoors.org; the *Trail Map and Guide to the White Mountain National Forest* for $7.95 from the DeLorme Publishing Company, 800/642-0970, website: www.DeLorme.com; or map 2 in the *Map and Guide to the Appalachian Trail in New Hampshire and Vermont,* an eight-map set for $19.95 ($14.95 for the maps alone) from the Appalachian Trail Conference (see address below). For a topographic area map, request Carter Dome from USGS Map Sales, Federal Center, Box 25286, Denver, CO 80225, 888/ASK-USGS (888/275-8747), website: http://mapping.usgs.gov.

**Directions:** The Nineteen-Mile Brook Trail begins at a turnout on Route 16, a mile north of the Mount Washington Auto Road.

**Contact:** White Mountain National Forest Supervisor, 719 North Main St., Laconia, NH 03246, 603/528-8721, TDD for the hearing impaired 603/528-8722, website: www.fs.fed .us/r9/white. Appalachian Trail Conference, 799 Washington St., P.O. Box 807, Harpers Ferry, WV 25425-0807, 304/535-6331, website: www.appalachiantrail.org.

## 28 CARTER NOTCH: WILDCAT RIVER TRAIL
8.6 mi/5 hrs

**in the White Mountain National Forest north of Jackson**

This relatively easy hike accesses spectacular Carter Notch via a trail less traveled than the popular Nineteen-Mile Brook Trail (see the

Mount Hight/Carter Dome/Carter Notch hike earlier in this chapter). It's arguably a more scenic outing on snowshoes in winter, when the leaves are down and you get better views of the mountains. For beginner snowshoers, it's also well protected from the severe winter weather that can pound the higher summits, though at 8.6 miles round-trip, you shouldn't underestimate how tiring it can be snowshoeing this entire route. The elevation gain is about 1,500 feet.

From the parking area, follow the Bog Brook Trail for 0.7 mile. Just after crossing the Wildcat River, which can be difficult at times of high water, the Bog Brook Trail bears right, but you will continue straight ahead onto the Wildcat River Trail. Follow it along the gorgeous river, then away from the river into the woods. It ascends steadily but gently except for brief, steep pitches, for 3.6 miles from the Bog Brook Trail junction to the Appalachian Mountain Club hut in Carter Notch. After exploring the notch a bit, return the way you came.

**User groups:** Hikers, snowshoers, skiers, and dogs. No wheelchair facilities. Bikes, horses, and hunting are prohibited.

**Access, fees:** No backcountry permit is needed, but a permit is required for day use or overnight parking at any White Mountain National Forest trailhead, as indicated by signs posted at most trailheads. Permits are available at several area stores and from the national forest (see address below) at a cost of $5 for seven consecutive days or $20 per year. A $3 one-day permit can be purchased at self-service stations at national forest trailheads, but the pass is good only for the trailhead at which it's purchased. Carry cash for camping overnight at the Appalachian Mountain Club hut in Carter Notch.

**Maps:** For a contour map of hiking trails, obtain the *Carter Range-Evans Notch/North Country-Mahoosuc* map, $7.95 in waterproof Tyvek, available in many stores and from the Appalachian Mountain Club, 800/262-4455, website: www.outdoors.org; or the *Trail Map and*

*Guide to the White Mountain National Forest* for $7.95 from the DeLorme Publishing Company, 800/642-0970. For a topographic area map, request Jackson and Carter Dome from USGS Map Sales, Federal Center, Box 25286, Denver, CO 80225, 888/ASK-USGS (888/275-8747), website: http://mapping.usgs.gov.

**Directions:** From Route 16A in Jackson, Route 16B loops through the north end of town, its two endpoints leaving Route 16A very near each other; take the left, or westernmost, endpoint of Route 16B and follow it uphill. Where Route 16B turns sharply right, continue straight ahead onto Carter Notch Road. Three miles after leaving Route 16B, just after a sharp left turn in the road, park at a turnout for the Bog Brook Trail.

**Contact:** White Mountain National Forest Supervisor, 719 North Main St., Laconia, NH 03246, 603/528-8721, TDD for the hearing impaired 603/528-8722, website: www.fs.fed .us/r9/white.

## 29 LOST POND
**2 mi/1 hr**
**in the White Mountain National Forest in Pinkham Notch**

While this pond is no more lost than the popular Lonesome Lake on the other side of the Whites is lonesome, this is a nice short hike that's flat and offers opportunities for wildlife viewing and a unique view of Mount Washington. Cross Route 16 from the Appalachian Mountain Club Visitor Center and follow the Lost Pond Trail, a section of the Appalachian Trail, around the pond. Immediately you will see signs of beaver activity—probably dams and a lodge—and, if you're lucky, a moose will be grazing in the swampy area to the left. About halfway around the pond, look across it to a fine view up at Washington above the still water. The trail ends at the Wildcat Ridge Trail, just minutes from Glen Ellis Falls, which can be reached by turning right (west) toward Route 16; in spring and early summer, crossing the Ellis River between this trail junction and Route 16 can be difficult and dangerous. You can also reach some nice views of this valley and Mount Washington by turning left at this junction and climbing less than a mile up the Wildcat Ridge Trail. This hike returns the way you came.

**User groups:** Hikers, dogs, skiers, and snowshoers. No wheelchair facilities. Bikes, horses, and hunting are prohibited.

**Access, fees:** No backcountry permit is needed, but a permit is required for day use or overnight parking at any White Mountain National Forest trailhead, as indicated by signs posted at most trailheads. Permits are available at several area stores and from the national forest (see address below) at a cost of $5 for seven consecutive days or $20 per year. A $3 one-day permit can be purchased at self-service stations at national forest trailheads, but the pass is good only for the trailhead at which it's purchased.

**Maps:** Contour maps covering this area include the *Presidential Range* map and *Carter Range-Evans Notch/North Country-Mahoosuc* map, both for $7.95 in waterproof Tyvek, available in many stores and from the Appalachian Mountain Club, 800/262-4455, website: www.outdoors.org. For topographic area maps, request Mount Washington, Carter Dome, Jackson, and Stairs Mountain from USGS Map Sales, Federal Center, Box 25286, Denver, CO 80225, 888/ASK-USGS (888/275-8747), website: http://mapping.usgs.gov.

**Directions:** The hike begins from the Appalachian Mountain Club Visitor Center on Route 16 in Pinkham Notch, at the base of Mount Washington, 12 miles south of the junction of Route 16 and U.S. 2 in Gorham and about eight miles north of Jackson. The trailhead is across the highway from the visitor center.

**Contact:** White Mountain National Forest Supervisor, 719 North Main St., Laconia, NH 03246, 603/528-8721, TDD for the hearing impaired 603/528-8722, website: www.fs.fed .us/r9/white. Appalachian Mountain Club Pinkham Notch Visitor Center, P.O. Box 298,

Gorham, NH 03581, 603/466-2721, website: www.outdoors.org.

## 30 GLEN ELLIS FALLS
**0.3 mi/0.75 hr**
**in the White Mountain National Forest south of Pinkham Notch**

Here's a scenic, short walk that's ideal for young children and enjoyable for adults—though it could be troublesome for people who have difficulty climbing steep steps. Follow the wide gravel trail through a tunnel under Route 16. It descends steeply at times, but there are rock steps and a handrail. The waterfall is less than a half-mile walk from the parking area and more than worth the effort: a 70-foot wall of water makes a sheer drop into a small pool at its base. This is a popular walk with tourists, and it's especially spectacular in late spring, when water flow is heaviest.

Special note: If you're coming from Lost Pond or Wildcat Mountain (see the hike listings in this chapter), be aware that the Wildcat River Trail makes a crossing of the Ellis River near Route 16 that can be treacherous in times of high water and unsafe for young children.

**User groups:** Hikers and dogs. No wheelchair facilities. This trail would be difficult to snowshoe and is not suitable for bikes, horses, or skis. Hunting is allowed in season.

**Access, fees:** No backcountry permit is needed, but a permit is required for day use or overnight parking at any White Mountain National Forest trailhead, as indicated by signs posted at most trailheads. Permits are available at several area stores and from the national forest (see address below) at a cost of $5 for seven consecutive days or $20 per year. A $3 one-day permit can be purchased at self-service stations at national forest trailheads, but the pass is good only for the trailhead at which it's purchased.

**Maps:** Although no map is needed for this hike, several maps cover it, including the Presidential Range for $10.95 (paper), and the

*Presidential Range* map and *Carter Range-Evans Notch/North Country-Mahoosuc* map, both for $7.95 in waterproof Tyvek, available in many stores and from the Appalachian Mountain Club, 800/262-4455, website: www.outdoors.org; and the *Trail Map and Guide to the White Mountain National Forest* for $7.95 from the DeLorme Publishing Company, 800/642-0970. For topographic area maps, request Mount Washington, Carter Dome, Jackson, and Stairs Mountain from USGS Map Sales, Federal Center, Box 25286, Denver, CO 80225, 888/ASK-USGS (888/275-8747), website: http://mapping.usgs.gov.

**Directions:** The trail begins at a parking lot for Glen Ellis Falls off Route 16, less than a mile south of the Appalachian Mountain Club Visitor Center in Pinkham Notch.

**Contact:** White Mountain National Forest Supervisor, 719 North Main St., Laconia, NH 03246, 603/528-8721, TDD for the hearing impaired 603/528-8722, website: www.fs.fed.us/r9/white. Appalachian Mountain Club Pinkham Notch Visitor Center, P.O. Box 298, Gorham, NH 03581, 603/466-2721, website: www.outdoors.org.

## 31 ZEALAND NOTCH/ WILLEY RANGE

**17 mi/2–3 days**

**in the White Mountain National Forest southeast of Twin Mountain**

This 17-mile loop, best spread over two or three days, passes through spectacular Zealand Notch and traverses the Willey Range, a less-well-known corner of the Whites with a pair of 4,000-foot peaks and rugged terrain, if limited views. Two friends and I made this trip one Thanksgiving weekend, hiking through the notch on a chilly but calm night under a full moon. We enjoyed views from Mount Willey of clouds swirling around the Presidentials before a storm blew in and dampened our spirits with a cold, driving rain. The cumulative elevation gained is less than 3,000 feet.

From the Zealand Road parking lot, follow the Zealand Trail south, paralleling the Zealand River. At 2.3 miles, the A-Z Trail enters from the left; you will return on that trail. The Zealand Trail reaches a junction with the Twinway and the Ethan Pond Trail at 2.5 miles. The AMC's Zealand Falls hut lies 0.2 mile uphill on the Twinway; on the way, you pass a short side path to a view of Zealand Falls, and there are views of the notch from the hut. Instead, this hike bears left onto the Ethan Pond Trail, which runs for two miles to the opposite end of the notch, passing numerous overlooks through the trees. Reaching the Thoreau Falls Trail at 4.6 miles, bear right and follow it for 0.1 mile to Thoreau Falls, which tumbles more than 100 feet down through several steps. Backtrack and turn right (east) on the Ethan Pond Trail, which follows level ground for 2.5 miles to the side path leading left less than 0.1 mile to Ethan Pond and the shelter just above the pond.

A mile beyond the junction, turn left (north) onto the Willey Range Trail, which soon begins a steep and sustained climb—employing wooden ladders in spots—of 1.1 miles up 4,285-foot Mount Willey, where there are some views from just below the summit. The trail continues north, dropping into a saddle, then ascending to the 4,340-foot summit of Mount Field—named for Darby Field, the first known person to climb Mount Washington—1.4 miles from Willey's summit. Field is wooded, with no views. Just beyond the summit, the Avalon Trail branches right, but stay left with the Willey Range Trail, descending steadily to the A-Z Trail, 0.9 mile from summit of Field. Turn left (west), descending easily for 2.7 miles to the Zealand Trail. Turn right (north) and walk 2.5 miles back to the Zealand Road parking lot.

**User groups:** Hikers and dogs. No wheelchair facilities. This trail may be difficult to snowshoe because of severe winter weather, and is not suitable for bikes, horses, or skis. Hunting is allowed in season, except along the Appalachian Trail, which coincides with the Twinway and the Ethan Pond Trail.

**Access, fees:** No backcountry permit is needed, but a permit is required for day use or overnight parking at any White Mountain National Forest trailhead, as indicated by signs posted at most trailheads. Permits are available at several area stores and from the national forest (see address below) at a cost of $5 for seven consecutive days or $20 per year. A $3 one-day permit can be purchased at self-service stations at national forest trailheads, but the pass is good only for the trailhead at which it's purchased. Zealand Road is not maintained in winter; the winter parking lot is on U.S. 302, immediately east of Zealand Road. The Appalachian Mountain Club operates the Zealand Falls hut year-round; it is on the Twinway, 0.2 mile from the junction of the Zealand, Twinway, and Ethan Pond Trails and 2.7 miles from the end of Zealand Road. Contact the AMC (see address below) for information on cost and reservations. The AMC also operates the first-come, first-served Ethan Pond shelter, located just off the Ethan Pond Trail, 7.3 miles from the Zealand Road parking lot along this hike's route. A caretaker collects the $6 per person nightly fee from late spring–fall.

**Maps:** Several maps cover this area's hiking trails, including the *Franconia-Pemigewasset Range* map and the *Crawford Notch-Sandwich Range/Moosilauke-Kinsman* map, each $7.95 in waterproof Tyvek, available in many stores and from the Appalachian Mountain Club, 800/262-4455, website: www.outdoors.org; the *Trail Map and Guide to the White Mountain National Forest* for $7.95 from the De-Lorme Publishing Company, 800/642-0970 and map 3 in the *Map and Guide to the Appalachian Trail in New Hampshire and Vermont,* an eight-map set and guidebook available for $19.95 ($14.95 for the maps alone) from the Appalachian Trail Conference (see address below). For a topographic area map, request Crawford Notch from USGS Map Sales, Federal Center, Box 25286, Denver, CO 80225, 888/ASK-USGS (888/275-8747), website: http://mapping.usgs.gov.

**Directions:** From the junction of U.S. 3 and U.S. 302 in Twin Mountain, drive east on U.S. 302 for 2.3 miles and turn right onto Zealand Road. Continue 3.5 miles to a parking lot at the end of the road.

**Contact:** White Mountain National Forest Supervisor, 719 North Main St., Laconia, NH 03246, 603/528-8721, TDD for the hearing impaired 603/528-8722, website: www.fs.fed .us/r9/white. Appalachian Mountain Club Pinkham Notch Visitor Center, P.O. Box 298, Gorham, NH 03581, 603/466-2721, website: www.outdoors.org. Appalachian Trail Conference, 799 Washington St., P.O. Box 807, Harpers Ferry, WV 25425-0807, 304/535-6331, website: www.appalachiantrail.org. New Hampshire Division of Parks and Recreation, Bureau of Trails, P.O. Box 1856, Concord, NH 03302-1856, 603/271-3254.

## 32 MOUNT HALE

**4.6 mi/2.5 hrs**

**in the White Mountain National Forest southeast of Twin Mountain**

Mount Hale, at 4,054 feet, is one of New Hampshire's 48 4,000-foot peaks—and one of the least-visited in that group because its summit isn't nearly as spectacular as many of the others. But from the tree-ringed clearing atop Hale, you do get views of the Sugarloafs to the north, the Presidential Range to the northeast, Zealand Notch to the southeast, and North and South Twin to the southwest. The elevation gain is about 2,200 feet, less than other 4,000-footers, but don't assume this is a walk in the park: The Hale Brook Trail presents a rugged, relentlessly steep 2.3-mile climb to the summit, passing cascades along the brook, including rocky sections that grow slick in the wet season. Some friends and I had an enjoyable hike up it one June day when intermittent, heavy rain and low clouds precluded attempting a peak that involved more exposure or time commitment. One curiosity about Hale is that rocks near its summit are magnetized and will interfere with a magnetic compass.

From the parking lot, follow the Hale Brook Trail all the way to the summit. This hike returns by descending the same trail, but another option is to create a loop of eight or nine miles—depending on whether you shuttle two vehicles—by descending on the Lend-a-Hand Trail from Hale's summit for 2.7 miles to the Twinway. Turn left on the Twinway, passing the Appalachian Mountain Club's Zealand Falls hut in 0.1 mile, and reaching the Zealand Trail 0.3 mile farther. Turn left (north) on the Zealand Trail and follow its fairly flat course 2.5 miles back to Zealand Road. Unless you've shuttled a second vehicle to the Zealand Trail parking area, walk just over a mile down the road back to the parking area for the Hale Brook Trail. You can make an enjoyable two-day outing of this loop—a great one for families—with a stay in the Zealand Falls hut.

**User groups:** Hikers, snowshoers, and dogs. No wheelchair facilities. Bikes and horses are prohibited, and the trail is not suitable for skis. Hunting is allowed in season.

**Access, fees:** No backcountry permit is needed, but a permit is required for day use or overnight parking at any White Mountain National Forest trailhead, as indicated by signs posted at most trailheads. Permits are available at several area stores and from the national forest (see address below) at a cost of $5 for seven consecutive days or $20 per year. A $3 one-day permit can be purchased at self-service stations at national forest trailheads, but the pass is good only for the trailhead at which it's purchased. Zealand Road is not maintained in winter. The Appalachian Mountain Club operates the Zealand Falls hut year-round; it is on the Twinway, 0.2 mile from the junction of the Zealand, Twinway, and Ethan Pond Trails and 2.7 miles from the end of Zealand Road. Contact the AMC (see address below) for information on cost and reservations.

**Maps:** For a map of hiking trails in this area, get the *Franconia-Pemigewasset Range* map, $7.95 in waterproof Tyvek, available in many stores and from the Appalachian Mountain

Club, 800/262-4455, website: www.outdoors.org; or the *Trail Map and Guide to the White Mountain National Forest* for $7.95 from the DeLorme Publishing Company, 800/642-0970. For a topographic area map, request Crawford Notch from USGS Map Sales, Federal Center, Box 25286, Denver, CO 80225, 888/ASK-USGS (888/275-8747), website: http://mapping.usgs.gov.

**Directions:** From the junction of U.S. 3 and U.S. 302 in Twin Mountain, drive east on U.S. 302 for 2.3 miles and turn right onto Zealand Road. Continue 2.4 miles to a parking lot on the right. The winter parking lot is on U.S. 302, 0.1 mile east of Zealand Road.

**Contact:** White Mountain National Forest Supervisor, 719 North Main St., Laconia, NH 03246, 603/528-8721, TDD for the hearing impaired 603/528-8722, website: www.fs.fed .us/r9/white. Appalachian Mountain Club Pinkham Notch Visitor Center, P.O. Box 298, Gorham, NH 03581, 603/466-2721, website: www.outdoors.org.

## 33 ZEALAND NOTCH
**7.6 mi/5 hrs**
**in the White Mountain National Forest southeast of Twin Mountain**

Partly due to the convenience provided by the Appalachian Mountain Club's Zealand Falls hut, but also simply because of its splendor, Zealand Notch ranks as one of the most-visited spots in the White Mountains year-round. Although the trail tends to be muddy and has a lot of slippery, exposed roots, this is a nice hike in summer and fall—and fairly easy, gaining only about 500 feet in elevation. On snowshoes or cross-country skis in winter, however, it's arguably even more beautiful. The Zealand Road is not maintained in winter—you have to ski or snowshoe up it—making the round-trip distance into the notch 14.6 miles, instead of 7.6 miles. On skis, the trail is easy to moderately difficult, though possible for an experienced cross-country skier to do in one day without metal-edged skis. Two friends and I skied to the hut one bitterly cold December Sunday after a series of storms had dumped at least a few feet of dry powder in the mountains. The forest wore a thick comforter of white that smothered all sound, and the skiing was fabulous.

From the end of Zealand Road, follow the Zealand Trail south, paralleling the Zealand River. At 2.3 miles, the A-Z Trail diverges left. Continuing on the Zealand Trail, you reach the junction with the Twinway and the Ethan Pond Trail at 2.5 miles. The AMC's Zealand Falls hut lies 0.2 mile to the right on the Twinway (adding 0.4 mile to this hike's distance). Continue straight ahead onto the Ethan Pond Trail into Zealand Notch. After about a mile, the trail breaks out of the woods and traverses a shelf across the boulder field left behind by an old rockslide on the side of Whitewall Mountain; the views of Zealand Notch are spectacular. Cross this open area to where the Ethan Pond Trail reenters the woods near the junction with the Zeacliff Trail, 1.3 miles from the Twinway/Zealand Trail junction. Return the way you came.

Special note: For the ambitious or those with more time because they are spending a night at the Zealand Falls hut, hiking all the way to Thoreau Falls would add 1.6 miles round-trip to this hike. Continue on the Ethan Pond Trail beyond the Zeacliff Trail junction for 0.7 mile, then bear right onto the Thoreau Falls Trail. In another 0.1 mile, the trail reaches the top of the falls, which drops more than 100 feet through several steps and creates a very impressive cascade of ice in winter.

**User groups:** Hikers, dogs, skiers, and snowshoers. No wheelchair facilities. Bikes and horses are prohibited. Hunting is allowed in season, except along the Appalachian Trail, which coincides with the Twinway and the Ethan Pond Trail.

**Access, fees:** No backcountry permit is needed, but a permit is required for day use or overnight parking at any White Mountain National Forest trailhead, as indicated by signs posted at most trailheads. Permits are available at several area stores and from the national forest (see address below) at a cost of $5 for seven consecutive days or $20 per year. A $3 one-day permit can be purchased at self-service stations at national forest trailheads, but the pass is good only for the trailhead at which it's purchased. Zealand Road is not maintained in winter. The Appalachian Mountain Club operates the Zealand Falls hut year-round; it is on the Twinway, 0.2 mile from the junction of the Zealand, Twinway, and Ethan Pond Trails and 2.7 miles from the end of Zealand Road. Contact the AMC (see address below) for information on cost and reservations.

**Maps:** Several maps cover this area's hiking trails, including the *Franconia-Pemigewasset Range* map, $7.95 in waterproof Tyvek, available in many stores and from the Appalachian Mountain Club, 800/262-4455, website: www.outdoors.org; the *Trail Map and Guide to the White Mountain National Forest* for $7.95 from the DeLorme Publishing Company, 800/642-0970; and map 3 in the *Map and Guide to the Appalachian Trail in New Hampshire and Vermont,* an eight-map set and guidebook available for $19.95 ($14.95 for the maps alone) from the Appalachian Trail Conference (see address below). For a topographic area map, request Crawford Notch from USGS Map Sales, Federal Center, Box 25286, Denver, CO 80225, 888/ASK-USGS (888/275-8747), website: http://mapping.usgs.gov.

**Directions:** From the junction of U.S. 3 and U.S. 302 in Twin Mountain, drive east on U.S. 302 for 2.3 miles and turn right onto Zealand Road. Continue 3.5 miles to a parking lot at the end of the road. The winter parking lot is on U.S. 302, 0.1 mile east of Zealand Road.

**Contact:** White Mountain National Forest Supervisor, 719 North Main St., Laconia, NH 03246, 603/528-8721, TDD for the hearing impaired 603/528-8722, website: www.fs.fed .us/r9/white. Appalachian Mountain Club Pinkham Notch Visitor Center, P.O. Box 298,

Gorham, NH 03581, 603/466-2721, website: www.outdoors.org. Appalachian Trail Conference, 799 Washington St., P.O. Box 807, Harpers Ferry, WV 25425-0807, 304/535-6331, website: www.appalachiantrail.org.

## 34 ZEALAND NOTCH/ TWINS LOOP

**16.1 mi one-way/2 days**

**in the White Mountain National Forest south of Twin Mountain**

This moderately difficult 16-mile trek was one of my first overnight trips in the White Mountains. With superb views, lots of relatively easy terrain, and a reasonable distance to cover in two days, it's a fairly popular weekend loop for backpackers. The cumulative elevation gained is about 3,500 feet. From the Zealand Road parking lot, follow the relatively easy Zealand Trail for 2.5 miles to its junction with the Ethan Pond Trail and the Twinway. Turn right onto the Twinway, which coincides with the Appalachian Trail, climbing 0.2 mile to the AMC's Zealand Falls hut.

Beyond the hut, the Twinway passes nice cascades and the Lend-a-Hand Trail junction, climbing high above Zealand Notch. Where the trail takes a right turn at 3.9 miles into this trip, a short side path loops out to the Zeacliff overlook, with a spectacular view of Zealand Notch and mountains—from Carrigain to the south to Mount Washington and the Presidential Range to the northeast. Just 0.1 mile farther up the Twinway, the Zeacliff Trail departs to the left, descending steeply into the notch. Continue along the Twinway, which traverses more level terrain on Zealand Mountain, passing a side path 4.4 miles into the hike that leads left 0.1 mile to Zeacliff Pond. After a short climb above the pond, the Twinway passes a side path at 5.6 miles that leads right a flat 0.1 mile to the summit of 4,260-foot Zealand Mountain. The Twinway then dips and climbs again to the flat, open summit of Mount Guyot, with views in every direction.

At 8.1 miles, the Twinway bears right and

the Bondcliff Trail diverges left (south); the Guyot campsite, a logical stop for the night, is 0.8 mile away along the Guyot, down a side path marked by a sign. (The 1.6 miles round-trip to the campsite is figured into this hike's total distance.) Following the Twinway, you will traverse easy terrain, then climb more steeply on the final short stretch up South Twin Mountain, 8.9 miles into this trek, at 4,902 feet the highest point on this trip and the eighth-highest mountain in New Hampshire. The views span much of the Pemigewasset Wilderness and stretch to the Presidential Range. Turn north off the Twinway onto the North Twin Spur, descending into a saddle, then climbing to the wooded and viewless summit of North Twin Mountain (4,761 feet), 1.3 miles from South Twin's summit and 10.2 miles into this trek. Turn right onto the North Twin Trail, soon emerging from the trees onto open ledges with one of the best views of the White Mountains on this trip. The trail descends, quite steeply for long stretches, for two miles to the Little River; it then swings left and follows an old railroad bed along the river for more than two miles to the parking area where your second vehicle awaits.

**User groups:** Hikers and dogs. No wheelchair facilities. This trail should not be attempted in winter except by hikers experienced in mountaineering and prepared for severe winter weather, and is not suitable for bikes, horses, or skis. Hunting is allowed in season except along the Appalachian Trail, which coincides with the Twinway.

**Access, fees:** No backcountry permit is needed, but a permit is required for day use or overnight parking at any White Mountain National Forest trailhead, as indicated by signs posted at most trailheads. Permits are available at several area stores and from the national forest (see address below) at a cost of $5 for seven consecutive days or $20 per year. A $3 one-day permit can be purchased at self-service stations at national forest trailheads, but the pass is good only for the trailhead at which it's purchased. Zealand Road is not maintained in winter; the winter parking lot is on U.S. 302 immediately east of Zealand Road. The Appalachian Mountain Club operates the Zealand Falls hut year-round; it is on the Twinway, 0.2 mile from the junction of the Zealand, Twinway, and Ethan Pond Trails and 2.7 miles from the end of Zealand Road. Contact the AMC (see address below) for information on cost and reservations. The AMC also operates the first-come, first-served Guyot campsite, with a shelter and several tent platforms, located just off the Bondcliff Trail 0.8 mile from the Twinway on Mount Guyot. A caretaker collects the $8 per person nightly fee from late spring–fall.

**Maps:** Several maps cover this area's hiking trails, including the *Franconia-Pemigewasset Range* map, $7.95 in waterproof Tyvek, available in many stores and from the Appalachian Mountain Club, 800/262-4455, website: www.outdoors.org; and the *Trail Map and Guide to the White Mountain National Forest* for $7.95 from the DeLorme Publishing Company, 800/642-0970. For topographic area maps, request Mount Washington, Bethlehem, South Twin Mountain, and Crawford Notch from USGS Map Sales, Federal Center, Box 25286, Denver, CO 80225, 888/ASK-USGS (888/275-8747), website: http://mapping.usgs.gov.

**Directions:** You will need to shuttle two vehicles for this trip. To reach this hike's endpoint from the junction of U.S. 302 and U.S. 3 in Twin Mountain, drive south on U.S. 3 for 2.5 miles and turn left onto Haystack Road (Fire Road 304). Or from I-93 north of Franconia Notch State Park, take Exit 35 for U.S. 3 north and continue about 7.5 miles, then turn right onto Fire Road 304. Follow Fire Road 304 to its end and a parking area at the trailhead. Leave one vehicle there. To reach the start of this hike from the junction of U.S. 3 and U.S. 302 in Twin Mountain, drive east on U.S. 302 for 2.3 miles and turn right onto Zealand Road. Continue 3.5 miles to a parking lot at the end of the road.

**Contact:** White Mountain National Forest Supervisor, 719 North Main St., Laconia, NH 03246, 603/528-8721, TDD for the hearing impaired 603/528-8722, website: www.fs.fed.us/r9/white. Appalachian Mountain Club Pinkham Notch Visitor Center, P.O. Box 298, Gorham, NH 03581, 603/466-2721, website: www.outdoors.org.

## 35 NORTH TWIN MOUNTAIN
**8.6 mi/6 hrs**

**in the White Mountain National Forest south of Twin Mountain**

Although it is the 12th-highest mountain in New Hampshire at 4,761 feet, North Twin lies sufficiently out of the way and attracts far fewer hikers than nearby Franconia Ridge and Zealand Notch. Every time I've stood atop this mountain, my only company was my own companions. But from open ledges just below the summit, you get a commanding view south over the Pemigewasset Wilderness, east toward the Presidential Range, and west to Franconia. The vertical ascent is about 2,800 feet.

Take the North Twin Trail for 4.3 miles to the summit. It follows an old railroad bed along the Little River for more than two miles, then turns sharply west, crosses the Little River—a daunting ford when the water is high—and makes a steep and sustained ascent of the mountain's east side. The trail may be heavily eroded in places. It emerges abruptly from the scrub forest onto the ledges more than four miles from the trailhead. Just a few hundred feet farther lies the summit, which is wooded, and the junction with the North Twin Spur Trail. Hike back the same way. For a scenic ridge walk to a summit with arguably better views, follow the North Twin Spur Trail to the 4,902-foot summit of South Twin Mountain, adding 2.6 miles round-trip to this hike's distance.

**User groups:** Hikers and dogs. No wheelchair facilities. This trail should not be attempted in winter except by hikers experienced in mountaineering and prepared for severe winter weather, and is not suitable for bikes, horses, or skis. Hunting is allowed in season.

**Access, fees:** No backcountry permit is needed, but a permit is required for day use or overnight parking at any White Mountain National Forest trailhead, as indicated by signs posted at most trailheads. Permits are available at several area stores and from the national forest (see address below) at a cost of $5 for seven consecutive days or $20 per year. A $3 one-day permit can be purchased at self-service stations at national forest trailheads, but the pass is good only for the trailhead at which it's purchased.

**Maps:** For a map of hiking trails, get the *Franconia-Pemigewasset Range* map, $7.95 in waterproof Tyvek, available in many stores and from the Appalachian Mountain Club, 800/262-4455, website: www.outdoors.org; or the *Trail Map and Guide to the White Mountain National Forest* for $7.95 from the DeLorme Publishing Company, 800/642-0970. For topographic area maps, request Bethlehem and South Twin Mountain from USGS Map Sales, Federal Center, Box 25286, Denver, CO 80225, 888/ASK-USGS (888/275-8747), website: http://mapping.usgs.gov.

**Directions:** From the junction of U.S. 302 and U.S. 3 in Twin Mountain, drive south on U.S. 3 for 2.5 miles and turn left onto Haystack Road/Fire Road 304, which may be marked only by a faded post reading "USFS 304." Or from I-93 north of Franconia Notch State Park, take Exit 35 for U.S. 3 north and continue about 7.5 miles; then turn right onto Fire Road 304. Follow Fire Road 304 to its end and a parking area at the trailhead for the North Twin Trail.

**Contact:** White Mountain National Forest Supervisor, 719 North Main St., Laconia, NH 03246, 603/528-8721, TDD for the hearing impaired 603/528-8722, website: www.fs.fed.us/r9/white.

# 36 GALEHEAD MOUNTAIN
**10.2 mi/7 hrs**
**in the White Mountain National Forest south of Twin Mountain**

Galehead Mountain, despite being an official 4,000-footer, attracts few hikers because trees cover its 4,024-foot summit, blocking any views. There is a good view of the tight valley of Twin Brook and a ridge of South Twin Mountain, however, from an overlook on the Frost Trail halfway between the Galehead hut and the summit. For visitors to the Galehead hut, the summit demands no more than a fairly easy one-mile hike—one that promises an opportunity for some quiet. This hike's elevation gain is about 2,400 feet.

From the parking area, follow the Gale River Trail, a wide and relatively flat path, until right before it crosses the north branch of the Gale River—over a wooden footbridge—at about 1.5 miles. For more than a mile beyond that bridge, the trail parallels the river, one of this 10-mile hike's most appealing stretches. It then makes a second river crossing on rocks, which could be difficult in high water. Four miles from the trailhead, the Gale River Trail ends at a junction with the Garfield Ridge Trail, which coincides with the Appalachian Trail. Bear left on the Ridge Trail and follow it another 0.6 mile to its junction with the Twinway. Turn right onto the Twinway for the Galehead hut. Behind the hut, pick up the Frost Trail, which leads a half mile to Galehead's summit. A short side path a quarter mile from the hut leads to the overlook described above. Descend the same way you came. For a longer hike combining Galehead and Mount Garfield, see the special note in the trail notes for Mount Garfield (described in this chapter).

**User groups:** Hikers and dogs. No wheelchair facilities. This trail may be difficult to snowshoe because of severe winter weather, and is not suitable for skis. Bikes, horses, and hunting are prohibited.

**Access, fees:** No backcountry permit is needed, but a permit is required for day use or overnight parking at any White Mountain National Forest trailhead, as indicated by signs posted at most trailheads. Permits are available at several area stores and from the national forest (see address below) at a cost of $5 for seven consecutive days or $20 per year. A $3 one-day permit can be purchased at self-service stations at national forest trailheads, but the pass is good only for the trailhead at which it's purchased. The Appalachian Mountain Club operates the Galehead hut, where a crew prepares meals and guests share bunkrooms and bathrooms. The hut lies at the western end of the trail called the Twinway, about 100 feet from the junction of the Twinway and the Garfield Ridge Trail; contact the AMC (see address below) for reservation and rate information.

**Maps:** For a contour map of hiking trails, get the *Franconia–Pemigewasset Range* map, $7.95 in waterproof Tyvek, available in many stores and from the Appalachian Mountain Club, 800/262-4455, website: www.outdoors.org; or the *Trail Map and Guide to the White Mountain National Forest* for $7.95 from the DeLorme Publishing Company, 800/642-0970. For topographic area maps, request South Twin Mountain and Bethlehem from USGS Map

Sales, Federal Center, Box 25286, Denver, CO 80225, 888/ASK-USGS (888/275-8747), website: http://mapping.usgs.gov.

**Directions:** From I-93 north of Franconia Notch State Park, take Exit 35 for U.S. 3 north. Drive about 4.8 miles and then turn right onto the dirt Fire Road 25 at a sign for the Gale River Trail. Or from the junction of U.S. 3 and U.S. 302 in Twin Mountain, drive south on U.S. 3 for 5.3 miles and turn left on Fire Road 25. Follow Fire Road 25 for 1.3 miles and turn right onto Fire Road 92. Continue 0.3 mile to a parking area on the left for the Gale River Trail.

**Contact:** White Mountain National Forest Supervisor, 719 North Main St., Laconia, NH 03246, 603/528-8721, TDD for the hearing impaired 603/528-8722, website: www.fs.fed.us/r9/white. Appalachian Mountain Club Pinkham Notch Visitor Center, P.O. Box 298, Gorham, NH 03581, 603/466-2721, website: www.outdoors.org.

## 37 MOUNT GARFIELD
**10 mi/7 hrs**

**in the White Mountain National Forest south of Twin Mountain**

Holding down the northwest corner of the Pemigewasset Wilderness in the White Mountains, the craggy, 4,500-foot summit of Garfield

a hiker on Mount Garfield, White Mountains

offers views in all directions, taking in Franconia Ridge to the southwest, the wooded mound of Owl's Head directly south, the Bonds and Mount Carrigain to the southeast, the valley of the Ammonoosuc River to the north, and Galehead Mountain, as well as the long ridge comprising North and South Twin Mountains, due east. When weather permits, you will see the peaks of the Presidential Range poking above the Twins. I had been hiking for years in the Whites before finally hoofing it up Garfield—and discovered views as nice as those offered by many of my favorite summits in these mountains. The hike up the Garfield Trail, while fairly long and gaining nearly 3,000 feet in elevation, never gets very steep or exposed.

From the parking area, follow the Garfield Trail, which for a short time parallels Spruce Brook on its steady ascent through the woods. The path is wide and obvious. At 4.8 miles, the trail terminates at the Garfield Ridge Trail, which is part of the white-blazed Appalachian Trail. To the left (east) on the Garfield Ridge Trail, it's 0.2 mile to the spur trail to the Garfield Ridge campsite. The summit lies 0.2 mile to the right (west), where you'll find the foundation of an old fire tower. Descend the same way you came.

Special note: Mount Garfield and Galehead Mountain (described in this chapter) can be combined on a loop of 13.5 miles, in which they are linked by hiking 2.7 miles along the Garfield Ridge Trail between the Garfield Trail and the Gale River Trail. The best way to do the loop is to begin on the Gale River Trail and descend the Garfield Trail; that way you will ascend, rather than descend, the often slick, steep, and rocky stretch of the Garfield Ridge Trail east of Mount Garfield. The Gale River Trail and Garfield Trail both begin on Fire Road 92, 1.6 miles apart (a distance not figured into the 13.5-mile loop).

**User groups:** Hikers and dogs. No wheelchair facilities. This trail should not be attempted in winter except by hikers experienced in mountaineering and prepared for severe winter weather, and is not suitable for skis. Bikes, horses, and hunting are prohibited.

**Access, fees:** No backcountry permit is needed, but a permit is required for day use or overnight parking at any White Mountain National Forest trailhead, as indicated by signs posted at most trailheads. Permits are available at several area stores and from the national forest (see address below) at a cost of $5 for seven consecutive days or $20 per year. A $3 one-day permit can be purchased at self-service stations at national forest trailheads, but the pass is good only for the trailhead at which it's purchased. The Appalachian Mountain Club (see address below) operates the Garfield Ridge campsite (a shelter and seven tent platforms), reached via a 200-yard spur trail off the Garfield Ridge Trail, 0.2 mile east of its junction with the Garfield Trail. A caretaker collects the $8 per person nightly fee from late springfall.

**Maps:** For a map of hiking trails, get the *Franconia-Pemigewasset Range* map, $7.95 in waterproof Tyvek, available in many stores and from the Appalachian Mountain Club, 800/262-4455, website: www.outdoors.org. Or the *Trail Map and Guide to the White Mountain National Forest* for $7.95 from the DeLorme Publishing Company, 800/642-0970. For topographic area maps, request South Twin Mountain and Bethlehem from USGS Map Sales, Federal Center, Box 25286, Denver, CO 80225, 888/ASK-USGS (888/275-8747), website: http://mapping.usgs.gov.

**Directions:** From I-93 north of Franconia Notch State Park, take Exit 35 for U.S. 3 north, continue about 4.5 miles, and then turn right on the dirt Fire Road 92. Or from the junction of U.S. 3 and U.S. 302 in Twin Mountain, drive south on U.S. 3 for 5.6 miles and turn left on Fire Road 92. Follow Fire Road 92 for 1.3 miles to a parking area on the right for the Garfield Trail.

**Contact:** White Mountain National Forest Supervisor, 719 North Main St., Laconia, NH

03246, 603/528-8721, TDD for the hearing impaired 603/528-8722, website: www.fs.fed.us/r9/white. Appalachian Mountain Club Pinkham Notch Visitor Center, P.O. Box 298, Gorham, NH 03581, 603/466-2721, website: www.outdoors.org.

## 38 ETHAN POND/ THOREAU FALLS

**10.4 mi/7 hrs**

in the White Mountain National Forest between Zealand Notch and Crawford Notch

This moderate day hike—much of it following a flat section of the Appalachian Trail—begins at one of New Hampshire's most spectacular notches and takes in a popular backcountry pond and towering waterfall. With a short, easy detour off this route, you can also take in a second notch. I like doing this hike on snowshoes in winter, when Thoreau Falls transforms into a giant staircase of ice; the trail may even be sufficiently packed down by other hikers that you won't need snowshoes, but carry them just in case. The total elevation gained on this hike is about 1,200 feet.

From the parking area in Crawford Notch State Park, follow the white blazes of the Appalachian Trail, which coincides here with the Ethan Pond Trail. After crossing railroad tracks, the trail climbs steadily. At 0.2 mile, in a stand of tall birch trees, the trail to Ripley Falls (a worthwhile side trip of 0.2 mile; see the Ripley Falls hike in this chapter) branches left. But veer right toward Ethan Pond. At 1.6 miles, the Willey Range Trail continues north; turn left (west) with the Ethan Pond Trail/AT, which soon flattens out. A mile farther, turn right onto the side path leading about 0.1 mile to scenic Ethan Pond and the Appalachian Mountain Club's Ethan Pond shelter. Back on the Ethan Pond Trail, continue west on flat ground another 2.5 miles, then turn left onto the Thoreau Falls Trail for the 0.1-mile walk to the waterfall. On the way back, you might want to add about a half mile to this hike by following the Ethan Pond Trail into the southern end of

spectacular Zealand Notch. Hike back along the same route.

**User groups:** Hikers, dogs, skiers, and snowshoers. No wheelchair facilities. Bikes, horses, and hunting are prohibited.

**Access, fees:** No backcountry permit is needed, but a permit is required for day use or overnight parking at any White Mountain National Forest trailhead, as indicated by signs posted at most trailheads. Permits are available at several area stores and from the national forest (see address below) at a cost of $5 for seven consecutive days or $20 per year. A $3 one-day permit can be purchased at self-service stations at national forest trailheads, but the pass is good only for the trailhead at which it's purchased. The Appalachian Mountain Club (see address below) operates the Ethan Pond shelter, located just off the Ethan Pond Trail, 2.6 miles from U.S. 302 in Crawford Notch. A caretaker collects the $6 per person nightly fee from late springfall.

**Maps:** Several maps cover this area's hiking trails, including the *Franconia-Pemigewasset Range* map and the *Crawford Notch-Sandwich Range/Moosilauke-Kinsman* map, $7.95 each in waterproof Tyvek, available in many stores and from the Appalachian Mountain Club, 800/262-4455, website: www.outdoors.org; the *Trail Map and Guide to the White Mountain National Forest* for $7.95 from the DeLorme Publishing Company, 800/642-0970; and map 3 in the *Map and Guide to the Appalachian Trail in New Hampshire and Vermont,* an eight-map set and guidebook available for $19.95 ($14.95 for the maps alone) from the Appalachian Trail Conference (see address below). For a topographic area map, request Crawford Notch from USGS Map Sales, Federal Center, Box 25286, Denver, CO 80225, 888/ASK-USGS (888/275-8747), website: http://mapping.usgs.gov.

**Directions:** From U.S. 302, 3.9 miles south of the Crawford Notch hostel, turn south onto a paved road at a sign for Ripley Falls. Drive 0.3 mile and park at the end of the road.

**Contact:** White Mountain National Forest Supervisor, 719 North Main St., Laconia, NH 03246, 603/528-8721, TDD for the hearing impaired 603/528-8722, website: www.fs.fed .us/r9/white. Appalachian Mountain Club Pinkham Notch Visitor Center, P.O. Box 298, Gorham, NH 03581, 603/466-2721, website: www.outdoors.org. Appalachian Trail Conference, 799 Washington St., P.O. Box 807, Harpers Ferry, WV 25425-0807, 304/535-6331, website: www.appalachiantrail.org. New Hampshire Division of Parks and Recreation, P.O. Box 1856, 172 Pembroke Rd., Concord, NH 03302, 603/271-3556, camping reservations 603/271-3628, website: www.nhstateparks.org.

## 39 MOUNT AVALON
**3.6 mi/2.5 hrs**

**in the White Mountain National Forest and Crawford Notch State Park north of Bartlett and south of Twin Mountain**

From various spots on Mount Avalon's 3,442-foot-high summit, you'll get views of the Whites in virtually every direction that are more than worth the 1,400-foot ascent. From the parking area, cross the railroad tracks behind the visitor center and pick up the Avalon Trail. At about 0.2 mile, turn left onto the Cascade Loop Trail, which passes scenic Beecher and Pearl cascades and rejoins the Avalon Trail about a half mile from the parking lot. (In fact, the cascades are a worthy destination for an easy hike of a mile; Beecher, an impressive flumelike cascade above a gorge, lies just 0.3 mile from the trailhead, and Pearl a short distance farther.) Turning left on the Avalon Trail, follow it another 0.8 mile to a junction with the A-Z Trail; bear left, staying on the Avalon, which grows very steep and rocky for the next half mile. Then turn left onto a spur trail that climbs 100 yards to Avalon's craggy summit. Follow the same route back.

**User groups:** Hikers and dogs. Dogs must be leashed. No wheelchair facilities. This trail is not suitable for bikes, horses, or skis, and may be difficult to snowshoe due to its steepness. Hunting is allowed in season.

**Access, fees:** Parking and access are free.

**Maps:** Several maps cover this area's hiking trails, including the *Franconia-Pemigewasset Range* map and the *Crawford Notch-Sandwich Range/Moosilauke-Kinsman* map, each $7.95 in waterproof Tyvek, available in many stores and from the Appalachian Mountain Club, 800/262-4455, website: www.outdoors.org; the *Trail Map and Guide to the White Mountain National Forest* for $7.95 from the DeLorme Publishing Company, 800/642-0970; and map 3 in the *Map and Guide to the Appalachian Trail in New Hampshire and Vermont,* an eight-map set and guidebook available for $19.95 ($14.95 for the maps alone) from the Appalachian Trail Conference (see address below). For a topographic area map, request Crawford Notch from USGS Map Sales, Federal Center, Box 25286, Denver, CO 80225, 888/ASK-USGS (888/275-8747), website: http://mapping.usgs.gov.

**Directions:** Park at the visitor center on U.S. 302 in Crawford Notch.

**Contact:** White Mountain National Forest Supervisor, 719 North Main St., Laconia, NH 03246, 603/528-8721, TDD for the hearing impaired 603/528-8722, website: www.fs.fed.us/r9/ white. Appalachian Trail Conference, 799 Washington St., P.O. Box 807, Harpers Ferry, WV 25425-0807, 304/535-6331, website: www.appalachiantrail.org. New Hampshire Division of Parks and Recreation, Bureau of Trails, P.O. Box 1856, Concord, NH 03302-1856, 603/271-3254.

## 40 MOUNT WILLARD
**2.8 mi/2 hrs**

**in Crawford Notch State Park north of Bartlett and south of Twin Mountain**

The view from the cliffs of Mount Willard is widely considered one of the best in the White Mountains for the relatively minor effort—a gradual ascent of less than 900 feet—required to reach it. From the parking area, cross the railroad tracks behind the visitor center and pick up the Avalon Trail. Within 100 yards, turn left onto the Mount Willard Trail, which ascends at a moderate grade. At 1.2 miles, a side path on the left leads 0.2 mile downhill to the Hitchcock Flume, a dramatic gorge worn into the mountainside by erosion. From that trail junction, it's just another 0.2 mile of flat walking on the Mount Willard Trail to Willard's summit. Its open ledges afford an excellent view from high above the notch, with the Webster Cliffs to the east (left) and the Willey Slide directly south (straight ahead). Hike back the same way.

**User groups:** Hikers, snowshoers, and dogs. Dogs must be leashed. No wheelchair facilities. This trail is not suitable for bikes, horses, or skis. Hunting is allowed in season.

**Access, fees:** Parking and access are free.

**Maps:** Several maps cover this area's hiking trails, including the *Franconia-Pemigewasset Range* map, the *Presidential Range* map, and the *Crawford Notch-Sandwich Range/Moosilauke-Kinsman* map, each $7.95 in waterproof Tyvek, available in many stores and from the Appalachian Mountain Club, 800/262-4455, website: www.outdoors.org; the *Trail Map and Guide to the White Mountain National Forest* for $7.95 from the DeLorme Publishing Company, 800/642-0970; and map 3 in the *Map and Guide to the Appalachian Trail in New Hampshire and Vermont,* an eight-map set and guidebook available for $19.95 ($14.95 for the maps alone) from the Appalachian Trail Conference (see address below). For a topographic area map, request Crawford Notch from USGS Map Sales, Federal Center, Box 25286, Denver, CO 80225, 888/ASK-USGS (888/275-8747), website: http://mapping.usgs.gov.

**Directions:** Park at the visitor center on U.S. 302 in Crawford Notch.

**Contact:** White Mountain National Forest Supervisor, 719 North Main St., Laconia, NH 03246, 603/528-8721, TDD for the hearing impaired 603/528-8722, website: www.fs.fed.us/r9/white. Appalachian Trail Conference, 799 Washington St., P.O. Box 807, Harpers Ferry, WV 25425-0807, 304/535-6331, website: www.appalachiantrail.org. New Hampshire Divi-

sion of Parks and Recreation, Bureau of Trails, P.O. Box 1856, Concord, NH 03302-1856, 603/271-3254.

## 41 MOUNTS PIERCE AND EISENHOWER

**10.8 mi/6.5 hrs**

**in the White Mountain National Forest and Crawford Notch State Park**

The Crawford Path is reputedly the oldest continuously maintained footpath in the country, dating back to 1819, when Abel Crawford and his son Ethan Allen Crawford cut the first section. It's also the easiest route onto the high ridge of the Presidential Range—the road sits at 2,000 feet, and the trail breaks out above the trees in less than three miles. Once on the ridge, you'll have sweeping views of the Whites; the 4,761-foot Mount Eisenhower itself is one of the more distinctive summits in the southern Presidentials. This can, however, be a difficult trail to follow down in foul weather, particularly when it comes to finding your way into the woods on Mount Pierce. The vertical ascent is more than 2,700 feet.

From the parking lot, the Crawford Connector spur leads 0.2 mile to the Crawford Path. (From there, a 45-minute, 0.8-mile round-trip detour on the Crawford Cliff Trail leads to a good view of the notch.) Less than a half mile up the Crawford Path, watch for a short side trail to Gibbs Falls. After emerging from the woods nearly three miles from the trailhead, the Crawford Path meets the Webster Cliffs Trail, which leads south 0.1 mile to the summit of 4,312-foot Mount Pierce. (The Webster Cliffs Trail and the Crawford Path from this junction north are part of the Appalachian Trail.) Turning back down the Crawford Path from Pierce makes a six-mile round-trip. This hike follows the Crawford Path—which from here coincides with the Appalachian Trail—north another two miles to the Eisenhower Loop Trail, then 0.4 mile up the loop trail to the Eisenhower summit, which has excellent views in every direction. To the north rises the Northeast's tallest peak,

6,288-foot Mount Washington. Stretching northwest from Washington are the northern Presidentials. The distinct hump in the ridge between Eisenhower and Washington is Mount Monroe. To the east you can see the Montalban Ridge running south from Washington—which includes Mount Isolation (see listing in this chapter), a rocky high point about midway along the ridge—and beyond the ridge into western Maine. To the southwest are the peaks and valleys of the Pemigewasset Wilderness, with Mount Carrigain (see listing in this chapter) the tallest among them. And in the distance, more west than south, rises Franconia Ridge, including Mounts Lincoln and Lafayette (see listing in this chapter) as well as Flume and Liberty (see listing in this chapter). Hike back along the same route.

**User groups:** Hikers and dogs. No wheelchair facilities. This trail should not be attempted in winter except by hikers experienced in mountaineering and prepared for severe winter weather, and is not suitable for skis. Bikes, horses, and hunting are prohibited.

**Access, fees:** No backcountry permit is needed, but a permit is required for day use or overnight parking at any White Mountain National Forest trailhead, as indicated by signs posted at most trailheads. Permits are available at several area stores and from the national forest (see address below) at a cost of $5 for seven consecutive days or $20 per year. A $3 one-day permit can be purchased at self-service stations at national forest trailheads, but the pass is good only for the trailhead at which it's purchased.

**Maps:** For a map of hiking trails, obtain the *Presidential Range* map for $7.95 in waterproof Tyvek, available in many stores and from the Appalachian Mountain Club, 800/262-4455, website: www.outdoors.org; the *Trail Map and Guide to the White Mountain National Forest* for $7.95 from the DeLorme Publishing Company, 800/642-0970, or map 2 in the *Map and Guide to the Appalachian Trail in New Hampshire and Vermont,* an eight-map set and guidebook available for $19.95 ($14.95

for the maps alone) from the Appalachian Trail Conference (see address below). For topographic area maps, request Crawford Notch and Stairs Mountain from USGS Map Sales, Federal Center, Box 25286, Denver, CO 80225, 888/ASK-USGS (888/275-8747), website: http://mapping.usgs.gov.

**Directions:** From U.S. 302 in Crawford Notch, turn onto Mount Clinton Road opposite the Crawford House site just north of Saco Lake. The trail begins at a parking area within 0.1 mile from U.S. 302.

**Contact:** White Mountain National Forest Supervisor, 719 North Main St., Laconia, NH 03246, 603/528-8721, TDD for the hearing impaired 603/528-8722, website: www.fs.fed .us/r9/white. Appalachian Trail Conference, 799 Washington St., P.O. Box 807, Harpers Ferry, WV 25425-0807, 304/535-6331, website: www.appalachiantrail.org. The Appalachian Mountain Club Pinkham Notch Visitor Center has up-to-date weather and trail information about the Whites; call 603/466-2725. New Hampshire Division of Parks and Recreation, Bureau of Trails, P.O. Box 1856, Concord, NH 03302-1856, 603/271-3254.

## 42 ELEPHANT HEAD
### 0.6 mi/0.5 hr

**in Crawford Notch State Park**
From the north end of Saco Lake in Crawford Notch, gaze south toward the short but prominent cliff at the far end of the pond; it resembles the head and trunk of an elephant. To hike an easy trail to the top of that cliff and a good view of the notch, cross U.S. 302 from the parking area to the Webster-Jackson Trail. After just 0.1 mile, turn right onto the Elephant Head Trail, and continue 0.2 mile to the top of the cliff. Return the way you came.

**User groups:** Hikers and snowshoers. Dogs must be leashed. No wheelchair facilities. This trail is not suitable for bikes, horses, or skis. Hunting is allowed in season.

**Access, fees:** Parking and access are free.

**Maps:** Several maps cover this area's hiking

trails, including the *Presidential Range* map and the *Franconia–Pemigewasset Range* map, each $7.95 in waterproof Tyvek, available in many stores and from the Appalachian Mountain Club, 800/262-4455, website: www.outdoors.org; and the *Trail Map and Guide to the White Mountain National Forest,* which is $7.95 from the DeLorme Publishing Company, 800/642-0970. For a topographic area map, request Crawford Notch from USGS Map Sales, Federal Center, Box 25286, Denver, CO 80225, 888/ASK-USGS (888/275-8747), website: http://mapping.usgs.gov.

**Directions:** Park in the turnout on the west side of U.S. 302, 0.3 mile south of the Crawford Notch hostel.

**Contact:** White Mountain National Forest Supervisor, 719 North Main St., Laconia, NH 03246, 603/528-8721, TDD for the hearing impaired 603/528-8722, website: www.fs.fed.us/r9/white. New Hampshire Division of Parks and Recreation, Bureau of Trails, P.O. Box 1856, Concord, NH 03302-1856, 603/271-3254.

## 43 WEBSTER CLIFFS
**9.4 mi/6.5 hrs**
**in the White Mountain National Forest and Crawford Notch State Park north of Bartlett and south of Twin Mountain**
This rugged, 9.4-mile hike along a spectacular

stretch of the Appalachian Trail follows the brink of the Webster Cliffs high above Crawford Notch and goes to 4,052-foot Mount Jackson, an open summit with views in every direction. In my opinion, only one other summit offers a better view of the southern Presidentials and Mount Washington, and that's Mount Isolation (described in this chapter). The elevation gain is about 2,700 feet.

From the parking area, cross U.S. 302 to a sign for the Webster Cliffs Trail/Appalachian Trail. The white-blazed trail ascends steadily with good footing at first, then grows steeper and rockier. The first good view comes within two miles, from a wide, flat ledge overlooking the notch and White Mountains to the south and west. (Just before that ledge is a smaller ledge with a less-expansive view.)

For a round-trip hike of just four miles, this ledge makes a worthwhile destination. But from there, you can see the next open ledge just 0.2 mile farther and a little higher along the ridge, beckoning you onward. The trail continues past several outlooks along the cliffs with sweeping views of the Whites, including the Willey Range across Crawford Notch and Mount Chocorua, the prominent horned peak to the southeast. At 3.3 miles, the AT passes over Mount Webster's 3,910-foot, partly wooded but craggy summit, with excellent views of the notch and

looking down on Crawford Notch from Webster Cliffs

mountains from Chocorua to Mount Carrigain and the Saco River Valley. Descending slightly off Webster, the trail crosses relatively flat and boggy terrain, then slabs up to the open summit of Jackson, 4.7 miles from the trailhead. Head back the same way.

**User groups:** Hikers and dogs. No wheelchair facilities. This trail should not be attempted in winter except by hikers experienced in mountaineering and prepared for severe winter weather, and is not suitable for skis. Bikes, horses, and hunting are prohibited.

**Access, fees:** Parking and access are free.

**Maps:** Several maps cover this area's hiking trails, including the *Franconia-Pemigewasset Range* map, the *Presidential Range* map, and the *Crawford Notch-Sandwich Range/Moosilauke-Kinsman* map, each $7.95 in waterproof Tyvek, available in many stores and from the Appalachian Mountain Club, 800/262-4455, website: www.outdoors.org; the *Trail Map and Guide to the White Mountain National Forest* for $7.95 from the DeLorme Publishing Company, 800/642-0970; and map 2 in the *Map and Guide to the Appalachian Trail in New Hampshire and Vermont,* an eight-map set and guidebook available for $19.95 ($14.95 for the maps alone) from the Appalachian Trail Conference (see address below). For a topographic area map, request Crawford Notch from USGS Map Sales, Federal Center, Box 25286, Denver, CO 80225, 888/ASK-USGS (888/275-8747), website: http://mapping.usgs.gov.

**Directions:** Park in the turnout on the west side of U.S. 302 3.9 miles south of the Crawford Notch hostel, at the access road to the Ripley Falls Trail and 1.3 miles north of the access road for Arethusa Falls.

**Contact:** White Mountain National Forest Supervisor, 719 North Main St., Laconia, NH 03246, 603/528-8721, TDD for the hearing impaired 603/528-8722, website: www.fs.fed.us/r9/white. Appalachian Trail Conference, 799 Washington St., P.O. Box 807, Harpers Ferry, WV 25425-0807, 304/535-6331, website: www

.appalachiantrail.org. New Hampshire Division of Parks and Recreation, Bureau of Trails, P.O. Box 1856, Concord, NH 03302-1856, 603/271-3254.

## 44 MOUNT ISOLATION
**20 mi one-way/2 days**

**in the White Mountain National Forest north of Jackson and east of Crawford Notch State Park**

In the heart of the Dry River Wilderness, south of Mount Washington, Mount Isolation's bald pate lies too far from any road for most day hikers—which translates into a true sense of isolation. A friend and I made this two-day traverse once in late spring and saw only four other backpackers in two days. The total elevation gain to Isolation's summit is about 3,000 feet.

Follow the Rocky Branch Trail west for 3.7 miles to the Rocky Branch, an aptly named tributary of the Saco River. Cross the stream and turn right (north) on the Isolation Trail (to the left is a lean-to, Rocky Branch shelter 2), which eventually swings west in its 2.5-mile climb onto the Montalban Ridge, where it meets the Davis Path. Find a place to camp well off the trail and leave your backpack behind for the one-mile hike south on the Davis Path to the short but steep spur trail to Mount Isolation's barren summit (4,005 feet). You'll have terrific views west and north to the southern Presidentials and Mount Washington, and to the southwest and south of the sprawling Whites. Return to your campsite.

On day two, hike north 0.3 mile on the Davis Path to where the Isolation Trail turns west (left) toward the valley of the Dry River; be careful, because this trail junction is easily overlooked—especially, I can tell you, when it lies under four feet of snow. In about 2.5 miles, turn left (south) on the Dry River Trail, paralleling the broad, boulder-choked river and crossing countless mountain brooks feeding into it. When the trees are bare, you get some fine views of Mount Washington directly upriver. It's nearly five miles from the Isolation Trail junction to U.S. 302.

**User groups:** Hikers and dogs. No wheelchair facilities. This trail should not be attempted in winter except by hikers prepared for severe winter weather, and is not suitable for bikes, horses, or skis. Hunting is allowed in season.

**Access, fees:** No backcountry permit is needed, but a permit is required for day use or overnight parking at any White Mountain National Forest trailhead, as indicated by signs posted at most trailheads. Permits are available at several area stores and from the national forest (see address below) at a cost of $5 for seven consecutive days or $20 per year. A $3 one-day permit can be purchased at self-service stations at national forest trailheads, but the pass is good only for the trailhead at which it's purchased. There is a lean-to shelter (Rocky Branch shelter 2) at the junction of the Rocky Branch Trail and Isolation Trail that is slated to be dismantled as soon as it needs major maintenance.

**Maps:** For a map of hiking trails, obtain the *Presidential Range* map for $7.95 in waterproof Tyvek, available in many stores and from the Appalachian Mountain Club, 800/262-4455, website: www.outdoors.org; or the *Trail Map and Guide to the White Mountain National Forest* for $7.95 from the DeLorme Publishing Company, 800/642-0970. For topographic area maps, request Jackson and Stairs Mountain from USGS Map Sales, Federal Center, Box 25286, Denver, CO 80225, 888/ASK-USGS (888/275-8747), website: http://mapping.usgs.gov.

**Directions:** You will need to shuttle two vehicles. Leave one at the roadside turnout at the Dry River Trailhead on U.S. 302, 0.3 mile north of the Dry River Campground and 4.5 miles south of the Crawford Notch hostel. Then drive south on U.S. 302 to Glen, turn left onto Route 16 north, and drive 8.1 miles to a large parking lot on the left for the Rocky Branch Trail.

**Contact:** White Mountain National Forest Supervisor, 719 North Main St., Laconia, NH 03246, 603/528-8721, TDD for the hearing impaired 603/528-8722, website: www.fs.fed.us/ r9/white. The Appalachian Mountain Club Pinkham Notch Visitor Center has up-to-date weather and trail information about the Whites; call 603/466-2725.

## 45 THE BALDIES LOOP
**9.7 mi/7 hrs**
**in the White Mountain National Forest near North Chatham**

As their names suggest, the pair of 3,500-foot peaks called the Baldies mimic higher mountains with their craggy summits, four miles of open ridge, and some of the best views this side of Mount Washington. This rugged hike is not to be underestimated. Besides its length of almost 10 miles and some 3,300 feet of vertical ascent, it climbs steep, exposed ledges on the way up South Baldface that may make some hikers uncomfortable. The Baldies can also attract harsh conditions—I've encountered winds up here strong enough to knock me around. Although it's probably the most popular hike in the Evans Notch area, I've done this loop without passing more than 10 other hikers—Evans Notch lies far enough from population centers that it attracts far fewer people than other areas of the Whites.

From the parking area, walk 50 yards north on Route 113 and cross the road to the start of the Baldface Circle Trail. It's a wide, easy trail for 0.7 mile to Circle Junction, where a side trail leads right 0.1 mile to Emerald Pool, a highly worthwhile detour (adding 0.2 mile to this hike) to a deep pool below a narrow gorge and a short falls along Charles Brook. From Circle Junction, bear left at a sign for South Baldface, following the loop clockwise because it's easier to ascend than descend the ledges on South Baldface. At 1.2 miles from the road, a side path marked by a sign leads a half mile to Chandler Gorge (adding a mile to this hike's distance).

Climbing steadily, the trail reaches the South Baldface shelter 2.5 miles from the road. Beyond the lean-to, the trail hits all the prominent ledges visible from the road, and for nearly a half mile winds up them, requiring steep, exposed scrambling. A bit more than three miles from the road, the trail reaches the level shoulder of South Baldface, where the Baldface Knob Trail leads left (south) to Baldface Knob and Eastman Mountain. From here, you'll get your first view into the broad glacial cirque, or ravine, bounded by North and South Baldface and the Bicknell Ridge. The Circle Trail continues a half mile west—and 500 feet up—to the 3,569-foot summit of South Baldface. The summit views extend to much of the White Mountains to the west and south, including Mounts Washington, Carrigain, and Chocorua, the triplet peaks of the Tripyramid above Waterville Valley, the distant Franconia Ridge, and the cliffs of Cathedral Ledge and Whitehorse Ledge near North Conway. To the north rise the Mahoosuc Range and a long chain of mountains reaching far into Maine. East lies a landscape of lakes and low hills, most prominently the long, low ridge of Pleasant Mountain.

Continue northwest on the Circle Trail another 1.2 miles, dropping into the woods and then ascending to the 3,591-foot summit of North Baldface, where the views are equally awesome. Descend north off North Baldy via the Circle Trail, and continue nearly a mile to the signed junction with the Bicknell Ridge Trail. Turn right (east) on Bicknell, a scenic alternative to completing the Circle Trail loop. The Bicknell descends an open ridge for about a mile before entering the forest and reaching its lower junction with the Circle Trail in 2.5 miles, at a stream crossing. Follow the Circle Trail another 0.7 mile to Circle Junction, from which it's 0.7 mile farther to the road.

**User groups:** Hikers and dogs. No wheelchair facilities. This trail is not suitable for bikes, horses, skis, or snowshoes. Hunting is allowed in season.

**Access, fees:** No backcountry permit is needed, but a permit is required for day use or overnight parking at any White Mountain National Forest trailhead, as indicated by signs posted at most trailheads. Permits are available at several area stores and from the national forest (see address below) at a cost of $5 for seven consecutive days or $20 per year. A $3 one-day permit can be purchased at self-service stations at national forest trailheads, but the pass is good only for the trailhead at which it's purchased.

**Maps:** For a map of trails, get the *Map of Cold River Valley and Evans Notch* for $6 from the Chatham Trails Association (see addresss below); the *Carter Range-Evans Notch/North Country-Mahoosuc* map, $7.95 in waterproof Tyvek, available in many stores and from the Appalachian Mountain Club, 800/262-4455, website: www.outdoors.org; or the *Trail Map and Guide to the White Mountain National Forest* for $7.95 from the DeLorme Publishing Company, 800/642-0970. For a topographic area map, request Chatham from USGS Map Sales, Federal Center, Box 25286, Denver, CO 80225, 888/ASK-USGS (888/275-8747), website: http://mapping.usgs.gov.

**Directions:** The trail begins near a large parking lot on the east side of Route 113, 2.7 miles north of the northern junction of Routes 113 and 113B, and 13 miles south of the junction of U.S. 2 and Route 113.

**Contact:** White Mountain National Forest Supervisor, 719 North Main St., Laconia, NH 03246, 603/528-8721, TDD for the hearing impaired 603/528-8722, website: www.fs.fed.us/r9/white. Chatham Trails Association, P.O. Box 605, Center Conway, NH 03813, website: http://chathamtrails.org/.

## 46 EMERALD POOL
**1.6 mi/1 hr**

**in the White Mountain National Forest near North Chatham**

The aptly named and gorgeous Emerald Pool is a deep hole below a narrow flume and gorge and a short falls along Charles Brook. It's a flat, easy walk to the pool, making this a good hike for young children. From the parking area, walk 50 yards north on Route 113 and cross the road to the start of the Baldface Circle Trail. Follow the wide, easy trail for 0.7 mile to Circle Junction, where a side trail leads right 0.1 mile to Emerald Pool. Return the same way you came in.

**User groups:** Hikers, dogs, snowshoers, and skiers. No wheelchair facilities. This trail is not suitable for bikes or horses. Hunting is allowed in season.

**Access, fees:** No backcountry permit is needed, but a permit is required for day use or overnight parking at any White Mountain National Forest trailhead, as indicated by signs posted at most trailheads. Permits are available at several area stores and from the national forest (see address below) at a cost of $5 for seven consecutive days or $20 per year. A $3 one-day permit can be purchased at self-service stations at national forest trailheads, but the permit is good only for the trailhead at which it's purchased.

**Maps:** For a contour map of trails, get the *Map of Cold River Valley and Evans Notch* for $6 from the Chatham Trails Association (see address below); the *Carter Range-Evans Notch/North Country-Mahoosuc* map, $7.95 in waterproof Tyvek, available in many stores and from the Appalachian Mountain Club, 800/262-4455, website: www.outdoors.org; or the *Trail Map and Guide to the White Mountain National Forest* for $7.95 from the DeLorme Publishing Company, 800/642-0970. For a topographic area map, request Chatham from USGS Map Sales, Federal Center, Box 25286, Denver, CO 80225, 888/ASK-USGS (888/275-8747), website: http://mapping.usgs.gov.

**Directions:** The trail begins near a large parking lot on the east side of Route 113, 2.7 miles north of the northern junction of Routes 113 and 113B, and 13 miles south of the junction of U.S. 2 and Route 113.

**Contact:** White Mountain National Forest Supervisor, 719 North Main St., Laconia, NH 03246, 603/528-8721, TDD for the hearing impaired 603/528-8722, website: www.fs.fed.us/r9/white. Chatham Trails Association, P.O.

Box 605, Center Conway, NH 03813, website: http://chathamtrails.org/.

## 47 MOUNT LAFAYETTE: SKOOKUMCHUCK TRAIL

**10 mi/8 hrs**

**in the White Mountain National Forest north of Franconia Notch State Park**

Compared to other routes up popular Mount Lafayette, the Skookumchuck is less traveled, a bit longer than some, and ascends more gradually. Still, it's 10 miles round-trip, and you will gain more than 3,500 feet in elevation, so it's a taxing hike. Some friends and I recently hiked this on a very chilly winter day, under a cobalt sky and through a forest blanketed thickly with clean snow. Once above tree line, though, it was a bitterly cold walk to the summit; this trail offers a nice winter outing on snowshoes, but turn around before reaching the Garfield Ridge Trail if you're not prepared for severe cold and wind. This is also a great hike for seeing woodland wildflowers in May. For more description about the views from atop Lafayette, see the Mounts Lincoln and Lafayette hike in this chapter.

From the parking lot, pick up the Skookumchuck Trail, which is sporadically marked with blue blazes (the trail corridor is fairly obvious). It contours southward around the west slope of a hill called Big Bickford Mountain, crossing an overgrown logging road a few times. Upon reaching Skookumchuck Brook at a little over a mile, the trail turns east to climb steadily along the brook for more than a half mile. It then leaves the brook and ascends a steep mountainside, passing through beautiful birch forest. Ascending into subalpine forest, you get your first views through the trees of the upper slopes of Lafayette. Shortly after breaking out of the forest, the Skookumchuck terminates at the Garfield Ridge Trail at 4.3 miles. Turn right (south) and follow the Garfield Ridge Trail another 0.7 mile along the exposed ridge to the summit of Lafayette. Return the way you came.

**User groups:** Hikers and dogs. Dogs must be leashed. No wheelchair facilities. This trail should not be attempted in winter except by hikers experienced in mountaineering and prepared for severe winter weather, and is not suitable for skis. Bikes, horses, and hunting are prohibited.

**Access, fees:** No backcountry permit is needed, but a permit is required for day use or overnight parking at any White Mountain National Forest trailhead, as indicated by signs posted at most trailheads. Permits are available at several area stores and from the national forest (see address below) at a cost of $5 for seven consecutive days or $20 per year. A $3 one-day permit can be purchased at self-service stations at national forest trailheads, but the pass is good only for the trailhead at which it's purchased.

**Maps:** For a map of hiking trails, get the *Franconia–Pemigewasset Range* map or the *Crawford Notch–Sandwich Range/Moosilauke–Kinsman* map, each $7.95 in waterproof Tyvek, available in many stores and from the Appalachian Mountain Club, 800/262-4455, website: www.outdoors.org; or the *Trail Map and Guide to the White Mountain National Forest* for $7.95 from the DeLorme Publishing Company, 800/642-0970. For a topographic area map, request Franconia from USGS Map Sales, Federal Center, Box 25286, Denver, CO 80225, 888/ASK-USGS (888/275-8747), website: http://mapping.usgs.gov.

**Directions:** The Skookumchuck Trail begins at a parking lot on Route 3, about 0.6 mile north of Exit 35 off I-93 in Franconia.

**Contact:** White Mountain National Forest Supervisor, 719 North Main St., Laconia, NH 03246, 603/528-8721, TDD for the hearing impaired 603/528-8722, website: www.fs.fed.us/r9/white.

## 48 CANNON MOUNTAIN: KINSMAN RIDGE TRAIL

**4.4 mi/3 hrs**

**in Franconia Notch State Park north of Lincoln and south of Franconia**

Cannon Mountain (4,077 feet) stands out at the north end of spectacular Franconia Notch because of the 1,000-foot cliff on its east face. That cliff is famous for the Old Man of the Mountain, a stone profile that for decades was visible from the notch's north end, but in early May 2003 finally succumbed to gravity and crumbled off the cliff. (Today, at the roadside parking area off I-93 where for many years tourists ogled the Old Man, there stands an information kiosk explaining why and how the stone profile fell.)

This moderate hike of 4.4 miles round-trip, climbing 2,100 feet in elevation, leads to the excellent views from Cannon's summit. Although popular, the Kinsman Ridge Trail has become severely eroded. A more pleasant trail up Cannon Mountain is the Hi-Cannon route (see following listing).

From the parking lot, follow the Kinsman Ridge Trail through a picnic area and briefly along a ski area trail before entering the woods. The trail ascends at a moderate grade, passing a short side path at 1.5 miles that leads to open ledges and a nice view across the notch to Franconia Ridge. The Kinsman Ridge Trail swings right, soon climbing more steeply to the summit, where there is an observation platform and the summit tramway station. To the east, the views extend to Mounts Lafayette and Lincoln. To the west, you can see Vermont's Green Mountains and New York's Adirondacks on a clear day. Head back along the same route.

**User groups:** Hikers and dogs. Dogs must be leashed. No wheelchair facilities. This trail should not be attempted in winter except by hikers prepared for severe winter weather, and is not suitable for bikes, horses, or skis. Hunting is allowed in season, but not near trails.

**Access, fees:** Parking and access are free.

**Maps:** For a map of hiking trails, get the *Franconia-Pemigewasset Range* map or the *Crawford Notch-Sandwich Range/Moosilauke-Kinsman* map, each $7.95 in waterproof Tyvek, available in many stores and from the Appalachian Mountain Club, 800/262-4455, website: www.outdoors.org; or the *Trail Map and Guide to the White Mountain National Forest* for $7.95 from the DeLorme Publishing Company, 800/642-0970. For a topographic area map, request Franconia from USGS Map Sales, Federal Center, Box 25286, Denver, CO 80225, 888/ASK-USGS (888/275-8747), website: http://mapping.usgs.gov.

**Directions:** The hike begins from the tramway parking lot at Exit 2 off I-93, at the north end of Franconia Notch. Look for a sign for the Kinsman Ridge Trail.

**Contact:** White Mountain National Forest Supervisor, 719 North Main St., Laconia, NH 03246, 603/528-8721, TDD for the hearing impaired 603/528-8722, website: www.fs.fed.us/r9/white. Franconia Notch State Park, Franconia, NH 03580, 603/745-8391, website: www.franconianotchstatepark.com. New Hampshire Division of Parks and Recreation, P.O. Box 1856, 172 Pembroke Rd., Concord, NH 03302, 603/271-3556, camping reservations 603/271-3628, website: www.nhstateparks.org.

## 49 CANNON MOUNTAIN: HI-CANNON TRAIL

**5.6 mi/3.5 hrs**

**in Franconia Notch State Park north of Lincoln and south of Franconia**

See the preceding hike's trail notes for more description of Cannon Mountain. This hike up Cannon is actually a far more pleasant route than the previous hike, on a more scenic trail that's in far better condition. I've done this hike in winter with friends, carrying telemark skis up the mountain on our packs, skiing down the Cannon Mountain Ski Area trails, then kicking and gliding down the Franconia Notch Bike Path (see listing in this chapter; watch out for snowmobiles) back to the parking lot. Snow

was caked to the trees and lots of blowdowns blocked the way—we had to climb around or over them and sometimes crawl on our hands and knees under them. But the trail is actually well protected from wind until you near the summit. This hike climbs about 2,300 feet.

From the parking lot, follow the Lonesome Lake Trail through the campground and ascend steadily toward Lonesome Lake (see listing in this chapter). At 0.4 mile, turn right onto the Hi-Cannon Trail. It climbs relentlessly through forest, gaining elevation quickly until you're traversing at the crest of towering cliffs high above Franconia Notch, with a great view across the notch toward Franconia Ridge. The trail features a wooden ladder to climb about 20 feet up a rock slab. After about 1.5 miles, the trail levels out, ascending at a more gentle angle through subalpine forest toward the summit. Two miles from the Lonesome Lake Trail, turn right on the Kinsman Ridge Trail and follow it 0.4 mile to Cannon's summit, with good views in every direction, most spectacularly toward Franconia Ridge. Return the way you came. To do the combined hike/ski outing I described above, from the Hi-Cannon Trail, walk directly across the Kinsman Ridge Trail, following an obvious trail a few hundred yards to the top of the Cannon Mountain Ski Area. Take your choice of ski trails to the bottom, then pick up the bike path in the parking lot and follow it south back to Lafayette Place. The entire outing might take five hours—with a stop for a hot chocolate at the ski area's summit restaurant.

**User groups:** Hikers and dogs. Dogs must be leashed. No wheelchair facilities. This trail should not be attempted in winter and is not suitable for bikes, horses, or skis. Hunting is allowed in season, but not near trails.

**Access, fees:** Parking and access are free.

**Maps:** For a map of hiking trails, get the *Franconia-Pemigewasset Range* map, or the *Crawford Notch-Sandwich Range/Moosilauke-Kinsman* map, each $7.95 in waterproof Tyvek, available in many stores and from the Appalachian Mountain Club, 800/262-4455, website:

www.outdoors.org; or the *Trail Map and Guide to the White Mountain National Forest* for $7.95 from the DeLorme Publishing Company, 800/642-0970. For a topographic area map, request Franconia from USGS Map Sales, Federal Center, Box 25286, Denver, CO 80225, 888/ASK-USGS (888/275-8747), website: http://mapping.usgs.gov.

**Directions:** Drive to one of the large parking lots on the east and west side of I-93 at the Lafayette Place Campground in Franconia Notch State Park. From the east side parking lot, hikers can cross under the highway to the Lafayette Place Campground on the west side, where the trail begins.

**Contact:** Franconia Notch State Park, Franconia, NH 03580, 603/745-8391, website: www.franconianotchstatepark.com. New Hampshire Division of Parks and Recreation, P.O. Box 1856, 172 Pembroke Rd., Concord, NH 03302, 603/271-3556, camping reservations 603/271-3628, website: www.nhstateparks.org. White Mountain National Forest Supervisor, 719 North Main St., Laconia, NH 03246, 603/528-8721, TDD for the hearing impaired 603/528-8722, website: www.fs.fed.us/r9/white.

# 50 LONESOME LAKE
**3.2 mi/2 hrs**
**in Franconia Notch State Park north of Lincoln and south of Franconia**

Lonesome Lake's name gives a newcomer to Franconia Notch no forewarning of the crowds that flock to this scenic mountain tarn; nonetheless, if you accept the likelihood of sharing this beautiful spot with dozens of other visitors, the view from the lake's southwest corner across its crystal waters to Mounts Lafayette and Lincoln on Franconia Ridge has no comparison. This trail passes through extensive boggy areas, which, combined with the heavy foot traffic it sees, can make for a muddy hike. It ascends about 1,000 feet in elevation.

From the parking lot, pick up the Lonesome Lake Trail, which crosses Lafayette Place Campground and ascends at a moderate grade for

1.2 miles to the northeast corner of the lake. Turn left (south) on the Cascade Brook Trail, following it nearly 0.3 mile to the south end of the lake. Turn right on the Fishin' Jimmy Trail, crossing the lake's outlet and reaching a small beach area where people often swim in the lake. The AMC hut lies a short distance off the lake, in the woods. Bear right off the Fishin' Jimmy Trail onto the Around-Lonesome-Lake Trail, which heads north along the lake's west shore, crossing boggy areas on boardwalks. In 0.3 mile, turn right (east) on the Lonesome Lake Trail and follow it 1.4 miles back to the campground.

**User groups:** Hikers and snowshoers. Dogs must be leashed. No wheelchair facilities. This trail is not suitable for bikes, horses, or skis. Hunting is allowed in season, but not near trails.

**Access, fees:** Parking and access are free. The Appalachian Mountain Club operates the Lonesome Lake hut on the Fishin' Jimmy Trail near Lonesome Lake; contact the AMC for reservation and rate information (see address below).

**Maps:** For a map of hiking trails, get the *Franconia–Pemigewasset Range* map or the *Crawford Notch–Sandwich Range/Moosilauke–Kinsman* map, each $7.95 in waterproof Tyvek, available in many stores and from the Appalachian Mountain Club, 800/262-4455, website: www.outdoors.org; the *Trail Map and Guide to the White Mountain National Forest* for $7.95 from the DeLorme Publishing Company, 800/642-0970, website: www.DeLorme.com; or map 3 in the *Map and Guide to the Appalachian Trail in New Hampshire and Vermont,* an eight-map set and guidebook available for $19.95 ($14.95 for the maps alone) from the Appalachian Trail Conference (see address below). For a topographic area map, request Franconia from USGS Map Sales, Federal Center, Box 25286, Denver, CO 80225, 888/ASK-USGS (888/275-8747), website: http://mapping.usgs.gov.

**Directions:** Drive to one of the large parking lots on the east and west side of I-93 at the Lafayette Place Campground in Franconia

Notch State Park. From the east side parking lot, hikers can cross under the highway to the Lafayette Place Campground on the west side, where the trail begins.

**Contact:** White Mountain National Forest Supervisor, 719 North Main St., Laconia, NH 03246, 603/528-8721, TDD for the hearing impaired 603/528-8722, website: www.fs.fed.us/r9/white. Franconia Notch State Park, Franconia, NH 03580, 603/745-8391, website: www.franconianotchstatepark.com. New Hampshire Division of Parks and Recreation, P.O. Box 1856, 172 Pembroke Rd., Concord, NH 03302, 603/271-3556, camping reservations 603/271-3628, website: www.nhstateparks.org. Appalachian Mountain Club Pinkham Notch Visitor Center, P.O. Box 298, Gorham, NH 03581, 603/466-2721, website: www.outdoors.org. Appalachian Trail Conference, 799 Washington St., P.O. Box 807, Harpers Ferry, WV 25425-0807, 304/535-6331, website: www.appalachiantrail.org.

## 51 NORTH AND SOUTH KINSMAN

**11.1 mi/8 hrs**

**in the White Mountain National Forest and Franconia Notch State Park north of Lincoln and south of Franconia**

Rising high above Franconia Notch, opposite the 5,000-foot peaks of Lafayette and Lincoln, Kinsman Mountain's two distinct peaks offer good views of the notch. But the more popular attractions on this 11.1-mile hike are the 1.5 miles of falls and cascades along Cascade Brook and the views across Lonesome Lake to Franconia Ridge. Many hikers, especially families with young children, explore only as far as the brook—a refreshing place on a hot summer day (steer clear of the drops). Most of the stream crossings on this hike utilize rocks or downed trees, and can be difficult at

times of high water. Also, the heavily used trails described here are often wet and muddy, making rocks and exposed roots slick and footing difficult. This hike ascends about 2,500 feet in elevation.

You can begin this hike on either side of I-93. From the parking lot on the northbound side of I-93, follow the signs to the Basin, passing beneath I-93 and crossing a footbridge over the Pemigewasset River. Beyond the bridge, the trail bends right; within 100 feet, bear left at a sign for the Basin-Cascades Trail. From the parking lot on the southbound side, follow the walkway south to the Basin. Turn right on the bridge over the Pemigewasset and watch for the Basin-Cascades Trail branching left. Hikers from either parking lot will converge at this trailhead at the Basin, a natural stone bowl carved out by the Pemigewasset River

Kinsman Pond

and a popular spot for tourists. Follow the Basin-Cascades Trail, where open ledges provide views to Franconia Ridge across the notch. Kinsman Falls lies a half mile up the trail and Rocky Glen Falls is 0.9 mile up, just 0.1 mile before the Basin-Cascades Trail meets the Cascade Brook Trail.

From this junction to the summit of 4,356-foot South Kinsman, the hike follows the white-blazed Appalachian Trail. Turn right (northwest) on the Cascade Brook Trail, immediately crossing the brook on stones or a downed tree. A half mile farther, the Kinsman Pond Trail bears left and crosses Cascade Brook; however, you should bear right and continue roughly north on the Cascade Brook Trail another mile to a junction with the Fishin' Jimmy Trail at the south end of Lonesome Lake. Turn left (west) on the Fishin' Jimmy, crossing a log bridge over the lake's outlet to a beachlike area popular for swimming. There's an outstanding view across Lonesome Lake to Franconia Ridge and Mounts Lafayette and Lincoln and Little Haystack (from left to right). Stay on the Fishin' Jimmy, passing the AMC's Lonesome Lake hut, which sits back in the woods just above the beach area. The trail rises and falls, passing over the hump separating Lonesome Lake from the upper flanks of Kinsman Mountain. After crossing a feeder stream to Cascade Brook, the trail ascends steeply, often up rock slabs into which wooden steps have been drilled in places. Two miles from Lonesome Lake, the Fishin' Jimmy Trail terminates at Kinsman Junction, a confluence of three trails—and a point you will return to on the descent.

Walk straight (west) onto the Kinsman Ridge Trail, climbing steep rock. Within 0.2 mile from Kinsman Junction, you begin to see views back toward Franconia Ridge; you reach the wooded summit of 4,293-foot North Kinsman at 0.4 mile. A side path leads 20 feet from the summit cairn to an open ledge with a sweeping view eastward that takes in Cannon Mountain, Lonesome Lake, Franconia Ridge, and the mountains above Waterville Valley. Continue south on the Kinsman Ridge Trail, descending past two open areas with good views. The trail drops into the saddle between the two peaks, then ascends steadily to the broad, flat summit of South Kinsman, nearly a mile from North Kinsman's summit. From various spots on South Kinsman's summit, you have views toward Franconia Ridge, North Kinsman, and Moosilauke to the south.

Backtrack to North Kinsman and descend to Kinsman Junction. Turn right (south) on the Kinsman Pond Trail, reaching the AMC shelter at Kinsman Pond in 0.1 mile. The trail follows the eastern shore of this scenic mountain tarn, below the summit cone of North Kinsman. It then hooks southeast into the forest, leading steadily downhill and making four stream crossings; this stretch of trail may be poorly marked, wet, and difficult to follow. It reaches the Cascade Brook Trail 2.5 miles from Kinsman Junction, right after crossing Cascade Brook. Bear right (southeast) onto the Cascade Brook Trail, following it a half mile. Immediately after crossing Cascade Brook again, turn left onto the Basin-Cascades Trail, which leads a mile back to the Basin.

Special note: Some hikers go just to the summit of North Kinsman, skipping the 1.8-mile round-trip hike from North to South Kinsman. That would make for a 9.3-mile hike along the route described here, reducing this hike's time by about 1.5 hours.

**User groups:** Hikers and dogs. No wheelchair facilities. This trail should not be attempted in winter except by hikers experienced in mountaineering and prepared for severe winter weather, and is not suitable for skis. Bikes, horses, and hunting are prohibited.

**Access, fees:** Parking and access are free. This hike begins in Franconia Notch State Park, but much of it lies within the White Mountain National Forest. The Appalachian Mountain Club operates the Kinsman Pond campsite, with a shelter and three tent platforms, located along the Kinsman Pond Trail, 0.1 mile from Kinsman Junction and 4.5 miles from the Basin. A caretaker collects the $8 per person nightly fee during the warmer months. The AMC also operates the Lonesome Lake hut, where a crew prepares meals, and guests share bunkrooms and bathrooms; contact the AMC (see address below) for reservation and rate information.

**Maps:** For a map of hiking trails, get the *Franconia-Pemigewasset Range* map or the *Crawford Notch-Sandwich Range/Moosilauke-Kinsman* map, each $7.95 in waterproof Tyvek, available in many stores and from the Appalachian Mountain Club, 800/262-4455, website: www.outdoors.org; the *Trail Map and Guide to the White Mountain National Forest* for $7.95 from the DeLorme Publishing Company, 800/642-0970; or map 3 in the *Map and Guide to the Appalachian Trail in New Hampshire and Vermont,* an eight-map set and guidebook available for $19.95 ($14.95 for the maps alone) from the Appalachian Trail Conference (see address below). For topographic area maps, request Franconia and Lincoln from USGS Map Sales, Federal Center, Box 25286, Denver, CO 80225, 888/ASK-USGS (888/275-8747), website: http://mapping.usgs.gov.

**Directions:** From I-93 in Franconia Notch, take the exit for the Basin. There are separate parking lots on the northbound and southbound sides of the highway; see trail notes above for details on locating the trailhead from each lot.

**Contact:** White Mountain National Forest Supervisor, 719 North Main St., Laconia, NH 03246, 603/528-8721, TDD for the hearing impaired 603/528-8722, website: www.fs.fed.us/r9/white. Franconia Notch State Park, Franconia, NH 03580, 603/745-8391, website: www.franconianotchstatepark.com. New Hampshire Division of Parks and Recreation, P.O. Box 1856, 172 Pembroke Rd., Concord, NH 03302, 603/271-3556, camping reservations 603/271-3628, website: www.nhstateparks.org. Appalachian Mountain Club Pinkham Notch Visitor Center, P.O. Box 298, Gorham, NH 03581, 603/466-2721, website: www.outdoors.org. Appalachian Trail Conference, 799 Washing-

ton St., P.O. Box 807, Harpers Ferry, WV 25425-0807, 304/535-6331, website: www .appalachiantrail.org.

## 52 FRANCONIA NOTCH: PEMI TRAIL

**5.5 mi one-way/2.5 hrs**

**in Franconia Notch State Park north of Lincoln and south of Franconia**

The Pemi Trail offers an easy and scenic 5.5-mile, one-way walk (a shuttling of cars is suggested) through Franconia Notch, with periodic views of the cliffs and peaks flanking the notch. The trail follows the west shore of Profile Lake, with excellent views across the water to Eagle Cliff on Mount Lafayette. When the light is right, you can distinguish a free-standing rock pinnacle in a gully separating two major cliffs on this shoulder of Lafayette; known as the Eaglet, this pinnacle is a destination for rock climbers and has been a nesting site in spring for peregrine falcons, which you might see flying around in spring. After crossing the paved bike path through the notch just south of Profile Lake and a second time just north of Lafayette Place Campground, the Pemi Trail follows a campground road along the west bank of the Pemigewasset River, then leaves the campground and parallels the river all the way to the water-sculpted rock at the Basin. It crosses the Basin-Cascades Trail, then meets the Cascade Brook Trail before crossing east beneath I-93 and finishing at the parking lot immediately north of the flume.

**User groups:** Hikers and snowshoers. Dogs must be leashed. No wheelchair facilities. This trail is not suitable for bikes, horses, or skis. Hunting is allowed in season, but not near trails.

**Access, fees:** Parking and access are free.

**Maps:** Obtain the free map of Franconia Notch State Park, available from the state park or the New Hampshire Division of Parks and Recreation (see address below); the *Franconia-Pemigewasset Range* map or the *Crawford Notch-Sandwich Range/Moosilauke-Kinsman* map, each $7.95 in waterproof Tyvek, available in many stores and from the Appalachian Mountain Club, 800/262-4455, website: www.outdoors.org. For topographic area maps, request Franconia and Lincoln from USGS Map Sales, Federal Center, Box 25286, Denver, CO 80225, 888/ASK-USGS (888/275-8747), website: http://mapping.usgs.gov. **Directions:** This one-way trail requires a shuttling of cars. The trail's endpoints are at the parking area off I-93 at the exit immediately north of the Flume near the south end of Franconia Notch State Park; and the parking area for the Kinsman Ridge Trail, reached via Exit 2 at the north end of the notch.

**Contact:** Franconia Notch State Park, Franconia, NH 03580, 603/745-8391, website: www.franconianotchstatepark.com. New Hampshire Division of Parks and Recreation, P.O. Box 1856, 172 Pembroke Rd., Concord, NH 03302, 603/271-3556, camping reservations 603/271-3628, website: www.nhstateparks.org.

## 53 MOUNT LAFAYETTE: OLD BRIDLE PATH

**8 mi/6.5 hrs**

**in the White Mountain National Forest and Franconia Notch State Park north of Lincoln and south of Franconia**

This eight-mile hike provides the most direct and popular route to the 5,260-foot summit of Mount Lafayette, the sixth-highest peak in the White Mountains. The elevation gain is about 3,500 feet, ranking this hike among the most difficult in New England, though it does not present the exposure of hikes like Mount Washington's Huntington Ravine. It is also a fairly well-traveled route in winter, often with a packed trough through the snow, but the route is completely exposed to weather once you venture beyond the Greenleaf hut. I've hiked it many times, including winter outings on days so cold we wore every stitch of clothing we'd brought—even while hiking uphill—and turned back before the summit because of strong, brutally cold winds pounding the upper mountain. The AMC's Greenleaf hut offers a scenic location

for making this hike a two-day trip and a way to catch the sunset high up the mountain. See the Mounts Lincoln and Lafayette hike listing in this chapter for more description of the views from the Old Bridle Path, Greenleaf Trail, and Lafayette's summit.

From the parking lot on the east side of I-93, follow the Falling Waters Trail and Old Bridle Path for 0.2 mile. Where the Falling Waters Trail turns sharply right, continue straight ahead on the Old Bridle Path. It climbs fairly easily at first through mostly deciduous forest, then grows steeper as it ascends the prominent west ridge hooking down from the summit of Lafayette. Once on the crest of that ridge, you'll get great views from a few open ledges of the summits of Lafayette to the left, and Mount Lincoln (5,089 feet) to the right of Lafayette. At 2.9 miles from the trailhead, the Old Bridle Path terminates at the Greenleaf Trail and Greenleaf hut. From there, follow the Greenleaf Trail as it dips down into a shallow basin, passes through subalpine forest, and soon emerges onto the rocky, open west slope of Lafayette, climbing another 1.1 miles and more than 1,000 feet in elevation to Lafayette's summit, where the views take in most of the White Mountains and New Hampshire's north country, and west to Vermont's Green Mountains. Return the way you came.

**User groups:** Hikers and dogs. Dogs must be leashed. No wheelchair facilities. This trail should not be attempted in winter except by hikers experienced in mountaineering and prepared for severe winter weather, and is not suitable for skis. Bikes, horses, and hunting are prohibited.

**Access, fees:** Parking and access are free. The Appalachian Mountain Club operates the Greenleaf hut at the junction of the Greenleaf Trail and Old Bridle Path; contact the AMC for reservation and rate information (see address below).

**Maps:** For a map of hiking trails, get the *Franconia-Pemigewasset Range* map or the *Crawford Notch-Sandwich Range/Moosilauke-Kinsman* map, each $7.95 in waterproof Tyvek, available in many stores and from the Appalachian Mountain Club, 800/262-4455, website: www.outdoors.org; the *Trail Map and Guide to the White Mountain National Forest* for $7.95 from the DeLorme Publishing Company, 800/642-0970; or map 3 in the *Map and Guide to the Appalachian Trail in New Hampshire and Vermont,* an eight-map set and guidebook available for $19.95 ($14.95 for the maps alone) from the Appalachian Trail Conference (see address below). For a topographic area map, request Franconia from USGS Map Sales, Federal Center, Box 25286, Denver, CO 80225, 888/ASK-USGS (888/275-8747), website: http://mapping.usgs.gov.

**Directions:** Drive to one of the large parking lots on the east and west side of I-93 at the Lafayette Place Campground in Franconia Notch State Park. From the west side parking lot, hikers can walk under the highway to the east side, where the trails begin.

**Contact:** White Mountain National Forest Supervisor, 719 North Main St., Laconia, NH 03246, 603/528-8721, TDD for the hearing impaired 603/528-8722, website: www.fs.fed.us/r9/white. Franconia Notch State Park, Franconia, NH 03580, 603/745-8391, website: www.franconianotchstatepark.com. New Hampshire Division of Parks and Recreation, P.O. Box 1856, 172 Pembroke Rd., Concord, NH 03302, 603/271-3556, camping reservations 603/271-3628, website: www.nhstateparks.org. Appalachian Mountain Club Pinkham Notch Visitor Center, P.O. Box 298, Gorham, NH 03581, 603/466-2721, website: www.outdoors.org. Appalachian Trail Conference, 799 Washington St., P.O. Box 807, Harpers Ferry, WV 25425-0807, 304/535-6331, website: www.appalachiantrail.org.

## 54 MOUNTS LINCOLN AND LAFAYETTE

**8.8 mi/6.5 hrs**

**in the White Mountain National Forest and Franconia Notch State Park north of Lincoln and south of Franconia**

For many New England hikers—myself included—this 8.8-mile loop over the sixth- and seventh-highest peaks in New Hampshire represented a dramatic introduction to the White Mountains and has become a favorite hike revisited many times over the years. With nearly two miles of continuous, exposed ridge-line high above the forest connecting Mounts Lincoln (5,089 feet) and Lafayette (5,260 feet), this hike lures hundreds of people on warm weekends in summer and fall. The views from Franconia Ridge encompass most of the White Mountains, spanning the peaks and valleys of the Pemigewasset Wilderness all the way to the Presidential Range, Vermont's Green Mountains, and, on a very clear day, New York's Adirondacks. The Falling Waters Trail passes several waterfalls and cascades, and the Old Bridle Path follows a long shoulder of Mount Lafayette over some open ledges that offer excellent views of Lincoln and Lafayette.

It's also a rugged hike, with some 3,600 feet of cumulative elevation gain and a considerable amount of steep, rocky trail. Because of the heavy foot traffic on Franconia Ridge and the fragility of the alpine flora, you should take care to walk only on the clearly marked trail or on bare rock.

From the parking lot on the east side of I-93, follow the Falling Waters Trail, which coincides for 0.2 mile with the Old Bridle Path, then turns sharply right and crosses Walker Brook on a bridge. The trail climbs steadily and steeply, crossing Dry Brook at 0.7 mile, which could be difficult in high water. Over the ensuing mile, it passes several cascades and waterfalls, including Cloudland Falls, with a sheer drop of 80 feet, and makes two more crossings of the brook.

At 2.8 miles, a side path leads to the right

a short distance to Shining Rock, a huge slab on the mountainside that appears to shimmer when viewed from the road far below. The views of the notch are excellent, but bear in mind that the shining is caused by running water, making the slab slippery and dangerous to scramble around on. Continue up the Falling Waters Trail, emerging above the trees about 0.1 mile before reaching the Franconia Ridge Trail (which is part of the Appalachian Trail) at the summit of Little Haystack Mountain, 3.2 miles from the trailhead. Turn left (north), following the cairns and white blazes of the Franconia Ridge Trail/AT along the open ridge.

Among the peaks in view as you head over Lincoln and Lafayette are the bald cap of Mount Garfield immediately northeast of Lafayette; North and South Twin Mountains, east of Garfield; Mount Washington and the high peaks of the Presidential Range in the more distant northeast; the wooded mound of Owl's Head, standing alone across the valley immediately east of Franconia Ridge; the Bonds and Bondcliff on the other side of Owl's Head; the towering mass of Mount Carrigain southeast of Owl's Head and the Bonds; the jumble of peaks above Waterville Valley farther south and east, including the three pointed summits of Mount Tripyramid; the distinct horn of Mount Chocorua in the distance between Carrigain and Waterville Valley; Cannon Cliff and Mountain to the west across Franconia Notch; the north and south peaks of Kinsman Mountain, south of and behind Cannon; and to the southwest, sprawling Mount Moosilauke. (This book describes hikes up all of the peaks listed here, except for the Owl's Head.)

From Haystack, the trail drops slightly but follows easy ground until climbing steeply to the summit of Lincoln, 0.7 mile from Haystack. It passes over a subsidiary summit of Lincoln immediately to the north, then drops into a saddle with the tallest scrub vegetation on the ridge before making the long ascent of Mount Lafayette, 0.9 mile from Lincoln's summit. This highest point on the ridge, predictably, tends to be the windiest and coldest spot as well, although there are sheltered places in the rocks on the summit's north side. Turn left (west) and descend the Greenleaf Trail, much of it over open terrain, for 1.1 miles to the AMC's Greenleaf hut. Just beyond the hut, bear left onto the Old Bridle Path, descending southwest over the crest of a long ridge, with occasional views of Franconia Ridge and the steep, green western slopes of Lafayette and Lincoln, before reentering the woods and eventually reaching the parking lot, 2.9 miles from the hut.

Special note: Under most conditions, it's desirable to hike this loop in the direction described here because the steep sections of the Falling Waters Trail are easier to ascend than descend, especially when, as often occurs, the trail is wet. But if you're doing the hike on a day with cold wind, consider reversing the direction; the wind generally comes from the northwest, and reversing this hike's direction would put it at your back while atop Franconia Ridge, rather than in your face.

**User groups:** Hikers and dogs. Dogs must be leashed. No wheelchair facilities. This trail should not be attempted in winter except by hikers experienced in mountaineering and prepared for severe winter weather, and is not suitable for skis. Bikes, horses, and hunting are prohibited.

**Access, fees:** Parking and access are free. The Appalachian Mountain Club operates the Greenleaf hut at the junction of the Greenleaf Trail and Old Bridle Path; contact the AMC for reservation and rate information (see address below).

**Maps:** For a map of hiking trails, get the *Franconia-Pemigewasset Range* map or the *Crawford Notch-Sandwich Range/Moosilauke-Kinsman* map, each $7.95 in waterproof Tyvek, available in many stores and from the Appalachian Mountain Club, 800/262-4455, website: www.outdoors.org; the *Trail Map and Guide to the White Mountain National Forest* for $7.95 from the DeLorme Publishing Company, 800/642-0970, website: www.DeLorme.com; or map 3 in the

*Map and Guide to the Appalachian Trail in New Hampshire and Vermont,* an eight-map set and guidebook available for $19.95 ($14.95 for the maps alone) from the Appalachian Trail Conference (see address below). For a topographic area map, request Franconia from USGS Map Sales, Federal Center, Box 25286, Denver, CO 80225, 888/ASK-USGS (888/275-8747), website: http://mapping.usgs.gov.

**Directions:** Drive to one of the large parking lots on the east and west sides of I-93 at the Lafayette Place Campground in Franconia Notch State Park. From the west side parking lot, hikers can walk under the highway to the east side, where the trails begin.

**Contact:** White Mountain National Forest Supervisor, 719 North Main St., Laconia, NH 03246, 603/528-8721, TDD for the hearing impaired 603/528-8722, website: www.fs.fed.us/r9/white. Franconia Notch State Park, Franconia, NH 03580, 603/745-8391, website: www.franconianotchstatepark.com. New Hampshire Division of Parks and Recreation, P.O. Box 1856, 172 Pembroke Rd., Concord, NH 03302, 603/271-3556, camping reservations 603/271-3628, website: www.nhstateparks.org. Appalachian Mountain Club Pinkham Notch Visitor Center, P.O. Box 298, Gorham, NH 03581, 603/466-2721, website: www.outdoors.org. Appalachian Trail Conference, 799 Washington St., P.O. Box 807, Harpers Ferry, WV 25425-0807, 304/535-6331, website: www.appalachiantrail.org.

## 55 FRANCONIA NOTCH LOOP
**14 mi/9 hrs or 1–2 days**

**in the White Mountain National Forest and Franconia Notch State Park north of Lincoln and south of Franconia**

While this loop of about 14 miles can be done in a day by fit hikers, I like to make an overnight trip of it, staying either in the Greenleaf hut or at the Liberty Springs campsite. Either place gives you a great high-elevation base from which to catch the sunset. I once spent a September evening sitting alone atop Mount Liberty, watch-

ing shadows grow long over the White Mountains and Franconia Notch while the setting sun fired long rays of light through the thin clouds, creating spectacular prisms of light that glowed luminously above Mount Moosilauke and the Kinsmans to the west. See the trail notes for the preceding hike, Mounts Lincoln and Lafayette, for more description of the views from Franconia Ridge. The cumulative elevation gained on this hike is about 4,700 feet.

From the parking lot on the east side of I-93, follow the Falling Waters Trail and the Old Bridle Path for 0.2 mile to where the trails split; then continue straight ahead on the Old Bridle Path. It climbs easily at first, then steeply, for 2.9 miles from the trailhead to a junction with the Greenleaf Trail at the Greenleaf hut. From the hut, continue east on the Greenleaf Trail as it dips down into a shallow basin, passes through subalpine forest, and soon emerges onto the rocky, open west slope of Lafayette, climbing another 1.1 miles and more than 1,000 feet in elevation to Lafayette's summit. Turn right (south) on the Franconia Ridge Trail, which coincides with the Appalachian Trail, and hike the rugged, open, and in places narrow Franconia Ridge—enjoying constant 360-degree views—for a mile to the 5,089-foot summit of Mount Lincoln, then another 0.7 mile to the summit of Little Haystack (4,780 feet), where the Falling Waters Trail turns right (west).

This hike continues south on the Franconia Ridge Trail, soon dropping into subalpine forest—although the forest cover is thin and the ridge narrow enough that you can see through the trees and know how abruptly the earth drops off to either side. At 1.8 miles past Little Haystack, the Liberty Spring Trail and AT turn right (west); you will eventually descend that way. But continue south on the Franconia Ridge Trail another 0.3 mile, climbing less than 300 feet to the rocky summit of Mount Liberty for excellent, 360-degree views of the Whites (see the trail notes for the preceding hike, Mounts Lincoln and Lafayette, for more description of these views).

From Liberty's summit, backtrack to the Liberty Spring Trail and descend it. Within 0.3 mile you'll reach the Liberty Spring campsite, where you can spend the night if backpacking. From the campsite, descend the Liberty Spring Trail another 2.6 miles to the Whitehouse Trail and the Franconia Notch Bike Path. Cross the Pemigewasset River on a bridge, and just beyond the bridge turn right onto the Pemi Trail. Walk under the highway, then stay to the right (north) on the Pemi Trail and follow it nearly a mile to the Basin, where the Pemigewasset River has carved impressive natural bowls and cascades into the granite bedrock. From the Basin, you can stay on the Pemi Trail, or follow the paved bike path, about two miles farther to the parking lot on the west side of the highway at Lafayette Place Campground. If you parked on the east side of the highway, you can walk under the highway to that parking lot.

**User groups:** Hikers and dogs. Dogs must be leashed. No wheelchair facilities. This trail should not be attempted in winter except by hikers experienced in mountaineering and prepared for severe winter weather, and is not suitable for skis. Bikes, horses, and hunting are prohibited.

**Access, fees:** Parking and access are free. The Appalachian Mountain Club operates the Greenleaf hut at the junction of the Greenleaf Trail and Old Bridle Path; contact the AMC for reservation and rate information (see address below). The AMC also manages the Liberty Spring campsite, with 12 tent platforms, located along the Liberty Spring Trail, 2.6 miles from the Whitehouse Trail and 0.3 mile from the Franconia Ridge Trail. A caretaker collects the $8 nightly fee during the warmer months.

**Maps:** For a map of hiking trails, get the *Franconia-Pemigewasset Range* map or the *Crawford Notch–Sandwich Range/Moosilauke–Kinsman* map, each $7.95 in waterproof Tyvek, available in many stores and from the Appalachian Mountain Club, 800/262-4455, website: www .outdoors.org; the *Trail Map and Guide to the White Mountain National Forest* for $7.95 from the DeLorme Publishing Company, 800/642-0970; or map 3 in the *Map and Guide to the Appalachian Trail in New Hampshire and Vermont,* an eight-map set and guidebook available for $19.95 ($14.95 for the maps alone) from the Appalachian Trail Conference (see address below). For a topographic area map, request Franconia from USGS Map Sales, Federal Center, Box 25286, Denver, CO 80225, 888/ASK-USGS (888/275-8747), website: http://mapping.usgs.gov.

**Directions:** Drive to one of the large parking lots on the east and west side of I-93 at the Lafayette Place Campground in Franconia Notch State Park. From the west side parking lot, hikers can walk under the highway to the east side, where the trails begin.

**Contact:** White Mountain National Forest Supervisor, 719 North Main St., Laconia, NH 03246, 603/528-8721, TDD for the hearing impaired 603/528-8722, website: www.fs.fed.us/ r9/white. Franconia Notch State Park, Franconia, NH 03580, 603/745-8391, website: www.franconianotchstatepark.com. New Hampshire Division of Parks and Recreation, P.O. Box 1856, 172 Pembroke Rd., Concord, NH 03302, 603/271-3556, camping reservations 603/271-3628, website: www.nhstateparks.org. Appalachian Mountain Club Pinkham Notch Visitor Center, P.O. Box 298, Gorham, NH 03581, 603/466-2721, website: www.outdoors.org. Appalachian Trail Conference, 799 Washington St., P.O. Box 807, Harpers Ferry, WV 25425-0807, 304/535-6331, website: www .appalachiantrail.org.

## 56 FRANCONIA NOTCH BIKE PATH

**8.5 mi/3.5 hrs**

**in the White Mountain National Forest and Franconia Notch State Park north of Lincoln and south of Franconia**

The Franconia Notch Bike Path runs like a stream, north/south for about 8.5 miles through Franconia Notch, providing a paved route for exploring one of the most spectacular notches in New England. Popular with families, it's great for cycling, walking, running, snowshoeing, and cross-country skiing. With several access points, you can do as much of the path as you like. Much of it is in the forest, but there are numerous views of the surrounding peaks from the path. There are some pretty steep, though short, hills along the path. The path may be accessible by wheelchairs provided the user can manage the short but steep climbs.

Its elevation begins at about 1,700 feet at the Skookumchuck trailhead, rises to around 2,000 feet at the base of Cannon Mountain and Profile Lake, then drops to about 1,100 feet at the Flume; going north to south is easier, especially from anywhere south of Profile Lake. Scenic points along it include the Flume, a natural cleavage in the mountainside; the Basin, where the still-small Pemigewasset River pours through natural bowls in the bedrock; a view of Cannon Cliff from a spot immediately north of Profile Lake; and the truck-sized boulder, estimated to weigh between 20 and 30 tons, lying right beside the paved path north of Lafayette Place campground, deposited there by a rockslide off Cannon Cliff on June 19, 1997.

**User groups:** Hikers, bikers, snowshoers, skiers, horses, wheelchairs. Dogs must be leashed. Hunting and in-line skating are prohibited.

**Access, fees:** Parking and access are free within Franconia Notch State Park, but the Skookumchuck Trail parking lot lies within the White Mountain National Forest, and a permit is required for day use or overnight parking. Permits are available at several area stores and from the national forest (see address below) at a cost of $5 for seven consecutive days or $20 per year. A $3 one-day permit can be purchased at self-service stations at national forest trailheads, but the pass is good only for the trailhead at which it's purchased.

**Maps:** For a map that shows the bike path, get the *Franconia-Pemigewasset Range* map, $7.95 in waterproof Tyvek, available in many stores and from the Appalachian Mountain Club, 800/262-4455, website: www.outdoors.org. For topographic area maps, request Franconia and Lincoln from USGS Map Sales, Federal Center, Box 25286, Denver, CO 80225, 888/ASK-USGS (888/275-8747), website: http://mapping.usgs.gov.

**Directions:** The bike path can be accessed from several points. Its northern end is at the parking lot for the Skookumchuck Trail, on Route 3 about 0.6 mile north of Exit 35 off I-93 in Franconia. Its southern end is at the Flume, reached via the exit for the Flume off I-93 in Franconia Notch. Other access points in Franconia Notch include the Cannon Mountain parking lot at Exit 2, the former Old Man of the Mountains viewpoint parking area (see the description of the Cannon Mountain: Kinsman Ridge Trail hike for details on the Old Man's demise), the Profile Lake parking lot, the Lafayette Place Campground, and the Basin parking lot.

**Contact:** Franconia Notch State Park, Franconia, NH 03580, 603/745-8391, website: www.franconianotchstatepark.com. New Hampshire Division of Parks and Recreation, P.O. Box 1856, 172 Pembroke Rd., Concord, NH 03302, 603/271-3556, camping reservations 603/271-3628, website: www.nhstateparks.org. White Mountain National Forest Supervisor, 719 North Main St., Laconia, NH 03246, 603/528-8721, TDD for the hearing impaired 603/528-8722, website: www.fs.fed.us/r9/white.

## 57 MOUNTS FLUME AND LIBERTY
**9.8 mi/7 hrs**

**in the White Mountain National Forest and Franconia Notch State Park north of Lincoln and south of Franconia**

If these two summits were located virtually anywhere else, this loop hike would enjoy enormous popularity. But the 5,000-footers to the north, Lafayette and Lincoln, are what captures the attention of most hikers venturing onto spectacular Franconia Ridge. Many people who call the Lafayette-Lincoln Loop (see the Mounts Lincoln and Lafayette listing in this chapter) their favorite hike in the Whites have never enjoyed the uninterrupted views from the rocky summits of 4,325-foot Flume or 4,459-foot Liberty: Franconia Notch, west to Mount Moosilauke and the Green Mountains, and a grand sweep of peaks to the east all the way to the Presidential Range. I hiked this loop on a March day when the sun felt like July—although the notion of summer approaching was dispelled by the cool wind, snow, and ice. This hike's cumulative elevation gain is nearly 2,500 feet.

From the parking lot, take the blue-blazed Whitehouse Trail north for nearly a mile (it coincides briefly with the Franconia Notch Bike Path). Pick up the white-blazed Liberty Spring Trail—a part of the Appalachian Trail—heading east. Within a half mile, signs mark where the Flume Slide Trail branches right. From that junction to the slide, the trail is somewhat overgrown, marked very sporadically with light-blue blazes and can be hard to follow. It grows steep on the upper part of the slide, and you will scramble over rocks that can be very slick when wet. (For a less exposed route to the summit of Mount Liberty, go up and down the Liberty Spring Trail.)

Where the Flume Slide Trail hits the ridge crest 3.3 miles from the Liberty Spring Trail, turn left onto the Osseo Trail, which leads a short distance to Mount Flume's summit. Continue over the summit on the Franconia Ridge Trail, dipping into the saddle between the peaks, then climbing to Liberty's summit a mile past the top of Flume. Another 0.3 mile beyond the summit, turn left onto the Liberty Spring Trail and descend for 2.9 miles to the Whitehouse Trail, following it back to the parking lot.

**User groups:** Hikers and dogs. Dogs must be leashed. No wheelchair facilities. This trail should not be attempted in winter except by hikers experienced in mountaineering and prepared for severe winter weather, and is not suitable for skis. Bikes, horses, and hunting are prohibited.

**Access, fees:** Parking and access are free. This hike begins in Franconia Notch State Park, but much of it lies within the White Mountain National Forest. The Appalachian Mountain Club (see address below) operates the Liberty Spring campsite, with 12 tent platforms, located along the Liberty Spring Trail, 2.6 miles from the Whitehouse Trail and 0.3 mile from the Franconia Ridge Trail. A caretaker collects the $8 nightly fee during the warmer months.

**Maps:** For a map of hiking trails, get the *Franconia-Pemigewasset Range* map or the *Crawford Notch-Sandwich Range/Moosilauke-Kinsman* map, each $7.95 in waterproof Tyvek, available in many stores and from the Appalachian Mountain Club, 800/262-4455, website: www.outdoors.org; the *Trail Map and Guide to the White Mountain National Forest* for $7.95 from the DeLorme Publishing Company, 800/642-0970; or map 3 in the *Map and Guide to the Appalachian Trail in New Hampshire and Vermont,* an eight-map set and guidebook available for $19.95 ($14.95 for the maps alone) from the Appalachian Trail Conference (see address below). For topographic area maps, request Franconia and Lincoln from USGS Map Sales, Federal Center, Box 25286, Denver, CO 80225, 888/ASK-USGS (888/275-8747), website: http://mapping.usgs.gov.

**Directions:** From I-93 in Franconia Notch, take the exit for the Flume. Follow the sign to trailhead parking for the Whitehouse Trail and the Appalachian Trail, which coincides with the Liberty Spring Trail and is reached via the Whitehouse.

**Contact:** Franconia Notch State Park, Franconia, NH 03580, 603/745-8391, website: www.franconianotchstatepark.com. New Hampshire Division of Parks and Recreation, P.O. Box 1856, 172 Pembroke Rd., Concord, NH 03302, 603/271-3556, camping reservations 603/271-3628, website: www.nhstateparks.org. White Mountain National Forest Supervisor, 719 North Main St., Laconia, NH 03246, 603/528-8721, TDD for the hearing impaired 603/528-8722, website: www.fs.fed.us/r9/white.

Appalachian Mountain Club Pinkham Notch Visitor Center, P.O. Box 298, Gorham, NH 03581, 603/466-2721, website: www.outdoors.org. Appalachian Trail Conference, 799 Washington St., P.O. Box 807, Harpers Ferry, WV 25425-0807, 304/535-6331, website: www .appalachiantrail.org.

## 58 TWINS-BONDS TRAVERSE
### 20 mi one-way/2.5–3 days
in the White Mountain National Forest between Twin Mountain and the Kancamagus Highway

Of the many good routes to backpack across the Pemigewasset Wilderness—the vast roadless area in the heart of the White Mountains—this ranks as my favorite because it traverses the spectacular Bondcliff Ridge, which splits the Pemi down the middle. The views are great from the summits of all five official 4,000-footers along this trek: North Twin (4,761 feet) and South Twin (4,902 feet), Bond (4,698 feet), Bondcliff (4,265 feet), and West Bond (4,540 feet), the last a wonderful knob of rock jutting above the dense scrub forest with terrific views of Franconia Ridge, Bondcliff, and the southern White Mountains. Two companions and I once caught a fabulous, burning-red sunrise from the shelter at the Guyot campsite.

Hiking north to south, follow the North Twin Trail 4.3 miles to the summit of North Twin, and the North Twin Spur 1.3 miles to South Twin. Turn left (southeast) on the Twinway and follow it for two miles. Turn right (south) onto the Bondcliff Trail. Within a half mile—a short distance beyond the spur trail leading left to Guyot campsite—turn right onto a spur trail for the one-mile round-trip to the summit of West Bond. Return to the Bondcliff Trail, and turn right (south) and continue about a half mile to the summit of Mount Bond, with excellent views in all directions, including Mount Washington to the east and the spectacular Bondcliff Ridge immediately south. Continuing south, you'll reach the ridge within a mile

and walk its open crest above tall cliffs. From Bondcliff's summit, it's 4.4 miles down through the woods to the Wilderness Trail. Turn right (west) and follow the Wilderness Trail 3.8 miles to the parking area at Lincoln Woods. If you're planning to camp at the Franconia Brook campsite, you will turn east (left) from the Bondcliff Trail onto the Wilderness Trail, and ultimately reach the Lincoln Woods trailhead via the trail known as the East Branch Road (see detailed notes on this in the "Access, fees" section below).

**User groups:** Hikers and dogs. No wheelchair facilities. The Wilderness Trail (see listing in this chapter) stretch of this hike is flat and is a popular day trip with skiers and snowshoers, but the rest of this route should not be attempted in winter except by hikers experienced in mountaineering and prepared for severe winter weather, and is not suitable for skis. Bikes and horses are prohibited. Hunting is allowed in season.

**Access, fees:** No backcountry permit is needed, but a permit is required for day use or overnight parking at any White Mountain National Forest trailhead, as indicated by signs posted at most trailheads. Permits are available at several area stores and from the national forest (see address below) at a cost of $5 for seven consecutive days or $20 per year. A $3 one-day permit can be purchased at self-service stations at national forest trailheads, but the pass is good only for the trailhead at which it's purchased. The Guyot campsite, operated by the Appalachian Mountain Club, 800/262-4455, has a shelter and six tent platforms and is reached via a short spur trail (marked by a sign) off the Bondcliff Trail about a quarter mile south of the Twinway junction. A caretaker collects the $8 per person nightly fee at Guyot from late spring-fall. The Franconia Brook campsite (16 tent platforms), operated by the White Mountain National Forest, costs $8 per person; it has been moved to the east side of the Pemigewasset River's East Branch, almost directly across the river from its former location at the river's confluence with Franconia Brook. The campsite is reached by hiking the trail known as East Branch Road for three miles from the Lincoln Woods trailhead. Hikers on this hike would reach this campsite by turning east (left) from the Bondcliff Trail onto the Wilderness Trail and following it for 0.7 mile to a bridge over the East Branch, crossing the bridge, following the Cedar Brook Trail west for a bit more than a half mile, then turning right onto the East Branch Road, which is overgrown and may be easily overlooked. The Guyot and Franconia Brook campsites are popular and often full on weekends. Camping in the forest is legal, provided you remain at least 200 feet from a trail and a quarter mile from established camping areas such as Guyot campsite.

**Maps:** For a map of hiking trails, get the *Franconia-Pemigewasset Range* map, $7.95 in waterproof Tyvek, available in many stores and from the Appalachian Mountain Club, 800/262-4455, website: www.outdoors.org. Or the *Trail Map and Guide to the White Mountain National Forest* for $7.95 from the DeLorme Publishing Company, 800/642-0970. For topographic area maps, request Bethlehem, South Twin Mountain, and Mount Osceola from USGS Map Sales, Federal Center, Box 25286, Denver, CO 80225, 888/ASK-USGS (888/275-8747), website: http://mapping.usgs.gov.

**Directions:** You will need to shuttle two vehicles for this trek. Leave one in the large parking lot at Lincoln Woods, where there is a White Mountain National Forest ranger station. It is along the Kancamagus Highway (Route 112) five miles east of McDonald's in Lincoln and just east of the bridge where the Kancamagus crosses the East Branch of the Pemigewasset River. The Wilderness Trail—also known for its initial three miles as the Lincoln Woods Trail—begins here.

The other trailhead—where this hike begins—is off U.S. 3. From the junction of U.S. 302 and U.S. 3 in Twin Mountain, drive south on U.S. 3 for 2.5 miles and turn left onto Haystack Road/Fire Road 304. Or from I-93 north of

Franconia Notch State Park, take Exit 35 for U.S. 3 north and continue approximately 7.5 miles, then turn right onto Fire Road 304. Follow this road to its end and a parking area at the North Twin Trail.

**Contact:** White Mountain National Forest Supervisor, 719 North Main St., Laconia, NH 03246, 603/528-8721, TDD for the hearing impaired 603/528-8722, website: www.fs.fed.us/r9/white.

## 59 PEMIGEWASSET WILDERNESS TRAVERSE

**19.5 mi one-way/10–12 hours or 1–2 days**

in the White Mountain National Forest between U.S. 302 near Twin Mountain and Route 112 east of Lincoln

The Pemigewasset Wilderness is the sprawling roadless area of mountains and wide valleys in the heart of the White Mountains. A federally designated wilderness area, the Pemi harbors spectacular big-mountain hikes such as the Twins-Bonds Traverse and Mount Carrigain (both in this chapter). This traverse, however, follows the valleys of the Pemi, much of it relatively easy hiking along routes once followed by the railroads of 19th-century logging companies. It could be done in a two-day backpacking trip. But I've included this mainly because it's considered a classic ski tour, feasible to accomplish in a day for experienced cross-country skiers also skilled in winter mountain travel. For that reason, I've included in this hike's distance the 3.5 miles you have to ski up Zealand Road, which is not plowed in winter. This hike is thus 3.5 miles shorter in the warmer months. The route may follow lower elevations and climb only about 1,000 feet in elevation over its course, but weather can change quickly in here, and 20 miles on skis is a long day. You may have to break trail through varied snow conditions much of the way, and not finish until after dark (which is what happened to three friends and me when we skied this route). Zealand Notch is even more wild in winter than in the warmer months, and there's some nice skiing along these other trails. The Thoreau Falls Trail presents significant amounts of steeper terrain; you will have to carry skis and hike intermittently for a mile or more. Depending upon the amount of snowfall and how much freezing has occurred, numerous brooks crossing the Thoreau trail may not be frozen, necessitating repeated removal of skis to cross the brooks. Do not underestimate how long or difficult a winter trip like this can be.

From the winter parking lot, follow the Zealand Road, climbing gradually for 3.5 miles to its end (where this hike begins in warmer months). Then pick up the blue-blazed Zealand Trail, winding through the forest on fairly flat ground, with some short, steep steps, for 2.5 miles to a trail junction. To the right, the Twinway leads 0.2 mile uphill to the AMC's Zealand Falls hut. This hike continues straight ahead onto the Ethan Pond Trail, which coincides with the Appalachian Trail. The Ethan Pond Trail contours along the west slope of Whitewall Mountain.

About 1.3 miles past the Zealand Trail, the Ethan Pond Trail emerges from the forest onto the open scar of an old rockslide on Whitewall, in the middle of Zealand Notch. Above loom the towering cliffs of the mountain; below, the rockslide's fallout, a broad boulder field. Across the notch rises Zealand Mountain, and straight ahead, to the south, stands Carrigain. The trail crosses the rockslide for about 0.2 mile, then reenters the woods. At 2.1 miles past the Zealand Trail, bear right onto the Thoreau Falls Trail, following easy terrain for 0.1 mile to Thoreau Falls, which tumbles more than 100 feet and forms an impressive cascade of ice in winter. The trail crosses the stream immediately above the brink of the falls. Be careful here in any season, but especially in winter do not assume that any snow or ice bridge is safe; two days before my friends and I skied through here in January 1997, someone had fallen through the ice.

Once across the stream, the trail climbs

steeply, angling across a wooded hillside, then dropping just as steeply down the other side. The trail may be difficult or impossible to ski for a mile or more, but it eventually reaches more level ground. At 4.7 miles from the Ethan Pond Trail, the trail crosses a bridge over the east branch of the Pemigewasset River. Just 0.4 mile past the bridge, turn right (west) onto the Wilderness Trail, which is the easiest trail on this route (making it the preferred way to finish if there's a chance of finishing after dark). The Wilderness Trail crosses the river again in 0.9 mile, on a 180-foot suspension bridge, then parallels the river for the remaining 5.4 flat miles to the Lincoln Woods parking lot on the Kancamagus Highway.

Special note: Skiers who do not want to wrestle their skis up and down the steep sections of the Thoreau Falls Trail might consider another option, two miles longer but easier. After passing through Zealand Notch, instead of turning right onto the Thoreau Falls Trail, continue left with the Ethan Pond Trail for a half mile, and then turn right (south) onto the Shoal Pond Trail. Follow it for four miles to a spot called Stillwater Junction, then turn right (west) onto the Wilderness Trail and follow it 8.9 miles to Lincoln Woods.

**User groups:** Hikers, dogs, skiers, and snowshoers. No wheelchair facilities. Bikes and horses are prohibited. This trail should only be attempted in winter by people prepared for severe winter weather. Hunting is allowed in season, except along the Appalachian Trail, which coincides with the Twinway and the Ethan Pond Trail.

**Access, fees:** No backcountry permit is needed, but a permit is required for day use or overnight parking at any White Mountain National Forest trailhead, as indicated by signs posted at most trailheads. Permits are available at several area stores and from the national forest (see address below) at a cost of $5 for seven consecutive days or $20 per year. A $3 one-day permit can be purchased at self-service stations at national forest trailheads, but the pass is good only for the trailhead at which it's purchased. Zealand Road is not maintained in winter. The Appalachian Mountain Club operates the Zealand Falls hut year-round; it is on the Twinway, 0.2 mile from the junction of the Zealand, Twinway, and Ethan Pond Trails and 2.7 miles from the end of Zealand Road. Contact the AMC (see address below) for information on cost and reservations. The Franconia Brook campsite (16 tent platforms), operated by the White Mountain National Forest, costs $8 per person and is open only during summer and fall; it has been moved to the east side of the Pemigewasset River's east branch, almost directly across the river from its former location at the river's confluence with Franconia Brook. The campsite is reached by hiking the trail known as East Branch Road for three miles from the Lincoln Woods trailhead. On this hike, you would reach this campsite by turning left (south) from the Wilderness Trail onto the Cedar Brook Trail right before the second bridge crossing of the east branch of the Pemigewasset River, and following the Cedar Brook Trail west for a little more than a half mile, then turning right onto the East Branch Road, which is overgrown and may be easily overlooked. Camping in the forest is legal, provided you remain at least 200 feet from a trail and a quarter mile from established camping areas such as Guyot campsite.

**Maps:** For a map of hiking trails, get the *Franconia-Pemigewasset Range* map, $7.95 in waterproof Tyvek, available in many stores and from the Appalachian Mountain Club, 800/262-4455, website: www.outdoors.org; the *Trail Map and Guide to the White Mountain National Forest* for $7.95 from the DeLorme Publishing Company, 800/642-0970; or map 3 in the *Map and Guide to the Appalachian Trail in New Hampshire and Vermont,* an eight-map set and guidebook available for $19.95 ($14.95 for the maps alone) from the Appalachian Trail Conference (see address below). For topographic area maps, request Bethlehem, Mount Washington, South

Twin Mountain, Crawford Notch, Mount Osceola, and Mount Carrigain from USGS Map Sales, Federal Center, Box 25286, Denver, CO 80225, 888/ASK-USGS (888/275-8747), website: http://mapping.usgs.gov.

**Directions:** You need to shuttle two vehicles for this one-way traverse. To go north to south, as described here, leave one vehicle in the Lincoln Woods parking lot, where there is a White Mountain National Forest ranger station. It is along the Kancamagus Highway (Route 112), five miles east of the McDonald's in Lincoln and just east of the bridge where the Kancamagus crosses the east branch of the Pemigewasset River. The Wilderness Trail—also known for its initial three miles as the Lincoln Woods Trail—begins here. To reach the start of this hike, from the junction of U.S. 3 and U.S. 302 in Twin Mountain, drive east on U.S. 302 for 2.3 miles and turn right onto Zealand Road, then continue 3.5 miles to a parking lot at the end of the road. In winter, park in the lot on the north side of U.S. 302, 0.1 mile east of Zealand Road, and ski or walk up Zealand Road.

**Contact:** White Mountain National Forest Supervisor, 719 North Main St., Laconia, NH 03246, 603/528-8721, TDD for the hearing impaired 603/528-8722, website: www.fs.fed.us/r9/white. Appalachian Mountain Club Pinkham Notch Visitor Center, P.O. Box 298, Gorham, NH 03581, 603/466-2721, website: www.outdoors.org. Appalachian Trail Conference, 799 Washington St., P.O. Box 807, Harpers Ferry, WV 25425-0807, 304/535-6331, website: www.appalachiantrail.org.

## 60 ARETHUSA FALLS AND FRANKENSTEIN CLIFF

4.7 mi/3 hrs

**in Crawford Notch State Park north of Bartlett and south of Twin Mountain**

This fairly easy loop of 4.7 miles takes in both New Hampshire's highest waterfall and the nice view from the top of Frankenstein Cliff, and ascends a total of about 1,200 feet in elevation. From the far end of the lower parking lot, you can pick up a connector trail to the upper lot. There, follow the Arethusa Falls Trail for 0.1 mile and then turn left onto the Bemis Brook Trail, which parallels the Arethusa Trail for a half mile and eventually rejoins it, but is more interesting for the short cascades it passes—Bemis Falls and Coliseum Falls—as well as Fawn Pool. After reaching the Arethusa Trail again, turn left and continue uphill another 0.8 mile to the base of the magnificent falls, which are more than 200 feet tall.

Many hikers return the same way, making a 2.8-mile round-trip. But this hike crosses the stream below the falls on rocks, following the Arethusa-Ripley Falls Trail, which crosses another stream on rocks within 0.3 mile (which could be difficult in high water). At 1.3 miles from Arethusa Falls, bear right onto the Frankenstein Cliff Trail and continue 0.8 mile to a ledge atop the cliffs with a view south to the lower end of Crawford Notch and the Saco Valley. Descend steeply another 1.3 miles on the Frankenstein Cliff Trail to the parking area. See the special note in the description of Ripley Falls (see following listing) for a loop hike incorporating both waterfalls.

**User groups:** Hikers, snowshoers, and dogs. Dogs must be leashed. No wheelchair facilities. This trail is not suitable for bikes, horses, or skis. Hunting is allowed in season.

**Access, fees:** Parking and access are free.

**Maps:** Several maps cover this area's hiking trails, including the *Franconia-Pemigewasset Range* map and the *Crawford Notch-Sandwich Range/Moosilauke-Kinsman* map, each $7.95 in waterproof Tyvek, available in many stores and from the Appalachian Mountain Club, 800/262-4455, website: www.outdoors.org; and the *Trail Map and Guide to the White Mountain National Forest* for $7.95 from the De-Lorme Publishing Company, 800/642-0970. For topographic area maps, request Crawford Notch and Stairs Mountain from USGS Map Sales, Federal Center, Box 25286, Denver, CO

80225, 888/ASK-USGS (888/275-8747), website: http://mapping.usgs.gov.

**Directions:** From U.S. 302, 5.2 miles south of the Crawford Notch hostel, turn west onto a paved road at a sign for Arethusa Falls. You can park in the lower lot immediately on the right, or drive 0.2 mile and park at the end of the road.

**Contact:** White Mountain National Forest Supervisor, 719 North Main St., Laconia, NH 03246, 603/528-8721, TDD for the hearing impaired 603/528-8722, website: www.fs.fed .us/r9/white. New Hampshire Division of Parks and Recreation, Bureau of Trails, P.O. Box 1856, Concord, NH 03302-1856, 603/271-3254.

## 61 RIPLEY FALLS

**1 mi/0.75 hr**

**in Crawford Notch State Park north of Bartlett and south of Twin Mountain**

This hike in Crawford Notch State Park begins on the Ethan Pond Trail, which coincides with the Appalachian Trail. Within 100 feet of the parking lot, cross railroad tracks and climb steadily uphill on an easy, wide trail. It passes through an area of tall birch trees at 0.2 mile, and then forks; the Ethan Pond Trail/AT bears right, but go left onto the Ripley Falls Trail. Continue 0.3 mile to the beautiful, cascading falls, which tumble from a height of more than 100 feet and are most impressive in late spring and early summer. Return the way you came.

Special note: You can combine this hike with the hike of Arethusa Falls (see prior listing) on a loop of 4.3 miles (about three hours); shuttling vehicles is necessary. Start by hiking to Arethusa. After passing that waterfall, bear left onto the Arethusa-Ripley Falls Trail (instead of right onto the Frankenstein Cliff Trail, as that hike describes) and follow it to Ripley Falls; then descend the Ripley Falls Trail.

**User groups:** Hikers, snowshoers, and dogs. No wheelchair facilities. This trail is not suitable for skis. Bikes, horses, and hunting are prohibited.

**Access, fees:** Parking and access are free.

**Maps:** Several maps cover this area's hiking trails, including the *Franconia-Pemigewasset Range* map and the *Crawford Notch-Sandwich Range/Moosilauke-Kinsman* map, each $7.95 in waterproof Tyvek, available in many stores and from the Appalachian Mountain Club, 800/262-4455; website: www.outdoors.org; the *Trail Map and Guide to the White Mountain National Forest* for $7.95 from the DeLorme Publishing Company, 800/642-0970; and map 3 in the *Map and Guide to the Appalachian Trail in New Hampshire and Vermont,* an eight-map set and guidebook available for $19.95 ($14.95 for the maps alone) from the Appalachian Trail Conference (see address below). For a topographic area map, request Crawford Notch from USGS Map Sales, Federal Center, Box 25286, Denver, CO 80225, 888/ASK-USGS (888/275-8747), website: http://mapping.usgs.gov.

**Directions:** From U.S. 302, 3.9 miles south of the Crawford Notch hostel, turn south onto a paved road at a sign for Ripley Falls. Drive 0.3 mile and park at the end of the road.

**Contact:** White Mountain National Forest Supervisor, 719 North Main St., Laconia, NH 03246, 603/528-8721, TDD for the hearing impaired 603/528-8722, website: www.fs.fed.us/r9/white. Appalachian Trail Conference, 799 Washington St., P.O. Box 807, Harpers Ferry, WV 25425-0807, 304/535-6331, website: www.appalachiantrail.org. New Hampshire Division of Parks and Recreation, Bureau of Trails, P.O. Box 1856, Concord, NH 03302-1856, 603/271-3254.

## 62 STAIRS MOUNTAIN
**9.2 mi/6 hrs**

**in the White Mountain National Forest north of Bartlett**

This hike can be done in a day or can be split up over a couple of days with a stay at the shelter. Stairs Mountain is so named because of the Giant Stairs, a pair of steplike ledges on the 3,463-foot mountain's south end. From the

cliffs atop the Giant Stairs, you get wide views of the mountains to the south. Although the Rocky Branch Trail attracts backpackers to the shelters along it, many of those people are headed for the 4,000-foot peaks farther north; you might find a little piece of solitude on Stairs Mountain. I snowshoed up Stairs once with a group of friends right after back-to-back blizzards in March—we were walking on several feet of snow, and it was an adventure just staying with the unbroken trail. This hike climbs about 2,100 feet.

From the end of Jericho Road, follow the Rocky Branch Trail north a flat two miles to the Rocky Branch shelter 1, where there is a lean-to and a tent site. Just beyond it, the Stairs Col Trail turns left (west) and ascends steadily for nearly two miles, passing below the Giant Stairs and through Stairs Col to the Davis Path. Turn right (north) on the Davis Path and follow it for a bit less than a half mile to a side path leading right for about 0.2 mile to the cliffs above the Giant Stairs. Return the way you came.

**User groups:** Hikers, snowshoers, and dogs. No wheelchair facilities. The Rocky Branch Trail is fairly easy to ski as far as the Stairs Col Trail junction. Bikes and horses are prohibited. Hunting is allowed in season.

**Access, fees:** No backcountry permit is needed, but a permit is required for day use or overnight parking at any White Mountain National Forest trailhead; signs indicating so are posted at most of them. Permits are available at several area stores and from the national forest (see address below) at a cost of $5 for seven consecutive days or $20 per year. A $3 one-day permit can be purchased at self-service stations at national forest trailheads, but the pass is good only for the trailhead at which it's purchased. Rocky Branch Shelter 1 consists of an open lean-to and tent site, reached via a short spur trail just south of the junction of the Rocky Branch Trail and the Stairs Col Trail (just outside the boundary of the Dry River Wilderness).

**Maps:** For a map of hiking trails, get the *Crawford Notch-Sandwich Range/Moosilauke-Kinsman* map, $7.95 in waterproof Tyvek, available in many stores and from the Appalachian Mountain Club, 800/262-4455, website: www.outdoors.org; or the *Trail Map and Guide to the White Mountain National Forest* for $7.95 from the DeLorme Publishing Company, 800/642-0970. For topographic area maps, request North Conway West, Bartlett, and Stairs Mountain from USGS Map Sales, Federal Center, Box 25286, Denver, CO 80225, 888/ASK-USGS (888/275-8747), website: http://mapping.usgs.gov.

**Directions:** From the junction of Route 16 and U.S. 302 in Glen, drive west on U.S. 302 for one mile and turn right onto Jericho Road/Rocky Branch Road. Follow that road, which is paved for about a mile and then becomes gravel (passable by car), for five miles to its end, where there is parking and the Rocky Branch Trail begins.

**Contact:** White Mountain National Forest Supervisor, 719 North Main St., Laconia, NH 03246, 603/528-8721, TDD for the hearing impaired 603/528-8722, website: www.fs.fed.us/r9/white. The Appalachian Mountain Club Pinkham Notch Visitor Center has up-to-date weather and trail information about the Whites; call 603/466-2725.

## 63 THE WILDERNESS TRAIL
**10.8 mi/5 hrs**
**in the White Mountain National Forest, east of Lincoln**

While this is a scenic hike or overnight backpacking trip along the east branch of the Pemigewasset River in any season, I've included it mainly for its popularity among cross-country skiers and snowshoers as a winter day trip. The season generally runs from December to March, and you can usually find ski tracks already laid down and a beaten path from previous snowshoers shortly after every fresh snowfall. Some visitors only go the nearly three miles out to the first bridge, over Franconia Brook, and return. This description covers the 5.4 miles out to the suspension bridge over the east branch of the Pemi at the junction with the Thoreau Falls Trail. The route is virtually flat the entire distance.

From the parking lot, take the bridge over the east branch of the Pemigewasset River, then turn right onto the Lincoln Woods Trail—the name given in recent years to the first three miles of what was formerly known entirely as the Wilderness Trail. The trail follows an old railroad grade from logging days, paralleling the river. At 2.6 miles, the Black Pond Trail branches left, leading 0.8 mile to this quiet little pond—a worthwhile detour where you will see far fewer people than on this popular trail. At 2.8 miles you reach the Franconia Brook campsite on the left. Just beyond it, the trail crosses a footbridge over Franconia Brook, and at 2.9 miles the Franconia Brook Trail branches left. Here the Lincoln Woods Trail enters the Pemigewasset Wilderness and becomes the Wilderness Trail. Continuing straight ahead on it, you reach a junction with the Bondcliff Trail, which branches left, at 4.7 miles. Continue on the Wilderness Trail, crossing Black Brook on a bridge near an old logging railroad bridge. From there, it's just another 0.7 mile to the suspension bridge over the Pemi's east branch at the junction with the Thoreau Falls Trail. Return the way you came.

Special note: You can make a loop of about the same distance from the Lincoln Woods trailhead by going out the trail known as the East Branch Road, which begins just beyond the ranger station and follows the Pemigewasset River's east branch on its east side. This trail can become obscure and is generally not nearly as well traveled as the Lincoln Woods/Wilderness Trail. Within four miles, you'll turn left (east) onto the Cedar Brook Trail; follow it about a half mile, cross the bridge over the east branch of the Pemi River, then turn left (west) and follow the Wilderness Trail back to the trailhead. If you're looking for a bigger adventure in this part of the Pemigewasset Wilderness, see either the Twins-Bonds

Traverse or the Pemigewasset Wilderness Traverse (both in this chapter).

**User groups:** Hikers, dogs, skiers, and snowshoers. No wheelchair facilities. Bikes and horses are prohibited. Hunting is allowed in season.

**Access, fees:** No backcountry permit is needed, but a permit is required for day use or overnight parking at any White Mountain National Forest trailhead, as indicated by signs posted at most trailheads. Permits are available at several area stores and from the national forest (see address below) at a cost of $5 for seven consecutive days or $20 per year. A $3 one-day permit can be purchased at self-service stations at national forest trailheads, but the pass is good only for the trailhead at which it's purchased. The Franconia Brook campsite (16 tent platforms), operated by the White Mountain National Forest, costs $8 per person and is open only during summer and fall; it has been moved to the east side of the Pemigewasset River's east branch, almost directly across the river from its former location at the river's confluence with Franconia Brook. The campsite is reached by hiking the trail known as East Branch Road for three miles from the Lincoln Woods trailhead. On this hike, you would reach this campsite from the Wilderness Trail by crossing the bridge over the east branch of the Pemigewasset River and turning right (west) onto the Cedar Brook Trail right before the second bridge crossing of the east branch of the Pemigewasset River, then following the Cedar Brook Trail west for a little more than a half mile before turning right onto the East Branch Road, which is overgrown and may be easily overlooked. Camping in the forest is legal, provided you remain at least 200 feet from a trail and a quarter mile from established camping areas such as Franconia Brook campsite.

**Maps:** For a map of hiking trails, get the *Franconia-Pemigewasset Range* map or the *Crawford Notch-Sandwich Range/Moosilauke-Kinsman* map, $7.95 each in waterproof Tyvek, available in many stores and from the Appalachian Moun-

tain Club, 800/262-4455, website: www.outdoors.org; or the *Trail Map and Guide to the White Mountain National Forest* for $7.95 from the DeLorme Publishing Company, 800/642-0970. For a topographic area map, request the Mount Osceola map from USGS Map Sales, Federal Center, Box 25286, Denver, CO 80225, 888/ASK-USGS (888/275-8747), website: http://mapping.usgs.gov.

**Directions:** Drive to the large parking lot at Lincoln Woods, along the Kancamagus Highway/Route 112, five miles east of the McDonald's in Lincoln, and just east of the bridge where the Kancamagus crosses the east branch of the Pemigewasset River. The Wilderness Trail–also known for its initial three miles as the Lincoln Woods Trail–begins here.

**Contact:** White Mountain National Forest Supervisor, 719 North Main St., Laconia, NH 03246, 603/528-8721, TDD for the hearing impaired 603/528-8722, website: www.fs.fed.us/r9/white.

## 64 MOUNT CARRIGAIN
**10 mi/7 hrs**

**in the White Mountain National Forest southwest of Crawford Notch State Park**

The tallest peak in this corner of the Whites, 4,700-foot Carrigain offers one of the finest—and unquestionably unique—views in these mountains from the observation tower on its summit. On a clear day, the panorama takes in Mount Washington and the Presidential Range, the vast sweep of peaks across the Pemigewasset Wilderness to Franconia Ridge, Moosilauke to the west, and the peaks above Waterville Valley and the distinctive horn of Chocorua to the south. Although 10 miles round-trip, with a vertical ascent of about 3,300 feet, this hike grows steep only for the ascent to the crest of Signal Ridge, which itself has spectacular views, including one toward the cliffs of Mount Lowell to the east.

Follow the Signal Ridge Trail, which follows Whiteface Brook at first, passing picturesque cascades. At 1.7 miles from the road, the Carrigain Notch Trail branches right; continue up the Signal Ridge Trail. Reaching the open terrain of Signal Ridge at about 4.5 miles, you enjoy excellent views, particularly east across Carrigain Notch to Mount Lowell's cliffs. The ridge ascends easily to the summit observation tower. Return the same way you came.

**User groups:** Hikers and dogs. No wheelchair facilities. This trail should not be attempted in winter except by hikers experienced in mountaineering and prepared for severe winter weather, and is not suitable for bikes, horses, or skis. Hunting is allowed in season.

**Access, fees:** No backcountry permit is needed, but a permit is required for day use or overnight parking at any White Mountain National Forest trailhead, as indicated by signs posted at most trailheads. Permits are available at several area stores and from the national forest (see address below) at a cost of $5 for seven consecutive days or $20 per year. A $3 one-day permit can be purchased at self-service stations at national forest trailheads, but the pass is good only for the trailhead at which it's purchased. Sawyer River Road (Fire Road 34) is usually closed to vehicles once the snow arrives.

**Maps:** For a map of hiking trails, get the *Franconia-Pemigewasset Range* map or the *Crawford Notch-Sandwich Range/Moosilauke-Kinsman* map, $7.95 each in waterproof Tyvek, available in many stores and from the Appalachian Mountain Club, 800/262-4455, website: www.outdoors.org. Or get the *Trail Map and Guide to the White Mountain National Forest* for $7.95 from the DeLorme Publishing Company, 800/642-0970. For topographic area maps, request Mount Carrigain and Bartlett from USGS Map Sales, Federal Center, Box 25286, Denver, CO 80225, 888/ASK-USGS (888/275-8747), website: http://mapping.usgs.gov.

**Directions:** From U.S. 302, 10.7 miles south of the visitor information center in Crawford Notch and 10.3 miles north of the junction of U.S. 302 and Route 16 in Glen, turn south onto Sawyer River Road/Fire Road 34. Follow it for two miles to the Signal Ridge Trail

on the right, just before a bridge over Whiteface Brook. There is parking on the left, just past the brook.

**Contact:** White Mountain National Forest Supervisor, 719 North Main St., Laconia, NH 03246, 603/528-8721, TDD for the hearing impaired 603/528-8722, website: www.fs.fed.us/r9/white.

## 65 MOUNT STANTON
**3 mi/2 hrs**

**in the White Mountain National Forest between Bartlett and Glen**

At just 1,716 feet above sea level, Mount Stanton offers spectacular views and the feel of a big mountain for relatively little work—just three miles and 1,000 feet of climbing. These factors make it a good hike for children or for a day when clouds descend upon the big mountains. The trail does have a few moderately steep stretches, but they are neither sustained nor very difficult; fit people could easily run up the path for a quick workout. Near Mount Stanton's summit, you will see open ledges to the left (south) worth exploring. Out on the ledges, you will find yourself on the brink of a 500-foot sheer drop, atop a cliff called White's Ledge (a wonderful technical rock climb for those with experience). You might see rock climbers reaching the top; be careful not to kick stones over the edge. The ledges offer broad views of the Saco River Valley. Follow the same route back.

**User groups:** Hikers, snowshoers, and dogs. No wheelchair facilities. This trail is not suitable for bikes, horses, or skis. Hunting is allowed in season.

**Access, fees:** Parking and access are free.

**Maps:** For a map of hiking trails, get the *Crawford Notch-Sandwich Range/Moosilauke-Kinsman* map, $7.95 in waterproof Tyvek, available in many stores and from the Appalachian Mountain Club, 800/262-4455, website: www.outdoors.org; or the *Trail Map and Guide to the White Mountain National Forest* for $7.95 from the DeLorme Publishing Company,

800/642-0970. For a topographic area map, request North Conway West from USGS Map Sales, Federal Center, Box 25286, Denver, CO 80225, 888/ASK-USGS (888/275-8747), website: http://mapping.usgs.gov.

**Directions:** From junction of U.S. 302 and Highway 16 in Glen, drive on U.S. 302 west toward Bartlett for about two miles. Just before the covered bridge, turn right onto Covered Bridge Lane (there is a small sign high on a tree). Follow the paved road 0.2 mile and bear right onto Oak Ridge Drive. Almost immediately, make a sharp right turn onto Hemlock Drive, which is dirt for a short distance before becoming paved, and continue for 0.3 mile. Park at a trail sign on the road. The trail begins just uphill on the left side of the driveway near the trail sign.

**Contact:** White Mountain National Forest Supervisor, 719 North Main St., Laconia, NH 03246, 603/528-8721, TDD for the hearing impaired 603/528-8722, website: www.fs.fed.us/r9/white.

## 66 MOUNT MOOSILAUKE: BEAVER BROOK TRAIL

**7.8 mi/5.5 hrs**

**west of North Woodstock**

A number of years ago, a friend invited me to hike Mount Moosilauke with a group of people—my first of many trips up this 4,802-foot massif in the southwest corner of the White Mountains. We went up the Beaver Brook Trail, past its numerous cascades and on to a summit with an extensive alpine area and views that span much of the White Mountains and extend west to the Green Mountains in Vermont and New York's Adirondacks. Moosilauke is one of the most popular peaks in the Whites, and the Beaver Brook Trail is a popular route up the mountain. But it is steep and rugged. This hike climbs about 3,000 feet.

The Beaver Brook Trail, which coincides with the Appalachian Trail, leaves Route 112 and soon begins the steep, sustained climb up the narrow drainage of Beaver Brook. At 0.3 mile, you may notice a side path that formerly led a short distance to the Dartmouth Outing Club's Beaver Brook lean-to. (The lean-to has been torn down and a new DOC shelter built farther up the trail, about 1.5 miles from the trailhead and less than a half mile from the Asquam-Ridge Trail junction.) Beyond there, the Beaver Brook Trail levels somewhat, and at 1.9 miles the Asquam-Ridge Trail branches left. The Beaver Brook Trail/AT then ascends over the wooded shoulder known as Mount Blue and finally emerges above the trees for the nearly flat final 0.2 mile to the summit. Visible to the northeast are Franconia Ridge and, much farther to the northeast, the Presidential Range. Hike back the way you came.

Special note: By shuttling two vehicles to the trailheads, this hike can be combined with the Glencliff Trail (see next listing) for a traverse of Moosilauke via the Appalachian Trail. Hike up the Beaver Brook Trail and descend the Glencliff.

**User groups:** Hikers and dogs. No wheelchair facilities. This trail should not be attempted in winter except by hikers experienced in mountaineering and prepared for severe winter weather, and is not suitable for skis. Bikes, horses, and hunting are prohibited.

**Access, fees:** No backcountry permit is needed, but a permit is required for day use or overnight parking at any White Mountain National Forest trailhead, as indicated by signs posted at most trailheads. Permits are available at several area stores and from the national forest (see address below) at a cost of $5 for seven consecutive days or $20 per year. A $3 one-day permit can be purchased at self-service stations at national forest trailheads, but the pass is good only for the trailhead at which it's purchased.

**Maps:** Several maps cover this area's hiking trails, including the *Crawford Notch–Sandwich Range/Moosilauke–Kinsman* map, $7.95 in waterproof Tyvek, available in many stores and from the Appalachian Mountain Club, 800/262-4455, website: www.outdoors.org; the *Trail Map and Guide to the White Mountain National Forest* for $7.95 from the DeLorme Publishing Company, 800/642-0970; and map 3 in the *Map and Guide to the Appalachian Trail in New Hampshire and Vermont,* an eight-map set and guidebook available for $19.95 ($14.95 for the maps alone) from the Appalachian Trail Conference (see address below). For a topographic area map, request Mount Moosilauke from USGS Map Sales, Federal Center, Box 25286, Denver, CO 80225, 888/ASK-USGS (888/275-8747), website: http://mapping.usgs.gov.

**Directions:** The Beaver Brook Trail, which coincides with the Appalachian Trail, begins from a parking lot along Route 112 at the height of land in Kinsman Notch, 6.2 miles west of North Woodstock and 4.8 miles south of the junction of Routes 112 and 116.

**Contact:** White Mountain National Forest Supervisor, 719 North Main St., Laconia, NH 03246, 603/528-8721, TDD for the hearing impaired 603/528-8722, website: www.fs.fed.us/r9/white. Appalachian Trail Conference, 799 Washington St., P.O. Box 807, Harpers Ferry, WV 25425-0807, 304/535-6331, website: www.appalachiantrail.org.

## 67 MOUNT MOOSILAUKE: GLENCLIFF TRAIL

**7.8 mi/5.5 hrs**

**north of Warren**

The Glencliff Trail, a section of the white-blazed Appalachian Trail, offers a difficult and very scenic route to the 4,802-foot summit of Mount Moosilauke, where an extensive alpine area offers panoramic views stretching across much of the White Mountains and west to Vermont's Green Mountains and New York's Adirondacks. This hike gains about 3,300 feet in elevation.

From the parking lot, follow the white blazes past a gate and along old farm roads through pastures before entering the woods at 0.4 mile, where a side path leads left to a Dartmouth

College cabin (not open to the public), and the Hurricane Trail diverges right. The Glencliff Trail ascends steadily but at a moderate grade for the next two miles, then grows steeper as it rises into the mountain's krummholtz, the scrub conifers that grow in the subalpine zone. At three miles the trail hits the old carriage road on Moosilauke. A spur path leads right (south) to Moosilauke's craggy south peak just 0.2 mile distant. This hike turns left (north) and follows the wide carriage road over easy ground along the open ridge—with great views—ascending gently to the summit at 3.9 miles. Return the way you came. For a full traverse of Moosilauke via the Appalachian Trail, see the special note in the description of the Mount Moosilauke: Beaver Brook Trail hike.

**User groups:** Hikers and dogs. No wheelchair facilities. This trail should not be attempted in winter except by hikers experienced in mountaineering and prepared for severe winter weather, and is not suitable for skis. Bikes, horses, and hunting are prohibited.

**Access, fees:** No backcountry permit is needed, but a permit is required for day use or overnight parking at any White Mountain National Forest trailhead, as indicated by signs posted at most trailheads. Permits are available at several area stores and from the national forest (see address below) at a cost of $5 for seven consecutive days or $20 per year. A $3 one-day permit can be purchased at self-service stations at national forest trailheads, but the pass is good only for the trailhead at which it's purchased.

**Maps:** Several maps cover this area's hiking trails, including the *Crawford Notch-Sandwich Range/Moosilauke-Kinsman* map, $7.95 in waterproof Tyvek, available in many stores and from the Appalachian Mountain Club, 800/262-4455, website: www.outdoors.org; the *Trail Map and Guide to the White Mountain National Forest* for $7.95 from the DeLorme Publishing Company, 800/642-0970; and map 3 in the *Map and Guide to the Appalachian Trail in New Hampshire and Vermont,* an eight-map set and guidebook available for $19.95 ($14.95 for the maps alone) from the Appalachian Trail Conference (see address below). For a topographic area map, request Mount Moosilauke from USGS Map Sales, Federal Center, Box 25286, Denver, CO 80225, 888/ASK-USGS (888/275-8747), website: http://mapping.usgs.gov.

**Directions:** From Route 25 in Glencliff Village, turn onto High Street, just past the sign for the Glencliff Home for the Elderly. Drive 1.2 miles to a dirt parking lot on the right.

**Contact:** White Mountain National Forest Supervisor, 719 North Main St., Laconia, NH 03246, 603/528-8721, TDD for the hearing impaired 603/528-8722, website: www.fs.fed .us/r9/white. Appalachian Trail Conference, 799 Washington St., P.O. Box 807, Harpers Ferry, WV 25425-0807, 304/535-6331, website: www.appalachiantrail.org.

## 68 MOUNT OSCEOLA
**6.4 mi/4 hrs**

**in the White Mountain National Forest, north of Waterville Valley and east of Lincoln**

One of the easiest 4,000-footers in New Hampshire to hike—with a vertical ascent of only about 2,000 feet—Osceola's summit ledges, rising 4,340 feet above sea level, give a sweeping view to the south and southeast of Waterville Valley and Mount Tripyramid, and northeast to the Pemigewasset Wilderness and the Presidential Range.

From the parking lot, follow the Mount Osceola Trail as it ascends at a moderate angle through numerous switchbacks and reaches the summit ledges at 3.2 miles. The trail continues one more mile to reach 4,156-foot East Osceola, which will add two miles and approximately 1.5 hours to this hike's distance and time. Hike back along the same route.

**User groups:** Hikers and dogs. No wheelchair facilities. This trail should not be attempted in winter except by hikers experienced in mountaineering and prepared for severe winter weather, and is not suitable for bikes, horses, or skis. Hunting is allowed in season.

**Access, fees:** No backcountry permit is needed, but a permit is required for day use or overnight parking at any White Mountain National Forest trailhead; signs indicating so are posted at most of them. Permits are available at several area stores and from the national forest (see address below) at a cost of $5 for seven consecutive days or $20 per year. A $3 one-day permit can be purchased at self-service stations at national forest trailheads, but the pass is good only for the trailhead at which it's purchased. Tripoli Road is generally not maintained in winter.

**Maps:** For a contour map of trails, get the *Franconia-Pemigewasset Range* map or the *Crawford Notch-Sandwich Range/Moosilauke-Kinsman* map, $7.95 each in waterproof Tyvek, available in many stores and from the Appalachian Mountain Club, 800/262-4455, website: www.outdoors.org; the *Trail Map and Guide to the White Mountain National Forest* for $7.95 from the DeLorme Publishing Company, 800/642-0970; or the map of the national forest, available by sending a check payable to White Mountain National Forest for $6 to the forest's main office (see address below). For topographic area maps, request Mount Osceola and Waterville Valley from USGS Map Sales, Federal Center, Box 25286, Denver, CO 80225, 888/ASK-USGS (888/275-8747), website: http://mapping.usgs.gov.

**Directions:** From I-93, take Exit 31 for Tripoli Road. Drive east on Tripoli Road for seven miles to a parking lot on the left for the Mount Osceola Trail.

**Contact:** White Mountain National Forest Supervisor, 719 North Main St., Laconia, NH 03246, 603/528-8721, TDD for the hearing impaired 603/528-8722, website: www.fs.fed .us/r9/white.

## 69 GREELEY PONDS NORTH
**4.4 mi/2 hrs**

**in the White Mountain National Forest on
the Kancamagus Highway/Route 112 between
Lincoln and Conway**

This fairly flat 4.4-mile hike offers the shortest
and easiest route to the two scenic Greeley
Ponds, ascending just a few hundred feet. It's
a nice hike in summer, better in the fall, but arguably best on snowshoes or cross-country skis
in winter. The ski trail begins at a separate parking area but eventually merges with the hiking
trail before reaching the first pond. From the
parking area, follow the Greeley Ponds Trail
as it winds southward through a mixed deciduous and conifer forest. At 1.3 miles, the Mount
Osceola Trail diverges to the right (east), soon
to climb steeply up East Osceola and Osceola,
a worthwhile side trip. This hike continues south
on the Greeley Ponds Trail for nearly another
half mile to the upper Greeley Pond, which sits
in a scenic basin below the dramatic cliffs of
East Osceola. Continuing another half mile on
the trail brings you to the lower pond. Return
the way you came.

**User groups:** Hikers, dogs, skiers, and snowshoers. No wheelchair facilities. This trail is
not suitable for bikes or horses. Hunting is allowed in season.

**Access, fees:** No backcountry permit is needed, but a permit is required for day use or
overnight parking at any White Mountain National Forest trailhead, as indicated by signs
posted at most trailheads. Permits are available
at several area stores and from the national forest (see address below) at a cost of $5 for seven
consecutive days or $20 per year. A $3 one-day
permit can be purchased at self-service stations
at national forest trailheads, but the pass is good
only for the trailhead at which it's purchased.
Camping and fires are prohibited within the
Greeley Ponds Scenic Area, the boundary of
which is marked by a sign along the trail.

**Maps:** For a contour map of trails, get the *Franconia-Pemigewasset Range* map or the *Crawford Notch-Sandwich Range/Moosilauke-Kinsman*

map, $7.95 each in waterproof Tyvek, available
in many stores and from the Appalachian Mountain Club, 800/262-4455, website: www.outdoors
.org; or the *Trail Map and Guide to the White
Mountain National Forest* for $7.95 from the De-
Lorme Publishing Company, 800/642-0970. For
a topographic area map, request the Mount
Osceola, Mount Carrigain, Mount Tripyramid,
and Waterville Valley maps from USGS Map
Sales, Federal Center, Box 25286, Denver, CO
80225, 888/ASK-USGS (888/275-8747), website: http://mapping.usgs.gov.

**Directions:** The hike begins at a small parking
area along the Kancamagus Highway/Route
112, 9.9 miles east of the McDonald's on Route
112 in Lincoln (Exit 32 off I-93), 3.4 miles west
of the sign at Kancamagus Pass and 25.6 miles
west of the junction of Routes 112 and 16 in
Conway. The ski trail begins at a parking lot
0.2 mile farther east.

**Contact:** White Mountain National Forest Supervisor, 719 North Main St., Laconia, NH
03246, 603/528-8721, TDD for the hearing impaired 603/528-8722, website: www.fs.fed.us/
r9/white.

## 70 GREELEY PONDS SOUTH
**7.4 mi/4 hrs**

**in Waterville Valley in the White Mountain
National Forest**

This 7.4-mile hike offers a route from popular
Waterville Valley to the two scenic Greeley
Ponds that is longer and climbs a little more
than the Greeley Ponds North hike. The total
vertical ascent on this hike is about 700 feet.
I love doing this trail on cross-country skis in
winter. The winter and summer parking area
is at the start of the Livermore Trail, a former
logging road that in winter is groomed and
tracked for skating and diagonal skiing by the
local ski touring center, although no touring
center pass is required because it's a national
forest trail.

From the parking lot, follow the wide road
for a quarter mile, then turn left at a sign onto
the Greeley Ponds Trail, a fairly wide hiking

trail that in winter is not groomed but is often packed and tracked by snowshoers and skiers. Flat at first, the trail begins to rise gradually as it parallels the Mad River, which up here is just a rambunctious stream. The trail grows fairly steep for the last 0.1 mile to the lower Greeley Pond—the one spot where some skiers may want to remove their skis—which can be reached by a short spur path. At one point the ski and hiking trails diverge, with the ski trail following the Mad River's right bank to the lower pond and the hiking trail crossing over the river to its left bank. At the lower pond, both trails cross to the pond's left shoreline, with the ski trail hugging the shore and the hiking trail running parallel a bit farther back into the woods. The trails lead all the way to the upper pond, below the cliffs of East Osceola. Return the way you came.

**User groups:** Hikers, dogs, skiers, and snowshoers. No wheelchair facilities. This trail is not suitable for bikes or horses. Hunting is allowed in season.

**Access, fees:** No backcountry permit is needed, but a permit is required for day use or overnight parking at any White Mountain National Forest trailhead, as indicated by signs posted at most trailheads. Permits are available at several area stores and from the national forest (see address below) at a cost of $5 for seven consecutive days or $20 per year. A $3 one-day permit can be purchased at self-service stations at national forest trailheads, but the pass is good only for the trailhead at which it's purchased. Camping and fires are prohibited within the Greeley Ponds Scenic Area, the boundary of which is marked by a sign along the trail.

**Maps:** For a contour map of trails, get the *Franconia-Pemigewasset Range* map or the *Crawford Notch–Sandwich Range/Moosilauke–Kinsman* map, $7.95 each in waterproof Tyvek, available in many stores and from the Appalachian Mountain Club, 800/262-4455, website: www.out-doors.org; or the *Trail Map and Guide to the White Mountain National Forest* for $7.95 from the DeLorme Publishing Company, 800/642-0970. For a topographic area map, request the Mount Osceola, Mount Carrigain, Mount Tripyramid, and Waterville Valley maps from USGS Map Sales, Federal Center, Box 25286, Denver, CO 80225, 888/ASK-USGS (888/275-8747), website: http://mapping.usgs.gov.

**Directions:** From I-93 in Campton, take Exit 28 onto Route 49 east. Drive about 11.4 miles into Waterville Valley and turn right onto Valley Road, which is still Route 49. Just 0.4 mile farther, turn left onto West Branch Road, in front of the Osceola Library. Drive another 0.7 mile and turn right (before the bridge) into the parking lot at the start of the Livermore Trail.

**Contact:** White Mountain National Forest Supervisor, 719 North Main St., Laconia, NH 03246, 603/528-8721, TDD for the hearing impaired 603/528-8722, website: www.fs.fed.us/r9/white.

## 71 CATHEDRAL LEDGE
**0.1 mi/0.25 hr**

**in Echo Lake State Park west of North Conway**
This is less a hike than an easy, five-minute walk to the top of Cathedral Ledge, a sheer, 400-foot cliff with a breaktaking view of the Mount Washington Valley. Popular with tourists when the access road is open from late spring–autumn, the lookout is protected by a fence to keep visitors from wandering too close to the brink. Cathedral is one of New Hampshire's most popular rock-climbing areas, so you're likely to see climbers pulling over the top of the cliff right in front of you. Obviously, you should not throw anything off the cliff, given the likelihood of there being people below. From the circle, follow a wide, obvious path to the east, a short distance through the woods to the top of the cliff. Return the same way.

**User groups:** Hikers, bikers, dogs, skiers, and snowshoers. No wheelchair facilities. Skiers and snowshoers must begin at the base of the access road, which adds about one mile to the round-trip mileage listed above and is a steep climb. Dogs must be leashed. Hunting is allowed in season.

**Access, fees:** Parking and access are free. The access road is not maintained in winter and is blocked by a gate.

**Maps:** Although no map is necessary for this hike, it is shown on the *Crawford Notch–Sandwich Range/Moosilauke–Kinsman* map, $7.95 in waterproof Tyvek, available in many stores and from the Appalachian Mountain Club, 800/262-4455, website: www.outdoors.org. For a topographic map of the area, request North Conway West from USGS Map Sales, Federal Center, Box 25286, Denver, CO 80225, 888/ASK-USGS (888/275-8747), website: http://mapping.usgs.gov.

**Directions:** From Route 16 in North Conway in front of the Eastern Slope Inn, turn west at traffic lights onto River Road. Continue 1.5 miles and turn left at a sign for Cathedral Ledge. Follow the road for more than a mile to its end at a circle near the cliff top.

**Contact:** New Hampshire Division of Parks and Recreation, P.O. Box 1856, 172 Pembroke Rd., Concord, NH 03302, 603/271-3556, camping reservations 603/271-3628, website: www.nhstateparks.org.

## 72 THE MOATS
**9.4 mi/6 hrs**
**in the White Mountain National Forest west of North Conway**

The 9.4-mile traverse of the Moats is one of the most scenic hikes that you can make in the White Mountains without going up a big peak. The highest of the three peaks, North Moat Mountain, is just 3,196 feet; the Middle and South peaks are both under 3,000 feet. Yet all three summits, and several open ledges along the ridge connecting them, offer broad views of the Saco Valley. From North Moat on a clear day, you can see Mount Washington almost due north. The full traverse of the Moats entails more than 3,000 feet of climbing. If you do not have two vehicles to shuttle, then park at the northern terminus of the Moat Moun-

tain Trail and hike up North Moat Mountain, which is an 8.4-mile round-trip that gains nearly 2,700 feet in elevation. You could also hike a loop to North Moat on the Moat Mountain Trail and Red Ridge Trail.

To hike the full traverse—which I strongly recommend—from south to north, pick up the Moat Mountain Trail on Dugway Road. As it also does at its northern end, the trail starts out here as an old woods road, eventually narrowing to a footpath. Watch for arrows marking the trail's direction at junctions. After starting out as an easy, flat walk, the trail begins climbing steadily, though never too steeply, up South Moat Mountain, reaching its 2,749-foot summit at 2.3 miles. It dips a bit, reentering the woods, but generally follows the gentle ridge top to the 2,805-foot summit of Middle Moat, just 0.6 mile farther. Behind the Middle, the hiking gets a little more strenuous—though not very difficult—dropping somewhat, passing a junction with the Red Ridge Trail at 3.8 miles from the trailhead, then climbing through dense forest and up rocky ledges to the summit of North Moat, at five miles. The descent is somewhat tiring on the knees—especially if the rock slabs along the trail are slick with water. Stay on the Moat Mountain Trail, passing junctions with the Attitash Trail at 6.8 miles and the other end of the Red Ridge Trail at 8.1 miles, and reaching the northern trailhead at 9.2 miles.

**User groups:** Hikers, snowshoers, and dogs. No wheelchair facilities. This trail is not suitable for bikes, skis, or horses. Hunting is allowed in season.

**Access, fees:** No backcountry permit is needed, but a permit is required for day use or overnight parking at any White Mountain National Forest trailhead, as indicated by signs posted at most trailheads. Permits are available at several area stores and from the national forest (see address below) at a cost of $5 for seven consecutive days or $20 per year. A $3 one-day permit can be purchased at self-service stations at national forest trailheads, but the pass is good only for the trailhead at which it's purchased.

**Maps:** For a map of hiking trails in this area, obtain the *Crawford Notch–Sandwich Range/Moosilauke-Kinsman* map, $7.95 in waterproof Tyvek, available in many stores and from the Appalachian Mountain Club, 800/262-4455, website: www.outdoors.org; or the *Trail Map and Guide to the White Mountain National Forest* for $7.95 from the DeLorme Publishing Company, 800/642-0970. For a topographic area map, request North Conway West from USGS Map Sales, Federal Center, Box 25286, Denver, CO 80225, 888/ASK-USGS (888/275-8747), website: http://mapping.usgs.gov.

**Directions:** From Route 16 in North Conway, turn west at the traffic lights in front of the Eastern Slope Inn onto River Road. Continue about 2.2 miles to a large parking area on the left for Diana's Baths. The trail begins on the west side of the parking area. To hike the complete traverse south to north, as described here, leave one vehicle here and drive a second vehicle back out, turning right (south) onto West Side Road. Continue for about 0.9 mile, taking Old West Side Road (at the three-way intersection with the road to Cathedral Ledge), which rejoins West Side Road. Turning right (south) onto West Side Road, continue for about 4.5 miles. Turn right onto Passaconaway Road (which becomes Dugway Road), and drive another 2.5 miles to roadside parking and the Moat Mountain Trail's southern end, on the right.

**Contact:** White Mountain National Forest Supervisor, 719 North Main St., Laconia, NH 03246, 603/528-8721, TDD for the hearing impaired 603/528-8722, website: www.fs.fed.us/r9/white.

## **73** SABBADAY FALLS
**0.8 mi/0.75 hr**

**in the White Mountain National Forest on the Kancamagus Highway/Route 112 between Lincoln and Conway**

 The early explorers of the Passaconaway Valley reached Sabbaday Falls on a Sun-

day, and thereafter the spectacular falls became a popular destination on the Sabbath. The falls drop twice through a narrow gorge so perfect in its geometry it seems the work of engineers. The gorge was formed from the gouging action of rocks and sand released by glacial melt-off 10,000 years ago. Below the gorge, Sabbaday Brook settles quietly, if briefly, in a clear pool. This easy hike is a great one for young children.

From the parking area, follow the wide gravel and dirt Sabbaday Brook Trail, which parallels the rocky brook. The trail ascends very little over its first 0.3 mile to where a side path leads left. This path loops past the lower pool and above the gorge and both falls before rejoining the Sabbaday Brook Trail. Turn right to return to the parking area.

**User groups:** Hikers, dogs, skiers, and snowshoers. No wheelchair facilities. This trail is not suitable for bikes or horses. Hunting is allowed in season.

**Access, fees:** No backcountry permit is needed, but a permit is required for day use or overnight parking at any White Mountain National Forest trailhead, as indicated by signs posted at most trailheads. Permits are available at several area stores and from the national forest (see address below) at a cost of $5 for seven consecutive days or $20 per year. A $3 one-day permit can be purchased at self-service stations at national forest trailheads, but the pass is good only for the trailhead at which it's purchased.

**Maps:** For a contour map of trails, get the *Franconia-Pemigewasset Range* map or the *Crawford Notch–Sandwich Range/Moosilauke-Kinsman* map, $7.95 each in waterproof Tyvek, available in many stores and from the Appalachian Mountain Club, 800/262-4455, website: www.outdoors.org; or the *Trail Map and Guide to the White Mountain National Forest* for $7.95 from the DeLorme Publishing Company, 800/642-0970. For a topographic area map, request Mount Tripyramid from USGS Map Sales, Federal Center, Box 25286, Denver, CO 80225,

888/ASK-USGS (888/275-8747), website: http://mapping.usgs.gov.

**Directions:** The hike begins at the Sabbaday Falls parking area along the Kancamagus Highway/Route 112, 19.9 miles east of the McDonald's on Route 112 in Lincoln, 6.6 miles east of the sign at Kancamagus Pass and 15.6 miles west of the junction of Routes 112 and 16 in Conway.

**Contact:** White Mountain National Forest Supervisor, 719 North Main St., Laconia, NH 03246, 603/528-8721, TDD for the hearing impaired 603/528-8722, website: www.fs.fed.us/r9/white.

## 74 MOUNT TRIPYRAMID
**11 mi/7 hrs**
**in the White Mountain National Forest east of Waterville Valley**

Tripyramid's three wooded summits offer little in the way of compelling views. But two friends and I spent a wonderful day mountain biking to the hiking trail loop and scrambling up and down Tripyramid's two rockslides. Although you can hike this entire route, I suggest mountain biking the Livermore Trail, an old logging road, then stashing your bikes in the woods and hiking the Mount Tripyramid Trail. And two of the three summits along this route, the North and Middle Peaks, are both official 4,000-footers. This hike ascends about 3,000 feet over its length and involves some exposed scrambling, especially going up the north slide of Tripyramid; it is not for the faint of heart or anyone not in good shape.

From the parking area, walk around the gate onto Livermore Road (also called the Livermore Trail), a rough road ascending gradually for 2.6 miles to the south end of the Tripyramid Trail, which loops over the mountain. If you have bikes, leave them here at the south end of the loop and walk another mile up the Livermore Trail, then turn right onto the Mount Tripyramid Trail at its north end. The trail ascends the north slide, which is more exposed and steeper than the south slide (mak-

ing this the preferred direction of travel on the loop) and dangerous when wet or icy. At 1.2 miles, the trail reaches the North Peak and true summit at 4,140 feet. There are limited views. Continue on the narrow path, passing a junction with the Sabbaday Brook Trail a half mile past the North Peak, and reaching Middle Peak (4,110 feet) 0.3 mile farther. A pair of outlooks just off the trail offer decent views. The trail continues to the South Peak (4,090 feet), which is wooded. Just beyond that peak, bear right where the Sleeper Trail branches left and descend the steep south slide, which has lots of loose rock. The trail enters the woods again and follows Slide Brook past nice pools to the Livermore Trail, 2.5 miles from South Peak. Turn left and hike (or bike) the 2.6 miles back to the parking area.

**User groups:** Hikers and dogs on the Mount Tripyramid Trail; hikers, bikers, dogs, and skiers on the Livermore Trail. No wheelchair facilities. The Mount Tripyramid Trail should not be attempted in winter except by hikers experienced in mountaineering and prepared for severe winter weather. It is not suitable for horses. Hunting is allowed in season.

**Access, fees:** No backcountry permit is needed, but a permit is required for day use or overnight parking at any White Mountain National Forest trailhead, as indicated by signs posted at most trailheads. Permits are available at several area stores and from the national forest (see address below) at a cost of $5 for seven consecutive days or $20 per year. A $3 one-day permit can be purchased at self-service stations at national forest trailheads, but the pass is good only for the trailhead at which it's purchased. In the winter months, you can ski or snowshoe up Livermore Trail, which is groomed and tracked for skating or diagonal skiing, without having to pay the trail fee for the cross-country ski touring center in Waterville Valley because Livermore Trail is within the national forest.

**Maps:** For a contour map of trails, get the *Franconia-Pemigewasset Range* map or the

Crawford Notch–Sandwich Range/Moosilauke-Kinsman map, $7.95 each in waterproof Tyvek, available in many stores and from the Appalachian Mountain Club, 800/262-4455, website: www.outdoors.org; or the *Trail Map and Guide to the White Mountain National Forest* for $7.95 from the DeLorme Publishing Company, 800/642-0970. For topographic area maps, request Mount Tripyramid and Waterville Valley from USGS Map Sales, Federal Center, Box 25286, Denver, CO 80225, 888/ASK-USGS (888/275-8747), website: http://mapping.usgs.gov.
**Directions:** From I-93 in Campton, take Exit 28 onto Route 49 east. Drive about 11.4 miles into Waterville Valley and turn right onto Valley Road, which is still Route 49 east. Just 0.4 mile farther, turn left onto West Branch Road, in front of the Osceola Library. Drive another 0.7 mile and turn right (before the bridge) into the parking lot at the start of the Livermore Trail (also called the Livermore Road).
**Contact:** White Mountain National Forest Supervisor, 719 North Main St., Laconia, NH 03246, 603/528-8721, TDD for the hearing impaired 603/528-8722, website: www.fs.fed.us/r9/white.

## 75 WELCH AND DICKEY
### 4.5 mi/3.5 hrs
in the White Mountain National Forest
southwest of Waterville Valley

My mom, an avid hiker, and I hiked this 4.5-mile loop over Welch (2,605 feet) and Dickey (2,736 feet) at the height of fall foliage color on a day when the higher mountains were swathed in clouds. Yet these lower summits remained clear, giving us colorful views from the many open ledges on this loop hike. Relatively easy, with just a few brief, steep stretches, it's a good hike for children, entailing only about 1,700 feet of uphill over 4.5 miles.

From the parking area, you can do the loop in either direction, but I recommend heading up the Welch Mountain Trail (hiking counterclockwise). Within a mile, the trail emerges onto open ledges just below the summit of Welch Mountain, with a wide view across the Mad River Valley to Sandwich Mountain. The trail turns left and ascends another mile to the summit, with broad views in every direction, including Dickey Mountain to the north. Continuing on the trail, you drop steeply into a shallow saddle, then climb up onto Dickey, a half mile from Welch. Watch for a sign pointing to nearby ledges, where there is a good view toward Franconia Notch. From Dickey's summit, follow an arrow onto an obvious trail north, which soon descends steeply to slab ledges above the cliffs of Dickey Mountain, overlooking a beautiful, narrow valley between Welch and Dickey that blazes with color during the peak of foliage. The Dickey Mountain Trail continues descending the ridge, reentering the woods, then reaching the parking area, two miles from Dickey's summit.

**User groups:** Hikers, snowshoers, and dogs. No wheelchair facilities. This trail is not suitable for bikes, horses, or skis. Hunting is allowed in season.

**Access, fees:** No backcountry permit is needed, but a permit is required for day use or overnight parking at any White Mountain National Forest trailhead, as indicated by signs posted at most trailheads. Permits are available at several area stores and from the national forest (see address below) at a cost of $5 for seven consecutive days or $20 per year. A $3 one-day permit can be purchased at self-service stations at national forest trailheads, but the pass is good only for the trailhead at which it's purchased.

**Maps:** For a contour map of trails, get the *Franconia-Pemigewasset Range* map or the *Crawford Notch-Sandwich Range/Moosilauke-Kinsman* map, $7.95 each in waterproof Tyvek, available in many stores and from the Appalachian Mountain Club, 800/262-4455, website: www.outdoors.org; or the *Trail Map and Guide to the White Mountain National Forest* for $7.95 from the DeLorme Publishing Company, 800/642-0970. For a topographic area map, request Waterville Valley from USGS Map Sales, Federal

Center, Box 25286, Denver, CO 80225, 888/ASK-USGS (888/275-8747), website: http://mapping.usgs.gov.

**Directions:** From I-93 in Campton, take Exit 28 onto Route 49 north, toward Waterville Valley. After passing through the traffic lights in Campton, drive another 4.4 miles on Route 49, then turn left onto Upper Mad River Road, immediately crossing the Mad River on Six Mile Bridge. Continue 0.7 mile from Route 49, then turn right onto Orris Road at a small sign reading Welch Mountain Trail. Drive another 0.7 mile to a parking area on the right, at the trailhead.

**Contact:** White Mountain National Forest Supervisor, 719 North Main St., Laconia, NH 03246, 603/528-8721, TDD for the hearing impaired 603/528-8722, website: www.fs.fed.us/r9/white.

## 76 SANDWICH MOUNTAIN
**8.3 mi/5.5 hrs**
**in Waterville Valley in the White Mountain National Forest**

At 3,993 feet, Sandwich Mountain is a tad short to attract the same attention among hikers as many of the 4,000-footers in the White Mountains. But from the small area of rocks jutting just above the forest at its summit, you get a wide view from the northwest to the east of most of the White Mountains—certainly more peaks are visible from here than from many of the smaller 4,000-footers in the Whites. I once caught an amazing sunset up here on a warm and calm autumn day at the peak of fall foliage. The elevation gained on this hike is about 2,500 feet.

The Drake's Brook Trail starts at the north end of the trailhead parking lot, the Sandwich Mountain Trail at the south end. This 8.3-mile loop can be done in either direction—both trails have steep sections that can be difficult to descend, particularly when wet. If the foliage is peaking, I would recommend deciding your direction of travel based on making sure you are on the lower half of the Sandwich Moun-

tain Trail when the sun is high, to enhance the color in the forest seen from open ledges along that trail; by midafternoon, the mountain shadow will fall over those views, dulling the color show. I will describe the hike clockwise.

Follow the old logging road of the Drake's Brook Trail for 0.4 mile to where the ski and bike trail to Fletcher's Cascades branches left (leading nearly a mile to these scenic cascades); bear right with the hiking trail. It soon crosses Drake's Brook, which can be difficult to cross at times of high water. The trail parallels the brook for about 2.5 miles, although it is often separated from the water by dense brush and a steep bank. It then swings right and climbs steeply for more than a half mile to a junction with the Sandwich Mountain Trail (SMT) at 3.2 miles. Turn left for the summit on the SMT. In 0.1 mile a side trail branches right, leading steeply uphill for 0.2 mile to Jennings Peak, a subsidiary summit of Sandwich Mountain with a good view from atop cliffs, taking in the summit of Sandwich Mountain, the valleys of the Mad and Pemigewasset Rivers, and the Lakes Region and Squam Mountains (see hike listing in the Central and Southern New Hampshire chapter) to the south.

Double back to the SMT, turn right, and continue 1.1 miles to the summit of Sandwich Mountain, where you break out of the spruce forest at a rock pile with a spectacular view in a wide sweep north. Jennings Peak lies to the immediate northwest and Waterville Valley in the near foreground, including the peaks surrounding it (left to right): Tecumseh, Osceola, and Tripyramid (the last two are described in this chapter) with its south slide visible. To the east stretches the broad ridge connecting Whiteface, Passaconaway, and Chocorua's bald knob beyond (all three described in this chapter). Massive Mount Moosilauke (described in this chapter) dominates the horizon to the west. The high Franconia Ridge, connecting Mounts Flume, Liberty, Lincoln, and Lafayette (all described in this chapter), rises above everything else in the distant northwest. Due north, the

Pemigewasset Wilderness covers the vast road-less area beyond Waterville Valley—and beyond the Kancamagus Highway, which is hidden from view—including the ridge of Mount Bond and Bondcliff, and Mount Carrigain, the prominent high mound at 1 o'clock (all described in this chapter). Finally, to Carrigain's right are the biggest peaks in the Whites, Mount Washington and the Presidential Range (also described in this chapter). Behind you, look for a somewhat hidden footpath through scrub trees that leads a few feet to a view south toward the Lakes Region. Descend the Sandwich Mountain Trail for 3.9 miles back to the parking area.

**User groups:** Hikers, snowshoers, and dogs. No wheelchair facilities. This trail is not suitable for bikes, horses, or skis. Hunting is allowed in season.

**Access, fees:** No backcountry permit is needed, but a permit is required for day use or overnight parking at any White Mountain National Forest trailhead, as indicated by signs posted at most trailheads. Permits are available at several area stores and from the national forest (see address below) at a cost of $5 for seven consecutive days or $20 per year. A $3 one-day permit can be purchased at self-service stations at national forest trailheads, but the pass is good only for the trailhead at which it's purchased.

**Maps:** For a contour map of trails, get the *Franconia-Pemigewasset Range* map or the *Crawford Notch-Sandwich Range/Moosilauke-Kinsman* map, $7.95 each in waterproof Tyvek, available in many stores and from the Appalachian Mountain Club, 800/262-4455, website: www.outdoors.org; or the *Trail Map and Guide to the White Mountain National Forest* for $7.95 from the DeLorme Publishing Company, 800/642-0970. For a topographic area map, request the Waterville Valley and Mount Tripyramid maps from USGS Map Sales, Federal Center, Box 25286, Denver, CO 80225, 888/ASK-USGS (888/275-8747), website: http://mapping.usgs.gov.

**Directions:** From Exit 28 off I-93 in Campton,

take Route 49 north for about 10.2 miles and turn right into a parking lot for the Drake's Brook and Sandwich Mountain Trails.

**Contact:** White Mountain National Forest Supervisor, 719 North Main St., Laconia, NH 03246, 603/528-8721, TDD for the hearing impaired 603/528-8722, website: www.fs.fed.us/r9/white.

## ⟨77⟩ MOUNT WHITEFACE
**8 mi/5.5 hrs**
**in the southern White Mountain National Forest north of Wonalancet**

While Whiteface, at 4,010 feet, is not among the best-known 4,000-footers in the Whites, the cliffs just below its summit offer dramatic views of the southern Whites, Mount Washington, and the Lakes Region to the south. The precipices along the upper Blueberry Ledge Trail are a great place to catch the fall foliage; I did one late September morning and also saw my first snowflakes of the season. All trails here are blazed in blue. The vertical ascent is about 3,800 feet. For a longer loop linking Whiteface with Passaconaway, see the special note in the description for the Mount Passaconaway hike.

From the parking lot, walk back to the road and turn right, following the road and signs for the trails for 0.3 mile. Turn left onto the Blueberry Ledge Trail, crossing over Wonalancet Brook on a bridge. Continue hiking on the single-lane dirt road to its end, where the Blueberry Ledge Trail enters the woods. The trail remains fairly easy at first, crossing slab ledges 1.5 miles from the parking lot.

At 3.2 miles, the Wiggin Trail diverges right (east), leading 1.1 miles to the Dicey's Mill Trail—the descent route for this hike. The best views begin at 3.6 miles, where the Blueberry Ledge Trail turns sharply right at a slab and the brink of a cliff that could be hazardous when wet or icy. In winter, you might want the security of roping up and belaying this section; a 60-foot rope would be long enough. To the south and southwest are the lakes of central

New Hampshire and Sandwich Mountain. Continue up the Blueberry Ledge Trail for another 0.3 mile; wooden steps on steep slabs along this stretch of the trail have been removed. You will pass ledges with terrific views down into the broad glacial cirque known as the Bowl (which is framed by Whiteface and neighboring Mount Passaconaway), east to Mount Chocorua, and north to Mount Washington. Bear right at a trail junction near open ledges onto the Rollins Trail, following it 0.2 mile to the wooded summit of Whiteface. To descend, return to the Wiggin Trail, turn left, and follow it to the Dicey's Mill Trail; turn right, and descend 1.9 miles to the parking area, the last half mile of hiking following Ferncroft Road.

**User groups:** Hikers only. No wheelchair facilities. This trail may be difficult to snowshoe because of severe winter weather, and is not suitable for bikes, dogs, horses, or skis. Hunting is allowed in season.

**Access, fees:** No backcountry permit is needed, but a permit is required for day use or overnight parking at any White Mountain National Forest trailhead, as indicated by signs posted at most trailheads. Permits are available at several area stores and from the national forest (see address below) at a cost of $5 for seven consecutive days or $20 per year. A $3 one-day permit can be purchased at self-service stations at national forest trailheads, but the pass is good only for the trailhead at which it's purchased. Trails in this part of the national forest are accessed through private land; be sure to stay on trails. Camping is permitted on the hardened ground at the former site of the Wonalancet Out Door Club's Camp Heermance (removed in 2002), 3.8 miles from the Ferncroft parking area via the Blueberry Ledge Trail. See the website of the Wonalancet Out Door Club (below) for current information.

**Maps:** For a map of trails, get the *Crawford Notch-Sandwich Range/Moosilauke-Kinsman* map, $7.95 in waterproof Tyvek, which is available in many stores and from the Appalachian Mountain Club, 800/262-4455, website:

www.outdoors.org; the Trail Map and Guide to the Sandwich Range Wilderness, on waterproof Tyvek, for $5 in local stores or from the Wonalancet Out Door Club (see address below); or the *Trail Map and Guide to the White Mountain National Forest* for $7.95 from the DeLorme Publishing Company, 800/642-0970. For topographic area maps, request Mount Chocorua and Mount Tripyramid from USGS Map Sales, Federal Center, Box 25286, Denver, CO 80225, 888/ASK-USGS (888/275-8747), website: http://mapping.usgs.gov.

**Directions:** From Route 113A in Wonalancet, turn north onto Ferncroft Road. Follow it for a half mile and bear right at a sign into the hiker parking lot.

**Contact:** Wonalancet Out Door Club, HCR 64 Box 248, Wonalancet, NH 03897, website: www.wodc.org. White Mountain National Forest Supervisor, 719 North Main St., Laconia, NH 03246, 603/528-8721, TDD for the hearing impaired 603/528-8722, website: www.fs.fed .us/r9/white.

## 78 MOUNT PASSACONAWAY
### 9.5 mi/6.5 hrs
**in the southern White Mountain National Forest north of Wonalancet**

Probably one of the least-visited of New Hampshire's 4,000-foot summits, the top of Passaconaway (4,060 feet) is wooded, with no views (unless you're standing on several feet of snow and can see over the low spruce trees). But there are two nice views near the summit. The trails are marked with blue blazes and the vertical ascent is about 3,800 feet.

From the parking lot, walk back to the road and turn right, following the road for 0.8 mile straight onto the Dicey's Mill Trail. Soon after entering the woods, the trail crosses into the national forest. It parallels and eventually crosses Wonalancet Brook at 2.3 miles (0.4 mile beyond the Wiggin Trail junction), then begins ascending more steeply. The trail passes the junction with the Rollins Trail, which comes in from the left (west) at 3.7 miles, then the

East Loop Trail departing right (east) at 3.9 miles. At around 4.5 miles, you'll get a view toward the peaks above Waterville Valley to the northwest. The junction with the Walden Trail is reached at 4.6 miles; from there, a spur path leads to the right about 50 yards to Passaconaway's summit. Follow the Walden Trail around the summit cone about 100 yards to the best view on this hike, from a ledge overlooking Mount Chocorua to the east and Mount Washington to the north. Continue descending the Walden Trail, dropping steeply to the East Loop, 0.6 mile from the summit spur path. Turn right (west) on the East Loop, which leads 0.2 mile back to the Dicey's Mill Trail. Turn left (south) and follow that trail 3.9 miles back to the Ferncroft Road parking area.

Special note: You can combine Passaconaway and Mount Whiteface on a rugged loop of nearly 12 miles, with more than 4,600 feet of climbing. Hike the Blueberry Ledge Trail up Whiteface, then the Rollins Trail for 2.3 miles over the high ridge connecting the two peaks; there are some views along the Rollins, though much of it is within the subalpine conifer forest. Turn left (north) on the Dicey's Mill Trail, and then complete the Passaconaway hike described above.

**User groups:** Hikers only. No wheelchair facilities. This trail could be difficult to snowshoe because of severe winter weather and is not suitable for bikes, dogs, horses, or skis. Hunting is allowed in season.

**Access, fees:** No backcountry permit is needed, but a permit is required for day use or overnight parking at any White Mountain National Forest trailhead, as indicated by signs posted at most trailheads. Permits are available at several area stores and from the national forest (see address below) at a cost of $5 for seven consecutive days or $20 per year. A $3 one-day permit can be purchased at self-service stations at national forest trailheads, but the pass is good only for the trailhead at which it's purchased. Trails in this part of the national forest are accessed through private land; be

sure to stay on the path. Camping is permitted on the hardened ground at the former site of the Camp Rich shelter, near the junction of the Rollins and Dicey's Mill Trails. See the website of the Wonalancet Out Door Club (below) for current information.

**Maps:** For a map of trails, get the *Crawford Notch-Sandwich Range/Moosilauke-Kinsman* map, $7.95 in waterproof Tyvek, which is available in many stores and from the Appalachian Mountain Club, 800/262-4455, website: www.outdoors.org; the Trail Map and Guide to the Sandwich Range Wilderness, on waterproof Tyvek, for $5 in local stores or from the Wonalancet Out Door Club (see address below); or the *Trail Map and Guide to the White Mountain National Forest* for $7.95 from the DeLorme Publishing Company, 800/642-0970. For topographic area maps, request Mount Chocorua and Mount Tripyramid from USGS Map Sales, Federal Center, Box 25286, Denver, CO 80225, 888/ASK-USGS (888/275-8747), website: http://mapping.usgs.gov.

**Directions:** From Route 113A in Wonalancet, turn north onto Ferncroft Road. Follow it for a half mile and bear right at a sign into the hiker parking lot.

**Contact:** Wonalancet Out Door Club, HCR 64 Box 248, Wonalancet, NH 03897, website: www.wodc.org. White Mountain National Forest Supervisor, 719 North Main St., Laconia, NH 03246, 603/528-8721, TDD for the hearing impaired 603/528-8722, website: www .fs.fed.us/r9/white.

## 79 MOUNT CHOCORUA: BROOK-LIBERTY LOOP

**7.4 mi/5 hrs**

**in the White Mountain National Forest north of Tamworth and east of Wonalancet**

Ⓕ Of the two routes described in this guide up the popular, 3,500-foot Mount Chocorua, this one is far less traveled—and, in my opinion, a better hike. Chocorua is a great place to bring children; I hiked this loop with my nephew Nicholas shortly before he turned seven, and he could not contain his excitement as we scrambled up the final slabs and ledges to the open, rocky summit. The summit attracts dozens of hikers on clear weekend days in summer and fall for good reason: The views north to Mount Washington, west across the White Mountains, south to the lakes region, and east over the hills and lakes of western Maine are among the finest attainable in the Whites without climbing a bigger peak. The foliage views are particularly striking. This hike climbs about 2,600 feet in elevation.

On this loop, hike up the Brook Trail, which is steeper, and descend the Liberty Trail—the easiest route on Chocorua. (Hikers looking for a less demanding route could opt to go up and down the Liberty Trail.) From the parking area, walk past the gate and follow the gravel woods road, which the Brook Trail leaves within a half mile. The trail passes a small waterfall along Claybank Brook less than two miles up and after some easy to moderately difficult hiking, emerges from the woods onto the bare rock of Chocorua's summit cone at three miles. The final 0.6 mile ascends steep slabs and ledges; the Liberty Trail coincides with the Brook Trail for the last 0.2 mile. To descend, follow the two trails down for that 0.2 mile, and then bear left onto the Liberty Trail. It traverses somewhat rocky ground high on the mountain, passing the U.S. Forest Service's Jim Liberty cabin within a half mile. The descent grows more moderate, eventually following an old bridle path back to the parking area, 3.8 miles from the summit.

**User groups:** Hikers and dogs. No wheelchair facilities. This trail should not be attempted in winter except by hikers experienced in mountaineering and prepared for severe winter weather, and is not suitable for bikes, horses, or skis. Hunting is allowed in season.

**Access, fees:** No backcountry permit is needed, but a permit is required for day use or overnight parking at any White Mountain National Forest trailhead, as indicated by signs posted at most trailheads. Permits are available at several area stores and from the national forest (see address below) at a cost of $5 for seven consecutive days or $20 per year. A $3 one-day permit can be purchased at self-service stations at national forest trailheads, but the pass is good only for the trailhead at which it's purchased. The national forest maintains the Jim Liberty cabin (which has a capacity of nine) on the Liberty Trail, a half mile below Chocorua's summit; a fee is charged and the water source is unreliable in dry seasons. Contact the White Mountain National Forest (see address below) for rate and reservation information.

**Maps:** For a map of trails, get the *Crawford Notch-Sandwich Range/Moosilauke-Kinsman* map, $7.95 in waterproof Tyvek, which is available in many stores and from the Appalachian Mountain Club, 800/262-4455, website: www.outdoors.org; or the *Trail Map and Guide to the White Mountain National Forest* for $7.95 from the DeLorme Publishing Company, 800/642-0970. For topographic area maps, request Mount Chocorua and Silver Lake from USGS Map Sales, Federal Center, Box 25286, Denver, CO 80225, 888/ASK-USGS (888/275-8747), website: http://mapping.usgs.gov.

**Directions:** From the junction of Routes 113 and 113A in Tamworth, drive west on Route 113A for 3.4 miles and turn right onto the dirt Fowler's Mill Road. Continue for 1.2 miles and turn left (at trail signs) onto Paugus Road/Fire Road 68. The parking area and trailhead lie 0.8 mile up the road.

**Contact:** White Mountain National Forest Supervisor, 719 North Main St., Laconia, NH 03246, 603/528-8721, TDD for the hearing impaired 603/528-8722, website: www.fs.fed.us/r9/white.

## 80 MOUNT CHOCORUA: PIPER TRAIL

**9 mi/6.5 hrs**

**in the White Mountain National Forest north of Chocorua and west of Conway**

 This is the most heavily used route up the popular, 3,500-foot Mount Chocorua, though at nine miles for the round-trip, it is not the shortest. It ascends some 2,700 feet. The trail suffers from erosion due to overuse, which can make the footing difficult in places.

From the parking area, the trail starts out on easy ground, entering the woods. About two miles out, it crosses the Chocorua River and ascends switchbacks up the steepening mountainside. At 3.1 miles, a short side path leads to the Camp Penacook shelter and tent sites. The final half mile of trail passes over open ledges with sweeping views and on to the summit, where the panoramic views take in Mount Washington to the north, New Hampshire's Lakes Region to the south, the hills and lakes of western Maine to the east, and the grand sweep of the White Mountains to the west and northwest. Descend the same trail.

**User groups:** Hikers and dogs. No wheelchair facilities. This trail should not be attempted in winter except by hikers experienced in mountaineering and prepared for severe winter weather and is not suitable for bikes, horses, or skis. Hunting is allowed in season.

**Access, fees:** No backcountry permit is needed, but a permit is required for day use or overnight parking at any White Mountain National Forest trailhead, as indicated by signs posted at most trailheads. Permits are available at several area stores and from the national forest (see address below) at a cost of $5 for seven consecutive days or $20 per year. A $3 one-day permit can be purchased at self-service stations at national forest trailheads, but the pass is good only for the trailhead at which it's purchased. The national forest maintains Camp Penacook, which consists of a lean-to shelter and four tent platforms, 3.1 miles up the Piper Trail and 1.4 miles below Chocorua's summit; there is no fee.

**Maps:** For a map of trails, get the *Crawford Notch-Sandwich Range/Moosilauke-Kinsman* map, $7.95 in waterproof Tyvek, which is available in many stores and from the Appalachian Mountain Club, 800/262-4455, website: www.outdoors.org; or the *Trail Map and Guide*

*to the White Mountain National Forest* for $7.95 from the DeLorme Publishing Company, 800/642-0970. For topographic area maps, request Mount Chocorua and Silver Lake from USGS Map Sales, Federal Center, Box 25286, Denver, CO 80225, 888/ASK-USGS (888/275-8747), website: http://mapping.usgs.gov.

**Directions:** The Piper Trail begins behind the Piper Trail Restaurant and Cabins on Route 16 between the towns of Chocorua and Conway, six miles south of the junction of Route 16 and Route 112 (the Kancamagus Highway). Follow the dirt road to the right of the store for a quarter mile to the trailhead parking area.

**Contact:** White Mountain National Forest Supervisor, 719 North Main St., Laconia, NH 03246, 603/528-8721, TDD for the hearing impaired 603/528-8722, website: www.fs.fed.us/r9/white.

## 81 MOUNT ISRAEL
**4.2 mi/2.5 hrs**

**in the southern White Mountain National Forest northwest of Center Sandwich**

Just 2,630 feet high, Mount Israel's summit ledges have nice views of the entire Sandwich Range to the north and Mount Moosilauke to the west. This is one of those hikes few people know about, which should be better known considering the relatively easy access to quality views and the ascent of just 1,600 feet. From the parking lot, walk past a sign reading "Israel," left of the main building of Mead Base, to the Wentworth Trail, which is marked by a sign. The trail climbs at a moderate grade for about 1.5 miles to a good overlook south to the Lakes Region. Two miles from the start, you emerge at the summit ledges and a wide view of the Sandwich Range (from left to right): Sandwich Mountain, Tripyramid, Whiteface with a cliff near its summit, Passaconaway immediately behind and to the right of Whiteface, and Chocorua far to the right, barely within sight. From a nearby ledge, you can look west to Moosilauke (see the listings for all of these peaks in this chapter). Descend the way you came.

**User groups:** Hikers, snowshoers, dogs. No wheelchair facilities. This trail is not suitable for bikes, horses, or skis. Hunting is allowed in season.

**Access, fees:** No backcountry permit is needed, but a permit is required for day use or overnight parking at any White Mountain National Forest trailhead, as indicated by signs posted at most trailheads. Permits are available at several area stores and from the national forest (see address below) at a cost of $5 for seven consecutive days or $20 per year. A $3 one-day permit can be purchased at self-service stations at national forest trailheads, but the pass is good only for the trailhead at which it's purchased.

**Maps:** For a map of trails, get the *Crawford Notch-Sandwich Range/Moosilauke-Kinsman* map, $7.95 in waterproof Tyvek, which is available in many stores and from the Appalachian Mountain Club, 800/262-4455, website: www.outdoors.org; or the *Trail Map and Guide to the White Mountain National Forest* for $7.95 from the DeLorme Publishing Company, 800/642-0970. The Squam Lakes Association (see address below)—which maintains 50 miles of trails in the area—also sells a trail map that covers this hike for $6, and an area guidebook and map for $6, plus $1.25 shipping per item (prices may change). For topographic area maps, request Squam Mountains and Center Sandwich from USGS Map Sales, Federal Center, Box 25286, Denver, CO 80225, 888/ASK-USGS (888/275-8747), website: http://mapping.usgs.gov.

**Directions:** From Route 113 in Center Sandwich, turn onto Grove Street at a sign for Sandwich Notch. At 0.4 mile, bear left on Diamond Ledge Road (don't be deceived by the name of the road bearing right—Mount Israel Road). At 2.5 miles from Route 113, bear right at a sign for Mead Base Camp. Follow that road another mile to its end at Mead Base Camp and parking on the right.

**Contact:** White Mountain National Forest Supervisor, 719 North Main St., Laconia, NH

03246, 603/528-8721, TDD for the hearing impaired 603/528-8722, website: www.fs.fed.us/r9/white. Squam Lakes Association, P.O. Box 204, Holderness, NH 03245, 603/968-7336, fax 603/968-7444, email: Info@squamlakes.org, website: www.squamlakes.org.

## 82 STINSON MOUNTAIN
**3.6 mi/2.5 hrs**

**north of Rumney in the White Mountain National Forest**

Tucked away in the very southwestern corner of the White Mountain National Forest is little Stinson Mountain (2,900 feet), a small mountain with a great summit view of the valley of the Baker River, the state college town of Plymouth, and the surrounding hills. It's a nice spot to catch the sunrise or foliage at its peak. This hike ascends 1,400 feet in a 1.8-mile uphill jaunt.

Follow the Stinson Mountain Trail, which begins quite easily, then grows moderately steep but never very difficult. Within a quarter mile, the trail crosses an old logging road, and in a half mile it bears right where an old wooden footbridge leads left on a former trail. Although the trail is generally an easy, wide, and obvious path, be careful not to be fooled into these wrong turns. Within a hundred yards of the summit, or 1.8 miles from the trailhead, the trail forks, with both branches leading to the summit ledges. Trees block the view somewhat to the north, but you can see Mount Moosilauke (see the two Moosilauke hike listings in this chapter). Immediately north of the summit ledges, a side path leads 200 feet to a better view of Stinson Lake and Moosilauke. Return the way you came.

**User groups:** Hikers, snowshoers, and dogs. No wheelchair facilities. This trail is not suitable for bikes, horses, or skis. Hunting is allowed in season.

**Access, fees:** No backcountry permit is needed, but a permit is required for day use or overnight parking at any White Mountain National Forest trailhead, as indicated by signs posted at most trailheads. Permits are available at several area stores and from the national forest (see address below) at a cost of $5 for seven consecutive days or $20 per year. A $3 one-day permit can be purchased at self-service stations at national forest trailheads, but the pass is good only for the trailhead at which it's purchased.

**Maps:** For a map of trails, get the *Crawford Notch-Sandwich Range/Moosilauke-Kinsman* map, $7.95 in waterproof Tyvek, which is available in many stores and from the Appalachian Mountain Club, 800/262-4455, website: www.outdoors.org. For a topographic area map, request Rumney from USGS Map Sales, Federal Center, Box 25286, Denver, CO 80225, 888/ASK-USGS (888/275-8747), website: http://mapping.usgs.gov.

**Directions:** From Route 25 in Rumney Village (3.5 miles north of the traffic circle at Routes 25 and 3A, 2.1 miles north of the Polar Caves Park, 7.7 miles west of I-93 Exit 26, and 4.2 miles south of the junction of Routes 25 and 118), turn at a blinking yellow light onto Main Street. In a mile, the street becomes Stinson Lake Road. At 5.1 miles from Route 25, bear right on Cross Road at a sign for Hawthorne Village. In 0.3 mile, bear right onto a gravel road, then drive another half mile and turn right at a sign for the Stinson Mountain Trail. Drive 0.3 mile farther to parking on the left and a trail sign.

**Contact:** White Mountain National Forest Supervisor, 719 North Main St., Laconia, NH 03246, 603/528-8721, TDD for the hearing impaired 603/528-8722, website: www.fs.fed.us/r9/white.

## Chapter 5

© MICHAEL LANZA

# Central and Southern
# New Hampshire

# Central and Southern New Hampshire

T he White Mountains may be the star attraction for hikers in the Granite State, but New Hampshire has several smaller peaks in the lower part of the state that are no less spectacular, and are easier to climb up and closer to where most people live. I've trekked up Mounts Monadnock and Cardigan more times than I know and never grown tired of them. Peaks like Kearsarge, Sunapee, Major, and Smarts are equally enjoyable, for adults and children. State parks scattered across the central and southern portion of the state offer great local hiking on miles of trails and old woods roads. Two long-distance trails in southern New Hampshire—the 21-mile Wapack Trail and the 50-mile Monadnock-Sunapee Greenway—offer scenic hiking over hills that see far fewer boots than popular corners of the Whites.

This chapter covers everything below the White Mountains, from hills along the Appalachian Trail in the Upper Connecticut Valley and the

Lakes Region to the Seacoast and Massachusetts border. The prime, snow-free hiking season in these places generally goes from April or May through October or November, with the exception of the Seacoast area, where snow is less frequent and the hiking season longer.

This chapter includes hikes along the Appalachian Trail in western New Hampshire (Moose Mountain, Smarts Mountain, and Holt's Ledge). Along the trail, dogs must be kept under control, and horses, bikes, hunting, and firearms are prohibited. Cross-country skiing and snowshoeing are allowed, though the trail is often too rugged for skiing.

In state parks and forests, dogs should remain under control, and many state lands post signs requiring leashes. Hunting is allowed in season in most state parks and forests. Mountain bikes, cross-country skiing, and snowshoeing are allowed on trails unless otherwise posted.

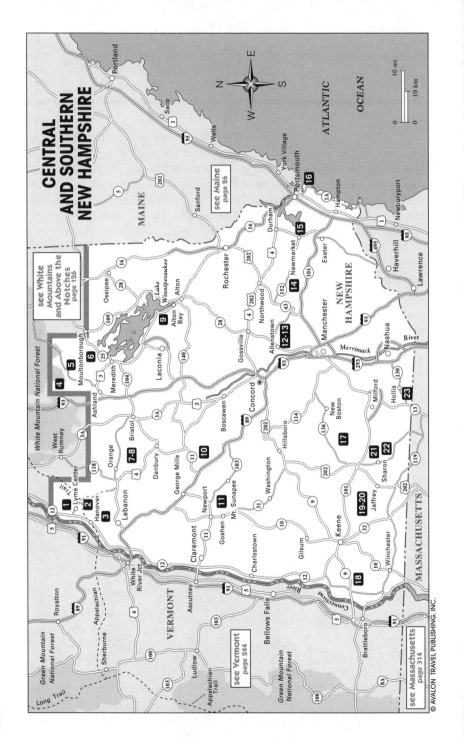

CENTRAL
AND SOUTHERN
NEW HAMPSHIRE

see Maine
page 26

see White
Mountains
and Above the
Notches
page 126

MAINE

ATLANTIC

OCEAN

Portland

Saco

Wells

York Village

Portsmouth

Hampton

Newburyport

Haverhill

Lawrence

NEW
HAMPSHIRE

White Mountain National Forest

West
Rumney

Lyme Center

Hanover

Lebanon

Orange

Bristol

Danbury

George Mills

Newport

Goshen

Claremont

White River Jct.

Ascutney

Bellows Falls

Brattleboro

VERMONT

Green Mountain
National Forest

Royalton

Sherburne

Ludlow

Long Trail

Appalachian
Trail

Appalachian Trail

Green Mountain
National Forest

see Vermont
page 244

see Massachusetts
page 314

MASSACHUSETTS

Ossipee

Moultonborough

Meredith

Ashland

Laconia

Lake
Winnipesaukee

Alton

Alton Bay

Rochester

Durham

Newmarket

Exeter

Northwood

Gossville

Allenstown

Concord

Boscawen

Manchester

Nashua

Merrimack River

Hollis

Milford

New
Boston

Hillsboro

Washington

Mt. Sunapee

Charlestown

Gilsum

Keene

Jaffrey

Sharon

Winchester

Connecticut River

Sanford

West Rumney

Connecticut River

© AVALON TRAVEL PUBLISHING, INC.

# **1** SMARTS MOUNTAIN
**7.5 mi/4.5 hrs**

**in Lyme**

New England's topography and weather sometimes collaborate to make a smaller peak feel like a bigger mountain. At 3,240 feet, Smarts is one of those peaks. This hike, not to be underestimated, blends nice walks in the woods and along the rocky crest of a ridge with a rigorous final push to the summit through the sort of evergreen forest usually found at higher elevations. A fire tower on the wooded summit offers a magnificent panorama of the upper Connecticut Valley, the Green Mountains, and the Whites on a clear day. The elevation gain is about 2,100 feet.

From the parking lot, pick up the Lambert Ridge Trail (signed), which is also the AT. (The unmarked but wide path at the end of the lot is the Ranger Trail, your route of descent.) Within the first 1.5 miles, the pleasant woods walk is enhanced by several views in various directions atop the rocky Lambert Ridge—itself a nice destination for a short hike. The trail then drops slightly, changes direction a few times—watch for white blazes—and then ascends the relentlessly steep west slope of Smarts, passing the unmarked junction (on the right) with the Ranger Trail 3.5 miles from the parking lot. A half mile farther, a side trail leads right to a tent site where the Smarts tent platform formerly stood. Continuing on the AT about 0.1 mile, watch on the left for a spur trail to the fire tower. Backtrack 0.6 mile and bear left to descend the Ranger Trail 3.5 miles to the trailhead. (The final 1.5 miles of the Ranger Trail, which ascends at a gentle angle, could be skied on an approach in winter, up to an abandoned garage where the trail crosses Grant Brook.)

**User groups:** Hikers, snowshoers, and dogs. No wheelchair facilities. This route is not suitable for skis, except for the final 1.5 miles of the Ranger Trail. Bikes, horses, and hunting are prohibited.

**Access, fees:** Parking and access are free. The Smarts tent site is located about four miles up the Lambert Ridge/Appalachian Trail and 0.1 mile below the summit.

**Maps:** A map of the Appalachian Trail between Pomfret, Vermont, and Kinsman Notch, New Hampshire, is available from the Dartmouth Outdoor Programs Office (see address below). This hike is also covered on map 4 in the *Map and Guide to the Appalachian Trail in New Hampshire and Vermont,* an eight-map set and guidebook available for $19.95 ($14.95 for the maps alone) from the Appalachian Trail Conference (see address below). For a topographic map of the area, request Smarts Mountain from USGS Map Sales, Federal Center, Box 25286, Denver, CO 80225, 888/ASK-USGS (888/275-8747), website: http://mapping.usgs.gov.

**Directions:** From Route 10 on the Green in Lyme, take Dorchester Road (at the white church), following signs for the Dartmouth Skiway. Two miles from the Green, you'll pass through the village of Lyme Center. In another 1.3 miles, bear left onto the gravel Lyme-Dorchester Road (across from where the Appalachian Trail emerges from the woods on the right). In another 1.8 miles, just before an iron bridge over Grant Brook, park in a small lot on the left, at the trailhead.

**Contact:** Appalachian Trail Conference, 799 Washington St., P.O. Box 807, Harpers Ferry, WV 25425-0807, 304/535-6331, website: www.appalachiantrail.org. Dartmouth Outdoor Programs Office, 119 Robinson Hall, Dartmouth College, Hanover, NH 03755, 603/646-2834, website: www.dartmouth.edu/~doc.

# **2** HOLT'S LEDGE
**2.2 mi/1.5 hrs**

**in Lyme**

Holt's Ledge, at the top of a tall, rugged cliff, lies at the end of a fairly easy walk through the woods along the Appalachian Trail. From Holt's Ledge you can see Smarts Mountain and Mount Cube (beyond and left of Smarts) to the north, Cardigan and Kearsarge to the east, and Ascutney in the distance to the south. Don't venture beyond the weathered fencing on the

the author's wife on Mount Cardigan's East Side Loop

ledge—the cliff's brink is quite crumbly and peregrine falcons nest below. The ascent gains about 1,000 feet.

From the trailhead, follow the white-blazed AT. At a half mile, it passes a side trail leading 0.2 mile to the Trapper John shelter, where you'll find water and an outhouse. After crossing a stream, the trail climbs a hillside to the cliffs; the AT swings right, and a side trail leads left to the open ledges. Return the same way; or from the ledges, turn left and descend the alpine ski trail.

**User groups:** Hikers, snowshoers, and dogs. No wheelchair facilities. This trail is not suitable for cross-country skis. Bikes, horses, and hunting are prohibited.

**Access, fees:** Parking and access are free. The Trapper John lean-to shelter is located 0.2 mile down a side path off the Appalachian Trail, a half mile south of this hike's start.

**Maps:** A map of the Appalachian Trail between Pomfret, VT, and Kinsman Notch, NH, is available from the Dartmouth Outdoor Programs Office (see address below). This hike is also covered on map 4 in the *Map and Guide to the Appalachian Trail in New Hampshire and Vermont,* an eight-map set and guidebook available for $19.95 ($14.95 for the maps alone) from the Appalachian Trail Conference (see address below). For a topographic map of the area, request Smarts Mountain from USGS Map Sales, Federal Center, Box 25286, Denver, CO 80225, 888/ASK-USGS (888/275-8747), website: http://mapping.usgs.gov.

**Directions:** From Route 10 on the Green in Lyme, take Dorchester Road (at the white church), following signs for the Dartmouth Skiway. Two miles from the Green, you pass through the village of Lyme Center. In another 1.3 miles, across from the gravel Lyme-Dorchester Road, the Appalachian Trail emerges from the woods on the right. Park either at the roadside or a short distance farther in the dirt lot for the Dartmouth Skiway.

**Contact:** Appalachian Trail Conference, 799 Washington St., P.O. Box 807, Harpers Ferry, WV 25425-0807, 304/535-6331, website: www.appalachiantrail.org. Dartmouth Outdoor Programs Office, 119 Robinson Hall, Dartmouth College, Hanover, NH 03755, 603/646-2834, website: www.dartmouth.edu/~doc.

## 3 MOOSE MOUNTAIN
**4.1 mi/3 hrs**
**in Hanover**

This loop, incorporating a stretch of the Appalachian Trail, passes over the south summit of Moose Mountain (2,290 feet), where a plane crashed in 1968. The ensuing rescue effort included a bulldozer clearing a route to the summit. The result is a lasting view east and southeast, taking in Goose Pond (in the foreground) and Clark Pond (in the distance) in the town of Canaan, and Mounts Cardigan and Kearsarge even farther in the distance. The hike climbs almost 1,000 feet.

From the parking area, cross the road to the east, following the white-blazed AT northbound. The trail crosses a brook, then the wide, two-track Harris Trail at 0.4 mile. It then begins the ascent of Moose Mountain, climbing at a moderate angle at first, leveling somewhat, then climbing again to the south summit at 1.8 miles. Continue north across the clearing, following the white blazes another half mile to a junction with the Clark Pond Loop. To the right, the Clark Pond Loop leads 0.2 mile to the Moose Mountain shelter. For this hike, turn left (west) onto the Clark Loop and descend 0.7 mile. Follow the gravel road to the left for about 50 feet, turn left (south) onto the Harris Trail, and follow it 0.7 mile to the AT. Turn right and walk the AT 0.4 mile back to Three Mile Road.

**User groups:** Hikers, snowshoers, and dogs. No wheelchair facilities. This trail is not suitable for skis. Bikes, horses, and hunting are prohibited.

**Access, fees:** Parking and access are free. The Moose Mountain shelter is located 0.2 mile off this loop, 2.3 miles into the hike.

**Maps:** This hike is covered on map 4 in the *Map and Guide to the Appalachian Trail in New Hampshire and Vermont,* an eight-map set and guidebook available for $19.95 ($14.95 for the maps alone) from the Appalachian Trail Conference (see address below). A map of the Appalachian Trail between Pomfret, VT, and Kinsman Notch, NH, is available from the Dartmouth Outing Club (see address below). For topographic area maps, request Hanover and Canaan from USGS Map Sales, Federal Center, Box 25286, Denver, CO 80225, 888/ASK-USGS (888/275-8747), website: http://mapping.usgs.gov.

**Directions:** From I-91, take Exit 13 in Norwich, VT. Head east, crossing the Connecticut River and driving up a long hill to the center of Hanover. Drive straight through the traffic lights (the Dartmouth College Green is to your left) onto East Wheelock Street and follow it 4.3 miles into the Hanover village of Etna. Turn left onto Etna Road, proceed 0.8 mile, and then turn right onto Ruddsboro Road. Continue 1.5 miles and then turn left onto Three Mile Road. Drive another 1.3 miles to a turnout on the left, where the white-blazed Appalachian Trail crosses the road.

**Contact:** Appalachian Trail Conference, 799 Washington St., P.O. Box 807, Harpers Ferry, WV 25425-0807, 304/535-6331, website: www.appalachiantrail.org. Outdoor Programs Office, 119 Robinson Hall, Dartmouth College, Hanover, NH 03755, 603/646-2834, website: www.dartmouth.edu/~doc.

## 4 SQUAM MOUNTAINS
**5.1 mi/3 hrs**
**between Holderness and Center Sandwich**

This very popular hike leads to views of Squam Lake and massive Lake Winnipesaukee from the low peaks of the Squam Mountains range. A friend and I made this loop on a sunny Saturday, the first weekend of October, when the fall foliage was at its peak. This is a fairly easy hike with only one short, difficult section—the cliffs on the Mount Morgan Trail—which can be avoided. The vertical ascent is about 1,400 feet.

From the parking lot, walk around the gate onto the Mount Morgan Trail. It ascends gently for more than a mile, then steepens somewhat. At 1.7 miles, the Crawford-Ridgepole Trail enters from the left and coincides with the Mount Morgan Trail for 0.2 mile. Where they split again, the Crawford-Ridgepole bears right for an easier route up Mount Morgan. This hike turns left with the Mount Morgan Trail, immediately scaling low cliffs on a wooden ladder, after which you crawl through a cavelike passage through rocks and emerge atop the cliffs with an excellent view of the big lakes to the south. Follow the blazes up the slabs to Morgan's open summit and extensive views south. Pick up the Crawford-Ridgepole Trail eastward along the Squam Mountains Ridge—with occasional views, including the distinctive horned summit of Mount Chocorua (see the White Mountains and Above the Notches chapter)—another 0.8 mile to the open summit of Mount Percival, which also has excellent views of the lakes. There are two options for descending off the summit of Percival. You can turn right and descend the Mount Percival Trail to the southeast (look for a small trail sign nailed to a tree at the base of the summit slabs). Or descend to the southwest on a path that passes through another boulder cave and rejoins the Mount Percival Trail in 0.1 mile. After a relatively easy descent of 1.9 miles to Route 113, turn right and walk the road for 0.3 mile back to the parking area.

Special note: Some hikers will find that hiking this loop in the opposite direction—and going up the steep section just below the summit of Mount Percival, rather than down it—will be easier on the knees.

**User groups:** Hikers, snowshoers, and dogs. No wheelchair facilities. This trail is not suitable for bikes, horses, or skis. Hunting is allowed in season.

**Access, fees:** Parking and access are free.

**Maps:** The Squam Lakes Association, which maintains 50 miles of trails in the area, sells a trail map that covers this hike for $6. Or get the *Crawford Notch-Sandwich Range/Moosilauke-Kinsman* map, $7.95 in waterproof Tyvek, which is available in many stores and from the Appalachian Mountain Club, 800/262-4455, website: www.outdoors.org. For a topographic area map, request Squam Mountains from USGS Map Sales, Federal Center, Box 25286, Denver, CO 80225, 888/ASK-USGS (888/275-8747), website: http://mapping.usgs.gov.

**Directions:** The trailhead parking lot is on Route 113, about 5.5 miles east of the junction of U.S. 3 and Route 113, and 6.3 miles west of the junction of Routes 109 and 113.

**Contact:** Squam Lakes Association, P.O. Box 204, Holderness, NH 03245, 603/968-7336, website: www.squamlakes.org.

## 5 WEST RATTLESNAKE
## 1.8 mi/1 hr

**between Holderness and Center Sandwich**

This easy hike, a good one for young children, follows a wide trail that rises gently for 0.9 mile to cliff-top views from several hundred feet above Squam Lake. From the parking area for the Mount Morgan Trail, cross Route 113 and walk west about 100 feet to the Old Bridle Path. Continue on the Old Bridle Path for 0.9 mile; where the main trail turns left, follow a side path to the right about 100 feet to the cliffs. At the summit, you may notice rock barriers surrounding Douglas' Knotweed, a threatened plant; avoid walking on the vegetation. Return the way you came.

**User groups:** Hikers, snowshoers, and dogs. No wheelchair facilities. This trail is not suitable for bikes, horses, or skis. Hunting is allowed in season.

**Access, fees:** Parking and access are free.

**Maps:** The Squam Lakes Association (see address below) sells a trail map that covers this hike for $6. Or get the *Crawford Notch-Sandwich Range/Moosilauke-Kinsman* map, $7.95 in waterproof Tyvek, which is available in many stores and from the Appalachian Mountain Club, 800/262-4455, website: www.outdoors.org. For a topographic area map, request Squam Mountains from USGS Map Sales, Federal Center, Box 25286, Denver, CO 80225, 888/ASK-USGS (888/275-8747), website: http://mapping.usgs.gov.

**Directions:** The trailhead parking lot is on Route 113, 5.6 miles east of the junction of U.S. 3 and Route 113, and 6.3 miles west of the junction of Routes 109 and 113.

**Contact:** Squam Lakes Association, P.O. Box 204, Holderness, NH 03245, 603/968-7336, website: www.squamlakes.org.

## 6 EAGLE CLIFF
**1.2 mi/0.75 hr**
**north of Center Harbor**

A few steps off the road and along the un-marked trail, you pass a small sign reading Eagle Cliff Trail. Rising moderately for much of its 0.6-mile climb, the trail grows steep for the final 0.2 mile (and should be avoided in icy conditions). Near the top, turn left to reach open ledges with a dramatic view from high above Squam Lake. Across the water rises the low ridge of the Squam Mountains. To the north lie the southern White Mountains; the most readily identifiable is the horn of Mount Chocorua to the northeast. Hike back along the same route, or descend the Teedie Trail from Eagle Cliff. The Teedie Trail is a much less steep ascent or descent, so it's the rec-ommended route if the ground is wet; or if you want to do a loop hike in dry conditions, the Teedie is a preferable descent route so hike up the Eagle Cliff Trail. The Teedie Trail will bring you back to Bean Road, next to a private ten-nis court at the Sandwich-Moltonborough town line, 0.4 mile from where you parked.

**User groups:** Hikers, snowshoers, and dogs. No wheelchair facilities. This trail is not suit-able for bikes, horses, or skis. Hunting is al-lowed in season.

**Access, fees:** Parking and access are free.

**Maps:** The Squam Lakes Association (see ad-dress below) sells a trail map that covers this hike for $6. Or get the *Crawford Notch-Sand-wich Range/Moosilauke-Kinsman* map, $7.95 in waterproof Tyvek, which is available in many stores and from the Appalachian Mountain Club, 800/262-4455, website: www.outdoors.org. For a topographic area map, request Squam Mountains from USGS Map Sales, Federal Center, Box 25286, Denver, CO 80225, 888/ASK-USGS (888/275-8747), website: http://mapping.usgs.gov.

**Directions:** In Center Harbor, immediately east of the junction of Routes 25 and 25B, turn north off Route 25 onto Bean Road. Follow it five miles. At 0.4 mile beyond the Sandwich-

Moltonborough town line—where the road be-comes Squam Lakes Road—look for roadside parking. The trail is marked by a small sign downhill from the road and not visible until you start down the path. The trail enters the woods across the road from a "Traffic turning and entering" sign (for southbound traffic).

**Contact:** Squam Lakes Association, P.O. Box 204, Holderness, NH 03245, 603/968-7336, website: www.squamlakes.org.

## 7 MOUNT CARDIGAN: WEST SIDE LOOP
**3.5 mi/2 hrs**
**in Cardigan State Park east of Canaan**

This loop, much easier than the Mount Cardigan East Side Loop, is probably the most popular route up this locally popu-lar mountain. See the trail notes for the next hike for more description about Mount Cardi-gan. While living nearby for four years, I en-joyed trail running this loop many times. The vertical ascent from this trailhead to the 3,121-foot summit is about 1,200 feet.

From the parking area, the orange blazes of the West Ridge Trail lead immediately up-hill, climbing steadily on a wide, well-main-tained, if sometimes rocky footpath. At a half mile, the South Ridge Trail enters from the right; you will eventually descend on this trail. Stay to the left on the West Ridge Trail, cross-ing a small brook on a wooden footbridge and passing a junction with the Skyland Trail. More than a mile from the trailhead, the West Ridge Trail emerges onto the nearly barren upper cone of Mount Cardigan, climbing steep slabs to the summit at 1.5 miles, where there is a fire tower. Turn around and descend about 100 feet on the West Ridge Trail, then turn left and follow the white blazes of the Clark Trail, which is marked by a sign. It descends the rock slabs generally southward, but watch carefully for the blazes, because it's easy to lose this trail above tree line. The trail be-comes briefly quite steep on slabs that can be a bit hazardous when wet, reaching the tiny warden's cabin 0.2 mile past Cardigan's summit. Turn right and follow the orange blazes of the South Ridge Trail past the cabin, moving in and out of low trees for 0.3 mile to South Peak, with good views to the south and west of the hills of central/western New Hampshire. The South Ridge Trail enters the forest and continues descending, very steeply in spots, for another mile to the West Ridge Trail. Turn left and descend another half mile to the parking lot.

**User groups:** Hikers and dogs. Dogs must be leashed. No wheelchair facilities. Snowshoeing is possible at lower elevations but may be difficult above tree line due to ice and harsh weather. This trail is not suitable for bikes, horses, or skis. Hunting is allowed in season unless otherwise posted.

**Access, fees:** Parking and access are free. The access road is maintained in winter only to a parking area about 0.6 mile before the summer parking lot.

**Maps:** A free, basic map of trails is available at the trailhead parking lot. Or get the *Monadnock/Cardigan* map, $7.95 in waterproof Tyvek, from the Appalachian Mountain Club, 800/262-4455, website: www.outdoors.org. For topographic area maps, request Mount Cardigan from USGS Map Sales, Federal Center, Box 25286, Denver, CO 80225, 888/ASK-USGS (888/275-8747), website: http://mapping.usgs.gov.

**Directions:** From the junction of Routes 4 and 118 in Canaan, drive north on 118 for 0.6 mile and then turn right at a sign for Cardigan State Park. Follow that road for 4.1 miles to a large dirt parking lot. The trail begins beside the parking lot.

**Contact:** New Hampshire Division of Parks and Recreation, P.O. Box 1856, Concord, NH 03302-1856, 603/271-3254. Trails on Mount Cardigan are maintained by the Cardigan Highlanders, P.O. Box 104, Enfield Center, NH 03749, 603/632-5640.

## 8 MOUNT CARDIGAN: EAST SIDE LOOP

**5.2 mi/3.5 hrs**

**in Cardigan State Park west of Alexandria**

Left bare by a fire in 1855, the 3,121-foot crown of Mount Cardigan affords long views in a 360-degree panorama of the Green and White Mountains, and prominent hills to the south such as Mounts Ascutney and Sunapee. It's a popular hike: Hundreds of people, many of them children, will climb Cardigan on sunny weekends during the warm months. This steep hike up the east side of Cardigan provided quite a big-mountain adventure for my two nephews and niece, ages six to nine at the time of our climb on a sunny, blustery September Saturday. As we scaled the mountain's upper slabs to the summit, they called out comments like, "Wow, this is steep!" and "Wow, look how high we are!" The upper portion of the trail does grow quite steep, involving exposed scrambling on open slabs that become dangerous when wet or icy—and on which I watched the kids closely even though the rock was dry. The vertical ascent on this loop hike is about 1,800 feet.

From the parking area, the Holt Trail at first follows a wide, nearly flat woods road for almost a mile. At 1.1 miles, the trail crosses Bailey Brook, then follows the brook (other trails branch left and right from the Holt). Growing steeper, the trail leaves the brook and ascends very steep, exposed rock slabs for the final 0.3 mile to the open summit, 2.2 miles from the parking area. Turn right (north) onto the Mowglis Trail and follow it off the summit, dropping sharply into the saddle between the main summit and Firescrew Mountain, a shoulder of Cardigan. The Mowglis Trail then climbs to the open top of Firescrew, with more long views, 0.6 mile from Cardigan's summit. Turn right (east) and follow the Manning Trail, descending steadily with good views for about 0.2 mile, then reentering the woods and reaching the Holt Trail nearly three miles from Cardigan's summit. Turn left and walk back to the parking lot.

**User groups:** Hikers and dogs. Dogs must be leashed. No wheelchair facilities. This trail may be difficult to snowshoe, in part because of severe winter weather, and is not suitable for bikes, horses, or skis. Hunting is allowed in season unless otherwise posted.

**Access, fees:** Parking and access are free. The access road is maintained in winter.

**Maps:** Get the *Monadnock/Cardigan* map, $7.95 in waterproof Tyvek, from the Appalachian Mountain Club, 800/262-4455, website: www.outdoors.org. For topographic area maps, request Mount Cardigan and Newfound Lake from USGS Map Sales, Federal Center, Box 25286, Denver, CO 80225, 888/ASK-USGS (888/275-8747), website: http://mapping.usgs.gov.

**Directions:** From the junction of Routes 3A and 104 in Bristol, drive north on Route 3A for 2.1 miles and turn left onto West Shore Road at a stone church at the south end of Newfound Lake. Continue 1.9 miles and proceed straight through a crossroads. Reaching a fork in 1.2 miles, bear right onto Fowler River Road, and then turn left 3.2 miles farther onto Brook Road. Continue another 1.1 miles and turn right onto the dirt Shem Valley Road; just 0.1 mile farther, bear right at a red schoolhouse. Drive 1.4 miles to the end of that road, where parking is available near the Appalachian Mountain Club's Cardigan Lodge. (At intersections along these roads, there are signs indicating the direction to the Cardigan Lodge.)

**Contact:** New Hampshire Division of Parks and Recreation, P.O. Box 1856, Concord, NH 03302-1856, 603/271-3254. Trails on Mount Cardigan are maintained by the Cardigan Highlanders, P.O. Box 104, Enfield Center, NH 03749, 603/632-5640.

## ⑨ MOUNT MAJOR
**3 mi/1.5 hrs**

**between West Alton and Alton Bay**
Perhaps the most popular hike in the lakes region, especially among families with young children, Mount Major has a bare summit that affords breathtaking views of Lake Win-

nipesaukee and north to the White Mountains on a clear day. From the parking lot, follow the wide, stone-littered trail climbing 1.5 miles and 1,100 feet to Major's summit. Descend the same way.

**User groups:** Hikers, snowshoers, and dogs. Dogs must be leashed. No wheelchair facilities. This trail is not suitable for bikes, horses, or skis. Hunting is allowed in season.

**Access, fees:** Parking and access are free. The state owns the summit area and maintains the parking lot, but the trail crosses private property.

**Maps:** For a topographic area map, request Squam Mountains from USGS Map Sales, Federal Center, Box 25286, Denver, CO 80225, 888/ASK-USGS (888/275-8747), website: http://mapping.usgs.gov.

**Directions:** The Mount Major Trail begins from a large parking area on Route 11, 2.4 miles south of the intersection of Routes 11 and 11A in West Alton, and 4.2 miles north of the junction of Routes 11 and 28A in Alton Bay.

**Contact:** New Hampshire Division of Parks and Recreation, P.O. Box 1856, 172 Pembroke Rd., Concord, NH 03302, 603/271-3556, camping reservations 603/271-3628, website: www.nhstateparks.org.

## ⑩ MOUNT KEARSARGE
**2.8 mi/2 hrs**

**in Winslow State Park in Wilmot**
The barren, 2,937-foot summit of Mount Kearsarge, offering views of the White Mountains, Green Mountains, and southern New Hampshire, makes this one of the finest short hikes in New England—and while steep, a great adventure for children. Previous editions of this book described the hike ascending and descending the Winslow Trail. But the state park has since opened a new trail, the Barlow Trail, which offers a less-steep descent route that's easier on the knees than the Winslow Trail. This hike climbs about 1,100 feet in elevation.

Walk to the upper end of the parking lot in Winslow State Park and pick up the red-blazed

Winslow Trail. The wide, well-beaten path rises quite steeply and relentlessly, and grows even more rugged the higher you go. At 0.8 mile, a large boulder on the left gives a good view north. A short distance farther, you break out of the trees onto the bald summit, with views in every direction, including Mount Sunapee and Lake Sunapee to the southwest, Mount Cardigan to the northwest, the Green Mountains to the west, and the White Mountains to the north. This is also a wonderful hike during the height of the fall foliage colors. A fire tower stands at the summit, and nearby are a pair of picnic tables—although on windy days it can be hard to linger up here for very long. Hike back along the same route.

Special note: In October 1997, the state allowed the construction of a 180-foot communications tower on the summit, something that offended many locals and prompted an effort to have the tower dismantled. Unfortunately, a Merrimack County Superior Court judge ruled in May 2000 that the tower does not violate any deed restriction for the property, as had been claimed by the land's previous owner, the Society for the Protection of New Hampshire Forests.

**User groups:** Hikers and dogs. Dogs must be leashed. No wheelchair facilities. This trail may be difficult to snowshoe, in part because of severe winter weather, and is not suitable for bikes, horses, or skis. Hunting is allowed in season.

**Access, fees:** Winslow State Park is open from 9 A.M.–8 P.M. from May 1–mid-November. There is a $3-per-person park entrance fee levied daily during the open season; children under 12 and New Hampshire residents 65 and older enter free. The last 0.6 mile of the entrance road is not maintained in winter (beyond the fork at the dead end sign).

**Maps:** A basic trail map of Winslow State Park is available at the park or from the New Hampshire Division of Parks and Recreation (see address below). For topographic area maps, request New London, Andover, Brad-

ford, and Warner from USGS Map Sales, Federal Center, Box 25286, Denver, CO 80225, 888/ASK-USGS (888/275-8747), website: http://mapping.usgs.gov.

**Directions:** Take I-89 to Exit 10 and follow the signs to Winslow State Park. From the tollbooth at the state park entrance, drive to the dirt parking lot at the end of the road.

**Contact:** Winslow State Park, P.O. Box 295, Newbury, NH 03255, 603/526-6168. New Hampshire Division of Parks and Recreation, P.O. Box 1856, 172 Pembroke Rd., Concord, NH 03302, 603/271-3556, camping reservations 603/271-3628, website: www.nhstateparks.org.

## 11 MOUNT SUNAPEE
**4 mi/2.5 hrs**
**in Mount Sunapee State Park in Newbury**
The Summit Trail up central New Hampshire's popular Mount Sunapee offers a fairly easy, four-mile round-trip route from the ski area parking lot to the 2,743-foot summit. Many hikers will be satisfied with that. But this description also covers the Monadnock-Sunapee Greenway Trail from Sunapee's summit to Lucia's Lookout on Sunapee's long southern ridge—an ambitious round-trip from the parking lot at 12.8 miles and about seven hours, but well worth the effort for the views along the ridge, particularly overlooking Lake Solitude. I walked this trail with an organizer of the Monadnock-Sunapee Greenway Trail Club one September afternoon, and we spotted several moose tracks. The climb to Sunapee's summit is about 1,300 feet.

From the parking lot, walk behind the North Peak Lodge about 100 feet to where two ski trails merge, and look to the right for a sign for the Summit Trail, marked by red blazes. Ascending easily but steadily through the woods for two miles, the trail emerges onto an open meadow, where to the right (south) you get a view toward Mount Monadnock. Turn left and walk to the summit lodge a short distance ahead. Some of the best views on the mountain are from the decks at the lodge, with

Mount Ascutney and the Green Mountains visible to the west, and Mounts Cardigan and Moosilauke and Franconia Ridge to the north. To complete this four-mile hike, return the way you came. To lengthen it with a walk along the somewhat rugged Sunapee Ridge, from where the trail emerges from the woods at the summit, trend right along the edge of the woods, behind the ski lift, then turn left and drop downhill a short distance, and turn right, looking for a sign and white blazes marking where the Monadnock-Sunapee Trail (which is also the trail to Lake Solitude) enters the woods off the ski trail.

After reentering the woods 0.2 mile from the summit, the greenway reaches the open White Ledges 0.9 mile from the summit; the trail swings left, but walking to the right will lead you to an open ledge with an excellent view of beautiful Lake Solitude, a small tarn tucked into the mountain's shoulder. Mount Monadnock is visible beyond the lake. Continuing south (left) on the greenway, you skirt the lake's shore within 0.2 mile. The trail passes over an open ledge 2.7 miles from the Sunapee summit before reaching Lucia's Lookout, 4.2 miles from the summit. Here, the views take in Mount Monadnock and Lovewell Mountain to the south, the Green Mountains to the west, and Mount Kearsarge and the White Mountains to the north. Hike back the way you came.

Special note: Future expansion at the Mount Sunapee ski area could affect access to the Summit Trail. Check with Mount Sunapee State Park or the New Hampshire Division of Parks and Recreation (see addresses below).

**User groups:** Hikers, snowshoers, and dogs. Dogs must be leashed. No wheelchair facilities. This trail is not suitable for bikes, horses, or skis. Hunting is allowed in season unless otherwise posted.

**Access, fees:** Parking and access are free.

**Maps:** A free map of trails is available at the state park or from the New Hampshire Division of Parks and Recreation (see address

below). A tear-proof, waterproof map of the entire Monadnock-Sunapee Greenway, a trail stretching 50 miles from Mount Monadnock to Mount Sunapee, costs $6, and The Greenway Trail Guide, which includes the map, costs $14; both can be purchased from the Monadnock-Sunapee Greenway Trail Club (MSGTC) or from area stores listed at the MSGTC website (see contact information below). For a topographic area map, request Newport from USGS Map Sales, Federal Center, Box 25286, Denver, CO 80225, 888/ASK-USGS (888/275-8747), website: http://mapping.usgs.gov.

**Directions:** From I-89 southbound, take Exit 12A. Turn right, drive about 0.6 mile, and turn right onto Route 11 west. Continue 3.5 miles and turn left onto Route 103B. (Or from I-89 northbound, take Exit 12, turn left, and follow Route 11 until turning left onto Route 103B.) Drive another 3.5 miles on Route 103B, go halfway around a traffic circle, and bear right at a sign for the state park. Continue to the end of the road and a large parking area at the base of the ski area.

**Contact:** Mount Sunapee State Park, P.O. Box 2021, Mount Sunapee, NH 03255, 603/763-3149. New Hampshire Division of Parks and Recreation, P.O. Box 1856, 172 Pembroke Rd., Concord, NH 03302, 603/271-3556, camping reservations 603/271-3628, website: www.nhstateparks.org. Monadnock-Sunapee Greenway Trail Club (MSGTC), P.O. Box 164, Marlow, NH 03456, website: www.msgtc.org.

## 12 CATAMOUNT HILL
**2.2 mi/1.5 hrs**

**in Bear Brook State Park in Allenstown**
This 2.2-mile hike ascends a few hundred feet to one of the park's highest points, 721-foot Catamount Hill, where a mostly wooded ridge offers limited views of the state park's rambling forest. From the parking lot, cross Deerfield Road and follow it briefly back toward Route 28. About 100 feet past the tollbooth, a trail marked One Mile Road enters the woods. Follow it for 0.2 mile, bearing left

where another dirt road enters from the right. In 0.1 mile from that junction, turn right onto the Catamount Hill Trail, which is marked by a sign. The trail climbs steadily, reaching the first lookout about 0.6 mile past the dirt road, just below the summit. Continue another 0.2 mile to the summit ridge, where another view is partially obscured by low trees. Return the way you came. At the bottom of the Catamount Hill Trail, turn left on One Mile Road; do not take the first trail on the right, which leads to a footbridge over Bear Brook. At the second junction, bear right to return to the tollbooth area.

**User groups:** Hikers, snowshoers, and dogs. No wheelchair facilities. This trail is not suitable for bikes, horses, or skis. Hunting is allowed in season.

**Access, fees:** An entrance fee of $3 per person is collected at the state park entrance. Children under 12 and New Hampshire residents 65 and older enter state parks free.

**Maps:** A free trail map is available at the park entrance and several other points within the park. For topographic area maps, request Suncook and Gossville from USGS Map Sales, Federal Center, Box 25286, Denver, CO 80225, 888/ASK-USGS (888/275-8747), website: http://mapping.usgs.gov.

**Directions:** The entrance to Bear Brook State Park is on Deerfield Road, off Route 28 in Allenstown, three miles north of the junction of Route 28 and U.S. 3. Turn left into a parking lot just past the entrance tollbooth on Deerfield Road.

**Contact:** Bear Brook State Park, 157 Deerfield Rd., Allenstown, NH 03275, 603/485-9874. New Hampshire Division of Parks and Recreation, P.O. Box 1856, 172 Pembroke Rd., Concord, NH 03302, 603/271-3556, camping reservations 603/271-3628, website: www.nhstateparks.org.

## 13 BEAR BROOK STATE PARK BIKE RACE LOOP

**12 mi/6 hrs**

**in Bear Brook State Park in Allenstown**

Bear Brook—the largest developed state park in New Hampshire—comprises nearly 10,000 acres and 40 miles of trails. The mostly moderate terrain makes for excellent mountain biking and cross-country skiing, and the difficulty ranges from relatively easy gravel roads to technically demanding single-track trails.

This loop—originally mapped out for a mountain bike race the park hosted, but also excellent for skiing—provides a good introduction to Bear Brook's varied offerings. Trails and roads are generally well marked with signs at intersections. Biking the somewhat hilly 12-mile trail takes about three hours.

From the parking lot, head across Podunk Road onto the narrow, winding Pitch Pine Trail. In a little more than a mile, the trail crosses the paved Campground Road. About a quarter mile farther, merge straight onto the Broken Boulder Trail (entering from the right). It passes a side path to a shelter at Smith Pond, then crosses the gravel Spruce Pond Road a half mile past Smith Pond. Continue nearly another mile on the Broken Boulder Trail, then take a sharp right and run straight onto Podunk Road, which is gravel here. Follow the gravel road about a mile, turn right onto the gravel Spruce Road, and then take an immediate left onto the Chipmunk Trail.

The Chipmunk Trail winds through the woods for nearly a mile, then you'll bear left onto the Bobcat Trail. Cross Podunk Road (gravel) and Hayes Field; bear left at a fork onto the Carr Ridge Trail. Cross two trails within a half mile, then bear right about a mile beyond the second trail, crossing onto the Cascade Trail. Reaching a junction in less than a quarter mile, turn right on the Lane Trail, following it over rough ground along Bear Brook. It eventually turns away from the brook and a mile farther reaches a junction with the Hayes Farm Trail; turn left, then left again within a half mile (before reaching the gravel Podunk Road) on the Little Bear Trail, which leads a mile back to the parking lot.

**User groups:** Hikers, bikers, dogs, horses, skiers, and snowshoers. No wheelchair facilities. Hunting is allowed in season.

**Access, fees:** An entrance fee of $3 per person is collected at the state park entrance. Children under 12 and New Hampshire residents 65 and older enter state parks free.

**Maps:** A free trail map is available in a box in the parking lot at the start of this hike and at other points in the park. For topographic area maps, request Suncook and Gossville from USGS Map Sales, Federal Center, Box 25286, Denver, CO 80225, 888/ASK-USGS (888/275-8747), website: http://mapping.usgs.gov.

**Directions:** The entrance to Bear Brook State Park is on Deerfield Road, off Route 28 in Allenstown, three miles north of the junction of Route 28 and U.S. 3. From the entrance tollbooth on Deerfield Road, drive another 2.2 miles and turn right on Podunk Road (at signs for the Public Camping Area). Continue another 0.3 mile and turn right into a parking lot for hikers and mountain bikers.

**Contact:** Bear Brook State Park, 157 Deerfield Rd., Allenstown, NH 03275, 603/485-9874. New Hampshire Division of Parks and Recreation, P.O. Box 1856, 172 Pembroke Rd., Concord, NH 03302, 603/271-3556, camping reservations 603/271-3628, website: www.nhstateparks.org.

## 14 PAWTUCKAWAY STATE PARK
### 7 mi/3.5 hrs
**in Raymond**

Pawtuckaway is far and away the most diverse natural area in southeastern New Hampshire. Many of its trails are ideal for hiking, mountain biking, or cross-country skiing, and you might be surprised by the extensive views from the ledges and fire tower atop South Mountain, though it rises less than 1,000 feet above sea level. Besides this hike, there are numerous trails to explore—try stretching this hike

into a 12-mile loop by combining Tower Road with the Shaw and Fundy Trails.

From the parking lot, follow the paved road around to the right for about a quarter mile. After passing a pond on your left, turn left at a sign onto the Mountain Trail. Where it forks, stay right. Almost three miles from the pond, you will reach junction 5 (marked by a sign); turn right and ascend the trail to the summit of South Mountain. (This trail is passable on bikes or skis until the steep final stretch.) Check out the views from the ledges to the left and right of the trail just below the summit; the east-facing trails to the right will be warmer on a sunny day when the breeze is cool.

**User groups:** Hikers, bikers, skiers, and snowshoers. No wheelchair facilities. Trails are closed to bikes during mud season, usually for the month of April. Dogs and horses are prohibited. Hunting is allowed in season.

**Access, fees:** The parking lot opens at 10 A.M. Monday–Thursday and at 9 A.M. Friday–Sunday. A daily $3 entrance fee is charged to people age 12 and older at the park entrance from mid-June–Labor Day, except for New Hampshire residents 65 and older, who enter free. There is no fee the rest of the year.

**Maps:** A noncontour map of park trails is available at the park's main entrance. For a topographic area map, request Mount Pawtuckaway from USGS Map Sales, Federal Center, Box 25286, Denver, CO 80225, 888/ASK-USGS (888/275-8747), website: http://mapping.usgs.gov.

**Directions:** From Route 101, take Exit 5 for Raymond (there is a sign for Pawtuckaway). Follow Route 156 north and turn left onto Mountain Road at the sign for Pawtuckaway State Park. Follow the road two miles to the state park entrance and a parking lot on the left.

**Contact:** Pawtuckaway State Park, 128 Mountain Rd., Nottingham, NH 03290, 603/895-3031. New Hampshire Division of Parks and Recreation, P.O. Box 1856, 172 Pembroke Rd., Concord, NH 03302, 603/271-3556, camping reservations 603/271-3628, website: www.nhstateparks.org.

## 15 GREAT BAY NATIONAL ESTUARINE RESEARCH RESERVE: SANDY POINT TRAIL

**1 mi/0.75 hr**

**in Stratham**

The Great Bay National Estuarine Research Reserve comprises a 4,500-acre tidal estuary and 800 acres of coastal land that provide a refuge for 23 species of endangered or threatened plant and animal species. Bald eagles winter here, osprey nest, and cormorants and great blue herons, among other birds, can be seen. Ecosystems range from salt marshes to upland forests and mud flats to tidal creeks, and three rivers empty into the bay. Great Bay also consistently has some of the finest sunsets I've ever seen. The Sandy Point Trail is one of two self-guided interpretive trails in the reserve; Adams Point in Durham, across the bay, also has an eagle-viewing platform. This trail largely follows a boardwalk for easy walking.

**User groups:** Hikers only. The boardwalk is wheelchair accessible. This trail is not suitable for bikes, dogs, horses, skis, or snowshoes. Hunting is prohibited.

**Access, fees:** Parking and access are free. Sandy Point Discovery Center is open to the public Wednesday–Sunday, 10 A.M.–4 P.M., May 1–September 30, and on weekends in October. The grounds are open daylight hours throughout the year.

**Maps:** An interpretive trail pamphlet available at the Sandy Point Discovery Center guides visitors along a boardwalk at the estuary's edge and offers information about natural history and the local environment. The pamphlet and other information can also be obtained through the Great Bay Reserve Manager (see address below). For topographic area maps, request Newmarket and Portsmouth from USGS Map Sales, Federal Center, Box 25286, Denver, CO 80225, 888/ASK-USGS (888/275-8747), website: http://mapping.usgs.gov.

**Directions:** From the Stratham traffic circle at the junction of Routes 108 and 33, drive 1.4 miles north on Route 33 and turn left onto Depot Road at a sign for the Sandy Point Discovery Center. At the end of Depot Road, turn left on Tidewater Farm Road. The Discovery Center is at the end of the road, and the trail begins behind the center.

**Contact:** Great Bay Reserve Manager, New Hampshire Fish and Game Department, Marine Fisheries Division, 225 Main St., Durham, NH 03824, 603/868-1095, website: www.greatbay.org. New Hampshire Division of Parks and Recreation, P.O. Box 1856, 172 Pembroke Rd., Concord, NH 03302, 603/271-3556, camping reservations 603/271-3628, website: www.nhstateparks.org.

## 16 ODIORNE POINT STATE PARK

**2 mi/1 hr**

**in Rye**

A relatively small park at 330 acres, Odiorne is still the largest tract of undeveloped land along New Hampshire's 18-mile shoreline. It has a rich history: Beginning about 400 years ago, the Pennacook and Abenaki tribes frequented the area. Later, several generations of descendants of settler John Odiorne farmed and fished here, and during World War II, the military acquired the property for the construction of Fort Dearborn. Ever since it became a state park in 1961, the point has offered the public a rugged shore and a great place to catch an ocean sunrise or watch storm-fattened waves crash against the rocks.

Head to the far end of the parking lot and pick up the paved walkway; bear right where it forks. You'll walk past the small grove of low trees known as the Sunken Forest on your right, and continue out to Odiorne Point and a picnic area. The paved walkway leads through the picnic area to form a loop leading back to the parking lot. From the picnic area, walk the rocky shore or a path just above the beach to the Seacoast Science Center; a paved path leads left back to the parking lot. Or continue on either the beach or a trail past the center all the way out to the jetty at Frost Point for a broad shoreline view. Turn inland again along a wide trail. Turn left in front of a high military bunker, bear right onto a trail around a freshwater marsh, and follow the shoreline trail back to the science center and the parking lot.

**User groups:** Hikers, bikers, skiers, and snowshoers. A portion of the trail is wheelchair accessible. Dogs, horses, and hunting are prohibited.

**Access, fees:** The park is open daily year-round. There is a $3-per-person park entrance fee levied daily from early May–late October and on weekends the rest of the year; children under 12 and New Hampshire residents 65 and older enter free. Admission to the park's Seacoast Science Center is $1 per person.

**Maps:** For a map with historical and natural information about Odiorne, contact the New Hampshire Division of Parks and Recreation (see address below). For a topographic area map, request Kittery from USGS Map Sales, Federal Center, Box 25286, Denver, CO 80225, 888/ASK-USGS (888/275-8747), website: http://mapping.usgs.gov.

**Directions:** The main entrance to Odiorne is on Route 1A, 1.6 miles north of Wallis Sands State Beach and three miles south of Portsmouth. Park in the lot to the right beyond the entrance gatehouse.

**Contact:** The New Hampshire Division of Parks and Recreation, East Region Office, 603/436-1552. The Seacoast Science Center, Audubon Society of New Hampshire, 603/436-8043. New Hampshire Division of Parks and Recreation, P.O. Box 1856, 172 Pembroke Rd., Concord, NH 03302, 603/271-3556, camping reservations 603/271-3628, website: www.nhstateparks.org.

# ◼17 NORTH PACK MONADNOCK
**3.2 mi/2 hrs**

**in Greenfield**

My nephews Stephen and Nicholas and niece Brittany were three, six, and four years old when I took them on this fairly easy 3.2-mile hike, which ascends less than 1,000 feet in elevation to the top of North Pack Monadnock. They gorged on the ripe blueberries along the

trail, and celebrated like mountaineers when they reached the summit, with its view west to Mount Monadnock.

From the parking area, walk south into the woods, following the yellow triangle blazes of the Wapack Trail. It ascends at an easy grade through the Wapack National Wildlife Refuge for a mile, then climbs steep ledges and passes over one open ledge with a view east before reaching the summit at 1.6 miles. From the 2,276-foot summit, the views of southern New Hampshire's wooded hills and valleys are excellent, especially to the west and north. Return the way you came.

**User groups:** Hikers, snowshoers, and dogs. No wheelchair facilities. This trail is not suitable for bikes, horses, or skis. Hunting is allowed in season.

**Access, fees:** Parking and access are free. Camping is allowed only at designated sites along the entire 21-mile Wapack Trail, but not along this hike. Fires are prohibited.

**Maps:** An excellent contour map of the Wapack Trail is available for $4 (including postage) from the Friends of the Wapack (see address below); the organization also sells a detailed guidebook to the entire trail for $11 (including postage). The *Guide to the Wapack Trail in Massachusetts & New Hampshire* three-color map costs $3.95 from New England Cartographics, 413/549-4124 or toll-free 888/995-6277, website: www.necartographics.com. For topographic area maps, request Peterborough South, Peterborough North, Greenfield, and Greenville from USGS Map Sales, Federal Center, Box 25286, Denver, CO 80225, 888/ASK-USGS (888/275-8747), website: http://mapping.usgs.gov.

**Directions:** The Wapack Trail begins at a parking area on Old Mountain Road in Greenfield, 2.6 miles west of Route 31 and 4.3 miles east of U.S. 202 in Peterborough (via Sand Hill Road).

**Contact:** Friends of the Wapack, Box 115, West Peterborough, NH 03468, website: www.wapack.org. New Hampshire Division of Parks and Recreation, P.O. Box 1856, 172 Pembroke Rd., Concord, NH 03302, 603/271-3556, camping reservations 603/271-3628, website: www.nhstateparks.org.

## 18 MOUNT PISGAH
**5 mi/3 hrs**
**in Pisgah State Park between Chesterfield and Hinsdale**

Tucked away in the state's rural southwest corner, New Hampshire's largest state park includes this big hill called Mount Pisgah, where open summit ledges afford nice views of rolling countryside and Mount Monadnock to the east, and toward Massachusetts and Vermont to the southwest. Key trail junctions are marked with signs, and there's just a few hundred feet of uphill. From the trailhead, follow the Kilburn Road Trail, bearing left at junctions with the Kilburn Loop Trail, eventually turning onto the Pisgah Mountain Trail. Double back from the summit on the same trails. This is a wonderful intermediate ski tour, though you may have to carry skis up the steep stretch of trail below the summit. Though mountain bikes are permitted in much of the park, they are prohibited on these trails.

Special note: Want a little added adventure? For a challenging ski tour, continue over the summit of Mount Pisgah, following the sporadically blazed Pisgah Mountain Trail to the Reservoir Trail (which sees snowmobile use). Turn left (north) and keep bearing left at trail junctions until you reach a sign that reads "to Baker Trail." Turn left and follow the Davis Hill Trail past the Baker Trail and Baker Pond on the left; it eventually winds southwest to your starting point, completing a loop of about 10 miles. Bear in mind that snowmobilers use the Reservoir Trail and other paths in the park during winter, as do hunters in late fall.

**User groups:** Hikers, snowshoers, and dogs. Dogs must be leashed. No wheelchair facilities. This trail may be difficult to snowshoe, in part because of severe winter weather, and difficult to ski due to the terrain's steepness. It is not suitable for bikes or horses. Hunting is allowed in season.

**Access, fees:** Parking and access are free.

**Maps:** For a map of park trails, contact the state park or the New Hampshire Division of Parks and Recreation (see address below). For topographic area maps, request Winchester and Keene from USGS Map Sales, Federal Center, Box 25286, Denver, CO 80225, 888/ASK-USGS (888/275-8747), website: http://mapping.usgs.gov.

**Directions:** From I-91 in Brattleboro, VT, take Exit 3 for Route 9 east. At Route 63, turn right (south), pass through Chesterfield, and continue three more miles to an entrance and parking area for Kilburn Road in Pisgah State Park.

**Contact:** Pisgah State Park, P.O. Box 242, Winchester, NH 03470-0242, 603/239-8153. New Hampshire Division of Parks and Recreation, P.O. Box 1856, 172 Pembroke Rd., Concord, NH 03302, 603/271-3556, camping reservations 603/271-3628, website: www.nhstateparks.org.

## 19 MOUNT MONADNOCK: WHITE ARROW TRAIL
**4.6 mi/3 hrs**
**in Monadnock State Park in Jaffrey**

Long one of my favorite mountains (see the Mount Monadnock: White Dot–White Cross Loop listing in this chapter), Monadnock is a peak I also hiked—via this route—with my niece Brittany and nephew Stephen when they were just six and five years old. They loved scrambling up the rocky trail, and did great on this ascent of 1,600 vertical feet. From the parking lot, walk past the gate onto the old toll road; you can either follow the wide road or immediately bear left onto the Old Halfway House Trail, which parallels the old carriage road for 1.2 miles to the meadow known as the Halfway House site. Cross the meadow to the White Arrow Trail, which ascends a rock-strewn but wide path for another 1.1 miles to the summit of Mount Monadnock. The final quarter mile is above the mountain's tree line and very exposed to harsh weather. White blazes are painted on the rocks above the trees. Just below the summit, the trail makes a sharp right turn, then ascends slabs to the summit. Hike back the same way.

**User groups:** Hikers only. No wheelchair facilities. This trail may be difficult to snowshoe, in part because of severe winter weather, and is not suitable for bikes, horses, or skis. Dogs are prohibited. Hunting is allowed in season, but not near trails.

**Access, fees:** There is a parking fee of $3 per person, usually from April–November, and the parking lot is not maintained in winter. Children under 12 enter for free.

**Maps:** A free map of trails is available from the state park or the New Hampshire Division of Parks and Recreation (see address below). Or get the *Monadnock/Cardigan* map, $7.95 in waterproof Tyvek, from the Appalachian Mountain Club, 800/262-4455, website: www.outdoors.org. For topographic area maps, request Monadnock Mountain and Marlborough from USGS Map Sales, Federal Center, Box 25286, Denver, CO 80225, 888/ASK-USGS (888/275-8747), website: http://mapping.usgs.gov.

**Directions:** This hike begins from a parking lot on the north side of Route 124, 7.1 miles east of the junction of Routes 101 and 124 in Marlborough, and 5.4 miles west of the junction of Route 124, Route 137, and U.S. 202 in Jaffrey.

**Contact:** Monadnock State Park, P.O. Box 181, Jaffrey, NH 03452-0181, 603/532-8862, website: www.nhstateparks.org/ParksPages/Monadnock/Monadnock.html. New Hampshire Division of Parks and Recreation, P.O. Box 1856, 172 Pembroke Rd., Concord, NH 03302, 603/271-3556, camping reservations 603/271-3628, website: www.nhstateparks.org.

## 20 MOUNT MONADNOCK: WHITE DOT–WHITE CROSS LOOP

**4.2 mi/3 hrs**

**in Monadnock State Park in Jaffrey**

At 3,165 feet high, majestic Mount Monadnock rises about 2,000 feet above the surrounding countryside of southern New Hampshire, making it prominently visible from many other lower peaks in the region. It was designated a National Natural Landmark in 1987. One of New England's most popular summits, it is said that Monadnock is hiked by more people than any peak in the world except Japan's Mount Fuji—although any ranger in the state park would tell you that's impossible to prove. Growing up not far from here, I soon adopted Monadnock as one of my favorite mountains in New England. I would estimate I've hiked it 50 or 60 times, in every season (conditions can be dangerous above tree line in winter). This can be a very crowded place from spring through fall, and this route may be the most commonly used on the mountain. Nonetheless, it's a scenic and moderately difficult two-mile route to the summit, climbing about 1,700 feet.

From the parking lot, walk up the road past the bathrooms and state park headquarters onto the White Dot Trail. The wide path dips slightly, crosses a brook, then ascends gently. At a half mile, the Spruce Link bears left, leading in 0.3 mile to the White Cross Trail, but stay to the right on the White Dot. At 0.7 mile, the White Cross turns left, leading a short distance to Falcon Spring, a good water source; this hike continues straight ahead on the White Dot. The trail climbs steeply for the next 0.4 mile, with some limited views, until emerging onto open ledges at 1.1 miles. It then follows more level terrain, enters a forest of low evergreens, and ascends again to its upper junction with the White Cross Trail at 1.7 miles. The trail climbs the open, rocky terrain of the upper mountain for the final 0.3 mile to the summit. Descend the same way, except bear right onto the White Cross Trail, which descends steeply, with occasional views, for a mile. Continue straight ahead onto the Spruce Link Trail, which rejoins the White Dot in 0.3 mile. Turn right and walk a half mile back to the trailhead.

**User groups:** Hikers only. No wheelchair facilities. This trail may be difficult to snowshoe, in part because of severe winter weather, and is not suitable for bikes, horses, or skis. Dogs are prohibited. Hunting is allowed in season, but not near trails.

**Access, fees:** An entrance fee of $3 per person is charged at the state park's main entrance year-round. Children under 12 enter for free.

**Maps:** A free map of trails is available from the state park or the New Hampshire Division of Parks and Recreation (see address below). Or get the *Monadnock/Cardigan* map, $7.95 in waterproof Tyvek, from the Appalachian Mountain Club, 800/262-4455, website: www.outdoors.org. For topographic area maps, request Mount Monadnock and Marlborough from USGS Map Sales, Federal Center, Box 25286, Denver, CO 80225, 888/ASK-USGS (888/275-8747), website: http://mapping.usgs.gov.

**Directions:** From Route 124, 10.4 miles east of the junction of Routes 101 and 124 in Marlborough, and 2.1 miles west of the junction of Route 124, Route 137, and U.S. 202 in Jaffrey, turn north at a sign for Monadnock State Park. Follow the state park signs to the large parking lot at the park's main entrance.

**Contact:** Monadnock State Park, P.O. Box 181, Jaffrey, NH 03452-0181, 603/532-8862, website: www.nhstateparks.org/ParksPages/Monadnock/Monadnock.html. New Hampshire Division of Parks and Recreation, P.O. Box 1856, 172 Pembroke Rd., Concord, NH 03302, 603/271-3556, camping reservations 603/271-3628, website: www.nhstateparks.org.

## 21 TEMPLE MOUNTAIN
**5.8 mi/3.5 hrs**
**in Sharon**

One of the more scenic stretches of the Wapack Ridge Trail, this hike traverses the long ridge of Temple Mountain all the way to the Temple Mountain Ledges, a 5.8-mile round-trip with, all told, more than 1,200 feet of climbing. But there are several nice views along the way that make worthwhile destinations for anyone seeking a shorter hike. I took my seven-year-old niece, Brittany, on this hike: She ran ahead much of the way and loved the wild blueberries on the Sharon Ledges.

From the parking area, cross Temple Road and follow the yellow triangle blazes of the Wapack Trail into the woods. About 0.1 mile from the road, the trail passes a dilapidated old house. At 0.3 mile, it reaches an open area at the start of the Sharon Ledges, and a view of Mount Monadnock. A sign points to an overlook 75 feet to the right with a view toward

the author's wife and niece on Temple Mountain

Mount Watatic. Continuing northeast, the Wapack follows the Sharon Ledges for 0.75 mile, with a series of views eastward toward the hills and woods of southern New Hampshire. The trail enters the woods again and 1.4 miles from the road passes over the wooded subsidiary summit known as Burton Peak. Nearly a half mile farther, a side path leads right to the top of cliffs and an unobstructed view to the east; on a clear day, the Boston skyline can be distinguished on the horizon. A short distance farther north on the Wapack lies an open ledge with a great view west to Monadnock—one of the nicest on this hike. The trail continues north 0.7 mile to the wooded summit of Holt Peak, another significant bump on the ridge. A half mile beyond Holt, watch through the trees on the left for a glimpse of an unusually tall rock cairn, then a side path leading to a flat, broad rock ledge with several tall cairns and good views in almost every direction. You've reached the Temple Mountain Ledges. The Wapack continues over Temple Mountain to Route 101, but this hike returns the same way you came.

**User groups:** Hikers, snowshoers, and dogs. No wheelchair facilities. This trail is fairly difficult to ski and is not suitable for bikes or horses. Hunting is allowed in season unless otherwise posted.

**Access, fees:** Parking and access are free. Camping is allowed only at designated sites along the entire 21-mile Wapack Trail; there are no designated sites along this hike. Fires are illegal without landowner permission and a permit from the town forest-fire warden.

**Maps:** An excellent contour map of the Wapack Trail is available for $4 (including postage) from the Friends of the Wapack (see address below); the organization also sells a detailed guidebook to the entire trail for $11 (including postage). The *Guide to the Wapack Trail in Massachusetts & New Hampshire* three-color map costs $3.95 from New England Cartographics, 413/549-4124 or toll-free 888/995-6277, website: www.necartographics.com. For topographic area maps, request Peterborough South and Greenville from USGS Map Sales, Federal Center, Box 25286, Denver, CO 80225, 888/ASK-USGS (888/275-8747), website: http://mapping.usgs.gov.

**Directions:** From the junction of Routes 101 and 123 (west of the Temple Mountain Ski Area), drive south four miles on Route 123 and turn left on Temple Road. Continue another 0.7 mile to a small dirt parking area on the right. Or from the junction where Routes 123 and 124 split, west of New Ipswich, drive north on Route 123 for a mile and turn right on Nashua Road. Continue another 0.6 mile and turn left on Temple Road. Drive 0.3 mile to the dirt parking area on the left.

**Contact:** Friends of the Wapack, Box 115, West Peterborough, NH 03468, website: www.wapack.org. New Hampshire Division of Parks and Recreation, Bureau of Trails, P.O. Box 1856, Concord, NH 03302-1856, 603/271-3254.

## 22 KIDDER MOUNTAIN
### 3 mi/2 hrs

**in New Ipswich**

This easy, three-mile hike gains less than 400 feet in elevation, yet the views from the open meadow atop 1,800-foot Kidder Mountain take in a grand sweep of this rural corner of southern New Hampshire. To the south, the Wapack Range extends to Mount Watatic in Massachusetts; behind Watatic rises Mount Wachusett. Two of us relaxed up here one July afternoon when there was just enough breeze to temper the heat and keep the bugs down, as we munched on the blueberries growing wild all over the meadow.

From the parking area, follow the yellow triangle blazes of the Wapack Trail into the woods, heading north. At 0.3 mile, the trail crosses a clearing and ascends a small hillside to the woods. At 0.6 mile from the road, the Wapack crosses a power line right-of-way. Turn right (east) at a sign onto the Kidder Mountain Trail. The trail follows a jeep road under the power line corridor for 0.1 mile, then turns left, crossing under the lines and entering the woods. It gradually ascends Kidder Mountain, reaching the open summit meadow nearly a mile from the Wapack Trail. Follow the same route back. **User groups:** Hikers, snowshoers, and dogs. No wheelchair facilities. This trail is not suitable for horses or skis. Hunting is allowed in season unless otherwise posted.

**Access, fees:** Parking and access are free. Camping is allowed only at designated sites along the entire 21-mile Wapack Trail; there are no designated sites along this hike. Fires are illegal without landowner permission and a permit from the town forest-fire warden.

**Maps:** An excellent contour map of the Wapack Trail is available for $4 (including postage) from the Friends of the Wapack (see address below); the organization also sells a detailed guidebook to the entire trail for $11 (including postage). The *Guide to the Wapack Trail in Massachusetts & New Hampshire* three-color map costs $3.95 from New England Cartographics, 413/549-4124 or toll-free 888/995-6277, website: www.necartographics.com. For topographic area maps, request Peterborough South and Greenville from USGS Map Sales, Federal Center, Box 25286, Denver, CO 80225, 888/ASK-USGS (888/275-8747), website: http://mapping.usgs.gov.

**Directions:** The trailhead parking area is on the north side of Route 123/124 in New Ipswich, 2.9 miles west of the junction with Route 123A and 0.7 mile east of where Route 123 and Route 124 split.

**Contact:** Friends of the Wapack, Box 115, West Peterborough, NH 03468, website: www.wapack.org. New Hampshire Division of Parks and Recreation, Bureau of Trails, P.O. Box 1856, Concord, NH 03302-1856, 603/271-3254.

## 23 BEAVER BROOK

**2.5 mi/1.5 hrs**

**in Hollis**

Chartered in 1964 by the state as an educational nonprofit organization, the Beaver Brook Association manages nearly 2,000 acres of land and about 35 miles of trails here at its main campus in Hollis. This place is a local jewel that attracts hikers, snowshoers, cross-country skiers, and mountain bikers from a wide radius. The terrain varies from flat wetlands that cover at least one-third of the land, to abrupt little-forested hills. Many of the trails are ideal for beginning skiers and bikers; some are appropriate for people with intermediate skills. This hike involves some trails that are closed to bikes and horses, but there are about 20 miles of trails here open to those activities. Do not overlook the trails on the north side of Route 130, in the area of Wildlife Pond; the Rocky Ridge and Mary Farley Trails also offer particularly nice hiking opportunities.

From the office, follow the wide woods road called Cow Lane. Turn onto the first trail on your left, Porcupine Trail, and follow it down to the wetlands. Turn right onto the Beaver Brook Trail, which parallels the broad marsh—a good place for bird-watching. Turn left and cross the boardwalk over the marsh, then continue straight onto Jason's Cutoff Trail. Turn right onto the wide forest road called Elkins Road and follow it to a right turn where a woods road crosses Beaver Brook, leading to the Brown Lane barn. Walk Brown Lane a short distance, and turn right onto the Tepee Trail, which leads back to Cow Lane. Turn left to return to your car.

**User groups:** Hikers, dogs, skiers, and snowshoers. Dogs must be leashed. No wheelchair facilities. This trail is not suitable for bikes or horses. Hunting is prohibited.

**Access, fees:** Parking and access are free.

**Maps:** A trail map is available at the Beaver Brook Association office. Office hours are weekdays, 9 A.M.–4 P.M. For a topographic area map, request Pepperell from USGS Map Sales, Federal Center, Box 25286, Denver, CO 80225, 888/ASK-USGS (888/275-8747), website: http://mapping.usgs.gov.

**Directions:** From the junction of Routes 130 and 122 in Hollis, drive south on Route 122 for 0.9 mile and turn right onto Ridge Road. Follow Ridge Road to the Maple Hill Farm and the office of the Beaver Brook Association. Once you become familiar with the trails here, another good access point to the Beaver Brook land is from the parking area off Route 130, west of the town center and across from the Diamond Casting and Machine Company.

**Contact:** Beaver Brook Association, 117 Ridge Rd., Hollis, NH 03049, 603/465-7787, website: www.beaverbrook.org.

**Vermont**

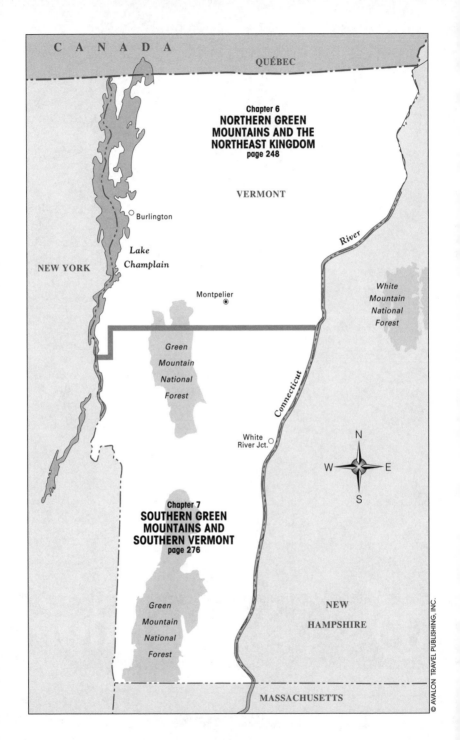

## Chapter 6

© MICHAEL LANZA

# Northern
# Green Mountains and the
# Northeast Kingdom

# Northern
# Green Mountains and the
# Northeast Kingdom

R oughly half of the 23 hikes in this chapter are along the northern portion of the 270-mile Long Trail (LT), which runs the length of the Green Mountains from Massachusetts to the Canadian border; the others include short, easy, and scenic walks along Lake Champlain and on lower hills with views of the Green Mountains, as well as a few hikes in the rural forests of the Northeast Kingdom. The northernmost hikes in this chapter—Jay Peak, Mounts Pisgah and Hor, Laraway Lookout, and Prospect Rock—are among the most remote and least-traveled trails in New England, and good places to escape the crowds.

Some of Vermont's highest, most rugged, and most challenging and enjoyable peaks—including Camel's Hump and Mount Mansfield—are featured in this chapter. Camel's Hump and several other summits lie along the famed Monroe Skyline, the LT's most spectacular stretch.

The Green Mountain Club (GMC) maintains the Long Trail and the numerous shelters and camping areas along it, including lean-to shelters with one open side, similar to those found along the Appalachian Trail, and the enclosed cabins, or lodges, most of which are on the trail's northern half. GMC caretakers collect an overnight fee for staying in its shelters; see individual hike listings for details. The water sources at most shelters and camping areas are usually reliable, though this is never guaranteed in a dry season. In the Green Mountain National Forest, no-trace camping is permitted, dogs must be leashed, and hunting is allowed in season, but not near trails.

The prime hiking season begins in late spring, when higher-elevation snows have melted away and lower-elevation mud has dried up, and lasts until the leaves hit the ground, usually in early October (though all of October can provide some great cool-weather hiking with a small chance of snow). To prevent erosion, parts of the Long Trail are closed to hiking during mud season, roughly mid-April through Memorial Day. Where the Long Trail crosses private land, camping is prohibited except at the GMC cabins and shelters. Winters are long and cold throughout Vermont—although there's great ski touring and snowshoeing to be had—and road access through the mountain passes is never assured (the Lincoln-Warren Highway through Lincoln Gap is not maintained in winter).

In Vermont's more than 50 state parks, trails are closed mid-April through mid-May (the lower-elevation state park trails dry out sooner than higher parts of the Long Trail). At all state park main entrances, an entrance fee of $2.50 per person age 14 and older, and $2 for children age 4 to 13, is collected from Memorial Day through Columbus Day. A free, basic trail map is available at virtually all state parks, or from the Vermont Department of Forests, Parks, and Recreation (see Resources appendix). Hunting is allowed in virtually all state parks and forests during hunting seasons, which are in the fall. Mountain bikes are allowed only on designated trails, which are few; consult with park officials for current designated trails. Dogs are not allowed in day-use areas such as picnic areas, but are unrestricted on trails.

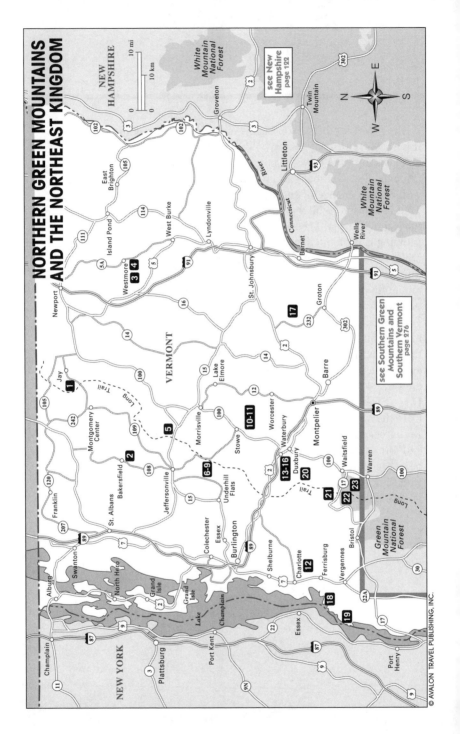

# 1 JAY PEAK

**3.4 mi/2.5 hrs**

**between Jay and Montgomery Center**

At 3,861 feet in elevation and just 10 trail miles from the Canadian border, Jay Peak is one of the more remote large mountains along the entire 270-mile length of the Long Trail. The views from the summit—where there are buildings belonging to the Jay Peak Ski Area—are of a vast North Country of mountains, forest, and few roads. And just about half of what you see lies in Canada. Remember that winter arrives earlier here than on peaks farther south. My wife, her dad, and I hiked up here once in the first week of November to find lots of ice and a snow dusting the trail. This hike climbs almost 1,700 feet.

From the turnout, cross the highway and follow the white blazes of the Long Trail northbound. You immediately pass the small lean-to known as Atlas Valley shelter—not designed for overnight use. In 0.1 mile, the Jay Loop Trail, also a part of the Catamount ski trail, branches left, leading 0.2 mile to the Jay Camp cabin. Just 0.3 mile farther up the LT, you pass the north end of the Jay Loop. The LT ascends steadily onto the mountain's southeast ridge. Just over a mile from the road, you start getting obstructed views to the south and west through the subalpine forest. The wooded peak to the west, connected to Jay by a high ridge, is Big Jay, at 3,800 feet one of New England's 100 highest summits and a destination for hikers seeking to tick off that list. In recent years, a trail was cut to Big Jay. At 1.5 miles from the highway, the LT crosses a ski resort trail and then climbs over open, rocky terrain the final 0.2 mile to the summit. Descend the way you came.

**User groups:** Hikers and dogs. Dogs must be leashed. No wheelchair facilities. This trail should not be attempted in winter except by hikers prepared for severe winter weather, and is not suitable for bikes, horses, or skis. Hunting is allowed in season unless otherwise posted.

**Access, fees:** Parking and access are free. This Long Trail section is on private land. Camping is prohibited except at the Green Mountain Club cabins and shelters. The Jay Camp cabin is located 0.3 mile north of Route 242 and 1.6 miles south of the Jay Peak summit, 0.2 mile off the Long Trail. The Laura Woodward shelter lies 1.5 miles north of Jay Peak, on the LT. The Atlas Valley shelter is a small lean-to a few steps north of Route 242 on the LT; exposed to winds, it does not provide good overnight shelter.

**Maps:** The waterproof *End-to-End Map of the Long Trail* is available for $8.95 from the Green Mountain Club (see address below). For a topographic area map, request Jay Peak from USGS Map Sales, Federal Center, Box 25286, Denver, CO 80225, 888/ASK-USGS (888/275-8747), website: http://mapping.usgs.gov.

**Directions:** Park in a large turnout where the Long Trail crosses Route 242, 6.5 miles east of the junction of Routes 242 and 118 in Montgomery Center, and 6.5 miles west of the junction of Routes 242 and 101 in Jay.

**Contact:** Green Mountain Club Inc., 4711 Waterbury-Stowe Rd., Waterbury Center, VT 05677, 802/244-7037, website: www.greenmountainclub.org.

# 2 LARAWAY LOOKOUT

**3.6 mi/2.5 hrs**

**between Waterville and Belvidere Junction**

I hiked to Laraway Lookout on an early November day that felt decidedly wintry, with an inch of snow on the ground and icicles hanging from cliffs along the trail. At the lookout, clouds obscured any view for several minutes. But patience rewarded me, for the clouds eventually separated, showing me the long view to the southwest and west of mountains and the Champlain Valley. This hike climbs about 1,500 feet.

From the parking area, follow the white-blazed Long Trail northbound. The wide path crosses a brook in 0.1 mile and then follows its opposite bank for about 200 yards, turning sharply left near picturesque cascades. The LT ascends gradually through woods, growing more rugged for the final 0.3 mile, passing beneath dramatically overhanging cliffs and climbing a narrow, rocky gully before reaching the open ledge at Laraway Lookout. The wooded summit of Laraway Mountain lies just 0.4 mile farther up the Long Trail, but this hike returns the way you came.

**User groups:** Hikers and dogs. Dogs must be leashed. No wheelchair facilities. This trail may be difficult to snowshoe, in part because of severe winter weather and is not suitable for bikes, horses, or skis. Hunting is allowed in season unless otherwise posted.

**Access, fees:** Parking and access are free. This Long Trail section is on private land. Camping is prohibited except at the Green Mountain Club cabins and shelters. The Corliss Camp is three miles north of Laraway Lookout on the Long Trail.

**Maps:** The waterproof *End-to-End Map of the Long Trail* is available for $8.95 from the Green Mountain Club (see address below). For a topographic area map, request Johnson from USGS Map Sales, Federal Center, Box 25286, Denver, CO 80225, 888/ASK-USGS (888/275-8747), website: http://mapping.usgs.gov.

**Directions:** From Route 109, 1.8 miles north of the Waterville Market in the town center and 8.8 miles south of the junction of Routes 109 and 118 in Belvidere Corners, turn east onto Codding Hollow Road. Drive 1.4 miles and bear left at a fork and a sign for Long Trail parking. A mile farther, the road narrows to a two-track that may not be passable in mud season. Follow that two-track for 0.2 mile to a dirt parking lot on the left.

**Contact:** Green Mountain Club Inc., 4711 Waterbury-Stowe Rd., Waterbury Center, VT 05677, 802/244-7037, website: www.greenmountainclub.org.

# 3 MOUNT HOR
## 2.8 mi/1.5 hrs

### in Willoughby State Forest

Lake Willoughby is a long finger of water embraced on both sides by the sheer cliffs of Mount Hor to the west and Mount Pisgah to the east. Tucked away in Vermont's remote Northeast Kingdom, Willoughby's topography inspires images of a Norwegian fjord more than it does the bucolic farmland and forests surrounding Willoughby State Forest. It certainly evoked that image for me one raw, rainy day I spent hiking Mounts Hor and Pisgah (see Mount Pisgah listing in this chapter). This is a great hike for viewing the fall foliage, which normally peaks by late September this far north. Although the views from 2,656-foot Mount Hor are not as nice as they are from Mount Pisgah, Hor does have beautiful views and is easier to hike than Mount Pisgah because much of the elevation is gained while driving the CCC Road to the trailhead. The actual hike climbs less than 500 feet.

From the parking area, walk 40 feet farther up the road and turn right onto the Herbert Hawkes Trail. In another 30 feet, turn right with the trail onto an old logging road. The hike is easy and nearly flat for the first 0.4 mile, passing through several wet, muddy areas. The road eventually narrows to a trail, then swings left, and ascends the mountainside. At 0.7 mile you reach a trail junction marked by signs: To the left it is 0.3 mile to the wooded, viewless summit of Mount Hor (not included in this hike's distance); for this hike, turn right and follow the fairly easy trail another half mile to the first overlook of Lake Willoughby and Mount Pisgah, and 0.1 mile beyond that to the second overlook. After you've taken in the views, hike back along the same route to the parking area.

**User groups:** Hikers and snowshoers. No wheelchair facilities. This trail is not suitable for bikes, horses, or skis. Dogs are not allowed in day-use areas such as picnic areas, but are not restricted on trails. Hunting is allowed in season.

**Access, fees:** Parking and access are free. Trails are closed during the spring mud season, usually mid-April–mid-May, and are posted when closed for peregrine falcon nesting in spring.

**Maps:** The *Northern Vermont Hiking Trail Map*, which covers Mount Mansfield, Camel's Hump, Lake Willoughby (including Mounts Hor and Pisgah), Cotton Brook, Little River, the Worcester Range (including Stowe Pinnacle and Mount Hunger), and Mount Elmore, is available from the Green Mountain Club (see address below) for $4.95. For a free, basic map of hiking trails, contact the Vermont Department of Forests, Parks, and Recreation (see address below). For topographic area maps, request Sutton and Westmore from USGS Map Sales, Federal Center, Box 25286, Denver, CO 80225, 888/ASK-USGS (888/275-8747), website: http://mapping.usgs.gov.

**Directions:** Take I-91 to Exit 25 for Barton. Turn right off the ramp onto Route 16 east. Drive one mile into Barton and turn right, then go 0.2 mile and turn left, staying on Route 16 east. Follow Route 16 for another 7.2 miles to the north end of Lake Willoughby and turn right onto Route 5A south. Drive 5.7 miles, beyond the foot of the lake, and turn right onto the gravel CCC Road beside a dirt parking lot. Follow that road for 1.8 miles to a parking area on the right.

**Contact:** Vermont Department of Forests, Parks, and Recreation, 103 South Main St., Waterbury, VT 05671-0601, 802/241-3655, website: www.state.vt.us/anr/fpr.

# ▋ MOUNT PISGAH
**3.8 mi/2.5 hrs**

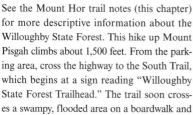

**in Willoughby State Forest**

See the Mount Hor trail notes (this chapter) for more descriptive information about the Willoughby State Forest. This hike up Mount Pisgah climbs about 1,500 feet. From the parking area, cross the highway to the South Trail, which begins at a sign reading "Willoughby State Forest Trailhead." The trail soon crosses a swampy, flooded area on a boardwalk and

then starts climbing a wide path well marked with blue blazes. After about 0.7 mile, you pass the first of three successive lookouts on the left with partly obstructed views of Lake Willoughby and Mount Hor, the third lookout being the best among them. At one mile, you reach a short side path leading left to Pulpit Rock, with an excellent view of the lake. Some hikers may choose to turn back from here, for a round-trip of two miles.

Continue up the trail, scrambling up rock slabs a half mile beyond Pulpit Rock, and then watch for a side path leading to the right about 100 feet to a view southeast to New Hampshire's White Mountains. Return to the South Trail, turn right, and continue to Mount Pisgah's 2,756-foot summit, 1.9 miles from the road. Three side paths around the wooded summit lead left to ledges atop tall cliffs with sweeping views of Lake Willoughby and Mount Hor. A sign points to the last side path, the north overlook. Head back the way you came.

**User groups:** Hikers and snowshoers. No wheelchair facilities. This trail is not suitable for bikes, horses, or skis. Dogs are not allowed in day-use areas such as picnic areas, but are not restricted on trails. Hunting is allowed in season.

**Access, fees:** Parking and access are free. Trails are closed during the spring mud season, usually mid-April–mid-May, and are posted when closed for peregrine falcon nesting, usually in spring.

**Maps:** *The Northern Vermont Hiking Trail Map*, which covers Mount Mansfield, Camel's Hump, Lake Willoughby (including Mounts Hor and Pisgah), Cotton Brook, Little River, the Worcester Range (including Stowe Pinnacle and Mount Hunger), and Mount Elmore, is available from the Green Mountain Club (see address below) for $4.95. For a free, basic map of hiking trails, contact the Vermont Department of Forests, Parks, and Recreation (see address below). For topographic area maps, request Sutton and Westmore from USGS Map Sales, Federal Center, Box 25286, Denver, CO 80225,

888/ASK-USGS (888/275-8747), website: http://mapping.usgs.gov.

**Directions:** Take I-91 to Exit 25 for Barton. Turn right off the ramp onto Route 16 east. Drive one mile into Barton and turn right, drive 0.2 mile, and turn left, staying on Route 16 east. Follow Route 16 for another 7.2 miles to the north end of Lake Willoughby and turn right onto Route 5A south. Drive 5.7 miles, beyond the foot of the lake, to a dirt parking lot on the right.

**Contact:** Vermont Department of Forests, Parks, and Recreation, 103 South Main St., Waterbury, VT 05671-0601, 802/241-3655, website: www.state.vt.us/anr/fpr.

# ⑤ PROSPECT ROCK
## 1.6 mi/1 hr

**in Johnson**

This relatively easy hike—it climbs about 500 feet over less than a mile—winds along a more remote Long Trail stretch, leading to a bucolic view of a northern Vermont farming valley and its surrounding hills. From the turnout, follow the Long Trail white blazes northbound up the dirt road for about 0.1 mile and then turn left with the trail into the woods. The LT follows an old woods road and then swings right onto a footpath winding uphill and reaching Prospect Rock, 0.8 mile from the parking area. Its open cliff-top ledges overlook the Lamoille River Valley and the Sterling Range to the south. Follow the same route back.

**User groups:** Hikers and dogs. Dogs must be leashed. No wheelchair facilities. This trail may be difficult to snowshoe and is not suitable for bikes, horses, or skis. Hunting is allowed in season unless otherwise posted.

**Access, fees:** Parking and access are free. This Long Trail section is on private land. Camping is prohibited except at the Green Mountain Club cabins and shelters. The Roundtop shelter is located 1.8 miles north of Prospect Rock on the Long Trail.

**Maps:** The waterproof *End-to-End Map of the Long Trail* is available for $8.95 from the Green

Mountain Club (see address below). For a topographic area map, request Johnson from USGS Map Sales, Federal Center, Box 25286, Denver, CO 80225, 888/ASK-USGS (888/275-8747), website: http://mapping.usgs.gov.

**Directions:** From Route 15, two miles west of the junction of Routes 15 and 100C in Johnson, and immediately east of the Lamoille River bridge, turn north onto a secondary road at signs for the Long Trail and Waterville. Continue 0.9 mile to a turnout on the right, across the road from the Ithiel Falls Camp Meeting Ground. You see the LT's white blazes on rocks at the turnout. Do not block the dirt road with your vehicle.

**Contact:** Green Mountain Club Inc., 4711 Waterbury-Stowe Rd., Waterbury Center, VT 05677, 802/244-7037, website: www.greenmountainclub.org.

# ⑥ SMUGGLER'S NOTCH
## 0.2 mi/0.25 hr

**in Smuggler's Notch State Park between Stowe and Jeffersonville**

Historically, the notch served as the route for illegal trade with Canada after President Thomas Jefferson's 1807 embargo forbade American trade with Great Britain and Canada, creating a hardship for northern Vermonters. It also was used as an escape route to Canada for fugitive slaves, and, once an improved road was built through the notch in 1922, served as a route for smuggling liquor from Canada during Prohibition.

During the warm months, this hike is an easy walk around the height of land in Smuggler's Notch, where massive boulders line the narrow, winding roadway and lie strewn throughout the woods. Tall cliffs flank the notch to either side, making it look more like the White Mountains than the usually more tame Green Mountains.

From the south end of the parking turnout, follow a short but obvious path about 200 feet back into the jumble of garage-sized boulders known as Smuggler's Cave, reputedly a stash for contraband during the War of 1812. Then wander around the notch; you'll see the white blazes of the Long Trail enter the woods across the road, a short distance uphill from the turnout. In winter, this hike transforms into a more involved outing, not to mention one typically accompanied by a frigid wind. With Route 108 not maintained through the notch, you have to hike or cross-country ski up to the height of land—about a mile at an easy to moderate grade from the Jeffersonville side, and about 2.3 miles from the Stowe side, which is much steeper. But the notch makes for a scenic ski tour and a fun descent.

**User groups:** Hikers, skiers, and snowshoers. No wheelchair facilities. This trail is not suitable for horses. Mountain bikes are allowed only on designated trails, which are few; consult with park officials for current designated trails. Dogs are not allowed in day-use areas such as picnic areas, but are not restricted on trails. Hunting is allowed in season.

**Access, fees:** Parking and access are free. Trails are closed during the spring mud season, usually mid-April–mid-May. Route 108 is not maintained through Smuggler's Notch once the snow falls. But the road often has a packed-snow surface in winter, making it possible to drive up from the Jeffersonville side with a four-wheel-drive vehicle, or ski or hike up from either side.

**Maps:** The *Northern Vermont Hiking Trail Map,* which covers Mount Mansfield, Camel's Hump, Lake Willoughby, Cotton Brook, Little River, the Worcester Range, and Mount Elmore, is available from the Green Mountain Club (see address below) for $4.95 for nonmembers; as is the waterproof End-to-End Map of the Long Trail, for $8.95. For a topographic area map, request Mount Mansfield from USGS Map Sales, Federal Center, Box 25286, Denver, CO 80225, 888/ASK-USGS (888/275-8747), website: http://mapping.usgs.gov.

**Directions:** Drive to the turnout immediately north of the height of land on Route 108 in Smuggler's Notch, south of Jeffersonville and north of Stowe.

**Contact:** Smuggler's Notch State Park, Box 7248, Mountain Rd., Stowe, VT 05672, 802/253-4014 in summer, 802/479-4280 in winter, or 800/658-6934. Vermont Department of Forests, Parks, and Recreation, 103 South Main St., Waterbury, VT 05671-0601, 802/241-3655, website: www.state.vt.us/anr/fpr. Green Mountain Club Inc., 4711 Waterbury-Stowe Rd., Waterbury Center, VT 05677, 802/244-7037, website: www.greenmountainclub.org.

## 7 MOUNT MANSFIELD: SUNSET RIDGE AND LAURA COWLES TRAILS

**6.2 mi/4.5 hrs**

**in Underhill State Park and Mount Mansfield State Forest in Underhill Center**

This 6.2-mile loop hike up Vermont's highest peak ascends the spectacular Sunset Ridge, much of it above the trees, with long views and rugged terrain more reminiscent of Mount Washington (White Mountains chapter) or Katahdin (North Woods chapter) than of most peaks here in the Green Mountains, few of which have alpine terrain. About half of the two-mile ridge ascent is over exposed ground. The sweeping views from the ridge to the south and north toward the Green Mountains—including the prominent summit of Camel's Hump to the south—and west toward Lake Champlain and the Adirondack Mountains are often accompanied by strong winds and harsh weather. Be prepared for wintry conditions any time of year. This hike passes over the Chin, Mansfield's true summit at 4,393 feet, with a 360-degree view encompassing the entire sweep of Vermont, as well as New Hampshire's White Mountains to the east. As with virtually any trail up Mansfield, this is a popular hike in summer and fall, and even attracts winter climbers (who should have the proper gear and skills). The trail gains about 2,100 feet in elevation from the state park to the summit. For more details, see the next listing in this chapter.

the author's wife on the Cliff Trail, Mount Mansfield

From the parking lot at the ranger station, hike up the dirt CCC Road for about a mile; just beyond a sharp right bend in the road, the blue-blazed Sunset Ridge Trail, marked by a sign, enters the woods. Follow the trail over two wooden footbridges spanning brooks to a junction just 0.1 mile from the road with the Laura Cowles Trail, branching right; you will descend that trail. Continuing up the Sunset Ridge Trail, ascending moderately, you'll see the first views through breaks in the forest within a half mile from the road. At 0.7 mile, turn left onto the Cantilever Rock Trail and follow it 0.1 mile to its namesake rock, a needlelike formation projecting horizontally about 40 feet from high up a cliff face. Backtrack to the Sunset Ridge Trail and continue climbing up through forest marked by occasional large boulders. About one mile from the road, the trail makes a short step up exposed rocks and emerges above tree line for the first broad views south and west.

The trail then follows the ridge upward, over rocky terrain where scrub spruce grow close to the ground in places, to a junction at about two miles with the Laura Cowles Trail, branching right—this hike's descent route. Continue another 0.2 mile up the Sunset Ridge Trail to its terminus at the Long Trail, on Mansfield's exposed summit ridge. Turn left (north) and follow the LT 0.2 mile to the Chin. Backtrack on the LT and Sunset Ridge Trail to the Laura Cowles Trail, and descend the Laura Cowles, reentering the woods within a half mile of the Sunset Ridge Trail. The Cowles Trail drops steadily for another 0.9 mile to its lower junction with the Sunset Ridge Trail. Turn left and walk 0.1 mile back to the CCC Road.

**User groups:** Hikers and dogs. Dogs must be leashed. No wheelchair facilities. This trail should not be attempted in winter except by hikers experienced in mountaineering and prepared for severe winter weather, and is not suitable for bikes, horses, or skis. Hunting is allowed in season.

**Access, fees:** From Memorial Day–Columbus Day, an entrance fee of $2.50 per person age 14 and older, and $2 for children age 4 to 13, is collected at the ranger station. Once the snow falls, the CCC Road is maintained only to a point about a half mile before the start of this hike, where winter visitors can park. Camping is prohibited except at the Green Mountain Club cabins and shelters.

**Maps:** The waterproof *End-to-End Map of the Long Trail* is available for $8.95 from the Green Mountain Club (see address below), as is the *Northern Vermont Hiking Trail Map,* which covers Mount Mansfield, Camel's Hump, Lake Willoughby, Cotton Brook, Little River, the Worcester Range, and Mount Elmore, for $4.95. For a topographic area map, request Mount Mansfield from USGS Map Sales, Federal Center, Box 25286, Denver, CO 80225, 888/ASK-USGS (888/275-8747), website: http://mapping.usgs.gov.

**Directions:** From Route 15 in Underhill Flats, drive east on the road to Underhill Center. In Underhill Center, three miles from Route 15, continue straight past the Underhill Country Store for one mile and turn right (at a sign for Underhill State Park) onto Mountain Road/TH2. Drive approximately two miles farther to a large parking lot at the ranger station.

**Contact:** Underhill State Park, P.O. Box 249, Underhill Center, VT 05490, 802/899-3022 in summer, 802/879-5674 in winter, or 800/252-2363. Vermont Department of Forests, Parks, and Recreation, Essex Junction District, 111 West St., Essex Junction, VT 05452, 802/879-6565. Vermont Department of Forests, Parks, and Recreation Commissioner's Office, 103 South Main St., Waterbury, VT 05671-0601, 802/241-3655, website: www.state.vt.us/anr/fpr. Green Mountain Club Inc., 4711 Waterbury-Stowe Rd., Waterbury Center, VT 05677, 802/244-7037, website: www.greenmountainclub.org.

### 8 MOUNT MANSFIELD: THE HELL BROOK AND CLIFF TRAILS

**5.8 mi/6 hrs**

**in Smuggler's Notch State Park and Mount Mansfield State Forest in Stowe**

This is one of the hardest routes I've hiked in New England, linking some of the steepest, most rugged trails on Vermont's highest peak, Mount Mansfield. This 5.8-mile hike can take even fit hikers six hours to complete because of the scrambling involved on parts of it—and the potential for harsh weather. My wife and I did this hike with two friends in early September one year, and ran into freezing fog and rime ice at Mansfield's higher elevations. This hike ascends more than 2,500 feet in elevation. Most trail junctions are marked by signs, and the Long Trail is marked by white blazes.

From the Big Spring parking area, cross the road and walk uphill 150 feet to the Hell Brook Trail (there may be no sign). It climbs very steeply, through dense and often wet forest where you find yourself grabbing roots and tree branches for aid in places. At 0.9 mile, the Hell Brook Cutoff branches left, but stay to the right on the Hell Brook Trail, at 1.3 miles reaching a junction with the Adam's Apple Trail on the left. The Bear Pond Trail heading north from this junction has been closed, although you may still be able to access scenic Lake of the Clouds on a short spur trail a very short distance down the former Bear Pond Trail. Climb the Adam's Apple Trail 0.1 mile to the rocky secondary summit of Mount Mansfield (known as the Adam's Apple) for excellent views of the true summit lying a stone's throw to the south. Descend over the Adam's Apple another 0.1 mile to rejoin the Hell Brook Trail and reach the Long Trail at Eagle Pass. Hikers looking to cut this loop short can descend the LT by turning left and hiking for two miles to Route 108; once reaching the road, turn left and walk a half mile to Big Spring.

This hike bears right at Eagle Pass onto the LT southbound, climbing the steep cliffs of Mansfield's summit for 0.3 mile onto the Chin, Mansfield's true summit at 4,393 feet. The Green Mountains reach to the north and south horizons; to the west is Lake Champlain and New York's Adirondack Mountains, and to the east you can see New Hampshire's White Mountains on a clear day. The LT continues south over Mansfield's long, exposed summit ridge, the most extensive of Vermont's few alpine areas, with fragile and rare vegetation; stay on the trail or walk on bare rock.

Stay on the LT southbound along the ridge for 0.4 mile, then turn left onto the Cliff Trail. Within 0.1 mile, a spur trail leads right 50 feet to the Cave of the Winds, a deep joint in the cliff. Continue along the Cliff Trail, descending over very rocky terrain below the imposing cliffs of the summit ridge to your right, and overlooking Smuggler's Notch and the ski area below on your left. Three-tenths of a mile down the trail, a path to the left leads 0.1 mile downhill to the top of the ski area gondola; hikers uncomfortable with the difficulty of the Cliff Trail can bail out here and hike down a ski trail, bearing in mind that the Cliff Trail's greatest challenges lie ahead.

Continuing on the Cliff Trail, in another 0.1 mile you'll reach Wall Street, where the trail squeezes through a claustrophobia-inducing gap between towering rock walls. For the next 0.7 mile, the Cliff Trail climbs up and down over rock and through dense subalpine forest, leading hikers up wooden ladders bolted into sheer rock. At trail's end, turn left onto the summit road and follow it downhill for nearly a half mile, then turn left onto the Haselton Trail, which coincides here with a ski trail called Nose Dive. This descends at a steep grade that is hard on the knees. Watch for where the Haselton Trail reenters the woods, within 0.3 mile, on the left. It's two miles from the Cliff Trail to the ski area parking lot via the Haselton Trail.

**User groups:** Hikers and dogs. Dogs must be leashed. No wheelchair facilities. This trail should not be attempted in winter except by hikers experienced in mountaineering and prepared for severe winter weather, and is not suitable for bikes, horses, or skis. Hunting is allowed in season.

**Access, fees:** Parking and access are free. Route 108 is not maintained through Smuggler's Notch once the snow falls, only to a point about a mile east of this hike's start. Camping is prohibited except at the Green Mountain Club cabins and shelters. The Taft Lodge cabin is located on the Long Trail, 1.7 miles south of Route 108.

**Maps:** The waterproof *End-to-End Map of the Long Trail* is available for $8.95 from the Green Mountain Club (see address below), as is the *Northern Vermont Hiking Trail Map,* which covers Mount Mansfield, Camel's Hump, Lake Willoughby, Cotton Brook, Little River, the Worcester Range, and Mount Elmore, for $4.95. For a topographic area map, request Mount Mansfield from USGS Map Sales, Federal Center, Box 25286, Denver, CO 80225, 888/ASK-USGS (888/275-8747), website: http://mapping.usgs.gov.

**Directions:** You will need to either shuttle two vehicles for this hike or hike an extra 1.6 miles along Route 108 between the ski area and the Hell Brook Trailhead. Another option is to shorten this hike by descending the Long Trail, which would require walking a half mile on Route 108 back to this hike's start. From the junction of Routes 108 and 100 in Stowe, drive 7.4 miles west on 108 and turn left into the gondola base station parking lot for the Mount Mansfield Ski Area; leave one vehicle there, turn back onto Route 108 west, and continue another 1.6 miles to the small dirt lot on the right at Big Spring, which is 1.2 miles east of the Route 108 height of land in Smuggler's Notch.

**Contact:** Vermont Department of Forests, Parks, and Recreation Region III-Northwest Vermont, 111 West St., Essex Junction, VT 05452, 802/879-5666. Vermont Department of Forests, Parks, and Recreation Commissioner's Office, 103 South Main St., Waterbury, VT 05671-0601, 802/241-3655, website: www.state.vt.us/anr/fpr. Green Mountain Club Inc., 4711 Waterbury-Stowe Rd., Waterbury Center, VT 05677, 802/244-7037, website: www.greenmountainclub.org.

# 9 MOUNT MANSFIELD: THE LONG TRAIL

**4.6 mi/3.5 hrs**

**in Smuggler's Notch State Park in Stowe**

Probably the most commonly hiked route up Vermont's highest peak, 4,393-foot Mount Mansfield, the Long Trail is a good trail of only moderate difficulty. And just 2.3 miles from the road in Smuggler's Notch—after an elevation gain of nearly 2,800 feet—you are standing atop the Chin, Mansfield's true summit, with a 360-degree view taking in all of northern Vermont, including much of the Green Mountains, and stretching to New Hampshire's White Mountains, New York's Adirondacks, and Quebec. Predictably, this is a very popular hike that sees many boots on nice weekends in summer and fall. But I once hiked up this trail on a bone-chilling November day, had Taft Lodge all to myself for a night, and then saw no one as I bagged the summit the next morning.

Numerous features on Mansfield's long, completely exposed ridge bear names that derive from the mountain's resemblance, especially from the east, to a man's profile: the Chin, the Nose, the Forehead, the Upper and Lower Lip, and the Adam's Apple. Mansfield is one of just two peaks in Vermont—the other being Camel's Hump (see the three Camel's Hump hikes in this chapter)—with a significant alpine area, or area above the tree line. The rare plants that grow in this tundralike terrain are fragile, so take care to walk only on the trail or rocks. Be aware also that alpine terrain signals frequent harsh weather: Mansfield can attract wintry weather in any month of the year, so come here prepared for the worst and be willing to turn back whenever conditions turn threatening. A Green Mountain Club caretaker is on duty during the prime hiking season to assist hikers and ensure the protection of the alpine area. There are also TV and radio stations at the summit, a toll road up the mountain, and a ski area operating on its east side.

From the parking area, walk a short distance south on Route 108 and turn right (southbound) onto the white-blazed Long Trail. The trail climbs steeply, crossing a brook and changing direction a few times before reaching Taft Lodge at 1.7 miles. From the clearing at the lodge, you can see the imposing cliffs below the summit. Continue up the LT. The trail emerges from the trees within 0.3 mile of the lodge and then climbs steeply another 0.3 mile to the summit. Return the way you came.

**User groups:** Hikers and dogs. Dogs must be leashed. No wheelchair facilities. This trail should not be attempted in winter except by hikers experienced in mountaineering and prepared for severe winter weather, and is not suitable for bikes, horses, or skis. Hunting is allowed in season.

**Access, fees:** Parking and access are free. Route 108 is not maintained through Smuggler's Notch once the snow falls, only to a point about a half mile east of this hike's start. Camping is prohibited except at the Green Mountain Club cabins and shelters. The Taft Lodge cabin is located on the Long Trail, 1.7 miles south of Route 108.

**Maps:** The waterproof *End-to-End Map of the Long Trail* is available for $8.95 from the Green Mountain Club (see address below), as is the *Northern Vermont Hiking Trail Map,* which covers Mount Mansfield, Camel's Hump, Lake Willoughby, Cotton Brook, Little River, the Worcester Range, and Mount Elmore, for $4.95. For a topographic area map, request Mount Mansfield from USGS Map Sales, Federal Center, Box 25286, Denver, CO 80225, 888/ASK-USGS (888/275-8747), website: http://mapping.usgs.gov.

**Directions:** Drive to the roadside parking area immediately north of where the Long Trail northbound from Mount Mansfield reaches Route 108, 8.5 miles west of the junction of Routes 108 and 100 in Stowe, and 1.7 miles east of the height of land in Smuggler's Notch.

**Contact:** Smuggler's Notch State Park, Box

7248, Mountain Rd., Stowe, VT 05672, 802/253-4014. Vermont Department of Forests, Parks, and Recreation Commissioner's Office, 103 South Main St., Waterbury, VT 05671-0601, 802/241-3655, website: www.state.vt.us/anr/fpr. Green Mountain Club Inc., 4711 Waterbury-Stowe Rd., Waterbury Center, VT 05677, 802/244-7037, website: www.greenmountainclub.org.

## 10 STOWE PINNACLE
### 2.3 mi/1.5 hrs

**in Putnam State Forest near Stowe**

This fairly easy round-trip hike of 2.3 miles leads to the open, craggy summit of Stowe Pinnacle, which is visible from the parking area. A great hike for young children—and quite popular with families—its summit offers excellent views, especially in a wide sweep from the northwest to the southwest, including Camel's Hump to the southwest, Mount Mansfield to the west, and the ski town of Stowe in the valley separating the pinnacle from Mansfield.

The trail begins at the rear of the parking area. Following easy terrain at first, the blue-blazed path traverses areas that are often muddy. It ascends moderately through the woods to a junction with the Skyline Trail (marked by a sign) just over a mile from the parking lot. Turn right and hike uphill another 0.1 mile to the Stowe Pinnacle summit. Return the way you came. See the special note in the Mount Hunger listing in this chapter for a way to link the two hikes on a nice ridge walk.

**User groups:** Hikers and snowshoers. No wheelchair facilities. This trail is not suitable for bikes, horses, or skis. Dogs are not allowed in day-use areas such as picnic areas, but are not restricted on trails. Hunting is allowed in season.

**Access, fees:** Parking and access are free. Trails are closed during the spring mud season, usually mid-April–mid-May.

**Maps:** The *Northern Vermont Hiking Trail Map,* which covers Mount Mansfield, Camel's Hump, Lake Willoughby (including Mounts Hor and Pisgah), Cotton Brook, Little River, the Worces-

ter Range (including Stowe Pinnacle and Mount Hunger), and Mount Elmore, is available from the Green Mountain Club (see address below) for $4.95. For a topographic area map, request Stowe from USGS Map Sales, Federal Center, Box 25286, Denver, CO 80225, 888/ASK-USGS (888/275-8747), website: http://mapping.usgs.gov.

**Directions:** Take I-89 to Exit 10 and turn north onto Route 100. Continue about 10 miles and turn right onto School Street. Drive 0.3 mile and bear right onto Stowe Hollow Road. In another 1.5 miles, drive straight onto Upper Hollow Road and continue 0.7 mile to a parking area for the Pinnacle Trail on the left.

**Contact:** Vermont Department of Forests, Parks, and Recreation, Barre District, 324 North Main St., Barre, VT 05641, 802/476-0170. Vermont Department of Forests, Parks, and Recreation Commissioner's Office, 103 South Main St., Waterbury, VT 05671-0601, 802/241-3655, website: www.state.vt.us/anr/fpr. Green Mountain Club Inc., 4711 Waterbury-Stowe Rd., Waterbury Center, VT 05677, 802/244-7037, website: www.greenmountainclub.org.

## 11 MOUNT HUNGER
### 4 mi/3 hrs

**in Putnam State Forest near Stowe**

One of the nicest hikes in Vermont, yet requiring less effort than higher Green Mountain peaks, Mount Hunger offers long views in virtually every direction from its 3,539-foot summit of bare rock. Dominating the western horizon is the long chain of the Green Mountains, with Camel's Hump the prominent peak to the southwest and Mount Mansfield, Vermont's highest, rising due west. Between Hunger and Mansfield lies a pastoral valley of open fields interspersed with sprawling forest. To the east, on a clear day, you can make out the White Mountains, particularly the towering wall of Franconia Ridge, and farther off, Mount Washington. Hike up here in late fall or winter and you may see the Whites

a hiker climbing Mount Hunger

Pinnacle end. From the Hunger summit, look for the cairns and blazes of the Skyline Trail heading north. The trail dips back into the woods and remains in the trees, but it's an interesting, if somewhat rugged, walk through a lush subalpine forest on a trail that experiences a fraction of the foot traffic seen on the primary trails up Hunger and Stowe Pinnacle. Some three miles or more from the top of Hunger, after the Skyline Trail passes over the wooded, 3,440-foot bump of Hogback Mountain, it descends, steeply in places, to a junction with the Pinnacle Trail. Bear left, reaching the top of Stowe Pinnacle in 0.1 mile. Descend the Pinnacle Trail 1.1 miles to the trailhead parking lot.

**User groups:** Hikers and snowshoers. No wheelchair facilities. This trail is not suitable for bikes, horses, or skis. Dogs are not allowed in day-use areas such as picnic areas, but are not restricted on trails. Hunting is allowed in season.

**Access, fees:** Parking and access are free. Trails are closed during the spring mud season, usually mid-April–mid-May.

**Maps:** The *Northern Vermont Hiking Trail Map,* which covers Mount Mansfield, Camel's Hump, Lake Willoughby (including Mounts Hor and Pisgah), Cotton Brook, Little River, the Worcester Range (including Stowe Pinnacle and Mount Hunger), and Mount Elmore, is available from the Green Mountain Club (see address below) for $4.95. For a topographic area map, request Stowe from USGS Map Sales, Federal Center, Box 25286, Denver, CO 80225, 888/ASK-USGS (888/275-8747), website: http://mapping.usgs.gov.

**Directions:** Take I-89 to Exit 10 and turn north onto Route 100. Drive about three miles and turn right onto Howard Avenue. Continue 0.4 mile and turn left onto Maple Street. In 0.1 mile, turn right onto Loomis Hill, then drive

capped in white. The ascent of Hunger is more than 2,200 feet. I hiked the longer loop described in the special note below, over Hunger and Stowe Pinnacle, with two friends on a fall day when the foliage was near its peak, and we enjoyed a colorful show.

From the parking lot, the blue-blazed Waterbury Trail makes a moderately difficult ascent, passing some cascades, for nearly two miles before emerging above tree line about 100 yards below the summit. After reaching the summit, head back the way you came.

Special note: A ridge trail links the Mount Hunger summit with Stowe Pinnacle (see listing in this chapter), and by shuttling cars to the parking lots at each trailhead, you can make this Worcester Range ridge walk of about seven miles (figure five hours). I recommend hiking up Mount Hunger and descending the Stowe two miles to the junction with Sweet and Riply Roads. Continue left onto Sweet Road. The parking entrance is roughly 1.4 miles farther on the right. There is a sign on the right.

**Contact:** Vermont Department of Forests, Parks, and Recreation, Barre District, 324 North Main St., Barre, VT 05641, 802/476-0170. Vermont Department of Forests, Parks, and Recreation Commissioner's Office, 103 South Main St., Waterbury, VT 05671-0601, 802/241-3655, website: www.state.vt.us/anr/fpr. Green Mountain Club Inc., 4711 Waterbury-Stowe Rd., Waterbury Center, VT 05677, 802/244-7037, website: www.greenmountainclub.org.

## 12 MOUNT PHILO
**2.2 mi/1.5 hrs**
**in Mount Philo State Park between North Ferrisburg and Charlotte**

The view from atop the cliffs of 968-foot Mount Philo far exceeds the expectations I had while driving toward this tiny hill. The bucolic Champlain Valley sprawls before you, flanked by the Green Mountains chain stretching far southward and the brooding Adirondack Mountains rising across Lake Champlain. This 2.2-mile loop over the summit is somewhat steep in places, although not difficult. When the road is open, you can drive to the top of Philo and walk about 0.1 mile to the cliff overlooks.

The blue-blazed trail begins just past the gate, on the left. The trail—which tends to be muddy and slippery in spring—winds up Mount Philo, crossing the summit road once, to the overlooks. After taking in the views, continue past the summit overlooks on a dirt road for 0.1 mile to a large parking lot and descend the paved park road 1.2 miles back to the hike's start.

**User groups:** Hikers, snowshoers, and dogs. Dogs must be leashed. No wheelchair facilities. This trail is not suitable for bikes, horses, or skis; bike riders and skiers should take the summit road up and down.

**Access, fees:** An entrance fee of $2.50 per person age 14 and older, and $2 for children age 4 to 13, is charged from Memorial Day through Columbus Day. Trails are closed during the spring mud season, usually mid-April–mid-May. The park road is not maintained in winter, making it a strenuous cross-country skiing route up the mountain.

**Maps:** While no map is necessary for this hike, a free, basic map is available at park entrances for virtually all state parks. For a topographic area map, request Mount Philo from USGS Map Sales, Federal Center, Box 25286, Denver, CO 80225, 888/ASK-USGS (888/275-8747), website: http://mapping.usgs.gov.

**Directions:** From U.S. 7, about 1.2 miles north of North Ferrisburg and 2.5 miles south of the junction of U.S. 7 and Route F5 in Charlotte, turn east onto State Park Road. Drive a half mile to a parking lot at the base of the mountain, just outside the gate.

**Contact:** Mount Philo State Park, 5425 Mount Philo Rd., Charlotte, VT 05445; or RD 1 Box 1049, North Ferrisburgh, VT 05473, 802/425-2390 in summer, 802/483-2001 in winter. Vermont Department of Forests, Parks, and Recreation Commissioner's Office, 103 South Main St., Waterbury, VT 05671-0601, 802/241-3655, website: www.state.vt.us/anr/fpr.

## 13 CAMEL'S HUMP: FOREST CITY/ BURROWS TRAILS LOOP
**6.4 mi/4.5 hrs**
**in Camel's Hump State Park in Huntington Center**

With the only undeveloped alpine area in the Green Mountain State and a skyline that sets itself apart from everything else for miles, 4,083-foot Camel's Hump may be Vermont's finest peak. The views from its distinctive summit are among the best in New England. To the west are the Adirondacks and Lake Champlain; the Green Mountains stretch out in a long chain to the south; to the southeast rises the prominent mound of Mount Ascutney; to the northeast lie Mount Hunger and

Stowe Pinnacle in the Worcester Range; far to the northeast, on a clear day, the White Mountains are visible; and to the north, when not smothered in clouds, are Bolton Mountain and Mount Mansfield.

Camel's Hump is one of the state's most popular peaks, too, attracting hundreds of hikers on nice weekend days in summer and fall. But twice I've had the summit all to myself, simply by hiking at times when other people don't hike. On one sunny, but bitterly cold, early spring afternoon (before mud season), I gazed through thin haze at the white caps of New Hampshire's Presidential Range and Franconia Ridge, seeming to float in the sky. The treeless summit of Camel's Hump hosts one of the state's few alpine vegetation zones, plants threatened by heavy hiker use. Help protect them by walking only on the trail or bare rock.

You can hike this loop in either direction, but I recommend going from Forest City to the Long Trail and down the Burrows because the exposed ascent of the LT up Camel's Hump's southern ridge is a wonderful climb that builds excitement for the summit. (For a shorter hike, the Burrows round-trip to the summit is 5.4 miles.) The vertical ascent on the loop is about 2,700 feet. The Forest City and Burrows Trails are well-worn paths and well marked with blue blazes; the Long Trail is blazed white. Trail junctions have been marked with signs in the past, but don't count on them. From the Burrows Trailhead, turn right onto the connector trail leading 0.1 mile to the Forest City Trail and then turn left onto it, hiking east. The trail ascends at a moderate grade, reaching the Long Trail about 1.6 miles from the Burrows Trailhead. Turn left (north) on the LT and follow it for nearly two miles to the summit, climbing below and around spectacular cliffs. Beyond the summit, stay on the LT for another 0.3 mile to the Camel's Hump hut clearing and then turn left (west) on the Burrows Trail, which leads 2.4 miles back to the trailhead.

**User groups:** Hikers and dogs. Dogs must be leashed above tree line. No wheelchair facilities. This trail should not be attempted in winter except by hikers experienced in mountaineering and prepared for severe winter weather, and is not suitable for bikes, horses, or skis. Hunting is allowed in season.

**Access, fees:** Parking and access are free. The trails are closed to hiking during mud season, mid-April–Memorial Day. Camping is prohibited except at the two Green Mountain Club cabins—Montclair Glen Lodge, near the Burrows and Long Trails junction, and Bamforth Ridge shelter 5.4 miles north of Montclair Glen Lodge on the Long Trail—and at the Hump Brook tenting area, just off the Dean Trail. From Memorial Day weekend–Columbus Day, a Green Mountain Club caretaker is on duty and a $6-per-person nightly fee is collected to stay at either cabin.

**Maps:** A basic trail map with state park information is sometimes available at the trailhead hiker register. The *Northern Vermont Hiking Trail Map,* which covers Mount Mansfield, Camel's Hump, Lake Willoughby (including Mounts Hor and Pisgah), Cotton Brook, Little River, the Worcester Range (including Stowe Pinnacle and Mount Hunger), and Mount Elmore, is available from the Green Mountain Club (see address below) and costs $4.95. For topographic area maps, request Huntington and Waterbury from USGS Map Sales, Federal Center, Box 25286, Denver, CO 80225, 888/ASK-USGS (888/275-8747), website: http://mapping.usgs.gov.

**Directions:** In Huntington Center, 2.5 miles south of the post office in Huntington Village, turn onto Camel's Hump Road at signs for Camel's Hump State Park. Follow the dirt road, bearing right at forks (state park signs point the way). At 2.8 miles from Huntington Center, there is a small parking area on the right at the Forest City Trailhead; you can start this loop from there (adding 1.5 miles to this hike's distance), or continue up the road another 0.7 mile to a larger parking area at the Burrows Trailhead.

**Contact:** Vermont Department of Forests, Parks, and Recreation Region III-Northwest Vermont, 111 West St., Essex Junction, VT 05452, 802/879-5666. Vermont Department of Forests, Parks, and Recreation Commissioner's Office, 103 South Main St., Waterbury, VT 05671-0601, 802/241-3655, website: www.state.vt.us/anr/fpr. Green Mountain Club Inc., 4711 Waterbury-Stowe Rd., Waterbury Center, VT 05677, 802/244-7037, website: www.greenmountainclub.org.

## 14 CAMEL'S HUMP: LONG TRAIL/ BAMFORTH RIDGE

**11.8 mi/8 hrs**

**in Camel's Hump State Park in North Duxbury**

See the Camel's Hump: Forest City/Burrows Trails Loop for more descriptive information about Camel's Hump. The Long Trail from the north constitutes the most arduous route to the 4,083-foot Camel's Hump summit: 11.8 miles round-trip and some 3,700 feet of ascent. The LT was relocated in 1996 onto this route, also known as the Bamforth Ridge Trail. (The former route of the LT, which passed the Honey Hollow tenting area, has been closed, as has the tenting area.) The LT ascends the rugged Bamforth Ridge, dipping and climbing repeatedly and often steeply, and traversing some boggy terrain. But open ledges at many points along the ridge offer the most sustained views of any routes up Camel's Hump.

From the parking lot, follow the LT's white blazes south. The trail climbs steadily to Camel's Hump clearing at 5.6 miles. From the clearing, the trail grows fairly steep and rugged to the summit, 5.9 miles from the road. Return the way you came.

**User groups:** Hikers and dogs. Dogs must be leashed above tree line. No wheelchair facilities. This trail should not be attempted in winter except by hikers experienced in mountaineering and prepared for severe winter weather,

and is not suitable for bikes, horses, or skis. Hunting is allowed in season.

**Access, fees:** Parking and access are free. The trails are closed to hiking during mud season, roughly mid-April–Memorial Day. Camping is prohibited except at the two Green Mountain Club cabins—Montclair Glen Lodge, near the Burrows and Long Trails junction, and Bamforth Ridge shelter 5.4 miles north of Montclair Glen Lodge on the Long Trail—and at the Hump Brook tenting area, just off the Dean Trail. From Memorial Day weekend–Columbus Day, a Green Mountain Club caretaker is on duty and a $6-per-person nightly fee is collected to stay at the two cabins.

**Maps:** A basic trail map with state park information is sometimes available at the trailhead hiker register. The waterproof *End-to-End Map of the Long Trail* is available for $8.95 from the Green Mountain Club (see address below), as is the *Northern Vermont Hiking Trail Map,* which covers Mount Mansfield, Camel's Hump, Lake Willoughby, Cotton Brook, Little River, the Worcester Range, and Mount Elmore, for $4.95. For topographic area maps, request Huntington and Waterbury from USGS Map Sales, Federal Center, Box 25286, Denver, CO 80225, 888/ASK-USGS (888/275-8747), website: http://mapping.usgs.gov.

**Directions:** From the south, take I-89 to Exit 10. Turn south, drive about a half mile to the end of the road, and turn left onto U.S. 2 east. Continue 1.3 miles and then turn right onto Route 100 south. Proceed just 0.2 mile and turn right at a sign for the Duxbury Elementary School. Just 0.2 mile farther, bear right onto a dirt road at a sign for Camel's Hump. Five miles down that road, continue straight ahead at a sign directing you left for Camel's Hump trails. The parking lot for the Long Trail/Bamforth Ridge Trail lies 2.7 miles farther down the road.

From the north, take I-89 to Exit 11 for U.S. 2 east. Drive about five miles into Jonesville, and just beyond the post office (on the left), turn right, crossing the bridge over the Winooski River. At 0.2 mile from U.S. 2, turn left onto Duxbury Road and continue 3.3 miles to the Long Trail/Bamforth Ridge Trail parking area on the right.

**Contact:** Vermont Department of Forests, Parks, and Recreation Region III-Northwest Vermont, 111 West St., Essex Junction, VT 05452, 802/879-5666. Vermont Department of Forests, Parks, and Recreation Commissioner's Office, 103 South Main St., Waterbury, VT 05671-0601, 802/241-3655, website: www.state.vt.us/anr/fpr. Green Mountain Club Inc., 4711 Waterbury-Stowe Rd., Waterbury Center, VT 05677, 802/244-7037, website: www.greenmountainclub.org.

## 🔟 CAMEL'S HUMP: MONROE/ ALPINE TRAILS LOOP

**6.6 mi/4.5 hrs**

**in Camel's Hump State Park in North Duxbury**

Ⓕ The Monroe Trail—renamed for Professor Will Monroe, father of the Monroe Skyline (see the listing in this chapter)—may be the most popular route up a very popular mountain. For more descriptive information about Camel's Hump, see the Camel's Hump: Forest City/Burrows Trails Loop in this chapter.

This 6.6-mile loop, which ascends about 2,600 feet, includes an interesting variation from the Monroe Trail onto the Alpine Trail. From the parking lot, the blue-blazed Monroe Trail ascends at a moderate grade at first but grows steeper as you climb higher. Trail sections are often wet, even into autumn. At 2.5 miles, turn left onto the yellow-blazed Alpine Trail, which is wooded and fairly rugged along this stretch. Within a half mile, you pass near the wing of a WWII bomber that crashed into the mountain during a wartime training flight at night.

Just beyond the wreckage, the Alpine Trail meets the Long Trail; turn right (north) on the white-blazed LT, quickly emerging from the trees for your first sweeping views from below

the towering cliffs on the Camel's Hump south face. The Long Trail swings left below the cliffs and ascends the mountain's west face to its open, 4,083-foot summit, 0.2 mile from the Alpine Trail. Continue on the Long Trail north over the summit, descending rocky terrain for 0.3 mile to the Camel's Hump hut clearing. Turn right onto the Monroe Trail, which takes you down 3.1 miles to the parking area.

**User groups:** Hikers and dogs. Dogs must be leashed above tree line. No wheelchair facilities. This trail should not be attempted in winter except by hikers experienced in mountaineering and prepared for severe winter weather and is not suitable for bikes, horses, or skis. Hunting is allowed in season.

**Access, fees:** Parking and access are free. The trails are closed to hiking during mud season, roughly mid-April–Memorial Day. Winter parking is in the lot for Camel's Hump View, a half mile before the Couching Lion site. Camping is prohibited except at the two Green Mountain Club cabins—Montclair Glen Lodge, near the Burrows and Long Trails junction, and Bamforth Ridge shelter 5.4 miles north of Montclair Glen Lodge on the Long Trail—and at the Hump Brook tenting area, just off the Dean Trail. From Memorial Day weekend–Columbus Day, a Green Mountain Club caretaker is on duty and a $6-per-person nightly fee is collected to stay at either cabin.

**Maps:** A basic trail map with state park information is sometimes available at the trailhead hiker register. The waterproof *End-to-End Map of the Long Trail* is available for $8.95 from the Green Mountain Club (see address below), as is the *Northern Vermont Hiking Trail Map,* which covers Mount Mansfield, Camel's Hump, Lake Willoughby, Cotton Brook, Little River, the Worcester Range, and Mount Elmore, for $4.95. For topographic area maps, request Huntington and Waterbury from USGS Map Sales, Federal Center, Box 25286, Denver, CO 80225, 888/ASK-USGS (888/275-8747), website: http://mapping.usgs.gov.

**Directions:** From the south, take I-89 to Exit

10. Turn south, drive about a half mile to the end of the road, and turn left onto U.S. 2 east. Continue 1.3 miles and then turn right onto Route 100 south. Proceed just 0.2 mile and turn right onto Duxbury Road; continue six miles down that road, then turn left at a sign for Camel's Hump trails. Drive 1.2 miles and bear left over a bridge. Continue another 2.4 miles to the parking lot at the end of the road, at the so-called Couching Lion site.

From the north, take I-89 to Exit 11 for U.S. 2 east. Drive about five miles into Jonesville, and just beyond the post office (on the left), turn right, crossing the bridge over the Winooski River. In 0.2 mile, turn left onto Duxbury Road and continue six miles to the sign for Camel's Hump trails. Turn right, cross the bridge at 1.2 miles, and continue 2.4 miles to the Couching Lion site.

**Contact:** Vermont Department of Forests, Parks, and Recreation Region III-Northwest Vermont, 111 West St., Essex Junction, VT 05452, 802/879-5666. Vermont Department of Forests, Parks, and Recreation Commissioner's Office, 103 South Main St., Waterbury, VT 05671-0601, 802/241-3655, website: www.state.vt.us/anr/fpr. Green Mountain Club Inc., 4711 Waterbury-Stowe Rd., Waterbury Center, VT 05677, 802/244-7037, website: www.greenmountainclub.org.

## 16 CAMEL'S HUMP VIEW
**0.2 mi/0.25 hr**
**in Camel's Hump State Park in North Duxbury**

Here is an easy walk of just 0.2 mile round-trip to a striking view of Camel's Hump for folks not inclined to actually climb the mountain. It's also a pleasant trail for hikers or cross-country skiers looking for an unusual angle on arguably Vermont's most recognizable peak. From the parking lot, walk up the left fork of the Camel's Hump View Trail, crossing over Sinnott Brook on a wooden bridge and reaching a wooden bench on the right at 0.1 mile. From the bench, look across a clear-

ing for a view of Camel's Hump. You can turn back from here or continue up the trail for a half-mile loop back to the parking lot. The Ridley Crossing ski trail diverges off this loop about halfway through it, leading to the Beaver Meadow Trail, where you would turn right to loop back to the main road just below the Couching Lion site.

**User groups:** Hikers, dogs, skiers, snowshoers, and wheelchair users. Dogs must be leashed. This trail is not suitable for bikes or horses. Hunting is allowed in season.

**Access, fees:** Parking and access are free. The trails in the park are closed to hiking during mud season, roughly mid-April–Memorial Day.

**Maps:** No map is necessary for this hike, although a basic trail map of Camel's Hump State Park is available at the trailhead hiker register at the Couching Lion site. For topographic area maps, request Huntington and Waterbury from USGS Map Sales, Federal Center, Box 25286, Denver, CO 80225, 888/ASK-USGS (888/275-8747), website: http://mapping.usgs.gov.

**Directions:** From the south, take I-89 to Exit 10. Turn south, drive about a half mile to the end of the road, and turn left onto U.S. 2 east. Continue 1.3 miles and then turn right onto Route 100 south. Proceed just 0.2 mile and turn right onto Duxbury Road; continue six miles down that road, then turn left at a sign for Camel's Hump trails. Drive 1.2 miles and bear left over a bridge. Continue another 1.9 miles, turn left (a half mile before the Couching Lion site), and drive another 0.2 mile to the Lewis Place parking area.

From the north, take I-89 to Exit 11 for U.S. 2 east. Drive about five miles into Jonesville, and just beyond the post office (on the left), turn right, crossing the bridge over the Winooski River. In 0.2 mile turn left onto Duxbury Road and continue six miles to the sign for Camel's Hump trails. Turn right, cross the bridge at 1.2 miles, and 1.9 miles past the bridge turn left for the Lewis Place parking area.

**Contact:** Vermont Department of Forests, Parks,

and Recreation Commissioner's Office, 103 South Main St., Waterbury, VT 05671-0601, 802/241-3655, website: www.state.vt.us/anr/fpr.

## 17 BIG DEER MOUNTAIN
**4.2 mi/3 hrs**
**in Groton State Forest**

I first discovered Groton State Forest, in Vermont's Northeast Kingdom, while on a bike tour several years ago; that time, I only spent a night in the campground. More recently, I returned with a friend to mountain bike its forest roads and hike up Big Deer Mountain, which has good views for a hill not even 2,000 feet high. This hike begins from different parking areas, depending upon whether the road into the New Discovery Campground is open. The elevation gained is about 300 feet.

In winter, parking at the gate, walk 0.1 mile past the gate to a field; in summer, backtrack the road from the Osmore Pond picnic area to the field. Facing that field (as you would in winter, walking from the gate), turn left onto an obvious dirt forest road and follow it 0.3 mile and turn right onto the Big Deer Mountain Trail (marked by a sign). Follow the blue blazes through the woods on a trail that's mostly flat for 1.1 miles. Then, at a trail junction, continue straight ahead, climbing about 200 feet in elevation over 0.6 mile of rocky trail onto Big Deer Mountain. The trail ends at open ledges with a view to the south, overlooking Lake Groton. Just before the trail's end, a side path leads left a short distance to another open ledge with a view east from high above Peacham Bog. On a clear day, you can see the White Mountains. Backtrack 0.6 mile to the junction and turn left onto the Big Deer Mountain Trail toward Osmore Pond. It descends gently, crosses a marshy area, passes over a slight rise, and then descends more steeply to a trail junction near the south end of Osmore Pond, 0.9 mile from the last junction. Turn right onto the Osmore Pond Hiking Loop, a rock-strewn but flat trail that parallels the pond's east shore and loops around its north end. In

winter, about 0.7 mile from the trail junction at the pond's south end, turn right again onto a connector trail leading back to the New Discovery Campground. In summer, follow the loop trail around the pond to the picnic area.

**User groups:** Hikers and snowshoers. No wheelchair facilities. This trail is not suitable for bikes, horses, or skis. Dogs are not allowed in day-use areas such as picnic areas, but are not restricted on trails. Hunting is allowed in season.

**Access, fees:** An entrance fee of $2.50 per person age 14 and older, and $2 for children age 4 to 13, is charged from a week before Memorial Day–Labor Day. Trails are closed during the spring mud season, usually mid-April–mid-May. The road into the New Discovery Campground is closed and blocked by a gate when the park is closed, from Labor Day–Memorial Day weekend.

**Maps:** A free, basic map is available at park entrances for virtually all state parks. For a topographic area map, request Marshfield from USGS Map Sales, Federal Center, Box 25286, Denver, CO 80225, 888/ASK-USGS (888/275-8747), website: http://mapping.usgs.gov.

**Directions:** From I-91, take Exit 17 onto U.S. 302 west. Drive about 8.8 miles and turn right onto Route 232 north. Drive 9.4 miles and turn right into the New Discovery Campground. From Memorial Day weekend–Labor Day, continue 0.1 mile past the open gate to a field, turn right, and drive to the picnic shelter on Osmore Pond to park. In winter, park at the gate without blocking it.

**Contact:** New Discovery Campground, 802/426-3042. Vermont Department of Forests, Parks, and Recreation Commissioner's Office, 103 South Main St., Waterbury, VT 05671-0601, 802/241-3655, website: www.state.vt.us/anr/fpr.

## 18 KINGSLAND BAY STATE PARK
**1 mi/0.75 hr**
**in Ferrisburg**

An unmarked but obvious trail begins behind the tennis courts and soon forks, creating a loop through the conifer woods on a point that juts into Lake Champlain; the loop can be done in either direction. Much of the one-mile, easy trail remains in the woods, with limited lake views; there is one clearing with a view northeast toward Camel's Hump and the Green Mountains.

**User groups:** Hikers and snowshoers. No wheelchair facilities. This trail is not suitable for bikes, horses, or skis. Dogs are not allowed in day-use areas such as picnic areas, but are not restricted on trails. Hunting is allowed in season.

**Access, fees:** An entrance fee of $2.50 is charged for persons 14 and older, and $2 for children age 4 to 13, from a week before Memorial Day–Labor Day. Trails are closed during the spring mud season, usually mid-April–mid-May. The park road is closed to traffic in the off-season, but you can walk the road, adding a mile round-trip to this hike's distance.

**Maps:** While no map is necessary for this hike, a free, basic map is available at park entrances for virtually all state parks. For a topographic area map, request Westport from USGS Map Sales, Federal Center, Box 25286, Denver, CO 80225, 888/ASK-USGS (888/275-8747), website: http://mapping.usgs.gov.

**Directions:** From the junction of U.S. 7 and Route 22A north of Vergennes, drive north on U.S. 7 for a half mile and then turn left (west) onto Tuppers Crossing Road. Proceed 0.4 mile and bear right onto Bottsford Road. Drive 0.8 mile and continue straight through a crossroads onto Hawkins Road. Or from North Ferrisburg, drive south on U.S. 7 for about four miles and turn right (west) onto Little Chicago Road. Continue a mile and turn right onto Hawkins. Follow Hawkins Road for 3.4 miles and then turn right at a sign into Kingsland Bay State Park. Follow the dirt park road about a half mile and park at the roadside near the tennis courts.

**Contact:** Kingsland Bay State Park, RR 1, Box 245, 787 Kingsland Bay State Park Rd., Ferrisburg, VT 05456, 802/877-3445 in summer, 802/483-2001 in winter, or 800/658-1622. Vermont Department of Forests, Parks, and Recreation Commissioner's Office, 103 South Main St., Waterbury, VT 05671-0601, 802/241-3655, website: www.state.vt.us/anr/fpr.

## 19 BUTTON BAY STATE PARK
**1 mi/0.75 hr**

**in Ferrisburg**

The park, named for the buttonlike concretions formed by clay deposits found along the shore, has been visited by such famous persons as Samuel De Champlain (in 1609), Ethan Allen (in 1776), Ben Franklin (also in 1776), and Benedict Arnold (in 1777). This flat walk of a mile round-trip along a wide gravel road leads to Button Point, where the land thrusts a finger of rocks into Lake Champlain and the views encompass a wide sweep from Camel's Hump and the Green Mountains to the east, to the Adirondacks across the lake. From the parking lots, walk the gravel road a half mile to its end at Button Point. Return the same way.

**User groups:** Hikers, bikers, skiers, and snowshoers. Wheelchair users can drive the dirt road beyond the public parking lots to wheelchair-accessible parking just 100 yards before the point on Lake Champlain. This trail is not suitable for horses. Dogs are not allowed in day-use areas such as picnic areas, but are not restricted on trails. Hunting is allowed in season.

**Access, fees:** An entrance fee of $2.50 per person age 14 and older, and $2 for children age 4 to 13, is charged from Memorial Day–Columbus Day. Trails are closed during the spring mud season, usually mid-April–Memorial Day. The park road is closed to traffic in the off-season, but you can walk the road, adding a mile round-trip to this hike's distance.

**Maps:** While no map is necessary for this hike, a free, basic map is available to virtually all state parks. For a topographic area map, request Westport from USGS Map Sales, Federal Center, Box 25286, Denver, CO 80225, 888/ASK-USGS (888/275-8747), website: http://mapping.usgs.gov.

**Directions:** From the green in the center of Vergennes, drive south on Route 22A for a half mile and turn right onto Panton Road. Proceed 1.4 miles and turn right onto Basin Harbor Road. Continue 4.5 miles, turn left onto Button Bay Road, and follow it 0.6 mile to the entrance on the right to Button Bay State Park. Drive about a half mile down the park road to two gravel parking lots on the left, across from the pavilion.

**Contact:** Button Bay State Park, RD 3, Box 4075, 5 Button Bay State Park Rd., Vergennes, VT 05491, 802/475-2377 in summer, 802/483-2001 in winter, or 800/658-1622. Vermont Department of Forests, Parks, and Recreation Commissioner's Office, 103 South Main St., Waterbury, VT 05671-0601, 802/241-3655, website: www.state.vt.us/anr/fpr.

## 20 THE LONG TRAIL: ROUTE 17, APPALACHIAN GAP, TO THE WINOOSKI RIVER

**18.4 mi one-way/2–3 days**

**between Appalachian Gap and North Duxbury**

This 18.4-mile leg of the Long Trail is arguably its most spectacular stretch. The hike's centerpiece is 4,083-foot Camel's Hump, but less well-known Burnt Rock Mountain offers one of the best views on the Long Trail; Molly Stark's Balcony is another choice spot, and the trail harbors some gems in the woods like Ladder Ravine. This is the northern section of the fabled Monroe Skyline (see listing, this chapter). The one-way traverse covers rugged terrain and involves more than 3,500 feet of climbing and much more descending (the descent from the summit of Camel's Hump to the Winooski River alone is about 3,700 feet); it can easily take three days.

This hike, especially the Camel's Hump area, is popular in summer and fall, and the shelters tend to fill up quickly on weekends. When above tree line, remember that the fragile alpine vegetation suffers under boots, so stay on the marked trail or rocks. Also be advised that water sources are few along the ridge and generally found only at the shelters.

From Route 17, the Long Trail northbound climbs steeply out of Appalachian Gap for 0.4 mile, descends steeply, and then climbs again to the top of Molly Stark Mountain at one mile from the road. At 1.3 miles, the trail passes over Molly Stark's Balcony, a rock outcropping atop a cliff rising above the trees, where you get a long view north toward Camel's Hump and northeast to the Worcester Range, which includes Mount Hunger and Stowe Pinnacle. Descending more easily, the LT reaches the Beane Trail at 2.6 miles, which leads left (west) about 100 feet to the Birch Glen Camp, and 0.9 mile to a road that travels 1.5 miles to Hanksville. The LT follows easier ground from here, ascending gradually to Cowles Cove shelter at 5.5 miles. Climbing slightly, the trail passes the Hedgehog Brook Trail at 6.4 miles, which descends right (east) 2.5 miles to a road two miles outside North Fayston. Then the Long Trail quickly grows more rugged, climbing to the open, rocky Burnt Rock Mountain summit seven miles into this hike. At 3,168 feet, the summit should be wooded, but it was denuded by fires years ago, and today offers long views of the Green Mountains arcing southward, the Worcester Range to the east and the White Mountains beyond, the Lake Champlain southern tip to the southwest, and New York's Adirondacks brooding darkly behind the lake.

Follow the blazes and cairns carefully as the trail makes numerous turns over Burnt Rock's bare crown. The LT reenters the lush, wild forest, reaching Ladder Ravine at 7.4 miles, a perpetually wet place where a wooden ladder is employed to descend a short cliff. Continuing over rough terrain, the trail climbs over the wooded humps of Ira Allen (at 8.5 miles) and Ethan Allen's two peaks (at 9.5 and 9.6 miles) and then descends past the Allis Trail at 10.4 miles; that trail leads straight ahead to Allis Lookout, where there is a view of the mountains to the north, and terminates at the Long Trail in 0.3 mile. The LT, meanwhile, swings left and descends to Montclair Glen Lodge at 10.6 miles. Just downhill from the cabin on the LT, the Forest City Trail departs left (west), dropping gradually for 2.2 miles to a road outside Huntington Center (see Camel's Hump: Forest City/Burrows Trails Loop, this chapter).

The LT then begins the ascent of Camel's Hump, passing the Dean Trail in Wind Gap (at 10.8 miles), which leads right (east) 2.3 miles to the Couching Lion site. Traversing open ledges on the east side of the Hump's southern ridge, the LT affords excellent views south along the Green Mountains and east in a wide sweep from Mount Ascutney to the Worcester Range. It then reenters the woods again briefly, climbing steeply to a junction at 12.3 miles with the Alpine Trail, which departs right (east) and provides an alternate route around the summit in bad weather, swinging north and reaching the Bamforth Ridge Trail/Long Trail in 1.7 miles. There is 0.2 mile more of steep, exposed hiking, with the trail swinging left around tall cliffs and ascending the west face up the rocky summit cone of Camel's Hump. For a more detailed summit description, see the Camel's Hump: Forest City/Burrows Trails Loop hike in this chapter.

Dropping north off the summit, the LT reaches the Camel's Hump hut clearing at 12.8 miles, where the Monroe Trail leaves right (east), descending 3.1 miles to the Couching Lion site, and the Burrows Trail leaves left (west), descending 2.6 miles to a road outside Huntington Center. Reentering the woods, the LT—since being re-routed in 1996—follows the old Bamforth Ridge Trail north. The descent is rugged, dipping and climbing repeatedly and often steeply, and traversing some boggy terrain. But open ledges at many points along the ridge offer the best views of any trail on Camel's Hump. The LT reaches the parking lot on River Road at 18.4 miles.

**User groups:** Hikers and dogs. Dogs must be leashed above tree line. No wheelchair facilities. This trail should not be attempted in winter except by hikers experienced in mountaineering and prepared for severe winter weather, and is not suitable for bikes, horses, or skis. Hunting is allowed in season.

**Access, fees:** Parking and access are free. The Long Trail is closed from Appalachian Gap to the Winooski River from mid-April–Memorial Day. Much of this Long Trail section is in Camel's Hump State Park; the remainder is on private land. Camping is prohibited except at the Green Mountain Club shelters and campsites: the Birch Glen Camp, 2.6 miles north of Route 17 and 100 feet off the LT on the Beane Trail; the Cowles Cove shelter, 5.5 miles north of Route 17; the Montclair Glen Lodge near the Forest City and Long Trails junction, 10.6 miles north of Route 17; and the Bamforth Ridge shelter 16 miles north of Route 17. From Memorial Day weekend–Columbus Day, a Green Mountain Club caretaker is on duty and a $6-per-person nightly fee is collected to stay at a cabin.

**Maps:** A basic trail map is available at trailheads in Camel's Hump State Park. The waterproof *End-to-End Map of the Long Trail* is available for $8.95 from the Green Mountain Club (see address below), as is the *Northern Vermont Hiking Trail Map,* which covers Mount Mansfield, Camel's Hump, Lake Willoughby, Cotton Brook, Little River, the Worcester Range, and Mount Elmore, for $4.95. For topographic area maps, request Mount Ellen, Huntington, and Waterbury from USGS Map Sales, Federal Center, Box 25286, Denver, CO 80225, 888/ASK-USGS (888/275-8747), website: http://mapping.usgs.gov.

**Directions:** You need to shuttle two vehicles for this one-way traverse. To hike south to north, as described here, leave one vehicle in the trailhead parking lot on River Road in North Duxbury (see Directions for Camel's Hump: Long Trail/Bamforth Ridge). Then drive to where the Long Trail crosses Route 17 in Appalachian Gap, three miles east of the Huntington Road and six miles west of Route 100 in Irasville.

**Contact:** Vermont Department of Forests, Parks, and Recreation Commissioner's Office, 103 South Main St., Waterbury, VT 05671-0601, 802/241-3655, website: www.state.vt.us/anr/fpr. Green Mountain Club Inc., 4711 Waterbury-Stowe Rd., Waterbury Center, VT 05677, 802/244-7037, website: www.greenmountainclub.org.

## 21 MOLLY STARK'S BALCONY
**2.6 mi/2 hrs**
**north of Appalachian Gap**

From Molly Stark's Balcony, a rocky ledge atop a cliff jutting above the woods, you get a long view north toward Camel's Hump and northeast to the Worcester Range, which includes Mount Hunger and Stowe Pinnacle. Though just a 2.6-mile round-trip climbing several hundred feet, this hike has very steep uphill stretches and descents. The Long Trail northbound climbs steeply out of Appalachian Gap for 0.4 mile, drops steeply, then climbs again to Molly Stark Mountain's highest point at one mile from the road. Continue north on the LT for 0.3 mile to the balcony, a small ledge on the right side of the trail immediately before another steep downhill. Return the way you came.

**User groups:** Hikers, snowshoers, and dogs. Dogs must be leashed. No wheelchair facilities. This trail is not suitable for bikes, horses, or skis. Hunting is allowed in season.

**Access, fees:** Parking and access are free. The Long Trail is closed from Appalachian Gap to the Winooski River from mid-April–Memorial Day. This stretch of the Long Trail passes through Camel's Hump State Park, and camping is prohibited except at the Green Mountain Club shelters. The Birch Glen Camp is 1.3 miles north of Molly Stark's Balcony and 100 feet off the LT on the Beane Trail.

**Maps:** The waterproof *End-to-End Map of the Long Trail* is available for $8.95 from the Green Mountain Club (see address below), as is the *Northern Vermont Hiking Trail Map,* which covers Mount Mansfield, Camel's Hump, Lake Willoughby, Cotton Brook, Little River, the Worcester Range, and Mount Elmore, for $4.95. For a topographic area map, request Mount Ellen from USGS Map Sales, Federal Center, Box 25286, Denver, CO 80225, 888/ASK-USGS (888/275-8747), website: http://mapping.usgs.gov.

**Directions:** Drive to where the Long Trail crosses Route 17 in Appalachian Gap, three miles east of the Huntington Road and six miles west of Route 100 in Irasville.

**Contact:** Vermont Department of Forests, Parks, and Recreation Commissioner's Office, 103 South Main St., Waterbury, VT 05671-0601, 802/241-3655, website: www.state.vt.us/anr/fpr. Green Mountain Club Inc., 4711 Waterbury-Stowe Rd., Waterbury Center, VT 05677, 802/244-7037, website: www.greenmountainclub.org.

## 22 THE MONROE SKYLINE
**47.4 mi one-way/5–6 days**
**between Middlebury Gap and North Duxbury**

When the nation's first long-distance hiking trail was in its formative years, this stretch of nearly 50 miles was not along the high mountain ridges it now traverses. It was mired down in the woods, where the state forestry officials who did much of the early trail work wanted it to be so they could access forest fires. Then along came Professor Will Monroe, a respected botanist and author, who over several years beginning in 1916 became the catalyst behind the Green Mountain Club's effort to move the Long Trail up onto the rugged chain of peaks between Middlebury Gap and the Winooski River. Now dubbed the Monroe Skyline, this 47.4-mile section is widely considered the soul of the Long Trail, and is a much-sought-after multiday trek. For backpackers who want to sample the best of the Long Trail and have a week or less, this is the trip to take.

The Monroe Skyline links three sections of the Long Trail described elsewhere in this book. For details, see the descriptions for the following three hikes: The Long Trail: Route 125, Middlebury Gap, to the Lincoln-Warren

Highway, Lincoln Gap; The Long Trail: Lincoln-Warren Highway, Lincoln Gap, to Route 17, Appalachian Gap; and The Long Trail: Route 17, Appalachian Gap, to the Winooski River.

**User groups:** Hikers and dogs. Dogs must be leashed. No wheelchair facilities. This trail should not be attempted in winter except by hikers experienced in mountaineering and prepared for severe winter weather, and is not suitable for bikes, horses, or skis. Hunting is allowed in season, but not near trails.

**Access, fees:** Parking and access are free. See specific access information for the Long Trail sections covered separately.

**Maps:** The waterproof *End-to-End Map of the Long Trail* is available for $8.95 from the Green Mountain Club (see address below), as is the *Northern Vermont Hiking Trail Map,* which covers Mount Mansfield, Camel's Hump, Lake Willoughby, Cotton Brook, Little River, the Worcester Range, and Mount Elmore, for $4.95. For topographic area maps, request Bread Loaf, Lincoln, Mount Ellen, Huntington, and Waterbury from USGS Map Sales, Federal Center, Box 25286, Denver, CO 80225, 888/ASK-USGS (888/275-8747), website: http://mapping.usgs.gov.

**Directions:** You need to shuttle two vehicles for this one-way traverse. To hike south to north, as described here, leave one vehicle in the trailhead parking lot on River Road in North Duxbury (see Directions for Camel's Hump: Long Trail/Bamforth Ridge). Then to reach the trailhead, drive to the large turnout on the south side of Route 125, immediately west of where the Long Trail crosses the road in Middlebury Gap, 5.6 miles east of Ripton and 6.4 miles west of Route 100 in Hancock.

**Contact:** Green Mountain Club Inc., 4711 Waterbury-Stowe Rd., Waterbury Center, VT 05677, 802/244-7037, website: www.green mountainclub.org.

## 23 THE LONG TRAIL: LINCOLN-WARREN HIGHWAY, LINCOLN GAP, TO ROUTE 17, APPALACHIAN GAP

**11.6 mi one-way/8.5 hrs**

**between Lincoln Gap and Appalachian Gap**

This 11.6-mile Long Trail stretch traverses the high, narrow ridge of Lincoln Mountain, passing over its several summits, including spectacular 4,006-foot Mount Abraham (see listing, Southern Green Mountains and Southern Vermont chapter) and two other summits with excellent views. One of the premier sections of the LT, it is also the middle portion of the fabled Monroe Skyline (see listing, this chapter). Although this hike can be done in a long day, many people make a two-day backpacking trip of it or hike it as a link in a longer outing on the LT. The cumulative elevation gain is nearly 2,500 feet.

This is a popular destination in summer and fall, and the shelters tend to fill up quickly on weekends. When above tree line, remember that the fragile alpine vegetation suffers under boots, so stay on the marked trail or rocks. Also be advised that water sources are few along the ridge and generally found only at the shelters (although the spring at the Theron Dean shelter is not reliable in dry seasons).

From the Lincoln-Warren Highway, follow the Long Trail white blazes northbound, gradually beginning the ascent of Mount Abraham. At 1.2 miles, the trail passes a pair of huge boulders named the Carpenters, after two trail workers. At 1.7 miles, the Battell Trail veers left (west), leading two miles to a road; at 0.1 mile farther, the LT reaches the Battell shelter. The trail then climbs more steeply, over rocky terrain and exposed slabs, until it emerges from the trees into the alpine zone atop Abraham, 2.6 miles from the road. The views stretch far down the Green Mountain chain to the south, east to the White Mountains, west to Lake Champlain and the Adirondacks, and north to Lincoln Mountain's other peaks.

At 3.3 miles, a sign indicates the wooded summit of Little Abe, and 0.1 mile farther the

LT crosses Lincoln Peak, at 3,975 feet, where an observation deck to the trail's right offers a panorama. The LT passes through a cleared area above the Sugarbush Valley Ski Area just past the observation deck, bears left, and reenters the forest. The hiking is fairly easy along the ridge, with little elevation shift. At four miles, the LT traverses the wooded summit of Nancy Hanks Peak, passes a Sugarbush chairlift at 4.7 miles, then climbs about 250 feet in elevation to the 4,022-foot Cutts Peak summit, which has good views, at 5.9 miles. Just 0.4 mile farther, the trail passes over the wooded and viewless Mount Ellen summit, at 4,083 feet tied with Camel's Hump for third-highest of Vermont's five official 4,000-footers. (Cutts does not qualify because there is not enough elevation gain and loss between it and Ellen.) The LT almost immediately passes a chairlift for the Sugarbush North Ski Area, bears left along a ski trail for 100 feet, and reenters the woods, descending very rocky ground where footing is difficult.

At 6.7 miles, the LT leaves the national forest, and at 8.1 miles reaches a junction with the Jerusalem Trail, which departs left (west) and continues 2.5 miles to a road. Just 0.1 mile farther, the LT reaches the Barton Trail, which leads to the right (east) 0.2 mile to the Glen Ellen Lodge. The LT then climbs steeply for a short distance to the height of General Stark Mountain (3,662 feet), at 8.5 miles, and reaches the Stark's Nest shelter at 9.1 miles. The LT follows a ski trail briefly, turns left into the woods, crosses a cross-country skiing trail, and then descends steeply to the Theron Dean shelter at 9.8 miles. A path leads a short distance past the shelter to a good view of the mountains to the north. From the shelter, the LT drops steeply, passes another chairlift station at 10 miles, and reaches Route 17 at 11.6 miles.

**User groups:** Hikers and dogs. Dogs must be leashed. No wheelchair facilities. This trail should not be attempted in winter except by hikers experienced in mountaineering and prepared for severe winter weather, and is not suitable for bikes, horses, or skis. Hunting is allowed in season, but not near trails.

**Access, fees:** Parking and access are free. The Long Trail is closed from Lincoln Gap to Appalachian Gap from mid-April–Memorial Day. The road through Lincoln Gap is not maintained during winter. No-trace camping is permitted within the Green Mountain National Forest, but north of the national forest boundary the Long Trail passes through private land, and camping is prohibited except at the Green Mountain Club's Glen Ellen Lodge cabin, located on the Barton Trail, 0.3 mile east of the Long Trail and 8.2 miles north of Lincoln Gap. From Memorial Day weekend–Columbus Day, a caretaker is on duty and a $6-per-person nightly fee is collected at the Battell shelter on the Long Trail, 1.8 miles north of Lincoln Gap. The Theron Dean shelter is on the LT 9.8 miles north of Lincoln Gap and 1.8 miles south of Appalachian Gap.

**Maps:** The waterproof *End-to-End Map of the Long Trail* is available for $8.95 from the Green Mountain Club (see address below). For topographic area maps, request Lincoln and Mount Ellen from USGS Map Sales, Federal Center, Box 25286, Denver, CO 80225, 888/ASK-USGS (888/275-8747), website: http://mapping.usgs.gov.

**Directions:** You need to shuttle two vehicles for this one-way traverse. To hike south to north, as described here, leave one vehicle where the Long Trail crosses Route 17 in Appalachian Gap, three miles east of the Huntington Road and six miles west of Route 100 in Irasville. Then drive to where the Long Trail crosses the Lincoln-Warren Highway in Lincoln Gap, 4.7 miles east of Lincoln and 4.1 miles west of Route 100 in Warren. There is parking 0.2 mile west of Lincoln Gap, as well as along the road near the trail crossing.

**Contact:** Green Mountain National Forest Supervisor, 231 North Main St., Rutland, VT 05701, 802/747-6700, fax 802/747-6766, website: www.fs.fed.us/r9/gmfl. Green Mountain Club Inc., 4711 Waterbury-Stowe Rd., Waterbury Center, VT 05677, 802/244-7037, website: www.greenmountainclub.org.

## Chapter 7

© MICHAEL LANZA

# Southern Green Mountains
# and Southern Vermont

# Southern Green Mountains and Southern Vermont

The southern Green Mountains do not rise as tall or as rugged as their neighbors to the north. But with relatively easy hiking through gorgeous woods, around scenic ponds, and to the top of occasional summits with long views, the bottom of Vermont is well worth exploring. The Long Trail is much gentler on the knees of hikers and backpackers here, and no less pleasant.

This is also a beautiful part of Vermont to hike in during the peak of fall foliage. And even though the summits aren't as high and most of the hiking here is deep in the woods with no long views, the memory of hiking to places like the Big Branch Wilderness, Baker Peak, Styles Peak, and along the southern Long Trail always triggers a special feeling for me. Plus, some of the higher peaks—Glastenbury Mountain, Stratton

Mountain, and Bromley Mountain—have summit towers offering incredible, long views.

This chapter also describes enduringly popular mountains such as Ascutney and secluded, special places such as Silent Cliff, Shrewsbury Peak, Rattlesnake Cliffs, and the Skyline Trail.

The Appalachian National Scenic Trail coincides with the Long Trail for more than 100 miles, from the Massachusetts line to just north of U.S. 4 in Sherburne Pass. Along the AT, dogs must be kept under control, and bikes, horses, hunting, and firearms are prohibited.

See the Northern Green Mountains and Northeast Kingdom chapter introduction for more information about the Long Trail and the Green Mountain Club.

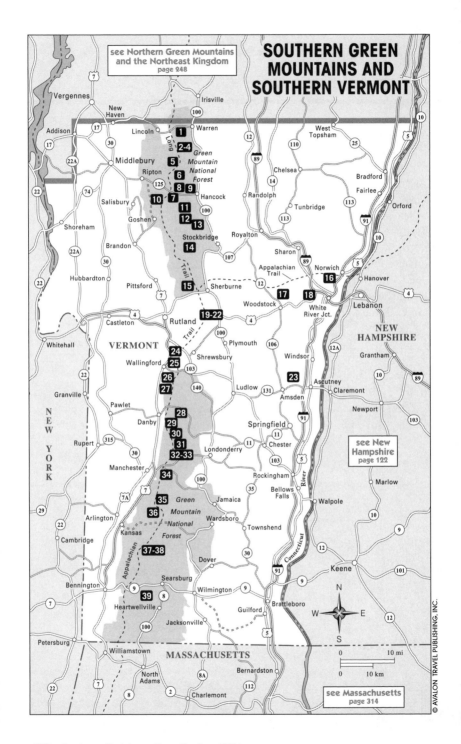

SOUTHERN GREEN
MOUNTAINS AND
SOUTHERN VERMONT

see Northern Green Mountains and the Northeast Kingdom page 248

see New Hampshire page 122

see Massachusetts page 314

© AVALON TRAVEL PUBLISHING, INC.

# ◼ MOUNT ABRAHAM
## 5.2 mi/4 hrs

**in the Green Mountain National Forest north of Lincoln Gap**

At 4,006 feet in elevation, Mount Abraham is one of just five Vermont summits that rise above 4,000 feet—and one of just four that thrust a rocky crown above the trees. For the other three, see Killington Peak (this chapter), Camel's Hump (previous chapter), and Mount Mansfield (previous chapter). The 360-degree view from the top of Abraham stretches south along the Green Mountain chain to Killington, west to the Champlain Valley and the Adirondacks, east to the White Mountains on a clear day, and north along this high ridge, anchored by Abraham at its south end. This hike ascends about 1,600 feet.

Remember that the fragile alpine vegetation above tree line suffers under boots, and stay on the marked trail or rocks. From Lincoln Gap, the hike to the summit is a steep, 5.2-mile round-trip. On the ascent, 1.2 miles from the road, the LT passes a pair of huge boulders known as the Carpenters, named for two trail workers. It passes the Battell Trail at 1.7 miles, which veers left (west), leading two miles to a road, and the Battell shelter, 1.8 miles from the road. From Abraham's summit, you can continue north along this level, high ridge to 3,975-foot Lincoln Peak (making this hike's round-trip distance 6.8 miles), where an observation deck just to the trail's right offers views in every direction.

Still feeling strong? Keep hiking north to Cutts Peak, which has good views, and then an easy 0.4 mile beyond Cutts to the wooded and viewless summit of another Vermont 4,000-footer (4,083-foot Mount Ellen), making this marathon hike a 12.6-mile round-trip from Lincoln Gap. Turn around and descend the way you came.

**User groups:** Hikers and dogs. Dogs must be leashed. No wheelchair facilities. This trail should not be attempted in winter except by hikers experienced in mountaineering and pre-pared for severe winter weather, and is not suitable for bikes, horses, or skis. Hunting is allowed in season, but not near trails.

**Access, fees:** Parking and access are free. The road through Lincoln Gap is not maintained during winter. No-trace camping is permitted within the Green Mountain National Forest. From Memorial Day weekend–Columbus Day, a Green Mountain Club caretaker is on duty and a $6-per-person nightly fee is collected to stay at the Battell shelter, which is on the Long Trail 1.8 miles north of Lincoln Gap. The Long Trail is closed from Lincoln Gap to Appalachian Gap from mid-April–Memorial Day.

**Maps:** The waterproof *End-to-End Map of the Long Trail* is available for $8.95 from the Green Mountain Club (see address below). For topographic area maps, request Lincoln and Mount Ellen from USGS Map Sales, Federal Center, Box 25286, Denver, CO 80225, 888/ASK-USGS (888/275-8747), website: http://mapping.usgs.gov.

**Directions:** Drive to where the Long Trail crosses the Lincoln-Warren Highway in Lincoln Gap, 4.7 miles east of Lincoln and 4.1 miles west of Route 100 in Warren. There is parking 0.2 mile west of Lincoln Gap, as well as along the road near the trail crossing.

**Contact:** Green Mountain National Forest Supervisor, 231 North Main St., Rutland, VT 05701, 802/747-6700, fax 802/747-6766, website: www.fs.fed.us/r9/gmfl. Green Mountain Club Inc., 4711 Waterbury-Stowe Rd., Waterbury Center, VT 05677, 802/244-7037, website: www.greenmountainclub.org.

# ◼ EASTWOOD'S RISE AND MOUNT GRANT
## 7.8 mi/5 hrs

**in the Green Mountain National Forest south of Lincoln Gap**

This one hike really presents the possibility of two different hikes, one a fairly easy round-trip of just 0.8 mile to Eastwood's Rise, a wide, flat ledge looking west all the way to New York's Adirondacks. Hikers seeking a longer outing can continue on to the Mount Grant summit (3,623 feet), with its view south to the Green Mountains' Bread Loaf Wilderness, for a 7.8-mile round-trip. This entire hike ascends about 1,500 feet.

From Lincoln Gap, follow the white blazes of the Long Trail southbound. The trail passes Eastwood's Rise at 0.4 mile, another overlook called Sunset Ledge at 1.1 miles, and then climbs steadily to Mount Grant at 3.9 miles. Hike back to the parking area along the same route.

**User groups:** Hikers and dogs. Dogs must be leashed. No wheelchair facilities. This trail may be difficult to snowshoe because of severe winter weather, and is not suitable for bikes, horses, or skis. Hunting is allowed in season, but not near trails.

**Access, fees:** Parking and access are free. The road through Lincoln Gap is not maintained during winter. No-trace camping is permitted within the Green Mountain National Forest. The Cooley Glen shelter is 0.8 mile south of Mount Grant on the Long Trail.

**Maps:** The waterproof *End-to-End Map of the Long Trail* is available for $8.95 from the Green Mountain Club (see address below). For a topographic area map, request Lincoln from USGS Map Sales, Federal Center, Box 25286, Denver, CO 80225, 888/ASK-USGS (888/275-8747), website: http://mapping.usgs.gov.

**Directions:** Drive to where the Long Trail crosses the Lincoln-Warren Highway in Lincoln Gap, 4.7 miles east of Lincoln and 4.1 miles west of Route 100 in Warren. There is parking 0.2 mile west of Lincoln Gap and along the road near the trail crossing.

**Contact:** Green Mountain National Forest Supervisor, 231 North Main St., Rutland, VT 05701, 802/747-6700, fax 802/747-6766, website: www.fs.fed.us/r9/gmfl. Green Mountain Club Inc., 4711 Waterbury-Stowe Rd., Waterbury Center, VT 05677, 802/244-7037, website: www.greenmountainclub.org.

## 3 MOUNT WILSON
### 8.6 mi/6 hrs

**in the Green Mountain National Forest near South Lincoln**

From the ledges just off the Long Trail, near the top of Mount Wilson (3,745 feet), one can take in the long chain of the Green Mountains stretching southward. It's one of the finest views on the LT between Middlebury Gap and Lincoln Gap. From the parking area, much of this hike's approximately 2,000 feet in elevation gain is accomplished on the Emily Proctor Trail, which largely follows an old logging road and crosses a tributary of the New Haven River three times, once on rocks. The crossings could be tricky in high water. The trail ascends moderately for much of its distance, becoming steeper just before reaching the Long Trail at the Emily Proctor shelter, 3.5 miles from the parking area. Turn left and follow the LT northbound for 0.8 mile to the summit of Mount Wilson. An obvious footpath leads a short distance to the overlook.

Returning the way you came, you might consider making the worthwhile side trip to 3,835-foot Bread Loaf Mountain for a sweeping view south and west of the Green Mountains, the Champlain Valley, and the Adirondack Mountains. From the LT junction with the Emily Proctor Trail, hike southbound on the LT for 0.7 mile to the wooded top of Bread Loaf Mountain. Here, the LT swings left, and a side path leads right for 0.1 mile to the overlook. Bagging Bread Loaf Mountain makes this hike's round-trip distance 10 miles. For another hiking option, see the special note with Skylight Pond (see listing, this chapter).

**User groups:** Hikers and dogs. Dogs must be leashed. No wheelchair facilities. This trail may be difficult to snowshoe because of severe winter weather, and is not suitable for bikes, horses, or skis. Hunting is allowed in season, but not near trails.

**Access, fees:** Parking and access are free. No-trace camping is permitted within the Green Mountain National Forest. The Emily Proctor shelter is located at the Long Trail and Emily Proctor Trail junction, 3.5 miles into this hike. The Skyline Lodge cabin is 0.1 mile east of the Long Trail via the Skylight Pond Trail, and 1.2 mile south of the Bread Loaf Mountain summit.

**Maps:** The waterproof *End-to-End Map of the Long Trail* is available for $8.95 from the Green Mountain Club (see address below). For topographic area maps, request Bread Loaf and Lincoln from USGS Map Sales, Federal Center, Box 25286, Denver, CO 80225, 888/ASK-USGS (888/275-8747), website: http://mapping.usgs.gov.

**Directions:** From the general store in the center of Lincoln, follow the road to South Lincoln for one mile and turn right at a sign for the Emily Proctor Trail. Drive 1.9 miles (it becomes a dirt road) and continue straight ahead onto South Lincoln Road for another two miles. Turn left onto USFS Road 201 and proceed 0.3 mile to parking on the left.

**Contact:** Green Mountain National Forest Supervisor, 231 North Main St., Rutland, VT 05701, 802/747-6700, fax 802/747-6766, website: www.fs.fed.us/r9/gmfl. Green Mountain Club Inc., 4711 Waterbury-Stowe Rd., Waterbury Center, VT 05677, 802/244-7037, website: www.greenmountainclub.org.

# ◢ COOLEY GLEN TRAIL/ EMILY PROCTOR TRAIL LOOP

## 12.5 mi/8.5 hrs

**in the Green Mountain National Forest near South Lincoln**

This 12.5-mile loop traverses three named 3,000-footers, Mounts Cleveland, Roosevelt, and Wilson, the last two of which have good views. The cumulative elevation gain is about 2,500 feet. From the parking area, take the Cooley Glen Trail, which climbs at a moderate grade east, then northeast, paralleling and crossing a stream before reaching the Long Trail at 3.4 miles. The Cooley Glen shelter lies at this trail junction. Turn right (south) on the white-blazed LT, climbing a half mile, steeply at times, to the wooded summit of 3,482-foot Mount Cleveland. The

Long Trail follows a ridge through several short dips and climbs for 3.1 miles to the Mount Roosevelt summit, at 3,528 feet, and a spot known as Killington View, with a good outlook south and west of the mountains.

Descending briefly off Roosevelt, the LT reaches the Clark Brook Trail in another 0.4 mile; that trail branches left (east), leading three miles to a road. The LT then ascends 0.8 mile to Mount Wilson (3,745 feet) and the best view on this hike; follow the obvious side path about 100 feet to the left to an open ledge with a long view south down the backbone of the Green Mountains. Just 0.8 mile farther south on the LT, turn right (north) onto the Emily Proctor Trail—near the shelter of the same name—and descend steadily for 3.5 miles to the parking area.

**User groups:** Hikers and dogs. Dogs must be leashed. No wheelchair facilities. This trail may be difficult to snowshoe because of severe winter weather, and is not suitable for bikes, horses, or skis. Hunting is allowed in season, but not near trails.

**Access, fees:** Parking and access are free. The access road is not maintained for winter access to the trailhead parking lot. No-trace camping is permitted within the Green Mountain National Forest. The Cooley Glen shelter is at the Long Trail and the Cooley Glen Trail junction, 3.4 miles into this hike. The Emily Proctor shelter is located at the Long Trail and Emily Proctor Trail junction, 5.6 miles south of the Cooley Glen shelter.

**Maps:** The waterproof *End-to-End Map of the Long Trail* is available for $8.95 from the Green Mountain Club (see address below). For topographic area maps, request Bread Loaf and Lincoln from USGS Map Sales, Federal Center, Box 25286, Denver, CO 80225, 888/ASK-USGS (888/275-8747), website: http://mapping.usgs.gov.

**Directions:** From the general store in the center of Lincoln, follow the road to South Lincoln for one mile and turn right at the Emily Proctor Trail sign. Go 1.9 miles (it becomes a dirt road) and continue straight on South

Lincoln Road for two miles. Turn left onto USFS Road 201 and drive 0.3 mile to parking on the left.

**Contact:** Green Mountain National Forest Supervisor, 231 North Main St., Rutland, VT 05701, 802/747-6700, fax 802/747-6766, website: www.fs.fed.us/r9/gmfl. Green Mountain Club Inc., 4711 Waterbury-Stowe Rd., Waterbury Center, VT 05677, 802/244-7037, website: www.greenmountainclub.org.

## 5 THE LONG TRAIL: ROUTE 125, MIDDLEBURY GAP, TO THE LINCOLN-WARREN HIGHWAY, LINCOLN GAP

### 17.4 mi one-way/2 days

in the Green Mountain National Forest between Middlebury Gap and Lincoln Gap

This fairly rugged Long Trail stretch passes over nine named 3,000-foot peaks in 17.4 miles. Although most of this ridge walk is wooded, there are several good, long views of the Green Mountains. This is also the southern section of the famous Monroe Skyline (see listing, previous chapter). Typical of New England's mountains, the Long Trail here takes you on a roller coaster ride up and down these peaks in a series of short, often steep steps that can seem endless— while no climb is more than about 500 feet, over the course of this traverse you'll walk some 4,500 feet uphill. But on my own extended Long Trail trek, this section whetted my appetite for the big peaks immediately north—especially the views from spots like Skylight Pond, Bread Loaf Mountain, and Mount Wilson.

From Route 125, the LT northbound climbs steeply for 0.4 mile to a junction with a blue-blazed trail branching right and leading 0.4 mile to Silent Cliff. This easy detour (which adds 0.8 mile to this hike's distance) takes only about 20–30 minutes round-trip and leads to a ledge jutting out over thin air atop Silent Cliff, with a view of Middlebury Gap and the Middlebury Snow Bowl Ski Area, and west to the Champlain Valley and the Adirondacks on a clear day. Immediately before the cliff, a foot-path veers right a few steps to Silent Cave, a passage beneath a massive boulder perched against the mountainside.

From the Silent Cliff Trail junction, the Long Trail swings left and ascends more moderately over 3,040-foot Burnt Hill at 2.1 miles from Route 125, passes the Burnt Hill Trail (which leads west 2.2 miles to a road), and then traverses up and down several summits along the ridge: Kirby Peak (3,140 feet) at 2.7 miles, Mount Boyce (3,323 feet) at 3.6 miles, and Battell Mountain (3,482 feet) at five miles from Route 125. Between Kirby and Boyce, the trail passes Boyce shelter at 3.2 miles. There are a few limited views of surrounding mountains and valleys from along this part of the ridge. At 5.3 miles, the LT is crossed by the Skylight Pond Trail, which leads left (west) 2.3 miles to a road and right (east) 0.1 mile to Skyline Lodge and Skylight Pond, one of the most picturesque spots on this hike. I awoke one morning in Skyline Lodge early enough to catch the predawn sky lit up with vivid red and yellow bands and fog filling the valleys between distant mountain ridges.

From the Skylight Pond Trail, the LT climbs about 400 feet in elevation to Bread Loaf Mountain, where at 6.4 miles a side path leads 0.1 mile to a good overlook south to the long Green Mountains chain and west to the Champlain Valley and Adirondack Mountains. At 7.1 miles, the LT passes the Emily Proctor shelter and the Emily Proctor Trail, which leads north 3.5 miles to a road outside South Lincoln. The LT then ascends about 300 feet to Mount Wilson at 7.9 miles. Do not pass up the obvious path that leads about 100 feet off the trail to ledges where you get a view south down the long backbone of the Greens. The LT descends to a junction with the Clark Brook Trail at 8.7 miles, which leads east three miles to a road; the LT then climbs less than 200 feet to reach the top of 3,528-foot Mount Roosevelt at 9.1 miles, and a spot called Killington View, with a good prospect south and west toward the mountains.

After several more short climbs and descents, the trail passes over the wooded Mount Cleveland summit (3,482 feet) at 12.2 miles and descends to the Cooley Glen shelter at 12.7 miles. From the shelter, the LT swings west and climbs 500 feet over 0.8 mile to the Mount Grant summit (3,623 feet) at 13.5 miles, where you get a view of the Green Mountains' Bread Loaf Wilderness to the south. The LT continues north along the ridge, passing through an interesting birch forest to a broad view west all the way to the Adirondacks from an open ledge at 17 miles called Eastwood's Rise. The trail drops fairly easily to the Lincoln-Warren Highway in Lincoln Gap.

**User groups:** Hikers and dogs. Dogs must be leashed. No wheelchair facilities. This trail may be difficult to snowshoe because of severe winter weather, and is not suitable for bikes, horses, or skis. Hunting is allowed in season, but not near trails.

**Access, fees:** Parking and access are free. The road through Lincoln Gap is not maintained during winter. No-trace camping is permitted within the Green Mountain National Forest. North from Route 125 on the Long Trail, it is 5.1 miles to the Skylight Pond Trail, which leads east 0.1 mile to the Skyline Lodge cabin; 6.9 miles to the Emily Proctor shelter; and 12.6 miles to the Cooley Glen shelter (the last is 4.7 miles south of the Lincoln-Warren Highway).

**Maps:** The waterproof *End-to-End Map of the Long Trail* is available for $8.95 from the Green Mountain Club (see address below). For topographic area maps, request Bread Loaf and Lincoln from USGS Map Sales, Federal Center, Box 25286, Denver, CO 80225, 888/ASK-USGS (888/275-8747), website: http://mapping.usgs.gov.

**Directions:** You need to shuttle two vehicles for this one-way traverse. To hike south to north, as described here, leave one vehicle where the Long Trail crosses the Lincoln-Warren Highway in Lincoln Gap, 4.7 miles east of Lincoln and 4.1 miles west of Route 100 in Warren. There is parking 0.2 mile west of Lincoln Gap, as well as along the road near the

trail crossing. Then drive to the large turnout on Route 125's south side, immediately west of where the Long Trail crosses the road in Middlebury Gap, 5.6 miles east of Ripton and 6.4 miles west of Route 100 in Hancock.

**Contact:** Green Mountain National Forest Supervisor, 231 North Main St., Rutland, VT 05701, 802/747-6700, fax 802/747-6766, website: www.fs.fed.us/r9/gmfl. Green Mountain Club Inc., 4711 Waterbury-Stowe Rd., Waterbury Center, VT 05677, 802/244-7037, website: www.greenmountainclub.org.

## 6 SKYLIGHT POND
**4.8 mi/3.2 hrs**

**in the Green Mountain National Forest between Middlebury Gap and Lincoln Gap**

I woke up alone in the Skyline Lodge one late October morning, before dawn, and saw fire through a musty window. I stepped outside and stood in the chill for about 45 minutes, watching a spectacular sunrise come to life on the distant eastern horizon, with mountain ridges and fog-filled valleys in the middle distance and the whole scene reflected in Skylight Pond. This is a popular spot, no doubt because the lodge is one of the nicest cabins along the entire trail. This 4.8-mile, round-trip hike can easily be done in a half day, but you just might be tempted to spend the night in the lodge and catch the sunrise. From the parking area, follow the Skylight Pond Trail, which ascends moderately for 2.3 miles to the Long Trail. It crosses the LT and continues 0.1 mile to the lodge, completing a climb of about 1,400 feet. Return the way you came.

Special note: Want to make a longer adventure of it? By shuttling two vehicles, you could combine this hike and Mount Wilson (see listing, this chapter) by taking the Skylight Pond Trail to the pond, the Long Trail north over Bread Loaf Mountain to Mount Wilson, then backtracking on the LT and descending the Emily Proctor Trail, a 9.4-mile trek. From the Skylight Pond Trail parking area, continue driving north on USFS Road 59, bear right onto USFS Road 54, and then turn right onto USFS Road 201 to reach the Emily Proctor Trail parking area.

**User groups:** Hikers and dogs. Dogs must be leashed. No wheelchair facilities. This trail may be difficult to snowshoe because of severe winter weather, and is not suitable for bikes, horses, or skis. Hunting is allowed in season, but not near trails.

**Access, fees:** Parking and access are free. USFS Road 59 is not maintained in winter. No-trace camping is permitted within the Green Mountain National Forest. The Skyline Lodge cabin is 0.1 mile off the Long Trail, 2.4 miles into this hike, at the Skylight Pond Trail's end.

**Maps:** The waterproof *End-to-End Map of the Long Trail* is available for $8.95 from the Green Mountain Club (see address below). For topographic area maps, request Bread Loaf and Lincoln from USGS Map Sales, Federal Center, Box 25286, Denver, CO 80225, 888/ASK-USGS (888/275-8747), website: http://mapping.usgs.gov.

**Directions:** From Route 125, nine miles west of the junction of Routes 125 and 100 in Hancock and 2.8 miles east of Ripton (or 0.8 mile east of the Robert Frost Interpretive Trail parking lot), turn north onto USFS Road 59 and drive about 3.5 miles to parking for the Skylight Pond Trail.

**Contact:** Green Mountain National Forest Supervisor, 231 North Main St., Rutland, VT 05701, 802/747-6700, fax 802/747-6766, website: www.fs.fed.us/r9/gmfl. Green Mountain Club Inc., 4711 Waterbury-Stowe Rd., Waterbury Center, VT 05677, 802/244-7037, website: www.greenmountainclub.org.

# 7 ROBERT FROST INTERPRETIVE TRAIL
**1 mi/0.75 hr**
**in the Green Mountain National Forest between Ripton and Hancock**

This interpretive trail, beginning from the parking lot, makes a flat, one-mile loop through various microenvironments, including forest, marsh, brooks, and an open meadow with a Green Mountains view. Along the trail are information boards identifying vegetation and containing snippets of verse from the famous New England poet for whom the trail is named. It's a tranquil place to visit under a blanket of snow, although the information boards may be covered by the white stuff, too.

**User groups:** Hikers, dogs, skiers, and snowshoers. A portion of this trail is wheelchair accessible. Dogs must be leashed. This trail is not suitable for bikes or horses. Hunting is allowed in season, but not near trails.

**Access, fees:** Parking and access are free.

**Maps:** No map is necessary for this hike. A brochure with information about this and other trails in the national forest's Middlebury and Rochester districts is available from the Green Mountain National Forest Supervisor (see address below). For a topographic area map, request Bread Loaf from USGS Map Sales, Federal Center, Box 25286, Denver, CO 80225, 888/ASK-USGS (888/275-8747), website: http://mapping.usgs.gov.

**Directions:** Drive to the parking area on the south side of Route 125, 9.8 miles west of the junction of Routes 125 and 100 in Hancock and two miles east of Ripton (also 0.1 mile west of the Robert Frost Wayside Area on Route 125).

**Contact:** Green Mountain National Forest Supervisor, 231 North Main St., Rutland, VT 05701, 802/747-6700, fax 802/747-6766, website: www.fs.fed.us/r9/gmfl.

# 8 SILENT CLIFF
**1.6 mi/1 hr**
**in the Green Mountain National Forest at Middlebury Gap**

The view from atop Silent Cliff, where a ledge juts out into thin air like a defiant chin, takes in a wide sweep of Middlebury Gap, the Middlebury Snow Bowl Ski Area across the gap, and west to the Champlain Valley and the Adirondacks on a clear day. While half the hike is steep, it's just 1.6 miles round-trip and about 400 feet uphill, and is a good trip for young children. From the parking area on Route 125, cross the road and follow the Long Trail northbound, climbing steeply for 0.4 mile. Turn right onto the blue-blazed Silent Cliff Trail, which leads 0.4 mile over much easier terrain to the cliff. Immediately before the cliff is Silent Cave, a steep and tight cavelike passage beneath a massive boulder perched against the mountainside—another attraction guaranteed to fascinate kids. Return the way you came. You might combine this with the Middlebury Gap hike (see listing, this chapter).

**User groups:** Hikers and dogs. Dogs must be leashed. No wheelchair facilities. This trail may be difficult to snowshoe because of severe winter weather, and is not suitable for bikes, horses, or skis. Hunting is allowed in season, but not near trails.

**Access, fees:** Parking and access are free. No-trace camping is permitted within the Green Mountain National Forest. The Boyce shelter is on the Long Trail, 3.1 miles north of Route 125 and 2.7 miles beyond the junction of the Long and Silent Cliff trails.

**Maps:** The waterproof *End-to-End Map of the Long Trail* is available for $8.95 from the Green Mountain Club (see address below). For a topographic area map, request Bread Loaf from USGS Map Sales, Federal Center, Box 25286, Denver, CO 80225, 888/ASK-USGS (888/275-8747), website: http://mapping.usgs.gov.

**Directions:** Drive to the large turnout on the south side of Route 125, immediately west of where the Long Trail crosses the road in Middlebury Gap, 5.6 miles east of Ripton and 6.4 miles west of Route 100 in Hancock.

**Contact:** Green Mountain National Forest Supervisor, 231 North Main St., Rutland, VT 05701, 802/747-6700, fax 802/747-6766, website: www.fs.fed.us/r9/gmfl. Green Mountain Club Inc., 4711 Waterbury-Stowe Rd., Waterbury Center, VT 05677, 802/244-7037, website: www.greenmountainclub.org.

# 🖪 TEXAS FALLS NATURE TRAIL
## 1 mi/1 hr

**in the Green Mountain National Forest between Ripton and Hancock**

Cross USFS Road 39 from the parking turnout, walk down a few steps, and you are at Texas Falls, where Texas Brook charges through a narrow, spectacular gorge. Cross the brook on a wooden bridge—with an excellent view of the gorge—to the start of the one-mile nature trail loop. Bearing left, the trail follows the brook upstream along a well-graded, easy path. Within a half mile, the trail swings right, ascends the hillside briefly, then swings right again, looping back to the start. It's a good hike for introducing young children to the national forest.

**User groups:** Hikers, snowshoers, and dogs. Dogs must be leashed. No wheelchair facilities. This trail is not suitable for bikes, horses, or skis. Hunting is allowed in season, but not near trails.

**Access, fees:** Parking and access are free. The Texas Falls Recreation Area is closed from 10 P.M.–6 A.M. From late fall into spring, USFS Road 39 can be hazardous from snow and ice.

**Maps:** No map is necessary for this hike. A brochure with information about this and other trails in the national forest's Middlebury and Rochester districts is available from the Green Mountain National Forest Supervisor (see address below). For a topographic area map, request Bread Loaf from USGS Map Sales, Federal Center, Box 25286, Denver, CO 80225, 888/ASK-USGS (888/275-8747), website: http://mapping.usgs.gov.

**Directions:** From Route 125, 3.1 miles west of the junction of Routes 125 and 100 in Hancock and 8.7 miles east of Ripton, turn north onto USFS Road 39 at a sign for Texas Falls. Drive a half mile to a turnout on the left.

**Contact:** Green Mountain National Forest Supervisor, 231 North Main St., Rutland, VT 05701, 802/747-6700, fax 802/747-6766, website: www.fs.fed.us/r9/gmfl.

## 10 FALLS OF LANA AND RATTLESNAKE CLIFFS

**4.8 mi/3 hrs**

**in the Green Mountain National Forest and Branbury State Park south of Middlebury**

On a crisp and clear mid-November day, with the leaves long dead on the ground, I made this 4.8-mile hike past the beautiful Falls of Lana and up to Rattlesnake Cliffs for a long, late-afternoon view stretching to New York's Adirondack Mountains. This moderate hike begins in Branbury State Park and enters the Green Mountain National Forest, ascending about 1,000 feet to Rattlesnake Cliffs.

From the parking area, follow the wide woods road a half mile to the Falls of Lana. Be sure to look for faint side paths leading left to various viewpoints above the falls, which tumble well over 100 feet through several picturesque cascades and pools. Many hikers turn back from the Falls of Lana for a round-trip of just one mile, but this hike continues past the falls, crossing Sucker Brook in another 0.1 mile. (To the right of the bridge is the Falls picnic area.) Beyond the bridge, walk straight ahead onto the North Branch Trail and then bear right within 100 feet at signs for Rattlesnake Cliffs and the North Branch Trail. Follow that trail for 0.1 mile, then turn left at a sign onto the Aunt Jennie Trail. The trail ascends, steeply in some places, about one mile until you reach the junction with the Rattlesnake Cliffs Trail. Turn left and follow that trail 0.1 mile to another junction. Bear left and hike 0.2 mile to the trail's end atop cliffs with a sweeping view that encompasses tiny Silver Lake, the bigger Lake Dunmore, and the Adirondacks in the distance. Backtrack up the trail about 50 yards to a side path branching to the right; a big tree and wooden post may be blown down across the path. Continue on the path downhill for 0.1 mile to another sweeping view, this one to the south. Backtrack again all the way to the Rattlesnake Cliffs Trail and descend to the parking area the same way you came.

**User groups:** Hikers, snowshoers, and dogs. Dogs must be leashed. No wheelchair facilities. This trail is not suitable for bikes, horses, or skis. Hunting is allowed in season, but not near trails.

**Access, fees:** Parking and access are free.

**Maps:** A basic trail map with state park information is available from the Vermont Department of Forests, Parks, and Recreation (see address below). A similar basic trail map with information about these and other trails in the national forest's Middlebury and Rochester districts is available from the Green Mountain National Forest Supervisor (see address below). For a topographic area map, request East Middlebury from USGS Map Sales, Federal Center, Box 25286, Denver, CO 80225, 888/ASK-USGS (888/275-8747), website: http://mapping.usgs.gov.

**Directions:** Drive to the parking area on the east side of Route 53, 5.3 miles north of the junction of Routes 53 and 73 in Forest Dale and 0.4 mile south of the Branbury State Park entrance.

**Contact:** Branbury State Park, 3570 Lake Dunmore Rd., Route 53, Salisbury, VT 05733, 802/247-5925 in summer, 802/483-2001 in winter, or 800/658-1622. Vermont Department of Forests, Parks, and Recreation Commissioner's Office, 103 South Main St., Waterbury, VT 05671-0601, 802/241-3655, website: www.state.vt.us/anr/fpr. Green Mountain National Forest Supervisor, 231 North Main St., Rutland, VT 05701, 802/747-6700, fax 802/747-6766, website: www.fs.fed.us/r9/gmfl.

## 11 MIDDLEBURY GAP

**6.4 mi/4.5 hrs**

**in the Green Mountain National Forest at Middlebury Gap**

Hiking the Long Trail south from Middlebury Gap will bring you past a series of views which, while neither sweeping nor grand, make for a pleasant jaunt on a relatively quiet section of the trail. The cumulative elevation gained hiking out and back approaches 2,000 feet. From the road, the trail climbs slightly for 0.4 mile to a side path on the right that leads 0.1 mile to Lake Pleiad and the site of a former shelter, where camping is now prohibited. Continuing south on the white-blazed Long Trail, you cross a pair of ski area trails, and soon reach the first viewpoint, Robert Frost Lookout. The LT goes through some short ups and downs to Monastery Lookout, 2.6 miles from Middlebury Gap. The wooded Worth Mountain summit lies just 0.1 mile farther, and then the trail descends for a half mile past other limited views to South Worth Lookout, 3.2 miles from the highway. Backtracking from here makes a 6.4-mile round-trip. For a slightly longer outing, combine this hike with Silent Cliff (see listing, this chapter).

**User groups:** Hikers and dogs. Dogs must be leashed. No wheelchair facilities. This trail may be difficult to snowshoe because of severe winter weather, and is not suitable for bikes, horses, or skis. Hunting is allowed in season, but not near trails.

**Access, fees:** Parking and access are free. No-trace camping is permitted within the Green Mountain National Forest. The Sucker Brook shelter is on the Long Trail, 4.4 miles south of Route 125 and 1.2 miles beyond the turnaround point for this hike.

**Maps:** The waterproof *End-to-End Map of the Long Trail* is available for $8.95 from the Green Mountain Club (see address below). For a topographic area map, request Bread Loaf from USGS Map Sales, Federal Center, Box 25286, Denver, CO 80225, 888/ASK-USGS (888/275-8747), website: http://mapping.usgs.gov.

**Directions:** Drive to the large turnout on the south side of Route 125, immediately west of where the Long Trail crosses the road in Middlebury Gap, 5.6 miles east of Ripton and 6.4 miles west of Route 100 in Hancock.

**Contact:** Green Mountain National Forest Supervisor, 231 North Main St., Rutland, VT 05701, 802/747-6700, fax 802/747-6766, website: www.fs.fed.us/r9/gmfl. Green Mountain Club Inc., 4711 Waterbury-Stowe Rd., Waterbury Center, VT 05677, 802/244-7037, website: www.greenmountainclub.org.

## 12 THE LONG TRAIL: ROUTE 73, BRANDON GAP, TO ROUTE 125, MIDDLEBURY GAP

**9.8 mi one-way/7.5 hrs**

in the Green Mountain National Forest between Brandon Gap and Middlebury Gap

The most significant natural feature along this 9.8-mile stretch of the Long Trail is the Great Cliff of Mount Horrid, but there are also views from points on the mostly wooded ridge north of Worth Mountain. The trail continues to grow more rugged, with repeated short but fairly steep climbs and descents and significant elevation gains and losses—the biggest being the climb of about 1,200 feet from the road in Brandon Gap to the 3,366-foot Gillespie Peak summit. The cumulative elevation gain on this hike approaches 2,500 feet.

From Route 73, follow the white blazes of the Long Trail northbound. The trail makes quick left and right turns, enters the woods, and begins a steep ascent of 0.6 mile to a junction with a blue-blazed side path leading right 0.1 mile to the view of the gap from the Great Cliff at Mount Horrid. From that junction, the LT ascends more moderately, passing over the wooded Mount Horrid summit (3,216 feet) at 1.2 miles. It then follows the forested ridge, with steep and rocky rises and dips, over Cape Lookoff Mountain at 1.7 miles, Gillespie Peak at 3.2 miles, and Romance Mountain's east summit (3,125 feet) at four miles, before descending to the Sucker Brook shelter at 5.4 miles. The trail then ascends, steeply at times, reaching Worth Mountain at 7.1 miles and follows the ridge north of the mountain past some views to the east and west.

Gradually descending, the LT passes a chairlift station for the Middlebury Snow Bowl, crosses a pair of ski trails, and then reaches a side path on the left at 9.4 miles that leads 0.1 mile to Lake Pleiad and the former site of a shelter; camping is prohibited here. The trail then descends slightly to Route 125 at 9.8 miles.

**User groups:** Hikers and dogs. Dogs must be leashed. No wheelchair facilities. This trail may be difficult to snowshoe because of severe winter weather, and is not suitable for bikes, horses, or skis. Hunting is allowed in season, but not near trails.

**Access, fees:** Parking and access are free. No-trace camping is permitted within the Green Mountain National Forest. The Sucker Brook shelter is on the Long Trail, 5.4 miles north of Route 73.

**Maps:** The waterproof *End-to-End Map of the Long Trail* is available for $8.95 from the Green Mountain Club (see address below). For topographic area maps, request Mount Carmel and Bread Loaf from USGS Map Sales, Federal Center, Box 25286, Denver, CO 80225, 888/ASK-USGS (888/275-8747), website: http://mapping.usgs.gov.

**Directions:** You need to shuttle two vehicles for this one-way traverse. To hike south to north, as described here, leave one vehicle in the large turnout on the south side of Route 125, immediately west of where the Long Trail crosses the road in Middlebury Gap, 5.6 miles east of Ripton and 6.4 miles west of Route 100 in Hancock. Then drive to the parking area immediately west of where the LT crosses Route 73 in Brandon Gap, 5.2 miles east of Forest Dale and 9.7 miles west of the Route 100 junction south of Rochester.

**Contact:** Green Mountain National Forest Supervisor, 231 North Main St., Rutland, VT 05701, 802/747-6700, fax 802/747-6766, website: www.fs.fed.us/r9/gmfl. Green Mountain Club Inc., 4711 Waterbury-Stowe Rd., Waterbury Center, VT 05677, 802/244-7037, website: www.greenmountainclub.org.

## 🔢 GREAT CLIFF OF MOUNT HORRID

**1.2 mi/1 hr**

**in the Green Mountain National Forest at Brandon Gap**

The Great Cliff of Mount Horrid scowls high above the highway in Brandon Gap, its scarred and crumbling face something of an anomaly in the rounded, generally heavily wooded Green Mountains. This hike, while just 1.2 miles round-trip, climbs quite steeply for about 600 feet to the excellent view of the gap and mountains from the cliff. From Route 73, follow the white blazes of the Long Trail northbound. The trail turns left and right, enters the woods, and climbs for 0.6 mile to a junction with a blue-blazed side path on the right. Follow that side trail 0.1 mile to the view from the cliff. Hike back the same way.

**User groups:** Hikers, snowshoers, and dogs. Dogs must be leashed. No wheelchair facilities. This trail is not suitable for bikes, horses, or skis. Hunting is allowed in season, but not near trails.

**Access, fees:** Parking and access are free. No-trace camping is permitted within the Green Mountain National Forest. The Sucker Brook shelter is on the Long Trail, 5.4 miles north of Route 73.

**Maps:** The waterproof *End-to-End Map of the Long Trail* is available for $8.95 from the Green Mountain Club (see address below). For a topographic area map, request Mount Carmel from USGS Map Sales, Federal Center, Box 25286, Denver, CO 80225, 888/ASK-USGS (888/275-8747), website: http://mapping.usgs.gov.

**Directions:** Drive to the parking area immediately west of where the Long Trail crosses Route 73 in Brandon Gap, 5.2 miles east of Forest Dale and 9.7 miles west of the Route 100 junction south of Rochester.

**Contact:** Green Mountain National Forest Supervisor, 231 North Main St., Rutland, VT 05701, 802/747-6700, fax 802/747-6766, website: www.fs.fed.us/r9/gmfl. Green Mountain Club Inc., 4711 Waterbury-Stowe Rd., Waterbury Center, VT 05677, 802/244-7037, website: www.greenmountainclub.org.

## 🔢 THE LONG TRAIL: U.S. 4 TO ROUTE 73, BRANDON GAP

**19.9 mi one-way/2 days**

**between Sherburne and Brandon Gap**

This nearly 20-mile Long Trail section is entirely within the woods and fairly flat, with only a few climbs and descents during which elevation gain or loss is no more than 500 or 600 feet—though the cumulative climbing over the entire hike nears 3,000 feet.

The Long Trail was rerouted in September 1999; where it previously crossed U.S. 4 in Sherburne Pass, near the Inn at Long Trail, it now crosses the highway one mile west of the pass. From U.S. 4, pick up the white-blazed Long Trail/Appalachian Trail northbound. It climbs to Willard Gap, rejoining the old route of the LT. To the right, the Appalachian Trail northbound heads toward New Hampshire; for the great view west from the cliff at Deer Leap Trail, walk 0.1 mile down that trail, turn right onto the Deer Leap Trail, and continue less than a mile (this distance is not included in this hike's total distance). This hike turns left and follows the LT northbound along the wooded ridge to Tucker Johnson shelter, 0.4 mile from Willard Gap. The LT continues on fairly easy ground, following an old logging road for awhile. Watch closely for blazes; if you lose the trail, you could find yourself in a maze of woods roads.

The trail crosses the abandoned Chittenden-Pittsfield Road at 3.7 miles, which leads right (east) 0.9 mile to Elbow Road (down which it's another 1.4 miles to Route 100). The LT reaches Rolston Rest shelter 5.4 miles from U.S. 4. The trail climbs over slight rises in the ridge; Chittenden Reservoir may be visible through the trees to the west. At 13.1 miles, the New Boston Trail departs left (west), reaching the David Logan shelter in 0.2 mile, and in 1.2 miles a public road that leads to Chittenden. The trail climbs and dips a bit more beyond this junction—over Mount Carmel without reaching its wooded, 3,361-foot summit, down through Wetmore Gap at 14 miles, over the Bloodroot Mountain east slope, and descending through Bloodroot Gap at 16.5 miles. Passing over one more hill, the Long Trail descends at a very easy grade to Sunrise shelter at 19.8 miles. The trail continues descending another 0.9 mile to Route 73; about 0.2 mile before the highway, you get a good view toward the Great Cliff of Mount Horrid.

**User groups:** Hikers and dogs. Dogs must be leashed. No wheelchair facilities. This trail should not be attempted in winter except by hikers prepared for severe winter weather, and is not suitable for bikes, horses, or skis. Hunting is allowed in season, but not near trails.

**Access, fees:** Parking and access are free. No-trace camping is permitted within the Green Mountain National Forest; elsewhere, camping is prohibited except at the Green Mountain Club cabins and shelters. The Long Trail is on private land from U.S. 4 to the New Boston Trail, and within the Green Mountain National Forest north of the New Boston Trail. The Tucker Johnson shelter is about 1.4 miles north of U.S. 4; the Rolston Rest shelter is 5.0 miles north of U.S. 4; the David Logan shelter is 0.2 mile south of the LT via the New Boston Trail, which leaves the LT 12.7 miles north of U.S. 4; and the Sunrise shelter is 19 miles north of U.S. 4 (or 0.9 mile south of Route 73).

**Maps:** The waterproof *End-to-End Map of the Long Trail* is available for $8.95 from the Green Mountain Club (see address below). For topographic area maps, request Pico Peak, Chittenden, Mount Carmel, and Rochester from USGS Map Sales, Federal Center, Box 25286, Denver, CO 80225, 888/ASK-USGS (888/275-8747), website: http://mapping.usgs.gov.

**Directions:** You need to shuttle two vehicles for this one-way traverse. To hike south to north, as described here, leave one vehicle in the parking area immediately west of where the Long Trail crosses Route 73 in Brandon Gap, 5.2 miles east of Forest Dale and 9.7 miles west of the Route 100 junction south of Rochester. Then drive to the Long Trail/Appalachian Trail crossing of U.S. 4, one mile west of Sherburne Pass.

**Contact:** Green Mountain National Forest Supervisor, 231 North Main St., Rutland, VT 05701, 802/747-6700, fax 802/747-6766, website: www.fs.fed.us/r9/gmfl. Green Mountain

Club Inc., 4711 Waterbury-Stowe Rd., Waterbury Center, VT 05677, 802/244-7037, website: www.greenmountainclub.org.

## 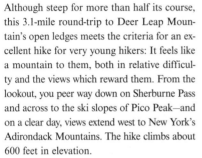 DEER LEAP MOUNTAIN
**3.1 mi/2 hrs**

**in Sherburne**

Although steep for more than half its course, this 3.1-mile round-trip to Deer Leap Mountain's open ledges meets the criteria for an excellent hike for very young hikers: It feels like a mountain to them, both in relative difficulty and the views which reward them. From the lookout, you peer way down on Sherburne Pass and across to the ski slopes of Pico Peak—and on a clear day, views extend west to New York's Adirondack Mountains. The hike climbs about 600 feet in elevation.

From the parking area, cross U.S. 4 and pick up the blue-blazed Sherburne Pass Trail (formerly the Long Trail northbound), entering the woods just east of the Inn at Long Trail. The trail immediately begins a steep, rocky, half-mile climb to a junction with the Appalachian Trail. Turn onto the AT southbound (actually walking north briefly), and within moments you'll reach the Deer Leap Trail, marked by blue blazes. Follow it up onto a small ridge and through birch forest for 0.9 mile, then turn left onto the Deer Leap Overlook Trail and follow it a quarter mile to the open ledges overlooking the Coolidge Range and Sherburne Pass.

Backtrack to the Deer Leap Trail. To complete a loop hike, turn north, descending steeply to a brook, then climbing over Big Deer Leap Mountain. The trail will return you to the AT. Turn right, following the AT northbound (though walking southward) back to the Sherburne Pass Trail, then follow the latter back to the trailhead.

**User groups:** Hikers and dogs. No wheelchair facilities. This trail may be difficult to snowshoe and is not suitable for skis. Bikes, horses, and hunting are prohibited.

**Access, fees:** Parking and access are free.

**Maps:** For a map of hiking trails, refer to map 5 in the *Map and Guide to the Appalachian Trail in New Hampshire/Vermont,* an eight-map set and guidebook available for $19.95 ($14.95 for the maps alone) from the Appalachian Trail Conference (see address below). Or get the waterproof *End-to-End Map of the Long Trail,* available for $8.95 from the Green Mountain Club (see address below). For a topographic area map, request Pico Peak from USGS Map Sales, Federal Center, Box 25286, Denver, CO 80225, 888/ASK-USGS (888/275-8747), website: http://mapping.usgs.gov.

**Directions:** Drive to the parking area across from the Inn at Long Trail, where the Sherburne Pass Trail crosses U.S. 4 at the height of land in Sherburne Pass.

**Contact:** Green Mountain Club Inc., 4711 Waterbury-Stowe Rd., Waterbury Center, VT 05677, 802/244-7037, website: www.greenmountainclub.org. Appalachian Trail Conference, 799 Washington St., P.O. Box 807, Harpers Ferry, WV 25425-0807, 304/535-6331, website: www.appalachiantrail.org.

##  GILE MOUNTAIN
**1.4 mi/1 hr**

**in Norwich**

With a group of friends, I mountain biked in the Gile Mountain area and hiked to the fire tower on its summit one September afternoon— an uphill climb of not more than 500 feet. From atop the tower, we enjoyed a sweeping panorama south to Mount Ascutney, west to Killington and Abraham, northwest to Camel's Hump, northeast to Mount Moosilauke and Franconia Ridge in the White Mountains, and east across the Connecticut River to the ridge that connects, from north to south, Mount Cube, Smarts Mountain, Holt's Ledge, and Moose Mountain. This is a great place to catch a sunset, especially with the fall foliage at its peak.

Unfortunately, the Town of Norwich Selectboard closed the fire tower in the fall of 2000 because it was in dangerous disrepair, rendering this hike almost absent of views (though there is a decent view to the south and east from the trail just below the fire ranger's cabin). The town's Conservation Commission was planning to seek grant money to repair the tower; check with town officials (see address below) about the status of those repairs.

Follow the Tower Trail, climbing steadily for 0.4 mile and then crossing power lines. At 0.7 mile, the trail reaches an abandoned fire ranger's cabin. Follow the trail a short distance beyond the cabin to the fire tower. Return the same way you came.

**User groups:** Hikers, snowshoers, and dogs. No wheelchair facilities. The last half of this trail is not suitable for bikes or skis, and the entire trail is not suitable for horses. Hunting is allowed in season.

**Access, fees:** Parking and access are free.

**Maps:** For a topographic area map, request Hanover from USGS Map Sales, Federal Center, Box 25286, Denver, CO 80225, 888/ASK-USGS (888/275-8747), website: http://mapping.usgs.gov.

**Directions:** From I-91, take Exit 13 and follow the signs into Norwich. From Dan and Whit's General Store in the town center, continue straight through town on Main Street for 0.6 mile and turn left onto Turnpike Road. Drive 0.9 mile and bear left at a fork. In another 1.7 miles, drive straight onto the dirt Lower Turnpike Road. Drive 2.6 miles farther to a turnout on the left for the Gile Mountain Trail.

**Contact:** Town of Norwich Selectboard, 802/649-0127, email: Selectboard@norwich.vt.us. Town of Norwich Conservation Commission, email: Conservation.Commission@norwich.vt.us.

## ⅒ THE SKYLINE TRAIL
### 6.3 mi one-way/3.5 hrs

**in Pomfret**

The Skyline Trail was conceived in the 1960s by Richard Brett, a local resident who wanted to build a ski trail connecting his homes in Barnard and Woodstock. By gaining the permission of landowners, Brett was able to cut a trail connecting abandoned woods roads, log-

ging roads, and pastures along a woodland ridge between Amity Pond and the Suicide Six Ski Area. Although efforts to complete the route to Woodstock have never succeeded, this trail offers a classic portrait of the Vermont countryside, ranging from dense, quiet woods to farm pastures with long views of green hills. It's a pleasant hike any time of year, but I recommend doing it on cross-country skis after a fresh snowfall, as my wife and I did with two friends a few years ago. There are two long, steep descents, but the tour can be done on standard touring skis by a nordic skier with intermediate skills. Just remember, you could be breaking fresh trail, so don't underestimate how long it can take to ski 6.3 miles. Also remember that the trail is not maintained and you are on private property; access and trail conditions can change at any time. And be careful driving on these Vermont back roads—after we finished skiing here, my wife slid her compact car into a snow bank on her way to retrieve the vehicle we'd left at the trail's start. Fortunately, no one was hurt and passersby helped push the car out of the snow. This trail has fairly short uphill sections, but actually drops about 1,000 in elevation over its course.

From the turnout at the start of the Skyline Trail, follow the trail toward Amity Pond. Where the trail branches left toward the lean-to, take the right fork. The trail soon crosses a broad meadow with long views of the mountains. Beyond the meadow, avoid the local side trails and follow the blue-blazed Skyline Trail. It can be difficult to detect in spots but is generally fairly obvious. It crosses several roads and descends one woods road near its end, before traversing an open hillside, then dropping steeply to Suicide Six.

**User groups:** Hikers, snowshoers, skiers, and dogs. No wheelchair facilities or bikes. Horses and hunting are prohibited along much of the trail.

**Access, fees:** Parking and access are free. The entire trail lies on private land, so stay on the trail. Access could change, so obey any no trespassing signs. Camping is allowed only in the lean-to shelter at Amity Pond. The trail is generally well marked, but not maintained.

**Maps:** For a topographic area map, request Woodstock North from USGS Map Sales, Federal Center, Box 25286, Denver, CO 80225, 888/ASK-USGS (888/275-8747), website: http://mapping.usgs.gov.

**Directions:** You need to shuttle two vehicles for this one-way traverse. To do it north to south, as described here, drive U.S. 4 into Woodstock. Just east of the village center, turn onto Route 12 north, turning right where Route 12 makes a dogleg within 0.2 mile. At 1.3 miles from Route 4, bear right, following signs for the Suicide Six Ski Area, and leave a vehicle in the parking lot. Turn right out of the parking lot, back onto Route 12 south, and drive a quarter mile to South Pomfret. Turn left onto County Road. Continue another five miles to Hewitt's Corner and take a left at a sign for Sharon. Within a quarter mile, turn left onto a gravel road. Follow it for roughly two miles; after it bends right and climbs a hill, park in the turnout on the right. The trail begins across the road and is marked by blue trail markers and a sign for the Amity Pond Natural Area.

**Contact:** The trail is not maintained, but Woodstock Ski Touring Center can provide information, 802/457-6674, website: www .woodstockinn.com.

# 🔟🔟 QUECHEE GORGE
## 2.2 mi/1.2 hrs

**in Quechee Gorge State Park**

This 150-foot-deep, narrow gorge along the Ottauquechee River has long attracted tourists to a bridge on U.S. 4 spanning the gorge. I first ventured into the gorge on cross-country skis several years ago, making this easy, 2.2-mile loop along the gorge and through the woods of tiny Quechee Gorge State Park. If you're skiing and interested in a longer outing, start from Wilderness Trails (see below), which maintains a ski trail system adjacent to this loop. From the parking area, walk down the

steps in front of the gift shop to the gorge trail and turn left (south), passing under the highway bridge. Follow the well-graded trail above the gorge downhill about a half mile to a bend in the river, where there is a bench. Turn left, continue about 0.2 mile along the river, walk up a small hill with good views of the river, and cross a small footbridge. Turn left onto the Beaver Dam Trail, marked by red wooden blocks on trees, which winds up through the state park, leaving the park boundaries briefly and crossing private property. The trail leads a mile to U.S. 4, at the state park campground entrance and a half mile east of the bridge. You can walk along the road back to the start of this hike or, especially if on skis, cross the highway and walk behind the Wildflowers Restaurant to an easy ski trail. Turn left and follow it a half mile back to the gorge trail. Turn left and continue a short distance back to the start of this hike.

**User groups:** Hikers, dogs, skiers, and snowshoers. No wheelchair facilities. This trail is not suitable for bikes or horses. Hunting is prohibited.

**Access, fees:** Parking and access are free, except that skiers must pay $5 per person at Wilderness Trails to cover costs of grooming the trails. Most of this hike is within Quechee Gorge State Park, but the Beaver Dam Trail briefly exits the state park onto private property; take care not to wander off the trail.

**Maps:** Get a map of ski trails at Wilderness Trails, behind the Marshland Farm. To reach Wilderness Trails, take Dewey's Mill Road, between the gift shops on the east side of the bridge, and follow it a mile; snowshoes and cross-country skis for adults and children can be rented there. For a topographic area map, request Quechee from USGS Map Sales, Federal Center, Box 25286, Denver, CO 80225, 888/ASK-USGS (888/275-8747), website: http://mapping.usgs.gov.

**Directions:** From I-89 southbound, take Exit 1 onto U.S. 4 west and drive 2.5 miles to the east side of the U.S. 4 bridge over Quechee

Gorge. From I-89 northbound, take Exit 1 and drive 3.2 miles to the gorge. Park at the gift shop or information booth on the bridge's east side.

**Contact:** Quechee Gorge State Park, 190 Dewey Mills Rd., White River Junction, VT 05001, 802/295-2990 in summer, 802/885-8891 in winter, or 800/299-3071. Vermont Department of Forests, Parks, and Recreation Commissioner's Office, 103 South Main St., Waterbury, VT 05671-0601, 802/241-3655, website: www.state.vt.us/anr/fpr. Friends of the Quechee Gorge, P.O. Box Q, Quechee, VT 05059.

## 19 KILLINGTON PEAK: BUCKLIN TRAIL

**7.4 mi/6 hrs**

**in Mendon and Sherburne**

This 7.4-mile hike provides a route of moderate distance and difficulty up Vermont's second-highest peak, 4,241-foot Killington, where the barren, rocky summit boasts one of the finest panoramas in the state. From the summit, where there are radio transmission facilities and a fire tower, the views extend to Mount Mansfield to the north, numerous other Green Mountains peaks to the north and south, Lake Champlain and the Adirondack Mountains to the west, Mount Ascutney to the southeast, and the White Mountains to the northeast. The vertical ascent is about 2,400 feet.

From the parking area, take the blue-blazed Bucklin Trail. It follows an abandoned logging road, first on the north bank of Brewers Brook, then the south bank, for nearly two miles. It grows steeper beyond the logging road, reaching the white-blazed Long Trail/Appalachian Trail at 3.3 miles. Continue uphill on the LT southbound, reaching the Cooper Lodge in 0.2 mile; just beyond it, the LT swings right, and the spur trail to Killington's summit continues straight ahead. Hike up the very steep and rocky spur trail for 0.2 mile to the summit. Hike back along the same route.

**User groups:** Hikers and dogs. No wheelchair facilities. This trail should not be attempted in winter except by hikers experienced in mountaineering and prepared for severe winter weather, and is not suitable for skis. Bikes, horses, and hunting are prohibited.

**Access, fees:** Parking and access are free. Most of this hike takes place on private land. Camping is prohibited except at the Green Mountain Club cabins and shelters. The Cooper Lodge cabin is located on the Long Trail, 0.1 mile south of the Bucklin Trail junction.

**Maps:** For a map of hiking trails, refer to map 6 in the *Map and Guide to the Appalachian Trail in New Hampshire/Vermont,* an eight-map set and guidebook available for $19.95 ($14.95 for the maps alone) from the Appalachian Trail Conference (see address below). Or get the waterproof *End-to-End Map of the Long Trail,* available for $8.95 from the Green Mountain Club (see address below). For a topographic area map, request Killington Peak from USGS Map Sales, Federal Center, Box 25286, Denver, CO 80225, 888/ASK-USGS (888/275-8747), website: http://mapping.usgs.gov.

**Directions:** From U.S. 4, 5.1 miles east of the northern junction of U.S. 4 and U.S. 7 in Rutland and 4.1 miles west of the Inn at Long Trail in Sherburne Pass, turn south onto Wheelerville Road. Follow it for 4.1 miles to a turnout on the left.

**Contact:** Green Mountain Club Inc., 4711 Waterbury-Stowe Rd., Waterbury Center, VT 05677, 802/244-7037, website: www.greenmountainclub.org. Appalachian Trail Conference, 799 Washington St., P.O. Box 807, Harpers Ferry, WV 25425-0807, 304/535-6331, website: www.appalachiantrail.org.

## 20 KILLINGTON PEAK: SHERBURNE PASS TRAIL

**11.2 mi/8 hrs**

**in Sherburne**

Although a fairly challenging hike of more than 11 miles, the Sherburne Pass Trail from Sherburne Pass presents a good route to the crown of Vermont's second-highest peak, 4,241-foot Killington. With the trailhead at 2,150 feet, the vertical ascent is about 2,100 feet, less than taking the Bucklin Trail up Killington (see the Killington Peak: Bucklin Trail listing, this chapter). And this hike also offers the option of bagging Pico Peak. On the craggy Killington summit, where there are radio transmission facilities and a fire tower, the 360-degree views encompass Mount Mansfield to the north, numerous other Green Mountains peaks to the north and south, Lake Champlain and the Adirondack Mountains to the west, Mount Ascutney to the southeast, and the White Mountains to the northeast.

From the parking area at Sherburne Pass, follow a short spur trail to the blue-blazed Sherburne Pass Trail southbound (this was a stretch of the Long Trail/Appalachian Trail until the national scenic trail was rerouted in September 1999 to the west side of Pico Mountain). Alternatively, you could walk east along U.S. 4 a short distance and turn right onto the Sherburne Pass Trail southbound. It climbs gradually for 0.6 mile to a side path that leads 0.1 mile right to a view from the top of a chairlift and an alpine slide at the Pico Ski Area. Continuing its steady ascent, the Sherburne Pass Trail reaches a ski trail at two miles and follows it for 300 yards before reentering the woods. At 2.5 miles from the pass, the Sherburne Pass Trail reaches Pico Camp. A side path, Pico Link, leads 0.4 mile up steep and rocky ground from behind Pico Camp to the 3,957-foot Pico Mountain summit, where there are good views (adding 0.8 mile to this hike's distance). Continue on the Sherburne Pass Trail southbound, mostly contouring along the rugged ridge to Killington Peak. About a half mile south of Pico Camp, you reach a junction with the white-blazed Long Trail/Appalachian Trail. Walk southbound on it. At about 5.5 miles from Sherburne Pass, the trail reaches Cooper Lodge and the junction with the spur trail to Killington's summit. Turn left and climb the very steep and rocky spur for 0.2 mile to the open summit. Return the way you came.

**User groups:** Hikers and dogs. No wheelchair facilities. This trail should not be attempted in winter except by hikers experienced in mountaineering and prepared for severe winter weather, and is not suitable for skis. Bikes, horses, and hunting are prohibited.

**Access, fees:** Parking and access are free. Parts of this hike are on private land. Camping is prohibited except at the Green Mountain Club cabins and shelters. The Pico Camp cabin is at the junction of the Sherburne Pass Trail and Pico Link, 2.5 miles south of Sherburne Pass and a half mile north of the junction of the Long Trail/Appalachian Trail and the Sherburne Pass Trail. The Cooper Lodge cabin is located on the Long Trail, 0.1 mile south of the Bucklin Trail junction and 2.5 miles south of the junction of the Sherburne Pass and Long Trails; from Cooper Lodge, it is 5.5 miles to Sherburne Pass and U.S. 4 via the Sherburne Pass Trail and 6.3 miles to U.S. 4 via the Long Trail.

**Maps:** For a map of hiking trails, refer to map 6 in the *Map and Guide to the Appalachian Trail in New Hampshire/Vermont,* an eight-map set and guidebook available for $19.95 ($14.95 for the maps alone) from the Appalachian Trail Conference (see address below). Or get the waterproof *End-to-End Map of the Long Trail,* available for $8.95 from the Green Mountain Club (see address below). For topographic area maps, request Killington Peak and Pico Peak from USGS Map Sales, Federal Center, Box 25286, Denver, CO 80225, 888/ASK-USGS (888/275-8747), website: http://mapping.usgs.gov.

**Directions:** Drive to the parking area across from the Inn at Long Trail, where the Sherburne Pass Trail (formerly the Long Trail/Appalachian Trail) crosses U.S. 4 at the height of land in Sherburne Pass.

**Contact:** Green Mountain Club Inc., 4711 Waterbury-Stowe Rd., Waterbury Center, VT 05677, 802/244-7037, website: www.greenmountainclub.org. Appalachian Trail Conference, 799 Washington St., P.O. Box 807, Harpers Ferry, WV 25425-0807, 304/535-6331, website: www.appalachiantrail.org.

## 21 THE LONG TRAIL: ROUTE 103 TO U.S. 4

**17.4 mi one-way/2 days**

**between Shrewsbury and Sherburne**

For someone hiking the entire Long Trail from south to north, this stretch is where the trail begins to metamorphose from a casual walk in the woods with occasional views to a more committing and rugged tromp through the mountains. The difference in elevation from Route 103 to the summit of Killington Peak—Vermont's second-tallest mountain at 4,241 feet—is about 3,400 feet. The views in every direction from the rocky, open Killington summit, where there are radio transmission facilities and a fire tower, encompass Mount Mansfield to the north, numerous other Green Mountains peaks to the north and south, Lake Champlain and the Adirondack Mountains to the west, Mount Ascutney to the southeast, and the White Mountains to the northeast. Remember that weather at the higher elevations can turn wintry in any month.

From the parking area on Route 103, the white-blazed Long Trail, which coincides here with the Appalachian Trail, crosses the highway and employs wooden stepladders to get over barbed wire fencing enclosing a field. Crossing the field into the woods, the trail follows a woods road and climbs steeply through a narrow, boulder-strewn ravine. Above the ravine, the LT passes a view to the south and west (0.4 mile from Route 103) and then descends to another woods road a mile from Route 103. To the right, a short distance down the road, is the Clarendon shelter. The LT crosses the road and a brook and ascends Beacon Hill at 1.5 miles, where there is a view south from an open area at the summit. The trail descends again, crossing Lottery Road at 1.9 miles and the dirt Keiffer Road at 3.6 miles. After following Northam Brook, it turns right onto Cold River Road (also called Lower Road), at 3.9 miles. The LT soon reenters the woods, following a ridge high above the Cold River, and descends steeply to cross the river's east branch on rocks, which could be tricky in times of high water. After paralleling the river's west branch, the trail crosses Upper Cold River Road at 5.4 miles.

At six miles, turn left onto a dirt road, walk over a bridge, and then turn immediately right into the woods. The trail crosses one more road before reaching the Governor Clement shelter at 6.9 miles from Route 103. Passing the shelter, the trail follows a flat woods road for less than a half mile and then starts the long climb up Little Killington and Killington Peak, becoming increasingly rockier, with difficult footing, as the trail narrows through a dense spruce forest. You gain nearly 2,400 feet in elevation. At nine miles, the LT crosses two small brooks that I've seen flowing well even during a dry autumn. The LT crosses a ski area trail on Killington and then reaches a junction at 9.8 miles with the Shrewsbury Peak Trail (see listing, this chapter), which bears right and leads two miles to Shrewsbury Peak, while the LT swings left.

After crossing another ski trail, the hiking grows easier, contouring around the south and west slopes of Killington Peak. At 10.9 miles, a side path bears right and climbs very steeply, over rocky terrain, 0.2 mile to the Killington summit (included in this hike's mileage). Leave your pack behind for this side trip. The LT passes the Cooper Lodge and descends for 0.2 mile before swinging north again. At 13.3 miles, the blue-blazed Sherburne Pass Trail diverges right, following the former route of the LT for a half mile to Pico Camp (there, a blue-blazed side trail, the Pico Link, leads steeply uphill for 0.4 mile to the Pico summit, where there are views and a chairlift station), and, beyond the Pico Camp, continues three more miles to U.S. 4 at Sherburne Pass.

This hike instead follows the new route of the LT/AT—opened in September 1999—a relocation done to avoid ski resort development on Pico Peak. Descending through a birch glade, the trail crosses a stream and a bridge across a brook. At 4.4 miles beyond Cooper

Lodge, a spur trail leads 0.1 mile to the Churchill Scott shelter, which sleeps 10 and has a tent platform nearby. It's another 2.4 miles on the LT/AT from Churchill Scott shelter to where the trail crosses Route 4 about a mile west of Sherburne Pass.

**User groups:** Hikers and dogs. No wheelchair facilities. This trail should not be attempted in winter except by hikers prepared for severe winter weather, and is not suitable for skis. Bikes, horses, and hunting are prohibited.

**Access, fees:** Parking and access are free. Except for a patch of state-owned land on Killington Peak, this hike is on private land; camping is prohibited except at the Green Mountain Club shelters. From Route 103, it is one mile north to the Clarendon shelter, reached via a short walk down a woods road from the Long Trail; 6.8 miles to the Governor Clement shelter; 11.1 miles to the Cooper Lodge cabin; and 15.5 miles to Churchill Scott shelter. The Pico Camp cabin is on the Sherburne Pass Trail, a half mile north of its junction with the LT and 3.0 miles south of U.S. 4.

**Maps:** For a map of hiking trails, refer to map 6 in the *Map and Guide to the Appalachian Trail in New Hampshire/Vermont,* an eight-map set and guidebook available for $19.95 ($14.95 for the maps alone) from the Appalachian Trail Conference (see address below). Or get the waterproof *End-to-End Map of the Long Trail* available for $8.95 from the Green Mountain Club (see address below). For topographic area maps, request Rutland, Killington Peak, and Pico Peak from USGS Map Sales, Federal Center, Box 25286, Denver, CO 80225, 888/ASK-USGS (888/275-8747), website: http://mapping.usgs.gov.

**Directions:** You need to shuttle two vehicles for this one-way traverse. To hike south to north, as described here, leave one vehicle where the Long Trail/Appalachian Trail crosses U.S. 4, one mile west of Sherburne Pass. Then drive to the parking area where the trail crosses Route 103, two miles east of U.S. 7 in Clarendon, and three miles west of Cuttingsville.

**Contact:** Green Mountain Club Inc., 4711 Waterbury-Stowe Rd., Waterbury Center, VT 05677, 802/244-7037, website: www.green-mountainclub.org. Appalachian Trail Conference, 799 Washington St., P.O. Box 807, Harpers Ferry, WV 25425-0807, 304/535-6331, website: www.appalachiantrail.org.

## 22 SHREWSBURY PEAK
**3.6 mi/2.5 hrs**
**in Coolidge State Forest outside North Shrewsbury**

On a mid-November day, with an inch of snow turning everything white, I hiked to the Shrewsbury Peak summit and enjoyed wonderfully long views in a wide sweep to the northeast, east, and south. In the clear air I saw all the way to Franconia Ridge in the White Mountains, Mount Ascutney to the east, Mount Monadnock to the southeast, and a long chain of the Green Mountains to the south. Through openings in the trees looking north, I even caught a glimpse of Killington (which can be reached via the Shrewsbury Peak Trail for a scenic if quite rugged round-trip hike of 10.2 miles). This hike climbs about 1,400 feet.

The Shrewsbury Peak Trail is unmarked but obvious and begins from the stone wall at the rear of the parking lot. Within 0.2 mile, it passes in front of a lean-to. Follow the blue blazes over moderate terrain, which grows steeper as the trail ascends into the subalpine hemlock and spruce forest. At 1.8 miles, you emerge at an open area at the summit. To complete this hike, return the way you came. To continue to Killington Peak, follow the Shrewsbury Peak Trail northward. In two miles, turn right (north) on the white-blazed Long Trail and follow it 1.1 miles to the Killington Peak Spur Trail. Turn right and climb very steeply 0.2 mile to the Killington summit.

**User groups:** Hikers, snowshoers, and dogs. Dogs must be leashed. No wheelchair facilities. This trail is not suitable for bikes, horses, or skis. Hunting is allowed in season.

**Access, fees:** Parking and access are free. The CCC Road can be difficult to drive, especially from the east, in muddy or icy conditions.

**Maps:** The waterproof *End-to-End Map of the Long Trail* is available for $8.95 from the Green Mountain Club (see address below). For a topographic area map, request Killington Peak from USGS Map Sales, Federal Center, Box 25286, Denver, CO 80225, 888/ASK-USGS (888/275-8747), website: http://mapping.usgs.gov.

**Directions:** From Route 100, 3.1 miles south of its junction with U.S. 4 in West Bridgewater, and 2.2 miles north of its junction with Route 100A in Plymouth Union, turn west onto the dirt CCC Road at a sign for Meadowsweet Herb Farm. Drive 3.4 miles to a parking area on the right at a sign for the Coolidge State Forest. Or from the center of North Shrewsbury, pick up the CCC Road (marked by a sign) heading east, which begins as pavement and turns to dirt. At 1.1 miles, bear right at a fork and continue 1.6 miles farther to the parking area on the left.

**Contact:** Vermont Department of Forests, Parks, and Recreation Commissioner's Office, 103 South Main St., Waterbury, VT 05671-0601, 802/241-3655, website: www.state.vt.us/anr/fpr. Green Mountain Club Inc., 4711 Waterbury-Stowe Rd., Waterbury Center, VT 05677, 802/244-7037, website: www.green-mountainclub.org.

## 23 MOUNT ASCUTNEY
**6.8 mi/4.5 hrs**

**in Ascutney State Park in Windsor**

Mount Ascutney, at 3,150 feet, belongs to a class of small New England mountains that rise much higher than any piece of earth surrounding them—peaks like Monadnock (see the Central and Southern New Hampshire chapter), Cardigan (see the Central and Southern New Hampshire chapter), and Wachusett (see the Central Massachusetts chapter). The eroded core of a volcano that once rose to 20,000 feet, Ascutney soars above the Connecticut River Valley. Its observation tower offers excellent views of the Green Mountains to the west, Monadnock to the southeast, Mounts Sunapee and Cardigan to the northeast, and the White Mountains beyond. The first trail up Ascutney was cut in 1825; today, several paths run up the mountain. This loop hike climbs about 2,400 feet in elevation.

Follow the Brownsville Trail's white blazes, climbing steadily along a wide woods path. At 1.1 miles, the trail passes by the Norcross Quarry remains on the right, where granite was mined until 1910. The trail continues upward, passing a short side path at 1.3 miles leading to an overlook. A second lookout is reached at two miles, offering a view eastward. At 2.3 miles, the trail crosses a grassy area atop wooded North Peak (2,660 feet). After reaching the Windsor Trail junction (on the left) at 2.9 miles, bear right for the summit. Just 0.1 mile beyond that junction, you reach the remains of the Stone Hut, a former shelter. An unmarked trail leads left 0.7 mile to the Ascutney auto road, and to the right, a short path leads to Brownsville Rock, which offers good views north.

Continue up the Windsor Trail 0.2 mile to the summit observation tower. Descend the same route for 0.3 mile and then turn right to follow the white-blazed Windsor Trail down. The trail crosses the two branches of Mountain Brook and then parallels the brook on a wide, old woods road through a wild drainage. At 2.6 miles below the summit, you reach Route 44A and the parking area for the Windsor Trail. If you have no vehicle here, turn left and follow 44A onto Route 44 west for 0.9 mile to the start of this hike.

**User groups:** Hikers and snowshoers. No wheelchair facilities. This trail is not suitable for bikes, horses, or skis. Dogs are not allowed in day-use areas such as picnic areas, but are not restricted on trails. Hunting is allowed in season.

**Access, fees:** Parking and access are free. Trails are closed during the spring mud season, usually mid-April–mid-May.

**Maps:** The Ascutney Trails Association (see

address below) publishes an Ascutney guidebook and map that costs $5. A free, basic map is available at park entrances for virtually all state parks. For a topographic area map, request Mount Ascutney from USGS Map Sales, Federal Center, Box 25286, Denver, CO 80225, 888/ASK-USGS (888/275-8747), website: http://mapping.usgs.gov.

**Directions:** If you have two vehicles, drive one to the Windsor Trail parking area at the end of this hike, reducing this hike's distance by the one mile of paved road separating the trailheads; otherwise, just note the location of the Windsor Trail on your way to the start of the Brownsville Trail. From the north, take I-91 to Exit 9 and then U.S. 5 south into the center of Windsor; from the south, take I-91 to Exit 8 and then U.S. 5 north into Windsor. At the junction of U.S. 5 and Route 44 in Windsor, turn west onto Route 44 and follow it for 3.3 miles to its junction with Route 44A. The Windsor Trail parking area is just 100 yards down Route 44A, on the right. Continue west on Route 44 for 0.9 mile to parking on the left side of the road for the Brownsville Trail.

**Contact:** Ascutney State Park, Box 186, HCR 71, 1826 Black Mountain Rd., Windsor, VT 05089, 802/674-2060 in summer, 802/885-8891 in winter, or 800/299-3071. Vermont Department of Forests, Parks, and Recreation Commissioner's Office, 103 South Main St., Waterbury, VT 05671-0601, 802/241-3655, website: www.state.vt.us/anr/fpr. Ascutney Trails Association, George Smith, Jr., P.O. Box 119, Hartland, VT 05048.

## 24 CLARENDON GORGE AND AIRPORT LOOKOUT

**1.8 mi/1.2 hrs**

**between Shrewsbury and Clarendon**

For the view down into Clarendon Gorge, one of the two attractions on this hike, you need only walk southbound on the white-blazed Long Trail/Appalachian Trail for 0.1 mile to the suspension bridge spanning the dramatic chasm. But the added uphill climb of less than a mile

and several hundred feet to Airport Lookout is worth the effort. Its open ledges atop low cliffs afford a view west to the Rutland Airport, the valley that U.S. 7 runs through, and the southern Adirondacks. Be careful scrambling around on these ledges; I nearly took a nasty fall there myself. From Airport Lookout, backtrack the way you came.

**User groups:** Hikers, snowshoers, and dogs. No wheelchair facilities. This trail is not suitable for skis. Bikes, horses, and hunting are prohibited.

**Access, fees:** Parking and access are free.

**Maps:** For a map of hiking trails, refer to map 6 in the *Map and Guide to the Appalachian Trail in New Hampshire/Vermont,* an eight-map set and guidebook available for $19.95 ($14.95 for the maps alone) from the Appalachian Trail Conference (see address below). Or get the waterproof *End-to-End Map of the Long Trail,* available for $8.95 from the Green Mountain Club (see address below). For a topographic area map, request Rutland from USGS Map Sales, Federal Center, Box 25286, Denver, CO 80225, 888/ASK-USGS (888/275-8747), website: http://mapping.usgs.gov.

**Directions:** Drive to the parking area on Route 103, three miles west of Cuttingsville and two miles east of U.S. 7 in Clarendon.

**Contact:** Green Mountain Club Inc., 4711 Waterbury-Stowe Rd., Waterbury Center, VT 05677, 802/244-7037, website: www.greenmountainclub.org. Appalachian Trail Conference, 799 Washington St., P.O. Box 807, Harpers Ferry, WV 25425-0807, 304/535-6331, website: www.appalachiantrail.org.

## 25 THE LONG TRAIL: ROUTE 140, WALLINGFORD GULF, TO ROUTE 103, CLARENDON GORGE

**6.3 mi one-way/3.5 hrs**

**between Shrewsbury and Clarendon**

In September 1999, the Long Trail was rerouted in this area and now ascends the south ridge of 2,262-foot Bear Mountain on this stretch, an improvement over the previous route because it now leads to a great view of the Otter Creek Valley. But this approximately 6.3-mile stretch of the Long and Appalachian Trails is still largely a pleasant walk in the woods and perhaps a safe and moderate route for a beginning winter hiker or snowshoer. The cumulative elevation gain is about 1,200 feet.

From Route 140, follow the LT northbound up Bear Mountain; don't miss the short spur trail to an open ledge overlooking the Otter Creek Valley to the south. The LT continues north, contouring just below the ridgeline, descends the steep north side of Bear Mountain, crosses a beaver meadow, and then follows a woods road to rejoin the old route of the LT just south of Minerva Hinchey shelter. At about 2.6 miles into this hike, a side path leads to the shelter. Beyond it, the LT climbs over a low, wooded hill and descends and passes through Spring Lake Clearing, 3.2 miles from Route 140. It follows a wooded ridge to Airport Lookout at 4.5 miles, where open ledges atop low cliffs offer a view west of the Rutland Airport, the valley that U.S. 7 runs through, and the southern Adirondacks. Descending, the trail reaches Clarendon Gorge, crossing the gorge on a suspension bridge that offers a dramatic view down into the chasm. Just 0.1 mile farther, you reach Route 103.

**User groups:** Hikers, snowshoers, and dogs. No wheelchair facilities. This trail is not suitable for skis. Bikes, horses, and hunting are prohibited.

**Access, fees:** Parking and access are free. Except for a patch of state-owned land at Clarendon Gorge, this hike is on private land; camping is prohibited except at the Green Mountain Club Minerva Hinchey shelter, reached via a short side path off the Long Trail, 2.6 miles north of Route 140.

**Maps:** For a map of hiking trails, refer to map 6 in the *Map and Guide to the Appalachian Trail in New Hampshire/Vermont,* an eight-map set and guidebook available for $19.95 ($14.95 for the maps alone) from the Appalachian Trail

Conference (see address below). Or get the waterproof *End-to-End Map of the Long Trail,* available for $8.95 from the Green Mountain Club (see address below). For topographic area maps, request Wallingford and Rutland from USGS Map Sales, Federal Center, Box 25286, Denver, CO 80225, 888/ASK-USGS (888/275-8747), website: http://mapping.usgs.gov.

**Directions:** You need to shuttle two vehicles for this one-way traverse. To hike south to north, as described here, leave one vehicle in the parking area on Route 103, two miles east of U.S. 7 in Clarendon, and three miles west of Cuttingsville. Then drive to where the Long Trail/Appalachian Trail crosses Route 140, about 2.8 miles east of U.S. 7 in Wallingford and about 3.7 miles west of the junction of Routes 140, 155, and 103 in East Wallingford.

**Contact:** Green Mountain Club Inc., 4711 Waterbury-Stowe Rd., Waterbury Center, VT 05677, 802/244-7037, website: www.greenmountainclub.org. Appalachian Trail Conference, 799 Washington St., P.O. Box 807, Harpers Ferry, WV 25425-0807, 304/535-6331, website: www.appalachiantrail.org.

## 26 WHITE ROCKS CLIFF
### 2.6 mi/2 hrs
**in the Green Mountain National Forest east of Wallingford**

From the White Rocks Recreation Area, follow the Keewaydin Trail steeply uphill. It soon passes a newly rerouted stretch of the northbound Long Trail bearing left; continue up the Keewaydin, and at 0.8 mile from the trailhead you'll reach a junction with the Greenwall Spur, a trail leading left a half mile to the Greenwall shelter. Turn right (south) on the Long Trail, hike 0.3 mile, and then turn right (west) on the White Rocks Cliff Trail. This trail descends steeply for 0.2 mile and ends at the top of the cliffs, with good views of the valley south of Wallingford. There are numerous footpaths around the cliffs, but take care because the rock is loose and footing can be dangerous. Return the way you came. The cumulative elevation gain on this hike is approximately 1,500 feet.

**User groups:** Hikers and dogs. Dogs must be leashed. No wheelchair facilities. This trail may be difficult to snowshoe and is not suitable for skis. Bikes, horses, and hunting are prohibited.

**Access, fees:** Parking and access are free. Camping is prohibited except at the Green Mountain Club cabins and shelters. The Greenwall shelter is located on the Greenwall Spur, a half mile north of the Keewaydin Trail and Long Trail junction.

**Maps:** For a map of hiking trails, refer to map 6 in the *Map and Guide to the Appalachian Trail in New Hampshire/Vermont,* an eight-map set and guidebook available for $19.95 ($14.95 for the maps alone) from the Appalachian Trail Conference (see address below). Or get the waterproof *End-to-End Map of the Long Trail,* available for $8.95 from the Green Mountain Club (see address below). For a topographic area map, request Wallingford from USGS Map Sales, Federal Center, Box 25286, Denver, CO 80225, 888/ASK-USGS (888/275-8747), website: http://mapping.usgs.gov.

**Directions:** From Route 140, 4.1 miles west of the junction of Routes 140 and 155 in East Wallingford and 2.1 miles east of the junction

of 140 and U.S. 7 in Wallingford, turn south onto the dirt Sugar Hill Road. Drive 0.1 mile and turn right onto the dirt USFS Road 52 at a sign for the White Rocks Picnic Area. Continue a half mile to the White Rocks Recreation Area.

**Contact:** Green Mountain National Forest Supervisor, 231 North Main St., Rutland, VT 05701, 802/747-6700, fax 802/747-6766, website: www.fs.fed.us/r9/gmfl. Green Mountain Club Inc., 4711 Waterbury-Stowe Rd., Waterbury Center, VT 05677, 802/244-7037, website: www.greenmountainclub.org. Appalachian Trail Conference, 799 Washington St., P.O. Box 807, Harpers Ferry, WV 25425-0807, 304/535-6331, website: www.appalachiantrail.org.

## ⓴ THE LONG TRAIL: USFS ROAD 10 TO ROUTE 140

**9 mi one-way/5.5 hrs**

**in the Green Mountain National Forest between Danby and Wallingford**

The highlights of this fairly easy and relatively flat nine-mile stretch of the Long Trail/Appalachian Trail are Little Rock Pond and the view from White Rocks Cliff (see previous listing for a shorter hike to the cliffs). From the parking area on

a backpacker on the Long Trail on Camel's Hump

USFS Road 10, cross the road onto the white-blazed LT northbound. The trail follows Little Black Brook, passing the Lula Tye shelter at 1.8 miles and reaching Little Rock Pond, a small mountain tarn, at two miles. A popular destination with hikers, the pond sits tucked beneath a low ridge; there's a nice view across the pond where the Long Trail first reaches it at its southeast corner. Following the pond's east shore, the LT reaches the short side path to Little Rock Pond shelter 0.1 mile beyond the pond, at 2.5 miles into this hike. The trail then climbs gently for 3.9 miles to a blue-blazed side path on the left that leads steeply downhill for 0.2 mile to White Rocks Cliff, with good views of the valley south of Wallingford. Continuing north, you reach a new section of the LT, where it was rerouted in September 1999 in order to avoid wet areas and to reduce the amount of hiking on roadway. Turn left onto the new LT, which coincides briefly with the Keewaydin Trail; the old LT leading to the right has been renamed Greenwall Spur, and it leads a half mile to the Greenwall shelter, dead-ending there. The LT now follows the Keewaydin Trail a short distance, then swings right, crosses Bully Brook, crosses Sugar Hill Road, and reaches Route 140 about 0.75 mile west of the former trail crossing.

**User groups:** Hikers, snowshoers, and dogs. Dogs must be leashed. No wheelchair facilities. This trail is not suitable for skis. Bikes, horses, and hunting are prohibited.

**Access, fees:** Parking and access are free. USFS Road 10 is not maintained in winter. No-trace camping is permitted within the Green Mountain National Forest, except at Little Rock Pond, where camping within 200 feet of shore is allowed at designated campsites only. From late May to late October, a Green Mountain Club caretaker is on duty and a nightly fee of $6 per person is collected to stay at the Little Rock Pond and Lula Tye shelters and campsites. From USFS Road 10, the Lula Tye shelter is 1.8 miles north, the Little Rock Pond tenting area two miles north, the Little Rock Pond shelter 2.5 miles, and the Greenwall shelter 7.2 miles.

**Maps:** For a map of hiking trails, refer to map 6 in the *Map and Guide to the Appalachian Trail in New Hampshire/Vermont,* an eight-map set and guidebook available for $19.95 ($14.95 for the maps alone) from the Appalachian Trail Conference (see address below). Or get the waterproof *End-to-End Map of the Long Trail,* available for $8.95 from the Green Mountain Club (see address below). For topographic area maps, request Danby and Wallingford from USGS Map Sales, Federal Center, Box 25286, Denver, CO 80225, 888/ASK-USGS (888/275-8747), website: http://mapping.usgs.gov.

**Directions:** You need to shuttle two vehicles for this one-way traverse. To hike south to north, as described here, leave one vehicle where the Long Trail/Appalachian Trail crosses Route 140, about 2.8 miles east of U.S. 7 in Wallingford and about 3.7 miles west of the junction of Routes 140, 155, and 103 in East Wallingford. This hike begins at the parking lot on USFS Road 10 at Big Black Branch, 3.5 miles west of U.S. 7 in Danby and 13.6 miles north of Route 11 in Peru.

**Contact:** Green Mountain National Forest Supervisor, 231 North Main St., Rutland, VT 05701, 802/747-6700, fax 802/747-6766, website: www.fs.fed.us/r9/gmfl. Green Mountain Club Inc., 4711 Waterbury-Stowe Rd., Waterbury Center, VT 05677, 802/244-7037, website: www.greenmountainclub.org. Appalachian Trail Conference, 799 Washington St., P.O. Box 807, Harpers Ferry, WV 25425-0807, 304/535-6331, website: www.appalachiantrail.org.

## 28 BIG BRANCH WILDERNESS
**14 mi/8.5 hrs or 1–2 days**     🥾 🏕

**in the Green Mountain National Forest east of Danby**

Ⓕ I pulled this hike out of the full segment of the Long Trail described in the Long Trail: Route 11/30 to USFS Road 10 hike to highlight a trail section I particularly enjoy, from the roaring, rock-strewn bed of the Big Branch and placid Griffith Lake to the craggy heights of Baker Peak. This full trek is a fairly easy, 14-mile, out-and-back hike on the Long Trail from USFS Road 10 to Griffith Lake, which could be done in a day but is better spread over two days to enjoy the scenery. But I could also envision going no farther than any of the shelters along the way—even staying at the Big Branch shelter, a mere 1.3 miles into this hike, and hanging out by the river all day. Along the Big Branch are deep holes for fishing native brook and rainbow trout. The cumulative elevation gained hiking all the way to Griffith Lake and back is about 1,500 feet.

From the parking lot on USFS Road 10, walk east on the road for 0.1 mile and turn right, entering the woods on the white-blazed Long Trail southbound, which coincides here with the Appalachian Trail. It's an easy hike to the Big Branch stream and shelter. The trail parallels the stream for 0.1 mile, turns right and crosses it on a suspension bridge, then swings immediately left to follow the stream for another 0.1 mile before turning right, away from the stream. Following an old woods road over flat terrain, the LT reaches the Lost Pond shelter via a short side path at three miles into this hike. The hiking remains relatively easy all the way to Baker Peak's open summit at five miles, where there is a wide view west toward the valley around the town of Danby and to Dorset Peak across the valley. Descending west off Baker Peak along a rock ridge for 0.1 mile, the LT swings sharply left at a junction with the Baker Peak Trail. It then descends at a gentle angle to the Griffith Lake east shore and the campsite there at seven miles. Nearby, the Old Job Trail departs east and the Lake Trail departs west. This hike backtracks on the Long Trail to the road.

Special note: There are a couple of options to this hike. A one- or two-day, one-way traverse of eight miles begins at USFS Road 10 and descends from Baker Peak via the Baker Peak and Lake Trails (see directions below). For a 13.7-mile loop of one–two days, hike the LT south from USFS Road 10 to Griffith Lake and then loop back to the Big Branch suspension bridge on the Old Job Trail.

**User groups:** Hikers and dogs. Dogs must be leashed. No wheelchair facilities. The trailhead is not accessible by road in winter for skiing or snowshoeing. Bikes, horses, and hunting are prohibited.

**Access, fees:** Parking and access are free. USFS Road 10 is not maintained during the winter. No-trace camping is permitted within the Green Mountain National Forest, except at Griffith Lake, where camping within 200 feet of shore is restricted to designated sites. The Griffith Lake campsite is on the Long Trail, seven miles south of USFS Road 10. The Peru Peak shelter lies 0.7 mile farther south. From Memorial Day weekend–Labor Day, a Green Mountain Club caretaker is on duty and a nightly fee of $6 per person is collected to stay at both sites. The Big Branch shelter is on the LT, 1.3 miles south of USFS Road 10, and the Lost Pond shelter is three miles south of the road.

**Maps:** For a map of hiking trails, refer to map 7 in the *Map and Guide to the Appalachian Trail in New Hampshire/Vermont,* an eight-map set and guidebook available for $19.95 ($14.95 for the maps alone) from the Appalachian Trail Conference (see address below). Or get the waterproof *End-to-End Map of the Long Trail,* available for $8.95 from the Green Mountain Club (see address below). For a topographic area map, request Danby from USGS Map Sales, Federal Center, Box 25286, Denver, CO 80225, 888/ASK-USGS (888/275-8747), website: http://mapping.usgs.gov.

**Directions:** Drive to the parking lot on USFS Road 10 at Big Black Branch, 3.5 miles west of U.S. 7 in Danby and 13.6 miles north of Route 11 in Peru. To finish this hike on the Baker Peak and Lake Trail, as described in the special note above, you must leave a vehicle at the start of the Lake Trail; from the crossroads in Danby, drive south on U.S. 7 for 2.1 miles and turn left onto Town Route 5. Drive a half mile to parking on the left.

**Contact:** Green Mountain National Forest Supervisor, 231 North Main St., Rutland, VT 05701, 802/747-6700, fax 802/747-6766, website: www.fs.fed.us/r9/gmfl. Green Mountain Club Inc., 4711 Waterbury-Stowe Rd., Waterbury Center, VT 05677, 802/244-7037, website: www.greenmountainclub.org. Appalachian Trail Conference, 799 Washington St., P.O. Box 807, Harpers Ferry, WV 25425-0807, 304/535-6331, website: www.appalachiantrail.org.

## 29 GRIFFITH LAKE AND BAKER PEAK

**8.5 mi/6 hrs**

**in the Green Mountain National Forest southeast of Danby**

Baker Peak, though just 2,850 feet high, thrusts a rocky spine above the trees for great views of the valley around the little town of Danby. And Griffith Lake is one of several scenic ponds and lakes along the Long Trail. This 8.5-mile loop incorporates both places and involves about 2,000 feet of climbing.

From the parking area, follow the Lake Trail. It ascends very gently at first, then steeply for two miles. Where the Baker Peak Trail bears left, stay to the right on the Lake Trail. It nearly levels off again before reaching the Long Trail—which coincides here with the Appalachian Trail—at 3.5 miles from the trailhead. Turning right (south), walk the LT for 0.1 mile to the Griffith Lake camping area and access views of the lake. Spin around and hike north on the LT for 1.8 relatively easy miles to the Baker Peak Trail junction. Here, turn right with the LT and scramble up the long rock ridge protruding from the earth for 0.1 mile to the open Baker Peak summit. Then backtrack, descending the Baker Peak Trail, past the Quarry View overlook, for a mile to the Lake Trail. Turn right (west) and descend another two miles to the parking area.

**User groups:** Hikers, snowshoers, and dogs. Dogs must be leashed. No wheelchair facilities. This trail is not suitable for skis. Bikes, horses, and hunting are prohibited.

**Access, fees:** Parking and access are free. Camping is prohibited except at the Green Mountain Club cabins and shelters. The Griffith Lake camping area, with tent sites, is located 0.1 mile south of the Lake and Long Trails junction. From Memorial Day weekend–Labor Day, a Green Mountain Club caretaker is on duty and a nightly fee of $6 per person is collected.

**Maps:** For a map of hiking trails, refer to map 7 in the *Map and Guide to the Appalachian Trail in New Hampshire/Vermont,* an eight-map set and guidebook available for $19.95 ($14.95 for the maps alone) from the Appalachian Trail Conference (see address below). Or get the waterproof *End-to-End Map of the Long Trail,* available for $8.95 from the Green Mountain Club (see address below). For a topographic area map, request Danby from USGS Map Sales, Federal Center, Box 25286, Denver, CO 80225, 888/ASK-USGS (888/275-8747), website: http://mapping.usgs.gov.

**Directions:** From the crossroads in Danby, drive south on U.S. 7 for 2.1 miles and turn left onto Town Route 5. Drive a half mile to parking on the left for the Lake Trail.

**Contact:** Green Mountain National Forest Supervisor, 231 North Main St., Rutland, VT 05701, 802/747-6700, fax 802/747-6766, website: www.fs.fed.us/r9/gmfl. Green Mountain Club Inc., 4711 Waterbury-Stowe Rd., Waterbury Center, VT 05677, 802/244-7037, website: www.greenmountainclub.org. Appalachian Trail Conference, 799 Washington St., P.O. Box 807, Harpers Ferry, WV 25425-0807, 304/535-6331, website: www.appalachiantrail.org.

## 30 THE LONG TRAIL: ROUTE 11/30 TO USFS ROAD 10

**17.3 mi one-way/2 days**

**in the Green Mountain National Forest east of Danby**

I have a personal bias regarding the mountains—I prefer hikes with good views and which inspire a sense of solitude. Those two features are not always mutually compatible in New

England. But when I hiked much of the Long Trail in October 1996, this fairly scenic stretch gave me just that sort of experience. Timing no doubt helped; I started my trip after the leaves had fallen off the trees. One of my favorite moments was standing alone on the Styles Peak summit at sunset. Another was sitting on big rocks beside the roaring, clear waters of the Big Branch, with no one around. I'd recommend this 17.3-mile stretch for a moderate, two-day backpacking trip. The cumulative elevation gain is nearly 3,000 feet, but spread over more than 17 miles.

From the parking lot on Route 11/30, follow the white blazes of the Long Trail northbound, which here coincides with the Appalachian Trail. Watch closely for the blazes; many unmarked trails cross the LT on this side of Bromley. At 0.8 mile into this hike, a spur trail leads 150 feet to the right to the Bromley tenting area. Two miles from the road, the LT grows steeper, and at 2.6 miles it emerges from the woods onto a wide ski trail. Hike up the ski trail 0.2 mile to the mountain's summit, where there are ski area buildings. To the right are an observation deck—which offers views in every direction—and the warming hut. The LT swings left from the ski trail just before a chairlift and descends a steep, rocky section. At 3.3 miles (a half mile beyond the summit), the LT climbs over the rugged, wooded north summit of Bromley and then descends to cross USFS Road 21 in Mad Tom Notch at 5.3 miles. There is a water pump at the roadside that may not be working. Continuing north, the LT makes a steady, though not difficult, ascent of nearly 1,000 feet in elevation to the 3,394-foot Styles Peak summit, at 6.7 miles. Although I mentioned enjoying the sunset from this summit, I couldn't actually see the sunset, but the wide view south and west showed me long shadows across the land, and Styles's own pyramidal shadow.

Following the ridge north, the LT dips slightly and then ascends slightly to the wooded Peru Peak summit (3,429 feet) at 8.4 miles, where

a side path leads 75 feet right to a largely obscured view eastward. Descending steeply, the trail reaches the Peru Peak shelter at 9.7 miles, with a good stream nearby. The LT crosses the stream on a wooden bridge and continues a flat 0.7 mile to Griffith Lake at 10.4 miles, where there are tent sites. The Old Job Trail leaves right (east), swinging north to loop 5.3 miles back to the Long Trail at a point 0.1 mile east of the Big Branch suspension bridge. The Lake Trail departs left (west) at 10.5 miles, descending 3.5 miles to Town Route 5 in Danby (a half mile from U.S. 7).

The Long Trail continues north over easy terrain and then climbs to a junction, at 12.2 miles, with the Baker Peak Trail (which descends west for 2.9 miles to Town Route 5 via the Lake Trail). Turn right with the LT and scramble up a spine of exposed rock for 0.1 mile to the open summit of 2,850-foot Baker Peak, with great views of the valley around the little town of Danby. The trail then reenters the forest and traverses fairly easy terrain, reaching and following an old woods road to a junction, at 14.3 miles, with a short side path leading left to the Lost Pond shelter.

Continuing on the woods road, the LT reaches the Big Branch at 15.8 miles, swings left along it for 0.1 mile, and then crosses the river on a suspension bridge. The trail swings left again, following the boulder-choked river to the Big Branch shelter at 16 miles. Easy hiking for another 1.2 miles brings you to USFS Road 10. Turn left and walk the road for 0.1 mile to the parking lot at this hike's north end.
**User groups:** Hikers and dogs. Dogs must be leashed. No wheelchair facilities. This trail is not suitable for skis. The north end of this trail is not accessible by road in winter for snowshoeing. Bikes, horses, and hunting are prohibited.
**Access, fees:** Parking and access are free. USFS Road 10 is not maintained during the winter. No-trace camping is permitted within the Green Mountain National Forest, except at Griffith Lake, where camping within 200 feet of shore

is restricted to designated sites. Backpackers can stay overnight in the warming hut on Bromley Mountain's summit, beside the observation deck; there is no water source. The Bromley tenting area is 0.7 mile north of Route 11/30, reached via a short spur trail off the Long Trail. The Peru Peak shelter sits beside the LT at 9.8 miles, the Griffith Lake campsite at 10.3 miles, the Lost Pond shelter at 14.5 miles, and the Big Branch shelter at 16.2 miles (the last 1.3 miles south of the parking lot on USFS Road 10). The Mad Tom shelter was removed in 1997. From Memorial Day weekend–Labor Day, a Green Mountain Club caretaker is on duty, and a nightly fee of $6 per person is collected to stay at the Peru Peak shelter and the Griffith Lake campsite.

**Maps:** For a map of hiking trails, refer to map 7 in the *Map and Guide to the Appalachian Trail in New Hampshire/Vermont,* an eight-map set and guidebook available for $19.95 ($14.95 for the maps alone) from the Appalachian Trail Conference (see address below). Or get the waterproof *End-to-End Map of the Long Trail,* available for $8.95 from the Green Mountain Club (see address below). For topographic area maps, request Peru and Danby from USGS Map Sales, Federal Center, Box 25286, Denver, CO 80225, 888/ASK-USGS (888/275-8747), website: http://mapping.usgs.gov.

**Directions:** You need to shuttle two vehicles for this one-way traverse. To hike south to north, as described here, leave one vehicle in the parking lot on USFS Road 10 at Big Black Branch, 3.5 miles west of U.S. 7 in Danby and 13.6 miles north of Route 11 in Peru. Drive to the parking lot on the north side of Route 11/30, six miles east of Manchester Center and 4.4 miles west of Peru.

**Contact:** Green Mountain National Forest Supervisor, 231 North Main St., Rutland, VT 05701, 802/747-6700, fax 802/747-6766, website: www.fs.fed.us/r9/gmfl. Green Mountain Club Inc., 4711 Waterbury-Stowe Rd., Waterbury Center, VT 05677, 802/244-7037, website: www.greenmountainclub.org. Appalachian

Trail Conference, 799 Washington St., P.O. Box 807, Harpers Ferry, WV 25425-0807, 304/535-6331, website: www.appalachiantrail.org.

## 31 STYLES PEAK
### 2.8 mi/2 hrs

**in the Peru Peak Wilderness in the Green Mountain National Forest west of Peru**

Styles Peak, 3,394 feet high, has a small crag of a summit that affords views to the east and south of the southern Green Mountains and the rumpled landscape of southeastern Vermont and southwestern New Hampshire. This quiet spot is a great place to catch the sunrise, and with just 1.4 miles to hike nearly 1,000 feet uphill to reach the summit, getting here before dawn is a reasonable objective.

From the parking area, walk east a few steps on the road to the junction with the LT and turn left (north). After passing a water pump (which may not be working), follow the white-blazed Long Trail, which coincides here with the Appalachian Trail as it climbs steadily and then steeply to the open rocks atop Styles Peak. Return the way you came.

**User groups:** Hikers, snowshoers, and dogs. Dogs must be leashed. No wheelchair facilities. Bikes, horses, and hunting are prohibited.

**Access, fees:** Parking and access are free. USFS Road 21 is maintained in winter only to a point about 2.5 miles from the Long Trail. No-trace camping is permitted within the Green Mountain National Forest. The Peru Peak shelter is on the Long Trail, 4.4 miles north of USFS Road 21 and three miles north of the Styles Peak summit. From Memorial Day weekend–Labor Day, a Green Mountain Club caretaker is on duty and collects a nightly fee of $6 per person.

**Maps:** For a trail map, see map 7 in the *Map and Guide to the Appalachian Trail in New Hampshire/Vermont,* an eight-map set and guidebook available for $19.95 ($14.95 for the maps alone) from the Appalachian Trail Conference (see address below). Or get the waterproof *End-to-End Map of the Long Trail,* available for

$8.95 from the Green Mountain Club (see address below). For a topographic area map, request Peru from USGS Map Sales, Federal Center, Box 25286, Denver, CO 80225, 888/ASK-USGS (888/275-8747), website: http://mapping.usgs.gov.

**Directions:** Drive to the parking area on USFS Road 21, immediately west of the height of land in Mad Tom Notch and the Long Trail crossing, and 4.3 miles west of Route 11 in Peru.

**Contact:** Green Mountain National Forest Supervisor, 231 North Main St., Rutland, VT 05701, 802/747-6700, fax 802/747-6766, website: www.fs.fed.us/r9/gmfl. Green Mountain Club Inc., 4711 Waterbury-Stowe Rd., Waterbury Center, VT 05677, 802/244-7037, website: www.greenmountainclub.org. Appalachian Trail Conference, 799 Washington St., P.O. Box 807, Harpers Ferry, WV 25425-0807, 304/535-6331, website: www.appalachiantrail.org.

## 32 BROMLEY MOUNTAIN FROM MAD TOM NOTCH
**5 mi/3.5 hrs**
**in the Green Mountain National Forest west of Peru**

This five-mile route from the north up 3,260-foot Bromley Mountain is a bit more wild and less trammeled than taking the Long Trail from the south (see the Bromley Mountain from Route 11/30 listing, this chapter, for more information). A ski area in winter, Bromley offers some of the better views along the southern Long Trail from its summit observation deck. This hike climbs about 800 feet.

From the parking lot, walk east on the road for a short stretch, then turn right and follow the white blazes of the Long Trail southbound, which here coincides with the Appalachian Trail. The trail ascends easily at first and then climbs more steeply, over rocky terrain, to Bromley's wooded north summit at two miles. After dipping slightly, it climbs to the open summit of Bromley Mountain, 2.5 miles from the road. Cross the clearing to the observation

deck and warming hut. Descend the same way you came.

**User groups:** Hikers and dogs. Dogs must be leashed. No wheelchair facilities. This trail may be difficult to snowshoe and is not suitable for skis. Bikes, horses, and hunting are prohibited.

**Access, fees:** Parking and access are free. USFS Road 21 is maintained in winter only to a point about 2.5 miles from the Long Trail. No-trace camping is permitted within the Green Mountain National Forest. Backpackers can stay overnight in the warming hut on Bromley's summit, beside the observation deck; there is no water source.

**Maps:** For a map of hiking trails, refer to map 7 in the *Map and Guide to the Appalachian Trail in New Hampshire/Vermont,* an eight-map set and guidebook available for $19.95 ($14.95 for the maps alone) from the Appalachian Trail Conference (see address below). Or get the waterproof *End-to-End Map of the Long Trail,* available for $8.95 from the Green Mountain Club (see address below). For a topographic area map, request Peru from USGS Map Sales, Federal Center, Box 25286, Denver, CO 80225, 888/ASK-USGS (888/275-8747), website: http://mapping.usgs.gov.

**Directions:** Drive to the parking area on USFS Road 21, immediately west of the height of land in Mad Tom Notch and the Long Trail crossing, and 4.3 miles west of Route 11 in Peru.

**Contact:** Green Mountain National Forest Supervisor, 231 North Main St., Rutland, VT 05701, 802/747-6700, fax 802/747-6766, website: www.fs.fed.us/r9/gmfl. Green Mountain Club Inc., 4711 Waterbury-Stowe Rd., Waterbury Center, VT 05677, 802/244-7037, fax 802/244-5867, website: www.greenmountainclub.org. Appalachian Trail Conference, 799 Washington St., P.O. Box 807, Harpers Ferry, WV 25425-0807, 304/535-6331, website: www.appalachiantrail.org.

## 33 BROMLEY MOUNTAIN FROM ROUTE 11/30

**5.6 mi/3.5 hrs**

**in the Green Mountain National Forest between Peru and Manchester Center**

Bromley Mountain, a ski area in winter, offers some of the better views along the southern Long Trail from the observation deck on its 3,260-foot summit. This 5.6-mile route up Bromley is a popular hike and suffers from erosion and muddy ground in many places. It ascends 1,460 feet.

From the parking lot, follow the white blazes of the Long Trail northbound, which here coincides with the Appalachian Trail. Watch closely for the blazes; numerous unmarked trails cross the LT on this side of Bromley. At two miles into this hike you reach the Bromley shelter, where there's a lean-to that sleeps 12 and four tent platforms. Beyond it, the LT grows steeper, and at 2.6 miles it emerges from the woods onto a wide ski trail. Hike up the ski trail 0.2 mile to the mountain's summit, where there are ski area buildings. Turn right and walk 100 feet to the observation deck. The views extend in every direction. Stratton Mountain looms prominently to the south. Beside the tower is the warming hut. Descend the way you came.

**User groups:** Hikers, snowshoers, and dogs. Dogs must be leashed. No wheelchair facilities. This trail is not suitable for skis. Bikes, horses, and hunting are prohibited.

**Access, fees:** Parking and access are free. No-trace camping is permitted within the Green Mountain National Forest. The Bromley shelter and tent platforms are two miles north of Route 11/30. Backpackers can stay overnight in the warming hut on Bromley's summit, beside the observation deck; there is no water source.

**Maps:** For a map of hiking trails, refer to map 7 in the *Map and Guide to the Appalachian Trail in New Hampshire/Vermont,* an eight-map set and guidebook available for $19.95 ($14.95 for the maps alone) from the Appalachian Trail

Conference (see address below). Or get the waterproof *End-to-End Map of the Long Trail,* available for $8.95 from the Green Mountain Club (see address below). For a topographic area map, request Peru from USGS Map Sales, Federal Center, Box 25286, Denver, CO 80225, 888/ASK-USGS (888/275-8747), website: http://mapping.usgs.gov.

**Directions:** Drive to the parking lot on the north side of Route 11/30, six miles east of Manchester Center and 4.4 miles west of Peru.

**Contact:** Green Mountain National Forest Supervisor, 231 North Main St., Rutland, VT 05701, 802/747-6700, fax 802/747-6766, website: www.fs.fed.us/r9/gmfl. Green Mountain Club Inc., 4711 Waterbury-Stowe Rd., Waterbury Center, VT 05677, 802/244-7037, website: www.greenmountainclub.org. Appalachian Trail Conference, 799 Washington St., P.O. Box 807, Harpers Ferry, WV 25425-0807, 304/535-6331, website: www.appalachiantrail.org.

## 34 SPRUCE PEAK

**4.4 mi/2.5 hrs**

**in the Green Mountain National Forest south of Peru**

This fairly easy hike of 4.4 miles takes you up to Spruce Peak, at 2,040 feet no more than a small bump along a wooded Green Mountain ridge, but a spot with a couple of good views west to the valley at Manchester Center and out to the Taconic Range. On my trip, I happened to time this hike perfectly, enjoying the view on a cloudless Indian summer day in October when the foliage in the valley below was at its peak.

From the parking area, cross Route 11/30 and follow the white blazes of the Long Trail southbound into the woods. The hiking is mostly easy, climbing only a few hundred feet in elevation, with the trail passing through an area of moss-covered boulders and rocks. At 2.2 miles from the road, turn right (west) onto a side path that leads about 300 feet to the Spruce Peak summit. There is a limited view west at the actual summit, but just below the summit, a few steps off the path, is a better view. Return the way you came.

**User groups:** Hikers, snowshoers, and dogs. Dogs must be leashed. No wheelchair facilities. Bikes, horses, and hunting are prohibited.

**Access, fees:** Parking and access are free. No-trace camping is permitted within the Green Mountain National Forest. The Spruce Peak shelter is 0.1 mile down a side path off the LT, 2.7 miles south of Route 11/30 and a half mile south of the side path to Spruce Peak.

**Maps:** For a map of hiking trails, refer to map 7 in the *Map and Guide to the Appalachian Trail in New Hampshire/Vermont,* an eight-map set and guidebook available for $19.95 ($14.95 for the maps alone) from the Appalachian Trail Conference (see address below). Or get the waterproof *End-to-End Map of the Long Trail,* available for $8.95 from the Green Mountain Club (see address below). For a topographic area map, request Peru from USGS Map Sales, Federal Center, Box 25286, Denver, CO 80225, 888/ASK-USGS (888/275-8747), website: http://mapping.usgs.gov.

**Directions:** Drive to the parking lot on the north side of Route 11/30, six miles east of Manchester Center and 4.4 miles west of Peru.

**Contact:** Green Mountain National Forest Supervisor, 231 North Main St., Rutland, VT 05701, 802/747-6700, fax 802/747-6766, website: www.fs.fed.us/r9/gmfl. Green Mountain Club Inc., 4711 Waterbury-Stowe Rd., Waterbury Center, VT 05677, 802/244-7037, website: www.greenmountainclub.org. Appalachian Trail Conference, 799 Washington St., P.O. Box 807, Harpers Ferry, WV 25425-0807, 304/535-6331, website: www.appalachiantrail.org.

## 35 THE LONG TRAIL: ARLINGTON– WEST WARDSBORO ROAD TO ROUTE 11/30

**16.3 mi one-way/ 11 hrs or 1–2 days**

**in the Green Mountain National Forest between Stratton and Peru**

The highlights of this 16.3-mile traverse of the

Long Trail's southern stretch are the 360-degree view from the observation tower on 3,936-foot Stratton Mountain, and beautiful Stratton Pond. But you also get a view from Spruce Peak, and the northern part of this trek will feel considerably more secluded than Stratton Pond or Stratton Mountain. The cumulative elevation gain is more than 2,500 feet, most of that involved in the 1,800-foot climb up Stratton Mountain.

From the parking area, head north on the white-blazed Long Trail (which coincides here with the Appalachian Trail). It rises gently through muddy areas, growing progressively steeper—and passing one outlook south—over the 3.4-mile climb to Stratton's summit. A Green Mountain Club caretaker cabin is located on the edge of the summit clearing, and a caretaker is on duty during the late spring–fall hiking season to answer questions and assist hikers. After climbing the observation tower (see Stratton Mountain and Stratton Pond listing for a description of the view from the tower), continue north on the LT, descending for 2.6 miles to Willis Ross Clearing on the east shore of Stratton Pond, the largest water body and one of the busiest spots on the Long Trail (see Access, for camping information). The Lye Brook Trail leads left while the LT swings right, passing a junction with the North Shore Trail within 0.1 mile. The LT contours, for easy hiking, to the Winhall River at 7.9 miles into this hike; the river is crossed on a bridge, and the trail enters the Lye Brook Wilderness.

At 10.3 miles, the Branch Pond Trail leads left (west) into the Lye Brook Wilderness to the William B. Douglas shelter. Crossing a brook, the LT turns left and follows a wide logging road. At 11.4 miles, an unmarked side path leads about 200 feet to Prospect Rock, with a good view of Downer Glen. The LT turns right (northeast) off the road and climbs steadily before descending again to a side path, at 13.6 miles, leading 0.1 mile to the Spruce Peak cabin. After more easy hiking, at 14.1 miles, a side path leads about 300 feet left to the Spruce Peak summit, where there is a limited view west. But just below the summit is a better view of the valley and the Taconic Mountains. Continuing north, the LT crosses easy ground for 2.2 miles, passing through an area of interesting, moss-covered boulders, to reach Routes 11/30 at 16.3 miles. Cross the highway to the parking lot.

**User groups:** Hikers and dogs. Dogs must be leashed. No wheelchair facilities. This trail is not suitable for skis. The south end of this trail is not accessible by road in winter for snowshoeing. Bikes, horses, and hunting are prohibited.

**Access, fees:** Parking and access are free. The Arlington–West Wardsboro Road is not maintained in winter. No-trace camping is permitted within the Green Mountain National Forest, except at Stratton Pond, where camping is restricted to the North Shore tenting area, which lies a half mile down the North Shore Trail from its junction with the Long Trail, 0.1 mile north of Willis Ross Clearing; and the new Stratton Pond shelter, located 100 yards down the Stratton Pond Trail from its junction with the LT/AT. From Memorial Day weekend–Columbus Day, a Green Mountain Club caretaker is on duty, and a nightly fee of $6 per person is collected to stay at the Stratton Pond shelter and the North Shore tenting area. Two Green Mountain Club shelters on Stratton Pond—Vondell shelter and Bigelow shelter—were removed in the fall of 2000 and 1997, respectively. Camping is prohibited on the upper slopes of Stratton Mountain, which is privately owned. The Williams B. Douglas shelter lies a half mile south of the LT on the Branch Pond Trail, 10.3 miles north of the Arlington–West Wardsboro Road. The Spruce Peak shelter lies 0.1 mile down a side path off the LT, at 13.6 miles into this hike.

**Maps:** For a map of hiking trails, refer to map 7 in the *Map and Guide to the Appalachian Trail in New Hampshire/Vermont,* an eight-map set and guidebook available for $19.95 ($14.95 for the maps alone) from the Appalachian Trail Conference (see address below). Or get the wa-

terproof *End-to-End Map of the Long Trail,* available for $8.95 from the Green Mountain Club (see address below). For topographic area maps, request Stratton Mountain, Manchester, and Peru from USGS Map Sales, Federal Center, Box 25286, Denver, CO 80225, 888/ASK-USGS (888/275-8747), website: http://mapping.usgs.gov.

**Directions:** You need to shuttle two vehicles for this one-way traverse. To hike south to north, as described here, leave one vehicle in the parking lot on the north side of Route 11/30, six miles east of Manchester Center and 4.4 miles west of Peru. Then drive to the large parking area on the Arlington–West Wardsboro Road, 13.3 miles east of U.S. 7 in Arlington and eight miles west of Route 100 in West Wardsboro.

**Contact:** Green Mountain National Forest Supervisor, 231 North Main St., Rutland, VT 05701, 802/747-6700, fax 802/747-6766, website: www.fs.fed.us/r9/gmfl. Green Mountain Club Inc., 4711 Waterbury-Stowe Rd., Waterbury Center, VT 05677, 802/244-7037, website: www.greenmountainclub.org. Appalachian Trail Conference, 799 Washington St., P.O. Box 807, Harpers Ferry, WV 25425-0807, 304/535-6331, website: www.appalachiantrail.org.

##  STRATTON MOUNTAIN AND STRATTON POND

**11 mi/7 hrs**

**in the Green Mountain National Forest between Arlington and West Wardsboro**

From the observation tower atop Stratton Mountain, you get one of the most sweeping panoramas on the LT. And merely climbing the tower will be an adventure for children, as well as adults not accustomed to heights. This 11-mile hike climbs about 1,500 feet. For a shorter hike—though with just as much climbing—you can make a 6.8-mile round-trip on the Long Trail to the 3,936-foot Stratton summit and return the same way.

From the parking area, follow the white-blazed Long Trail north (which coincides here

a long view from Vermont's Long Trail

with the Appalachian Trail). It rises steadily, through muddy areas at the lower elevations, and passes one outlook south in the 3.4-mile climb—the last stretch of which grows steeper. On the 3,936-foot summit is the Green Mountain Club's caretaker cabin, and a caretaker is on duty during the late spring–fall hiking season to answer questions and assist hikers. Climb the fire tower, where the views take in Somerset Reservoir and Mount Greylock to the south, the Taconic Range to the west, Mount Ascutney to the northeast, and Mount Monadnock to the southeast.

Return the same way, or make an 11-mile loop by continuing north on the LT, descending for 2.6 miles to beautiful Stratton Pond, the largest body of water and one of the busiest areas on the Long Trail. The Long Trail reaches the east shore of Stratton Pond at Willis Ross Clearing. From here, a loop of about 1.5 miles around the pond is possible, taking the Lye Brook Trail along the south shore, and the North Shore Trail back to the Long Trail, 0.1 mile north of Willis Ross Clearing; this distance is not included in this hike's mileage. From the clearing, backtrack 0.1 mile south on the LT, turn right onto the Stratton Pond

Trail, and follow it for an easy 3.8 miles back to the Arlington–West Wardsboro Road. Turn left (east) and walk the road 1.1 miles back to the parking area.

**User groups:** Hikers and dogs. Dogs must be leashed. No wheelchair facilities. This trail is not suitable for skis. The trailhead is not accessible by road in winter for snowshoeing. Bikes, horses, and hunting are prohibited.

**Access, fees:** Parking and access are free. The Arlington–West Wardsboro Road is not maintained in winter. No-trace camping is permitted within the Green Mountain National Forest, except at Stratton Pond, where camping is restricted to the North Shore tenting area, which lies a half mile down the North Shore Trail from its junction with the Long Trail, 0.1 mile north of Willis Ross Clearing; and the new Stratton Pond shelter, located 100 yards down the Stratton Pond Trail from its junction with the LT/AT. From Memorial Day weekend–Columbus Day, a Green Mountain Club caretaker is on duty, and a nightly fee of $6 per person is collected to stay at the Stratton shelter and the North Shore tenting area. Two Green Mountain Club shelters on Stratton Pond—Vondell shelter and Bigelow shelter—

were removed in the fall of 2000 and in 1997, respectively. Camping is prohibited on the upper slopes of Stratton Mountain, which is privately owned.

**Maps:** For a map of hiking trails, refer to map 7 in the *Map and Guide to the Appalachian Trail in New Hampshire/Vermont,* an eight-map set and guidebook available for $19.95 ($14.95 for the maps alone) from the Appalachian Trail Conference (see address below). Or get the waterproof *End-to-End Map of the Long Trail,* available for $8.95 from the Green Mountain Club (see address below). For a topographic area map, request Stratton Mountain from USGS Map Sales, Federal Center, Box 25286, Denver, CO 80225, 888/ASK-USGS (888/275-8747), website: http://mapping.usgs.gov.

**Directions:** The hike begins from a large parking area on the Arlington–West Wardsboro Road, 13.3 miles east of U.S. 7 in Arlington and eight miles west of Route 100 in West Wardsboro.

**Contact:** Green Mountain National Forest Supervisor, 231 North Main St., Rutland, VT 05701, 802/747-6700, fax 802/747-6766, website: www.fs.fed.us/r9/gmfl. Green Mountain Club Inc., 4711 Waterbury-Stowe Rd., Waterbury Center, VT 05677, 802/244-7037, website: www.greenmountainclub.org. Appalachian Trail Conference, 799 Washington St., P.O. Box 807, Harpers Ferry, WV 25425-0807, 304/535-6331, website: www.appalachiantrail.org.

## 37 THE LONG TRAIL: ROUTE 9 TO ARLINGTON–WEST WARDSBORO ROAD

**22.3 mi one-way/2–3 days**

**in the Green Mountain National Forest between Woodford and Stratton**

While much of this 22.3-mile stretch of the Long Trail/Appalachian Trail remains in the woods, it makes for a nice walk along a wooded ridge, on a relatively easy backpacking trip that can be done in two days without extreme effort. And there are a few breathtaking views, most particularly from the fire tower on the

3,748-foot Glastenbury Mountain summit, which offers one of the finest panoramas I've seen on the Long Trail. The cumulative elevation gain over the course of this hike exceeds 4,000 feet.

From the parking lot, follow the white blazes of the Long Trail northbound. The trail parallels City Stream briefly and then crosses it on a wooden bridge. Climbing steadily, the trail crosses an old woods road 0.2 mile from the highway and then passes between the twin halves of Split Rock, formerly one giant boulder, at 0.6 mile. At 1.5 miles, a side path leads right a short distance to the Nauheim shelter. Ascending north from the shelter, the trail crosses a power line atop Maple Hill at two miles, which affords a view toward Bennington. The trail then traverses the more level terrain of a wooded ridge and crosses Hell Hollow Brook, a reliable water source, on a bridge at three miles.

Passing through a stand of beech trees, the LT reaches Little Pond Lookout at 5.7 miles, with a good view east, then Glastenbury Lookout at 7.4 miles, with its view of Glastenbury Mountain. The trail then ascends about 600 feet at a moderate angle to Goddard shelter, at 9.8 miles. From the shelter, it's a not-too-rigorous, 0.3-mile walk uphill on the LT to the Glastenbury summit. From the fire tower, the 360-degree view encompasses the Berkshires—most prominently Mount Greylock—to the south, the Taconic Range to the west, Stratton Mountain to the north, and Somerset Reservoir to the east. Continuing north, the LT descends about 500 feet in elevation and then follows a wooded ridge, with slight rises and dips, for about four miles, finally descending at a moderate angle to a side path on the right at 14 miles, which leads 0.1 mile to the Kid Gore shelter. About 0.1 mile farther north on the LT, the other end of that side loop reaches the LT near the Caughnawaga shelter. The LT then goes through more slight ups and downs before reaching the Story Spring shelter, 18.7 miles north of

Route 9 and 3.6 miles south of the Arlington–West Wardsboro Road. The LT crosses USFS Road 71 at 20.3 miles, passes beaver ponds, traverses an area often wet and muddy, and then crosses Black Brook, a reliable water source, on a wooden bridge at 21.3 miles. Paralleling the east branch of the Deerfield River, the trail reaches the Arlington–West Wardsboro Road at 22.3 miles. Turn right (east) and walk 200 feet to the parking area.

**User groups:** Hikers, snowshoers, and dogs. Dogs must be leashed. No wheelchair facilities. This trail is not suitable for skis. Bikes, horses, and hunting are prohibited.

**Access, fees:** Parking and access are free. The Arlington–West Wardsboro Road is not maintained in winter. No-trace camping is permitted within the Green Mountain National Forest. The Green Mountain Club Melville Nauheim shelter is located 1.6 miles north of Route 9 on the Long Trail, the Goddard shelter at 10.1 miles, the Kid Gore shelter at 14.2 miles, the Caughnawaga shelter at 14.4 miles, and the Story Spring shelter at 19 miles (or 3.6 miles south of the Arlington–West Wardsboro Road).

**Maps:** For a map of hiking trails, refer to map 8 in the *Map and Guide to the Appalachian Trail in New Hampshire/Vermont,* an eight-map set and guidebook available for $19.95 ($14.95 for the maps alone) from the Appalachian Trail Conference (see address below). Or get the waterproof *End-to-End Map of the Long Trail,* available for $8.95 from the Green Mountain Club (see address below). For topographic area maps, request Woodford, Sunderland, and Stratton Mountain from USGS Map Sales, Federal Center, Box 25286, Denver, CO 80225, 888/ASK-USGS (888/275-8747), website: http://mapping.usgs.gov.

**Directions:** You need to shuttle two vehicles for this one-way traverse. To hike south to north, as described here, leave one vehicle in the roadside parking area where the Long Trail/Appalachian Trail crosses the Arlington–West Wardsboro Road, 13.3 miles east of U.S. 7 in Arlington and eight miles west of Route 100 in

West Wardsboro. Then drive to the large parking lot at the Long Trail/Appalachian Trail crossing of Route 9, 5.2 miles east of Bennington and 2.8 miles west of Woodford.

**Contact:** Green Mountain National Forest Supervisor, 231 North Main St., Rutland, VT 05701, 802/747-6700, fax 802/747-6766, website: www.fs.fed.us/r9/gmfl. Green Mountain Club Inc., 4711 Waterbury-Stowe Rd., Waterbury Center, VT 05677, 802/244-7037, website: www.greenmountainclub.org. Appalachian Trail Conference, 799 Washington St., P.O. Box 807, Harpers Ferry, WV 25425-0807, 304/535-6331, website: www.appalachiantrail.org.

## 38 GLASTENBURY MOUNTAIN
### 20.2 mi/2 days

**in the Green Mountain National Forest between Bennington and Woodford**

While much of the southern third of the Long Trail, which coincides with the Appalachian Trail, remains in the woods, the fire tower on the 3,748-foot Glastenbury Mountain summit offers a superb panorama of the gently rolling, southern Green Mountains wilderness. Other views include the Berkshires, particularly Mount Greylock, due south, the Taconic Range to the west, Stratton Mountain to the north, and Somerset Reservoir to the east. I stood up here one afternoon at the height of the fall foliage, and it turned out to be one of the finest views I had in my lengthy Long Trail trek.

This 20.2-mile round-trip—which involves nearly 4,000 feet of uphill—is best spread over two days, with an overnight stay at the spacious Goddard shelter (or tenting in the area). Goddard, which has a nice view south to Greylock, can be a popular place on temperate weekends in summer and fall. See the trail notes for the Long Trail: Route 9 to Arlington–West Wardsboro Road for the description of this hike from Route 9 to the Goddard shelter. At the shelter, leave your packs behind for the 0.3-mile walk uphill on the LT to the Glastenbury summit and the fire tower. On the second day, you can return the same way you came. Or to avoid backtracking, hike the West Ridge Trail from God-dard shelter, a fairly easy route that leads 7.7 miles to the Bald Mountain summit and a junc-tion at 7.8 miles with the Bald Mountain Trail. Turn left on that trail and descend 1.9 miles to a public road. Turning right on the road, you reach Route 9 in 0.8 mile, 1.2 miles west of the parking lot where you began this hike.

**User groups:** Hikers, snowshoers, and dogs. Dogs must be leashed. No wheelchair facili-ties. This trail is not suitable for skis. Bikes, horses, and hunting are prohibited.

**Access, fees:** Parking and access are free. No-trace camping is permitted within the Green Mountain National Forest. The Green Moun-tain Club Melville Nauheim shelter is located 1.6 miles north of Route 9 on the Long Trail, and the Goddard shelter 10.1 miles north of the highway.

**Maps:** For a map of hiking trails, refer to map 8 in the *Map and Guide to the Appalachian Trail in New Hampshire/Vermont,* an eight-map set and guidebook available for $19.95 ($14.95 for the maps alone) from the Appalachian Trail Conference (see address below). Or get the wa-terproof *End-to-End Map of the Long Trail,* available for $8.95 from the Green Mountain Club (see address below). For a topographic area map, request Woodford from USGS Map Sales, Federal Center, Box 25286, Denver, CO 80225, 888/ASK-USGS (888/275-8747), web-site: http://mapping.usgs.gov.

**Directions:** Drive to the large parking lot at the Long Trail/Appalachian Trail crossing of Route 9, 5.2 miles east of Bennington and 2.8 miles west of Woodford.

**Contact:** Green Mountain National Forest Su-pervisor, 231 North Main St., Rutland, VT 05701, 802/747-6700, fax 802/747-6766, web-site: www.fs.fed.us/r9/gmfl. Green Mountain Club Inc., 4711 Waterbury-Stowe Rd., Water-bury Center, VT 05677, 802/244-7037, website: www.greenmountainclub.org. Appalachian Trail Conference, 799 Washington St., P.O. Box 807, Harpers Ferry, WV 25425-0807, 304/535-6331, website: www.appalachiantrail.org.

## 39 THE LONG TRAIL: MASSACHUSETTS LINE TO ROUTE 9

**14.2 mi one-way/2 days**

**in the Green Mountain National Forest between Clarksburg, Massachusetts, and Woodford**

This southernmost stretch of the Long Trail—here coinciding with the Ap-palachian Trail—is for the most part an easy hike along a mostly flat, wooded ridge. The cumulative elevation gain is well under 1,000 feet per day. The southern Green Mountains are not known for spectacular views, although there are few on this hike. But this would be a good overnight backpacking trip for hikers who prefer a woods walk or for a beginner backpacker. Because the Long Trail's south-ern terminus lies in the forest on the Vermont-Massachusetts border, you have to access this hike via one of two trails, adding either 3.6 miles or 4 miles to this hike's distance.

The Pine Cobble Trail, the more interesting and slightly shorter of the two access trails, reaches the LT in 3.6 miles; from the parking area, walk east on Brooks Road for 0.2 mile and turn left on Pine Cobble Road. The trail begins 0.1 mile up the road on the right and is marked by a sign. (See the Pine Cobble list-ing in the Berkshires and Western Massachu-setts chapter for details about this trail.)

The white-blazed Appalachian Trail takes four miles to reach the border of the two states, passing a view south to Mount Greylock from an old rock slide 2.4 miles from Route 2. From the state border, the Long Trail follows level, wooded terrain, crossing some old logging roads, for 2.6 miles to a junction with the Broad Brook Trail, which branches left (west) and leads four miles to a road outside Williamstown. At 2.8 miles, the Seth Warner Trail leads left (west) 0.2 mile to the Seth Warner shelter. Con-tinuing north, the LT crosses the dirt County Road at 3.1 miles, which connects Pownal and Stamford and may be passable by motor ve-hicle as far as the Long Trail. The LT ascends several hundred feet over a 3,000-foot hill, drops down the other side, and then makes an easier climb over Consultation Peak (2,810 feet) before reaching Congdon Camp at 10 miles. At 10.5 miles, the LT crosses the Dunville Hollow Trail, which leads left (west) 0.7 mile to a rough woods road (turning right onto that road leads 1.8 miles to houses on Burgess Road and four miles to Route 9, a mile east of Bennington). The LT follows more easy terrain before climbing slightly to the top of Harmon Hill (2,325 feet) at 12.5 miles, from which there are some views west toward Bennington and north toward Glastenbury Mountain. Continuing north, the trail descends at an easy grade for a mile, then drops steeply over the final half mile to Route 9.

**User groups:** Hikers, snowshoers, and dogs. Dogs must be leashed. No wheelchair facilities. This trail is not suitable for skis. Bikes, horses, and hunting are prohibited.

**Access, fees:** Parking and access are free. No-trace camping is permitted within the Green Mountain National Forest. The Seth Warner shelter is 300 yards west of the Long Trail, reached via a side path off the LT, 2.8 miles north of the Massachusetts border. The Congdon Camp shelter is on the Long Trail, 10 miles north of the Massachusetts border and 4.3 miles south of Route 9.

**Maps:** For a map of hiking trails, refer to map 8 in the *Map and Guide to the Appalachian Trail in New Hampshire/Vermont,* an eight-map set and guidebook available for $19.95 ($14.95 for the maps alone) from the Appalachian Trail Conference (see address below). Or get the waterproof *End-to-End Map of the Long Trail,* available for $8.95 from the Green Mountain Club (see address below). For topographic area maps, request Pownal, Stamford, Bennington, and Woodford from USGS Map Sales, Federal Center, Box 25286, Denver, CO 80225, 888/ASK-USGS (888/275-8747), website: http://mapping.usgs.gov.

**Directions:** You need to shuttle two vehicles for this one-way traverse. To hike south to north, as described here, leave one vehicle in the large parking lot at the Long Trail/Appalachian Trail crossing of Route 9, 5.2 miles east of Bennington and 2.8 miles west of Woodford. Then drive to one of two possible starts for this hike, both in Massachusetts. For the Pine Cobble start, from U.S. 7 in Williamstown, a mile south of the Vermont line and 0.3 mile north of the Hoosic River bridge, turn east on North Housac Road. Drive a half mile and turn right on Brooks Road. Drive 0.7 mile and park in a dirt lot on the left marked by a sign reading, "Parking for Pine Cobble Trail." For the Appalachian Trail start, drive to the AT footbridge over the Hoosic River (where there is no convenient parking) on Route 2, 2.9 miles east of Williamstown center and 2.5 miles west of North Adams center.

**Contact:** Green Mountain National Forest Supervisor, 231 North Main St., Rutland, VT 05701, 802/747-6700, fax 802/747-6766, website: www.fs.fed.us/r9/gmfl. Green Mountain Club Inc., 4711 Waterbury-Stowe Rd., Waterbury Center, VT 05677, 802/244-7037, website: www.greenmountainclub.org. Appalachian Trail Conference, 799 Washington St., P.O. Box 807, Harpers Ferry, WV 25425-0807, 304/535-6331, website: www.appalachiantrail.org.

# Massachusetts

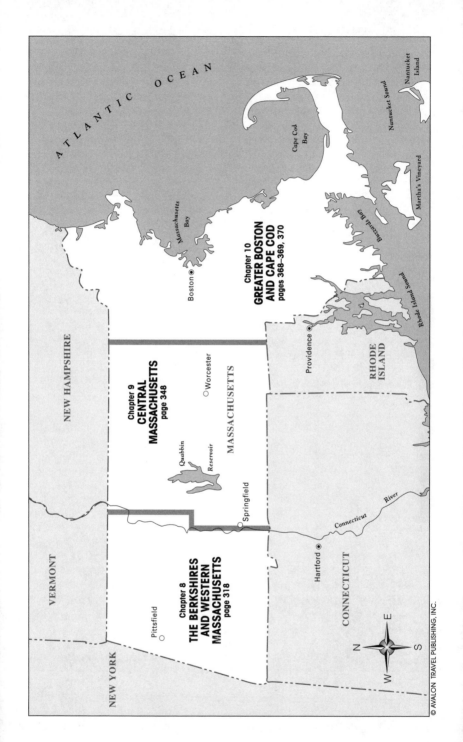

© MICHAEL LANZA

# The Berkshires and Western Massachusetts

# The Berkshires and Western Massachusetts

The rural hills west of the Connecticut River harbor the best opportunities in Massachusetts for longer day hikes and backpacking trips. The Bay State's highest peak, 3,491-foot Mount Greylock, and other summits in the Berkshires offer scenic, sometimes rugged trails with occasional far-reaching views of these green, rounded hills.

The Appalachian Trail runs for 89 miles through the Berkshires, with such highlights as Mount Greylock and the beautiful Riga Plateau; both are popular destinations for day hiking and backpacking, especially from July through September, when camping areas tend to fill up quickly on weekends. But both are also far enough south and low enough that the prime hiking season often begins by mid-spring and lasts through late autumn. I backpacked the Riga Plateau one May and found the trees in full, leafy bloom, the temperature comfortably warm, the bugs barely noticeable, and few other people on the trail. Winters are typically cold and see plenty of snow in the hills, and several of these hikes make excellent, easy-to-moderate outings on snowshoes or cross-country skis.

The AT does tend to draw the heaviest hiker traffic, though, and there's plenty of other fine hiking in western Massachusetts, from state forests with hidden gems like Alander Mountain and the Hubbard River Gorge to private reserves like Monument Mountain, and one of New England's most beautiful waterfalls, Bash Bish Falls.

Along the AT, dogs must be kept under control, and bikes, horses, hunting, and firearms are prohibited. In state parks and forests, dogs must be leashed; horses are allowed in most state forests and parks, as is hunting in season.

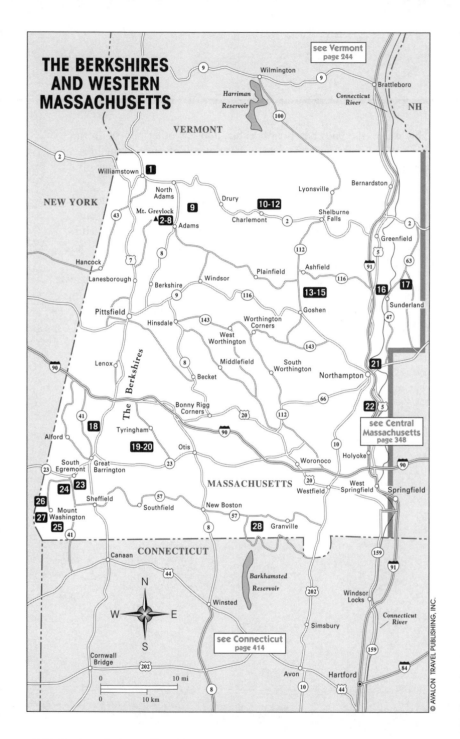

THE BERKSHIRES
AND WESTERN
MASSACHUSETTS

see Vermont
page 244

VERMONT

Harriman
Reservoir

Connecticut
River

NH

Wilmington

Brattleboro

NEW YORK

Williamstown **1**

North
Adams
Lyonsville

Bernardston

Drury

**10-12**

Mt. Greylock
**2-8**
**9**
Charlemont
Shelburne
Falls

Adams

Greenfield

Hancock

Plainfield
Ashfield
**16** **17**

Lanesborough

Berkshire
Windsor
Sunderland

Pittsfield

Hinsdale
Worthington
Corners
Goshen

West
Worthington
**13-15**

Lenox
The Berkshires
Middlefield
South
Worthington
**21**
Northampton

Becket

Bonny Rigg
Corners
**22**

see Central
Massachusetts
page 348

**18**
Tyringham

Alford
**19-20**
Otis
Woronoco
Holyoke

South
Egremont
Great
Barrington
MASSACHUSETTS
West
Springfield
Springfield

**24** **23**
Sheffield
Westfield

**26**
Mount
Washington
Southfield
New Boston
**25**
**28** Granville

**27**

CONNECTICUT

Barkhamsted
Reservoir

Canaan

Winsted
Windsor
Locks

Connecticut
River

Simsbury

see Connecticut
page 414

N
W E
S

Cornwall
Bridge
Avon
Hartford

0        10 mi
0        10 km

© AVALON TRAVEL PUBLISHING, INC.

# 1 PINE COBBLE

**3.2 mi/2 hrs**

**in Williamstown**

I began backpacking Vermont's Long Trail from this access trail rather than using the Appalachian Trail (which crosses MA 2 in the North Adams Blackinton section) because the view from Pine Cobble makes for a much more auspicious start to a long hike. Here in Massachusetts's northwest corner, the extensive quartzite ledges on the top of 1,894-foot Pine Cobble offer excellent views of the Hoosic Valley, the low, green hills flanking the river, and towering Mount Greylock (see hikes 2–8 in this chapter). Ascending at an easy to moderate grade, this 3.2-mile trek is popular with students at nearby Williams College and is a good outing for young children. It climbs about 900 feet in elevation.

From the parking area, walk across Pine Cobble Road to the trail. Follow the trail's blue blazes and well-worn path. In less than a mile, a side path on the right leads 350 feet downhill to Bear Spring. At 1.5 miles from the parking area, the blue blazes hook sharply left and a spur path leads to the right 0.1 mile to Pine Cobble's summit. Take the spur path, soon reaching a ledge that offers a view west to the Taconic Range. About 100 feet farther uphill is the summit. The best views are from the open ledges about 30 feet beyond the summit. Looking south (right) you see Mount Greylock; east lie the Clarksburg State Forest's woods and hills, and to the north extends an array of hills traversed by Appalachian Trail hikers on their way into Vermont. Return the same way you came.

Special note: Hikers interested in a longer outing can continue north on the Pine Cobble Trail 0.5 mile to the Appalachian Trail, turn left (north), and hike another 0.5 mile to a view south of Mount Greylock from Eph's Lookout. The added distance makes the entire round-trip 5.2 miles.

**User groups:** Hikers, snowshoers, and dogs. No wheelchair facilities. This trail is not suitable for bikes, horses, or skis. Hunting is prohibited.

**Access, fees:** Parking and access are free.

**Maps:** For a map of hiking trails, refer to map 1 in the *Map and Guide to the Appalachian Trail in Massachusetts and Connecticut,* a five-map set and guidebook available for $19.95 ($14.95 for the maps alone) from the Appalachian Trail Conference (see address below). For a topographic area map, request North Adams from USGS Map Sales, Federal Center, Box 25286, Denver, CO 80225, 888/ASK-USGS (888/275-8747), website: http://mapping.usgs.gov.

**Directions:** From the junction of U.S. 7 and MA 2 in Williamstown, drive east on MA 2 for 0.6 mile, then turn left on Cole Avenue at the first traffic light. Drive another 0.8 mile, crossing a bridge over the Hoosic River and crossing railroad tracks, then turn right on North Housac Road. Follow it 0.4 mile to a left turn onto Pine Cobble Road and continue to the parking area 0.2 mile up on the left, across the street from the trailhead.

**Contact:** Appalachian Trail Conference, 799 Washington St., P.O. Box 807, Harpers Ferry, WV 25425-0807, 304/535-6331, website: www.appalachiantrail.org.

# 2 MOUNT GREYLOCK: MONEY BROOK FALLS

**5 mi/3 hrs**

**in Mount Greylock State Reservation in Williamstown, North Adams, Adams, and Lanesborough**

Money Brook Falls tumbles from an impressive height into a ravine choked with trees that haven't survived the steep, erosive terrain. Despite being one of the most spectacular natural features on the biggest hill in the Bay State, it may be Massachusetts's best-kept secret. The trail makes several stream crossings, some of which could be difficult in high water.

From the parking area, walk past the gate onto the Hopper Trail and follow a flat, grassy lane 0.2 mile. Where the Hopper Trail diverges right, continue straight ahead on the Money Brook Trail. It ascends gently at first, but after passing the Mount Prospect Trail junction at 1.5 miles, it goes through some short, steep stretches. At 2.4 miles, turn right onto a side path that leads 0.1 mile to the falls. Hike back the way you came.

**User groups:** Hikers, snowshoers, and dogs. Dogs must be leashed. No wheelchair facilities. This trail is not suitable for horses or skis. Bikes are prohibited. Hunting is allowed in season.

**Access, fees:** A daily fee of $2 is collected from mid-May–mid-October at some parking areas. From the mid-December close of hunting season through mid-May, roads within the state reservation are closed to vehicles (and groomed for snowmobiles), but Hopper Road is maintained to this trailhead. There is a lean-to and a dispersed backcountry camping zone along the Money Brook Trail.

**Maps:** A free trail map of Mount Greylock State Reservation is available at the visitor center or at the Massachusetts Division of State Parks and Recreation website (see below). The *Northern Berkshires/Southwestern Massachusetts/Wachusett Mountain* map costs $5.95 in paper from the Appalachian Mountain Club, 800/262-4455, website: www.outdoors.org. The *Mount Greylock Reservation Trail Map* is $3.95 from New England Cartographics, 413/549-4124 or toll-free 888/995-6277, website: www.necartographics.com. These trails are also covered on map 1 in the *Map and Guide to the Appalachian Trail in Massachusetts and Connecticut,* a five-map set available for $19.95 ($14.95 for the maps alone) from the Appalachian Trail Conference (see address below). For topographic area maps, request North Adams and Cheshire from USGS Map Sales, Federal Center, Box 25286, Denver, CO 80225, 888/ASK-USGS (888/275-8747), website: http://mapping.usgs.gov.

**Directions:** From Route 43, 2.5 miles south of the junction of Routes 43 and 2 in Williamstown and 2.3 miles north of the junction of Route 43 and U.S. 7, turn east onto Hopper Road at

a sign for Mount Hope Park. Drive 1.4 miles and bear left onto a dirt road. Continue 0.7 mile to the parking area on the right.

**Contact:** Mount Greylock State Reservation, P.O. Box 138, Rockwell Rd., Lanesborough, MA 01237, 413/499-4262 or 499-4263. Massachusetts Division of State Parks and Recreation, 251 Causeway St., Suite 600, Boston, MA 02114-2104, 617/626-1250, website: www.state.ma.us/dem/forparks.htm. Appalachian Trail Conference, P.O. Box 807, Harpers Ferry, WV 25425, 304/535-6331, website: www.appalachiantrail.org.

## 3 MOUNT GREYLOCK CIRCUIT
### 12 mi/8 hrs
**in Mount Greylock State Reservation in Williamstown, North Adams, Adams, and Lanesborough**

Wanting to hike a loop around Massachusetts's highest peak, 3,491-foot Mount Greylock, taking in as many of its best features as possible on a day hike, I devised this 12-mile circuit. It climbs through and loops around the spectacular glacial cirque known as the Hopper, passes two waterfalls, travels over the summit, follows a stretch of the Appalachian Trail, and then descends through the rugged ravine of beautiful Money Brook. You could shave this distance by two miles by skipping the side trail to March Cataract Falls, and another mile by skipping Robinson Point. This entire hike gains more than 2,500 feet in elevation.

From the parking area, walk past the gate onto the Hopper Trail and follow a flat, grassy lane 0.2 mile to where the Money Brook Trail leads straight ahead. Bear right with the Hopper Trail, ascending an old logging road, somewhat steeply at times, another two miles until you reach Sperry Road. Turn left and walk the road 0.1 mile; just before the parking area on the right, turn left on a dirt campground road. Walk about 200 feet, past the Chimney Group Camping Area, and turn left at a sign for the March Cataract Falls Trail. It leads a mile, descending through switchbacks, to March

Cataract Falls, a 30-foot falls that usually maintains a flow even during dry seasons.

Backtrack to Sperry Road, turn left, walk about 100 yards past the parking area, and then turn left at a sign onto the Hopper Trail. The wide path climbs at a moderate grade past a short falls. Where the Deer Hill Trail diverges right, bear left. Within a mile of Sperry Road, where the Hopper Trail makes a sharp right, turn left onto the Overlook Trail. You reach the first view of the Hopper within minutes, though trees partially obstruct it. A half mile down the Overlook Trail lies the second view, which is better; Stony Ledge is visible across the Hopper to the west. Continue on the Overlook Trail to the paved Notch Road, 1.2 miles from the Hopper Trail junction. Turn left and walk the road downhill 0.1 mile, past a day-use parking turnout, then turn left onto a trail marked by blue blazes. It descends steeply 0.2 mile to Robinson Point and a view of the Hopper superior to anything on the Overlook Trail. Double back to the Overlook Trail, cross Notch Road, and follow the Overlook uphill for 0.4 mile to the white-blazed Appalachian Trail. Turn left on the AT, following it across the parking lot to the summit, where you find the War Memorial Tower and the Bascom Lodge. The best views are to the east from the meadow beyond the tower; there are also good views to the west.

From the tower, follow the AT north. About a mile from the summit is a good eastern view. About 2.4 miles from the summit, a side trail leads left to Notch Road, but continue 0.2 mile straight ahead on the AT over Mount Williams, one of Greylock's summits. The AT swings left here, descending easily 0.9 mile to Notch Road. Cross the road and, 0.1 mile into the woods, turn left onto the Money Brook Trail; in 0.2 mile, pass a short side path leading to the Wilbur's Clearing shelter. The trail reaches a side path 0.7 mile beyond the shelter that leads a short distance to spectacular Money Brook Falls. Backtrack from the falls on the side path and continue on the Money Brook Trail, following the brook through a wild, narrow valley, with a few crossings that could be tricky in high water. Nearly a mile past the falls, the Mount Prospect Trail branches right; stay on the Money Brook Trail another 1.5 miles to the Hopper Trail—passing a dispersed camping zone just before reaching the Hopper Trail—then continue straight ahead 0.2 mile to return to the parking area.

**User groups:** Hikers and dogs. Dogs must be leashed. No wheelchair facilities. This trail should not be attempted in winter except by hikers prepared for severe winter weather, and is not suitable for horses or skis. Bikes are prohibited. Hunting is allowed in season.

**Access, fees:** A daily fee of $2 is collected from mid-May–mid-October at some parking areas. From the mid-December close of hunting season through mid-May, roads within the state reservation are closed to vehicles (and groomed for snowmobiles), but Hopper Road is maintained to this trailhead. There is a lean-to and a dispersed backcountry camping zone along the Money Brook Trail. Contact the Mount Greylock State Reservation about whether the Bascom Lodge on the mountain's summit is open; it was formerly managed by the Appalachian Mountain Club.

**Maps:** A free, basic trail map of Mount Greylock State Reservation is available at the visitor center or at the Massachusetts Division of State Parks and Recreation website (see below). The *Northern Berkshires/Southwestern Massachusetts/Wachusett Mountain* map costs $5.95 in paper from the Appalachian Mountain Club, 800/262-4455, website: www.outdoors.org. The *Mount Greylock Reservation Trail Map* is $3.95 from New England Cartographics, 413/549-4124 or toll-free 888/995-6277, website: www.necartographics.com. These trails are also covered on map 1 in the *Map and Guide to the Appalachian Trail in Massachusetts and Connecticut,* a five-map set available for $19.95 ($14.95 for the maps alone) from the Appalachian Trail Conference (see address below). For topographic area maps, request North

Adams and Cheshire from USGS Map Sales, Federal Center, Box 25286, Denver, CO 80225, 888/ASK-USGS (888/275-8747), website: http://mapping.usgs.gov.

**Directions:** From Route 43, 2.5 miles south of the junction of Routes 43 and 2 in Williamstown and 2.3 miles north of the junction of Route 43 and U.S. 7, turn east onto Hopper Road at a sign for Mount Hope Park. Drive 1.4 miles and bear left onto a dirt road. Continue 0.7 mile to the parking area on the right.

**Contact:** Mount Greylock State Reservation, P.O. Box 138, Rockwell Rd., Lanesborough, MA 01237, 413/499-4262 or 499-4263. Massachusetts Division of State Parks and Recreation, 251 Causeway St., Suite 600, Boston, MA 02114-2104, 617/626-1250, website: www.state.ma.us/dem/forparks.htm. Appalachian Trail Conference, P.O. Box 807, Harpers Ferry, WV 25425, 304/535-6331, website: www.appalachiantrail.org.

## ④ MOUNT GREYLOCK: ROBINSON POINT

**0.4 mi/0.5 hr**

**in Mount Greylock State Reservation in Williamstown, North Adams, Adams, and Lanesborough**

The high ledge at Robinson Point offers one of the best views on Greylock of the Hopper, the huge glacial cirque carved out of the mountain's northwest flank. Visible are Stony Ledge, at the end of the ridge forming the Hopper's western wall; Williamstown, in the valley beyond the Hopper's mouth; and the Taconic Range on the horizon. From the turnout, walk downhill just a few steps and then turn left onto a trail marked by blue blazes. It descends steeply 0.2 mile to Robinson Point. Return the same way.

**User groups:** Hikers and dogs. Dogs must be leashed. No wheelchair facilities. This trail is not suitable for horses or skis. The trailhead is not accessible by road in winter for snowshoeing. Bikes are prohibited. Hunting is allowed in season.

**Access, fees:** A daily fee of $2 is collected from mid-May–mid-October at some parking areas. From the mid-December close of hunting season through mid-May, roads within the state reservation are closed to vehicles (and groomed for snowmobiles). This trailhead is not accessible by car in the winter months.

**Maps:** A free, basic trail map of Mount Greylock State Reservation is available at the visitor center or at the Massachusetts Division of State Parks and Recreation website (see below). The *Northern Berkshires/Southwestern Massachusetts/Wachusett Mountain* map costs $5.95 in paper from the Appalachian Mountain Club, 800/262-4455, website: www.outdoors.org. The *Mount Greylock Reservation Trail Map* is $3.95 from New England Cartographics, 413/549-4124 or toll-free 888/995-6277, website: www.necartographics.com. These trails are also covered on map 1 in the *Map and Guide to the Appalachian Trail in Massachusetts and Connecticut*, a five-map set available for $19.95 ($14.95 for the maps alone) from the Appalachian Trail Conference (see address below). For topographic area maps, request North Adams and Cheshire from USGS Map Sales, Federal Center, Box 25286, Denver, CO 80225, 888/ASK-USGS (888/275-8747), website: http://mapping.usgs.gov.

**Directions:** From MA 2, 3.7 miles east of the junction of Routes 2 and 43 in Williamstown and 1.3 miles west of the junction of Routes 2 and 8A in North Adams, turn south onto Notch Road. Follow Notch Road up the mountain for 7.4 miles to a turnout for day-use parking on the right. From U.S. 7 in Lanesborough, 1.3 miles north of town center and 4.2 miles south of the Lanesborough/New Ashford line, turn east onto North Main Street. Drive 0.7 mile and turn right onto Quarry Road. Continue 0.6 mile and bear left at a sign reading "Rockwell Road to Greylock." The Greylock Visitor Center is 0.6 mile farther up that road. From the visitor center, follow Rockwell Road up the mountain for 7.2 miles, turn left onto

Notch Road, and continue 0.9 mile to the day-use parking turnout on the left.

**Contact:** Mount Greylock State Reservation, P.O. Box 138, Rockwell Rd., Lanesborough, MA 01237, 413/499-4262 or 499-4263. Massachusetts Division of State Parks and Recreation, 251 Causeway St., Suite 600, Boston, MA 02114-2104, 617/626-1250, website: www.state.ma.us/dem/forparks.htm. Appalachian Trail Conference, P.O. Box 807, Harpers Ferry, WV 25425, 304/535-6331, website: www.appalachiantrail.org.

# 5 MOUNT GREYLOCK: DEER HILL TRAIL

**2.2 mi/1.5 hrs**

**in Mount Greylock State Reservation in Williamstown, North Adams, Adams, and Lanesborough**

A friend and I actually backpacked this fairly easy two-mile loop past Deer Hill Falls and an interesting grove of tall hemlocks one weekend, and spent the night at the lean-to along the way, listening to coyotes in the darkness. If you have time, walk or drive the mile to the end of Sperry Road for the view from Stony Ledge of the huge glacial cirque on Greylock known as the Hopper. It is perhaps the finest view on the mountain.

From the parking area, walk back up Sperry Road (south) for 0.4 mile and turn right onto the Deer Hill Trail. The flat, wide path crosses a brook and within 0.4 mile makes a right turn, descending past a dark grove of tall hemlocks on the left and reaching the lean-to one mile from the road. Just beyond the lean-to, the trail descends abruptly, crosses over a stream on a wooden bridge, and then climbs steeply up to Deer Hill Falls. About 0.2 mile above the falls, make a right turn onto the Roaring Brook Trail, which leads back to the parking area in 0.1 mile.

**User groups:** Hikers, snowshoers, and dogs. Dogs must be leashed. No wheelchair facilities. This trail is not suitable for horses or skis. Bikes are prohibited. Hunting is allowed in season.

**Access, fees:** A daily fee of $2 is collected from mid-May–mid-October at some parking areas. From the mid-December close of hunting season through mid-May, roads within the state reservation are closed to vehicles (and groomed for snowmobiles). This trailhead is not accessible by car in winter. There is a lean-to for overnight camping along the Deer Hill Trail.

**Maps:** A free, basic trail map of Mount Greylock State Reservation is available at the visitor center or at the Massachusetts Division of State Parks and Recreation website (see below). The *Northern Berkshires/Southwestern Massachusetts/Wachusett Mountain* map costs $5.95 in paper from the Appalachian Mountain Club, 800/262-4455, website: www.outdoors.org. The *Mount Greylock Reservation Trail Map* is $3.95 from New England Cartographics, 413/549-4124 or toll-free 888/995-6277, website: www.necartographics.com. These trails are also covered on map 1 in the *Map and Guide to the Appalachian Trail in Massachusetts and Connecticut,* a five-map set available for $19.95 ($14.95 for the maps alone) from the Appalachian Trail Conference (see address below). For topographic area maps, request North Adams and Cheshire from USGS Map Sales, Federal Center, Box 25286, Denver, CO 80225, 888/ASK-USGS (888/275-8747), website: http://mapping.usgs.gov.

**Directions:** From MA 2, 3.7 miles east of the junction of Routes 2 and 43 in Williamstown and 1.3 miles west of the junction of Routes 2 and 8A in North Adams, turn south onto Notch Road. Follow Notch Road up the mountain for 8.3 miles and turn right onto Rockwell Road. Continue 1.7 miles, turn right onto Sperry Road, and drive 0.6 mile to the roadside parking. From U.S. 7 in Lanesborough, 1.3 miles north of the town center and 4.2 miles south of the Lanesborough/New Ashford line, turn east onto North Main Street. Drive 0.7 mile and turn right onto Quarry Road. Continue 0.6 mile and bear left at a sign reading "Rockwell Road to Greylock." The Greylock Visitor Center is 0.6 mile farther up that road.

From the visitor center, follow Rockwell Road up the mountain for 5.5 miles, turn left onto Sperry Road, and continue 0.6 mile to the parking area.

**Contact:** Mount Greylock State Reservation, P.O. Box 138, Rockwell Rd., Lanesborough, MA 01237, 413/499-4262 or 499-4263. Massachusetts Division of State Parks and Recreation, 251 Causeway St., Suite 600, Boston, MA 02114-2104, 617/626-1250, website: www.state.ma.us/dem/forparks.htm. Appalachian Trail Conference, P.O. Box 807, Harpers Ferry, WV 25425, 304/535-6331, website: www.appalachiantrail.org.

## 6 MOUNT GREYLOCK: MARCH CATARACT FALLS
**2 mi/1.5 hrs**

**in Mount Greylock State Reservation in Williamstown, North Adams, Adams, and Lanesborough**

March Cataract Falls is a 30-foot-high water curtain at the end of a fairly easy one-mile trail beginning in the Sperry Road Campground. From the parking area, cross the road onto a dirt campground road. Walk that short half-circle road to the March Cataract Falls Trail, marked by a sign. It starts out on easy ground and then descends through switchbacks, reaching March Cataract Falls a mile from the campground. Head back along the same route.

**User groups:** Hikers and dogs. Dogs must be leashed. No wheelchair facilities. This trail is not suitable for horses or skis. The trailhead is not accessible by road in winter for snowshoeing. Bikes are prohibited. Hunting is allowed in season.

**Access, fees:** A daily fee of $2 is collected from mid-May–mid-October at some parking areas. From the mid-December close of hunting season through mid-May, roads in the state reservation are closed to vehicles (and groomed for snowmobiles). This trailhead is not accessible by car in winter.

**Maps:** A free, basic trail map of Mount Greylock State Reservation is available at the visitor center or at the Massachusetts Division of State Parks and Recreation website (see below). The *Northern Berkshires/Southwestern Massachusetts/Wachusett Mountain* map costs $5.95 in paper from the Appalachian Mountain Club, 800/262-4455, website: www.outdoors.org. The *Mount Greylock Reservation Trail Map* is $3.95 from New England Cartographics, 413/549-4124 or toll-free 888/995-6277, website: www.necartographics.com. These trails are also covered on map 1 in the *Map and Guide to the Appalachian Trail in Massachusetts and Connecticut,* a five-map set available for $19.95 ($14.95 for the maps alone) from the Appalachian Trail Conference (see address below). For topographic area maps, request North Adams and Cheshire from USGS Map Sales, Federal Center, Box 25286, Denver, CO 80225, 888/ASK-USGS (888/275-8747), website: http://mapping.usgs.gov.

**Directions:** From MA 2, 3.7 miles east of the junction of Routes 2 and 43 in Williamstown and 1.3 miles west of the junction of Routes 2 and 8A in North Adams, turn south onto Notch Road. Follow Notch Road up the mountain for 8.3 miles and turn right onto Rockwell Road. Continue 1.7 miles, turn right onto Sperry Road, and drive 0.6 mile to the roadside parking. From U.S. 7 in Lanesborough, 1.3 miles north of the town center and 4.2 miles south of the Lanesborough/New Ashford line, turn east onto North Main Street. Drive 0.7 mile and turn right onto Quarry Road. Continue 0.6 mile and bear left at a sign reading "Rockwell Road to Greylock." The Greylock Visitor Center is 0.6 mile farther up that road. From the visitor center, follow Rockwell Road up the mountain for 5.5 miles, turn left onto Sperry Road, and continue 0.6 mile to the parking area.

**Contact:** Mount Greylock State Reservation, P.O. Box 138, Rockwell Rd., Lanesborough, MA 01237, 413/499-4262 or 499-4263. Massachusetts Division of State Parks and Recreation, 251 Causeway St., Suite 600, Boston, MA 02114-2104, 617/626-1250, website:

www.state.ma.us/dem/forparks.htm. Appalachian Trail Conference, P.O. Box 807, Harpers Ferry, WV 25425, 304/535-6331, website: www.appalachiantrail.org.

## 7 MOUNT GREYLOCK: JONES NOSE

**1 mi/0.75 hr**

**in Mount Greylock State Reservation in Williamstown, North Adams, Adams, and Lanesborough**

Jones Nose is an open ledge on Greylock's southern ridge that offers a broad view of the mountains to the south and west—a nice spot to catch a sunset. From the parking area, walk north on the Jones Nose Trail. It passes through woods, crosses a meadow, and then ascends steeply to a side path on the left, a half mile from the parking lot. Follow that path 40 feet to the viewpoint. Return the way you came.

**User groups:** Hikers and dogs. Dogs must be leashed. No wheelchair facilities. This trail is not suitable for horses or skis. The trailhead is not accessible by road in winter for snowshoeing. Bikes are prohibited. Hunting is allowed in season.

**Access, fees:** A daily fee of $2 is collected from mid-May–mid-October at some parking areas. From the mid-December close of hunting season through mid-May, roads in the state reservation are closed to vehicles (and groomed for snowmobiles). This trailhead is not accessible by car in winter.

**Maps:** A free, basic trail map of Mount Greylock State Reservation is available at the visitor center or at the Massachusetts Division of State Parks and Recreation website (see below). The *Northern Berkshires/Southwestern Massachusetts/Wachusett Mountain* map costs $5.95 in paper from the Appalachian Mountain Club, 800/262-4455, website: www.outdoors.org. The *Mount Greylock Reservation Trail Map* is $3.95 from New England Cartographics, 413/549-4124 or toll-free 888/995-6277, website: www.necartographics.com. These trails are also covered on map 1 in the *Map and Guide to the*

*Appalachian Trail in Massachusetts and Connecticut,* a five-map set available for $19.95 ($14.95 for the maps alone) from the Appalachian Trail Conference (see address below). For topographic area maps, request North Adams and Cheshire from USGS Map Sales, Federal Center, Box 25286, Denver, CO 80225, 888/ASK-USGS (888/275-8747), website: http://mapping.usgs.gov.

**Directions:** From MA 2, 3.7 miles east of the junction of Routes 2 and 43 in Williamstown and 1.3 miles west of the junction of Routes 2 and 8A in North Adams, turn south onto Notch Road. Follow Notch Road up the mountain for 8.3 miles and turn right onto Rockwell Road. Continue 3.5 miles to the Jones Nose parking lot on the left. From U.S. 7 in Lanesborough, 1.3 miles north of the town center and 4.2 miles south of the Lanesborough/New Ashford line, turn east onto North Main Street. Drive 0.7 mile and turn right onto Quarry Road. Continue 0.6 mile and bear left at a sign reading "Rockwell Road to Greylock." The Greylock Visitor Center is 0.6 mile farther up that road. From the visitor center, follow Rockwell Road up the mountain for 3.7 miles to the Jones Nose parking lot on the right.

**Contact:** Mount Greylock State Reservation, P.O. Box 138, Rockwell Rd., Lanesborough, MA 01237, 413/499-4262 or 499-4263. Massachusetts Division of State Parks and Recreation, 251 Causeway St., Suite 600, Boston, MA 02114-2104, 617/626-1250, website: www.state.ma.us/dem/forparks.htm. Appalachian Trail Conference, P.O. Box 807, Harpers Ferry, WV 25425, 304/535-6331, website: www.appalachiantrail.org.

## 8 MOUNT GREYLOCK: ROUNDS ROCK

**1 mi/0.75 hr**

**in Mount Greylock State Reservation in Williamstown, North Adams, Adams, and Lanesborough**

This easy one-mile loop to a pair of ledges offers some of the most dramatic views on Mount Greylock—for little effort. This is a terrific hike with young children or for catching a sunset or the fall foliage. From the turnout, cross the road to the Rounds Rock Trail. Follow it through woods and across blueberry patches about a half mile to where a side path (at a sign that reads "scenic vista") leads left about 75 yards to a sweeping view south from atop a low cliff. Backtrack and turn left on the main trail, following it 0.1 mile to another, shorter side path and a view south and west. Complete the loop on the Rounds Rock Trail by following it out to Rockwell Road. Turn right and walk the road about 150 yards back to the turnout.

**User groups:** Hikers and dogs. Dogs must be leashed. No wheelchair facilities. This trail is not suitable for horses or skis. The trailhead is not accessible by road in winter for snowshoeing. Bikes are prohibited. Hunting is allowed in season.

**Access, fees:** A daily fee of $2 is collected from mid-May–mid-October at some parking areas. From the mid-December close of hunting season through mid-May, roads in the state reservation are closed to vehicles (and groomed for snowmobiles). This trailhead is not accessible by car in winter.

**Maps:** A free, basic trail map of Mount Greylock State Reservation is available at the visitor center or at the Massachusetts Division of State Parks and Recreation website (see below). The *Northern Berkshires/Southwestern Massachusetts/Wachusett Mountain* map costs $5.95 in paper from the Appalachian Mountain Club, 800/262-4455, website: www.outdoors.org. The *Mount Greylock Reservation Trail Map* is $3.95 from New England Cartographics, 413/549-4124 or toll-free 888/995-6277, website: www.necartographics.com. These trails are also covered on map 1 in the *Map and Guide to the Appalachian Trail in Massachusetts and Connecticut,* a five-map set available for $19.95 ($14.95 for the maps alone) from the Appalachian Trail Conference (see address below). For topographic area maps, request North

Adams and Cheshire from USGS Map Sales, Federal Center, Box 25286, Denver, CO 80225, 888/ASK-USGS (888/275-8747), website: http://mapping.usgs.gov.

**Directions:** From MA 2, 3.7 miles east of the junction of Routes 2 and 43 in Williamstown and 1.3 miles west of the junction of Routes 2 and 8A in North Adams, turn south onto Notch Road. Follow Notch Road up the mountain for 8.3 miles and turn right onto Rockwell Road. Continue 4.2 miles to a turnout on the left, across from the Rounds Rock Trail. From U.S. 7 in Lanesborough, 1.3 miles north of the town center and 4.2 miles south of the Lanesborough/New Ashford line, turn east onto North Main Street. Drive 0.7 mile and turn right onto Quarry Road. Continue 0.6 mile and bear left at a sign reading "Rockwell Road to Greylock." The Greylock Visitor Center is 0.6 mile farther up that road. From the visitor center, follow Rockwell Road up the mountain for three miles to a turnout on the right, across from the Rounds Rock Trail.

**Contact:** Mount Greylock State Reservation, P.O. Box 138, Rockwell Rd., Lanesborough, MA 01237, 413/499-4262 or 499-4263. Massachusetts Division of State Parks and Recreation, 251 Causeway St., Suite 600, Boston, MA 02114-2104, 617/626-1250, website: www.state.ma.us/dem/forparks.htm. Appalachian Trail Conference, P.O. Box 807, Harpers Ferry, WV 25425, 304/535-6331, website: www.appalachiantrail.org.

## 9 SPRUCE HILL
**3 mi/1.5 hrs**

**in Savoy Mountain State Forest near North Adams and Adams**

This easy, three-mile hike provides some of the most attractive views possible in the state for a relatively minor effort; only the last stretch turns somewhat steep, and only briefly at that. Spruce Hill's summit is at 2,566 feet. The total elevation gained is about 1,200 feet. I camped out just below the Spruce Hill summit one night in early December. After dark, I hiked up onto the hill under a sky full of stars, overlooking the lights of the Hoosic Valley. The Savoy Mountain State Forest has about 48 miles of trails and roads for hiking, snowshoeing, mountain biking, and cross-country skiing. It is the fourth-largest piece, but one of the least-known pieces, of Bay State public land.

Walk 100 feet up the forest road and turn right onto a trail signed for "Spruce Hill, Hawk Lookout." Within 150 yards, the trail crosses a power line easement. About a quarter mile farther, it crosses a second set of power lines; just beyond those lines, continue straight onto the Busby Trail (marked by a sign), going uphill and following blue blazes. In a quarter mile or so, the trail crosses an old stone wall. Then, within the span of about a quarter mile, you cross a small brook, pass an old stone foundation on your right, and then pass over a stone wall. On the other side of that wall, another trail branches left, but continue straight ahead, still following the blue blazes. About 0.1 mile farther, the trail forks; both forks go to the summit, but the right option is easier and more direct, reaching the bare top of Spruce Hill within a quarter mile.

Though a few low trees grow in isolated groves on the hilltop, the hill's several open areas provide excellent views in all directions. To the west lies the Hoosic River Valley, where Route 8 runs through the towns of Adams and North Adams. Farther northwest you can see Williamstown. Across the valley rises the highest peak in Massachusetts, 3,491-foot Mount Greylock (hikes 2–8 in this chapter), with a prominent war memorial tower on its summit. The Appalachian Trail follows the obvious northern ridge on Greylock—and you might consider how busy that trail can be while you are enjoying the top of Spruce Hill by yourself. Descend the way you came.

**User groups:** Hikers and dogs. Dogs must be leashed. No wheelchair facilities. This trail is not suitable for horses or skis. Bikes are prohibited. Hunting is allowed in season.

**Access, fees:** A daily parking fee of $5 is collected from mid-May–mid-October.

**Maps:** A free, basic trail map of Savoy Mountain State Forest is available at the state forest headquarters (see address below) or at the Massachusetts Division of State Parks and Recreation website (see below). For topographic area maps, request North Adams, Cheshire, and Ashfield from USGS Map Sales, Federal Center, Box 25286, Denver, CO 80225, 888/ASK-USGS (888/275-8747), website: http://mapping.usgs.gov.

**Directions:** From MA 2 in Florida, 6.9 miles west of the Florida/Savoy town line and 0.4 mile east of the Florida/North Adams line, turn south onto Central Shaft Road. Continue 2.9 miles, following signs for the Savoy Mountain State Forest, to the headquarters on the right (where maps are available). Less than 0.1 mile beyond the headquarters, park at a turnout on the right at the Old Florida Road, an unmaintained, wide forest road.

**Contact:** Savoy Mountain State Forest, 260 Central Shaft Rd., Florida, MA 01247, 413/663-8469. Massachusetts Division of State Parks and Recreation, 251 Causeway St., Suite 600, Boston, MA 02114-2104, 617/626-1250, website: www.state.ma.us/dem/forparks.htm.

## 🔟 MOHAWK TRAIL
**5 mi/3.5 hrs**

**in Mohawk Trail State Forest in Charlemont**
This mostly wooded ridge walk follows a historical route: the original Mohawk Trail, used for hundreds of years by the area's Native Americans. There is one good view along the ridge, from Todd Mountain ledge overlooking the Cold River Valley. This hike ascends about 700 feet. From the parking area, continue up the paved road, bearing left toward the camping area where the road forks, then bearing right at a sign for the Indian Trail at 0.7 mile. The trail remains flat for only about 200 feet, then turns right, and begins the steep and relentless ascent a half mile to the ridge. This trail is not well marked and can be easy to lose

in a few places. Once atop the ridge, the walking grows much easier. Turn right onto the Todd Mountain Trail, following it a half mile to an open ledge with a good view. Double back to the Indian Trail and continue straight ahead on the Clark Mountain Trail; you will see disks on trees indicating that this is the old Mohawk Trail. This easy, wide path predates European settlement here by hundreds of years. About 0.8 mile past the Todd Mountain Trail, the Clark Mountain/Mohawk Trail swings right and begins descending; double back from here and descend the Indian Trail back to the start.

**User groups:** Hikers and dogs. Dogs must be leashed. No wheelchair facilities. This trail would be difficult to snowshoe, and is not suitable for bikes, horses, or skis. Hunting is allowed in season.

**Access, fees:** A daily parking fee of $5 is collected from mid-May–mid-October.

**Maps:** A free, basic trail and contour map of Mohawk Trail State Forest is available at the state forest headquarters (see address below) or at the Massachusetts Division of State Parks and Recreation website (see below). For a topographic area map, request Rowe from USGS Map Sales, Federal Center, Box 25286, Denver, CO 80225, 888/ASK-USGS (888/275-8747), website: http://mapping.usgs.gov.

**Directions:** The main entrance to the Mohawk Trail State Forest is on MA 2, 3.7 miles west of the junction of Routes 2 and 8A in Charlemont and one mile east of the Savoy/Charlemont line. Drive the state forest road for 0.2 mile, through a gate, and park just beyond the gate on the left, behind the headquarters building.

**Contact:** Mohawk Trail State Forest, P.O. Box 7, MA 2, Charlemont, MA 01339, 413/339-5504. Massachusetts Division of State Parks and Recreation, 251 Causeway St., Suite 600, Boston, MA 02114-2104, 617/626-1250, website: www.state.ma.us/dem/forparks.htm.

## 🔢 GIANT TREES OF CLARK RIDGE

**1 mi/2 hrs**

**in Mohawk Trail State Forest in Charlemont**

If you're wondering how it could take two hours to walk a mile, then consider this: You may not even walk a mile, yet you may spend even longer in here. Unlike the other hikes in this book, this one doesn't follow an established trail. It begins on an abandoned, somewhat overgrown logging road and becomes a bushwhack. But the steep, rugged terrain you encounter on the north flank of Clark Ridge is probably a big part of the reason loggers left so many giant trees untouched here over the past few centuries—a time period during which most of New England was deforested. Within an area of about 75 acres are an uncounted number of sugar maple, red oak, white ash, beech, and other hardwoods reaching more than 120 feet into the sky, and aged 200 to 300 years. One respected regional expert has identified a 160-foot white pine here as the tallest living thing in New England. It would be impossible for me to direct you to particular trees, and equally difficult for you to identify any individual tree by its height without the proper equipment. But, just as I did, I think you will find walking around in this cathedral of bark to be a rare and stirring experience.

From either parking area, walk across the bridge and immediately turn left, following a faint footpath down across a wash and a cleared area and onto a distinct trail—actually an abandoned logging road. The road dissipates within about a half mile, but you need only walk a quarter mile or so, then turn right, and bushwhack uphill. You soon find yourself craning your neck constantly. Be sure to remember how to find your way back to the logging road.

**User groups:** Hikers, snowshoers, and dogs. Dogs must be leashed. No wheelchair facilities. This trail is not suitable for bikes, horses, or skis. Hunting is allowed in season.

**Access, fees:** A daily parking fee of $5 is collected from mid-May–mid-October at some trailheads.

**Maps:** A free, basic trail and contour map of the Mohawk Trail State Forest is available at the state forest headquarters (reached via the state forest's main entrance; see directions below) or at the Massachusetts Division of State Parks and Recreation website (see below). For a topographic area map, request Rowe from USGS Map Sales, Federal Center, Box 25286, Denver, CO 80225, 888/ASK-USGS (888/275-8747), website: http://mapping.usgs.gov.

**Directions:** From MA 2, 1.6 miles west of the junction of Routes 2 and 8A in Charlemont and 2.1 miles east of the Mohawk Trail State Forest entrance, turn right at the Rowe/Monroe sign. Proceed 2.2 miles, bear left, and continue another 0.8 mile to the Zoar picnic area on the left, where there is parking, or to parking 0.1 mile farther on the right, immediately before the bridge over Deerfield River.

**Contact:** Mohawk Trail State Forest, P.O. Box 7, MA 2, Charlemont, MA 01339, 413/339-5504. Massachusetts Division of State Parks and Recreation, 251 Causeway St., Suite 600, Boston, MA 02114-2104, 617/626-1250, website: www.state.ma.us/dem/forparks.htm.

## 12 THE LOOKOUT
### 2.2 mi/1.5 hrs

**in Mohawk Trail State Forest in Charlemont**
Here's an easy 2.2-mile walk through the quiet woods of Mohawk Trail State Forest to a lookout with a good view east toward the Deerfield River Valley and Charlemont. Some friends and I encountered a ruffed grouse on this trail one snowless March day. From the parking area, cross the Route to the Totem Trail, which begins behind a stone marker for the state forest. The trail is obvious and well marked, crossing a small brook and reaching the overlook in 1.1 miles. Hike back along the same route. This hike climbs about 600 feet.

**User groups:** Hikers, snowshoers, and dogs. Dogs must be leashed. No wheelchair facilities. The trail is not suitable for bikes, horses, or skis. Hunting is allowed in season.

**Access, fees:** A daily parking fee of $5 is collected from mid-May–mid-October at some trailheads.

**Maps:** A free, basic trail and contour map of Mohawk Trail State Forest is available at the state forest headquarters (see address below) or at the Massachusetts Division of State Parks and Recreation website (see below). For a topographic area map, request Rowe from USGS Map Sales, Federal Center, Box 25286, Denver, CO 80225, 888/ASK-USGS (888/275-8747), website: http://mapping.usgs.gov.

**Directions:** The trail begins opposite a turnout and picnic area on MA 2 in Charlemont, 0.9 mile west of the Mohawk Trail State Forest main entrance and 0.1 mile east of the Charlemont/Savoy line.

**Contact:** Mohawk Trail State Forest, P.O. Box 7, MA 2, Charlemont, MA 01339, 413/339-5504. Massachusetts Division of State Parks and Recreation, 251 Causeway St., Suite 600, Boston, MA 02114-2104, 617/626-1250, website: www.state.ma.us/dem/forparks.htm.

## 13 FIRE TOWER HIKE
### 3 mi/2 hrs

**in D.A.R. State Forest in Goshen**
This 1,500-acre state forest has a network of fun forest roads for mountain biking or cross-country skiing, hiking trails through interesting woodlands, and a hilltop fire tower that affords 360-degree views of the countryside. (See this chapter's D.A.R. State Forest Ski Touring Loop and Balancing Rock hikes for two other possibilities.) This hike follows the Long Trail (not to be confused with the trail running the length of Vermont), which begins between the boat launch and the night registration office and makes a circuitous route of about 1.5 miles through the state forest to the fire tower. Climbing the tower's steps, you get a panorama of the surrounding countryside, with views stretching to Mount Monadnock (see listings, Central and Southern New Hampshire chapter) to the northeast, the Holyoke Range (see listing, Central Massachusetts chapter) and Mount Tom (see listing, this chapter)

to the southeast, and Mount Greylock (see listings, this chapter) to the northwest. Descend the same way you hiked up.

**User groups:** Hikers, snowshoers, and dogs. Dogs must be leashed. No wheelchair facilities. This trail is not suitable for bikes, horses, or skis. Hunting is prohibited.

**Access, fees:** A daily parking fee of $5 is collected from mid-May–mid-October.

**Maps:** A free trail map is available at the state forest (see address below) or at the Massachusetts Division of State Parks and Recreation website (see below).

**Directions:** From I-91 northbound, take Exit 19 onto Route 9 west. In Goshen, turn right onto Route 112 north. The park entrance is on your right. From I-91 southbound, take Exit 25 for Route 116 west. In Ashfield, turn left onto Route 112 south. The park entrance is on your left. In summer, park in the second lot along Moore Hill Road, located just past the left turn for the boat launch and nature center. In winter, park in the first lot, near the restrooms and warming hut (Moore Hill Road is not maintained beyond that point).

**Contact:** D.A.R. State Forest, Route 112, Goshen, MA, 413/268-7098; or mail to 555 East St., RFD 1, Williamsburg, MA 01096. Massachusetts Division of State Parks and Recreation, 251 Causeway St., Suite 600, Boston, MA 02114-2104, 617/626-1250, website: www.state.ma.us/dem/forparks.htm.

## 14 D.A.R. STATE FOREST SKI TOURING LOOP
**6 mi/3.5 hrs**

**in D.A.R. State Forest in Goshen**

I've included this loop for cross-country skiers looking for a moderate ski tour and a nice view from a fire tower. The approximately six-mile route largely follows state forest roads that are not maintained in winter; a friend and I skied this one winter when we could not find snow in much of Massachusetts and southern New Hampshire, and we found plenty of it in D.A.R. State Forest. From spring through fall, the road

that this route follows is maintained for vehicular traffic; the better choice for a hike during that time would be the Fire Tower Hike (see previous listing).

Head out from the first parking lot on Moore Hill Road, ascending to the fire tower; a sign directs you to it. If you climb the tower's steps, you enjoy a panorama of the surrounding countryside, with views stretching to Mount Monadnock (see listings, Central and Southern New Hampshire chapter) to the northeast, the Holyoke Range (see listing, Central Massachusetts chapter) and Mount Tom (see listing, this chapter) to the southeast, and Mount Greylock (see listings, this chapter) to the northwest. Backtrack from the tower, but before reaching Moore Hill Road, turn right onto another woods road, Oak Hill Road, which descends steeply to a junction with Wing Hollow Road. Turn left and continue until you reach pavement; carry your skis about a quarter mile, turn left onto Moore Hill Road, and take the long climb back over the hill and down to the parking area. You could also combine this with the hike to Balancing Rock, though short trail sections might be difficult on skis (we skied out there and had a ball, though). Don't expect many signs marking roads or trails.

**User groups:** Hikers, bikers, dogs, horses, skiers, and snowshoers. Dogs must be leashed. No wheelchair facilities. Hunting is prohibited.

**Access, fees:** A daily parking fee of $5 is collected from mid-May–mid-October.

**Maps:** A free trail map is available at the state forest (see address below) or at the Massachusetts Division of State Parks and Recreation website (see below).

**Directions:** From I-91 northbound, take Exit 19 onto Route 9 west. In Goshen, turn right onto Route 112 north. The park entrance is on your right. From I-91 southbound, take Exit 25 for Route 116 west. In Ashfield, turn left onto Route 112 south. The park entrance is on your left. In summer, park in the second lot along Moore Hill Road, located just past the left turn for the boat launch and nature center. In winter, park in the first lot, near the restrooms and warming hut (Moore Hill Road is not maintained beyond that point).

**Contact:** D.A.R. State Forest, Route 112, Goshen, MA, 413/268-7098; or mail to 555 East St., RFD 1, Williamsburg, MA 01096. Massachusetts Division of State Parks and Recreation, 251 Causeway St., Suite 600, Boston, MA 02114-2104, 617/626-1250, website: www.state.ma.us/dem/forparks.htm.

## 15 BALANCING ROCK
**1 mi/0.75 hr**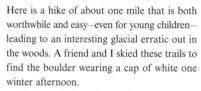
**in D.A.R. State Forest in Goshen**
Here is a hike of about one mile that is both worthwhile and easy—even for young children—leading to an interesting glacial erratic out in the woods. A friend and I skied these trails to find the boulder wearing a cap of white one winter afternoon.

Head south along the woods road opposite the second parking lot, following the blue blazes. At the intersection of several trails, turn left onto the trail with orange blazes and follow it all the way to Balancing Rock, a truck-size boulder in the woods. Continue to follow the orange blazes past Balancing Rock, paralleling a stone wall at one point, back to a wide trail in the dark woods where you'll turn right and return shortly to the start of the orange-blazed trail. At this point, turn left on the blue-blazed trail back to the parking lot.

**User groups:** Hikers, dogs, skiers, and snowshoers. Dogs must be leashed. No wheelchair facilities. This trail is not suitable for horses. Hunting is prohibited.

**Access, fees:** A daily parking fee of $5 is collected from mid-May–mid-October.

**Maps:** A free trail map is available at the state forest (see address below) or at the Massachusetts Division of State Parks and Recreation website (see below).

**Directions:** From I-91 northbound, take Exit 19 onto Route 9 west. In Goshen, turn right onto Route 112 north. The park entrance is

on your right. From I-91 southbound, take Exit 25 for Route 116 west. In Ashfield, turn left onto Route 112 south. The park entrance is on your left. In summer, park in the second lot along Moore Hill Road, located just past the left turn for the boat launch and nature center. In winter, park in the first lot, near the restrooms and warming hut (Moore Hill Road is not maintained beyond that point).

**Contact:** D.A.R. State Forest, Route 112, Goshen, MA, 413/268-7098; or mail to 555 East St., RFD 1, Williamsburg, MA 01096. Massachusetts Division of State Parks and Recreation, 251 Causeway St., Suite 600, Boston, MA 02114-2104, 617/626-1250, website: www.state.ma.us/dem/forparks.htm.

## 16 SOUTH SUGARLOAF MOUNTAIN
**1.5 mi/1.5 hrs**
**in Mount Sugarloaf State Reservation in South Deerfield**
At just 652 feet above sea level, South Sugarloaf is barely a hill—but one that rises abruptly from the flat valley, its cliffs looming over the wide Connecticut River. Reached via this short but steep hike, the South Sugarloaf summit offers some of the best Massachusetts views of the Connecticut Valley. The vertical ascent is about 300 feet.

From the parking lot, the wide (though unmarked) West Side Trail leads into the woods. A side trail branches right immediately, soon leading across the Summit Road to the start of the Pocumtuck Ridge Trail, marked by a wooden post without a sign. (The Pocumtuck Ridge Trail can also be reached by walking up the Summit Road about 100 feet inside the gate.) Follow the blue blazes straight up the steep hillside under power lines; the trail finally makes several switchbacks just below the summit. It follows the fence edge, with sweeping views from atop the cliffs. An observation tower on the summit provides a panorama.

Cross the summit to the lower parking lot,

looking down on the Connecticut River Valley from South Sugarloaf Mountain, Massachusetts

where the blue-blazed Pocumtuck Ridge Trail reenters the woods and follows the cliff top, descending steeply and passing a fenced overlook. After crossing the Summit Road's hairpin turn, descend an old woods road to where the trail forks and turn left onto the sporadically red-blazed West Side Trail. Just before reaching a dead-end paved road, the trail turns left, skirting the edges of fields and returning to the parking lot. If hiking a loop isn't important to you, go up the West Side Trail and the Pocumtuck Ridge Trail to the summit and return the same way; though somewhat longer, it's a more pleasant hike than the lower stretch of the Pocumtuck Ridge Trail.

**User groups:** Hikers and dogs. Dogs must be leashed. No wheelchair facilities. This trail would be difficult to snowshoe, and is not suit-

able for bikes, horses, or skis. Hunting is prohibited.

**Access, fees:** A daily parking fee of $2 is collected from mid-May–mid-October.

**Maps:** For a free, basic map of hiking trails, contact the Mount Sugarloaf State Reservation or see the Massachusetts Division of State Parks and Recreation website (see below). *The Mount Toby Reservation Trail Map,* which covers the Mount Sugarloaf State Reservation, is $3.95 from New England Cartographics, 413/549-4124 or toll-free 888/995-6277, website: www.necartographics.com. For a topographic area map, request Williamsburg from USGS Map Sales, Federal Center, Box 25286, Denver, CO 80225, 888/ASK-USGS (888/275-8747), website: http://mapping.usgs.gov.

**Directions:** From the junction of Routes 47 and 116 in Sunderland, drive 0.7 mile west on Route 116 and turn right onto Sugarloaf Road. The Mount Sugarloaf State Reservation Summit Road begins immediately on the right; park in the dirt lot along Sugarloaf Road just beyond the turn for the Summit Road.

**Contact:** Mount Sugarloaf State Reservation, Sugarloaf St./Route 116, South Deerfield, MA 01373, 413/545-5993. Massachusetts Division of State Parks and Recreation, 251 Causeway St., Suite 600, Boston, MA 02114-2104, 617/626-1250, website: www.state.ma.us/dem/forparks.htm.

## ⓱ MOUNT TOBY

**5 mi/2.5 hrs**
**in Sunderland**

The well-maintained Summit Road provides a route to the top of Mount Toby that can be hiked easily—or biked or skied by anyone seeking a fairly challenging climb and a fast descent. The hike described here ascends the

Summit Road but descends the steeper Telephone Line Trail to complete a loop; skiers or bikers should double back at the top and descend the Summit Road instead. Toby's 1,269-foot summit is wooded, but a fire tower open to the public offers a panorama with views stretching 50 miles across five states on a clear day. This hike climbs about 800 feet in elevation.

The Summit Road begins behind the Mount Toby Forest sign (don't turn right onto the orange-blazed Robert Frost Trail, although that is an alternate route). Frequent white blazes begin a short distance down the road. After less than a mile, the Telephone Line Trail (which you'll follow on the descent) diverges right. Approaching the summit, the road coincides with the orange-blazed Robert Frost Trail. From the fire tower, follow the Telephone Line Trail down Mount Toby. The Telephone Line Trail eventually reaches the Summit Road near the start of the hike; turn left and follow the Summit Road back to the trailhead. Another option for the return trip is to pick up the Robert Frost Trail, which diverges left about halfway down the Telephone Line Trail and also leads back to the Summit Road start.

**User groups:** Hikers, snowshoers, and dogs. Dogs must be leashed. No wheelchair facilities. Parts of the trail are not suitable for bikes, horses, or skis, but Summit Road is open to them (see the trail notes above). Hunting is allowed in season.

**Access, fees:** Parking and access are free.

**Maps:** The Mount Toby Reservation Trail Map is $3.95 from New England Cartographics, 413/549-4124 or toll-free 888/995-6277, website: www.necartographics.com. For topographic area maps, request Greenfield and Williamsburg from USGS Map Sales, Federal Center, Box 25286, Denver, CO 80225, 888/ASK-USGS (888/275-8747), website: http://mapping.usgs.gov.

**Directions:** The Mount Toby Summit Road is off Reservation Road, which comes off Route 47 0.9 mile south of its junction with Route 63 and just north of the Sunderland town line

(there may not be a sign for Reservation Road). Follow it for a half mile and park in a dirt lot on the right, just past the sign for the Mount Toby Forest.

**Contact:** Mount Toby Reservation is owned by the University of Massachusetts, but there is no contact for this hike.

## 18 MONUMENT MOUNTAIN
### 1.6 mi/1.2 hrs
**in Great Barrington**

 Perhaps the finest hike in an area that rivals the Mount Greylock region for the best hiking in southern New England, Monument Mountain thrusts a spectacular gray-white quartzite ridge into the sky. Its summit, Squaw Peak, rises to 1,640 feet and offers three-state views in all directions. Arguably even more dramatic, though, are the cliffs south of Squaw Peak and the detached rock pinnacle known as Devil's Pulpit. A good time to come here is mid-June, when the mountain laurel blooms. This unique hill has been popular since at least the 19th century: In 1850, so legend goes, Nathaniel Hawthorne, Oliver Wendell Holmes, and Herman Melville picnicked together on Monument's summit. And William Cullen Bryant wrote a poem titled "Monument Mountain" relating the tale of an Indian maiden who, spurned in love, leapt to her death from the cliffs. Your hike may be less historic and less traumatic than either of those, but Monument Mountain is one not to miss.

This fairly easy, 1.6-mile hike ascends and descends the Hickey Trail, but you may enjoy making a loop hike, going up the Hickey and coming down the 1.3-mile Indian Monument Trail, which joins up with the Hickey below the summit. At the picnic area, a sign describes the trail heading south, the Indian Monument, as easier, and the Hickey, which heads north, as steeper. The Hickey actually grows steep for only a short section below the summit and is otherwise a well-graded and well-maintained trail. Following the white blazes, you parallel a brook with a small waterfall. Nearing the summit ridge, watch for a trail entering on the right; that's the Indian Monument Trail, and you want to be able to distinguish it from the Hickey on your way back down. From the summit, continue following the white blazes south about a quarter mile, passing a pile of rocks, until you reach the cliffs. Devil's Pulpit is the obvious pinnacle at the far end of the cliffs.

**User groups:** Hikers and snowshoers. No wheelchair facilities. Bikes, dogs, horses, hunting, and skis are prohibited.

**Access, fees:** Parking and access are free. Monument Mountain is open to the public from sunrise–sunset year-round.

**Maps:** A map of trails is posted on an information board at the picnic area, and a paper map is available at the trailhead. A map is also available from The Trustees of Reservations (see address below). For topographic area maps, request Great Barrington and Stockbridge from USGS Map Sales, Federal Center, Box 25286, Denver, CO 80225, 888/ASK-USGS (888/275-8747), website: http://mapping.usgs.gov.

**Directions:** The trails begin at a large turnout and picnic area along Route 7 in Great Barrington, 1.1 miles south of the Stockbridge town line and 1.7 miles north of the junction with Route 183.

**Contact:** The Trustees of Reservations Western Management Region, Mission House, P.O. Box 792, Sergeant St., Stockbridge, MA 01262-0792, 413/298-3239, website: www.thetrustees.org.

## 19 WILDCAT LOOP
### 9.5 mi/6 hrs
### in Beartown State Forest in Monterey

I included this trail primarily for mountain bikers looking for a challenging bounce up and down a heavily rutted and rock-strewn old woods road (a 2.5-hour ride). I emerged from this ride covered with a thick paste of mud and sweat—and with a new-found respect for Beartown's hills. As a hike, it represents a rugged, six-hour outing through quiet woods, though it tends to get muddy in some spots.

From the campground, head up Beartown Road a short distance and turn left onto the Wildcat Trail, which is marked by a sign and is just beyond a right bend in the road. This old woods road rolls up and down a few hills, passing through areas that tend to be muddy, especially in spring. After about 3.5 miles, the trail reaches paved Beartown Road. Turn right, cross over West Brook, and turn left onto Beebe Trail, another woods road marked by a sign. The Beebe loops less than two miles back to Beartown Road. Turn left and follow the paved road back to the campground. For a longer route, you can link up with the Sky Peak and Turkey Trails, both of which are clearly labeled on the map (see below).

**User groups:** Hikers, bikers, snowshoes, skis, and dogs. Dogs must be leashed. No wheelchair facilities. Horses are prohibited. Hunting is allowed in season.

**Access, fees:** A daily parking fee of $5 is collected from mid-May–mid-October. Beartown State Forest is closed from dusk to a half hour before sunrise year-round.

**Maps:** A contour map of trails (designating uses allowed on each trail) is available in boxes at the state forest headquarters, at the parking area for hiking, at a trail information kiosk at the swimming area and restrooms, and at the campground. You can also find one at the Massachusetts Division of State Parks and Recreation website (see below). For topographic area maps, request Great Barrington and Otis from USGS Map Sales, Federal Center, Box 25286, Denver, CO 80225, 888/ASK-USGS (888/275-8747), website: http://mapping.usgs.gov.

**Directions:** Beartown State Forest is on Blue Hill Road, which runs north off Route 23, 2.4 miles west of the Monterey General Store and 1.8 miles east of the junction with Route 57. Follow Blue Hill Road 0.7 mile to the forest headquarters on the left. Continuing north on Blue Hill Road, you pass the Appalachian Trail crossing at 1.3 miles from the headquarters; at 1.5 miles, turn right onto Benedict Pond Road (shown as Beartown Road on the park map). Follow signs past the hiking trailhead and swimming area to the campground parking area.

**Contact:** Beartown State Forest, 69 Blue Hill Rd., P.O. Box 97, Monterey, MA 01245-0097, 413/528-0904. Massachusetts Division of State Parks and Recreation, 251 Causeway St., Suite 600, Boston, MA 02114-2104, 617/626-1250, website: www.state.ma.us/dem/forparks.htm.

## 20 BENEDICT POND AND THE LEDGES

### 2.5 mi/1.5 hrs

**in Beartown State Forest in Monterey**

This hike makes a loop around pristine Benedict Pond, a place with rich bird life—I heard three or four woodpeckers hard at work one morning and saw one fairly close up. When I stopped to eat by the pond's shore, a pair of Canada geese with two goslings in tow swam up and waddled ashore not eight feet from me as I sat quietly; the gander stood sentry over me while his family grazed on grass.

From the trailhead, follow the Pond Loop Trail to the pond's eastern end, where it merges with the white-blazed Appalachian Trail. Turn left. The trails soon reach a woods road and split again. Turn right onto the AT, ascending a low hillside. Where the AT hooks right and crosses a brook, continue straight ahead on a short side path to an impressive beaver dam that has flooded a swamp. Backtrack, cross the brook on the AT, and within several minutes you reach The Ledges, with a view west toward East Mountain and Mount Everett. Backtrack on the AT to the woods road and turn right onto the Pond Loop Trail. Watch for where the trail bears left off the woods road (at a sign and blue blazes). The trail passes through the state forest campground on the way back to the parking area.

**User groups:** Hikers, snowshoers, and dogs. Dogs must be leashed. No wheelchair facilities. Bikes, horses, and skis are prohibited. Hunting is allowed in season.

**Access, fees:** A daily parking fee of $5 is collected from mid-May–mid-October. Beartown State Forest is closed from dusk to a half hour before sunrise year-round.

**Maps:** A contour map of trails (designating uses allowed on each trail) is available in boxes at the state forest headquarters, at the trailhead parking area, at a trail information kiosk at the swimming area and restrooms, and at the campground. You can also find one at the Massachusetts Division of State Parks and Recreation website (see below). This Appalachian Trail section is covered on map 3 in the *Map and Guide to the Appalachian Trail in Massachusetts and Connecticut,* a five-map set for $19.95 ($14.95 for the maps alone) from the Appalachian Trail Conference (see address below). For topographic area maps, request Great Barrington and Otis from USGS Map Sales, Federal Center, Box 25286, Denver, CO 80225, 888/ASK-USGS (888/275-8747), website: http://mapping.usgs.gov.

**Directions:** Beartown State Forest is on Blue Hill Road, which runs north off Route 23, 2.4 miles west of the Monterey General Store and 1.8 miles east of the junction with Route 57. Follow Blue Hill Road 0.7 mile to the forest headquarters on the left. Continuing north on Blue Hill Road, you pass the Appalachian Trail crossing 1.3 miles from the headquarters; at 1.5 miles, turn right onto Benedict Pond Road (shown as Beartown Road on the park map). Follow signs to the trailhead in a dirt parking area; a sign marks the Pond Loop Trail. A short distance farther up the road are public restrooms and a state forest campground.

**Contact:** Beartown State Forest, Blue Hill Rd., P.O. Box 97, Monterey, MA 01245-0097, 413/528-0904. Massachusetts Division of State Parks and Recreation, 251 Causeway St., Suite 600, Boston, MA 02114-2104, 617/626-1250, website: www.state.ma.us/dem/forparks.htm. Appalachian Trail Conference, P.O. Box 807, Harpers Ferry, WV 25425, 304/535-6331, website: www.appalachiantrail.org.

## 21 NORWOTTUCK TRAIL
**10.1 mi one-way/5 hrs**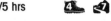
**in Northampton**

The 10.1-mile-long Norwottuck Trail is a paved bike path that follows a former railroad bed from Northampton, through Hadley and Amherst, into Belchertown. Its flat course provides a linear recreation area for walkers, runners, bicyclists, in-line skaters, cross-country skiers, snowshoers, and people in wheelchairs. As with any bike or pedestrian path, it is popular with families because it provides a refuge from traffic. The place from which many users access the trail is the large parking lot at its western end; this lot is often full, so it's wise to try one of the other access points among those listed below in the directions. Park officials are hoping to eventually complete an extension of the Norwottuck to Woodmont Road in Northampton, or possibly as far as the University of Massachusetts campus in Amherst.

**User groups:** Hikers, bikers, dogs, skiers, snowshoers, and wheelchair users. Dogs must be leashed. Horses and hunting are prohibited.

**Access, fees:** Parking and access are free.

**Maps:** A brochure/map is available at both trailheads. The *Western Massachusetts Bicycle Map,* a detailed bicycling map covering the state from the New York border to the Quabbin Reservoir, including the Norwottuck Trail, is available for $4.25 from Rubel BikeMaps, P.O. Box 401035, Cambridge, MA 02140, 617/776-6567, website: www.bikemaps.com, and from area stores listed at the website. For topographic area maps, request Easthampton and Holyoke from USGS Map Sales, Federal Center, Box 25286, Denver, CO 80225, 888/ASK-USGS (888/275-8747), website: http://mapping.usgs.gov.

**Directions:** To reach the trail's western end from the south, take I-91 to Exit 19. Down the off-ramp, drive straight through the intersection and turn right into the Connecticut River Greenway State Park/Elwell Recreation Area. From the north, take I-91 to Exit 20. Turn left at the traffic lights and drive 1.5 miles to the Elwell Recreation Area on the left. The trail can also be accessed from four other parking areas: behind the Bread and Circus store in the Mountain Farms Mall on Route 9 in Hadley, 3.7 miles from the Elwell Recreation Area parking lot; near the junction of Mill Lane and Southeast Street, off Route 9 in Amherst; on Station Road in Amherst (reached via Southeast Street off Route 9), 1.6 miles from the trail's eastern terminus; and on Warren Wright Road in Belchertown, the trail's eastern terminus.

**Contact:** Connecticut River Greenway State Park/Elwell Recreation Area, 136 Damon Rd., Northampton, MA 01060, 413/586-8706, ext. 12. Massachusetts Division of State Parks and Recreation, 251 Causeway St., Suite 600, Boston, MA 02114-2104, 617/626-1250, website: www.state.ma.us/dem/forparks.htm.

## 22 MOUNT TOM
**5.4 mi/2.5 hrs**
**in Mount Tom State Reservation in Holyoke**

One of the most popular stretches of the 98-mile Metacomet-Monadnock Trail is the traverse of the Mount Tom Ridge. A steep mountainside capped by tall basalt cliffs defines Mount Tom's west face, and the trail follows the brink of that precipice for nearly two miles, treating hikers to commanding views west as far as the Berkshires on a clear day. This hike climbs less than 500 feet.

From the parking area, walk up the paved road toward the stone house for about 75 yards. Turn right and enter the woods at a trail marked by white rectangular blazes and a triangular marker for the Metacomet-Monadnock Trail. Within minutes, the trail veers right and climbs steeply toward Goat Peak. Pass a good view westward and then reach the open clearing of Goat Peak, where the lookout tower offers a panorama. Double back to Smiths Ferry Road, turn right, walk about 75 yards, and then enter the woods on the left, following the white blazes of the Metacomet-Monadnock. It crosses the Quarry Trail and then ascends the ridge. Numerous side paths lead to the right to great views from the cliffs, with each view better than the last until you reach the Mount Tom summit, where there are radio and television transmission stations. Retrace your steps on the Metacomet-Monadnock Trail to your car.

**User groups:** Hikers and snowshoers. Dogs must be leashed. No wheelchair facilities. This trail is not suitable for skis. Bikes, horses, and hunting are prohibited.

**Access, fees:** A daily parking fee of $2 is collected from mid-May–mid-October.

**Maps:** A free map of hiking trails is available at the reservation headquarters and the stone house, or at the Massachusetts Division of State Parks and Recreation website (see below). The *Blue Hills Reservation/Mount Tom/Holyoke Range* map costs $5.95 in paper from the Appalachian Mountain Club, 800/262-4455, website: www.outdoors.org. The *Mount Tom Reservation Trail Map* costs $3.95 from New England Cartographics, 413/549-4124 or toll-free 888/995-6277, website: www.necarto-graphics.com. For topographic area maps, request Mount Tom, Easthampton, Mount Holyoke, and Springfield North from USGS Map Sales, Federal Center, Box 25286, Denver, CO 80225, 888/ASK-USGS (888/275-8747), website: http://mapping.usgs.gov.

**Directions:** Take I-91 to Exit 18 and then U.S. 5 south for roughly 3.3 miles. Turn right onto Smiths Ferry Road, at the entrance to Mount Tom State Reservation. Follow the road for nearly a mile, passing under I-91 (immediately after which the reservation headquarters are on the right), to a horseshoe-shaped parking area on the right. The parking area is about 0.2 mile before the stone house interpretive center, where Smiths Ferry Road meets Christopher Clark Road, just beyond a paved, dead-end road.

**Contact:** Mount Tom State Reservation, 125 Reservation Rd., Route 5, Holyoke, MA 01040, 413/534-1186. Massachusetts Division of State Parks and Recreation, 251 Causeway St., Suite 600, Boston, MA 02114-2104, 617/626-1250, website: www.state.ma.us/dem/forparks.htm.

## 23 JUG END
**2.2 mi/2 hrs**
**in Egremont**

I hiked up to Jug End on a morning when a leaden sky threatened rain and clouds hung low on many of the bigger hills in this part of the southern Berkshires. I considered not even making the hike of barely more than two miles—but ultimately went up and encountered some exciting conditions. At the summit, I stood in an icy wind watching low clouds drift across the valley between rounded mountains. The view from the open ledges above cliffs at Jug End is well worth the short, if steep, hike of more than 500 feet uphill.

From the turnout, follow the Appalachian Trail steeply uphill. Within 0.3 mile, the trail starts up the steep ridge side, reaching the first open views at about 0.7 mile from the road. Jug End's summit, with good views northward toward the valley and the surrounding green hills of the southern Berkshires, is 1.1 miles from the road. After you've taken in the views, head back to the parking area the same way you hiked up.

**User groups:** Hikers, snowshoers, and dogs. No wheelchair facilities. This trail is not suitable for skis. Bikes, horses, and hunting are prohibited.

**Access, fees:** Parking and access are free.

**Maps:** Refer to map 3 in the *Map and Guide to the Appalachian Trail in Massachusetts and Connecticut,* a five-map set and guidebook available for $19.95 ($14.95 for the maps alone) from the Appalachian Trail Conference (see address below). For topographic area maps, request Ashley Falls and Great Barrington from USGS Map Sales, Federal Center, Box 25286, Denver, CO 80225, 888/ASK-USGS (888/275-8747), website: http://mapping.usgs.gov.

**Directions:** From the junction of Routes 23 and 41 in Egremont, drive south on Route 41 for 0.1 mile and turn right onto Mount

Washington Road. Continue 0.8 mile and turn left on Avenue Road. At a half mile, bear left onto Jug End Road and continue 0.3 mile to a turnout on the right where the Appalachian Trail emerges from the woods. Park in the turnout.

**Contact:** Appalachian Trail Conference, 799 Washington St., P.O. Box 807, Harpers Ferry, WV 25425-0807, 304/535-6331, website: www.appalachiantrail.org.

## 24 MOUNT EVERETT
**5.4 mi/3.5 hrs**
**in Mount Washington**

Mount Everett, at 2,602 feet, is among the taller of those little hills in southwestern Massachusetts with the green, rounded tops and steep flanks that seem close enough for someone standing in the valley to reach out and touch. Long views east from atop Everett suggest that it's a good place to catch the sunrise. As a bonus, you pass several waterfalls on the way to the peak. This hike climbs about 1,900 feet.

From the kiosk, follow the Race Brook Trail. Not far up the trail, a sign marks a side path leading right to a view of the lower falls along Race Brook. The main trail bears left and grows steeper just before crossing the brook below upper Race Brook Falls, some 80 feet high—an impressive sight at times of high runoff, most common in the spring. Above the falls, you reach a ledge with a view east. The trail then descends slightly to a third crossing of the brook.

At the Appalachian Trail, marked by signs, turn right (north) for the summit of Everett, 0.7 mile distant. You are walking on bare rock exposed by the footsteps of the many hikers who have come before you—hundreds of whom were backpacking the entire AT from Georgia to Maine. Notice how thin the soil is beside the trail and you will understand how hiker traffic has eroded soil on the trail. The views eastward begin before the summit, where only stunted trees and vegetation grow; in this rural southwest corner of Massachusetts, you survey the valley and an expanse of wooded hills with few signs of human presence. An abandoned fire tower marks the summit; walk toward it to a spot with views toward the Catskills. Hike down along the same route.

**User groups:** Hikers, snowshoers, and dogs. No wheelchair facilities. This trail is not suitable for skis. Bikes, horses, and hunting are prohibited.

on Mount Everett

© MICHAEL LANZA

**Access, fees:** Parking and access are free.

**Maps:** A free trail map of Mount Washington State Forest, which covers Mount Everett, is available at the state forest headquarters or at the Massachusetts Division of State Parks and Recreation website (see below). The *Northern Berkshires/Southwestern Massachusetts/Wachusett Mountain* map costs $5.95 in paper from the Appalachian Mountain Club, 800/262-4455, website: www.outdoors.org. These trails are also covered on map 4 in the *Map and Guide to the Appalachian Trail in Massachusetts and Connecticut,* a five-map set and guidebook available for $19.95 ($14.95 for the maps alone) from the Appalachian Trail Conference (see address below). For a topographic area map, request Ashley Falls from USGS Map Sales, Federal Center, Box 25286, Denver, CO 80225, 888/ASK-USGS (888/275-8747), website: http://mapping.usgs.gov.

**Directions:** From the junction where Routes 23 and 41 split in Egremont, follow Route 41 south for 5.2 miles to a turnout on the right. A kiosk and blue blazes mark the start of the Race Brook Trail.

**Contact:** Mount Washington State Forest, RD 3 East St., Mount Washington, MA 01258, 413/528-0330. Massachusetts Division of State Parks and Recreation, 251 Causeway St., Suite 600, Boston, MA 02114-2104, 617/626-1250, website: www.state.ma.us/dem/forparks.htm. Appalachian Trail Conference, 799 Washington St., P.O. Box 807, Harpers Ferry, WV 25425-0807, 304/535-6331, website: www.appalachiantrail.org.

## 25 THE RIGA PLATEAU
**17 mi/2 days**

**between Egremont, MA, and Salisbury, CT**

This very popular Appalachian Trail stretch offers easy hiking along a low ridge with numerous long views of the green hills and rural countryside. In my opinion, it's the nicest stretch of the AT south of New Hampshire's Mount Moosilauke. Expect to see lots of day hikers and backpackers on warm weekends here, with shelters and camping areas tending to fill to overflowing. I backpacked this once midweek, though, when I saw just three other backpackers in two days and shared the Bear Rock Falls campsite with only a group of well-behaved teens. It was May, and the trail and woods had already dried out from spring, yet there were very few bugs and the temperature was quite mild. I fell in love with this section of the AT and can't wait to get back again. The cumulative elevation gained over the course of this hike is about 3,500 feet.

From the turnout on Jug End Road, follow the AT southbound. You follow the AT's white blazes for this entire hike. The trail ascends gently, then steeply through the woods to Jug End at 1.1 miles, the northern tip of the so-called Riga Plateau, with wide views northward to the Berkshire Mountains. On a clear day, Mount Greylock (hikes 2–8, this chapter), the highest peak in Massachusetts, is visible in the distance. Now you're on the ridge, with only fairly easy climbs and dips ahead. The trail passes several open ledges on the Mount Bushnell ascent, reaching its 1,834-foot summit at 2.3 miles. Easy woods walking leads you into the Mount Everett State Reservation, crossing a road at 3.9 miles; a short distance to the right is Guilder Pond, the second-highest in Massachusetts. The trail steepens a bit to a fire tower at 4.3 miles, and Everett's summit (2,602 feet) at 4.6 miles, with views in all directions.

The AT descends off Everett at an easy slope and heads back into the woods, then climbs slightly to the open, rocky Race Mountain crown, 6.4 miles into this hike and 2,365 feet above the ocean. The trail follows the crest of cliffs with wide views northeast to southeast of the Housatonic Valley. At 8.1 miles, you pass near Bear Rock Falls (on the left) and its namesake camping area. Beyond here, the trail descends steadily, then a bit more steeply into the dark defile of Sages Ravine, another camping area at 9.5 miles, as the AT enters Connecticut.

The AT follows the ravine, then leaves it for

the most strenuous part of this hike, the 1.4-mile climb to the 2,316-foot Bear Mountain summit, the highest peak in Connecticut—though not the highest point, which is actually on a slope of nearby Mount Frissell. On the way up Bear Mountain, you pass the Paradise Lane Trail at 10.3 miles into this hike. From the top of Bear, at 10.9 miles, the trail descends steadily, if easily, over open terrain with long views of Connecticut's northwestern corner before reentering the woods. The Undermountain Trail turns sharply left at 11.8 miles; continue straight ahead on the AT, soon passing the Brassie Brook, Ball Brook, and Riga camping areas (see the Access section for this hike). The forest along here is bright, and although trees block the views, you're on the ridge and it feels high. I once hiked this at night under a brilliant moon, seeing a sky riddled with stars overhead.

Stay southbound on the AT, soon climbing more steeply to reach the open ledges of the Lion's Head at 14.2 miles, with some of the hike's best views of a bucolic countryside, including the town of Salisbury and Prospect Mountain straight ahead. Double back a short distance from the Lion's Head ledges and descend on the AT, passing a junction with the Lion's Head Trail. The trail now descends at a steady grade through quiet woods, reaching the parking lot on Route 41 at 17 miles from Jug End Road.

**User groups:** Hikers, snowshoers, and dogs. No wheelchair facilities. This trail is not suitable for skis. Bikes, horses, and hunting are prohibited.

**Access, fees:** Parking and access are free. Camping is permitted only at designated shelters and campsites along this section of the Appalachian Trail. From north to south, they are: Glen Brook shelter, reached via a short side trail off the AT, 3.4 miles into this hike; a campsite 0.4 mile off the AT down the Race Brook Falls Trail, 5.3 miles into this hike; the Bear Rock Falls campsite, beside the AT at 8.1 miles; Sages Ravine at 9.9 miles; the Brassie Brook shelter

and campsites at 12.3 miles; the Ball Brook campsite at 12.9 miles; the Riga camping area at 13.5 miles; and the Plateau campsite at 13.7 miles, a short distance from the hike's end. Campfires are prohibited from Bear Rock Falls campsite south to the Plateau campsite. Campers must cook with portable camp stoves.

**Maps:** See maps 3 and 4 in the *Map and Guide to the Appalachian Trail in Massachusetts and Connecticut,* a five-map set and guidebook available for $19.95 ($14.95 for the maps alone) from the Appalachian Trail Conference (see address below). For topographic area maps, request Great Barrington, Ashley Falls, and Sharon from USGS Map Sales, Federal Center, Box 25286, Denver, CO 80225, 888/ASK-USGS (888/275-8747), website: http://mapping.usgs.gov.

**Directions:** You need to shuttle two vehicles to make this one-way traverse. To hike north to south, as described here, leave one vehicle in the Appalachian Trail parking lot on Route 41 in Salisbury, CT, 0.8 mile north of the junction of Routes 44 and 41. To reach this hike's start, drive your second vehicle north on Route 41 to Egremont Just before reaching Route 23, turn left onto Mount Washington Road. Continue 0.8 mile and turn left on Avenue Road. At a half mile, bear to the left onto Jug End Road and continue 0.3 mile to a turnout on the right where the Appalachian Trail emerges from the woods. Park in the turnout.

**Contact:** Appalachian Trail Conference, 799 Washington St., P.O. Box 807, Harpers Ferry, WV 25425-0807, 304/535-6331, website: www.appalachiantrail.org.

## 26 BASH BISH FALLS
**0.5 mi/0.75 hr**

**in Bash Bish Falls State Park in Mount Washington**

After driving one of the most winding Massachusetts roads, you hike this short trail to what may be the state's most spectacular waterfall. The stream tumbles down through a vertical stack of giant boulders—splitting into twin columns of water around one huge, triangular block—then settles briefly in a clear, deep pool at the base of the falls before dropping in a foaming torrent through the water-carved rock walls of Bash Bish Gorge. The falls are, predictably, enhanced by spring rains and snowmelt and much thinner in fall. The Bash Bish Falls Trail is well marked with blue triangles, and a quarter-mile walk downhill from the roadside turnout leads to the falls.

**User groups:** Hikers, snowshoers, and dogs. Dogs must be leashed. No wheelchair facilities. This trail is not suitable for bikes, horses, or skis. Hunting is allowed in season.

**Access, fees:** Parking and access are free.

**Maps:** Although no map is needed for this hike, a free area trail map is available at the Mount Washington State Forest headquarters or at the Massachusetts Division of State Parks and Recreation website (see below). This area is covered in the *Northern Berkshires/Southwestern Massachusetts/Wachusett Mountain* map, $5.95 in paper, available in many stores and from the Appalachian Mountain Club, 800/262-4455, website: www.outdoors.org. For a topographic area map, request Ashley Falls from USGS Map Sales, Federal Center, Box 25286, Denver, CO 80225, 888/ASK-USGS (888/275-8747), website: http://mapping.usgs.gov.

**Directions:** From the junction of Routes 23 and 41 in Egremont, drive south on Route 41 for 0.1 mile and turn right onto Mount Washington Road, which becomes East Street. Follow the signs several miles to Bash Bish Falls State Park and a turnout on the left. To reach the Mount Washington State Forest headquarters, follow the signs from East Street.

**Contact:** Mount Washington State Forest, RD 3 East St., Mount Washington, MA 01258, 413/528-0330. Massachusetts Division of State Parks and Recreation, 251 Causeway St., Suite 600, Boston, MA 02114-2104, 617/626-1250, website: www.state.ma.us/dem/forparks.htm.

## 27 ALANDER MOUNTAIN

**5.6 mi/3 hrs**

**in Mount Washington State Forest in Mount Washington**

Less than a mile from the New York border and a few miles from Connecticut, Alander Mountain (2,240 feet) has two broad, flat summits, the westernmost having the best views of the southern Berkshires and of the New York hills and farmland all the way to the Catskill Mountains. An open ridge running south from the summit offers sweeping views for a fairly easy climb (500 feet in elevation gain). I rode my mountain bike as far as I could up the Alander Mountain Trail one spring afternoon and then hiked to the summit. Dark storm clouds drifted over the hills to the east, and shafts of sunlight daubed bright splotches over the green mountainsides while hawks floated on thermals overhead. While this is a wonderful hike, I think biking or skiing as far as possible up the trail adds another dimension to this little adventure.

From the kiosk behind the headquarters, the Alander Mountain Trail gradually ascends a woods road for much of its distance, then narrows to a trail and grows steeper. Just past the cabin, a sign points left to the east loop and right to the west loop; both loops take just minutes to walk. The west loop offers great views to the north, east, and south; three old concrete blocks, probably the foundation of a former fire tower, sit at the summit. Continue over the summit on the white-blazed South Taconic Trail for views westward into New York. Turn back and descend the way you came.

Special note: By hiking northbound from Alander's summit on the scenic South Taconic Trail, you can reach Bash Bish Falls (see previous listing), then return to Alander, adding four miles round-trip to this hike's distance.

**User groups:** Hikers, bikers, dogs, horses, skiers, and snowshoers. Dogs must be leashed. No wheelchair facilities. Hunting is allowed in season. During the winter, watch out for snowmobiles.

**Access, fees:** Parking and access are free. Backcountry camping is available in the Mount Washington State Forest, at 15 wilderness campsites just off this trail at 1.5 miles from the trailhead, and in a cabin that sleeps six just below Alander's summit. The cabin (which has a wood-burning stove) and the campsites are filled on a first-come, first-served basis.

**Maps:** The *Northern Berkshires/Southwestern Massachusetts/Wachusett Mountain* map costs $5.95 in paper and is available in many stores and from the Appalachian Mountain Club, 800/262-4455, website: www.outdoors.org. A free map of Mount Washington State Forest is available at the state forest headquarters or at the Massachusetts Division of State Parks and Recreation website (see below). For a topographic area map, request Ashley Falls from USGS Map Sales, Federal Center, Box 25286, Denver, CO 80225, 888/ASK-USGS (888/275-8747), website: http://mapping.usgs.gov.

**Directions:** From the junction of Routes 23 and 41 in Egremont, drive south on Route 41 for 0.1 mile and turn right onto Mount Washington Road, which becomes East Street. Follow the signs about nine miles to the Mount Washington State Forest headquarters on the right. The blue-blazed Alander Mountain Trail begins behind the headquarters.

**Contact:** Mount Washington State Forest, RD 3 East St., Mount Washington, MA 01258, 413/528-0330. Massachusetts Division of State Parks and Recreation, 251 Causeway St., Suite 600, Boston, MA 02114-2104, 617/626-1250, website: www.state.ma.us/dem/forparks.htm.

## 28 HUBBARD RIVER GORGE
**6 mi/2.5 hrs**

**in Granville State Forest in Granville**
This out-and-back hike features the highlight of this out-of-the-way state forest—the Hubbard River Gorge, which drops 450 feet over 2.5 miles through numerous falls. I've done this hike in winter, when ice made the going treacherous and beautiful in places, and in a spring rain and hailstorm when the river swelled with runoff.

From the dirt lot, backtrack over the bridge and turn right onto the paved road leading a half mile to the now-closed Hubbard River Campground; the Hubbard River Trail begins at the road's end. Follow the trail, an old woods road marked by blue triangles bearing a hiker symbol, southeast along the Hubbard River. After turning briefly away from the river, the road hugs the rim of the spectacular gorge, passing many spots that afford views of the river. Follow the trail as far as you like, then turn around and return the same way. If you go all the way to an old woods road marked on the map as Hartland Hollow Road before turning back, the round-trip is six miles. If you'd like to see another area similar to the Hubbard River Gorge, turn left and hike upstream (north) along Hartland Hollow Road. Watch for the stream through the trees to your right; you'll discover a small gorge and pools in there within less than a half mile from the Hubbard River Trail.

Special note: If you want to cross-country ski elsewhere in the state forest, check out the short but scenic Beaver Pond Loop beyond the forest headquarters on West Hartland Road, or the loop from the headquarters on the CCC and Corduroy Trails. One last note: This quiet corner of Massachusetts is a wonderful area to drive through or, better yet, bicycle. The villages of Granville and West Granville are both on the National Register of Historic Districts.

**User groups:** Hikers, bikers, dogs, skiers, and snowshoers. Dogs must be leashed. No wheelchair facilities. Sections of the trail would be difficult on a bike or skis and could be icy in winter. Horses are allowed. Hunting is allowed in season, except on Sundays or within 150 feet of a paved road or bike trail. Swimming in the Hubbard River is prohibited under penalty of fine.

**Access, fees:** Parking and access are free.

**Maps:** A free map of hiking trails is available at the state forest headquarters or at the Massachusetts Division of State Parks and Recreation website (see below). For a topographic

Hubbard River Gorge, Granville State Forest

area map, request Southwick from USGS Map Sales, Federal Center, Box 25286, Denver, CO 80225, 888/ASK-USGS (888/275-8747), website: http://mapping.usgs.gov.

**Directions:** From the junction of Routes 189 and 57, drive six miles west on Route 57 and turn left onto West Hartland Road. In another 0.6 mile, you pass a sign for the Granville State Forest; the rough dirt road heading left from that point is where this loop hike will emerge. Continue another 0.3 mile, cross the bridge over the Hubbard River, and park in the dirt lot on the left. The state forest headquarters is on West Hartland Road, 0.6 mile beyond the bridge.

**Contact:** Granville State Forest, 323 West Hartland Rd., Granville, MA 01034, 413/357-6611. Massachusetts Division of State Parks and Recreation, 251 Causeway St., Suite 600, Boston, MA 02114-2104, 617/626-1250, website: www.state.ma.us/dem/forparks.htm.

## Chapter 9

© MICHAEL LANZA

# Central Massachusetts

# Central Massachusetts

This chapter covers central Massachusetts from the Connecticut River east to I-495, from Douglas in the south to Ashburnham in the north. The state's midsection is a rumpled blanket of rolling hills and thick forest with some low but craggy summits that rise above the trees to give long views, most notable among them Mount Holyoke, Wachusett Mountain, and Mount Watatic. Beyond these hills, you will mostly find pleasant woods walks that are easy to moderately difficult and make for enjoyable outings of anywhere from an hour to half a day. Many of them are also quiet, uncrowded, and easy to reach. These hikes are great for beginners as well as serious hikers and backpackers trying to get their legs in shape for more strenuous trips elsewhere.

Central Massachusetts has two long-distance trails, both of which are largely used by day hikers. The Metacomet-Monadnock Trail

(Crag Mountain, Mount Holyoke) bounces along the Holyoke Range and through the hills of north-central Massachusetts on its 117-mile course from the Massachusetts/Connecticut line near Agawam and Southwick to the summit of Mount Monadnock in Jaffrey, New Hampshire. The Midstate Trail extends 92 miles from Douglas (on the Rhode Island border) to the New Hampshire line in Ashburnham. Significant stretches of both trails are on private land, so be aware of and respect any closures.

The trails in this chapter usually become free of snow sometime between mid-March and mid-April, though they often will be muddy for a few weeks after the snow melts. Many of the hikes in this chapter are in state parks and forests, where dogs must be leashed; horses are allowed in most state forests and parks, as is hunting in season.

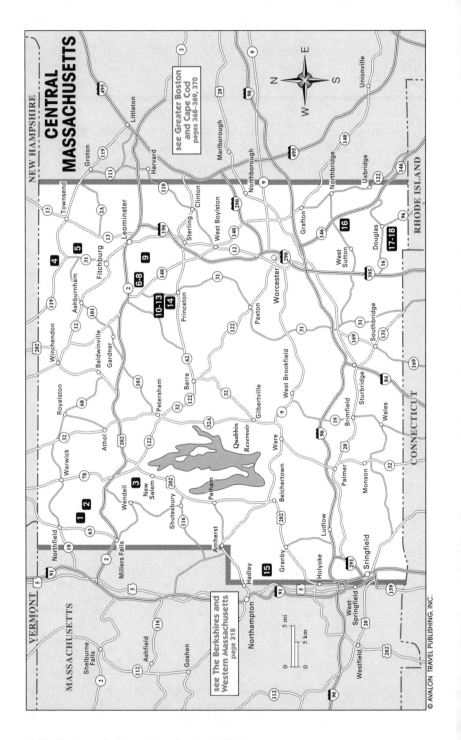

## CENTRAL MASSACHUSETTS

see Greater Boston and Cape Cod pages 368-369, 370

see The Berkshires and Western Massachusetts page 318

© AVALON TRAVEL PUBLISHING, INC.

# 1 NORTHFIELD MOUNTAIN: ROSE LEDGE

**5.5 mi/3.5 hrs**

**in Northfield**

Owned by Northeast Utilities, the Northfield Mountain Recreation and Environmental Center's 25 miles of hiking and multiuse trails comprise one of the best trail systems open year-round in Massachusetts. The Metacomet-Monadnock Trail is not far from this system and can be reached via a marked trail off the 10th Mountain Trail, near Bugaboo Pass on Northfield Mountain. Other activities, including orienteering, canoeing on the nearby Connecticut River, and educational programs, are conducted through the center. This hike takes in some of the mountain's best features—including the Rose Ledge cliffs and a view of the reservoir at the 1,100-foot summit—but many other loop options are possible here. The route described here climbs about 600–700 feet in elevation.

From the parking lot, follow the wide carriage road of the 10th Mountain Trail to the right. At the sign, turn left onto a footpath, the Rose Ledge Trail (marked here by blue diamonds). Follow the trail across a carriage road and then turn right where the trail follows orange blazes. Cross two carriage roads, Hemlock Hill and Jug End. The Rose Ledge Trail forks here: The left branch traverses above the cliffs and the right branch below them. Either is a nice hike, and both branches link at the opposite end of the cliffs.

The left branch begins above the cliffs, with some views of nearby wooded hills, then drops below them for close-up views of the cliffs themselves. Bear left at the fork, and just before reaching the wide carriage road called Rock Oak Ramble, turn right at an easily overlooked trail leading downhill (parallel to Rock Oak Ramble). Reaching the Lower Ledge Trail, turn left and cross Rock Oak Ramble. You're soon walking below the cliffs and may see rock climbers on them; be careful of loose rock falling from above if you venture near the cliff

base. After rejoining the Rose Ledge Trail, continue straight on the Mariah Foot Trail to the Hill 'n Dale carriage road; turn right and then left onto the 10th Mountain carriage road. At a junction marked number 32 (corresponding to the trail map), turn right for the summit, which has a reservoir viewing platform. Descend back to Junction 32 and turn left on 10th Mountain, right on Hill 'n Dale, right at Junction 16 onto Rock Oak Ramble, left at Junction 8 onto Hemlock Hill, and then right onto the orange-blazed Rose Ledge Trail, backtracking to the parking lot.

**User groups:** Hikers, snowshoers, and dogs. Dogs must be leashed. No wheelchair facilities. Bikes, horses, hunting, and skis are prohibited from parts of this trail.

**Access, fees:** No fee is charged for parking or trail use, with the exception of a trail fee for cross-country skiing. Bikers must register once per season at the visitor center, and horseback riders must check in for parking and trail information; helmets are required for both biking and horseback riding. Trails are often closed to bikes and horses during mud season, usually until late April.

**Maps:** A trail map is available at the visitor center. For topographic area maps, request Northfield and Orange from USGS Map Sales, Federal Center, Box 25286, Denver, CO 80225, 888/ASK-USGS (888/275-8747), website: http://mapping.usgs.gov.

**Directions:** The Northfield Mountain Visitor Center is off Route 63, 5.8 miles south of its junction with Route 10 and 2.5 miles north of Route 2. The visitor center is open from 9 A.M.–5 P.M. Wednesday–Sunday, spring–fall. The cross-country center is open 9 A.M.– 5 P.M. every day during the ski season.

**Contact:** Northfield Mountain Recreation and Environmental Center, 99 Millers Falls Rd./Route 63, Northfield, MA 01360, 413/659-3714, website: www.tiac.com/users/erving/cyber/skiing.html.

## 2 CRAG MOUNTAIN
**3.4 mi/2 hrs**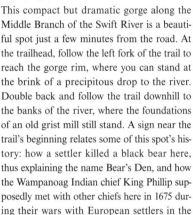
in Northfield

This easy hike—ascending only a few hundred feet—leads to Crag Mountain, a rocky outcropping on the ridge with excellent views. Follow the white-blazed Metacomet-Monadnock Trail south. The trail crosses one wet area, rises gently through a mixed deciduous and conifer forest, and reaches Crag's open summit 1.7 miles from the road. The views take in the Berkshires and the southern Green Mountains of Vermont to the west and northwest, Mount Monadnock (See Central and Southern New Hampshire chapter) to the northeast, the central Massachusetts hills to the east, and the Northfield Mountain Reservoir, Mount Toby (see listing in Berkshires and Western Massachusetts chapter), and South Sugarloaf Mountain (see listing in Berkshires and Western Massachusetts chapter) to the south. Hike back along the same route.

**User groups:** Hikers, snowshoers, and dogs. No wheelchair facilities. The trail is not suitable for bikes, horses, or skis. This hike is on private land; assume that hunting is allowed unless otherwise posted.

**Access, fees:** Parking and access are free.

**Maps:** For a topographic area map, request Northfield from USGS Map Sales, Federal Center, Box 25286, Denver, CO 80225, 888/ASK-USGS (888/275-8747), website: http://mapping.usgs.gov.

**Directions:** From Route 10/63 in Northfield, about 0.2 mile south of the town center and 0.3 mile north of the southern junction of Routes 10 and 63, turn west onto Maple Street, which becomes Gulf Road. Drive 3.1 miles to a turnout on the right, where the white blazes of the Metacomet-Monadnock Trail enter the woods.

**Contact:** There is no contact organization for this hike.

## 3 BEAR'S DEN
**0.2 mi/0.5 hr**
in New Salem

This compact but dramatic gorge along the Middle Branch of the Swift River is a beautiful spot just a few minutes from the road. At the trailhead, follow the left fork of the trail to reach the gorge rim, where you can stand at the brink of a precipitous drop to the river. Double back and follow the trail downhill to the banks of the river, where the foundations of an old grist mill still stand. A sign near the trail's beginning relates some of this spot's history: how a settler killed a black bear here, thus explaining the name Bear's Den, and how the Wampanoag Indian chief King Phillip supposedly met with other chiefs here in 1675 during their wars with European settlers in the Connecticut Valley.

**User groups:** Hikers, snowshoers, and dogs. No wheelchair facilities. This trail is not suitable for bikes, horses, or skis. Hunting is prohibited.

**Access, fees:** Parking and access are free. The reservation is open to the public from sunrise–sunset year-round.

**Maps:** No map is necessary for this short and easy walk.

**Directions:** From the junction of Routes 202 and 122 in New Salem, follow Route 202 south for 0.4 mile. Turn right onto Elm Street, drive 0.7 mile, and then turn left onto Neilson Road. Drive a half mile and park at the roadside. The entrance is on the right, where a short trail leads to the gorge.

**Contact:** The Trustees of Reservations Central Region Office, Doyle Reservation, 325 Lindell Ave., Leominster, MA 01453-5414, 978/840-4446, website: www.thetrustees.org.

## 4 MOUNT WATATIC AND NUTTING HILL
**2.8 mi/1.5 hrs**
in Ashburnham

Mount Watatic's 1,832-foot elevation barely qualifies it as anything but a big hill. But the pair of barren, rocky summits offer excellent views of nearby peaks such as Wachusett Mountain (see hikes 10–14, this chapter) and Monadnock (Central and Southern New Hampshire chapter, hikes 19–20), as well as the entire Wapack Range (see North Pack Monadnock, Kidder Mountain, and Temple Mountain, in the Central and Southern New Hampshire chapter) extending north and, on a clear day, landmarks as distant as Mount Greylock (Berkshires and Western Massachusetts chapter, hikes 2–8), New Hampshire's White Mountains, and the Boston skyline. Watatic can feel like a bigger mountain, especially when the wind kicks up on its exposed crown. This loop encompasses Nutting Hill, where the flat, open summit offers some views. The Midstate Trail was rerouted in recent years to coincide with the Wapack Trail over Watatic's summit; both are well blazed with yellow triangles.

From the parking area, follow an old woods road north, ascending gradually. At 0.3 mile, the Wapack/Midstate Trail turns right (east), reaching the Watatic summit in another mile. Instead, this hike continues straight ahead on the blue-blazed State Line Trail (following the former route of the Midstate Trail). A half mile farther, you reach a junction where the State Line Trail forks left; continue straight ahead onto the Midstate Trail, which itself rejoins the Wapack Trail within another 0.2 mile. It is nearly a mile to Watatic's summit from this point. Turn right (southeast), soon passing over Nutting Hill's open top; watch for cairns leading directly over the hill and into the woods. Climbing Watatic's northwest slope, you pass somewhat overgrown trails of the former Mount Watatic ski area. Just below the summit stands an abandoned fire tower, now closed and unsafe. From the summit, an unmarked path leads to the lower, southeast summit. Double back to the fire tower, turn left, and follow the Wapack, passing an open ledge with views and, farther down, an enormous split boulder. At the Midstate Trail junction, turn left for the parking area.

**User groups:** Hikers, snowshoers, and dogs. No wheelchair facilities. This trail is not suitable for bikes, horses, or skis. Hunting is allowed in season.

**Access, fees:** Parking and access are free.

**Maps:** An excellent map of the Wapack Trail is available for $4 (including postage) from the Friends of the Wapack (see address below); the organization also sells a detailed guidebook to the entire trail for $11 (including postage). The *Guide to the Wapack Trail in Massachusetts & New Hampshire,* a three-color map, costs $3.95 from New England Cartographics, 413/549-4124 or toll-free 888/995-6277, website: www.necartographics.com. For a topographic area map, request Ashburnham from USGS Map Sales, Federal Center, Box 25286, Denver, CO 80225, 888/ASK-USGS (888/275-8747), website: http://mapping.usgs.gov.

**Directions:** The trailhead parking area is on the north side of Route 119 in Ashburnham, 1.4 miles west of its junction with Route 101.

**Contact:** Friends of the Wapack, P.O. Box 115, West Peterborough, NH 03468, website: www.wapack.org.

# ⑤ WILLARD BROOK

**2 mi/1 hr**

**in Willard Brook State Forest in Ashby**

This easy walk hugs the rock-strewn Willard Brook through its tight valley, winding through hemlock groves and among huge boulders. This is a good, gentle hike for introducing very young children to the woods. The trail begins from either side of the stone bridge over Willard Brook, just below Damon Pond. Toward the other (northeast) end of the trail, it ascends a hillside and reaches a forest road; turning left brings you shortly to the state forest headquarters. Most people just double back to the start. There are several miles of woods roads in the state forest open to other activities, such as mountain biking or horseback riding.

**User groups:** Hikers, dogs, skiers, and snowshoers. Dogs must be leashed. No wheelchair facilities. Bikes and horses are prohibited. Hunting is allowed in season.

**Access, fees:** A daily parking fee of $5 is collected from mid-May–mid-October.

**Maps:** A free, basic trail map of the state forest is available at the headquarters on Route 119 in West Townsend, just before the Ashby town line, or at the Massachusetts Division of State Parks and Recreation website (see below). For a topographic area map, request Ashburnham from USGS Map Sales, Federal Center, Box 25286, Denver, CO 80225, 888/ASK-USGS (888/275-8747), website: http://mapping.usgs.gov.

**Directions:** Park at the Damon Pond entrance off Route 119 in Ashby, 1.3 miles west of the Willard Brook State Forest headquarters and 0.2 mile east of the junction of Routes 119 and 31. The gate is closed in winter, so park in the roadside pullout.

**Contact:** Willard Brook State Forest, Route 119, West Townsend, MA 01474, 978/597-8802. Massachusetts Division of State Parks and Recreation, 251 Causeway St., Suite 600, Boston, MA 02114-2104, 617/626-1250, website: www.state.ma.us/dem/forparks.htm.

## 6 CROW HILLS

**0.7 mi/0.75 hr**

**in Leominster State Forest in Westminster**

The hike up Crow Hills, at the western edge of the more than 4,000-acre Leominster State Forest, is a short loop that can be done with young children, though it gets steep and rocky in brief sections (where you would have to remove snowshoes and watch for ice in winter). Despite its brevity and the climb of just a few hundred feet, it is one of the most dramatic walks in central Massachusetts, traversing the top of tall cliffs with commanding views of the wooded hills and ponds of the state forest and of Wachusett Mountain (see hikes 10–14, this chapter).

From the parking lot, cross Route 31 to a wide, well-marked trail entering the woods. Within 100 feet, the trail turns sharply left, then swings right and climbs steeply to the base of cliffs, 100 feet high in places. The trail then diverges right and left, with both branches looping up to the cliff tops. You can hike the loop in either direction; this description leads to the right (counterclockwise). Walk below the cliff to where stones arranged in

two of the author's nieces enjoying Crow Hills

steps lead steeply uphill to a junction with the Midstate Trail, marked by yellow triangular blazes. Turn left, carefully following the trail atop the cliffs past several spots that offer sweeping views; the best views are at the far end of the cliffs. Wachusett Mountain, with its ski slopes, is visible to the southwest. Take care not to kick any loose stones or wander near the cliff's edge; there are often rock climbers and hikers below. From the last open ledges, the Midstate Trail swings right, entering the woods again and continuing about 75 yards, then turning left and descending a steep, rocky gully. At its bottom, turn left again and, diverging from the Midstate, walk the trail around the base of the cliffs to this loop's beginning. Turn right and descend to the parking lot.

**User groups:** Hikers, snowshoers, and dogs. Dogs must be leashed. No wheelchair facilities. This trail is not suitable for bikes, horses, or skis. Hunting is allowed in season.

**Access, fees:** From May–October, a $5 parking fee is collected; a season pass costs $35. The parking lot may not always be plowed in winter; call the state forest headquarters for more information.

**Maps:** A free, basic trail map of Leominster State Forest is available at the state forest headquarters or at the Massachusetts Division of State Parks and Recreation website (see below). The *Mount Wachusett and Leominster State Forest Trail Map* costs $3.95 from New England Cartographics, 413/549-4124 or toll-free 888/995-6277, website: www.necartographics.com. For a topographic area map, request Fitchburg from USGS Map Sales, Federal Center, Box 25286, Denver, CO 80225, 888/ASK-USGS (888/275-8747), website: http://mapping.usgs.gov.

**Directions:** The hike begins from a large parking lot at the Crow Hills Pond Picnic Area along Route 31 on the Westminster/Princeton line, 2.2 miles south of the junction of Routes 31 and 2 and 1.5 miles north of the junction of Routes 31 and 140.

**Contact:** Leominster State Forest, Route 31,

Princeton, MA 01541, 978/874-2303. Massachusetts Division of State Parks and Recreation, 251 Causeway St., Suite 600, Boston, MA 02114-2104, 617/626-1250, website: www.state.ma.us/dem/forparks.htm.

## 7 BALL HILL LOOP
### 3.5 mi/2.5 hrs

**in Leominster State Forest in Westminster, Princeton, and Leominster**

Leominster State Forest has a network of marked trails and less-distinct footpaths weaving throughout, most in its northern half, north of Rocky Pond Road/Parmenter Road. (South of that dirt road, which is open to bikes but not motor vehicles, the state forest is crossed mainly by old woods roads.) This hike ascends one of the low, wooded hills in the state forest, into an area I've wandered into countless times—having grown up in Leominster—but where I still run across trails I don't recognize or end up someplace I did not expect to end up. There are myriad trails through here, and it's easy to get lost once you venture over Ball Hill. Nonetheless, it's a quiet woodlands that's fun to explore. This hike ascends small hills but never climbs more than a few hundred feet.

From the parking area, walk across the earthen dike between the two halves of Crow Hills Pond and then turn right, following a blazed trail south along the shore of the pond. Within a half mile, turn left (east) onto the Rocky Pond Trail, which climbs Ball Hill, steeply for short stretches. Near the hilltop, about one mile from the hike's start, is a spot where the trees thin enough to allow a partially obstructed view of the hills to the west. Anyone concerned about getting lost might want to turn back from here. Otherwise, continue over the hill, through quiet woods crossed by the occasional stone wall.

Descending the back side of the hill, ignore the trails branching off to the right. Turn left at the first opportunity; about 2.5 miles from the parking area, you see a landfill through the trees at the state forest edge. The trail swings north, then west; continue bearing left at trail junctions. On your way back, you pass through a wet area, over a low hillock, and eventually reach the paved parking lot at the public beach at the Crow Hills Pond north end. Cross the parking lot to the south (left), picking up the trail again for the short walk back to the dike across the pond.

**User groups:** Hikers, snowshoers, and dogs. Dogs must be leashed. No wheelchair facilities. This trail is not suitable for bikes, horses, or skis. Hunting is allowed in season.

**Access, fees:** From May–October, a $5 parking fee is collected; a season pass costs $35. The parking lot may not always be plowed in winter; call the state forest headquarters for more information.

**Maps:** A free, basic trail map of Leominster State Forest is available at the state forest headquarters or at the Massachusetts Division of State Parks and Recreation website (see below). The *Mount Wachusett and Leominster State Forest Trail Map* costs $3.95 from New England Cartographics, 413/549-4124 or toll-free 888/995-6277, website: www.necartographics.com. For a topographic area map, request Fitchburg from USGS Map Sales, Federal Center, Box 25286, Denver, CO 80225, 888/ASK-USGS (888/275-8747), website: http://mapping.usgs.gov.

**Directions:** The hike begins from a large parking lot at the Crow Hills Pond Picnic Area along Route 31 on the Westminster-Princeton line, 2.2 miles south of the junction of Routes 31 and 2 and 1.5 miles north of the junction of Routes 31 and 140.

**Contact:** Leominster State Forest, Route 31, Princeton, MA 01541, 978/874-2303. Massachusetts Division of State Parks and Recreation, 251 Causeway St., Suite 600, Boston, MA 02114-2104, 617/626-1250, website: www.state.ma.us/dem/forparks.htm.

## 8 LEOMINSTER FOREST ROADS LOOP

**5.5 mi/3 hrs**

**in Leominster State Forest in Westminster, Princeton, and Leominster**

This loop of approximately 5.5 miles largely follows old forest roads through the southern half of Leominster State Forest, making it particularly fun on cross-country skis or a mountain bike. I've skied this loop and other roads in here many times; I especially enjoy coming to this state forest in winter. There are small hills along these roads—nothing that is difficult to hike, but which can make skiing or biking moderately difficult.

From the parking lot, cross the picnic area and the earthen dike dividing the two halves of Crow Hills Pond. Across the dike, turn right (south), following the trail along the pond and past it about 0.7 mile to the dirt Rocky Pond Road (which is not open to motor vehicles). Cross Rocky Pond Road onto Wolf Rock Road and continue about a half mile. Where the road forks, bear right and then watch for an unmarked footpath diverging left within 0.2 mile (if you reach the state forest boundary near private homes, you've gone too far). Follow that winding, narrow path through the woods—I've seen tracks of deer, rabbit, and other animals here in winter—less than a half mile to Wolf Rock Road and turn right. You descend a steep hill on the road, turn left onto Center Road, and follow it about 1.2 miles to Parmenter Road. Turn left (west), climbing a hill and crossing from Leominster into Princeton, where the road becomes Rocky Pond Road. From the road's high point, continue west for less than a mile to the junction of Rocky Pond Road, Wolf Rock Road, and the trail from Crow Hills Pond; turn right on the trail to return to this hike's start.

Special note: Short sections of this loop follow hiking trails that would be difficult on a bike. Cyclists might instead begin this loop from the dirt parking area and gate where Rocky Pond Road crosses Route 31, 0.6 mile south of the main parking area described in the directions below. Pedal east on Rocky Pond Road for about 0.4 mile and then turn right onto the wide Wolf Rock Road. A half mile farther, where the road forks, bear left, staying on Wolf Rock, which leads to Center Road and the continuation of this hike.

**User groups:** Hikers, bikers, dogs, skiers, and snowshoers. Dogs must be leashed. No wheelchair facilities. Horses are prohibited. Hunting is allowed in season.

**Access, fees:** From May–October, a $5 parking fee is collected; a season pass costs $35. The parking lot may not always be plowed in winter; call the state forest headquarters for more information.

**Maps:** A free, basic trail map of Leominster State Forest is available at the state forest headquarters or at the Massachusetts Division of State Parks and Recreation website (see below). The *Mount Wachusett and Leominster State Forest Trail Map* costs $3.95 from New England Cartographics, 413/549-4124 or toll-free 888/995-6277, website: www.necartographics.com. For a topographic area map, request Fitchburg from USGS Map Sales, Federal Center, Box 25286, Denver, CO 80225, 888/ASK-USGS (888/275-8747), website: http://mapping.usgs.gov.

**Directions:** The hike begins from a large parking lot at the Crow Hills Pond Picnic Area along Route 31 on the Westminster/Princeton line, 2.2 miles south of the junction of Routes 31 and 2 and 1.5 miles north of the junction of Routes 31 and 140.

**Contact:** Leominster State Forest, Route 31, Princeton, MA 01541, 978/874-2303. Massachusetts Division of State Parks and Recreation, 251 Causeway St., Suite 600, Boston, MA 02114-2104, 617/626-1250, website: www.state.ma.us/dem/forparks.htm.

# ⑨ MONOOSNOC RIDGE TRAIL
**9 mi/4 hrs**
**in Leominster**

My parents hiked this trail after it opened in 2000 and promptly informed me that it belonged in this book. After a reconnaissance with them, I agreed. This pleasant nine-mile hike across public land in my hometown came about thanks to the Leominster Land Trust, with assistance from the Trustees of Reservations Central Region Office, and the cooperation of the city of Leominster. It traverses hilltops with some ups and downs and occasional views, and makes for a great, quiet stroll in the woods or winter outing on snowshoes. The Leominster Land Trust is working on developing a network of trails and linking the Monoosnoc Ridge Trail and others with the trails of nearby Leominster State Forest (hikes 6–8 in this chapter).

The Monoosnoc Ridge Trail is well marked with blue blazes and signs at the trailheads and road crossings. It intersects other trails and forest roads, so watch for the blazes. You can hike it end to end from either the May Street or West Street trailhead (see Directions below), or hike a section of it by leaving a second vehicle at one of the road crossings. The Wachusett Street and Elm Street crossings divide the trail in approximate thirds, so you can hike about three miles on any one section, or combine two sections for a six-mile walk. The trail begins behind gates across old forest roads at both trailheads.

**User groups:** Hikers, bikers, snowshoers, and dogs. Parts of this trail would be difficult to ski (probably requiring more than a foot of snow coverage). No wheelchair facilities. Horses are prohibited. Hunting is allowed in season.

**Access, fees:** Parking and access are free.

**Maps:** A free trail map is available through the Leominster Land Trust, Trustees of Reservations Central Region Office, and the Leominster Recreation Department (see addresses below). The Leominster Land Trust also plans to install trailhead kiosks with maps. For a topographic area map, request Fitchburg from USGS Map Sales, Federal Center, Box 25286, Denver, CO 80225, 888/ASK-USGS (888/275-8747), website: http://mapping.usgs.gov.

**Directions:** The trail's endpoints are at a turnout at the end of West Street (which begins in the center of Leominster), and at the end of May Street. To reach the latter, drive out Pleasant Street from the center of Leominster to a quarter mile beyond the intersection of Pleasant, Union, and Wachusett Streets in Leominster, turn right onto May Street, and drive 0.1 mile to its end. The trail can be accessed easily from the two paved streets it crosses, Wachusett Street and Elm Street. The northbound trail crosses Elm Street about 0.1 mile (or less) west of the power lines crossing the street, and enters the woods southbound about 0.2 mile west of the power lines. The trail crosses Wachusett Street less than 0.1 mile west of a small reservoir. It also crosses the dirt, upper portion of Granite Street, which can be walked from the end of the pavement. For directions to these streets, see a road map of Leominster.

**Contact:** Leominster Land Trust, 14 Monument Square, Suite 300, Leominster, MA 01453, 978/537-7451. Trustees of Reservations Central Region Office, Doyle Reservation, 325 Lindell Ave., Leominster, MA 01453-5414, 978/840-4446, website: www.thetrustees.org. Leominster Recreation Department, 978/534-7529.

## 🔟 WACHUSETT MOUNTAIN: BALANCED ROCK

**0.6 mi/0.5 hr**

**in Wachusett Mountain State Reservation in Princeton**

Balanced Rock is a glacial-erratic boulder that well lives up to its name. Pick up the Midstate Trail's yellow triangular blazes from the parking lot, behind and to the right of the lodge. Here the trail is also known as the Balanced Rock Trail. Follow it, climbing gently, for 0.3 mile to Balanced Rock. To finish this hike, return the way you came. Hikers looking for a bit more of an outing can continue on the Midstate Trail to the Wachusett summit via the Semuhenna and Harrington Trails and then descend the Old Indian Trail back to the Mid-

state to return—a loop of several miles. Consult the map and inquire at the visitor center for specific distances.

**User groups:** Hikers, snowshoers, and dogs. Dogs must be leashed. No wheelchair facilities. This trail is not suitable for skis. Bikes and horses are prohibited. Hunting is allowed in season.

**Access, fees:** A daily parking fee of $2 is collected from mid-May–mid-October.

**Maps:** A free contour map of hiking trails is available at the visitor center or at the Massachusetts Division of State Parks and Recreation website (see below). The *Northern Berkshires/Southwestern Massachusetts/Wachusett Mountain* costs $5.95 in paper from the Appalachian Mountain Club, 800/262-4455, website: www.outdoors.org. The *Mount Wachusett and Leominster State Forest Trail Map* is $3.95 from New England Cartographics, 413/549-4124 or toll-free 888/995-6277, website: www.necartographics.com. For topographic area maps, request Sterling and Fitchburg from USGS Map Sales, Federal Center, Box 25286, Denver, CO 80225, 888/ASK-USGS (888/275-8747), website: http://mapping.usgs.gov.

**Directions:** From Route 140, 2.2 miles south of the junction of Routes 140 and 2 in Westminster and 1.8 miles north of the junction of Routes 140 and 31, turn onto Mile Hill Road, following signs to the Wachusett Mountain Ski Area. Drive a mile, turn right into the ski area parking lot, and then cross to the rear of the lot, behind the lodge. The Wachusett Mountain State Reservation Visitor Center is farther up Mile Hill Road.

**Contact:** Wachusett Mountain State Reservation, Mountain Rd., P.O. Box 248, Princeton, MA 01541, 978/464-2987. Massachusetts Division of State Parks and Recreation, 251 Causeway St., Suite 600, Boston, MA 02114-2104, 617/626-1250, website: www.state.ma.us/dem/forparks.htm.

## 11 WACHUSETT MOUNTAIN: PINE HILL TRAIL

**2 mi/1.5 hrs**

**in Wachusett Mountain State Reservation in Princeton**

At 2,006 feet and the biggest hill in central Massachusetts, Wachusett may be better known for its downhill ski area. But the state reservation has a fairly extensive network of fine hiking trails, including a section of the Midstate Trail that passes over the summit. The summit offers views in all directions—on a clear day, you can see Mount Monadnock (Central and Southern New Hampshire chapter, hikes 19–20) to the north and the Boston skyline 40 miles to the east. Trail junctions are marked with signs. The Pine Hill Trail is a steep, rocky climb that could be dangerous in snowy or icy conditions.

From the visitor center parking lot, follow the Bicentennial Trail about 0.1 mile to the first trail branching off to the right, the Pine Hill Trail—actually an old ski trail and the most direct route to the summit, about a half mile. The trail ascends at a moderate grade over fairly rocky terrain. After checking out the views from various spots on the broad summit, cross to its southwest corner and look for the Harrington Trail sign. Descending the Harrington, you soon cross the paved summit road; after reentering the woods, take a short side path left off the Harrington to enjoy a long view west over the sparsely populated hills and valleys of central Massachusetts. Backtrack and descend the Harrington to the Link Trail, turning left. Turn right onto the Mountain House Trail, descend briefly, and then bear left onto the Loop Trail, which descends to the Bicentennial. Turn left for the visitor center.

**User groups:** Hikers and dogs. Dogs must be leashed. No wheelchair facilities. This trail would be difficult to snowshoe or ski. Bikes and horses are prohibited. Hunting is allowed in season.

**Access, fees:** A daily parking fee of $2 is collected from mid-May–mid-October.

**Maps:** A free contour map of hiking trails is available at the visitor center at the Massachusetts Division of State Parks and Recreation website (see below). The *Northern Berkshires/Southwestern Massachusetts/Wachusett Mountain* map costs $5.95 in paper from the Appalachian Mountain Club, 800/262-4455, website: www.outdoors.org. The *Mount Wachusett and Leominster State Forest Trail Map* is $3.95 from New England Cartographics, 413/549-4124 or toll-free 888/995-6277, website: www.necartographics.com. For topographic area maps, request Sterling and Fitchburg from USGS Map Sales, Federal Center, Box 25286, Denver, CO 80225, 888/ASK-USGS (888/275-8747), website: http://mapping.usgs.gov.

**Directions:** From Route 140, 2.2 miles south of the junction of Routes 140 and 2 in Westminster and 1.8 miles north of the junction of Routes 140 and 31, turn onto Mile Hill Road, following signs to the Wachusett Mountain State Reservation Visitor Center.

**Contact:** Wachusett Mountain State Reservation, Mountain Rd., P.O. Box 248, Princeton, MA 01541, 978/464-2987. Massachusetts Division of State Parks and Recreation, 251 Causeway St., Suite 600, Boston, MA 02114-2104, 617/626-1250, website: www.state.ma.us/dem/forparks.htm.

## 12 WACHUSETT MOUNTAIN LOOP

**5 mi/3 hrs**

**in Wachusett Mountain State Reservation in Princeton**

See the trail notes for the Wachusett Mountain: Pine Hill Trail hike for more description about Wachusett Mountain. This hike takes a much more circuitous—and in many respects more enjoyable—route around the mountain than the previous hike, taking advantage of the extensive trail network here. Although sections of this route are somewhat rocky and steep for brief stretches, it's not very difficult, ascending about 700 feet in elevation. I've run it numerous times, and on parts of this loop you can escape the crowds that congregate at the summit and on the trails nearer to the visitor center. You can easily shorten or lengthen this hike as well; check out the trail map and improvise from this description. A scenic alternative is the Jack Frost Trail, which passes through dense hemlock forest.

From the visitor center parking lot, follow the Bicentennial Trail for about a mile as it contours around the mountain's base, passing three trail junctions, then bear left onto the High Meadow Trail. Follow it across an open meadow and then back into the woods again before reaching Echo Lake. Stay to the left on the gravel road beside the lake for about 0.1 mile, turn left on the Echo Lake Trail, and follow it less than a half mile to a parking lot. Crossing the small lot, pick up the Stage Coach Trail, climbing steadily up an old carriage road, which narrows to a footpath. After more than a half mile, bear right on the Harrington Trail. It crosses West Road, then the Administration Road, before suddenly growing much steeper as it makes a direct line for the summit. But right before that steep part begins, turn left on the Semuhenna Trail, staying on it for about a half mile. Cross the paved summit road, reenter the woods, and then immediately turn right on the West Side Trail. You're on that path for less than a half mile before turning right again on the Old Indian Trail, the steepest part of this hike, as you climb to the summit, passing a ski area chairlift station right before reaching the top. Cross the summit to the paved road that heads down, follow it about 100 feet, and then bear right into the woods on the Mountain House Trail. Descend about a quarter mile, turn left, continue another quarter mile or less, and turn left again on the Loop Trail, descending over rocks to the Bicentennial Trail. Turn left for the visitor center.

**User groups:** Hikers, snowshoers, and dogs. Dogs must be leashed. No wheelchair facilities. This trail is not suitable for skis. Bikes and horses are prohibited. Hunting is allowed in season.

**Access, fees:** A daily parking fee of $2 is collected from mid-May–mid-October.

**Maps:** A free contour map of hiking trails is available at the visitor center or at the Massachusetts Division of State Parks and Recreation website (see below). The *Northern Berkshires/Southwestern Massachusetts/Wachusett Mountain* map costs $5.95 in paper from the Appalachian Mountain Club, 800/262-4455, website: www.outdoors.org. The *Mount Wachusett and Leominster State Forest Trail Map* is $3.95 from New England Cartographics, 413/549-4124 or toll-free 888/995-6277, website: www.necartographics.com. For topographic area maps, request Sterling and Fitchburg from USGS Map Sales, Federal Center, Box 25286, Denver, CO 80225, 888/ASK-USGS (888/275-8747), website: http://mapping.usgs.gov.

**Directions:** From Route 140, 2.2 miles south of the junction of Routes 140 and 2 in Westminster and 1.8 miles north of the junction of Routes 140 and 31, turn onto Mile Hill Road, following signs to the Wachusett Mountain State Reservation Visitor Center.

**Contact:** Wachusett Mountain State Reservation, Mountain Rd., P.O. Box 248, Princeton, MA 01541, 978/464-2987. Massachusetts Division of State Parks and Recreation, 251 Causeway St., Suite 600, Boston, MA 02114-2104, 617/626-1250, website: www.state.ma.us/dem/forparks.htm.

## 🔢 REDEMPTION ROCK TO WACHUSETT MOUNTAIN

**1.8 mi/1 hr**

**in Princeton**

When I was a young boy, an uncle and aunt took my brothers, a sister, and me to Redemption Rock, a massive, flat-topped granite boulder just off the roadside. We climbed around on it, thinking we were on some great adventure—which, of course, we were. Years later, I took my young nephew and niece to Redemption Rock and let them have their own little adventure. Legend has it that a Concord settler named John Hoar sat atop this boulder with members of a band of King Phillip's Indians in 1676 to negotiate the release of Mary Rowlandson, wife of the minister in the nearby town of Lancaster, whom the Indians abducted and held captive for 11 weeks.

Redemption Rock is a fun spot for young children, and the walk through the woods to the base of Wachusett Mountain and back follows a fairly quiet Midstate Trail stretch where you might see a deer or grouse. After exploring Redemption Rock, which sits beside the parking area, follow the Midstate Trail's yellow triangular blazes into the woods. Watch closely for the blazes; several side trails branch off the Midstate. It proceeds generally westward through the woods, climbing slightly and traversing some rocky trail stretches and some wet areas, reaching Mountain Road and the parking lot for the Wachusett Mountain Ski Area in 0.9 mile. Turn around and return the way you came, or combine this with the Wachusett Mountain: Balanced Rock hike, which begins across the ski area parking lot.

**User groups:** Hikers, snowshoers, and dogs. No wheelchair facilities. The trail is not suitable for bikes, horses, or skis. Hunting is allowed in season on the Midstate Trail, but is prohibited at Redemption Rock, which is a quarter-mile preserve owned by The Trustees of Reservations.

**Access, fees:** Parking and access are free. Redemption Rock is open to the public from sunrise–sunset year-round.

**Maps:** The *Mount Wachusett and Leominster State Forest Trail Map* is $3.95 from New England Cartographics, 413/549-4124 or toll-free 888/995-6277, website: www.necartographics.com. For topographic area maps, request Fitchburg and Sterling from USGS Map Sales, Federal Center, Box 25286, Denver, CO 80225, 888/ASK-USGS (888/275-8747), website: http://mapping.usgs.gov.

**Directions:** The hike begins from the small parking lot at Redemption Rock along Route 140 in Princeton, 3.1 miles south of the junction of Routes 140 and 2 in Westminster and 0.9 mile north of the junction of Routes 140 and 31 in Princeton.

**Contact:** The Trustees of Reservations Central Region Office, Doyle Reservation, 325 Lindell Ave., Leominster, MA 01453-5414, 978/840-4446, website: www.thetrustees.org.

## 14 WACHUSETT MEADOW TO WACHUSETT MOUNTAIN
**6.2 mi/3.5 hrs**
**in Princeton**

Much of this Midstate Trail stretch is relatively easy, ascending less than 1,000 feet in elevation, much of that over the steep final 0.3-mile climb to the Wachusett Mountain summit, where there are long views in every direction. Visitors to Wachusett Meadow, a 977-acre nature preserve, might want to check out the loop of about 1.5 miles over Brown Hill, where the open crown affords 360-degree views. You also shouldn't miss the 300-year-old Crocker maple, one of the largest sugar maples in the country, with a trunk circumference of more than 15 feet. It sits on the west edge of the meadow, a very short detour off this hike's route, and it is guaranteed to awe children.

From the parking area, walk north into the meadow on the Mountain Trail and then turn left in the middle of the meadow at post six, heading for the woods and reaching a junction with the Midstate Trail about 0.2 mile from the parking lot. Turn right (north), following the Midstate over easy terrain through the woods. The trail crosses a dirt road about a mile from the hike's start, passes over a small hill, and then crosses paved Westminster Road at 1.8 miles. After crossing a field, the trail enters the woods again, ascending a low hill and passing just below the summit. (You can bushwhack a short distance off trail to the hilltop and see a wind farm of windmills, then double back to the trail.) After crossing paved Administration Road, the Midstate Trail—here also called the Harrington Trail—reaches a junction with the Semuhenna Trail one mile from Westminster Road. The Semuhenna/Midstate turns left, but this hike continues straight up the Harrington another 0.3 mile to the Wachusett Mountain summit. Hike back the way you came.

Special note: To avoid backtracking, and for a somewhat shorter hike, shuttle vehicles to Wachusett Meadow and the Wachusett Mountain State Reservation Visitor Center and do this hike one-way; then descend the Pine Hill Trail and Bicentennial Trail to the Wachusett Mountain Visitor Center, as described in the Redemption Rock to Wachusett Mountain hike. **User groups:** Hikers and snowshoers. No wheelchair facilities. This trail is not suitable for horses. Bikes, dogs, hunting, and skis are prohibited. **Access, fees:** A fee of $4 per adult and $3 per child age 3–12 and seniors is charged at Wachusett Meadow to nonmembers of the Massachusetts Audubon Society. The Wachusett Meadow Visitor Center trails are open dawn–dusk, Tuesday–Sunday and on Monday holidays. The Nature Center is open Tuesday–Saturday, 10 A.M.–2 P.M. A daily parking fee of $2 is collected from mid-May–mid-October at Wachusett Mountain State Reservation.

**Maps:** A map of Wachusett Meadow is available at an information board beside the parking lot. A free contour map of hiking trails in the Wachusett Mountain State Reservation is available at the state reservation or at the Massachusetts Division of State Parks and Recreation website (see below). The *Northern Berkshires/Southwestern Massachusetts/Wachusett Mountain* map costs $5.95 in paper from the Appalachian Mountain Club, 800/262-4455, website: www.outdoors.org. The *Mount Wachusett and Leominster State Forest Trail Map* is $3.95 from New England Cartographics, 413/549-4124 or toll-free 888/995-6277, website: www.necartographics.com. For a topographic area map, request Sterling from USGS Map Sales, Federal Center, Box 25286, Denver, CO 80225, 888/ASK-USGS (888/275-8747), website: http://mapping.usgs.gov.

**Directions:** From the junction of Routes 62 and 31 in Princeton center, drive west on Route 62 for a half mile and turn right onto Goodnow Road at a sign for the Wachusett Meadow Sanctuary. Continue a mile to the end of the paved road and park at the sanctuary visitor center.

**Contact:** Massachusetts Audubon Society Wachusett Meadow Wildlife Sanctuary, 113 Goodnow Rd., Princeton, MA 01541, 978/464-2712, email: wachusett@massaudubon.org. Massachusetts Audubon Society, 208 South Great Rd., Lincoln, MA 01773, 781/259-9500 or 800/AUDUBON, website: www.massaudubon.org. Wachusett Mountain State Reservation, Mountain Rd., P.O. Box 248, Princeton, MA 01541, 978/464-2987. Massachusetts Division of State Parks and Recreation, 251 Causeway St., Suite 600, Boston, MA 02114-2104, 617/626-1250, website: www.state.ma.us/dem/forparks.htm.

## 15 MOUNT HOLYOKE

**3.2 mi/2 hrs**

**in Skinner State Park in Hadley**

Along the up-and-down ridge of 878-foot Mount Holyoke, the Summit House stands out prominently, easily visible to I-91 motorists several miles to the west. Although mostly wooded, this rugged ridgeline has several overlooks that afford splendid views west to the Connecticut Valley and the Berkshires, and some views southward. This hike climbs about 700 feet in elevation.

Follow the Metacomet-Monadnock Trail east from the road, immediately climbing a steep hillside; the trail soon swings north and ascends the ridge, reaching the first views in just over a half mile. At 1.6 miles, the trail passes by the historic Summit House, once a fashionable mountaintop hotel and now part of the state park; it's open weekends from Memorial Day to Columbus Day for tours and programs; there are picnic grounds. The Connecticut Valley views from here are excellent. You can return the way you came or continue over the summit, crossing the paved Mountain Road and turning right (south) in Taylor's Notch onto the red-blazed Dry Brook Trail. Follow it down the small valley, trending to the southwest and finally to the west and back to your vehicle.

**User groups:** Hikers, snowshoers, and dogs. Dogs must be leashed. No wheelchair facilities. This trail is not suitable for bikes, horses, or skis. Hunting is prohibited.

**Access, fees:** Parking and access are free.

**Maps:** A free trail map of Skinner State Park is available at the Halfway House on Mountain Road (off Route 47) when a staff person is there; at the Notch Visitor Center on Route 116, where the Metacomet-Monadnock Trail crosses the road and enters Holyoke Range State Park in Amherst; or at the Massachusetts Division of State Parks and Recreation website (see below). The *Blue Hills Reservation/Mount Tom/Holyoke Range* map costs $5.95 in paper from the Appalachian Mountain Club, 800/262-4455, website: www.outdoors.org. The *Holyoke Range/Skinner State Park Trail Map (Western Section)* costs $3.95 from New England Cartographics, 413/549-4124 or toll-free 888/995-6277, website: www.necartographics.com. For a topographic area map, request Mount Holyoke from USGS Map Sales, Federal Center, Box 25286, Denver, CO 80225, 888/ASK-USGS (888/275-8747), website: http://mapping.usgs.gov.

**Directions:** From the junction of Routes 47 and 9 in Hadley, drive south on Route 47 for 4.9 miles (you'll see the Summit House on the Mount Holyoke ridge straight ahead). Across from the Hockanum Cemetery, turn left, continue 0.1 mile, and park at the roadside where the white blazes of the Metacomet-Monadnock Trail enter the woods on the right. Or from the junction of Routes 47 and 116 in South Hadley, drive north on Route 47 for 2.7 miles, turn right at Hockanum Cemetery, and then continue 0.1 mile to the trailhead.

**Contact:** Skinner State Park, Route 47, Box 91, Hadley, MA 01035, 413/586-0350 or 413/253-

2883. Massachusetts Division of State Parks and Recreation, 251 Causeway St., Suite 600, Boston, MA 02114-2104, 617/626-1250, website: www.state.ma.us/dem/forparks.htm.

## 16 PURGATORY CHASM
**0.5 mi/0.5 hr**
**in Purgatory Chasm State Reservation in Sutton**

On this adventure, you scramble over rocks into the mouth of a chasm stretching a quarter mile before you, its floor littered with huge boulders. The air is often at least 10 degrees cooler than in the parking lot you've just left behind. Rock walls rise as high at 70 feet on either side of this narrow defile, which geologists theorize was created by catastrophic force after melting glacial ice suddenly released torrents of flood water that shattered this gap through the granite bedrock. As if clinging to its prehistoric roots, Purgatory Chasm today is known to harbor pockets of ice into May and June. Although the scrambling can be difficult for people who are uncomfortable moving over rocks, this half-mile loop is mostly flat and a good one for children.

From the information kiosk, walk toward the pavilion, but before reaching it turn right where the blue-blazed Chasm Loop Trail leads down through the chasm; you may see rock climbers on the walls. At the chasm's far end, poke your head inside the aptly named Coffin, a tight space among the boulders to the trail's right. Then turn left and follow the Chasm Loop Trail's blue blazes uphill onto the rim above the chasm, past deep cracks that have been given such names as Fat Man's Misery and the Corn Crib. The trail leads back to the parking lot.

**User groups:** Hikers and dogs. Dogs must be leashed. No wheelchair facilities. The trail may be difficult to snowshoe, depending on snow conditions, and is not suitable for bikes, horses, or skis. Hunting is allowed in season.

**Access, fees:** Parking and access are free. Purgatory Chasm State Reservation is open sunrise–sunset daily, year-round.

**Maps:** A free map of hiking trails is available at the information kiosk and at the Massachusetts Division of State Parks and Recreation website (see below). For topographic area maps, request Milford and Worcester South from USGS Map Sales, Federal Center, Box 25286, Denver, CO 80225, 888/ASK-USGS (888/275-8747), website: http://mapping.usgs.gov.
**Directions:** From Route 146 in Northbridge, take the exit for Purgatory Road. Turn west on Purgatory Road and drive 0.6 mile to parking on the left, beside a pavilion and information kiosk.
**Contact:** Purgatory Chasm State Reservation, Purgatory Rd., Sutton, MA 01590, 508/234-3733. Massachusetts Division of State Parks and Recreation, 251 Causeway St., Suite 600, Boston, MA 02114-2104, 617/626-1250, website: www.state.ma.us/dem/forparks.htm.

## 17 MIDSTATE TRAIL LOOP
**6.5 mi/3.5 hrs**

**in Douglas State Forest in Douglas**
This loop, mostly on forest roads, uses the Midstate Trail to explore the big piece of Douglas State Forest that lies south of Route 16. The state forest also extends north of Route 16 and is worth exploring further. The loop sections that employ forest roads are easy or moderately difficult for mountain bikers; however, the stretches that follow a rougher trail are more difficult. The Midstate is fairly flat but crosses some streams and gets rocky in places. It's a well-blazed trail with yellow triangles, yet most other forest roads are not marked; use the map.

The Midstate Trail is accessed via the Coffeehouse Loop's southern arm, a forest road beginning at the south end of the parking lot. When you reach the Midstate, turn right (north) onto it. The Midstate makes several turns and, three miles out, reaches a T intersection at a forest road; you'll probably hear traffic on Route 16 to the left. This loop turns right, following the forest road south. At a fork, bear right and cross the dirt Southwest Main Street

(where, if you turned left, you would shortly reach the intersection of Cedar Road and Wallum Street). The next intersection reconnects you with the Midstate Trail; backtrack on the Midstate southbound to return.
**User groups:** Hikers, bikers, dogs, horses, skiers, and snowshoers. Dogs must be leashed. No wheelchair facilities. Hunting is allowed in season.
**Access, fees:** A daily parking fee of $5 is collected from mid-May–mid-October. The fee can be avoided by accessing the state forest at other roadside parking areas. Consult the map for other access points.
**Maps:** A free trail map and informational brochure are available at the park entrance or at the Massachusetts Division of State Parks and Recreation website (see below). For a topographic area map, request Webster from USGS Map Sales, Federal Center, Box 25286, Denver, CO 80225, 888/ASK-USGS (888/275-8747), website: http://mapping.usgs.gov.
**Directions:** From I-395, take Exit 2 for Route 16 east. Drive 5.1 miles and turn right onto Cedar Road (there may be no street sign) at the sign for Douglas State Forest. Drive 1.8 miles to a crossroads at Southwest Main Street and proceed straight through onto Wallum Street. At 0.9 mile farther, turn right into the state forest and drive 0.7 mile to an information panel where a box contains maps. Bear right and continue a short distance to a parking lot.
**Contact:** Douglas State Forest, 107 Wallum Lake Rd., Douglas, MA 01516, 508/476-7872. Massachusetts Division of State Parks and Recreation, 251 Causeway St., Suite 600, Boston, MA 02114-2104, 617/626-1250, website: www.state.ma.us/dem/forparks.htm.

## 18 COFFEEHOUSE LOOP
**2.2 mi/1.5 hrs**

**in Douglas State Forest in Douglas**
This relatively flat trail makes an easy loop through peaceful woods, with the terrain growing slightly rocky in some places. Easy to follow, with trail junctions clearly signed, this hike

also offers access to a longer outing on the Midstate Trail for those with extra time and energy. The loop begins at the parking lot's north end, eventually reaches and coincides for a short distance with the Midstate Trail southbound, then diverges left from the Midstate Trail and returns to the parking lot via a forest road.

**User groups:** Hikers, dogs, skiers, and snowshoers. Dogs must be leashed. No wheelchair facilities. Bikes and horses are prohibited on part of this loop. Hunting is allowed in season.

**Access, fees:** A daily parking fee of $5 is collected from mid-May–mid-October. The fee can be avoided by accessing the state forest at other roadside parking areas. Consult the map for other access points.

**Maps:** A free trail map and informational brochure are available at the park entrance or at the Massachusetts Division of State Parks and Recreation website (see below). For a topo-graphic area map, request Webster from USGS Map Sales, Federal Center, Box 25286, Denver, CO 80225, 888/ASK-USGS (888/275-8747), website: http://mapping.usgs.gov.

**Directions:** From I-395, take Exit 2 for Route 16 east. Drive 5.1 miles and turn right onto Cedar Road (there may be no street sign) at the sign for Douglas State Forest. Drive 1.8 miles to a crossroads at Southwest Main Street and proceed straight through onto Wallum Street. At 0.9 mile farther, turn right into the state forest and drive 0.7 mile to an information panel where a box contains maps. Bear right and continue a short distance to a parking lot.

**Contact:** Douglas State Forest, 107 Wallum Lake Rd., Douglas, MA 01516, 508/476-7872. Massachusetts Division of State Parks and Recreation, 251 Causeway St., Suite 600, Boston, MA 02114-2104, 617/626-1250, website: www.state.ma.us/dem/forparks.htm.

## Chapter 10

© MICHAEL LANZA

# Greater Boston and Cape Cod

# Greater Boston and Cape Cod

The Greater Boston area has a tremendous variety of hiking. The rocky and scenic Blue Hills and Middlesex Fells are oases of quiet, wooded hills amid metropolitan Boston, making them rare and cherished recreation areas. The unique coastal trails of the Cape Cod National Seashore put hikers in unusual microenvironments. Premier state lands like Bradley Palmer State Park and Myles Standish State Forest are sprawling, four-season recreation centers for thousands of local residents. Likewise, the Trustees of Reservations properties—Noanet Woodlands, Rocky Woods, and World's End—provide valuable local places to walk, exercise, and sightsee. Maudslay State Park and Walden Pond State Park Reservation not only are great places to walk, but preserve invaluable pieces of local history. Great Meadows, Plum Island, and Caratunk are on the must-see destinations list of many bird-watchers. And to keep things interesting, this chapter even tosses in a few paved recreation paths.

Winter weather is erratic but generally milder in this area than much of New England, opening up opportunities for visiting many of these places year-round without having to deal with snow or extreme cold. More commonly, visitors must deal with wind and, in certain seasons, biting insects and traffic. Do a little research before you go. Regulations vary widely under these different land-management agencies; be aware of and respect them always.

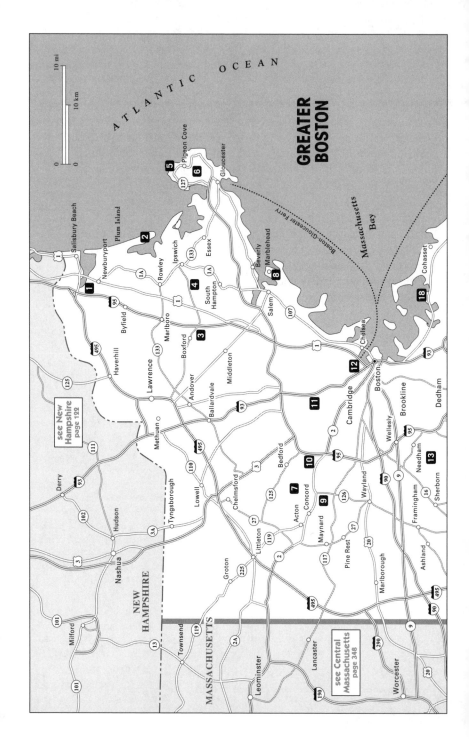

ATLANTIC OCEAN

GREATER BOSTON

Massachusetts Bay

Boston-Gloucester Ferry

Pigeon Cove

see New Hampshire page 122

see Central Massachusetts page 348

NEW HAMPSHIRE

MASSACHUSETTS

Salisbury Beach
Plum Island
Newburyport
Rowley
Ipswich
Essex
Gloucester
Marblehead
Beverly
Salem
Cohasset
Byfield
Marlboro
South Hampton
Boxford
Haverhill
Lawrence
Andover
Middleton
Ballardvale
Chelsea
Boston
Cambridge
Brookline
Dedham
Methuen
Tyngsborough
Chelmsford
Bedford
Wellesly
Needham
Sherborn
Derry
Hudson
Lowell
Concord
Acton
Wayland
Framingham
Ashland
Nashua
Littleton
Maynard
Pine Rest
Marlborough
Milford
Groton
Townsend
Lancaster
Worcester
Leominster

368    Foghorn Outdoors New England Hiking

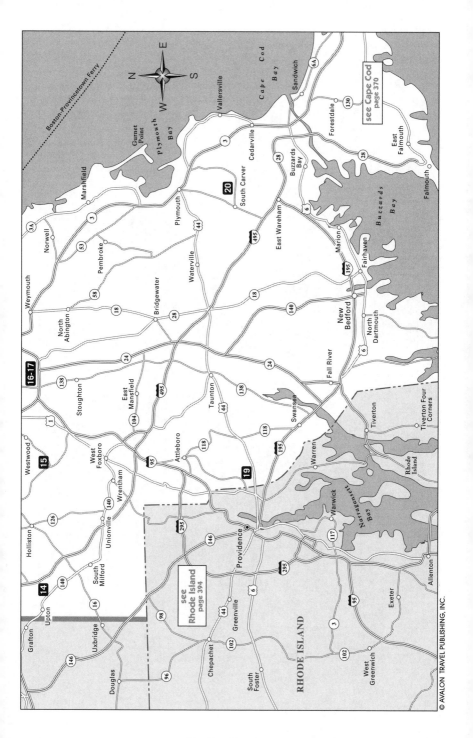

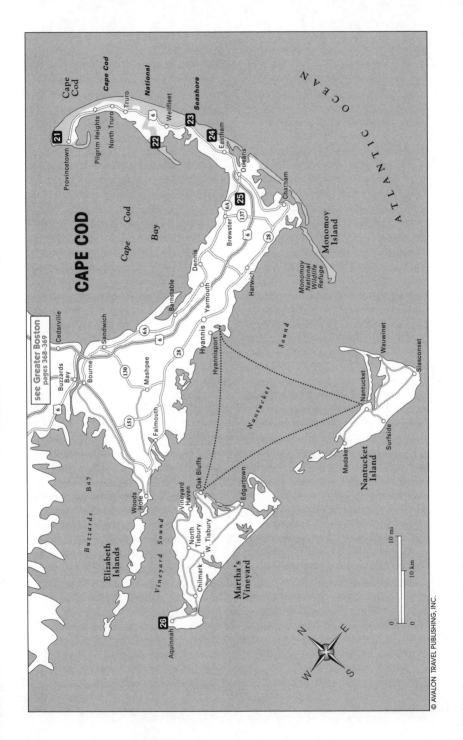

© AVALON TRAVEL PUBLISHING, INC.

# ◼ MAUDSLAY STATE PARK
**2.5 mi/1.5 hrs**
**in Newburyport**

    This 480-acre park on the Merrimack River was the 19th-century estate of the Moseleys, one of New England's wealthiest families. George Washington visited this area in 1789, and a regular ferry crossed the river here in the 17th century. Today you can hike trails through its many gardens and one of the largest naturally occurring mountain laurel stands in eastern Massachusetts, and stroll grounds where more flowers and plants bloom than I could begin to list. Mid-June is the time to catch the brilliant white flowers of the mountain laurel. The park sponsors numerous educational and recreational events. This hike is relatively flat.

    From the parking lot, walk past the headquarters and turn right at a green gate onto Hedge Drive, a dirt road lined with trees and hedges. Near a small building, turn left and follow that road a short distance to its intersection with another road. You are across from the vegetable garden. Turn left, walk past buildings, and enter the Italian Garden. Walk straight through it onto a path that passes an old well, cross the dirt Main Road, and walk through a courtyard to the Merrimack River Trail, which is marked by blue, white, and green blazes. Straight ahead is the Merrimack River. Turn right onto the Merrimack River Trail, following it along the hilltop and down into woods. After crossing two brooks on wooden bridges, the trail bears left onto another road and crosses over a dam at the end of the Flowering Pond. Here you reach the Laurel Walk, where the Merrimack River Trail branches right and left. The area to the left is closed from November 1–March 31; take the right branch during these months. Otherwise, turn left and follow the Merrimack River Trail along the riverbank. When it meets the Castle Hill Trail (and the Merrimack River Trail's other branch), turn left and stay with the Merrimack River Trail until you reach the end of a tree-lined road on

your right; the Castle Hill Trail follows it up onto Castle Hill, where there are views of the state park and this corner of the Merrimack Valley. Over the hilltop, turn right onto one road, quickly left onto another, and then right onto Line Road. It leads straight onto the Main Road (backtracking over the Merrimack River Trail's right branch). Take the stone bridge over the Flowering Pond, turn left onto the Pasture Trail, and follow it back to the parking lot.

**User groups:** Hikers, bikers, dogs, horses, skiers, and snowshoers. Dogs must be leashed. No wheelchair facilities. Hunting is prohibited.

**Access, fees:** A daily parking fee of $2 is collected year-round. The park is open from 8 A.M.–sunset. Picnickers are welcome. A special-use permit is required for weddings, family reunions, and school groups.

**Maps:** A free, good trail map, including historical information and the seasons for viewing various park flora in bloom, is available at park headquarters (see address below). A basic map is also available at the Massachusetts Division of State Parks and Recreation website (see below). For a topographic area map, request Newburyport from USGS Map Sales, Federal Center, Box 25286, Denver, CO 80225, 888/ASK-USGS (888/275-8747), website: http://mapping.usgs.gov.

**Directions:** From I-95, take Exit 57 in Newburyport for Route 113 west. Drive a half mile and then turn right onto Hoyt's Lane/Gypsy Lane. At the road's end, turn right (in front of the park headquarters) onto Pine Hill Road and right again into the parking lot.

**Contact:** Maudslay State Park, Curzon's Mill Rd., Newburyport, MA 01950, 978/465-7223. Massachusetts Division of State Parks and Recreation, 251 Causeway St., Suite 600, Boston, MA 02114-2104, 617/626-1250, website: www.state.ma.us/dem/forparks.htm.

## ② BAR HEAD DRUMLIN/ PLUM ISLAND

**3 mi/1.5 hrs**

**in Sandy Point State Reservation in Ipswich**

Ⓕ This easy hike combines a walk along a sandy beach and a rocky shoreline with a hike onto the glacial drumlin, an oval mound of earth deposited by a receding glacier 10,000 years ago. Today several plant and animal species rarely found near a sandy beach thrive on Bar Head Drumlin. Fifty feet high and covering 15 acres, the drumlin is shrinking under constant erosion by the ocean. Nearby, the sprawling Parker River National Wildlife Refuge is home to numerous bird species in summer, including cormorants, herons, kingfishers, and ducks. The refuge also offers hiking opportunities. Nearly across from the parking area is an observation tower with a view of the refuge's marshlands. Bring bug repellent in summer—there are lots of biting insects, especially on the overgrown road along the refuge boundary. Inspect your skin and clothing afterward for ticks.

From the parking lot, pass through a gate onto the beach and turn right for the drumlin. Below the eroded cliffs of Bar Head, you walk a rock-strewn beach. Beyond the drumlin, the beach again becomes sandy. Follow the waterline around to the right until you reach a fence at the wildlife refuge boundary. Turn right and follow an overgrown road along the refuge boundary to a parking lot for the state reservation. Cross the lot to an unmarked, overgrown trail leading up onto Bar Head. Although the trees and brush atop the drumlin are too dense and high to afford views, a few side trails to the cliffs permit beach and ocean views. The trail leads over Bar Head and back to the beach near the boardwalk where you started.

**User groups:** Hikers and snowshoers. No wheelchair facilities. This trail rarely receives enough snow for skis or snowshoes and is not suitable for horses. Bicycles are permitted only on the refuge road and in designated parking areas.

Dogs are prohibited. Waterfowl hunting is permitted during fall and winter in designated salt marsh areas, and in fall, there is a controlled deer hunt on the island area of the refuge, with hunters chosen by lottery.

**Access, fees:** Open daily sunrise–sunset. Walk only on trails, boardwalks, roads, parking areas, observation areas, and the beach; all other areas, including the dunes, are closed to the public. The beach is closed April 1 through at least July 1, portions possibly through late August, to protect nesting areas for the threatened piping plover. The fee for entering the Parker River National Wildlife Refuge is $5 per vehicle or $2 for anyone entering on foot or bike, year-round. During the warmer months, the refuge often fills to capacity and the entrance closes temporarily, even to visitors on foot. Arrive early to avoid this inconvenience.

**Maps:** No map is really needed for this hike, but two different maps are available at the refuge's website (see below). For topographic area maps, request Ipswich and Newburyport from USGS Map Sales, Federal Center, Box 25286, Denver, CO 80225, 888/ASK-USGS (888/275-8747), website: http://mapping.usgs.gov.

**Directions:** From Route 95 take exit 57 and travel east on Route 113, then continue straight onto Route 1A South to the intersection with Rolfe's Lane for a total of 3.5 miles. Turn left onto Rolfe's Lane and travel 0.5 mile to its end. Turn right onto the Plum Island Turnpike and travel 2.0 miles crossing the Sgt. Donald Wilkinson Bridge to Plum Island. Take your first right onto Sunset Drive and travel 0.5 mile to the refuge entrance. From the entrance, drive 6.5 miles to a dirt lot at the end of the road and park.

**Contact:** Parker River National Wildlife Refuge, 6 Plum Island Turnpike, Newburyport, MA 01950, 978/465-5753 or 800/877-8339 for the hearing impaired, website: http://parkerriver.fws.gov/. Refuge headquarters is located at the north end of Plum Island near the Newburyport Harbor Lighthouse and is open Monday–Friday, 8 A.M.–4:30 P.M., except on federal holidays. U.S. Fish and Wildlife Service, 800/344-WILD, website: www.fws.gov.

# 3 BALD HILL
## 3 mi/2 hrs

**in Boxford State Forest**

Here is yet another sizable chunk of state land on the North Shore with a wealth of trails ideal for many activities. This loop takes you through the forest's southeast corner and over Bald Hill, but there's a lot more to this place worth checking out. You may stumble across old gravestones or home foundations from when this was farmland. This loop largely follows forest roads, is hilly, and the terrain can be rocky and rugged—a challenge on a mountain bike. Many trail intersections have numbered markers that correspond to numbers on the trail map. The forest tends toward the soggy, meaning a plague of mosquitoes in spring and early summer. This is a primo mountain biking destination during summer and fall, but avoid digging up the trails with bikes in mud season.

From the turnout, head past the gate onto the dirt Bald Hill Road. Past Crooked Pond, bear left at Intersection 14, and left again at Intersection 13. Farther along, turn right, climbing fairly steeply up Bald Hill. On its open summit, cross the field to the left and pick up a forest road heading back down. Bear right and you'll pass a stone foundation at the former Russell-Hooper farmhouse site (marked by a small sign). Just beyond it, to the right of the trail, is the Russell-Hooper barn site. Follow the trail around to the right. At Intersection 8A, turn right; eventually you follow white blazes. At Intersection 26, turn right again and follow this trail back to Intersection 13.

**User groups:** Hikers, bikers, dogs, horses, skiers, and snowshoers. Dogs must be leashed. No wheelchair facilities. Hunting is allowed in season.

**Access, fees:** Parking and access are free.

**Maps:** A trail map is available at the Massachusetts Division of State Parks and Recreation website (see below).

**Directions:** From I-95 in Boxford, take Exit 51 for Endicott Road. Drive west and turn right onto Middleton Road. After passing Fuller Lane on the right, continue on Middleton Road another 0.8 mile. Park at a roadside turnout on the left.

**Contact:** Boxford State Forest, c/o Harold Parker State Forest, 1951 Turnpike Rd., North Andover, MA 01845-6326, 978/686-3391. Massachusetts Division of State Parks and Recreation, 251 Causeway St., Suite 600, Boston, MA 02114-2104, 617/626-1250, website: www.state.ma.us/dem/forparks.htm.

# 4 BRADLEY PALMER STATE PARK
## 2.5 mi/1.5 hrs

**in Topsfield**

Bradley Palmer was a famous attorney in the early 1900s who represented Sinclair Oil in the Teapot Dome Scandal and President Wilson at the Versailles Peace Conference after World War I. This park, named for Palmer, is a great multiuse recreational area. I lived on the North Shore a number of years ago, and this park was my favorite local place to cross-country ski. Its moderately sloping hills, wide forest roads, and rugged trails also offer very interesting and varied mountain biking and hiking. And the wildlife here might surprise you: Two friends of mine were mountain biking here when an owl with a squirrel in its talons swept just over their heads. This hike merely introduces you to this park; explore it further on your own.

From the parking area, cross the paved road and head onto a broad forest road. Bear left and start climbing Blueberry Hill (a rigorous climb on a bike). Take the third right onto another forest road and then the second left to reach the open hilltop. If you imagine entering the hilltop meadow at six o'clock, cross the hilltop and turn right, toward a road entering the woods at about three o'clock. Watch for a narrower trail exiting left off that road and follow it down a steep hill. Bear right onto another trail, which leads down to the Ipswich

River and land in the Essex County Greenbelt. Turn left along a trail paralleling the river; you'll begin seeing the blue blazes, with a paw print on them, of the Discover Hamilton Trail. Where a footbridge leads right over the river, turn left up a forest road. At a long, wide meadow, turn right and continue onto a forest road back to the park headquarters.

**User groups:** Hikers, bikers, dogs, horses, skiers, and snowshoers. Dogs must be leashed. No wheelchair facilities. Hunting is allowed in season.

**Access, fees:** A daily parking fee of $5 is collected from mid-May–mid-October.

**Maps:** A free trail map is available at the park headquarters or at the Massachusetts Division of State Parks and Recreation website (see below).

**Directions:** From U.S. 1 in Topsfield, turn east onto Ipswich Road (at a traffic light). Drive 1.2 miles and turn right onto Asbury Street. The state park entrance is on the left, a short distance down the road. Park in a dirt area just before the state park headquarters.

**Contact:** Bradley Palmer State Park, Asbury St., Topsfield, MA 01983, 978/887-5931. Massachusetts Division of State Parks and Recreation, 251 Causeway St., Suite 600, Boston, MA 02114-2104, 617/626-1250, website: www.state.ma.us/dem/forparks.htm.

## ⑤ HALIBUT POINT
### 0.5 mi/0.5 hr
**in Halibut Point State Park and Reservation in Rockport**

Halibut Point consists of Halibut Point Reservation and Halibut Point State Park and is jointly managed by The Trustees of Reservations and the state. The state park surrounds the site of the former Babson Farm granite quarry, which operated for nearly a century and is now filled with water, creating a small pond ringed by the sheer cliffs of the quarry walls. I visited late one spring day, when the low sun was highlighting thin clouds, creating beautiful reflections in the pond. The park's name derives from "Haul About Point," the name given to the 50-foot granite cliff at the ocean's edge by sailors tacking around the point to approach Cape Ann.

From the parking lot, cross Gott Avenue, following signs to the park entrance. A short trail through trees leads to the quarry. The park headquarters is to the left. Take the trail that goes around the quarry to the right. You pass a mooring stone—an enormous granite slab sunk underwater that anchors an oak post used as a mooring for fishermen's boats. Turn onto a trail branching to the right, toward the ocean, to reach The Trustees of Reservations property. The shore here is very rocky, an extremely wild place when the surf is high; be sure not to get too close to the water because the riptide is powerful. Walk to the left along the shore and then follow a trail back up toward the quarry. To return, walk around the quarry to the left, which takes you back to the entrance trail.

**User groups:** Hikers and dogs. Dogs must be leashed. No wheelchair facilities. This trail very rarely receives enough snow for skis or snowshoes, and is not suitable for bikes or horses. Hunting is prohibited.

**Access, fees:** Halibut Point is open to the public from sunrise–sunset year-round. From mid-May–mid-October, hours are 8 A.M.–8 P.M. and a $2 fee is charged for parking. For the rest of the year, the park is open at no charge during the daylight hours. The Trustees of Reservations members park for free.

**Maps:** A free trail map is available at the park. A map is also available at the Massachusetts Division of State Parks and Recreation website (see below).

**Directions:** From the junction of Routes 128 and 127, follow Route 127 north (on Eastern Avenue) toward Rockport. After three miles, turn left onto Railroad Avenue, which is still Route 127. After another 2.4 miles, turn right onto Gott Avenue. The parking lot is on the right a short distance up the road.

**Contact:** Halibut Point State Park, Gott Ave.,

Rockport, MA 01966, 978/546-2997. The Trustees of Reservations, Long Hill, 572 Essex St., Beverly, MA 01915-1530, 978/921-1944, website: www.thetrustees.org. Massachusetts Division of State Parks and Recreation, 251 Causeway St., Suite 600, Boston, MA 02114-2104, 617/626-1250, website: www.state.ma.us/dem/forparks.htm.

## 6 DOGTOWN

**8.8 mi/5 hrs**

**in Gloucester and Rockport**

This patch of untamed woods in the heart of Cape Ann has become a favorite among local hikers and mountain bikers for its rugged trails, glacial-erratic boulders scattered through the forest, and the legacy of a wealthy financier named Roger Babson. Earlier in this century, Babson hired stonecutters to carve sayings into rocks here like "Get a Job" and "Never Try Never Win." The old woods roads along this hike carry names but are not maintained thoroughfares for motor vehicles; many are very difficult to negotiate, even for experienced mountain bikers. This rolling, nearly nine-mile route through Dogtown could take five hours hiking, three to four hours on bikes.

From the parking area, go around the gate and follow the rough dirt Dogtown Road for 1.2 miles, passing old cellar holes on the left, to Dogtown Square, a junction of trails where a rock is inscribed "D.T. SQ." From Dogtown Square, turn right onto a rock-strewn dirt road and follow it for 0.1 mile, then turn right again (where the red blazes of the Beaver Dam Trail branch left) onto the Tent Rock Trail, sometimes called the Boulder Trail. It continues for a mile to Babson Reservoir, along the way passing the large boulders inscribed with messages such as "Truth," "Industry," and "Help Mother." From the view of the reservoir, the trail turns left, crosses railroad tracks, and reaches the rough dirt Old Rockport Road behind Blackburn Industrial Park, 1.4 miles from Dogtown Square. Turn left and follow the road 1.2 miles to the Babson Museum on Eastern Av-

enue/Route 127. Behind the museum, turn left onto the red-blazed Beaver Dam Trail. Crossing the railroad tracks, then a brook four times, the trail passes over a small hill, takes a sharp right, and reaches Dogtown Square, 1.4 miles from the museum. Turn right onto Wharf Road and follow it 0.4 mile to Common Road. Turn right onto the Whale's Jaw Trail, pass a huge boulder called Peter's Pulpit at about 0.3 mile, and reach the Whale's Jaw, another massive boulder, at 0.8 mile. Backtrack the same way to Dogtown Square and follow Dogtown Road back to the parking area.

**User groups:** Hikers, bikes, and dogs. No wheelchair facilities. This trail rarely receives enough snow for skis or snowshoes, and is not suitable for horses. Hunting is permitted in season.

**Access, fees:** Parking and access are free.

**Maps:** A free trail map of Dogtown is available from the Gloucester Chamber of Commerce (see address below). For a topographic area map, request Rockport from USGS Map Sales, Federal Center, Box 25286, Denver, CO 80225, 888/ASK-USGS (888/275-8747), website: http://mapping.usgs.gov.

**Directions:** From the Grant Circle Rotary on Route 128 in Gloucester, take Route 127/Washington Street north for 0.9 mile and turn right onto Reynard Street. Follow Reynard to a left onto Cherry Street. Then turn right onto the access road to Dogtown, 1.5 miles from Grant Circle Rotary. Drive less than a half mile to a parking area and a gate.

**Contact:** Cape Ann Chamber of Commerce, 33 Commercial St., Gloucester, MA 01930, 978/283-1601, website: www.capeannvacations.com.

## 7 GREAT MEADOWS NATIONAL WILDLIFE REFUGE

**2 mi/1.5 hrs**

**in Concord**

Although most visitors here are birdwatchers, even the casual walker can't help but be impressed by the profusion of winged creatures on this 3,000-acre refuge, stretching

© MICHAEL LANZA

Great Meadows National Wildlife Refuge

along 12 miles of the Concord River. From great blue herons and osprey to songbirds and wood ducks, 221 bird species have been observed here. The Dike Trail around the broad wetlands is considered one of the best birding sites in the state. I watched a great blue not 50 feet away slowly stalking a meal across a shallow marsh. Bring binoculars if you have them. Besides birds, animals such as deer, muskrats, foxes, raccoons, cottontail rabbits, and weasels call the refuge home. With all the standing water here, you can bet there are lots of bugs too, especially in spring. Interestingly, relics of human habitation here date back to 5500 B.C.

Before you begin your hike, check out the view from the observation tower beside the parking lot. Then pick up the Dike Trail, to the right of the tower, which traverses the meadows between Upper Pool and Lower Pool. On the other side, the trail reaches the Concord

River banks (where canoeists pull ashore to walk the trail). Turn left, following the trail along the Upper Pool about a quarter mile to the refuge boundary, marked by signs. Turn back and follow the trail around the Lower Pool. You can either double back or, where the Lower Pool ends, take the Edge Trail through the woods back to the entrance road. Turn right on the road to return to the parking lot.

Special note: You can canoe the gentle Sudbury and Concord Rivers through the refuge and put ashore here to walk this trail. Depending on how long a day trip you want, put in along either Route 27, Route 117, or Route 62 and take out along Route 225 on the Carlisle/Bedford line.

**User groups:** Hikers, dogs, skiers, snowshoers, and wheelchair users. Dogs must be leashed. Bikes, horses, and hunting are prohibited.

**Access, fees:** Parking and access are free.

**Maps:** A map of hiking trails and a number of brochures about Great Meadows, including a list of bird species sighted here, are available at the trailhead. For a topographic area map, request Maynard from USGS Map Sales, Federal Center, Box 25286, Denver, CO 80225, 888/ASK-USGS (888/275-8747), website: http://mapping.usgs.gov.

**Directions:** From Route 2 (0.9 mile east of Emerson Hospital and one mile West of Route 126), turn right onto Sudbury Road and continue across Route 117 (2.1 miles). At the stop sign (2.4 miles from Route 117), turn left onto Concord Road. Follow it 0.7 mile to Lincoln-Sudbury Regional High School, then turn left onto Lincoln Road. Continue 1.4 miles to the Great Meadows NWR sign. Turn left onto Weir Hill Road and follow signs to visitor center and headquarters.

**Contact:** Great Meadows National Wildlife Refuge, Refuge Manager, 73 Weir Hill Rd.,

Sudbury, MA 01776, 978/443-4661, website: http://greatmeadows.fws.gov/.

## 8 CHANDLER HOVEY PARK
**0.2 mi/0.25 hr**
**in Marblehead**

This town park on Marblehead Neck is a postage stamp–sized parcel of public land amid some of the most stately houses on Massachusetts's North Shore. The sea crashes up against a classic New England rocky shoreline, a beautiful place at any time of year, in any weather. I especially like coming out here on a stormy day when no one else is around. There is no trail; from the parking lot, simply wander out onto the rocks.

**User groups:** Hikers only. No wheelchair facilities. This trail rarely receives enough snow for skis or snowshoes and is not suitable for bikes or horses. Dogs and hunting are prohibited.

**Access, fees:** Parking and access are free.

**Maps:** No map is necessary for this short walk, but for topographic area maps, request Lynn and Salem from USGS Map Sales, Federal Center, Box 25286, Denver, CO 80225, 888/ASK-USGS (888/275-8747), website: http://mapping.usgs.gov.

**Directions:** From the junction of Routes 114 and 129 in Marblehead, turn east onto Route 129. Drive one block to where Route 129 turns right and continue straight ahead onto Ocean Avenue. Follow it nearly a mile, passing Devereaux Beach, onto Marblehead Neck. Bear left onto Harbor Avenue and follow it nearly a mile; it merges onto Ocean Avenue again. Continue 0.2 mile, turn left onto Follett Street, and proceed 0.1 mile to the parking lot at the road's end. If the gate is closed, park on the street.

**Contact:** Marblehead Parks and Recreation Department, 781/631-3350.

## 9 WALDEN POND
**1.7 mi/1 hr**
**in Walden Pond State Park Reservation in Concord**

In 1845, a 27-year-old former schoolteacher named Henry David Thoreau came to Walden Pond to live on 14 acres owned by his friend, Ralph Waldo Emerson. Thoreau built a small one-room cabin and began his "experiment in simplicity," living a sustenance lifestyle on the pond. At the time, much of Concord was already deforested and the land converted to farms, but the woods around Walden Pond had remained untouched because the sandy soil was not very fertile. Two years, two months, and two days later, Thoreau closed up his house and returned to village life in Concord. Emerson sold the cabin to his gardener. (The cabin no longer stands, but a replica can be seen beside the parking lot.) In 1854, Thoreau published *Walden, or Life in the Woods*—still considered a classic of American literature. Ever since, Walden

Walden Pond

Pond has stood as a symbol of the American conservation movement.

Today, Walden Pond sits in the middle of a small patch of woods within earshot of busy state routes and a railroad line, yet it remains popular with hikers and cross-country skiers, as well as fishermen and canoeists (a boat launch is on the right side of Route 126, just beyond the parking area). Songbirds, Canada geese, and ducks are commonly seen here.

From the parking lot, cross Route 126 and walk downhill to the pond. From either end of the beach, the Pond Path circles the pond, usually staying just above the shoreline but offering almost constant pond views. It's a wide, mostly flat trail and is easy to ski. A short side trail, marked by a sign along the Pond Path, leads to Thoreau's house site. Stay on the trails—erosion is a problem here.

**User groups:** Hikers, skiers, and snowshoers. Wheelchair users can access the beginning of this trail above the beach on Walden Pond. Bikes, dogs, horses, and hunting are prohibited.

**Access, fees:** A daily parking fee of $5 is collected year-round. Park officials may close the entrance if the park reaches capacity. The park is open to the public from 5 A.M.–sunset; check for the closing time posted in the parking lot.

**Maps:** A free map and an informational brochure about Walden Pond are available outside the Shop at Walden Pond, next to the park office at the parking lot's south end. The map can also be obtained at the Massachusetts Division of State Parks and Recreation website (see below). For a topographic area map, request Maynard from USGS Map Sales, Federal Center, Box 25286, Denver, CO 80225, 888/ASK-USGS (888/275-8747), website: http://mapping.usgs.gov.

**Directions:** From the junction of Routes 2 and 126 in Concord, drive south on Route 126 for 0.3 mile to the Walden Pond State Reservation entrance and parking lot on the left.

**Contact:** Walden Pond State Park Reservation, 915 Walden St./Route 126, Concord, MA 01742, 978/369-3254. Massachusetts Division of State

Parks and Recreation, 251 Causeway St., Suite 600, Boston, MA 02114-2104, 617/626-1250, website: www.state.ma.us/dem/forparks.htm. The Shop at Walden Pond, 508/287-5477.

## 10 MINUTEMAN BIKEWAY
**11 mi/5.5 hrs**
**in Somerville, Cambridge, Arlington, Lexington, and Bedford**

This paved bikeway follows a former railroad bed and is popular with walkers, runners, bicyclists, families, in-line skaters, and—when there's snow—cross-country skiers. Many people, particularly students, use the bikeway to commute to work and classes. The bikeway passes mainly through forest in Bedford and Lexington, and through a wetland in Lexington as well. From Arlington into Cambridge and Somerville, the bikeway becomes increasingly an urban recreation path. It is flat and can be done in sections of short lengths, which is why this receives an easy difficulty rating despite its 11-mile total length.

**User groups:** Hikers, bikers, dogs, and wheelchair users. This trail does not usually receive enough snow for skis or snowshoes, and is not suitable for horses. Hunting is prohibited.

**Access, fees:** Parking and access are free.

**Maps:** A brochure and map of the bikeway is available from the Arlington Planning Department (see address below). Boston's Bikemap, a detailed bicycling map of the metropolitan area, which includes the Minuteman Bikeway, is available for $4.25 from Rubel BikeMaps, P.O. Box 401035, Cambridge, MA 02140, website: www.bikemaps.com, and from area stores listed at the website. For topographic area maps, request Boston South, Boston North, and Maynard from USGS Map Sales, Federal Center, Box 25286, Denver, CO 80225, 888/ASK-USGS (888/275-8747), website: http://mapping.usgs.gov.

**Directions:** The Minuteman Bikeway can be accessed from numerous points for walks or rides of virtually any distance. Its endpoints are behind the T station in Davis Square, between Holland Street and Meacham Road in Somerville; and at the junction of Railroad Avenue and Loomis Street in Bedford. Access points include Massachusetts Avenue in Cambridge at Cameron Avenue and Harvey Street, 0.4 mile south of Route 16; the Alewife T station at the junction of Routes 2 and 16; a parking lot on Lake Street in Arlington, just west of the Brooks Avenue traffic lights; Swan Place and Mystic Street in Arlington center, near the junction of Routes 2A and 60 (where the bikeway crosses Massachusetts Avenue); Park Avenue in Arlington (via a stairway), just north of Massachusetts Avenue; Maple Street (Route 2A) in Lexington; Woburn Street in Lexington, just west of Massachusetts Avenue; Hancock and Meriam Streets (at a large parking lot), off Bedford Street (Route 4 and Route 225) and the Lexington Battle Green; and Bedford Street (Route 4 and Route 225) between North Hancock and Revere Streets in Lexington.

**Contact:** The Friends of the Minuteman Bikeway, website: http://users.rcn.com/hwbingham/lexbike/friends.htm. Rails to Trails Conservancy, 1100 17th St. Northwest, 10th floor, Washington, DC 20036, 202/331-9696, website: www.railtrails.org.

## 11 MIDDLESEX FELLS SKYLINE TRAIL

**7 mi/4 hrs**

**in Middlesex Fells Reservation in Medford, Malden, Winchester, Melrose, and Stoneham**
This may be the premier hiking circuit in the Fells, a 2,000-acre piece of woods in an urban wilderness. ("Fells" is a Saxon word for rocky hills.) You can actually find quiet and solitude along parts of this trail—although traffic on the interstate can be heard at times, and the Fells as a whole sees heavy recreational use. The trail loops around the Winchester Reservoirs, passing through forest and traversing countless rocky ledges, some with good views of the Fells and, occasionally, the Boston skyline. Perhaps the best view is from

atop Pine Hill, near the start of this loop, which overlooks Boston's skyline and the Blue Hills to the south; climb the stone Wright's Tower on the hill. The white blazes of the Skyline Trail are generally easy to follow, but it crosses many other paths and forest roads, which can cause confusion. The trail dries out fairly quickly after the snow melts—it's a glorious hike on the first warm day of spring. Bikes are prohibited from this trail, and it's not suited to skiing, but there are many forest roads and trails forming a network through the Fells that offer good mountain biking and cross-country skiing.

From the parking lot, walk along the right side of Bellevue Pond and onto a wide forest road at the opposite end of the pond. Look for the white-blazed trail leading to the right, up Pine Hill. The loop eventually brings you back to this intersection.

**User groups:** Hikers and dogs. Dogs must be leashed. No wheelchair facilities. This trail rarely receives enough snow for snowshoes, and is not suitable for horses or skis. Bikes are prohibited from the Skyline Trail. Mountain biking in groups of five or fewer is permitted on fire roads and the designated Mountain Bike Loop from mid-April–mid-December. Mountain biking is not permitted on single-track (hiking) trails and is prohibited in all parts of the reservation from January 1–April 15 to protect trails and fire roads from erosion damage during this often-muddy season. Hunting is prohibited throughout the Middlesex Fells Reservation.

**Access, fees:** Parking and access are free. The reservation is open year-round from sunrise–sunset.

**Maps:** A trail map of the Middlesex Fells Reservation is available for $5 via mail (with SASE) from The Friends of Middlesex Fells Reservation (see address below), and sometimes at Bookends Bookstore, at 559 Main St., Winchester, 781/721-5933; The Map Shack, 253 North Ave., Wakefield, 781/213-7989; The Book Oasis, 297 Main St., Stoneham, 781/438-0077;

and Best Sellers Café, 24 High St., Medford Square, 781/391-7171.

**Directions:** Take I-93 to Exit 33 in Medford. From the traffic circle, turn onto South Border Road. Drive 0.2 mile and turn into a parking area on the right, at Bellevue Pond.

**Contact:** Middlesex Fells Reservation, 781/322-2851 or 781/662-5230. Massachusetts Division of Urban Parks and Recreation, Commissioner's Office, 20 Somerset St., Boston, MA 02108, 617/722-5000, website: www.state.ma.us/mdc/mdc_home. The Friends of the Middlesex Fells Reservation, 4 Woodland Rd., Stoneham, MA 02180, 781/662-2340, website: www.fells.org.

## 12 PAUL DUDLEY WHITE CHARLES RIVER BIKE PATH
**14 mi/6 hrs**

**in the Charles River Reservation, Boston, Cambridge, and Watertown**

The paved Paul Dudley White Bike Path along both banks of the Charles River teems with activity weekday evenings and weekends: walkers, runners, in-line skaters, bicyclists, skateboarders, people of all ages out getting exercise in the middle of the city. It is easily reached from such colleges as MIT, Boston University, and Harvard, and it accesses riverside attractions like the Esplanade and Hatch Shell. The bike path provides a more convenient, more pleasant, and often faster means of getting around the city than driving or using public transportation. It also has great skyline views of Boston from the Cambridge side. For the 20th anniversary Earth Day concert several years ago, when hundreds of thousands of concertgoers jammed the Esplanade and Storrow Drive was closed to motor vehicles, a friend and I easily biked to the show, then left without getting stuck in the crowds afterward. Some sections of the path are quite wide, others no wider than a pair of bikes; likewise, some stretches see much heavier use than others. Bicycling quickly can be difficult when the path is crowded, and numerous crossings of busy streets necessitate frequent stops. The entire path forms a 14-mile loop between the Museum of Science and Watertown Square and can be traveled in either direction and done in smaller sections, which is why this trail receives such an easy difficulty rating.

**User groups:** Hikers, bikers, dogs, and wheelchair users. Dogs must be leashed. This path rarely receives enough snow for skis, and is not suitable for snowshoeing. Horses and hunting are prohibited.

**Access, fees:** Parking and access are free.

**Maps:** *Boston's Bikemap,* a detailed bicycling map of the metropolitan area, which covers the Paul Dudley White Charles River Bike Path, is available for $4.25 from Rubel BikeMaps, P.O. Box 401035, Cambridge, MA 02140, website: www.bikemaps.com, and from area stores listed at the website. For a topographic area map, request Boston South from USGS Map Sales, Federal Center, Box 25286, Denver, CO 80225, 888/ASK-USGS (888/275-8747), website: http://mapping.usgs.gov.

**Directions:** The bike path runs for seven miles along both sides of the Charles River, from the Boston Museum of Science on the O'Brien Route/Route 28 to Watertown Square in Watertown (the junction of Routes 16 and 20), forming a 14-mile loop. It is accessible from numerous points in Boston, Cambridge, and Watertown, including the footbridges over Storrow Drive in Boston, although not from the Longfellow and Boston University bridges on the Boston side.

**Contact:** Massachusetts Division of Urban Parks and Recreation, Commissioner's Office, 20 Somerset St., Boston, MA 02108, 617/722-5000, website: www.state.ma.us/mdc/mdc_home.

## 13 NOANET WOODLANDS
**4 mi/2 hrs**

**in Dover**

The 695-acre Noanet Woodlands is a surprisingly quiet and secluded-feeling forest patch plunked down in the middle of suburbia. I suspect it comes as a shock to many first-time hikers of 387-foot Noanet Peak to find that virtually the only sign of civilization visible from this rocky knob is the Boston skyline 20 miles away—floating on the horizon like the Emerald City. You have to scan the unbroken forest and rolling hills for a glimpse of another building. And you may hear no other sounds than the breeze and singing of birds.

The yellow-blazed Caryl Trail begins at one end of the parking lot. Follow it to Junction 6 (trail junction signs are on trees) and turn left onto an unmarked trail. Pass a trail entering on the right. At the next junction, turn right and then left up a hill. You soon reach the open ledge atop Noanet Peak. After enjoying the view, walk to your right a short distance onto a trail that follows a wooded ridge crest, slowly descending to the Caryl Trail; turn left (you'll almost immediately recross the trail leading to Noanet's summit, but do not turn onto it). Follow the Caryl Trail to Junction 18 and walk straight onto the blue-blazed Peabody Trail. Pass ponds and the site of an old mill on the right. (From 1815 to 1840, Noanet Brook powered the Dover Union Iron Company. A flood breached the huge dam at Noanet Falls in 1876. In 1954, then-owner Amelia Peabody rebuilt the dam.) Bear left through Junction 4 and turn right onto the Caryl Trail again, which leads back to the parking lot.

**User groups:** Hikers, skiers, snowshoers, and horses. No wheelchair facilities. Bikes are allowed by permit only (see below); the price of the permit is discounted for The Trustees of Reservations members. Dogs are prohibited at Caryl Park, but visitors who walk to Noanet Woodlands can bring their dog. Hunting is prohibited.

**Access, fees:** Parking and access are free. Noanet Woodlands is open to the public from sunrise–sunset year-round. A biking permit can be obtained at the Noanet Woodlands ranger station at the Caryl Park entrance on weekends and holidays, or from the Southeast Region office of The Trustees of Reservations (see address below).

**Maps:** A trail map is posted on an informa-

tion board at the trailhead, and one is available free from The Trustees of Reservations, either at the trailhead or through The Trustees headquarters (see address below). Major trail junctions in Noanet are marked with numbered signs that correspond to markings on the map. For topographic area maps, request Boston South, Framingham, Medfield, and Norwood from USGS Map Sales, Federal Center, Box 25286, Denver, CO 80225, 888/ASK-USGS (888/275-8747), website: http://mapping.usgs.gov.

**Directions:** From I-95/Route 128, take Exit 17 onto Route 135 west. Drive about 0.6 mile and turn left at the traffic lights onto South Street. Drive 0.7 mile and bear left at a fork. After another 0.4 miles, turn left onto Chestnut Street. Cross the Charles River and enter Dover; turn right onto Dedham Street. Two miles past the river, turn left into Caryl Park; the sign is hard to see, but the parking lot is next to tennis courts.

**Contact:** The Trustees of Reservations Southeast/Cape Cod Regional Office, The Bradley Estate, 2468B Washington St., Canton, MA 02021-1124, 781/821-2977, website: www .thetrustees.org.

## 14 WHISTLING CAVE
**3 mi/1.5 hrs**
**in Upton State Forest in Upton**

Whistling Cave is not a cave but two large boulders, one leaning against the other, with a small passageway beneath them. It's located in an interesting little wooded stream valley littered with such boulders. Trails are well blazed, the forest road intersections are marked by signs, and the state forest has many more miles of both trails and roads. This hike has some hills but is relatively easy.

From the parking lot, head past the gate on a dirt forest road to the junction of Loop Road and Park Road. Bear right on Park Road, passing one blue-blazed trail on the left (which may not appear on the map). Continue up a gentle hill to a pullout on the left. The Whistling Cave Trail, marked by a sign and blazed with blue triangles, begins there. It soon drops over ledges and down a steep embankment, then levels out. You cross a couple of small brooks and then enter the area of boulders. Whistling Cave is right on the trail at this area's far end, shortly after you start up a hillside. Just beyond it, the trail ends at the junction of Middle Road and Loop Road. (To reach Whistling Cave on bikes, horses, or skis, take Loop Road to this intersection, walk or attempt to ski to the boulders, and double back.) You can return on either Loop Road or Middle Road; the former remains a forest road, while the latter eventually narrows to an easy trail marked by blue triangles.

**User groups:** Hikers, snowshoers, and dogs. Dogs must be leashed. No wheelchair facilities. Bikes, horses, and skis are prohibited. Hunting is allowed in season.

**Access, fees:** Parking and access are free.

**Maps:** A free map is available at the state forest entrance or at the Massachusetts Division of State Parks and Recreation website (see below). For a topographic area map, request Milford from USGS Map Sales, Federal Center, Box 25286, Denver, CO 80225, 888/ASK-USGS (888/275-8747), website: http://mapping.usgs.gov.

**Directions:** From I-495, take Exit 21B for West Main Street, Upton, and drive 3.7 miles south to the junction of High Street, Hopkinton Road, and Westboro Road; there is a pond to the left. (The junction can be reached in the other direction from Route 140 in Upton center by taking North Main Street for a half mile.) Turn north onto Westboro Road, drive two miles, and then turn right at the sign for Upton State Forest. Bear right onto a dirt road and stop at the map box. Continue down that dirt road a short distance to a parking lot at a gate.

**Contact:** Upton State Forest, 205 Westboro Rd., Upton, MA 01568, 508/278-6486. Massachusetts Division of State Parks and Recreation, 251 Causeway St., Suite 600, Boston, MA 02114-2104, 617/626-1250, website: www.state.ma.us/dem/forparks.htm.

## 15 ROCKY WOODS
**2.3 mi/1.5 hrs**

**in Medfield**

This 491-acre patch of woodlands boasts more than 12 miles of cart paths and foot trails and is popular with locals for activities from walking and cross-country skiing to fishing (catch-and-release only). There are many more loop possibilities besides the one described here.

Walk down the entrance road to the Quarry Trail and follow it 0.1 mile along the shore of Chickering Pond. Bear left at Junction 2, continue 0.1 mile, and then continue straight through Junction 3. At Junction 4, a half mile from Junction 3, cross the Harwood Notch Trail diagonally, staying on the Quarry Trail. A quarter mile farther, at Junction 7, turn right on the Ridge Trail and walk 0.7 mile. Bear right at Junction 6, turn left immediately after that at Junction 5, and follow the cart path more than a half mile back to Junction 2. The pond and parking area lie straight ahead.

**User groups:** Hikers, bikers, horses, skiers, and snowshoers. No wheelchair facilities. Dogs and hunting are prohibited, although the moratorium on walking dogs may eventually be lifted.

**Access, fees:** There's an entrance fee of $3 per person age 12 and older, with The Trustees of Reservations members entering free. The reservation is open daily from sunrise–sunset year-round.

**Maps:** A free trail map is available from the ranger on duty weekends and holidays. Trail intersections numbered on the map correspond to numbered trail signs. For topographic area maps, request Medfield and Norwood from USGS Map Sales, Federal Center, Box 25286, Denver, CO 80225, 888/ASK-USGS (888/275-8747), website: http://mapping.usgs.gov.

**Directions:** From I-95/Route 128 in Westwood, take Exit 16B onto Route 109, driving west for 5.7 miles. Take a sharp right onto Hartford Street and continue 0.6 mile to the reservation entrance on the left. Or from the junction of Routes 27 and 109 in Medfield, drive 1.7 miles east on Route 109 and bear left on Hartford Street and park along that street.

**Contact:** The Trustees of Reservations Southeast/Cape Cod Regional Office, The Bradley Estate, 2468B Washington St., Canton, MA 02021-1124, 781/821-2977, website: www.thetrustees.org.

## 16 BLUE HILLS: SKYLINE TRAIL LOOP

**4.5 mi/2.5 hrs**

**in the Blue Hills Reservation in Canton**

With 5,800 forest acres spread over 20 hilltops, the Blue Hills Reservation in Quincy, Braintree, Randolph, Canton, and Milton comprises the largest tract of open space in Greater Boston. It hosts a broad diversity of flora and fauna, including the timber rattlesnake, which you are extremely unlikely to encounter given the snake's fear of people. The reservation harbors an extensive network of trails and carriage roads—but be aware that some are unmarked and confusing, and many are rocky and surprisingly rugged. At 635 feet, Great Blue Hill, near the reservation's western end, is the park's highest point and probably its most popular hike.

This 4.5-mile loop on the north and south branches of the Skyline Trail passes over Great Blue and four other hills, climbing a cumulative total of about 1,200 feet. It incorporates several good views—the best being the panorama from the stone tower on Great Blue, reached near this hike's end. In fact, while the native granite tower is less than 50 years old, it symbolizes this high point's long history. Patriots used Great Blue as a lookout during the Revolutionary War, lighting beacons up here to warn of any British attack, and for several hundred years, fires have been lit on Great Blue to celebrate historic occurrences, beginning with the repeal of the Stamp Act and including the signing of the Declaration of Independence.

From the parking lot, walk back toward the Howard Johnson's, watching for blue blazes that cross the road within 100 feet, and enter the woods at a granite post inscribed with the words "Skyline Trail." The trail ascends steeply for a half mile, reaching open ledges and the carriage road just below the summit. Turn right on the carriage road, where blue blazes are often marked on stones (which may be covered by snow in winter). Pass the path leading to the summit (there aren't any views, and the observatory is private property), and within 0.1 mile turn right with the blue blazes onto a footpath marked by a post inscribed "South Skyline Trail." It descends ledges with good views of the Boston skyline and Houghton Pond, enters the woods, and, within a mile of Great Blue, reaches wooded Houghton Hill. Descend a short distance to Hillside Street, cross it, turn left, and follow the blue blazes about 150 feet to where the blazes direct you back across the street toward the reservation headquarters (passing a post marked "North Skyline Trail"). Walk up the driveway and left of the headquarters onto a carriage path. In about 75 feet, turn right at a sign onto the North Skyline Trail. In minutes you reach an open ledge on Hancock Hill with a view of Great Blue Hill.

Continuing over Hemenway Hill and Wolcott Hill in the next mile, watch for side paths leading right to views of Boston. The Skyline Trail drops downhill, crosses a carriage path, and then climbs the north side of Great Blue to the stone tower. Climb the stairs to the tower for a sweeping view of woods, city, and ocean. From the tower's observation deck looking west (out over the stone building beside the tower), you may see Mount Wachusett (see hikes 10–14, Central Massachusetts chapter). Standing on the side of the tower facing Boston, look left: On a clear day, you'll spy Mount Monadnock (Central and Southern New Hampshire chapter, hikes 19–20) between two tall radio towers in the distance. Descend the stone tower and turn right on the Skyline Trail, circling around Great Blue, past the posts marking the south and north Skyline Trail branches.

Make a left turn at the third Skyline Trail post and descend a half mile to Route 138, where you began this hike.

**User groups:** Hikers and dogs. Dogs must be leashed. No wheelchair facilities. This trail is not suitable for skis or snowshoes. Bikes and hunting are prohibited, though bikes are permitted on some other specifically marked trails in the Blue Hills.

**Access, fees:** Parking and access are free.

**Maps:** A trail map of the Blue Hills is available at the reservation headquarters or the Massachusetts Audubon Society Blue Hills Trailside Museum (see addresses below). The *Blue Hills Reservation/Mount Tom/Holyoke Range* map costs $5.95 in paper from the Appalachian Mountain Club, 800/262-4455, website: www.outdoors.org. For a topographic area map, request Norwood from USGS Map Sales, Federal Center, Box 25286, Denver, CO 80225, 888/ASK-USGS (888/275-8747), website: http://mapping.usgs.gov.

**Directions:** From I-93, take Exit 2B onto Route 138 north. Continue for nearly a half mile, passing the Howard Johnson's, to a commuter parking lot on the left. The reservation headquarters is at 695 Hillside Street in Milton, reached via the reservation entrance on Route 138, before the Howard Johnson's, or from Randolph Avenue (I-93 Exit 5).

**Contact:** Blue Hills Reservation Headquarters, 695 Hillside St., Milton, MA 02186, 617/698-1802, website: www.state.ma.us/mdc/blue.htm. Friends of the Blue Hills, P.O. Box 416, Milton, MA 02186, 781/828-1805, website: www.friendsofthebluehills.org. Massachusetts Audubon Society Blue Hills Trailside Museum, 1904 Canton Ave./Route 138, Milton, MA 02186, 781/333-0690, website: www.massaudubon.org/Nature_Connection/Sanctuaries/Blue_Hills.

## 17 BLUE HILLS: RATTLESNAKE AND WAMPATUCK HILLS

**2.2 mi/1.5 hrs**

**in the Blue Hills Reservation in Braintree**

While many hikers flock to the west side of the reservation and to Great Blue Hill, the east side of the reservation remains a fairly well-kept secret—and the views from there are arguably better than those from Great Blue Hill. Standing in a warm summer breeze on Rattlesnake Hill one afternoon, gazing out over an expanse of woods to the Boston skyline in the distance, I listened, and listened . . . and realized I couldn't hear any traffic. I heard only the breeze and the singing of birds, despite having left the interstate behind just a half hour earlier and hiking merely a half mile.

From the roadside parking area, follow the Skyline Trail, which quickly ascends a short but steep hillside to a view of the thickly forested, rolling hills of the reservation and the Boston skyline beyond. The trail bends around an old quarry now filled with water, and about a half mile from the road reaches the rocky top of Rattlesnake Hill, with excellent views of the hills and skyline. Wampatuck Hill, with more good views, lies less than a half mile farther. There is a short, rocky scramble along the trail between Rattlesnake and Wampatuck that may be intimidating for some inexperienced hikers. Return the same way.

**User groups:** Hikers and dogs. Dogs must be leashed. No wheelchair facilities. This trail is not suitable for skis or snowshoes. Bikes and hunting are prohibited, though bikes are permitted on some other specifically marked trails in the Blue Hills.

**Access, fees:** Parking and access are free. This trail is closed from 8 P.M.–dawn.

**Maps:** A trail map of the Blue Hills is available at the reservation headquarters or the Massachusetts Audubon Society Blue Hills Trailside Museum (see addresses below). The *Rhode Island NW–SW/Blue Hills Map* costs $5.95 in waterproof Tyvek or $2.95 paper from the Appalachian Mountain Club, 800/262-4455, website: www.outdoors.org. For a topographic area map, request Norwood from USGS Map Sales, Federal Center, Box 25286, Denver, CO 80225, 888/ASK-USGS (888/275-8747), website: http://mapping.usgs.gov.

**Directions:** From I-93 in Braintree, take Exit 6 and follow signs to Willard Street. About a mile from I-93, watch for the ice rink on the left. Drive 0.2 mile beyond the rink, turn left on Hayden Street, and then immediately left again on Wampatuck Road. Drive another 0.2 mile and park at the roadside on the right, where a post marks the Skyline Trail. The reservation headquarters is at 695 Hillside Street in Milton, reached via the reservation entrance on Route 138, before the Howard Johnson's, or from Randolph Avenue (I-93 Exit 5).

**Contact:** Blue Hills Reservation Headquarters, 695 Hillside St., Milton, MA 02186, 617/698-1802, website: www.state.ma.us/mdc/blue.htm. Friends of the Blue Hills, P.O. Box 416, Milton, MA 02186, 781/828-1805, website: www.friendsofthebluehills.org. Massachusetts Audubon Society Blue Hills Trailside Museum, 1904 Canton Ave./Route 138, Milton, MA 02186, 781/333-0690, website: www.massaudubon.org/Nature_Connection/Sanctuaries/Blue_Hills.

## 🔟8️⃣ WORLD'S END
### 2.9 mi/1.5 hrs

**in Hingham**

This 251-acre peninsula in Hingham nearly became a community of 163 homes in the late 1800s, when then-landowner John Brewer hired none other than the famous landscape architect Frederick Law Olmsted to design a landscape of carriage paths lined by English oaks and native hardwoods. That much was accomplished, but the Brewer family continued to farm the land rather than develop it. Today, thanks to The Trustees of Reservations, this string of four low hills rising above Hingham Harbor provides local people with a wonderful recreation area for

walking, running, or cross-country skiing. Bird-watchers flock here, particularly in spring and fall, to observe migratory species. From various spots, you'll enjoy views of the Boston skyline, Hingham Harbor, and across the Weir River to Hull. This hike loops around the property's perimeter, but four miles of carriage paths and three miles of foot trails, all interconnected, offer many other possible routes for exploration.

From the entrance, walk straight (northwest) along the flat carriage path for a quarter mile and then bear left around the west flank of Planter's Hill. A quarter mile past Planter's, cross the narrow land bar between the harbor and river, and turn left onto another carriage road. This follows a half-mile curve around a hillside; turn left at the next junction of carriage paths. After another half mile, bear left again, reaching the land bar a quarter mile farther. Bear left, continue 0.3 mile, then turn right and walk nearly 0.4 mile back to the entrance.

**User groups:** Hikers, dogs, skiers, and snowshoers. Dogs must be leashed. No wheelchair facilities. Horses are allowed by permit. Bikes and hunting are prohibited.

**Access, fees:** There is an entrance fee of $4.50 per person age 12 and older, except for members of The Trustees of Reservations, who enter free. The reservation is open daily from 8 A.M.–sunset year-round.

**Maps:** A map of the carriage paths and trails is available free at the entrance. For a topographic area map, request Hull from USGS Map Sales, Federal Center, Box 25286, Denver, CO 80225, 888/ASK-USGS (888/275-8747), website: http://mapping.usgs.gov.

**Directions:** From the junction of Routes 228 and 3A, drive north on 3A for 0.6 mile. Turn right on Summer Street, drive 0.3 mile, proceed straight through the traffic lights, and then continue another 0.8 mile to the World's End entrance.

**Contact:** The Trustees of Reservations Southeast/Cape Cod Regional Office, The Bradley Estate, 2468B Washington St., Canton, MA

02021-1124, 781/821-2977, website: www
.thetrustees.org.

## 19 CARATUNK WILDLIFE REFUGE

2 mi/1 hr

**in Seekonk**

Bird-watchers will want to visit here during April and May or from late August–October to catch the migratory birds, but this easy, two-mile walk mostly through woods is a satisfying outing any time of year. There are a few trail options in the refuge, all of them well blazed; this loop, mostly on the blue trail, is the longest, winding through much of the property, past open fields, wetlands, and two small ponds.

From the parking lot, walk to the right of the building, past the information kiosk and along the field's right edge. Soon a short side path loops into the woods to the right, bringing you along a bog, then back out to the field. Walk a short distance farther along the field, then turn right onto the red trail. After passing through a pine grove and skirting the far edge of the same field where you began, turn right onto the yellow trail and then bear left onto the blue trail. At the edge of Muskrat Pond, turn right, staying on blue past Ice Pond, crossing power lines, passing another pond, and continuing through the beech woods and a hemlock stand; you'll pass several trail junctions and loop back to the bog, where you begin backtracking on the blue trail. After crossing the power lines and passing Ice Pond in the other direction, stay on the blue trail past one junction with the yellow trail and then bear left onto the yellow trail at the next junction. Upon reaching the field, turn right on the red trail and follow it around the field back to the refuge office and parking lot.

**User groups:** Hikers, skiers, and snowshoers. No wheelchair facilities. Bikes, dogs, horses, and hunting are prohibited.

**Access, fees:** A donation of $1 is requested for nonmembers of the Audubon Society. The refuge is open daily, sunrise–sunset. Visitors should stay on trails.

**Maps:** A map is available at the refuge. For a topographic area map, request Providence from USGS Map Sales, Federal Center, Box 25286, Denver, CO 80225, 888/ASK-USGS (888/275-8747), website: http://mapping.usgs.gov.

**Directions:** From I-95 in Attleboro, take Exit 2 onto Newport Avenue southbound/Route 1A. Drive 1.8 miles from the interstate, turn left onto Armistice Boulevard/Route 15, and follow it 1.2 miles to its end. Turn right onto Route 152 south, continue 0.6 mile, and then turn left at a church onto Brown Avenue. Proceed 0.8 mile farther to the refuge entrance on the right.

**Contact:** Caratunk Wildlife Refuge, 301 Brown Ave., Seekonk, MA 02771, 508/761-8230. The Audubon Society of Rhode Island, 12 Sanderson Rd., Smithfield, RI 02917, 401/949-5454, website: www.asri.org.

## 20 MYLES STANDISH STATE FOREST LOOP

11 mi/6 hrs

**in Carver**

Myles Standish State Forest sprawls over more than 14,000 acres, making it one of the largest public lands in Massachusetts. A grid work of old woods roads cuts through this pine barrens, along with a hiking trail and a paved bicycle path. This loop from the forest headquarters, which I did one November afternoon on my mountain bike, connects several dirt woods roads, and much of its course is reserved for skiers in winter (who have to watch out for snowmobiles on other roads in Myles Standish). The grid pattern of roads and the signs at many intersections makes navigating through this vast landscape easier than it might be otherwise, but bring a map. Although the terrain is mostly flat, there are slight rises and dips that can make the workout a little harder on a bike or skis. Also, sand traps crop up periodically, spanning the roads, and I found a few of them impossible to pedal across; fortunately, none of them were very big. Distances in this description are estimates based on the map provided by the state.

From the parking lot, head back out onto Cranberry Road, turn right, and then immediately right again past the headquarters building onto paved Lower College Pond Road into the state forest. Within a half mile, bicyclists and skiers can turn left onto the paved bike path, which leads to the dirt Halfway Pond Road; others will continue a quarter mile on Lower College Pond Road to the Halfway Pond Road intersection. Turn left onto Halfway Pond Road, follow it a half mile to a crossroads, and turn right onto Jessup Road. Continue about 0.7 mile and bear right at a sign reading "Ebeeme Road," which is shown as Jessup Road on the state map. A half mile farther, turn right at a crossroads onto Federal Pond Road. Follow it a mile, crossing the bridle trail, a gas line right-of-way, and Kamesit Way, and then turn right onto Sabbatia Road. Continue a mile and then turn left onto Three Cornered Pond Road. Reaching the paved Lower College Pond Road within a quarter mile, turn right, then bear left immediately and proceed straight onto the bridle path (don't turn left onto another bridle path branch), marked by a horse symbol. In a quarter mile, at the next intersection, turn left onto Negas Road, continue a half mile, and then turn left onto paved Upper College Pond Road. Proceed nearly a half mile and turn right onto Three Cornered Pond Road. Three-quarters of a mile farther, turn right again onto Cobb Road and follow it 0.75 mile to its end. Turn right onto Halfway Pond Road, go about 0.2 mile, and then take the first left. In about 0.3 mile, turn left again onto Doctor's Pond Road, go a half mile, and then turn right onto Webster Springs Road. Follow it nearly a mile, crossing paved Circuit Drive, a dirt road, the bike path, and the bridle path before reaching Upper College Pond Road. Turn left, following the paved road nearly a half mile to its end. Turn right on paved Fearing Pond Road

and continue a half mile back to the forest headquarters.

**User groups:** Hikers, bikers, dogs, skiers, and snowshoers. The paved bike path is wheelchair accessible. Dogs must be leashed. Horses are prohibited. Hunting is allowed in season.

**Access, fees:** A daily parking fee of $5 is collected from mid-May–mid-October.

**Maps:** A free, basic trail map of Myles Standish State Forest is available at the state forest headquarters (see address below) or at the Massachusetts Division of State Parks and Recreation website (see below). For topographic area maps, request Plymouth and Wareham from USGS Map Sales, Federal Center, Box 25286, Denver, CO 80225, 888/ASK-USGS (888/275-8747), website: http://mapping.usgs.gov.

**Directions:** From I-495, take Exit 2 on the Middleborough-Wareham line onto Route 58 north. Drive 2.5 miles to where Route 58 turns left, but continue straight ahead, following signs for the state forest. Proceed another 0.8 mile, turn right onto Cranberry Road, and then drive 2.8 miles to the state forest headquarters and a parking lot on the left.

**Contact:** Myles Standish State Forest, Cranberry Rd., P.O. Box 66, South Carver, MA 02366, 508/866-2526. Massachusetts Division of State Parks and Recreation, 251 Causeway St., Suite 600, Boston, MA 02114-2104, 617/626-1250, website: www.state.ma.us/dem/forparks.htm.

## 21 PROVINCE LANDS TRAIL
**6 mi/3 hrs**
**in the Cape Cod National Seashore in Provincetown**

This paved path is popular with bikers, hikers, runners, in-line skaters, and others, and it's good for wheelchairs, too. The paved bikeway makes a circuitous loop through forest, past ponds, and over sprawling sand dunes—it may be the most interesting bike path I've ever pedaled. Be sure to take the spur path a half mile out to Race Point (included in the mileage), which is near the very tip of Massachusetts and a great place for whale-watching during the seasonal migrations, when the whales often swim close to shore. Heed the center dividing line on this path, especially around its many blind corners. Pick up the bike path from the Beech Forest parking lot; the loop returns here.

**User groups:** Hikers, bikers, dogs, and wheelchair users. Dogs must be leashed. This trail rarely receives enough snow for skis or snowshoes. Horses and hunting are prohibited.

**Access, fees:** Parking and access are free. Trails are closed to the public between midnight–6 A.M. The Province Lands Visitor Center on Race Point Road is open daily from 9 A.M.–4:30 P.M.

**Maps:** A guide to national seashore bike trails is available at the Province Lands and Salt Pond Visitor Centers in Eastham (see addresses below). The *Cape Cod & North Shore Bicycle Map,* a detailed map of roads and bike paths on Cape Cod and the Islands and Cape Ann and the North Shore, is available for $4.25 from Rubel BikeMaps, P.O. Box 401035, Cambridge, MA 02140, website: www.bikemaps.com, and from area stores listed at the website. The waterproof/tearproof *Cape Cod National Seashore Map 250* costs $9.95 from Trails Illustrated, 800/962-1643, website: http://maps.nationalgeographic.com/trails/. For a topographic area map, request Provincetown from USGS Map Sales, Federal Center, Box 25286, Denver, CO 80225, 888/ASK-USGS (888/275-8747), website: http://mapping.usgs.gov.

**Directions:** Drive U.S. 6 east to Provincetown. At the traffic lights on U.S. 6, turn right onto Race Point Road. Continue to the Beech Forest parking area on the left; the Province Lands Visitor Center is a short distance farther on the right.

**Contact:** Cape Cod National Seashore, 99 Marconi Station Site Rd., Wellfleet, MA 02667, 508/349-3785, website: www.nps.gov/caco/index.htm. Salt Pond Visitor Center (corner of Nauset Road and Route 6, Eastham), 508/255-3421. Province Lands Visitor Center (on Race Point Road, off Route 6, at the north-

ern end of Cape Cod National Seashore and approximately one mile from Provincetown), 508/487-1256.

## 22 GREAT ISLAND TRAIL
**6 mi/3.5 hrs**
**in the Cape Cod National Seashore in Wellfleet**

A friend and I took this hike in late afternoon on a warm spring day as the sinking sun ignited the dunes a vivid yellow that contrasted sharply with the cobalt sky. We watched dozens of tiny crabs scatter from us in a wave of motion that for an instant made me think the sand was inexplicably sliding away. We watched high, thin cirrus clouds create a rainbow halo around the sun. We saw no one else in three hours on this trail—except a lone sea kayaker paddling the glassy waters of the bay far offshore. The beach here is a great place to watch the sun set over Cape Cod Bay.

a hiker on the Great Island Trail, Cape Cod National Seashore

From the parking lot, the trail enters the woods, following a wide forest road. An optional side loop (adding two miles to the hike) leads to the Tavern Site, so named because fragments of a 17th-century tavern were excavated there; nothing remains today, however. The main trail leads over Great Beach Hill—which has no views—and out to the grasslands separating the beach from the forest. Follow that old road around to Jeremy Point overlook, where the dunes end abruptly and you reach the beach on Cape Cod Bay. At low tide, the long spit out to Jeremy Point may be walkable, but be aware that it disappears under the ocean when the tide rises. Return the way you came.

**User groups:** Hikers only. No wheelchair facilities. This trail rarely receives enough snow for skis or snowshoes. Bikes, dogs, horses, and hunting are prohibited.

**Access, fees:** Parking and access are free. Trails are closed to the public between midnight–6 A.M. The Salt Pond Visitor Center is open daily from 9 A.M.–4:30 P.M.

**Maps:** An information board is at the trailhead, and trail information is available at the Salt Pond Visitor Center (see address below). The *Cape Cod & North Shore Bicycle Map,* a detailed map of roads and bike paths on Cape Cod and the Islands and Cape Ann and the North Shore, is available for $4.25 from Rubel BikeMaps, P.O. Box 401035, Cambridge, MA 02140, 617/776-6567, website: www .bikemaps.com, and from area stores listed at the website. The waterproof/tearproof *Cape Cod National Seashore Map 250* costs $9.95 from Trails Illustrated, 800/962-1643, website: http://maps.nationalgeographic.com/trails/. For a topographic area map, request Wellfleet from USGS Map Sales, Federal Center, Box 25286, Denver, CO 80225, 888/ASK-USGS (888/275-8747), website: http://mapping.usgs.gov.

**Directions:** From the Salt Pond Visitor Center at the Doane Road Exit in Eastham, drive U.S. 6 east for 8.2 miles. Turn left at the sign for Wellfleet Center and Harbor. Drive 0.4

mile and turn left at the sign for Blue Harbor. In another 0.6 mile you reach the marina; turn right, following the road (with the water on your left) for 2.5 miles to the Great Island parking lot on the left.

**Contact:** Cape Cod National Seashore, 99 Marconi Station Site Rd., Wellfleet, MA 02667, 508/349-3785, website: www.nps.gov/caco/index.htm. Salt Pond Visitor Center (corner of Nauset Road and Route 6, Eastham), 508/255-3421. Province Lands Visitor Center, 508/487-1256.

## 23 ATLANTIC WHITE CEDAR SWAMP

1 mi/0.75 hr

**in the Cape Cod National Seashore in South Wellfleet**

I consider this one of the highlights of the national seashore—and almost as much for the site's historic significance as for this short but uniquely beautiful swamp trail. It was from this spot, on January 18, 1903, that the Italian Guglielmo Marconi transmitted a 48-word message to England and received an immediate reply—the first two-way transoceanic communication and first wireless telegram between America and Europe. The four huge towers that once stood here are long gone; in fact, more than half the land where they stood has since eroded into the sea. Considering the way the ocean and wind continually batter this narrowest section of Cape Cod—the peninsula is barely a mile across here—one has to wonder how many years will elapse before the sea cuts the outer cape off completely from the mainland.

The Atlantic White Cedar Swamp Trail begins among stunted oak and pine trees. But as you descend at a very gentle grade, the trees grow taller—they are more protected from the harsh ocean climate in this hollow of sorts. Pitch pine, black and white oak, golden beachheather, and broom crowberry thrive here, though many are still twisted in the manner characteristic of a place buffeted by almost constant winds. A boardwalk winds through the swamp—an eerie depression formed, like other kettles on the cape, by a melting glacial ice block. The swamp's peat floor reaches down 24 feet. Cedars crowd in on the boardwalk, some leaning over it, creating an almost overwhelming sense of intimacy in this odd little forest. The trail emerges abruptly from the swamp onto an old sand road that leads back to the parking lot.

**User groups:** Hikers only. The Marconi station is wheelchair accessible. This trail rarely receives enough snow for skis or snowshoes. Bikes, dogs, horses, and hunting are prohibited.

**Access, fees:** Parking and access are free. Trails are closed to the public between midnight–6 A.M. The Salt Pond Visitor Center is open daily from 9 A.M.–4:30 P.M.

**Maps:** A trail guide is available at the trailhead. Maps and information about the national seashore are available at the Salt Pond Visitor Center (see address below). The *Cape Cod & North Shore Bicycle Map,* a detailed map of roads and bike paths on Cape Cod and the Islands and Cape Ann and the North Shore, is available for $4.25 from Rubel BikeMaps, P.O. Box 401035, Cambridge, MA 02140, website: www.bikemaps.com, and from area stores listed at the website. The waterproof/tearproof *Cape Cod National Seashore Map 250* costs $9.95 from Trails Illustrated, 800/962-1643, website: http://maps.nationalgeographic.com/ trails/. For a topographic area map, request Wellfleet from USGS Map Sales, Federal Center, Box 25286, Denver, CO 80225, 888/ASK-USGS (888/275-8747), website: http://mapping .usgs.gov.

**Directions:** Drive U.S. 6 east to Eastham. Five miles beyond the Doane Road exit for the Salt Pond Visitor Center, turn right at signs for the Marconi station and continue to the parking lot. The Marconi station, which has historical displays, is between the lot and the beach. The trail begins at the parking lot.

**Contact:** Cape Cod National Seashore, 99 Marconi Station Site Rd., Wellfleet, MA 02667,

508/349-3785, website: www.nps.gov/caco/ index.htm. Salt Pond Visitor Center (corner of Nauset Road and Route 6, Eastham), 508/255-3421. Province Lands Visitor Center, 508/487-1256.

## 24 NAUSET MARSH
1.2 mi/0.75 hr
**in the Cape Cod National Seashore in Eastham**

This easy-to-follow trail has numerous interpretive signs with information about its abundant flora and a good view of Nauset Marsh. From the visitor center parking lot, start out on the Buttonbush Trail for the Blind, which leads shortly to the Nauset Marsh Trail. The Marsh Trail passes through pitch pine, black cherry, and eastern red cedar trees, then follows the edge of Salt Pond. (The pond was created when a glacier receded and left behind enormous salt blocks, which eventually melted, leaving kettle ponds such as this one in their wake. The ocean later broke through a land barrier to infiltrate Salt Pond.) The trail then turns away from the channel connecting pond to ocean and enters a forest of honeysuckle and cedar. It passes an open overlook above Nauset Marsh, which at one time was navigable. After entering a forest of red cedar and bayberry, the trail passes a side path leading nearly a mile to a good view of the marsh at a spot marked by the Doane Memorial, a plaque paying tribute to a family that once owned land here. The loop culminates near the visitor center parking lot.

**User groups:** Hikers only. No wheelchair facilities. This trail rarely receives enough snow for skis or snowshoes. Bikes, dogs, horses, and hunting are prohibited.

**Access, fees:** Parking and access are free. Trails are closed to the public between midnight–6 A.M. The Salt Pond Visitor Center is open daily from 9 A.M.–4:30 P.M.

**Maps:** A trail guide is available in a box at the trailhead, and maps and information about the national seashore are available in the visitor center. The *Cape Cod & North Shore Bicycle*

*Map,* a detailed map of roads and bike paths on Cape Cod and the Islands and Cape Ann and the North Shore, is available for $4.25 from Rubel BikeMaps, P.O. Box 401035, Cambridge, MA 02140, website: www.bikemaps.com, and from area stores listed at the website. The waterproof/tearproof *Cape Cod National Seashore Map 250* costs $9.95 from Trails Illustrated, 800/962-1643, website: http://maps.nationalgeographic.com/trails/. For a topographic area map, request Orleans from USGS Map Sales, Federal Center, Box 25286, Denver, CO 80225, 888/ASK-USGS (888/275-8747), website: http://mapping.usgs.gov.

**Directions:** Drive U.S. 6 east to Eastham. Take the exit for Doane Road, following signs for national seashore information to the Salt Pond Visitor Center.

**Contact:** Cape Cod National Seashore, 99 Marconi Station Site Rd., Wellfleet, MA 02667, 508/349-3785, website: www.nps.gov/caco/index.htm. Salt Pond Visitor Center (corner of Nauset Road and Route 6, Eastham), 508/255-3421. Province Lands Visitor Center, 508/487-1256.

## 25 CAPE COD RAIL TRAIL
### 25 mi one-way/12 hrs
**in Dennis, Harwich, Brewster, Orleans, Eastham, and Wellfleet**

Following a former railroad bed, the paved Cape Cod Rail Trail extends for 25 miles from Route 134 in South Dennis to Lecount Hollow Road in South Wellfleet, near the Cape Cod National Seashore's Marconi Visitor Center, making for about a two-hour bike ride. The mostly flat, paved trail crosses cranberry bogs, forests, and several roads, providing numerous access and egress points, including at the entrance to Nickerson State Park on Route 6A in Brewster, and at Locust Road in Eastham, which is off U.S. 6 near the Cape Cod National Seashore's Salt Pond Visitor Center on Doane Road. The trail passes through Nickerson, which has its own hiking trail system and a bike path, and it connects with bike paths

at the national seashore. The rail trail is very much a citizen's path—every time I've biked on it, it has been busy with cyclists, in-line skaters, walkers, adults, and children. As such, it can be difficult to bike at a fast pace, but it's a scenic and safe outing for a family. You can do sections of varying length rather than the entire 25-mile distance, which is why this receives such an easy difficulty rating.

**User groups:** Hikers, bikers, dogs, horses, and wheelchairs users. Dogs must be leashed. This trail rarely receives enough snow for skis or snowshoes. Hunting is prohibited.

**Access, fees:** Parking and access are free.

**Maps:** The *Cape Cod & North Shore Bicycle Map,* a detailed map of roads and bike paths on Cape Cod and the Islands and Cape Ann and the North Shore, is available for $4.25 from Rubel BikeMaps, P.O. Box 401035, Cambridge, MA 02140, website: www.bikemaps.com, and from area stores listed at the website. Or get the waterproof *Cape Cod National Seashore Map 250* for $9.95 from Trails Illustrated, 800/962-1643, website: http://maps.nationalgeographic.com/trails/. For topographic area maps, request Dennis, Harwich, and Orleans from USGS Map Sales, Federal Center, Box 25286, Denver, CO 80225, 888/ASK-USGS (888/275-8747), website: http://mapping.usgs.gov.

**Directions:** To reach the trail's western end, from U.S. 6 in Dennis, take Exit 9 onto Route 134 south. Proceed through two traffic signals to a large parking lot on the left for the Cape Cod Rail Trail. The eastern terminus is at Lecount Hollow Road in South Wellfleet, near the Cape Cod National Seashore's Marconi Visitor Center and off U.S. 6. The trail can be accessed at numerous points along its path.

**Contact:** Cape Cod Rail Trail/Nickerson State Park, P.O. Box 787, Brewster, MA 02631, 508/896-3491, website: www.state.ma.us/dem/parks/ccrt.htm. Massachusetts Division of Forests and Parks, 100 Cambridge St., 19th Floor, Boston, MA 02202, 800/831-0569 (in-state only) or 617/626-1250 ext. 1451, website: www.state.ma.us/dem/forparks.htm. Rails to

Trails Conservancy, 1100 17th St. NW, 10th floor, Washington, DC 20036, 202/331-9696, website: www.railtrails.org.

## 26 AQUINNAH

**3 mi/1.5 hrs**

**in Aquinnah on Martha's Vineyard**

The vibrant pastels of the clay cliffs at Aquinnah, the westernmost point of Martha's Vineyard island, are an eye-catching attraction at any time of day, but particularly striking at sunset, when the sun's low, long rays bring out the layered browns, yellows, reds, whites, and deep grays. This hike is an easy walk along Moshup Beach and is popular with tourists. From the parking lot, follow the sandy trail, sometimes crossing a boardwalk, which parallels Moshup Road. Within minutes you are on the beach; turn right and follow the beach to the cliffs. At high tide, you may have difficulty walking to the far end of the cliffs. Head back the way you came.

**User groups:** Hikers only. No wheelchair facilities. This trail rarely receives enough snow for skis or snowshoes, and is not suitable for bikes or horses. Dogs and hunting are prohibited.

**Access, fees:** A parking fee of $5 per hour, or $15 maximum for a day, is charged from Memorial Day weekend–mid-October, although cyclists, walkers, or anyone not parking a vehicle can access the beach free. Three seasonal ferry services make regular trips, from May–October, to Vineyard Haven or Oak Bluffs from Falmouth, 508/548-4800, and Hyannis, 508/778-2600, on Cape Cod as well as from New Bedford, MA, 508/997-1688. The Steamship Authority, 508/477-8600, carries vehicles and passengers from Woods Hole on Cape Cod to Vineyard Haven year-round and Woods Hole to Oak Bluffs from May 15–October 15.

**Maps:** Although no map is needed for this hike, for a topographic area map, request Squibnocket from USGS Map Sales, Federal Center, Box 25286, Denver, CO 80225, 888/ASK-USGS (888/275-8747), website: http://mapping.usgs.gov.

**Directions:** The cliffs at Aquinnah are on Moshup Beach at the western tip of Martha's Vineyard, in the town of Aquinnah, and at the end of the State Road, which crosses the island from Vineyard Haven. Ferry services make regular trips to Vineyard Haven and Oak Bluffs from Falmouth and Hyannis on Cape Cod, as well as from New Bedford, MA (see additional ferry information above).

**Contact:** Aquinnah Town Hall, 65 State Rd., Aquinnah, MA 02535, 508/645-2300. Martha's Vineyard Chamber of Commerce, P.O. Box 1698, Vineyard Haven, MA 02568, 508/693-0085, website: www.mvy.com/islandinfo/townAquinnah.html.

# Rhode Island

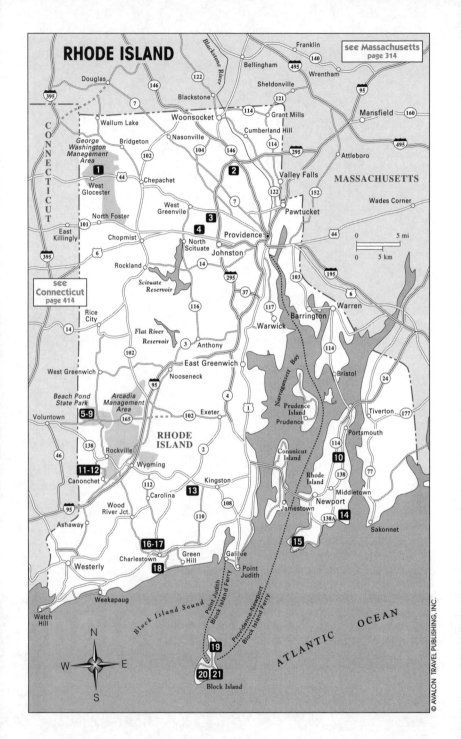

# Rhode Island

# Rhode Island

The country's smallest state and one of its flattest, Rhode Island doesn't entice hikers and backpackers to travel great distances in order to sample its trails, as do states like Maine, New Hampshire, and Vermont. But locals enjoy its relatively shorter and easier hikes, which are scattered across the Ocean State in an abundance that surprised me when I first visited.

Most of the hikes here are in either state parklands or private preserves. Each state park's management creates regulations specific to its property, and many impose restrictions on bikes and require that dogs be leashed. The two premier public lands are the George Washington Management Area, in the state's northwest corner, and the Arcadia Management Area, in the southwest corner.

Several hikes covered in this guide are in bird sanctuaries or other places known among bird-watchers; the state's woods and waters are a popular stop for migratory birds along the Atlantic Flyway. The private preserves are often open only to hikers, and some require a small fee.

Rhode Island's winters rarely see enough snow for cross-country skiing or snowshoeing. But many public lands, like the Arcadia Management Area, harbor a wealth of dirt roads perfect for mountain biking. Respect postings that prohibit bikes from certain trails. Hunting is generally allowed in season on any land that is not posted with signs specifically prohibiting it. The Arcadia Management Area requires trail users to wear fluorescent orange during the hunting season.

## 1 WALKABOUT TRAIL

**2–8 mi/1–4 hrs**

**in the George Washington Management Area in Chepachet**

The George Washington Management Area is one of the two nicest backcountry parklands in Rhode Island, and the Walkabout is its signature hiking trail. Mostly flat, it winds along the shores of largely undeveloped ponds and through quiet woodlands punctuated by glacial-erratic boulders, crossing myriad brooks and streams. In fact, the first view of Bowdish Reservoir occurs not far down the trail, at a large rock. This is a wet place that can be buggy in spring.

The trail offers three options—the eight-mile orange loop, the six-mile red loop, and the two-mile blue loop—all well blazed and beginning from the same parking lot. The possibilities in this remote corner of tiny Rhode Island begin with the Walkabout, but the forest roads here open up much more terrain for easy hiking, skiing, or mountain biking.

**User groups:** Hikers, dogs, horses, and snowshoers. Dogs must be leashed. No wheelchair facilities. Bikes and skis are prohibited. Hunting is allowed in season.

**Access, fees:** Parking and access are free.

**Maps:** A trail map is available at the park headquarters on U.S. 44 in Glocester. For a topographic area map, request Thompson, CT, from USGS Map Sales, Federal Center, Box 25286, Denver, CO 80225, 888/ASK-USGS (888/275-8747), website: http://mapping.usgs.gov.

**Directions:** The entrance is off U.S. 44, 0.8 mile east of its junction with Route 94, at a sign for the George Washington Camping Area. Proceed past the gatehouse; at 0.3 mile from U.S. 44, turn left across from a trail marked by orange, red, and blue blazes—this hike's terminus. The Walkabout Trail begins a short distance farther, on the right, across from a parking area.

**Contact:** George Washington Management Area, 2185 Putnam Pike, Chepachet, RI 02814, 401/568-2248. Rhode Island Division of Forest Environment, 1037 Hartford Pike, North Scituate, RI 02857, 401/647-1439, website: www.state.ri.us/dem.

## 2 LIME ROCK PRESERVE

**2 mi/1.5 hrs**

**in Lincoln**

This nature preserve in Lincoln boasts a variety of distinctive regional habitats—rich woodlands, forested swamps, streams, open water, and calcareous ledges. Lime Rock is considered one of Rhode Island's top natural areas, harboring more rare plant species than any other site in the state. Records of notable botanists visiting the area date back over 100 years. This hike offers a pleasant walk in the woods along a long-abandoned electric railroad bed and around a pond. From the dirt driveway, follow the railroad bed. Initially, it sits low and may be flooded—you can easily hike the higher ground to either side—but it gradually rises high above the surrounding terrain. Within about a half mile, just before you reach a point where the railroad bed passes above a little stream valley, turn onto a trail diverging right (the first you encounter on that side). It leads to the far end of the pond, which soon becomes visible through the trees, and across an earthen dam where you get a good view of the pond. Across the dam, ledges rise high up a hillside. Turn left with the trail, circling the pond and eventually reaching the railroad bed again, where turning left returns you to the parking area.

**User groups:** Hikers, bikers, dogs, horses, skiers, and snowshoers. No wheelchair facilities. Hunting is allowed in season.

**Access, fees:** Parking and access are free. The preserve is open to hikers year-round from dawn–dusk.

**Maps:** For a topographic area map, request Attleboro from USGS Map Sales, Federal Center, Box 25286, Denver, CO 80225, 888/ASK-USGS (888/275-8747), website: http://mapping.usgs.gov.

**Directions:** From Route 146 northbound, take the exit for Route 123 westbound, proceed to the traffic lights, and turn right. Drive 1.7 miles; at the Blackstone Valley Historical Society building, turn left onto Wilbur Road and drive another half mile. Watch closely for a small dirt parking area on the right, across from the Just Right Printing Company; there's no sign, but information boards are set back from the road. From Route 146 southbound, take the Route 246 exit, turn right, drive 0.3 mile, and then turn left on Wilbur Road.

**Contact:** The Nature Conservancy Rhode Island Chapter, 159 Waterman St., Providence, RI 02906, 401/331-7110, website: http://nature.org, email: ri@tnc.org.

## ❸ POWDER MILL LEDGES
**2 mi/1 hr**

**in Smithfield**

 The three well-marked loop trails through this bird sanctuary lead you along open meadows, a small pond and boggy areas, and through pine forest. The orange loop offers a self-guided tour of its vegetation; pick up a pamphlet at the visitor center. Although at times the traffic sounds from nearby U.S. 44 are audible, the birdsong is constant. This is an attractive local walk, not to mention a good place for birding. A lengthy list of the month's bird sightings is posted on an information board outside the visitor center. On the spring day of my visit, species checked off the list included the red-tailed hawk, downy woodpecker, black-capped chickadee, and white-breasted nuthatch. The center conducts regular educational and children's programs as well.

Pick up the trail behind the information board. This hike links all three loops around the refuge perimeter—the first blazed orange, the second blue, and the third yellow—but you can easily make a shorter loop. The yellow loop, the longest and outermost of the three, follows power lines for a time and can be very hot on a sunny summer day.

**User groups:** Hikers only. No wheelchair facilities. These trails rarely receive enough snow for snowshoes and are not suitable for skis. Bikes, dogs, horses, and hunting are prohibited.

**Access, fees:** Parking and access are free. Trails are open to the public from dawn–dusk every day.

**Maps:** A map is available in the Audubon Society Visitor Center, which is open Tuesday–Friday from noon–5 P.M., and Saturday from noon–4 P.M. For a topographic area map, request North Scituate from USGS Map Sales, Federal Center, Box 25286, Denver, CO 80225, 888/ASK-USGS (888/275-8747), website: http://mapping.usgs.gov.

**Directions:** From U.S. 44 in Smithfield, turn south on Route 5. Immediately on the left is the entrance to Powder Mill Ledges, at the Audubon Society of Rhode Island headquarters. From I-295, take exit 7B onto Route 44 West. At the fourth set of lights, turn left onto Route 5 (Sanderson Road). Turn left at the second driveway into the parking lot.

**Contact:** The Audubon Society of Rhode Island, 12 Sanderson Rd., Smithfield, RI 02917, 401/949-5454, website: www.asri.org.

## ❹ SNAKE DEN
**0.5 mi/0.5 hr**

**in Snake Den State Park in Johnston**

The Snake Den is a narrow defile in the woods, barely more than 100 yards long, with broken rock ledges rising as much as 40 feet above the trail on one side. A short, easy walk, it's a good place to bring young children, though you'll want to watch out for loose rock on the ledges. From the pullout, follow the wide trail into the woods, bearing right where it forks. Within minutes, you drop down into the Snake Den; the trail leads straight through and continues into the woods beyond. It is possible—exercising appropriate caution—to scramble up through natural breaks, or gullies, in the ledges and get atop these low cliffs; then take a trail that loops back to where you started hiking; or you can access the trail over the ledges from the opposite end of the cliffs.

**User groups:** Hikers, dogs, skiers, and

snowshoers. No wheelchair facilities. This trail is not suitable for bikes or horses. Hunting is prohibited.

**Access, fees:** Parking and access are free.

**Maps:** For a topographic area map, request North Scituate from USGS Map Sales, Federal Center, Box 25286, Denver, CO 80225, 888/ASK-USGS (888/275-8747), website: http://mapping.usgs.gov.

**Directions:** From U.S. 44, follow Route 5 southbound for 0.6 mile, turn right onto Brown Avenue, and drive 0.4 mile to a pullout on the right, across from a wide, unmarked trail blocked by large rocks. From U.S. 6, 2.6 miles west of I-295, turn north onto Brown Avenue and drive two miles to the pullout on the left.

**Contact:** Rhode Island Division of Parks and Recreation, 2321 Hartford Ave., Johnston, RI 02919-1719, 401/222-2632, website: www.riparks.com.

## ⑤ STEPSTONE FALLS
**3.4 mi/2.5 hrs**

**in the Arcadia Management Area in Exeter**

The Ben Utter Trail, marked by a sign at the back of the parking area, parallels Falls River, actually a small, stone-littered brook. Relatively flat, the trail follows the brook for 1.7 miles to Stepstone Falls, where water tumbles through a series of short ledges, the highest about two feet tall. I walked this trail on a beautiful Saturday morning in August and, surprisingly, had it all to myself. Follow the yellow blazes and the obvious footpath all the way to the falls and then double back. The trail actually ends at the dirt Falls River Road, just beyond the falls, which is reached via Escoheag Hill Road; by shuttling cars, you could make this a 1.7-mile walk and not have to double back.

Special note: For a longer hike, link this one with Penny Hill (see next listing), which begins from the same parking area.

**User groups:** Hikers, dogs, skiers, and snowshoers. Dogs must be leashed from March 1–August 15. No wheelchair facilities. Bikes and horses are prohibited. Hunting is allowed

in season; all trail users are required to wear at least 200 square inches of fluorescent orange, as a cap and vest, during the hunting season (from the second Saturday of October–the last day of February).

**Access, fees:** Parking and access are free. Austin Farm Road is closed to motor vehicles at Escoheag Hill Road during the winter. Other roads open to traffic in summer but closed in winter include Brook Trail, Barber Trail, and Blitzkrieg Trail.

**Maps:** A free trail map is available at the Arcadia headquarters (see address below) and in various parking lots in the management area. For topographic area maps, request Hope Valley and Voluntown from USGS Map Sales, Federal Center, Box 25286, Denver, CO 80225, 888/ASK-USGS (888/275-8747), website: http://mapping.usgs.gov.

**Directions:** From the junction of Routes 3 and 165 in Exeter, drive west on Route 165 for about 5.5 miles and turn right onto the paved Escoheag Hill Road. Continue another mile and turn right onto the dirt Austin Farm Road. Two roads diverge here; take the left one, drive past a former ranger station, and pull into a parking area on the left about a mile from Escoheag Hill Road, immediately before the bridge over Falls River. To reach the Arcadia Management Area headquarters from the junction of Routes 3 and 165, drive west on Route 165 for 1.5 miles and turn left onto Arcadia Road. Continue 2.5 miles to a T intersection, turn left, and drive 0.6 mile to the headquarters on the right.

**Contact:** Arcadia Management Area headquarters, 260 Arcadia Rd., Richmond, RI 02832, 401/539-1052. Rhode Island Division of Forest Environment, 1037 Hartford Pike, North Scituate, RI 02857, 401/647-1439, website: www.state.ri.us/dem.

## ⑥ PENNY HILL
**1.6 mi/1 hr**

**in the Arcadia Management Area in Exeter**

Although trees largely block any view from the

370-foot Penny Hill summit, this hike offers an appealing walk through the woods to hilltop ledges that young kids would enjoy scrambling around on. From the parking area, cross the bridge over Falls River and ignore the first yellow-blazed trail entering the woods on the right. About 75 feet past the bridge, turn right into the woods on the yellow-blazed Breakheart Trail. The trail crosses a brook in an area that is often muddy, emerges from the woods within a half mile of the start to cross Austin Farm Road again, and then ascends moderately to the craggy height of Penny Hill. From here, the Breakheart Trail descends to the east, but this hike returns the way you came.

Special note: For a combination of hikes, link this one with Stepstone Falls (see previous listing), which begins from the same parking area.

**User groups:** Hikers, snowshoers, and dogs. Dogs must be leashed from March 1–August 15. No wheelchair facilities. Bikes and horses are prohibited. Hunting is allowed in season; all trail users are required to wear at least 200 square inches of fluorescent orange, as a cap and vest, during the hunting season (from the second Saturday of October–the last day of February).

**Access, fees:** Parking and access are free. Austin Farm Road is closed to motor vehicles at Escoheag Hill Road during the winter. Other roads open to traffic in summer but closed in winter include Brook Trail, Barber Trail, and Blitzkrieg Trail.

**Maps:** A free trail map is available at the Arcadia headquarters (see address below) and in various parking lots in the management area. For topographic area maps, request Hope Valley and Voluntown from USGS Map Sales, Federal Center, Box 25286, Denver, CO 80225, 888/ASK-USGS (888/275-8747), website: http://mapping.usgs.gov.

**Directions:** From the junction of Routes 3 and 165 in Exeter, drive west on Route 165 for about 5.5 miles and turn right onto the paved Escoheag Hill Road. Continue another mile and turn right onto the dirt Austin Farm Road. Two roads diverge here; take the left one, drive past a former ranger station, and pull into a parking area on the left about a mile from Escoheag Hill Road, immediately before the bridge over Falls River. To reach the Arcadia Management Area headquarters from the junction of Routes 3 and 165, drive west on Route 165 for 1.5 miles and turn left onto Arcadia Road. Continue 2.5 miles to a T intersection, turn left, and drive 0.6 mile to the headquarters on the right.

**Contact:** Arcadia Management Area headquarters, 260 Arcadia Rd., Richmond, RI 02832, 401/539-1052. Rhode Island Division of Forest Environment, 1037 Hartford Pike, North Scituate, RI 02857, 401/647-1439, website: www.state.ri.us/dem.

## ❼ BREAKHEART POND LOOP
### 1.5 mi/1 hr
**in the Arcadia Management Area in Exeter**

This relatively flat, 1.5-mile loop around Breakheart Pond provides a good introduction to hiking in Arcadia. The pond views are better from the trail on its west bank, which you reach during the second half of this hike. From the parking area, pick up the Breakheart Trail— marked by a sign—and follow its yellow blazes counterclockwise around the pond. Water views are few here, though you could bushwhack off the trail to the shore. Reaching the pond's north end in about 0.7 mile, turn left with the blazed trail, cross a brook on a wooden footbridge beside a small beaver dam, and reach a junction of trails. Turn left and you soon come upon the pond's west shore, with decent views of Breakheart Pond. The loop finishes in the parking area.

**User groups:** Hikers, dogs, skiers, and snowshoers. Dogs must be leashed. No wheelchair facilities.from March 1–August 15. Bikes and horses are prohibited. Hunting is allowed in season; all trail users are required to wear at least 200 square inches of fluorescent orange, as a cap and vest, during the hunting season (from the second Saturday of October–the last day of February).

**Access, fees:** Parking and access are free. Austin Farm Road is closed to motor vehicles at Escoheag Hill Road during the winter. Other roads open to traffic in summer but closed in winter include Brook Trail, Barber Trail, and Blitzkrieg Trail.

**Maps:** A free map of trails and roads is available at the Arcadia headquarters (see address below) and in various parking lots in the management area. For topographic area maps, request Hope Valley and Voluntown from USGS Map Sales, Federal Center, Box 25286, Denver, CO 80225, 888/ASK-USGS (888/275-8747), website: http://mapping.usgs.gov.

**Directions:** From the junction of Routes 3 and 165 in Exeter, drive west on Route 165 for 2.9 miles and turn right at the sign for Camp E-Hun-Tee onto the dirt Frosty Hollow Road. Follow that road for 1.6 miles and turn right onto the dirt Austin Farm Road. Continue another half mile to the road's end at Breakheart Pond. Park in the lot to the right. To reach the Arcadia Management Area headquarters from the junction of Routes 3 and 165, drive west on Route 165 for 1.5 miles and turn left onto Arcadia Road. Continue 2.5 miles to a T intersection, turn left, and drive 0.6 mile to the headquarters on the right.

**Contact:** Arcadia Management Area headquarters, 260 Arcadia Rd., Richmond, RI 02832, 401/539-1052. Rhode Island Division of Forest Environment, 1037 Hartford Pike, North Scituate, RI 02857, 401/647-1439, website: www.state.ri.us/dem.

# 8 FOREST ROADS LOOP
## 8 mi/4 hrs

**in the Arcadia Management Area in Exeter**

I've included this eight-mile loop on dirt roads through Arcadia less for hikers than as a fairly easy outing for novice mountain bikers, including children, and—on those rare occasions when snow falls—cross-country skiers. I biked this loop to reach the foot trails I wanted to hike: Breakheart Pond, Penny Hill, and Stepstone Falls (see listings for all three hikes, this chapter). In fact, the start of the trail to the Mount Tom Cliffs (see next listing) lies just a half mile west, on Route 165, of the parking area where this loop begins and ends. Be aware that some of these dirt roads are open to motor vehicles.

From the parking area, follow the dirt Brook Trail a short distance north and turn right on the first dirt road you encounter, passing a gate. Within a quarter mile, pass another gate and turn left on the dirt Frosty Hollow Road. Continue about 1.5 miles to the dirt Austin Farm Road and turn right, reaching the foot of Breakheart Pond in a half mile, where you have a good view of the pond. Retrace that half mile and continue west on Austin Farm Road for another 2.2 miles, cross a bridge over the Falls River (where the Penny Hill and Stepstone Falls hikes begin), and go another half mile before turning left on the dirt Barber Road. Within two miles, the road leads to a T intersection; turn left, cross Falls River again, then turn right on the Brook Trail and follow it about a half mile back to the parking area.

**User groups:** Hikers, bikers, dogs, horses, skiers, and snowshoers. Dogs must be leashed. No wheelchair facilities.from March 1–August 15. Hunting is allowed in season; all trail users are required to wear at least 200 square inches of fluorescent orange, as a cap and vest, during the hunting season (from the second Saturday of October–the last day of February).

**Access, fees:** Parking and access are free. Austin Farm Road is closed to motor vehicles at Escoheag Hill Road during the winter. Other roads open to traffic in summer but closed in winter include Brook Trail, Barber Trail, and Blitzkrieg Trail.

**Maps:** A free trail map is available at the Arcadia headquarters (see address below) and in various parking lots in the management area. For topographic area maps, request Hope Valley and Voluntown from USGS Map Sales, Federal Center, Box 25286, Denver, CO 80225,

888/ASK-USGS (888/275-8747), website: http://mapping.usgs.gov.

**Directions:** From the junction of Routes 3 and 165 in Exeter, drive west on Route 165 for three miles and turn right onto the dirt road marked Brook Trail. Park in the large dirt lot immediately on the right. To reach the Arcadia Management Area headquarters from the junction of Routes 3 and 165, go west on Route 165 for 1.5 miles and turn left onto Arcadia Road. Drive 2.5 miles to a T intersection, turn left, and drive 0.6 mile to the headquarters on the right.

**Contact:** Arcadia Management Area headquarters, 260 Arcadia Rd., Richmond, RI 02832, 401/539-1052. Rhode Island Division of Forest Environment, 1037 Hartford Pike, North Scituate, RI 02857, 401/647-1439, website: www.state.ri.us/dem.

## 9 MOUNT TOM CLIFFS
### 2.8 mi/1.5 hrs
**in the Arcadia Management Area in Exeter**
The cliffs that form the low ridge of Mount Tom offer what are probably Arcadia's most sweeping views. From the back of the parking lot, follow the Mount Tom Trail's white blazes into the woods. The trail is flat and wide at first, passing several giant anthills, maybe a foot high and two feet across, best observed from a comfortable distance. In about a half mile, turn left onto the dirt road called Blitzkrieg Trail (watch closely for the white blazes), which reenter the woods on the right within 0.1 mile, where the road crosses Parris Brook. The trail ascends easily for less than a mile until it reaches the open crest of the Mount Tom cliffs and a 270-degree view of gently rolling forest. Walk the trail over the ledges for about 0.1 mile, until the trail begins descending into the woods again, and then backtrack.

**User groups:** Hikers, snowshoers, and dogs. Dogs must be leashed from March 1–August 15. No wheelchair facilities. Bikes and horses are prohibited. Hunting is allowed in season; all trail users are required to wear at least 200 square inches of fluorescent orange, as a cap and vest, during the hunting season (from the second Saturday of October–the last day of February).

**Access, fees:** Parking and access are free. Austin Farm Road is closed to motor vehicles at Escoheag Hill Road during the winter. Other roads open to traffic in summer but closed in winter include Brook Trail, Barber Trail, and Blitzkrieg Trail.

**Maps:** A free trail map is available at the Arcadia headquarters (see address below) and in various parking lots in the management area. For topographic area maps, request Hope Valley and Voluntown from USGS Map Sales, Federal Center, Box 25286, Denver, CO 80225, 888/ASK-USGS (888/275-8747), website: http://mapping.usgs.gov.

**Directions:** From the junction of Routes 3 and 165 in Exeter, drive west on Route 165 for 3.6 miles. Immediately after crossing the bridge over the Wood River, turn left at the sign for the hunter checking station into a large dirt parking lot beside a Quonset hut. To reach the Arcadia Management Area headquarters from the junction of Routes 3 and 165, drive west on Route 165 for 1.5 miles and turn left onto Arcadia Road. Continue 2.5 miles to a T intersection, turn left, and drive 0.6 mile to the headquarters on the right.

**Contact:** Arcadia Management Area headquarters, 260 Arcadia Rd., Richmond, RI 02832, 401/539-1052. Rhode Island Division of Forest Environment, 1037 Hartford Pike, North Scituate, RI 02857, 401/647-1439, website: www.state.ri.us/dem.

## 10 NORMAN BIRD SANCTUARY
### 2 mi/1.5 hrs
**in Middletown**
This private sanctuary, established in 1949, comprises 450 acres and is home to creatures ranging from pheasants to foxes. It has eight miles of trails through forests, old fields, pastures, and swamps. The most popular trail here is the Hanging Rock Trail, which traverses

the narrow crest of a rock spine that seems wholly out of place rising 40 to 50 feet above the surrounding woods and marsh. Stunted trees, characteristic of high mountains, grow atop it. Although parts of the ridge are somewhat exposed, it's a fairly easy walk and great for kids. The sanctuary, as the name implies, is also a good spot for birding.

From the parking lot, walk past the visitor center (housed in a 125-year-old barn) onto the main path and follow it a short distance. Turn left onto the Quarry Trail, passing a field with bird feeders. Turn right on the Blue Dot Trail, going by a former slate quarry on the left, now filled with water. Cross a boardwalk, climb a short hill past ledges, and turn left at a T junction. Beyond the views of Gardner Pond, the trail turns sharply uphill onto the Hanging Rock Trail. Go left, following the increasingly open ridge to its end, where it terminates abruptly at a short cliff with Narragansett Bay views. Double back, staying with the Hanging Rock Trail to its beginning, then turn right and follow signs back to the barn.

**User groups:** Hikers only. No wheelchair facilities. The trail is not suitable for bikes, horses, skis, or snowshoes. Dogs and hunting are prohibited.

**Access, fees:** There is an entrance fee of $4 for adults, $3 for seniors, and $1 for children. Members of the private sanctuary and children under three are admitted free. The sanctuary is open seven days a week, 9 A.M.–5 P.M., except Thanksgiving and Christmas.

**Maps:** A map and trail guide is available at the visitor center. For a topographic area map, request Prudence Island from USGS Map Sales, Federal Center, Box 25286, Denver, CO 80225, 888/ASK-USGS (888/275-8747), website: http://mapping.usgs.gov.

**Directions:** From Route 114, at the Middletown-Portsmouth town line, turn east onto Mitchell's Lane at a small sign for the Norman Bird Sanctuary. At 1.4 miles, turn left at a stop sign. Drive a half mile, then bear right at a fork and proceed another 0.3 mile to a four-way stop at a crossroads. Drive straight through the intersection and go another 0.8 mile to the sanctuary entrance on the right.

**Contact:** Norman Bird Sanctuary, 583 Third Beach Rd., Middletown, RI 02842, 401/846-2577, website: www.normanbirdsanctuary.org, email: info@normanbirdsanctuary.org. Ask about guided group tours and workshops for adults and children.

## 11 GREEN FALLS POND
**2 mi/1 hr**
**in Rockville**

Here's a relatively easy two-mile walk through the woods—which happens to include some interesting, if brief, scrambling over rock ledges—to a scenic little pond. The Narragansett Trail actually follows the Rhode Island–Connecticut state line for a short distance before turning west into Connecticut and reaching the shore of Green Falls Pond. Although the blue-blazed trail continues west around the pond, my companion and I found it difficult to follow and returned the way we'd hiked in—but not until we had enjoyed the pond views for a while.

**User groups:** Hikers only. No wheelchair facilities. This trail rarely receives enough snow for snowshoes and is not suitable for bikes, horses, or skis. A portion of this hike lies on private land, and use restrictions can change. Dogs are not allowed unless otherwise posted. Hunting is permitted in season unless otherwise posted.

**Access, fees:** Parking and access are free.

**Maps:** For a topographic area map, request Voluntown from USGS Map Sales, Federal Center, Box 25286, Denver, CO 80225, 888/ASK-USGS (888/275-8747), website: http://mapping.usgs.gov.

**Directions:** From Route 138 in Rockville, turn onto Camp Yawgoog Road, drive 3.8 miles, passing Camp Yawgoog, and park in a turnout on the right.

**Contact:** Connecticut Forest and Park Association Inc., 16 Meriden Rd., Rockfall, CT 06481-2961, 860/346-2372, website: www.ctwoodlands.org, email: conn.forest.assoc@Dnet .net. Pachaug State Forest, RFD 1, Voluntown, CT 06384, 860/376-4075.

## 🖸 LONG AND ELL PONDS
**0.5 mi/0.5 hr**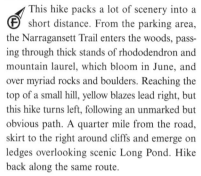
**in Rockville**

This hike packs a lot of scenery into a short distance. From the parking area, the Narragansett Trail enters the woods, passing through thick stands of rhododendron and mountain laurel, which bloom in June, and over myriad rocks and boulders. Reaching the top of a small hill, yellow blazes lead right, but this hike turns left, following an unmarked but obvious path. A quarter mile from the road, skirt to the right around cliffs and emerge on ledges overlooking scenic Long Pond. Hike back along the same route.

**User groups:** Hikers only. No wheelchair facilities. This trail rarely receives enough snow for snowshoes, and is not suitable for skis. Bikes, dogs, horses, and hunting are prohibited.

**Access, fees:** Parking and access are free. The refuge is open from a half hour before sunrise–a half hour after sunset.

**Maps:** No map is needed for this short hike. For a topographic area map, request Voluntown from USGS Map Sales, Federal Center, Box 25286, Denver, CO 80225, 888/ASK-USGS (888/275-8747), website: http://mapping.usgs.gov.

**Directions:** From Route 138 in Rockville, turn onto Winchek Road, follow it for 0.1 mile, and then turn onto Canonchet Road. Continue a half mile, bear right, and drive another mile to a small parking area on the left. There is also space for cars at the roadside just beyond the parking area.

**Contact:** The Long Pond Woods Refuge is jointly managed by two conservation organizations and a state agency: The Nature Conservancy Rhode Island Chapter, 159 Waterman St., Providence, RI 02906, 401/331-7110, email: ri@tnc.org, website: http://nature.org; the Audubon Society of Rhode Island, 12 Sanderson Rd., Smithfield, RI 02917, 401/949-5454,

website: www.asri.org; and the Rhode Island Department of Environmental Management, 235 Promenade St., Providence, RI 02908-5767, 401/222-6800, website: www.state.ri.us/dem.

## 🖽 GREAT SWAMP MANAGEMENT AREA
**5.5 mi/2.5 hrs**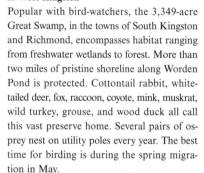
**in West Kingston**

Popular with bird-watchers, the 3,349-acre Great Swamp, in the towns of South Kingston and Richmond, encompasses habitat ranging from freshwater wetlands to forest. More than two miles of pristine shoreline along Worden Pond is protected. Cottontail rabbit, white-tailed deer, fox, raccoon, coyote, mink, muskrat, wild turkey, grouse, and wood duck all call this vast preserve home. Several pairs of osprey nest on utility poles every year. The best time for birding is during the spring migration in May.

This loop follows relatively flat, wide woods roads that make for easy biking or skiing (although snow is rare here), as well as hiking. From the parking area, go around the gate and follow the woods road straight (avoiding the side roads leading right) for a bit more than a mile until you reach an old hangar and the scenic Worden Pond shore. Double back on the woods road and take the second left onto another dirt road, which loops around the perimeter of the Great Swamp Impoundment, a man-made marsh of more than 130 acres and a good place for birding. Where that woods road ends beyond the swamp, turn left, and then left again at the next junction to return to the parking area.

**User groups:** Hikers, bikers, dogs, horses, skiers, and snowshoers. Dogs must be leashed. No wheelchair facilities. Hunting is allowed in season.

**Access, fees:** Parking and access are free.

**Maps:** A trail map is available at the management area headquarters (see address below). For a topographic area map, request Kingston from USGS Map Sales, Federal Center, Box

25286, Denver, CO 80225, 888/ASK-USGS (888/275-8747), website: http://mapping.usgs.gov. **Directions:** From Route 138 in West Kingston, just west of the junction with Route 110, turn west onto Liberty Lane. Drive a mile to the road's end and then turn left onto the dirt Great Neck Road. Within a mile, you pass the headquarters on the right. The dirt road ends one mile from Liberty Lane, at a big parking area.

**Contact:** Great Swamp Management Area, P.O. Box 218, West Kingston, RI, 401/789-0281. Rhode Island Division of Fish and Wildlife, Stedman Government Center, 4808 Tower Hill Rd., Wakefield, RI 02879, 401/789-3094, fax 401/783-4460, website: www.state.ri.us/dem.

## 14 NEWPORT CLIFF WALK
**6 mi/3 hrs**
**in Newport**

Come here during the height of the summer tourist season, and the experience of your walk suffers from the crowds, which often form a conga line along the trail's length. But come here in the off-season—during the spring or fall—and you gain much more enjoyment from this scenic walk atop cliffs that fall away dramatically to the ocean. What is probably Rhode Island's most famous walk passes mansions built by some of the nation's wealthiest families in the late 19th and early 20th centuries—including Rosecliff, the house used in the filming of *The Great Gatsby.*

This hike brings you along the Cliff Walk and then down Bellevue Avenue for mansion views that are often better than the views from the Cliff Walk. Follow the wide walkway along the cliff tops; do not stray onto private property. Though the walk begins on flat and level ground, parts of it become rocky. After about three miles, you emerge at the end of a side street, Ledge Road. Turn right and follow Ledge Road straight onto Bellevue Avenue. Walk down Bellevue, past the mansions, back to Memorial Boulevard, and then turn right to return to Easton Beach.

**User groups:** Hikers only. No wheelchair facilities. This trail is not suitable for bikes, dogs, horses, skis, or snowshoes. Hunting is prohibited.

**Access, fees:** Parking and access are free. The Cliff Walk is closed to the public between 9 P.M.–6 A.M.

**Maps:** No map is necessary for this walk, but for a topographic area map, request Newport from USGS Map Sales, Federal Center, Box 25286, Denver, CO 80225, 888/ASK-USGS (888/275-8747), website: http://mapping.usgs.gov. **Directions:** Take Route 114 to Route 138 to Route 138A in Newport (Memorial Boulevard). Follow it to Easton Beach and park. On foot, continue up Memorial Boulevard in the town center's direction, walking a short distance to a large sign on the median strip indicating the start of the Cliff Walk, behind Cliff Walk Manor.

**Contact:** Newport County Convention and Visitor Bureau, 23 America's Cup Ave., Newport, RI 02840, 401/849-8098 or 800/976-5122, website: www.gonewport.com.

## 15 BRENTON POINT STATE PARK
**2 mi/1 hr**
**in Newport**

This easy walk follows the rocky, wind-battered shoreline at Brenton Point. The land once belonged to the Budlong family, but before World War II the federal government took it over and built military facilities here. Later the feds turned the land over to the state for this park. I recommend driving to the farthest parking lot on the right—beside a field popular among kite flyers—then crossing the road and walking along the shore back in the direction you came by car. Clamber up onto a crooked stone jetty jutting a short distance into the ocean. Continue along the shore, walking for about a mile, and then double back to your car.

**User groups:** Hikers and dogs. A wheelchair-accessible paved sidewalk parallels the shoreline. This trail is not suitable for bikes, horses, skis, or snowshoes. Hunting is prohibited.

**Access, fees:** Parking and access are free.

**Maps:** No map is necessary for this short walk, but for a topographic area map, request Newport from USGS Map Sales, Federal Center, Box 25286, Denver, CO 80225, 888/ASK-USGS (888/275-8747), website: http://mapping.usgs.gov.

**Directions:** Take Route 114 or Route 138 into Newport. Turn left onto Thames Street and then bear right into the through-lanes. Turn right (remaining on Thames) at the Newport Bay Club and Hotel. Turn right onto Wellington Street; follow it to its end and then turn right onto Harrison Street, passing Fort Adams State Park. At the end of the road, turn right onto Ocean Drive. Brenton Point State Park lies a short distance ahead, with several places to park.

**Contact:** Rhode Island Division of Parks and Recreation, 2321 Hartford Ave., Johnston, RI 02919-1719, 401/222-2632, website: www.ri-parks.com.

## 16 VIN GORMLEY TRAIL
**8 mi/4 hrs**

**in Burlingame State Park in Charlestown**

The Vin Gormley Trail makes a big loop around Watchaug Pond in the state park. Although the flat terrain here doesn't offer any compelling views, this trail is a nice walk along narrow footpaths, woods roads, and a stretch of paved road for a short distance. You cross several brooks and boardwalks through boggy areas. The entire trail is well blazed and easy to follow. In spring 2001, a covered bridge with benches was built across Perry Healy Brook along this hike, about 1.5 miles from the Prosser Trail road; it makes a nice spot for a rest break.

**User groups:** Hikers and bikes. No wheelchair facilities. This trail rarely receives enough snow for skis or snowshoes. Dogs, horses, and hunting are prohibited.

**Access, fees:** Parking and access are free.

**Maps:** A map of the Vin Gormley Trail is available at the state park campground office off Klondike Road in Charlestown, which is open

weekdays year-round, and at the picnic area off Prosser Trail, which is open from Memorial Day–Labor Day. For a topographic area map, request Carolina from USGS Map Sales, Federal Center, Box 25286, Denver, CO 80225, 888/ASK-USGS (888/275-8747), website: http://mapping.usgs.gov.

**Directions:** Take U.S. 1 to Charlestown and the exit for Burlingame State Park. Drive 0.6 mile to the park entrance on the left. Watch for the yellow blazes of the Vin Gormley Trail, which crosses the parking lot.

**Contact:** Burlingame State Park, Sanctuary Rd., Charlestown, RI 02813, 401/322-8910. Rhode Island Division of Parks and Recreation, 2321 Hartford Ave., Johnston, RI 02919-1719, 401/222-2632, website: www.riparks.com.

## 17 KIMBALL WILDLIFE SANCTUARY
**1.5 mi/0.75 hr**

**in Charlestown**

Owned by the Audubon Society of Rhode Island, this 29-acre woodlands parcel on Watchaug Pond, abutting Burlingame State Park, has three well-marked loop trails through the woods. This hike makes a loop around the refuge, incorporating sections of all three trails. Begin behind the information kiosk, turning left onto the red trail and then left at each successive junction with the orange, green, and blue trails. Spring, when flowers bloom and the songbirds return, is the time to visit this refuge.

**User groups:** Hikers only. No wheelchair facilities. The trails rarely receive enough snow for snowshoes, and are not suitable for skis. Bikes, dogs, horses, and hunting are prohibited.

**Access, fees:** Parking and access are free.

**Maps:** A basic trail map is available at the information kiosk next to the parking area. For a topographic area map, request Carolina from USGS Map Sales, Federal Center, Box 25286, Denver, CO 80225, 888/ASK-USGS (888/275-8747), website: http://mapping.usgs.gov.

**Directions:** Take U.S. 1 to Charlestown and

the exit for Burlingame State Park. Take the first left at a small sign for the Kimball Wildlife Refuge. Drive to the end of the road, turn left again, and proceed to a dirt parking lot near an information kiosk.

**Contact:** Kimball Wildlife Sanctuary, 180 Sanctuary Rd., Charlestown, RI 02813. The Audubon Society of Rhode Island, 12 Sanderson Rd., Smithfield, RI 02917, 401/949-5454, website: www.asri.org.

## 18 NINIGRET NATIONAL WILDLIFE REFUGE
**1.4 mi/1 hr**
**in Charlestown**

Established in 1971, the refuge occupies 407 acres of shrublands, grasslands, freshwater ponds, salt marshes, and a barrier beach around a former naval training site. This is a stopover area for migrating birds and a wintering spot for some bird species. Call the refuge headquarters (see number below) for a list of bird species found at Rhode Island's national wildlife refuges, including Ninigret. This hike follows wide dirt roads through marsh and out to the shore of the saltwater Ninigret Pond and is a good place to see herons, cormorants, geese, and migrating songbirds. Hiking here one spring day, we saw a sea kayaker in the distance paddling surreptitiously out toward a group of swans.

From the parking lot, walk on the runway to the left until you reach the kiosk at the start of the Grassy Point Nature Trail, which consists of two loops totaling 1.4 miles. Take the shorter loop first, beginning to the left of the kiosk and following the arrows, eventually returning to the kiosk. The second loop begins to the right. A wide spur road, not marked by arrows, diverges left from this trail out to Grassy Point, where an observation deck offers good views of the pond and its birds. At the end of the loop, walk down a runway back to the kiosk.

**User groups:** Hikers only. No wheelchair facilities. This trail rarely receives enough snow for snowshoes, and is not suitable for bikes,

horses, or skis. Dogs and hunting are prohibited.

**Access, fees:** Parking and access are free.

**Maps:** A map is posted in an information kiosk at the trailhead, and a look at it is really all that's needed for this hike. For topographic area maps, request Carolina and Quonochontaug from USGS Map Sales, Federal Center, Box 25286, Denver, CO 80225, 888/ASK-USGS (888/275-8747), website: http://mapping.usgs.gov.

**Directions:** Take U.S. 1 to Charlestown and the exit for Ninigret Park. Follow signs to the park, turn left into it, and then follow signs to the nature trails and a parking lot on an old runway.

**Contact:** The U.S. Fish and Wildlife Service refuge headquarters is in Shoreline Plaza on Old Post Road/Route 1 in Charlestown, 401/364-9124. For information by mail, write to P.O. Box 307, Charlestown, RI 02813. The office is open from 8 A.M.–4:30 P.M. weekdays. Friends of the Rhode Island National Wildlife Refuges, P.O. Box 553, Charlestown, RI 02813, 401/364-9124, website: www.friendsnwr-ri.org/.

## 19 BLOCK ISLAND: CLAY HEAD TRAIL AND THE MAZE
**0.7 mi/0.75 hr**
**in Clay Head Preserve, Block Island**

As with the other trails on Block Island, the best way to explore this one is to ride a bicycle from the ferry landing in Old Harbor to the trailhead. Reasonably fit people could easily link this hike with the two other Block Island hikes in this chapter, Rodman's Hollow and Mohegan Bluffs, in a day. Bikes can be brought over on the ferry or rented in Old Harbor when you get off the ferry. The best times to go are spring and fall, when hundreds of thousands of birds representing some 150 species descend on the island during their seasonal migrations—the Nature Conservancy describes Clay Head as one of the best spots in the Northeast to see migratory songbirds in autumn. Tourists jam the island in July and August, the months to avoid.

a view from the Clay Head Trail, Block Island

The Clay Head Trail follows the bluff top, passing Clay Head Swamp, the edge of the Littlefield Farm, and numerous views of the bluffs and seashore. At first, several trails leading left into the dense scrub brush and forest are posted as private property. Once beyond these, however, you'll see many unmarked trails diverging off the Clay Head Trail and weaving through a cooked-spaghetti tangle of footpaths called the Maze. These trails are fun to explore, though they can get confusing.

**User groups:** Hikers and dogs. Dogs must be leashed. No wheelchair facilities. This trail rarely receives enough snow for skis or snow-shoes, and is not suitable for horses. Bikes and hunting are prohibited.

**Access, fees:** Access to hiking trails on the island is free.

**Maps:** Get a basic map of the island and its hiking trails at the Chamber of Commerce, which operates an information booth at the ferry landing in Old Harbor and a visitor center around the corner on Water Street. Bike shops within walking distance of the ferry landing have maps of island roads. For a topographic area map, request Block Island from USGS Map Sales, Federal Center, Box 25286, Denver, CO 80225, 888/ASK-USGS (888/275-8747), website: http://mapping.usgs.gov.

**Directions:** The Interstate Navigation Co. (see below) operates ferries year-round from Point Judith, RI, and during the summer from New London, CT. The Island Hi-Speed Ferry (see below) operates between Point Judith and Block Island from May–October. From the island's ferry landing in Old Harbor, turn right on Water Street along the waterfront strip, left on Dodge Street, and then right at the post office onto Corn Neck Road. Continue about 3.5 miles to a dirt road on the right marked by a post indicating the Clay Head Trail. Follow the dirt road about a half mile to the trailhead (there is a bike rack).

**Contact:** Block Island Chamber of Commerce, P.O. Box D, Block Island, RI 02807, 401/466-2982 or 800/383-2474, website: www.blockislandchamber.com, email: BIchamber@biri.com. Block Island Tourism Council, Dept. B, 23 Water St., P.O. Box 356, Block Island, RI 02807, 800/383-BIRI, fax 401/466-5286, website: www.blockislandinfo.com. Interstate Navigation Company, 401/783-4613, website: www.blockislandferry.com, email: interstate@edgenet.net. The Island Hi-Speed Ferry, 877/733-9425, website: www.blockislandhighspeedferry.com, email: contact@islandhighspeedferry.com. For information about trails on conservation land, visit The Nature Conservancy's Block Island office on High Street near the harbor, 401/466-2129. The Nature Conservancy Rhode Island Chapter, 159 Waterman St., Providence, RI 02906, 401/331-7110, email: ri@tnc.org, website: http://nature.org.

## 20 BLOCK ISLAND: RODMAN'S HOLLOW
**0.5 mi/0.75 hr**
**on Block Island**

A depression left by a receding glacier, Rodman's Hollow is a wild little corner of the island overgrown with dense brush. A loop trail cuts through it, cresting one small hill with sweeping views of the homes and rolling hills at the southern end of the island. Rodman's Hollow was the inspiration for the 1970s conservation movement that helped protect a quarter of Block Island from development. It's also part of the Greenway, a network of interconnecting trail systems that includes the Enchanted Forest, Turnip Farm, and Fresh Swamp Preserve. The shadbush bloom in early to mid-May is a beautiful sight.

I recommend bicycling from the ferry landing in Old Harbor to this and other Block Island trails in this chapter: Mohegan Bluffs, and Clay Head Trail and the Maze. Bikes can be brought over on the ferry or rented in Old Harbor when you get off the ferry. The best times to visit are spring and fall, when hundreds of thousands of birds representing some 150 species descend on the island during their seasonal migrations. Avoid coming in July and August, when tourists crowd the island.

From just beyond the turnstile, follow the loop trail to the right; a sign indicates a "short loop" and a "long loop," but it's all one trail. The trail crests a hill at a wooden bench. From here, the path forks; following the right fork brings you back to Black Rock Road (where you would turn right to return to the trailhead).

Bear left instead, following the trail through the hollow and eventually back to the spot where the path first split.

**User groups:** Hikers and dogs. Dogs must be leashed. No wheelchair facilities. This trail rarely receives enough snow for skis or snowshoes, and is not suitable for horses. Bikes and hunting are prohibited.

**Access, fees:** Access to hiking trails on the island is free.

**Maps:** Get a basic map of the island and its hiking trails at the Chamber of Commerce, which operates an information booth at the ferry landing in Old Harbor and a visitor center around the corner on Water Street. Bike shops within walking distance of the ferry landing have maps of island roads. For a topographic map, request Block Island from USGS Map Sales, Federal Center, Box 25286, Denver, CO 80225, 888/ASK-USGS (888/275-8747), website: http://mapping.usgs.gov.

**Directions:** The Interstate Navigation Co. (see below) operates ferries year-round from Point Judith, RI, and during the summer from New London, CT. The Island Hi-Speed Ferry (see below) operates between Point Judith and Block Island from May–October. From the island's ferry landing in Old Harbor, turn left on Water Street and head straight through an intersection, passing the First Baptist Church on your left, onto Spring Street. It runs straight onto Southeast Light Road, passing two trails leading to the Mohegan Bluffs. The road becomes Mohegan Trail, then hooks right and becomes Lakeside Drive. About four miles from Old Harbor, turn left onto Cooneymus Road. The road doglegs left, then right, and then passes a stone wall and a sign on the left overlooking Rodman's Hollow. Just beyond that point, turn left onto the dirt Black Rock Road. A quarter mile farther is the trailhead, marked by a bike rack and a wooden turnstile. The road continues to a trail leading down to the beach.

**Contact:** Block Island Chamber of Commerce, P.O. Box D, Block Island, RI 02807, 401/466-2982 or 800/383-2474, website: www.blockislandchamber.com, email: BIchamber@biri.com. Block Island Tourism Council, Dept. B, 23 Water St., P.O. Box 356, Block Island, RI 02807, 800/383-BIRI, fax 401/466-5286, website: www.blockislandinfo.com. Interstate Navigation Company, 401/783-4613, website: www.block-islandferry.com, email: interstate@edgenet.net. The Island Hi-Speed Ferry, 877/733-9425, website: www.blockislandhighspeedferry.com, email: contact@islandhighspeedferry.com. For information about trails on conservation land, visit The Nature Conservancy's Block Island office on High Street near the harbor, 401/466-2129. The Nature Conservancy Rhode Island Chapter, 159 Waterman St., Providence, RI 02906, 401/331-7110, email: ri@tnc.org, website: http://nature.org.

## 21 BLOCK ISLAND: MOHEGAN BLUFFS

**0.5 mi/0.75 hr**

**on Block Island**

Dubbed one of the Last Great Places in the Western Hemisphere by the Nature Conservancy, Block Island has evolved as a unique microenvironment since a glacier left 12 miles of ocean between it and mainland New England 10,000 years ago. More than 40 of its indigenous species are listed as rare or endangered. Just seven miles long and three miles wide, it has 32 miles of hiking trails.

The best way to explore Block Island's trails is to ride a bicycle from the ferry landing in Old Harbor to the trailheads. This way you see more trails and enjoy some scenic cycling on country roads through a landscape of rolling hills and open fields crisscrossed by an uncanny 2,042 miles of stone walls. Reasonably fit people could easily link this hike with the two other Block Island hikes in this chapter (Rodman's Hollow, and Clay Head Trail and the Maze) in a day, by biking between them. Bikes can be brought over on the ferry or rented in Old Harbor when you get off the ferry. The best times to go are spring and fall, when hundreds of thousands of birds representing some 150 species descend on the island during their seasonal migrations. In May, the white blossoms of the shadblow are in bloom. Tourists jam the island in July and August, the months to avoid. Winters tend to be cold and windy.

This hike is actually two short walks near one another. The first leads to Southeast Lighthouse and great views of the spectacular Mohegan Bluffs. The lighthouse, built in 1873 on the eroding cliffs 150 feet above the sea, had to be moved back 200 feet in 1993 because the ocean had chewed away nearly all the land

Mohegan Bluffs, Block Island

between it and the sea. Legend has it that in 1590 the island's first inhabitants, the Narragansett Indians—also known as the Manisses tribe, for the name they gave the island—drove a party of invading Mohegan Indians over the cliffs here.

From the second trailhead, a trail leads to a wooden staircase that drops steeply down to the rocky beach, a nice place to walk below the bluffs. Don't try scrambling around on the cliffs themselves, though—the soil and rocks are as loose as they appear, and dangerous rockslides occur frequently.

**User groups:** Hikers and dogs. Dogs must be leashed. No wheelchair facilities. This trail rarely receives enough snow for skis or snowshoes, and is not suitable for horses. Bikes and hunting are prohibited.

**Access, fees:** Access to hiking trails on the island is free.

**Maps:** Get a basic map of the island and its hiking trails at the Chamber of Commerce, which operates an information booth at the ferry landing in Old Harbor and a visitor center around the corner on Water Street. Bike shops within walking distance of the ferry landing have maps of island roads. For a topographic map, request Block Island from USGS Map Sales, Federal Center, Box 25286, Denver, CO 80225, 888/ASK-USGS (888/275-8747), website: http://mapping.usgs.gov.

**Directions:** The Interstate Navigation Co. (see below) operates ferries year-round from Point Judith, RI, and during the summer from New London, CT. The Island Hi-Speed Ferry (see below) operates between Point Judith and Block Island from May–October. From the island's ferry landing in Old Harbor, turn left on Water Street and head straight through an intersection, passing the First Baptist Church on your left, onto Spring Street, which runs straight onto Southeast Light Road. About two miles from the ferry landing, a footpath on the left leads a short distance to Southeast Lighthouse, above the Mohegan Bluffs. A short distance up the road is a trailhead (with a rack for parking bicycles) leading to stairs that descend the bluffs to the beach.

**Contact:** Block Island Chamber of Commerce, P.O. Box D, Block Island, RI 02807, 401/466-2982 or 800/383-2474, website: www.blockislandchamber.com, email: BIchamber@biri.com. Block Island Tourism Council, Dept. B, 23 Water St., P.O. Box 356, Block Island, RI 02807, 800/383-BIRI, fax 401/466-5286, website: www.blockislandinfo.com. Interstate Navigation Company, 401/783-4613, website: www.blockislandferry.com, email: interstate@edgenet.net. The Island Hi-Speed Ferry, 877/733-9425, website: www.blockislandhighspeedferry.com, email: contact@islandhighspeedferry.com. For information about trails on conservation land, visit The Nature Conservancy's Block Island office on High Street near the harbor, 401/466-2129. The Nature Conservancy Rhode Island Chapter, 159 Waterman St., Providence, RI 02906, 401/331-7110, email: ri@tnc.org, website: http://nature.org.

# Connecticut

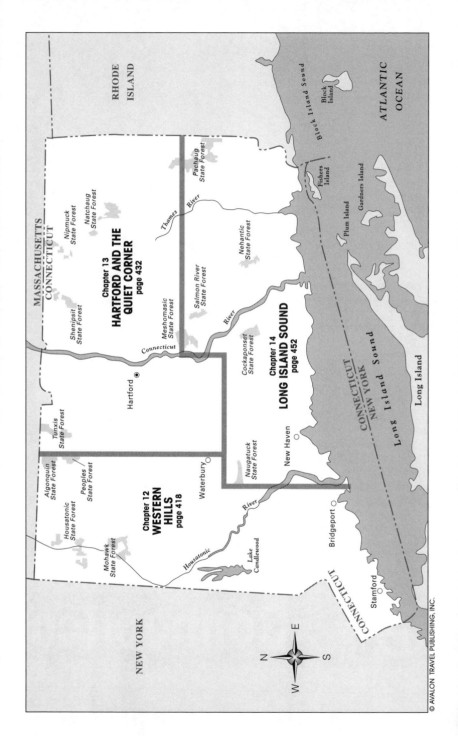

## Chapter 12

© MICHAEL LANZA

# Western Hills

# Western Hills

In the state's rural northwestern corner, the Appalachian Trail follows a chain of green hills above the beautiful Housatonic River valley for 52 miles in Connecticut, from the New York border to the Massachusetts line. In the eyes of many hikers, this part of Connecticut harbors the state's best hiking—and certainly its biggest hills and best opportunities for longer day hikes and multiday backpacking trips.

The hikes up Bear Mountain and Lion's Head probably have no rivals in the state. Most of the hikes in this chapter are along the AT, though the others are worth a visit, including Mount Tom State Park, a great hike for young kids. All of the hikes in this chapter lie in the state's northwestern corner.

The prime hiking season begins by April and extends into October or November, but winters are also milder than in northern New England; at certain times in winter you may find some of these trails with little or no snow on them.

Along the Appalachian Trail, dogs must be kept under control, and horses, mountain bikes, hunting, and firearms are prohibited—although that rule does not preclude hunters inadvertently wandering near the AT. Cross-country skiing and snowshoeing are permitted on the AT, and much of the trail in Connecticut presents easy to moderate terrain for snowshoeing.

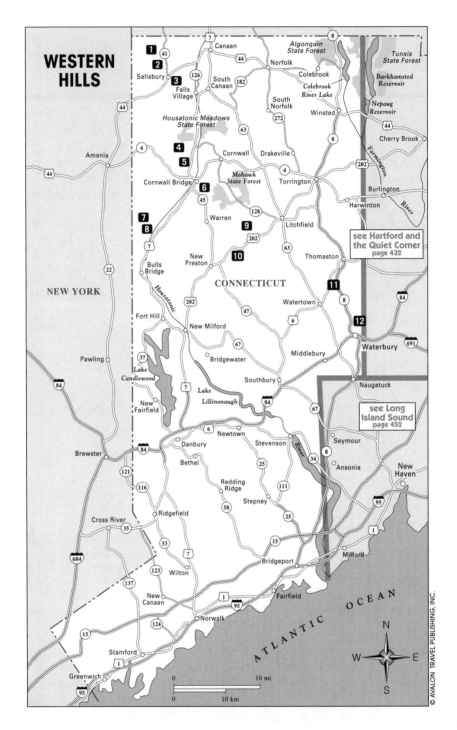

see Hartford and
the Quiet Corner
page 432

see Long
Island Sound
page 452

© AVALON TRAVEL PUBLISHING, INC.

# 1 BEAR MOUNTAIN
**6.5 mi/4 hrs**

**in Salisbury**

This loop over the state's highest peak, 2,316-foot Bear Mountain, is one of the most popular Connecticut hikes and a busy place on a nice weekend. Youth groups and backpackers make frequent use of the few campsites along the Appalachian Trail just south of Bear's summit. Still, even here you can avoid the crowds with an early start—or a well-planned late one. I started up this loop with a backpack at dusk one Saturday, as the last few day hikers were returning to their cars. A nearly full moon lit the trail for me, making for a beautiful, and solitary, 2.4-mile walk to the Brassie Brook shelter camping area. Come morning, I hit the trail early and had the summit to myself. This hike gains more than 1,600 feet in elevation. An interesting footnote, by the way, is that the summit of the state's highest mountain is not the highest point in Connecticut; that's actually on the southern slope of Mount Frissell, whose summit lies just over the line into Massachusetts, northwest of Bear Mountain.

From the trailhead, follow the Undermountain Trail for 1.9 miles to its junction with the Appalachian Trail, marked by a sign. To the left (south), three camping areas are spread out along the AT, from a half mile to 1.7 miles distant. Turn right (north) on the AT for the Bear summit. You break out of the trees for sweeping views of the hills, dense forest, and tiny towns that makes up this rural northwest corner of Connecticut. The views are also excellent from the enormous stone pile on the summit. The AT steeply descends the north side of Bear Mountain, and the rocks may be slippery with water or even ice in late fall or early spring. A half mile beyond the summit, turn right onto Paradise Lane Trail, walk two miles to the Undermountain Trail, and turn left for the parking area.

**User groups:** Hikers, snowshoers, and dogs. No wheelchair facilities. This trail is not suitable for skis. Bikes, horses, and hunting are prohibited.

**Access, fees:** Parking and access are free. Camping is prohibited except in designated shelters and campsites along the Appalachian Trail. Campfires are prohibited; campers must cook with portable camp stoves.

**Maps:** For a trail map, refer to map 4 in the *Map and Guide to the Appalachian Trail in Massachusetts and Connecticut,* a five-map set and guidebook available for $19.95 ($14.95 for the maps alone) from the Appalachian Trail Conference (see address below). For topographic area maps, request Ashley Falls and Sharon from USGS Map Sales, Federal Center, Box 25286, Denver, CO 80225, 888/ASK-USGS (888/275-8747), website: http://mapping.usgs.gov.

**Directions:** From the junction of U.S. 44 and Route 41 in Salisbury, drive north on Route 41 for three miles to a parking area on the left for the Undermountain Trail.

**Contact:** Appalachian Trail Conference, 799 Washington St., P.O. Box 807, Harpers Ferry, WV 25425-0807, 304/535-6331, website: www.appalachiantrail.org. Connecticut Forest and Park Association Inc., 16 Meriden Rd., Rockfall, CT 06481-2961, 860/346-2372, website: www.ctwoodlands.org. Appalachian Mountain Club, 5 Joy St., Boston, MA 02108, 617/523-0636, website: www.outdoors.org.

# 2 LION'S HEAD
**4.6 mi/2.5 hrs**

**in Salisbury**

The ridge shared by Bear Mountain (see previous listing) and Lion's Head in Connecticut's northwestern corner may harbor the most pleasant stretch of the Appalachian Trail through Connecticut—and the view from Lion's Head nearly rivals that from the enormously popular Bear Mountain just a few miles to the north. After a pleasant walk through the woods for 2.3 miles, you turn abruptly upward, scramble over exposed rock the last 50 feet to the Lion's Head summit, and step up to wide views of hills, forest, and pastures. On our hike, we shared the summit with just a few Appalachian Trail through-hikers—people who had already walked more than 1,000 miles, yet stood awed by this view. This hike climbs about 1,000 feet.

From the trailhead, follow the white blazes of the Appalachian Trail as it heads west, then swings northward. After you've gone about two miles, the blue-blazed Lion's Head Trail enters from the left; stay on the AT as it swings right and climbs steeply but briefly to the 1,738-foot Lion's Head summit. A ledge about 30 feet south of the actual summit offers the best view, encompassing the Twin Lakes, Prospect Mountain, and the Housatonic Valley. Return the way you came.

**User groups:** Hikers, snowshoers, and dogs. No wheelchair facilities. This trail is not suitable for skis. Bikes, horses, and hunting are prohibited.

**Access, fees:** Parking and access are free. Camping is prohibited except in designated shelters and campsites along the Appalachian Trail. Campfires are prohibited; campers must cook with portable camp stoves.

**Maps:** For a map of hiking trails, refer to map 4 in the *Map and Guide to the Appalachian Trail in Massachusetts and Connecticut,* a five-map set and guidebook available for $19.95 ($14.95 for the maps alone) from the Appalachian Trail Conference (see address below). For topographic area maps, request Ashley Falls and Sharon from USGS Map Sales, Federal Center, Box 25286, Denver, CO 80225, 888/ASK-USGS (888/275-8747), website: http://mapping.usgs.gov.

**Directions:** From the junction of U.S. 44 and Route 41 in Salisbury, drive north on Route 41 for 0.8 mile to a somewhat hidden parking area on the left for the Appalachian Trail.

**Contact:** Appalachian Trail Conference, 799 Washington St., P.O. Box 807, Harpers Ferry, WV 25425-0807, 304/535-6331, website: www.appalachiantrail.org. Connecticut Forest and Park Association Inc., 16 Meriden Rd., Rockfall, CT 06481-2961, 860/346-2372, website: www.ctwoodlands.org. Appalachian Mountain Club, 5 Joy St., Boston, MA 02108, 617/523-0636, website: www.outdoors.org.

## 3 PROSPECT MOUNTAIN AND RAND'S VIEW

**5.2 mi/2.5 hrs**

**in Salisbury**

Rand's View has been praised as the most scenic view along the Appalachian Trail in Con-

the famous Rand's View toward the Riga Plateau, along the Appalachian Trail in Connecticut

© MICHAEL LANZA

necticut. That's a big claim, but a hiker standing at Rand's gazes north across a classic New England countryside of broad pastures and hills. In the left foreground rises the low ridge of Wetauwanchu Mountain. In the distance, from left to right, are Bear Mountain (see listing, this chapter), Mount Everett in Massachusetts, and the abrupt end of the ridge at Jug End (both described in the Berkshires and Western Massachusetts chapter)—a look into the future for an AT through-hiker reaching this spot, because the trail traverses that prominent ridge. On a clear day, you can see Mount Greylock, 50 miles away, on the center-right horizon. The cumulative elevation gained on this hike is about 2,000 feet.

From the parking area, cross Housatonic River Road to the left and pick up the white-blazed Appalachian Trail. The trail is gentle here, so you can quickly walk the two miles to Prospect Mountain's 2,690-foot summit, with its view of the Housatonic Valley and Canaan Mountain. Continue over Prospect another half mile to where the AT turns sharply right and a blue-blazed trail (marked by a sign) leads left a half mile to Limestone shelter. A second sign points to the right toward Rand's View, just 500 feet farther down the Appalachian Trail. Hike back along the same route.

**User groups:** Hikers, snowshoers, and dogs. No wheelchair facilities. Trail sections would be difficult to ski. Bikes, horses, and hunting are prohibited.

**Access, fees:** Parking and access are free. Camping is prohibited except in designated shelters and campsites along the Appalachian Trail. Campfires are prohibited; campers must cook with portable camp stoves.

**Maps:** For a map of hiking trails, refer to map 4 in the *Map and Guide to the Appalachian Trail in Massachusetts and Connecticut,* a five-map set and guidebook available for $19.95 ($14.95 for the maps alone) from the Appalachian Trail Conference (see address below). For topographic area maps, request South Canaan and Sharon from USGS Map Sales,

Federal Center, Box 25286, Denver, CO 80225, 888/ASK-USGS (888/275-8747), website: http://mapping.usgs.gov.

**Directions:** From the junction of U.S. 7 and Route 126 in Falls Village, take Route 126 north for 0.6 mile and turn left on Point of Rocks Road. Drive 0.1 mile and turn right on Water Street. Drive another 0.3 mile, cross the famous Iron Bridge (look for the white blazes of the Appalachian Trail, which crosses this bridge and enters the woods on the right), bear right after the bridge, and then take an immediate right onto Housatonic River Road. Continue 0.4 mile to a parking area on the right marked by a sign reading "Cartop boat launch/Historic Trail." Park on the left, away from the boat launch area.

**Contact:** Appalachian Trail Conference, 799 Washington St., P.O. Box 807, Harpers Ferry, WV 25425-0807, 304/535-6331, website: www.appalachiantrail.org. Connecticut Forest and Park Association Inc., 16 Meriden Rd., Rockfall, CT 06481-2961, 860/346-2372, website: www.ctwoodlands.org. Appalachian Mountain Club, 5 Joy St., Boston, MA 02108, 617/523-0636, website: www.outdoors.org.

## 4 PINE KNOB LOOP
### 2.5 mi/1.5 hrs
**in Housatonic Meadows State Park in Sharon**

This loop hike leads to a pair of scenic views of the hills lining the Housatonic River Valley. The vertical ascent is about 500 feet. From the parking area, follow the blue-blazed Pine Knob Loop Trail. The trail ascends gradually over Pine Knob, arriving at the first view, among low pine trees, about one mile from the trailhead. Another 0.2 mile past that view, turn left (south) on the Appalachian Trail (marked by a sign), now following both white and blue blazes. The next view lies about a half mile beyond the trail junction, and it also looks southeast over the Housatonic Valley. Continuing south on the Appalachian Trail, you reach a junction (marked by a sign) in 0.3 mile where the AT leads straight ahead and this hike turns left, descending the blue-blazed Pine Knob Loop Trail to the parking area.

**User groups:** Hikers, snowshoers, and dogs. Dogs must be leashed. No wheelchair facilities. This trail is not suitable for skis. Bikes, horses, and hunting are prohibited.

**Access, fees:** Parking and access are free. Camping is prohibited except in designated shelters and campsites along the Appalachian Trail. Campfires are prohibited; campers must cook with portable camp stoves.

**Maps:** For a map of hiking trails, refer to map 4 in the *Map and Guide to the Appalachian Trail in Massachusetts and Connecticut,* a five-map set and guidebook available for $19.95 ($14.95 for the maps alone) from the Appalachian Trail Conference (see address below). For topographic area maps, request Ellsworth and Cornwall from USGS Map Sales, Federal Center, Box 25286, Denver, CO 80225, 888/ASK-USGS (888/275-8747), website: http://mapping.usgs.gov.

**Directions:** The trail begins at a parking area marked by a sign on U.S. 7 in Housatonic Meadows State Park, between the towns of Cornwall Bridge and West Cornwall, one mile north of the junction with Route 4 and 0.4 mile south of the state park campground entrance.

**Contact:** Appalachian Trail Conference, 799 Washington St., P.O. Box 807, Harpers Ferry, WV 25425-0807, 304/535-6331, website: www.appalachiantrail.org. Connecticut Forest and Park Association Inc., 16 Meriden Rd., Rockfall, CT 06481-2961, 860/346-2372, website: www.ctwoodlands.org. Appalachian Mountain Club, 5 Joy St., Boston, MA 02108, 617/523-0636, website: www.outdoors.org. Housatonic Meadows State Park, c/o Macedonia Brook State Park, 159 Macedonia Brook Rd., Kent, CT 06757, 860/927-3238. Connecticut State Parks Division, 79 Elm St., Hartford, CT 06106-5127, 860/424-3200, fax 860/424-4070, website: www.dep.state.ct.us/stateparks/index.htm.

# 5 BREADLOAF MOUNTAIN
**1 mi/0.75 hr**
**in Housatonic Meadows State Park in Sharon**

I awoke one morning in the campground at Housatonic Meadows State Park to the sound of rain drumming on my tent, and poked my head out to discover a steady but light shower. So I headed for the Mohawk Trail leading up Breadloaf Mountain. This easy hike promised me a quick escape back to my car if the rain really intensified into a downpour—and possibly some interesting foul-weather views of the Housatonic River Valley. Sure enough, before long I stood on the Breadloaf Mountain summit looking out over heavily wooded hillsides cloaked in gray, with wisps of clouds rising off them like a thousand question marks. This hike climbs some 500 feet in elevation.

From the trailhead, follow the blue-blazed Breadloaf Mountain Trail all the way up to the 1,050-foot Breadloaf summit. The Appalachian Trail is located just 0.1 mile beyond the summit, but this hike returns down the Breadloaf Mountain Trail to the parking area.

**User groups:** Hikers, snowshoers, and dogs. Dogs must be leashed. No wheelchair facilities. This trail is not suitable for skis. Bikes, horses, and hunting are prohibited.

**Access, fees:** Parking and access are free. Camping is prohibited except in designated shelters and campsites along the Appalachian Trail. Campfires are prohibited; campers must cook with portable camp stoves.

**Maps:** For a map of hiking trails, refer to map 4 in the *Map and Guide to the Appalachian Trail in Massachusetts and Connecticut,* a five-map set and guidebook available for $19.95 ($14.95 for the maps alone) from the Appalachian Trail Conference (see address below). For topographic area maps, request Ellsworth and Cornwall from USGS Map Sales, Federal Center, Box 25286, Denver, CO 80225, 888/ASK-USGS (888/275-8747), website: http://mapping.usgs.gov.

**Directions:** The trail begins at a parking area marked by a sign for the Mohawk Trail, on U.S. 7 in Housatonic Meadows State Park, between the towns of Cornwall Bridge and West Cornwall, 0.1 mile north of the junction with Route 4 and 1.4 miles south of the state park campground entrance.

**Contact:** Connecticut Forest and Park Association Inc., 16 Meriden Rd., Rockfall, CT 06481-2961, 860/346-2372, website: www.ctwoodlands.org. Housatonic Meadows State Park, c/o Macedonia Brook State Park, 159 Macedonia Brook Rd., Kent, CT 06757, 860/927-3238. Connecticut State Parks Division, 79 Elm St., Hartford, CT 06106-5127, 860/424-3200, website: www.dep.state.ct.us/stateparks/index.htm. Appalachian Trail Conference, 799 Washington St., P.O. Box 807, Harpers Ferry, WV 25425-0807, 304/535-6331, website: www.appalachiantrail.org.

## 6 ECHO ROCK AND DUDLEYTOWN

**5 mi/2.5 hrs**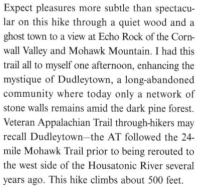

**in Cornwall**

Expect pleasures more subtle than spectacular on this hike through a quiet wood and a ghost town to a view at Echo Rock of the Cornwall Valley and Mohawk Mountain. I had this trail all to myself one afternoon, enhancing the mystique of Dudleytown, a long-abandoned community where today only a network of stone walls remains amid the dark pine forest. Veteran Appalachian Trail through-hikers may recall Dudleytown—the AT followed the 24-mile Mohawk Trail prior to being rerouted to the west side of the Housatonic River several years ago. This hike climbs about 500 feet.

This hike is on private land, and the Dudleytown area has apparently drawn increased interest since the release of the movie *The Blair Witch Project*. The Connecticut Forest and Park Association has been working with the landowners to preserve hiking access, and has agreed to a closure of the trail from prior to Halloween until after All Souls Day in November. Please

respect the closure in order to help maintain access to this hike.

This trail is well marked with blue blazes but goes through enough twists and turns that you can lose it easily if you're not watching closely for the blazes. From the parking area, walk back toward the green. At the Mohawk Trail sign, turn left up paved Dark Entry Road (there may not be a street sign), following blue blazes. The road becomes dirt and ends about a half mile from Route 4. Turn left onto an old woods road. The trail crosses Bonney Brook nearly a mile from Route 4, then parallels the gentle brook. About 1.5 miles out, cross the brook again, entering Dudleytown. A mile past Dudleytown, you reach Echo Rock, a slab on the right. Return the way you came.

**User groups:** Hikers and snowshoers. No wheelchair facilities. Portions of this trail lie on private land, and use restrictions can change. Assume that bikes, dogs, and horses are not allowed unless a trail is specifically marked for them (although many landowners do not object to dogs). Most trails are open to cross-country skiing. Assume that hunting is allowed in season unless otherwise posted.

**Access, fees:** Parking and access are free. There is no parking on Dark Entry Road. This hike is on private land and closed to public access from mid-October–mid-November. Camping and fires are prohibited.

**Maps:** For a topographic area map, request Cornwall from USGS Map Sales, Federal Center, Box 25286, Denver, CO 80225, 888/ASK-USGS (888/275-8747), website: http://mapping.usgs.gov.

**Directions:** At the junction of U.S. 7 and Route 4 in Cornwall Bridge, look for the sign marking the Mohawk Trail on the east side of the green, just north of Baird's General Store. Park in a turnout 75 yards farther east on Route 4.

**Contact:** Connecticut Forest and Park Association Inc., 16 Meriden Rd., Rockfall, CT 06481-2961, 860/346-2372, website: www.ctwoodlands.org.

## 7 COBBLE MOUNTAIN AND PINE HILL

**2.5 mi/2 hrs**

**in Macedonia Brook State Park in Kent**

This loop in Macedonia Brook State Park offers a range of hiking, from easy walking down a flat forest road to steep, rocky stretches and summit views of hills unblemished by signs of development. It's a good hike for young children, ascending only about 500 feet in elevation.

From the parking area, cross the road and pick up the Cobble Mountain Trail (marked by a sign). Follow its white blazes a quarter mile and turn right onto the wide CCC Road (a grassy woods road). Watch for the blazes turning left into the woods again in another quarter mile. The trail then ascends Cobble Mountain, taking you over rock slabs as you near the top. About a half mile from the CCC Road, turn right (north) on the blue-blazed Macedonia Ridge Trail (formerly the route of the Appalachian Trail) and walk 0.1 mile to the Cobble Mountain summit, where open ledges offer views west all the way to the Catskills in New York. The trail follows these ledges for about 100 yards, then enters the woods again and descends steeply over rocky ground to a junction with the Pine Hill Trail (entering from the right) within a half mile. Bear left, staying on the Ridge Trail; you soon reach the top of Pine Hill, where ledges offer a view eastward. A quarter mile past Pine Hill, turn right onto the Old CCC Road and follow it straight for about a mile. Turn left on the white-blazed Cobble Mountain Trail to return to the pavilion parking area.

**User groups:** Hikers, snowshoers, and dogs. Dogs must be leashed. No wheelchair facilities. This trail is not suitable for skis. Bikes, horses, and hunting are prohibited.

**Access, fees:** Parking and access are free. Macedonia Brook State Park is open from 8 A.M.–sunset year-round.

**Maps:** A basic map of hiking trails with park information is available at the park office (see address below). For topographic area maps, request Amenia, Ellsworth, Dover Plains, and Kent from USGS Map Sales, Federal Center, Box 25286, Denver, CO 80225, 888/ASK-USGS (888/275-8747), website: http://mapping.usgs.gov.

**Directions:** From the junction of U.S. 7 and Route 341 in Kent, drive west on Route 341 for 1.8 miles. Turn right at the sign for Macedonia Brook State Park and then follow the signs to the park office, which is two miles from Route 341. Park in the pavilion lot on the right, 0.1 mile beyond the office.

**Contact:** Macedonia Brook State Park, 159 Macedonia Brook Rd., Kent, CT 06757, 860/927-3238. Connecticut State Parks Division, 79 Elm St., Hartford, CT 06106-5127, 860/424-3200, website: www.dep.state.ct.us/stateparks/index.htm. Connecticut Forest and Park Association Inc., 16 Meriden Rd., Rockfall, CT 06481-2961, 860/346-2372, website: www.ctwoodlands.org.

## 8 ST. JOHNS LEDGES AND CALEB'S PEAK

**2.4 mi/2 hrs**

**in Kent**

From atop St. Johns Ledges, you enjoy a broad view of the bucolic Housatonic Valley to the east; I stood there one morning watching a hawk float on the warm breezes. Caleb's Peak offers a decent, if somewhat more limited, view to the south. This AT section includes a very steep 0.1-mile stretch up large rocks laid out as steps by trail crews, and easy walking along the ridge from St. Johns Ledges to Caleb's Peak. This hike's vertical ascent is about 750 feet.

From the turnout, head west into the woods. Within about 0.1 mile, an unmarked side path diverges left to low cliffs frequented by rock climbers. The white-blazed AT continues straight, turns left (southwest), ascends below slab cliffs, and then turns steeply upward, reaching St. Johns Ledges 0.6 mile from the road. Continue another 0.6 mile south on the AT to Caleb's Peak. Hike back along the same route.

**User groups:** Hikers, snowshoers, and dogs.

No wheelchair facilities. This trail is not suitable for skis. Bikes, horses, and hunting are prohibited.

**Access, fees:** Parking and access are free. Camping is prohibited except in designated shelters and campsites along the Appalachian Trail. Campfires are prohibited; campers must cook with portable camp stoves. The dirt access road to the Appalachian Trail closes at sunset.

**Maps:** For a map of hiking trails, refer to map 5 in the *Map and Guide to the Appalachian Trail in Massachusetts and Connecticut,* a five-map set and guidebook available for $19.95 ($14.95 for the maps alone) from the Appalachian Trail Conference (see address below). For topographic area maps, request Ellsworth and Kent from USGS Map Sales, Federal Center, Box 25286, Denver, CO 80225, 888/ASK-USGS (888/275-8747), website: http://mapping.usgs.gov.

**Directions:** From Route 341 on the west side of the Housatonic River in Kent, turn north onto Skiff Mountain Road. Drive 1.1 miles and bear right onto a dirt road marked by a sign for the Appalachian National Scenic Trail. Continue another 1.6 miles to a turnout on the left where the Appalachian Trail's white blazes enter the woods.

**Contact:** Appalachian Trail Conference, 799 Washington St., P.O. Box 807, Harpers Ferry, WV 25425-0807, 304/535-6331, website: www.appalachiantrail.org. Connecticut Forest and Park Association Inc., 16 Meriden Rd., Rockfall, CT 06481-2961, 860/346-2372, website: www.ctwoodlands.org. Appalachian Mountain Club, 5 Joy St., Boston, MA 02108, 617/523-0636, website: www.outdoors.org.

# 🛈 PROSPECT MOUNTAIN
## 2.5 mi/1.5 hrs
**in the Bantam section of Litchfield**

Although the start of this hike lacks much scenic appeal, ledges in two spots offer decent views of western Connecticut's forested hills, including Mount Tom, with its distinctly visible observation tower. The trail also passes between interesting rock ledges just below the summit, which is only about 400 feet higher than the trailhead. Follow the blue blazes of the Mattatuck Trail through an area recovering from tornado damage, ascending steadily. The trail reaches a ridge crest, dips briefly through the ledges, and then emerges from the woods onto a broad, open ledge with good views west to Mount Tom. Continue another 0.1 mile; where the trail turns sharply left, a footpath leads to the right up onto the summit ledges with some views of the surrounding hills. Return the way you came.

**User groups:** Hikers and snowshoers. No wheelchair facilities. Portions of this trail lie on private land, and use restrictions can change. Assume that bikes, dogs, and horses are not allowed unless a trail is specifically marked for them (although many landowners do not object to dogs). Most trails are open to cross-country skiing. Assume that hunting is allowed in season unless otherwise posted.

**Access, fees:** Parking and access are free.

**Maps:** For topographic area maps, request New Preston and Litchfield from USGS Map Sales, Federal Center, Box 25286, Denver, CO 80225, 888/ASK-USGS (888/275-8747), website: http://mapping.usgs.gov.

**Directions:** From the junction of U.S. 202 and Route 209 in Bantam (west of Litchfield), drive west on U.S. 202 for 0.6 mile and turn right onto Cathole Road. Drive 1.6 miles to a turnout on the left. There is no trail sign, but look for a rock with a blue blaze (difficult to see from the road) marking the trail.

**Contact:** Connecticut Forest and Park Association Inc., 16 Meriden Rd., Rockfall, CT 06481-2961, 860/346-2372, website: www.ctwoodlands.org.

# 🛈 MOUNT TOM STATE PARK TOWER
## 1 mi/0.75 hr
**in Mount Tom State Park in Litchfield and Washington**

Ⓕ This short hike—a good one for young children—climbs easily to a stone tower on Mount Tom's summit that you can climb to enjoy a panorama of the western Connecticut countryside. From the parking lot, head up a dirt road to where it forks at a sign directing you up the right fork for the Tower Trail. At the next fork, bear right, following yellow blazes through a few more turns. The trail skirts a wet area, then turns right, and climbs to the summit. Be careful not to turn onto a different trail on the descent.

**User groups:** Hikers and snowshoers. No wheelchair facilities. This trail is not suitable for skis. Bikes, dogs, horses, and hunting are prohibited.

**Access, fees:** On weekends from Memorial Day–Labor Day, a $7 parking fee is charged for Connecticut vehicles, $10 to nonresidents; on weekdays during this period, residents pay $6 and nonresidents $7.

**Maps:** A trail map is available free from the Connecticut State Parks Division (see address below). For a topographic area map, request New Preston from USGS Map Sales, Federal Center, Box 25286, Denver, CO 80225, 888/ASK-USGS (888/275-8747), website: http://mapping.usgs.gov.

**Directions:** The Mount Tom State Park entrance is along U.S. 202 between Woodville and Bantam and is marked by signs. Inside the park entrance, turn right into a parking lot marked by a sign for the picnic area and Tower Trail.

**Contact:** Mount Tom State Park, c/o Lake Waramaug State Park, 30 Lake Waramaug Rd., New Preston, CT 06777, 860/868-2592. Connecticut State Parks Division, 79 Elm St., Hartford, CT 06106-5127, 860/424-3200, fax 860/424-4070, website: www.dep.state.ct.us/stateparks/index.htm.

## ■11■ LEATHERMAN'S CAVE/ CRANE LOOKOUT

**2 mi/1 hr**

**in Watertown**

Leatherman's Cave is the sort of place that excites both children and adults: a jumble of giant boulders that have fallen from the cliff below Crane Lookout over the centuries. And the Mattatuck Trail sends hikers crawling through a dark, cool 50-foot passageway among the boulders. Though there are little hills, the elevation gain on this hike is negligible.

From the turnout, cross the highway and follow Mattatuck Trail's blue blazes into the woods. You soon scramble up exposed rock and traverse a classic Connecticut rock ridge with views of rolling, wooded hills. Descending the other end, cross an unmarked trail. Reaching a woods road, turn left, following it a short distance through a sometimes wet area. Bear right, then take the far left trail of the three before you, an eroded gully that ascends through a burned area. At the next trail junction, turn left and walk out onto Crane Lookout, which offers views of the craggy hills to the north and of the industrial areas to the east. Leatherman's Cave is below you, out of sight. Double back and veer down and left with the blue blazes (the trail you followed onto Crane Lookout bears right). Take a left at the first of two successive trail junctions, descending quickly to Leatherman's Cave. Return to U.S. 6 the same way you came.

**User groups:** Hikers and snowshoers. No wheelchair facilities. Portions of this trail lie on private land, and use restrictions can change. Assume that bikes, dogs, and horses are not allowed unless a trail is specifically marked for them. Most trails are open to cross-country skiing. Assume that hunting is allowed in season unless otherwise posted.

**Access, fees:** Parking and access are free.

**Maps:** For a topographic area map, request Thomaston from USGS Map Sales, Federal Center, Box 25286, Denver, CO 80225, 888/ASK-USGS (888/275-8747), website: http://mapping.usgs.gov.

**Directions:** Take Route 8 to Exit 39 and then take U.S. 6 west. From the traffic lights at the junction of U.S. 6 and Route 109, drive 0.9 mile farther west on U.S. 6 to a turnout on the right at a small sign for the Mattatuck Trail.

**Contact:** Connecticut Forest and Park Association Inc., 16 Meriden Rd., Rockfall, CT

06481-2961, 860/346-2372, website: www.ct-woodlands.org.

## 12 HANCOCK BROOK/LION HEAD LOOP

**2.5 mi/1.5 hrs**

**in the Waterville section of Waterbury**

Okay, so after driving through industrial Waterville and parking next to a gravel pit, your expectations for this hike may be a bit modest. But after leaving the gravel pit behind, this actually becomes a decent little hike. The highlight is Hancock Brook, which I had the opportunity to see running full and rambunctious with spring runoff.

The trail begins at a post marked with a blue blaze. Walk the right edge of the gravel pit's property. At a rock where a blue arrow directs you into the woods, stop and look left; the gravel road leading uphill is where this loop finishes. Soon after entering the woods, the sound of heavy machinery is replaced by the sound of running water—or rather, falling water—as Hancock Brook drops steeply through a narrow ravine. Follow the wide and flat path of what resembles an old rail bed (watch on the right for a cascade tumbling into the brook on its opposite bank). Abundant hardwoods create a shady, cool corridor along the brook. Although it lies well down a steep embankment at the outset, the brook gradually rises nearly to trail level. After the brook becomes more

placid, the well-blazed trail turns left and ascends steeply up a small hill onto the open Lion's Head ledge, with decent views in all directions of central Connecticut's rolling hills and the surrounding communities. Backtrack, following the blazes to the gravel pit.

**User groups:** Hikers and snowshoers. No wheelchair facilities. Portions of this trail lie on private land, and use restrictions can change. Assume that bikes, dogs, and horses are not allowed unless a trail is specifically marked for them (although many landowners do not object to dogs). Most trails are open to cross-country skiing. Assume that hunting is allowed in season unless otherwise posted.

**Access, fees:** Parking and access are free.

**Maps:** For a topographic area map, request Waterbury from USGS Map Sales, Federal Center, Box 25286, Denver, CO 80225, 888/ASK-USGS (888/275-8747), website: http://mapping.usgs.gov.

**Directions:** Take Exit 37 off Route 8 and head east a short distance to Thomaston Avenue (old Route 8). Turn right and drive 1.9 miles into Waterville, then turn left onto Sheffield Street. Follow it to the end and park at the roadside on the right just before the sand and gravel pit.

**Contact:** Connecticut Forest and Park Association Inc., 16 Meriden Rd., Rockfall, CT 06481-2961, 860/346-2372, website: www.ct-woodlands.org.

## Chapter 13

© MICHAEL LANZA

# Hartford and the Quiet Corner

# Hartford and the Quiet Corner

There's a good reason northeastern Connecticut is known as "The Quiet Corner": It's off the beaten tourist path of western Connecticut and away from the urban centers along I-91 and in the state's southwestern corner. Although the hikes in this chapter are generally flat and wooded, they also present the opportunity—more than anyplace else in the Constitution State—to get away from it all.

From Mashamoquet Brook State Park to Nipmuck and Natchaug State Forests, there's a wealth of uncrowded trails awaiting you here. Breakneck Pond—one of my favorite hikes in Connecticut—is a gem tucked away in a big patch of quiet forest—some of it part of Nipmuck State Forest—where I wouldn't be surprised to learn that moose are beginning to hang out since in recent years they have been seen migrating farther south. In addition, the Jessie Girard Trail in Peoples State Forest offers breathtaking views of the Farmington River Valley from several lookouts.

Some of Connecticut's most dramatic hiking is along the traprock ridges rising above the Connecticut River Valley in the middle of the state. Though rarely more than a few hundred feet high, ridges like those at Talcott Mountain, Tariffville Gorge, Ragged Mountain, Lamentation Mountain, and others jut abruptly above the valley, often in cliffs with open ledges offering long views of the countryside. Although the trails leading up onto them can be very steep, the climbs are relatively short; many of these hikes are at most a half-day outing, often shorter. Some hikes are on state lands, some in private reserves, and many on private land where access is granted by the landowner and can be revoked at any time.

While central Connecticut sees occasional heavy snowstorms, winters are milder than northern New England, and it's possible to hike beyond the prime April–November season.

In Connecticut state parks and forests, dogs must be leashed and horses are allowed on some trails and forest roads. Hunting is allowed in season in state forests, but not in state parks, and is prohibited on Sundays. Access fees are levied at some state lands, but most allow free entrance year-round.

For more information about regulations concerning Blue Trails, see the Long Island Sound chapter introduction.

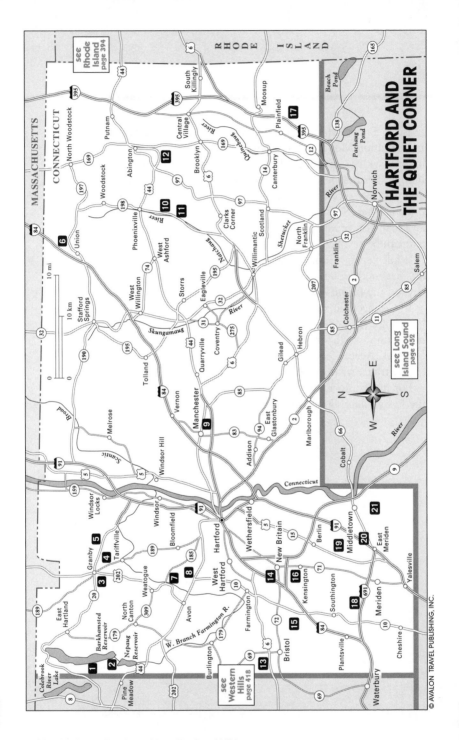

# ■ JESSIE GERARD TRAIL

**3 mi/2 hrs**

**in Peoples State Forest in Barkhamsted**

This hike leads to open ledges at the Overlook and Chaugham Lookout, which offer spectacular views of the Farmington River Valley—and a largely undeveloped landscape, a somewhat rare treat in Connecticut. You may catch a fog over the river in the early morning when conditions are right, and the fall foliage show is five-star.

From the turnout, cross the road and follow the yellow-blazed trail on a steep and strenuous climb of the famous stone stairway known as the 299 Steps, paralleling the cascades of a brook. Shortly after a brook crossing, where the trail hooks right, look for trees with large woodpecker holes beside the trail on the right. Pass a waterfall and then follow the trail as it ascends more moderately. A little more than

a mile from the trailhead lies the Overlook, with this hike's best views. Another 0.3 mile ahead is Chaugham Lookout; shortly beyond that, the trail passes between enormous, twin glacial erratics called the Veeder Boulders. This hike doubles back from the boulders, though Greenswoods Road lies just 0.3 mile beyond them.

**User groups:** Hikers and dogs. Dogs must be leashed. No wheelchair facilities. This trail may be difficult to snowshoe because of steepness and ice, and is not suitable for bikes, horses, or skis. Hunting is prohibited.

**Access, fees:** Peoples State Forest has a weekend and holiday entrance fee of $7 per vehicle with a Connecticut registration and $10 per out-of-state vehicle.

**Maps:** A free, noncontour map of hiking trails in the Peoples and American Legion State Forests is available at several locations, including boxes at the Peoples State Forest office and museum (see address below), the Austin F. Hawes Campground on West River Road (which runs north from the junction of Routes 318 and 181 in Barkhamsted), and the field office on West River Road. You can also try the Pleasant Valley Store or the Riverton Store (both located in the center of those towns). For topographic area maps, request Winsted and New Hartford from USGS Map Sales, Federal Center, Box 25286, Denver, CO 80225, 888/ASK-USGS (888/275-8747), website: http://mapping.usgs.gov.

**Directions:** From the junction of Routes 318 and 181 in Pleasant Valley/Barkhamsted, drive east over the Farmington River bridge and take an immediate left onto East River Road. Proceed another 2.4 miles (passing a road on the right, marked by a sign, which leads to the state forest office), and park in the turnout on

© MICHAEL LANZA

a view from the Jessie Gerard Trail

the left, across from a sign marking the Jessie
Gerard Trail.

**Contact:** Peoples State Forest, P.O. Box 1, Pleasant Valley State Park, CT 06063, 860/379-2469.
Connecticut State Parks Division, 79 Elm St.,
Hartford, CT 06106-5127, 860/424-3200, website: www.dep.state.ct.us/stateparks/index.htm.

## ❷ BRAILLE TRAIL
**0.3 mi/0.5 hr**
**in Barkhamsted**

Opened in 1994 on the scenic Lake McDo-
nough shores, this short, paved loop is designed
for people with visual and other physical im-
pairments and walkers who prefer a gentle
grade. Managed by the Metropolitan District
Commission, it has information signs in English and Braille, a guide rope for visitors to follow to each station, and signs that point out
various features of geology, vegetation, and
wildlife. And it's right on the water, with views
of the lake and hills.

**User groups:** Hikers, dogs, and wheelchair
users. This trail is closed in the winter. Bikes,
horses, and hunting are prohibited.

**Access, fees:** Parking and access are free. The
recreation area is open daily from 8 A.M.–8
P.M., beginning April 1 until the first snowfall.

**Maps:** No map is needed for this short walk, but
for a topographic area map, request New Hartford from USGS Map Sales, Federal Center, Box
25286, Denver, CO 80225, 888/ASK-USGS
(888/275-8747), website: http://mapping.usgs.gov.

**Directions:** From the junction of Routes 318
and 181 in Pleasant Valley/Barkhamsted, drive
east over the Farmington River bridge and follow Route 181 past the Pleasant Valley firehouse. Turn right onto Goosegreen Road, which
is the first paved road on the right. Drive about
0.1 mile and turn left into the Metropolitan
District Commission's Goosegreen Recreation
Area. Follow signs to the Braille Trail.

**Contact:** Metropolitan District Commission,
Supply Division, 39 Beachrock Rd., Pleasant
Valley, CT 06063, 860/379-0938; or the MDC's
main office in Hartford, 860/278-7850.

## ❸ MCLEAN GAME REFUGE SUMMIT HIKE LOOP
**2.6 mi/1.5 hrs**
**in Granby**

Former Senator George P. McLean created
the 3,480-acre refuge that bears his name in
an act of his will when he died in 1932. Woods
roads and foot trails meander through the gently rolling, forested terrain. Several loops are
possible.

This hike takes you to an overlook atop the
Barndoor Hills with a view of a bucolic valley
and wooded hills. From the parking lot, walk
past the wooden gate and follow the woods
road across a wooden bridge over Bissell Brook.
Just beyond the bridge, turn right onto the
Blue Loop. Follow the blue blazes through a
mixed forest with slight ups and downs. At an
intersection with a woods road, the Blue Loop
turns left to return to the start, but you turn
right, following the road through a dark hemlock grove. At a junction of woods roads, with
a hillside of shattered rock on your left, a sign
directs you to turn left for the Barndoor Hills
summit. Do not go straight onto Barndoor Hill
Road. Go left and follow the road steadily uphill and then turn right onto the blue-blazed
summit trail, which soon leads to the open
ledge with unobstructed views. Backtrack down
the summit trail and turn left on the woods
road, returning the way you came. But at the
next road's junction, bear right into the woods
onto a trail marked by faded blue blazes. Within minutes, turn left onto another trail, which
deposits you onto the same woods road where
the Blue Loop emerged earlier. Turn right to
return to the parking lot, passing scenic Trout
Pond on the way. On my hike by the pond, I
happened upon a fuzzy little yellow gosling
that fled, squeaking in panic, at my approach.
Moments later, three honking geese flew low
overhead in perfect V formation.

**User groups:** Hikers, dogs, skiers, and snowshoers. Dogs must be leashed. No wheelchair
facilities. Bikes, horses, and hunting are prohibited.

**Access, fees:** Parking and access are free. The refuge trails are open daily from 8 A.M.–dusk.

**Maps:** A map of hiking trails is posted with refuge regulations on an information board in the parking lot. For a topographic area map, request Tariffville from USGS Map Sales, Federal Center, Box 25286, Denver, CO 80225, 888/ASK-USGS (888/275-8747), website: http://mapping.usgs.gov.

**Directions:** From the junction in Granby of Routes 20, 10, and 189 and U.S. 202, drive south on Route 10/U.S. 202 for one mile and turn right onto the entrance road (which is 1.6 miles north of the Simsbury town line). Park in the lot at the end of the road.

**Contact:** Trustees of the McLean Fund, 75 Great Pond Rd., Simsbury, CT 06070, 860/653-7869.

## 🄯 TARIFFVILLE GORGE
**0.4 mi/0.5 hr**

**near East Granby, Bloomfield, and Simsbury**
This short hike climbs a steep hillside to one of the Metacomet Trail's finest views: looking out over the village of Tariffville, the Farmington River, and the surrounding hills from an open ledge hundreds of feet above the river. Because this hike is so short and ascends only a couple hundred feet in elevation, you can do it at odd times of day—perhaps early morning, with a fog over the river, or toward evening if a nice sunset is starting to take shape. Follow the blue blazes. Once you gain the ridge top, it's a short walk to the open ledge overlooking the river. Return the same way.

**User groups:** Hikers only. No wheelchair facilities. This trail would be difficult to snowshoe, and is not suitable for bikes, dogs, horses, or skis. Hunting is prohibited.

**Access, fees:** Parking and access are free.

**Maps:** For topographic area maps, request Tariffville and Windsor Locks from USGS Map Sales, Federal Center, Box 25286, Denver, CO 80225, 888/ASK-USGS (888/275-8747), website: http://mapping.usgs.gov.

**Directions:** Take Route 189 north into Tariffville. Pass the town center, cross the Farm-

ington River, and park on the other side of the bridge. The Metacomet Trail's blue blazes enter the woods on the east side of the road.

**Contact:** Connecticut Forest and Park Association Inc., 16 Meriden Rd., Rockfall, CT 06481-2961, 860/346-2372, website: www.ctwoodlands.org.

## 🄯 PEAK MOUNTAIN
**2 mi/1 hr**

**in East Granby**
Some might say that Peak Mountain, at 672 feet, is neither a peak nor a mountain. But the open ledges at its summit offer long views to the west and make an attractive local spot to catch the sunset—and they're easily reached on a one-mile uphill climb that gains about 300 feet. From the turnout, follow the blue-blazed Metacomet Trail as it ascends a steep hillside, quickly reaching the ridge. Then turn left (north), following the blue blazes to the broad rock outcropping a mile from the trailhead. Either double back from here or continue north along the ridge for nearly another mile to enjoy two more long views of the Granby area and the hills farther west, one from an open area and another from an outcropping. Follow the Metacomet Trail back to the trailhead.

**User groups:** Hikers and snowshoers. No wheelchair facilities. Portions of this trail lie on private land, and use restrictions can change. Assume that bikes, dogs, and horses are not allowed unless a trail is specifically marked for them (although many landowners do not object to dogs). Most trails are open to cross-country skiing. Assume that hunting is allowed in season unless otherwise posted.

**Access, fees:** Parking and access are free.

**Maps:** For topographic area maps, request Tariffville and Windsor Locks from USGS Map Sales, Federal Center, Box 25286, Denver, CO 80225, 888/ASK-USGS (888/275-8747), website: http://mapping.usgs.gov.

**Directions:** On Route 20 in East Granby, 0.7 mile west of the junction with Route 187 and 2.6 miles east of the junction in Granby of Routes 20, 10, and 189 and U.S. 202, turn north onto Newgate Road (there is a sign for the Old Newgate Prison, which is open to visitors). Pull into the turnout on the right; the blue-blazed Metacomet Trail enters the woods there.

**Contact:** Connecticut Forest and Park Association Inc., 16 Meriden Rd., Rockfall, CT 06481-2961, 860/346-2372, website: www.ctwoodlands.org.

## 6 BREAKNECK POND
**6.5 mi/4.5 hrs**

**in Bigelow Hollow State Park and Nipmuck State Forest in Union**

Located in one of the more rural parts of Connecticut, this relatively flat, 6.5-mile loop through Bigelow Hollow State Park and Nipmuck State Forest circles around picturesque Breakneck Pond, a long, narrow, and—notable in the Constitution State—undeveloped finger of fresh water hidden away in quiet woods. For its relative sense of remoteness, scenic qualities, and even a bit of rugged trail along the pond's west shore, this is one of my favorite hikes in the state.

From the parking area, cross the road to the information board at the trailhead, where maps are available. The trail immediately splits; bear right onto the white-blazed East Ridge Trail. Within 0.1 mile, it reaches and turns left onto an old logging road, following it 1.1 miles to a trail junction near the south end of Breakneck Pond. Turn left onto the Breakneck Pond View Trail, marked by blue blazes with white dots. The trail crosses a wet area and emerges at the pond's southern end, where you get your first almost complete view of the 1.5-mile-long pond. I first stood at this spot while accompanying a trail maintenance crew from the Connecticut Forest and Park Association. More than a year later, eager to hike around the pond, I returned with my wife and we made this loop in later afternoon without encountering another soul.

The trail then bears right off the logging road onto a footpath, still following the blue-

white blazes. The footpath hugs the pond's western shore for the next two miles, traversing rocky ground in a thick forest with almost constant pond views—the most difficult stretch of this hike. Near the pond's north end (where beaver activity may necessitate bushwhacking or eventual trail rerouting), turn right at a trail junction, following the View Trail across an outlet stream (on rocks and a log), and turn right (south) again onto the blue-blazed Nipmuck Trail. The Nipmuck soon bears right off a logging road and becomes a footpath for two miles along the pond's eastern shore. Now you have nearly constant views in the other direction, looking west across the pond, giving you a whole new perspective. At the next trail junction, turn right with the East Ridge Trail's white blazes, walk about 0.1 mile to the first trail junction you reached on this hike, then turn left, and follow the East Ridge Trail along the logging road for the 1.1 miles back to the trailhead.

**User groups:** Hikers, snowshoers, and dogs. Dogs must be leashed. No wheelchair facilities. horses can access the woods roads on this hike. This trail is not suitable for bikes. Hunting is allowed in season in state forests, but not in state parks, and is prohibited on Sundays. This hike begins in Bigelow Hollow State Park, but most of it is within Nipmuck State Forest.

**Access, fees:** From Memorial Day–Labor Day, a parking fee of $7 is charged for Connecticut vehicles, $10 for out-of-state vehicles, on weekends and holidays; weekdays are free. Bigelow Hollow State Park closes at sunset.

**Maps:** A basic trail map is available free at the trailhead and from the Connecticut State Parks Division (see address below). For topographic area maps, request Eastford, Westford, and Southbridge from USGS Map Sales, Federal Center, Box 25286, Denver, CO 80225, 888/ASK-USGS (888/275-8747), website: http://mapping.usgs.gov.

**Directions:** From the north, take I-84 to Exit 74. Follow Route 171 east for 2.4 miles to the junction with Route 190. Turn left, staying on Route 171; proceed 1.4 miles and then turn left into Bigelow Hollow State Park. Continue 0.7 mile to the picnic area parking lot and trailhead. From the south, take I-84 to Exit 73. Turn right onto Route 190 east, follow it for two miles, turn right onto Route 171, and continue 1.4 miles to the state park entrance.

**Contact:** Bigelow Hollow State Park, c/o Shenipsit State Forest, 166 Chestnut Hill Rd., Stafford Springs, CT 06076, 860/684-3430. Connecticut State Parks Division, 79 Elm St., Hartford, CT 06106-5127, 860/424-3200, fax 860/424-4070, website: www.dep.state.ct.us/stateparks/index.htm. Connecticut Forest and Park Association Inc., 16 Meriden Rd., Rockfall, CT 06481-2961, 860/346-2372, website: www.ctwoodlands.org.

## ⑦ TALCOTT MOUNTAIN
**5 mi/3 hrs**

**in Talcott Mountain State Park in Bloomfield**
This five-mile round-trip hike takes in the quarter mile of the Metacomet Trail along the exposed ridge in Talcott Mountain State Park—the most scenic stretch of what may be the state's premier trail—and the Heublein Tower, which offers a panorama of the surrounding countryside. The vertical ascent is about 400 feet.

From the parking lot, follow the blue-blazed Metacomet south across Route 185 and into the woods. Within 0.2 mile, the trail crosses power lines; don't cross straight onto a woods road, but bear right across the power lines, looking for a footpath and a blue blaze at the forest's edge. The Metacomet then zigs and zags along various woods roads for nearly a mile, ascending gently to the ridge and more interesting hiking along a footpath through eastern hemlock trees. At 2.3 miles from the parking lot, the trail emerges onto an open ledge with a view stretching for miles out to the western Connecticut hills. Just 0.1 mile farther south, the trail passes by the impressive 165-foot tower built in 1914 by Gilbert Heublein and used as his summer home until 1937. Continue 0.1 mile

past the tower to a traprock ledge to the left of the picnic area for Farmington River Valley views. Hike back the way you came.

**User groups:** Hikers, snowshoers, and dogs. Dogs must be leashed. No wheelchair facilities. The trail is not suitable for bikes, horses, or skis. Hunting is prohibited.

**Access, fees:** Parking and access are free. The Heublein Tower and the small museum at the summit are open daily from June 1–November 1 and on weekends in May.

**Maps:** For a topographic area map, request Avon from USGS Map Sales, Federal Center, Box 25286, Denver, CO 80225, 888/ASK-USGS (888/275-8747), website: http://mapping.usgs.gov.

**Directions:** This hike begins from the parking lot 0.1 mile inside the entrance to Penwood State Park on Route 185, 1.2 miles west of the junction of Routes 178 and 185 in Bloomfield and 1.7 miles east of the junction of Route 185 and Route 10/U.S. 202 in Simsbury.

**Contact:** Talcott Mountain State Park, c/o Penwood State Park, 57 Gun Mill Rd., Bloomfield, CT 06002, 860/242-1158. Connecticut State Parks Division, 79 Elm St., Hartford, CT 06106-5127, 860/424-3200, website: www.dep.state.ct.us/stateparks/index.htm. Connecticut Forest and Park Association Inc., 16 Meriden Rd., Rockfall, CT 06481-2961, 860/346-2372, website: www.ctwoodlands.org.

## ⑧ WEST HARTFORD RESERVOIR
**8 mi/4 hrs**

**in West Hartford**
This roughly eight-mile loop is great for hiking, mountain biking, cross-country skiing, or trail running. With an extensive network of trails and old woods roads weaving through the forest and around the water bodies here, the West Hartford Reservoir area is a popular local recreation spot. This loop encircles the southern half of the water district land, and there's a lot more exploration potential here. Trail maps are posted at several strategic junctions, but it's a good idea to carry one. This route climbs some

small hills, but has relatively little elevation gain and loss.

The hike's first half is on the blue-blazed Metacomet Trail. From the turnout on U.S. 44, follow the blue blazes up onto the earthen dike and turn right (west), following the dike about 200 yards to a gate beside the highway on your right. Turn left with the Metacomet, continuing along an old woods road until the trail hooks left, crossing a brook onto a footpath. The trail then passes through fairly open woods and over occasional rock ledges for more than two miles before emerging on the rough Finger Rock Road. Turn right on the road, still following the Metacomet, and descend a steep slope of broken rock. Within a half mile, bear left with the blue blazes, off the woods road and onto a path. About half a mile farther, turn left onto a paved section of Finger Rock Road and then right onto the paved Red Road. In about 0.3 mile, turn left onto a wide woods road and then take the next left, near a map board, onto the dirt Overlook Road.

Stay on Overlook for about 1.2 miles and cross Reservoir Number 5 on a bridge, where you enjoy the nicest views along this route of forest tightly embracing the reservoir waters on both sides of the bridge. Then take two lefts in rapid succession. You are on the paved Reservoir Road Extension; follow it to the left around the end of the reservoir, through a quiet woods, and then turn right onto the paved Northwest Road, which becomes dirt within about 0.3 mile. Continue about another 0.3 mile and take the first trail on the right. Stay left through the next two trail intersections and then bear right twice, the second time at the edge of an open meadow. Follow the obvious path, which leads onto the earthen dike, about 1.2 miles back to the U.S. 44 turnout.

**User groups:** Hikers, bikers, dogs, horses, skiers, and snowshoers. Dogs must be leashed. No wheelchair facilities. Hunting is prohibited. The Metropolitan District Commission issues tickets for illegal mountain biking on trails with postings indicating no bikes.

**Access, fees:** Parking and access are free. The reservoir is open from 8 A.M.–8 P.M. from mid-April–late October, and 8 A.M.–6 P.M. during the rest of the year.

**Maps:** A good map of the West Hartford Reservoir Area (also called the Talcott Mountain Reservoir Area) can be ordered for $2 from the Metropolitan District Commission; call 860/278-7850 and ask for West Hartford Filters. For a topographic area map, request Avon from USGS Map Sales, Federal Center, Box 25286, Denver, CO 80225, 888/ASK-USGS (888/275-8747), website: http://mapping.usgs.gov.

**Directions:** This loop begins from a dirt turnout on the south side of U.S. 44 in West Hartford, 2.1 miles east of the easternmost junction of U.S. 44 and Route 10 in Avon and 0.1 mile west of a large paved parking lot and entrance to the reservoir area. You could also park in the paved lot and walk (or bike) up U.S. 44 to access this loop.

**Contact:** Metropolitan District Commission, Supply Division, 39 Beachrock Rd., Pleasant Valley, CT 06063, 860/379-0938.

# 9 CASE MOUNTAIN
## 2 mi/1 hr
**in the Highland Park section of Manchester**
This fairly easy two-mile hike incorporates the Shenipsit and other trails through the Case Mountain Open Space to loop over the Lookout, a cleared area with limited views west toward Hartford. For the most part, this hike remains in the woods, but it's a nice refuge for a short hike in the midst of a fairly populous urban area. Trails are well blazed and generally easy to follow, and distances between junctions described here are rarely more than 0.3 mile.

From the parking area, walk past the gate, following the wide path of the white-blazed Carriage Road Trail about 150 yards, and then turn right onto the red-blazed Highland Park Trail at a sign that reads "Trail to Lookout." Follow the red trail past a junction where the orange-blazed Boulder Trail diverges left and then turn right, following the white trail uphill 0.1 mile to the Lookout. Turn left on the yellow-blazed Lookout Trail, which coincides briefly with the blue-blazed Shenipsit Trail; bear right on the yellow trail after the two split again. After crossing the white trail, turn left onto a newer trail blazed blue and yellow (watch closely for it). Turn left on the blue and yellow trail, walk 100 yards, and then turn right on the white trail, which soon bears left off the woods road onto a footpath leading straight onto the red trail. Upon rejoining the white trail, turn right and follow it back to the parking area.

**User groups:** Hikers, bikers, dogs, skiers, and snowshoers. Dogs must be leashed. No wheelchair facilities. Horses and hunting are prohibited.

**Access, fees:** Parking and access are free.

**Maps:** A trail map is posted at several major trail junctions, and a free copy of the map is available through the Manchester Parks and Recreation Department (see address below). For topographic area maps, request Manchester and Rockville from USGS Map Sales, Federal Center, Box 25286, Denver, CO 80225, 888/ASK-USGS (888/275-8747), website: http://mapping.usgs.gov.

**Directions:** From I-384 westbound, take Exit 4 in Manchester. Turn right onto Highland Street, drive 0.3 mile, and then turn right again onto Spring Street. Continue another 0.3 mile to a parking turnout on the left just over a bridge. From I-384 eastbound, take Exit 4 in Manchester and turn right onto Spring Street. Continue 0.2 mile to the same parking turnout on the left.

**Contact:** Manchester Parks and Recreation Department, P.O. Box 191, Manchester, CT 06045-0191, 860/647-3084, fax 860/647-3083. Connecticut Forest and Park Association Inc., 16 Meriden Rd., Rockfall, CT 06481-2961, 860/346-2372, website: www.ctwoodlands.org.

## 🔟 NATCHAUG STATE FOREST ROAD LOOP

**4 mi/2 hrs**
**in Eastford**

This loop, ideal for mountain bikers, cross-country skiers, or hikers looking for an easy woods walk, introduces you to a 12,500-acre expanse of state forest cut by several trails and forest roads, including the Natchaug Trail. Get a map and explore. Some major trail junctions are marked by numbered signs. There is very little elevation gain.

From the parking area, double back on the park road a short distance to where it hooks right; continue straight onto the gravel Kingsbury Road. Go past trail junction 5, where a gas line right-of-way leads left, to junction 6, where you turn left. Bear right around a horse camp and then bear left at the next fork. The trail descends, and just before crossing a brook, you turn left. You're now on the gas line right-of-way, which leads back to junction 5 on Kingsbury Road. Bear in mind that snowmobilers use these trails in winter, as do hunters in late fall.

**User groups:** Hikers, bikers, dogs, horses, skiers, and snowshoers. Dogs must be leashed. No wheelchair facilities. Hunting is allowed in season.

**Access, fees:** Parking and access are free.

**Maps:** A free trail map is available at the park, outside the maintenance building across from the parking area, or from the Connecticut State Parks Division (see address below). For a topographic area map, request Hampton from USGS Map Sales, Federal Center, Box 25286, Denver, CO 80225, 888/ASK-USGS (888/275-8747), website: http://mapping.usgs.gov.

**Directions:** From I-395, take Exit 93 for Dayville onto Route 101 west. In Phoenixville, turn right (south) onto Route 198. Watch for a sign and the park entrance on the left. Follow the main park road to the headquarters building and park at a roadside pullout across from the large maintenance building.

**Contact:** Natchaug State Forest, c/o Mashamoquet Brook State Park, 147 Wolf Den Dr., Pomfret Center, CT 06259, 860/928-6121. Connecticut

State Parks Division, 79 Elm St., Hartford, CT 06106-5127, 860/424-3200, fax 860/424-4070, website: www.dep.state.ct.us/stateparks/index.htm.

## 11 ORCHARD HILL LOOKOUT
**2 mi/1 hr**

**in Chaplin**

This hike does not lead to any spectacular views, or to orchards for that matter. It's simply a pleasant little stroll through the woods to a lookout where, when the leaves are down, the view of the valley to the west is only partly obscured by trees. The trail is well blazed, so you're not likely to even need a map. It does cross one brook and a stone wall where skiers might have to walk, but the slope is very gentle. I hiked this late one winter Monday afternoon when there was no one else around. The forest was quiet, and the low-angle light from the sun was throwing long shadows behind bare trees and giving the snow subtle yellow highlights.

**User groups:** Hikers, dogs, skiers, and snowshoers. No wheelchair facilities. This trail is not suitable for horses. Hunting is allowed in season.

**Access, fees:** Parking and access are free.

**Maps:** For topographic area maps, request Hampton and Spring Hill from USGS Map Sales, Federal Center, Box 25286, Denver, CO 80225, 888/ASK-USGS (888/275-8747), website: http://mapping.usgs.gov.

**Directions:** From the junction of U.S. 44 and Route 198 in Eastford, drive south on Route 198, past the entrance to Natchaug State Forest, into Chaplin. Turn left onto Morey Road, cross a bridge over a stream, and turn right onto Marcy Road. About 0.2 mile farther, the blue-blazed Natchaug Trail crosses Marcy Road. Park here along the roadside.

**Contact:** Connecticut Forest and Park Association Inc., 16 Meriden Rd., Rockfall, CT 06481-2961, 860/346-2372, website: www.ct-woodlands.org.

## 12 MASHAMOQUET BROOK STATE PARK
**3.5 mi/2 hrs**

**in Mashamoquet**

Mashamoquet dispels any suggestion that Connecticut's northeast corner is flat. This hike almost immediately ascends a hillside, then winds through forested hills and a classic, glacier-scoured landscape of rocky ledges and boulders. (Short sections will be very difficult on skis; I had to remove and carry mine a few

the wolf den in Mashamoquet Brook State Park

times.) This is a great hike for young children. All trails are well marked.

From the first picnic area, head a short distance up the road and cross Mashamoquet Brook on a wooden bridge. Follow the trail to the right and uphill. The blue-blazed trail branches to the right; stay on the red-blazed trail. Shortly after crossing Wolf Den Drive, you see Table Rock on the left, two flat boulders stacked like a table. Beyond it, the blue and red trails converge and enter an area of rocky ledges. A rock-mounted plaque on the right marks the Wolf Den site, where in 1742 Israel Putnam crept into the cavelike channel in the boulders and shot what was reputedly the last wolf in Connecticut, an animal suspected of killing numerous sheep in the area. Continue following the blue blazes to the Indian Chair—another unique rock formation—through more ledges, across an open field, and finally to the first junction with the red-blazed trail.

**User groups:** Hikers, bikers, dogs, skiers, and snowshoers. No wheelchair facilities. Bikes are not allowed during the spring mud season, from April–mid-May. Dogs must be leashed. This trail is not suitable for horses. Hunting is prohibited.

**Access, fees:** From Memorial Day–Labor Day, a parking fee of $7 is charged for Connecticut vehicles, $10 for out-of-state vehicles, on weekends and holidays; weekdays are free. Parking is free at the state park office on Wolf Den Road, more than a mile east of the park main entrance and picnic area; from the office, you can pick up a blue-blazed trail leading a mile to the red-blazed trail described above.

**Maps:** A free trail map is available from the park office or the Connecticut State Parks Division (see addresses below). For a topographic area map, request Danielson from USGS Map Sales, Federal Center, Box 25286, Denver, CO 80225, 888/ASK-USGS (888/275-8747), website: http://mapping.usgs.gov.

**Directions:** From I-395, take Exit 93 for Dayville onto Route 101 west. In Pomfret, beyond the junction with Route 169 and U.S. 44, watch for a sign and the park main entrance and picnic area on the left.

**Contact:** Mashamoquet Brook State Park, 147 Wolf Den Dr., Pomfret Center, CT 06259, 860/928-6121. Connecticut State Parks Division, 79 Elm St., Hartford, CT 06106-5127, 860/424-3200, fax 860/424-4070, website: www.dep.state.ct.us/stateparks/index.htm.

## 13 BUTTERMILK FALLS
### 0.2 mi/0.25 hr

**in Plymouth**

As soon as you step out of your car, the sound of Buttermilk Falls reaches your ears. It's a short, relatively flat walk to the waterfall, which plummets about 100 feet through several drops. A popular place to bring young children, Buttermilk sees lots of visitors, especially on weekends in summer, so parking here can be difficult at times. The preserve also, unfortunately, attracts illegal after-hours activity. Lend a hand by picking up trailside litter on your visit here.

From the roadside parking area, the trail leads into the woods, traversing fairly level terrain a short distance to the falls, where you can easily walk up or downhill for various waterfall views.

**User groups:** Hikers and snowshoers. No wheelchair facilities. This trail is not suitable for skis. Bikes, dogs, horses, and hunting are prohibited.

**Access, fees:** Parking and access are free.

**Maps:** No map is needed for this short walk, but for a topographic area map, request Thomaston from USGS Map Sales, Federal Center, Box 25286, Denver, CO 80225, 888/ASK-USGS (888/275-8747), website: http://mapping.usgs.gov.

**Directions:** Take U.S. 6 into Terryville/Plymouth. Turn south onto South Main Street, which makes a right turn in 0.2 mile and again in another 1.2 miles. After the second right, drive 1.3 miles and turn left onto Lane Hill Road. Drive 0.2 mile to a small turnout on the right marked by a sign for the Nature Conservancy, where the Mattatuck Trail's blue blazes enter the woods. There are also turnouts along the road just before and beyond the trailhead.

**Contact:** The Nature Conservancy Connecticut Chapter, 55 High St., Middletown, CT 06457-3788, 860/344-0716, website: http://nature.org, email: ct@tnc.org. Connecticut Forest and Park Association Inc., 16 Meriden Rd., Rockfall, CT 06481-2961, 860/346-2372, website: www.ctwoodlands.org.

## 14 RATTLESNAKE MOUNTAIN
**5.4 mi/3.5 hrs**
**in Plainville**

Here's another relatively easy ridge walk that begins in a heavily industrialized area, yet leads to some pretty good views from two cliff tops. The cumulative elevation gain is less than 1,000 feet.

Follow the blue-blazed Metacomet Trail along a fence and then up a hillside into the woods. The trail makes numerous turns, finally reaching and following the western side of the low ridge past a couple of rock outcroppings with views west. At 1.7 miles, you reach Pinnacle Rock's bare top, with views in all directions. You may see or hear rock climbers below; be careful not to dislodge any loose stones, and certainly do not walk toward the cliff edge. Continue north, descending past an old stone foundation and crossing a dirt road. The trail turns left and reenters the woods. It eventually reaches Rattlesnake Mountain, ascending a slope of loose rocks and traversing below its vertical cliffs (another popular spot for climbers), passing through a tunnel-like passage in rocks.

The trail ascends the end of the cliffs to the open ledges atop them, with good views to the north, east, and south (including Hartford's skyline to the northeast). A short distance farther along the Metacomet Trail lies Will Warren's Den, an area of huge boulders worth checking out before you retrace your steps on the return hike. (A local legend, which dates back to colonial times, has it that a man named Will Warren was flogged for not going to church, and in a fit of vengeance, he tried to

burn down the entire Farmington village. As a result, he was chased by the villagers into the nearby hills, where an Indian woman hid him in this cave.)

**User groups:** Hikers and snowshoers. No wheelchair facilities. Portions of this trail lie on private land, and use restrictions can change. Assume that bikes, dogs, and horses are not allowed unless a trail is specifically marked for them (although many landowners do not object to dogs). Most trails are open to cross-country skiing. Assume that hunting is allowed in season unless otherwise posted.

**Access, fees:** Parking and access are free.

**Maps:** For a topographic area map, request New Britain from USGS Map Sales, Federal Center, Box 25286, Denver, CO 80225, 888/ASK-USGS (888/275-8747), website: http://mapping.usgs.gov.

**Directions:** This hike begins along Route 372 in Plainville at a sign for the Metacomet Trail, 1.5 miles east of the junction with Route 10 and two miles west of Exit 7 off Route 72. Parking here is difficult. Heed the "No Trespassing" signs. You might ask permission to park at one of the gas stations just east of the trailhead on Route 372.

**Contact:** Connecticut Forest and Park Association Inc., 16 Meriden Rd., Rockfall, CT 06481-2961, 860/346-2372, website: www.ctwoodlands.org.

## 15 COMPOUNCE RIDGE
**2.5 mi one-way/2 hrs**
**in Southington**

This local ridge walk brings you to a pair of fine, open ledges—Norton Outlook and Julian's Rock—with views east. From Panthorn Trail, the Steep Climb Trail does indeed ascend steeply, crossing two brooks. At a half mile, turn right onto the Compounce Ridge Trail (CRT)—a part of the Tunxis Trail—and watch for a side path that leads right to an overlook. Continue uphill on the CRT to the bald cap of Norton Outlook, at 931 feet the ridge's actual high point. On a clear day, you might see as far as Long Island to the south and Mount Tom in Massachusetts to the north. Norton is a mile from Panthorn Trail and is a logical turnaround point if you have just one vehicle parked here. The distance for hiking the trail in a loop is 3.7 miles, and this hike climbs less than 500 feet.

The one-way hike continues north on the CRT, descending to an unmarked trail junction and turning right. Soon you pass a low, overhanging cliff on your left and reach signs at the place where the Bobcat Trail crosses the CRT. Make a diagonal right on the CRT toward Julian's Rock, 0.4 mile from Norton Outlook, an open rock ridge with expansive views east to the city of Southington and, in the background to the northeast, Hartford's skyline. At the next trail junction, turn left. The trail descends a slab into the woods. Where two streams meet in a little wooded drainage, turn right onto the Compounce Cascade Trail, which parallels scenic Cussgutter Brook for much of the descent to the Cussgutter parking area. Watch the blazes and look for a log bridge where the trail crosses the stream.

**User groups:** Hikers and snowshoers. No wheelchair facilities. Portions of this trail lie on private land, and use restrictions can change. Assume that bikes, dogs, and horses are not allowed unless a trail is specifically marked for them (although many landowners do not object to dogs). Most trails are open to cross-country skiing. Assume that hunting is allowed in season unless otherwise posted.

**Access, fees:** Parking and access are free.

**Maps:** For a topographic area map, request Bristol from USGS Map Sales, Federal Center, Box 25286, Denver, CO 80225, 888/ASK-USGS (888/275-8747), website: http://mapping.usgs.gov.

**Directions:** Take two vehicles if possible. From the junction of Routes 72 and 229 in Bristol, drive south on Route 229 for 0.3 mile and turn right onto Lake Road. Drive 1.4 miles to the unmarked, dirt Cussgutter parking area on the right, just before the amusement park; leave a vehicle here, where this hike ends. Drive a second vehicle another 1.4 miles south on Route

229 and turn right onto Panthorn Trail, a paved residential street; at its end, the blue blazes of the Steep Climb Trail enter the woods. If you don't have two vehicles, you have to walk about 1.3 miles of road between the trailheads.

**Contact:** Connecticut Forest and Park Association Inc., 16 Meriden Rd., Rockfall, CT 06481-2961, 860/346-2372, website: www.ctwoodlands.org.

## 16 RAGGED MOUNTAIN PRESERVE TRAIL

**6 mi/4 hrs**

**in Southington**

I did this six-mile loop on a blustery November afternoon when the leaves were down, giving me far more open views along the ridge than you have during summer or early fall. I also saw just three other hikers—and one deer. This is a great foliage hike, too, and much of the loop would be a satisfying ski tour, provided you don't mind lugging skis through the several short, difficult sections. The vertical ascent is about 600 feet.

From the turnout, walk the woods road 0.1 mile to the Ragged Mountain Preserve Trail loop. Follow its blue blazes with red dots to the left. Within half a mile you reach the tall cliff tops high above Hart Ponds, with wide views to the southeast. The trail follows the cliff tops along the southern edge of Ragged Mountain for the next mile or so, passing one cliff, at about 1.5 miles out, where a wall stands completely detached from the main cliff. Turn right onto the blue-blazed Metacomet Trail, which follows the west ridge of Ragged Mountain, high above Shuttle Meadow Reservoir, with excellent views to the south, west, and northwest. After dropping off the ridge, the Metacomet heads north; bear to the right (east) on the blue-red Ragged Mountain Preserve Trail, which eventually turns south through the woods, at one point climbing a slope of loose stones. The loop trail ends where you started; turn left and walk 0.1 mile back to your vehicle.

**User groups:** Hikers, snowshoers, and dogs. Dogs must be leashed. No wheelchair facilities. This trail is not suitable for bikes, horses, or skis. Hunting is prohibited.

**Access, fees:** Parking and access are free. Ragged Mountain Preserve closes at dusk.

**Maps:** For topographic area maps, request New Britain and Meriden from the USGS Map Sales, Federal Center, Box 25286, Denver, CO 80225, 888/ASK-USGS (888/275-8747), website: http://mapping.usgs.gov.

**Directions:** From Route 71A in Berlin, 1.2 miles south of the junction of 71A and Route 372 and 1.2 miles north of the junction of 71A and Route 71, turn west onto West Lane. Proceed 0.6 mile to a turnout on the right at Ragged Mountain Preserve's gated entrance.

**Contact:** Ragged Mountain Foundation, P.O. Box 948, Southington, CT 06489, website: www.raggedmtn.org. Connecticut Forest and Park Association Inc., 16 Meriden Rd., Rockfall, CT 06481-2961, 860/346-2372, website: www.ctwoodlands.org.

## 17 DEVIL'S DEN
**1 mi/0.5 hr**
**in Plainfield**

This relatively flat hike follows a rough woods road for a half mile to a faint side path on the right. The path—easily overlooked—leads 30 feet downhill to ledges in the woods that feature cavelike cavities and a narrow passageway known as Devil's Den. Although unspectacular and lacking any views, this is a peaceful, enjoyable local walk.

From the parking area, walk out via the road (now impassable by car), which here is the blue-blazed Quinebaug Trail. Watch for a faint path on the right, just after walking a slight downhill over a slab in the road and before the road levels out. If you reach the yellow-blazed Pachaug-Quinebaug Trail, you have gone about 0.1 mile past Devil's Den. Return the way you came.

**User groups:** Hikers and snowshoers. No wheelchair facilities. Portions of this trail lie on private land, and use restrictions can change.

Assume that bikes, dogs, and horses are not allowed unless a trail is specifically marked for them (although many landowners do not object to dogs). Most trails are open to cross-country skiing. Assume that hunting is allowed in season unless otherwise posted.

**Access, fees:** Parking and access are free.

**Maps:** Although a map is not necessary for this hike, for topographic area maps, request Plainfield and Oneco from USGS Map Sales, Federal Center, Box 25286, Denver, CO 80225, 888/ASK-USGS (888/275-8747), website: http://mapping.usgs.gov.

**Directions:** From I-395, take Exit 88 in Plainfield and follow Route 14A east for 1.6 miles. Turn right on Spaulding Road and drive two miles to its end. Turn left on Flat Rock Road and continue another 0.7 mile; just beyond where the road becomes pavement, park in a turnout on the left.

**Contact:** Connecticut Forest and Park Association Inc., 16 Meriden Rd., Rockfall, CT 06481-2961, 860/346-2372, website: www.ctwoodlands.org.

## 18 CASTLE CRAG AND WEST PEAK
**6 mi/3.5 hrs**
**in Hubbard Park in Meriden**

This popular six-mile hike to a small, castlelike stone tower is one of the area's nicest, and a great adventure for children because it follows the crest of high cliffs for much of its distance. You can cut the hike in half by just going to Castle Crag. This entire hike involves about 600 feet of uphill walking.

From the parking area, walk across the dam bridge. At its far end, pick up the blue-blazed Metacomet Trail, which turns left into a rock-strewn gully, then immediately left again, climbing a hillside out of the gully. An easy hike, with a few short, steep sections, brings you to the crest of the ridge high above Merimere Reservoir, with sweeping views of the surrounding hills and the city of Meriden. Follow the trail along the ridge, passing several viewpoints. At 1.5 miles, you will reach Castle Crag, where the castle stands atop cliffs; you can climb its stairs for a 360-degree panorama. To make this a three-mile round-trip, return the way you came.

To continue on to West Peak for the full hike, cross the parking lot at Castle Crag to a blue arrow marking the Metacomet Trail, which follows the edge of woods along the tops of cliffs with almost constant views. The trail parallels the road to Castle Crag for about 0.3 mile, then turns left and descends fairly steeply for 0.2 mile. At the bottom of the hill, turn right onto an old woods road for about 50 feet, then right onto a footpath (watch for the blue blazes), slabbing uphill. Within 0.1 mile, you pass below cliffs, then ascend a short hillside to a woods road. Turn left and walk the road about 75 yards to where it terminates atop high cliffs with a commanding view. To the south lies the profile of the Sleeping Giant, a chain of low hills just north of New Haven that resembles a man lying on his back. To return to this hike's start, you can backtrack the way you came (or follow the paved West Peak Road for an easier descent) by following the woods road, past the trail to the end of the paved road (there are transmission towers to the left). Follow the woods road downhill, passing the right turn that leads to Castle Crag, all the way back to the reservoir dam, about an hour's walk (roughly three miles).

**User groups:** Hikers and snowshoers. No wheelchair facilities. Portions of this trail lie on private land, and use restrictions can change. Assume that bikes, dogs, and horses are not allowed unless a trail is specifically marked for them (although many landowners do not object to dogs). Most trails are open to cross-country skiing. Assume that hunting is allowed in season unless otherwise posted.

**Access, fees:** Parking and access are free.

**Maps:** For a topographic area map, request Meriden from USGS Map Sales, Federal Center, Box 25286, Denver, CO 80225, 888/ASK-USGS (888/275-8747), website: http://mapping.usgs.gov.

**Directions:** Take I-691 to Exit 4. Turn east, continue 0.8 mile, and take a left into Hubbard Park. Continue 0.2 mile and bear right, then go another 0.1 mile to a stop sign and turn left. Follow that road 0.3 mile to its end, passing under the highway. Turn left and drive another 1.1 miles, along the Merimere Reservoir, and park at a barricade at the end of the reservoir.

**Contact:** Connecticut Forest and Park Association Inc., 16 Meriden Rd., Rockfall, CT 06481-2961, 860/346-2372, website: www.ctwoodlands.org.

## 19 CHAUNCEY PEAK/ LAMENTATION MOUNTAIN
**4.2 mi/3 hrs**
**in Giuffrida Park and Lamentation Mountain State Park in Middletown**

Chauncey Peak and Lamentation Mountain comprise one of the finest hikes along the Mattabesett Trail, if not among all the traprock ridge walks of the Connecticut River Valley. Although it entails some steep hiking for brief periods, and involves some 750 feet of uphill hiking, this 4.2-mile trip amply rewards you for the modest effort.

From the parking lot, cross the field below the dam and bear right onto a flat trail, following it 0.1 mile to the blue-blazed Mattabesett. Turn left, soon climbing steeply to the summit of Chauncey at 0.4 mile, where you walk along the brink of a sheer cliff overlooking a pastoral countryside of fields and woods. Continue along the Mattabesett around the upper edge of a quarry to the open ridge and a view at 0.8 mile from high above Crescent Lake—I stood up here one afternoon, watching the glasslike water perfectly mirror the sky. Walk the open ridge with long views, mostly to the west, for about 0.2 mile, then descend a steep hillside of loose rocks. At 1.2 miles, cross a small brook, then begin climbing Lamentation, reaching the first view at 1.7 miles. From here, walk the ridge for 0.4 mile—with nearly constant views south, west, and north—to the summit, or high point on the ridge, at 2.1 miles.

Visible are the Sleeping Giant to the south and Castle Crag to the west. Hike back along the same route.

**User groups:** Hikers and snowshoers. No wheelchair facilities. Portions of this trail lie on private land, and use restrictions can change. Assume that bikes, dogs, and horses are not allowed unless a trail is specifically marked for them (although many landowners do not object to dogs). Most trails are open to cross-country skiing. Assume that hunting is allowed in season unless otherwise posted.

**Access, fees:** Parking and access are free.

**Maps:** A map of Giuffrida Park trails is available at the caretaker's house across the road from the parking lot. For a topographic area map, request Meriden from USGS Map Sales, Federal Center, Box 25286, Denver, CO 80225, 888/ASK-USGS (888/275-8747), website: http://mapping.usgs.gov.

**Directions:** Take I-91 to Exit 20 in Middletown. Head west on Country Club Road, which becomes Westfield Road; 2.5 miles from the highway—where the Mattabesett Trail enters the woods on the right—bear right and continue 0.1 mile to the parking area on the right at Giuffrida Park.

**Contact:** Connecticut Forest and Park Association Inc., 16 Meriden Rd., Rockfall, CT 06481-2961, 860/346-2372, website: www.ctwoodlands.org. Connecticut State Parks Division, 79 Elm St., Hartford, CT 06106-5127, 860/424-3200, website: www.dep.state.ct.us/stateparks/index.htm.

## 20 HIGBY MOUNTAIN
**2.4 mi/1.5 hrs**
**in Middlefield**

Unfortunately, you never escape the traffic sounds on this fairly easy, 2.4-mile walk, but it leads through a forest to a good spot to catch the sunset over the Meriden cityscape. The hike goes up about 250 feet.

From the parking lot, pick up the trail marked by blue blazes with purple dots, which begins beside the restaurant. (Don't take the trail from

the rear of the lot marked only with a sign reading "no snowmobiles.") This connector trail follows flat ground for nearly 0.4 mile to the blue-blazed Mattabesett Trail (by turning left here, you could reach Route 66 in 0.1 mile). Bear right onto the Mattabesett and continue 0.3 mile to where it turns sharply right and climbs steeply onto the ridge, an ascent that is brief but can leave you short of breath. About 1.2 miles from the parking lot, you reach the Pinnacle, a tall rock outcropping offering long views in nearly every direction, especially to the west. Return the way you came.

**User groups:** Hikers and snowshoers. No wheelchair facilities. Portions of this trail lie on private land, and use restrictions can change. Assume that bikes, dogs, and horses are not allowed unless a trail is specifically marked for them (although many landowners do not object to dogs). Most trails are open to cross-country skiing. Assume that hunting is allowed in season unless otherwise posted.

**Access, fees:** Parking and access are free.

**Maps:** For a topographic area map, request Middletown from USGS Map Sales, Federal Center, Box 25286, Denver, CO 80225, 888/ASK-USGS (888/275-8747), website: http://mapping.usgs.gov.

**Directions:** From the north, take exit 19 off I-91 southbound, turn left off the exit and take the first left onto Preston Avenue. From the east, drive west on Route 66 to I-691, take the first exit (#13 for East Main Street, a left exit), turn right at the first light onto Preston Avenue, then drive 1.1 miles and turn right onto Preston Avenue. From the south, take I-91 to exit 16 (Main Street), turn right onto Main Street, turn left on Preston Avenue just before the Route 66 east on-ramp, then drive 1.1 miles and turn right onto Preston Avenue. Park at the end of Preston Avenue. Enter the preserve through a gate; a Nature Conservancy sign is about a two-minute walk beyond the gate.

**Contact:** The Nature Conservancy Connecticut Chapter, 55 High St., Middletown, CT 06457-3788, 860/344-0716, website: http://nature.org, email: ct@tnc.org. Connecticut Forest and Park Association Inc., 16 Meriden Rd., Rockfall, CT 06481-2961, 860/346-2372, website: www.ctwoodlands.org.

## 21 WADSWORTH FALLS STATE PARK

**3.2 mi/1.5 hrs**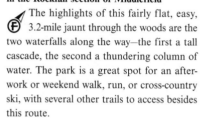

**in the Rockfall section of Middlefield**

The highlights of this fairly flat, easy, 3.2-mile jaunt through the woods are the two waterfalls along the way—the first a tall cascade, the second a thundering column of water. The park is a great spot for an after-work or weekend walk, run, or cross-country ski, with several other trails to access besides this route.

Behind the restrooms off the parking lot, pick up the orange-blazed Main Trail, a wide, mostly flat path. In a half mile, opposite a park map board, grows a giant mountain laurel. Continue on the Main Trail for 0.2 mile and then bear right at a sign for Little Falls, following a blue trail 0.2 mile to where the Coginchaug River tumbles 40 feet through a series of ledges. Rejoining the Main Trail above Little Falls, turn right. At 1.5 miles from the start, the Main Trail ends at a paved road. Turn right and follow the road 0.1 mile to a parking area on the right, then follow the sound of crash-ing water about 100 yards to the Big Falls. Retrace your steps back to the parking lot.

**User groups:** Hikers, skiers, and snowshoers. Dogs must be leashed. No wheelchair facilities. The blue side trail is not suitable for bikes, horses, or skis (see trail notes above). Hunting is prohibited.

**Access, fees:** From Memorial Day–mid-September, a parking fee of $7 is charged for Connecticut vehicles, $10 for out-of-state vehicles, on weekends and holidays. On weekdays the fee is $6 for residents and $7 for nonresidents. Access is free the rest of the year. The state park is open from 8 A.M.–sunset.

**Maps:** Trail maps are available at the information board beside the parking lot. For a topographic area map, request Middletown from USGS Map Sales, Federal Center, Box 25286, Denver, CO 80225, 888/ASK-USGS (888/275-8747), website: http://mapping.usgs.gov.

**Directions:** From the junction of Routes 66 and 157 in Middletown, drive south on Route 157 for 1.5 miles and turn left into the state park entrance and parking lot.

**Contact:** Wadsworth Falls State Park, c/o Chatfield Hollow State Park, 381 Route 80, Killingworth, CT 06419, 860/663-2030. Connecticut State Parks Division, 79 Elm St., Hartford, CT 06106-5127, 860/424-3200, website: www.dep.state.ct.us/stateparks/index.htm.

## Chapter 14

© MICHAEL LANZA

# Long Island Sound

# Long Island Sound

This chapter continues coverage of hiking along the traprock ridges and south to the coast. This region also features excellent hikes in Pachaug State Forest and Devil's Hopyard State Park.

Most Blue Trails across Connecticut are on private land, and the Connecticut Forest and Park Association has secured landowner permission only for hiker access. Changes in everything from land use to ownership constantly threaten the Blue Trail System, making it imperative that hikers respect any closures of trails, whether temporary or permanent. Although uses can vary, assume that dogs, horses, and mountain bikes are not allowed unless a trail is specifically marked for them. Most Blue Trails are open to cross-country skiing. Assume that hunting is permitted in season unless the land is posted with signs prohibiting it. Fires must not be lit except where officially designated fireplaces have been provided.

In Connecticut state parks and forests, dogs must be leashed, and horses are allowed on some trails and forest roads. Hunting is allowed in season in state forests, but not in state parks, and is prohibited on Sundays. Access fees are levied at some state lands, but most allow free entrance year-round.

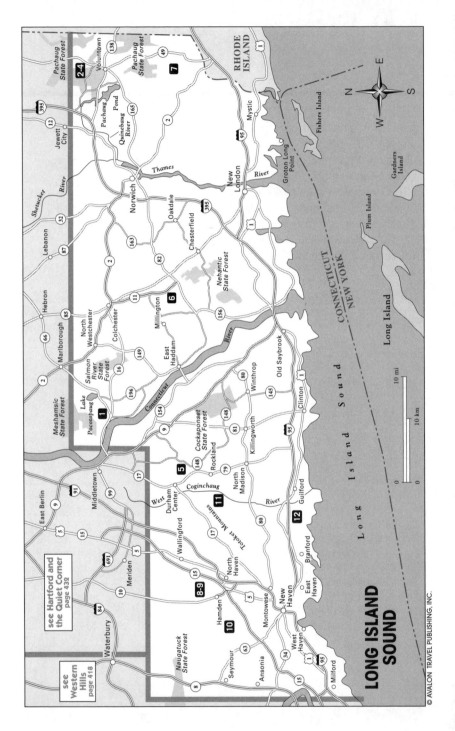

# 1 GREAT HILL

**1 mi/0.75 hr**

**in East Hampton**

This fairly easy hike of just one mile round-trip and a few hundred feet uphill leads to interesting quartz ledges with a good view over Great Hill Pond and the Connecticut River Valley. On the way to the ledges, the trail passes below low, rugged cliffs that young children can have a little adventure on.

From the parking area, cross the road and follow the blue-blazed Shenipsit Trail into the woods. The trail is easy at first, then begins slabbing up Great Hill, traversing ledges. Atop the hill, the Shenipsit makes a hairpin turn with two quick, sharp right turns; at the second of those, a white-blazed side trail leads to the left about 0.1 mile to the quartz ledges. Return the way you came.

**User groups:** Hikers and snowshoers. No wheelchair facilities. Portions of this trail lie on private land, and use restrictions can change. Assume that bikes, dogs, and horses are not allowed unless a trail is specifically marked for them (although many landowners do not object to dogs). Most trails are open to cross-country skiing. Assume that hunting is allowed in season unless otherwise posted.

**Access, fees:** Parking and access are free.

**Maps:** For a topographic area map, request Middle Haddam from USGS Map Sales, Federal Center, Box 25286, Denver, CO 80225, 888/ASK-USGS (888/275-8747), website: http://mapping.usgs.gov.

**Directions:** From the junction of Routes 66 and 151 in Cobalt/East Hampton, turn north onto Depot Hill Road, drive 0.1 mile, then bear right, uphill, following the road another 0.1 mile. Turn right onto Gadpouch Road and proceed a half mile (the road becomes dirt) to a small dirt parking area on the right.

**Contact:** Connecticut Forest and Park Association Inc., 16 Meriden Rd., Rockfall, CT 06481-2961, 860/346-2372, website: www.ct-woodlands.org.

# 2 PACHAUG STATE FOREST RHODODENDRON SANCTUARY

**0.5 mi/0.25 hr**

**in Pachaug State Forest in Voluntown**

This short, easy walk begins to the right of the field parking area, at the Rhododendron Sanctuary sign. A wheelchair-accessible trail leads into the forest, home to a stand of huge wild rhododendrons sprawling over the forest floor. Blussoms usually arrire in July. The trail winds a quarter mile through the woods. Return the way you came. Just down the road is the start of the blue-blazed Pachaug Trail hike up Mount Misery (see next listing).

**User groups:** Hikers, snowshoers, wheelchair users, and dogs. Dogs must be leashed. This trail is not suitable for bikes, horses, or skis. Hunting is allowed in season.

**Access, fees:** Parking and access are free.

**Maps:** A free map of Pachaug State Forest is available at the state forest headquarters (see contact information, below) or from the Connecticut State Parks Division (see addresses below). For topographic area maps, request Voluntown, Jewett City, Oneco, and Plainfield from USGS Map Sales, Federal Center, Box 25286, Denver, CO 80225, 888/ASK-USGS (888/275-8747), website: http://mapping.usgs.gov.

**Directions:** The main entrance to Pachaug State Forest is Headquarters Road, which is off Route 49, 7.9 miles south of its junction with Route 14A and 0.6 mile north of Route 138 in Voluntown. Follow Headquarters Road 0.8 mile, bear left at a fork, and drive another 0.1 mile to a field and parking; to the right is a sign at the Rhododendron Sanctuary entrance. To reach the state forest headquarters, follow Headquarters Road for 0.3 mile from Route 49, turn right, and continue another 0.1 mile to the office on the left.

**Contact:** Pachaug State Forest, P.O. Box 5, Voluntown, CT 06384, 860/376-4075. Connecticut State Parks Division, 79 Elm St., Hartford, CT 06106-5127, 860/424-3200, website: www.dep.state.ct.us/stateparks/index.htm.

Connecticut Forest and Park Association Inc., 16 Meriden Rd., Rockfall, CT 06481-2961, 860/346-2372, website: www.ctwoodlands.org.

## ❸ MOUNT MISERY
### 1 mi/0.75 hr

**in Pachaug State Forest in Voluntown**

Not expecting to find any real views from a 441-foot hill in eastern Connecticut, I scrambled over rocks to the Mount Misery summit—and was surprised by a sweeping view of forested countryside from atop low cliffs. This one-mile round-trip hike is fairly flat for much of its length and a good one for young children. The Pachaug Trail enters the woods diagonally across Cutoff Road from the turnout, about 50 feet before the turnout and 75 feet beyond the road to the campground. Follow its blue blazes up Mount Misery and then explore the views from atop Misery's ridge of low cliffs. Return the way you came. This hike is very near the Rhododendron Sanctuary (see previous listing); in fact, you can park at the Rhododendron Sanctuary trailhead and walk a short distance down the road (which the Pachaug Trail follows) to this hike.

**User groups:** Hikers, snowshoers, and dogs. Dogs must be leashed. No wheelchair facilities. The trail is not suitable for bikes, horses, or skis. Hunting is allowed in season.

**Access, fees:** Parking and access are free.

**Maps:** A free map of Pachaug State Forest is available at the state forest headquarters, or from the Connecticut State Parks Division (see addresses below). For topographic area maps, request Voluntown, Jewett City, Oneco, and Plainfield from USGS Map Sales, Federal Center, Box 25286, Denver, CO 80225, 888/ASK-USGS (888/275-8747), website: http://mapping.usgs.gov.

**Directions:** The main entrance to Pachaug State Forest is Headquarters Road, which is off Route 49, 7.9 miles south of its junction with Route 14A and 0.6 mile north of Route 138 in Voluntown. Follow Headquarters Road 0.8 mile, bear left at a fork, and drive another 0.1 mile to a field. Bear right on the dirt Cutoff Road and drive another 0.2 mile to a turnout on the right, about 125 feet beyond a left turn for the campground. To reach the state forest headquarters, follow Headquarters Road for 0.3 mile from Route 49, turn right, and continue another 0.1 mile to the office on the left.

**Contact:** Pachaug State Forest, Route 49, Box 5, Voluntown, CT 06384, 860/376-4075. Connecticut State Parks Division, 79 Elm St., Hartford, CT 06106-5127, 860/424-3200, website: www.dep.state.ct.us/stateparks/index.htm. Connecticut Forest and Park Association Inc., 16 Meriden Rd., Rockfall, CT 06481-2961, 860/346-2372, website: www.ctwoodlands.org.

## ❹ PACHAUG STATE FOREST ROADS LOOP
### 9 mi/4.5 hrs

**in Pachaug State Forest in Voluntown**

With miles of dirt roads laced throughout the sprawling Pachaug State Forest, the area is fertile ground for a long, flat hike or loop ride on a mountain bike. The loop described here covers about nine miles and much of the state forest—including, somewhat surprisingly, a few pretty good hills and a 20-minute side hike over 441-foot Mount Misery, which offers a sweeping view of forested countryside from atop low cliffs. This loop would make a good outing on skis as well, but there are better options in Pachaug.

From the picnic area, head out Trail 1 Road, which becomes dirt within about 150 feet. Pass a dirt road entering from the right and cross Gardner Road within the first mile. Follow Trail 1 Road another mile or more to a paved road and turn left. In about a half mile, turn left at a four-way intersection onto the dirt Breakneck Hill Road. Within a mile, turn left onto the first major dirt road, Lawrence Road, and begin a long descent. Reaching a T intersection, turn right on Forest Road, climb a hill, and then turn left on Cutoff Road, descending again. Turn onto the first dirt road on the right (watch for it), Firetower Road, and follow it a half mile to a gate. Before passing the gate, turn left down the side dirt road, which ends within a few hundred feet at a pair of trails leading up Mount Misery.

Hike the trail on the right, which traverses below low cliffs, circles around Mount Misery, and then turns left (uphill) on the blue-blazed Pachaug Trail heading toward the summit. After checking out the view, continue over the top of Mount Misery, following the blue blazes back. Go back to the gate and turn left past it, following Firetower Road another half mile or more to another gate. Continue around the gate and turn left; this is Trail 1 Road. Follow it more than a mile back to the picnic area.

**User groups:** Hikers, bikers, dogs, horses, skiers, and snowshoers; check with state forest authorities in winter to find out which roads are open to skiers. Dogs must be leashed. No wheelchair facilities. Hunting is allowed in season.

**Access, fees:** Parking and access are free.

**Maps:** A free map of Pachaug State Forest is available at the state forest headquarters, or from the Connecticut State Parks Division (see addresses below). For topographic area maps, request Voluntown, Jewett City, Oneco, and Plainfield from USGS Map Sales, Federal Center, Box 25286, Denver, CO 80225, 888/ASK-USGS (888/275-8747), website: http://mapping.usgs.gov.

**Directions:** The main entrance to Pachaug State Forest is Headquarters Road, which is off Route 49, 7.9 miles south of its junction with Route 14A and 0.6 mile north of Route 138 in Voluntown. Follow Headquarters Road 0.8 mile, bear right at a fork onto Trail 1 Road, and drive another 0.1 mile to parking on the right at a picnic area. To reach the state forest headquarters, follow Headquarters Road for 0.3 mile from Route 49, turn right, and continue another 0.1 mile to the office on the left.

**Contact:** Pachaug State Forest, Route 49, Box 5, Voluntown, CT 06384, 860/376-4075. Connecticut State Parks Division, 79 Elm St., Hartford, CT 06106-5127, 860/424-3200, website:

www.dep.state.ct.us/stateparks/index.htm. Connecticut Forest and Park Association Inc., 16 Meriden Rd., Rockfall, CT 06481-2961, 860/346-2372, website: www.ctwoodlands.org.

## 5 COGINCHAUG CAVE
**1.4 mi/1 hr**
**in Durham**

This quiet Mattabesett Trail stretch leads to a huge overhanging rock wall known as Coginchaug Cave—an easy round-trip of 1.4 miles with minimal uphill walking. Many years ago the cave supposedly sheltered Indians.

From the parking area, follow the rough jeep road 100 feet and turn right with the blue blazes onto a footpath into the woods. The trail crosses one small brook, makes a very short but steep hillock climb, and circles around exposed ledges in the forest to the cave, 0.7 mile from the hike's start. Return the way you came.

**User groups:** Hikers and snowshoers. No wheelchair facilities. Portions of this trail lie on private land, and use restrictions can change. Assume that bikes, dogs, and horses are not allowed unless a trail is specifically marked for them (although many landowners do not object to dogs). Most trails are open to cross-country skiing. Assume that hunting is allowed in season unless otherwise posted.

**Access, fees:** Parking and access are free.

**Maps:** For a topographic area map, request Durham from USGS Map Sales, Federal Center, Box 25286, Denver, CO 80225, 888/ASK-USGS (888/275-8747), website: http://mapping.usgs.gov.

**Directions:** From the junction of Routes 17 and 79 in Durham, drive south on Route 79 for 0.8 mile and turn left onto Old Blue Hills Road. Bear right immediately, following blue blazes on the utility poles for 0.7 mile to the end of the road, where there is limited parking.

**Contact:** Connecticut Forest and Park Association Inc., 16 Meriden Rd., Rockfall, CT 06481-2961, 860/346-2372, website: www.ctwoodlands.org.

## 6 DEVIL'S HOPYARD STATE PARK VISTA TRAIL LOOP

**2.5 mi/1.5 hrs**

**in East Haddam**

This 2.5-mile loop hike through Devil's Hopyard State Park, in a more rural section of central Connecticut, is mostly wooded, but it begins with spectacular Chapman Falls, which thunders loudly as it crashes down, frothing white, 40 or 50 feet over several rock ledges. The trail then passes a beautiful view from an open ledge—be sure to take the time to enjoy the vistas, including a dark gorge along the Eight Mile River. I enjoyed a very peaceful, late-afternoon walk through here one cool autumn day. The hills are small, with just a few hundred feet of elevation gain.

From the parking lot, cross the road to the map board beside Chapman Falls. Follow the footpath past the falls for 0.1 mile to the picnic area and the covered bridge. Once over the bridge, turn left, following the orange blazes of the Vista Trail. Within the first half mile you cross a brook on stones, which could be tricky in high water. The trail passes through a hemlock grove and some wet areas, and at 1.3 miles reaches an open ledge with a pastoral view to the south. The trail, which can be tricky to follow from here, descends to the right through mountain laurel and then mixed forest, reaching the Eight Mile River just downstream from a gorge. Before the gorge, the trail turns right, climbing a hillside and eventually reaching an old woods road that leads back to the covered bridge. Backtrack from here to the parking lot.

**User groups:** Hikers, snowshoers, and dogs. Dogs must be leashed. No wheelchair facilities. This trail is not suitable for bikes or skis. Horses and hunting are prohibited.

**Access, fees:** Parking and access are free. The park closes at sunset.

**Maps:** A map of the state park is posted at an information board across the street from the parking lot. For topographic area maps, request Colchester and Hamburg from USGS Map Sales, Federal Center, Box 25286, Denver, CO 80225, 888/ASK-USGS (888/275-8747), website: http://mapping.usgs.gov.

**Directions:** From the center of Millington, north of the state park, drive east on Haywardville Road for 0.7 mile and turn right onto Hopyard Road at a sign for Devil's Hopyard State Park. Continue 0.8 mile and turn left at a sign for Chapman Falls (0.1 mile beyond the park headquarters). Turn immediately left into the parking lot. Or from the junction of Routes 82 and 158 in East Haddam, south of the park, drive 0.2 mile east on Route 82 and turn left onto Hopyard Road. Continue 3.5 miles, turn right at the sign for Chapman Falls, and left into the parking lot.

**Contact:** Devil's Hopyard State Park, 366 Hopyard Rd., East Haddam, CT 06423, 860/873-8566. Connecticut State Parks Division, 79 Elm St., Hartford, CT 06106-5127, 860/424-3200, website: www.dep.state.ct.us/stateparks/index.htm.

## 7 HIGH AND BULLET LEDGES

**4.4 mi/2.5 hrs**

**in North Stonington**

This relatively easy hike—with just a couple of steep, if short, climbs—on a 2.2-mile stretch of the blue-blazed Narragansett Trail brings you to two very different ledges hidden away in the woods. Neither offers any views; the appeal here lies in a quiet walk through the forest and a pair of interesting rock formations.

From the parking lot, continue 0.1 mile farther down the road to where blue blazes turn left onto a woods road. Follow it a quarter mile and then continue straight ahead with the blue blazes, while the woods road bears left. The trail ascends a steep hillside, turns right, and reaches High Ledge just 0.8 mile from the parking area. The trail circles the small ledge and follows another woods road, descending somewhat and passing below the base of a cliff some 40 feet high. At the cliff's far side, the trail turns right, ascends left of the cliff, and reaches its top—Bullet Ledge, 2.2 miles from the parking area. Head back to the parking lot the same way you came.

**User groups:** Hikers and snowshoers. No wheelchair facilities. Portions of this trail lie on private land, and use restrictions can change. Assume that bikes, dogs, and horses are not allowed unless a trail is specifically marked for them (although many landowners do not object to dogs). Most trails are open to cross-country skiing. Assume that hunting is allowed in season unless otherwise posted.

**Access, fees:** Parking and access are free.

**Maps:** Although a map is not necessary for this hike, for topographic area maps, request Old Mystic and Ashaway from USGS Map Sales, Federal Center, Box 25286, Denver, CO 80225, 888/ASK-USGS (888/275-8747), website: http://mapping.usgs.gov.

**Directions:** Drive Route 2 to North Stonington and turn off the highway onto Main Street at the village sign. Drive 0.4 mile and turn onto Wyassup Road. Continue 3.1 miles, turn left onto Wyassup Lake Road, and follow it 0.7 mile to parking at a boat launch area on the right.

**Contact:** Connecticut Forest and Park Association Inc., 16 Meriden Rd., Rockfall, CT 06481-2961, 860/346-2372, website: www.ctwoodlands.org.

## ⑧ SLEEPING GIANT STATE PARK BLUE-WHITE LOOP

**5.6 mi/4.5 hrs**

**in Hamden**

The Sleeping Giant is a chain of low hills which, from a distance, resemble a giant lying on his back. Sleeping Giant State Park consists of 1,500 acres and has more than 30 trail miles, although the Sleeping Giant Park Association's goal is to expand the park to 2,000 acres.

This fairly rugged, 5.6-mile loop on the blue and white trails passes over all of the major features of the giant—including the towering cliffs at his chin—and numerous ledges with excellent views. It is one of the most scenic hikes in the state. Besides the Tower Trail (see next listing), the blue-blazed Quinnipiac Trail is the only park trail that leads to the stone tower, which can be climbed for panoramic

views of the countryside and New Haven Harbor. Although the loop could be done in either direction, I suggest hiking it counterclockwise, starting on the white trail. The only drawback of going in this direction is that you have to descend—rather than climb, which is easier—the steep, exposed slabs on the Head's south slope (via the blue trail); this section can be hazardous when wet. (To avoid the slabs descent, backtrack north on the blue trail from the chin's cliff tops to the wide Tower Trail, which provides an easy descent to the parking area.) On the other hand, hiking this loop counterclockwise allows you to finish this hike with the cliff walks over the Head, which boasts the most striking and precipitous cliffs in the park. I won't bother describing every turn on this hike—they are myriad—but the trails are well blazed and the state park trail map is good. This hike's cumulative elevation gain is hard to calculate, but probably not more than 500 feet.

From the parking lot, follow the paved road about 0.1 mile to the picnic grounds and watch for the white-blazed trail branching to the right. Follow the white trail eastward across the park for nearly three miles to where it crosses the blue-blazed trail near Hezekiah's Knob. Turn left onto the blue trail and follow it back, passing by the stone tower and finishing over the Head. After descending steeply to the south off the Head, watch for a connector trail leading to the left (east) back to the picnic area. If you miss the first connector trail and start seeing Mount Carmel Avenue through the woods, take the violet-blazed trail, which also leads you back to the picnic area.

**User groups:** Hikers, snowshoers, and dogs. Dogs must be leashed. No wheelchair facilities. Bikes, horses, hunting, and skis are prohibited.

**Access, fees:** From April 1–November 1, a parking fee of $7 is charged for Connecticut vehicles, $10 for out-of-state vehicles, on weekends and holidays, while weekdays are free. The park closes at sunset.

**Maps:** A basic trail map is available at the state park and from the Connecticut State Parks Division (see address below). For topographic area maps, request Mount Carmel and Wallingford from USGS Map Sales, Federal Center, Box 25286, Denver, CO 80225, 888/ASK-USGS (888/275-8747), website: http://mapping.usgs.gov.

**Directions:** From Route 10 in Hamden, about 1.4 miles north of the junction of Routes 10 and 40, turn east onto Mount Carmel Avenue. Continue 0.2 mile to the state park entrance and parking on the left, across from Quinnipiac College.

**Contact:** Sleeping Giant State Park, 200 Mount Carmel Ave., Hamden, CT 06518, 203/789-7498. Connecticut State Parks Division, 79 Elm St., Hartford, CT 06106-5127, 860/424-3200, website: www.dep.state.ct.us/stateparks/index.htm. Connecticut Forest and Park Association Inc., 16 Meriden Rd., Rockfall, CT 06481-2961, 860/346-2372, website: www.ct-woodlands.org.

## 9 SLEEPING GIANT STATE PARK TOWER TRAIL

**3.2 mi/1.5 hrs**

**in Hamden**

This relatively easy, 3.2-mile round-trip climbs about 500 feet and leads to Sleeping Giant State Park's stone tower, which has stairs leading to its top and panoramic views of the countryside and, to the south, New Haven Harbor. This hike is shorter and easier than the Sleeping Giant State Park Blue-White Loop hike (see previous listing).

From the parking area, walk the paved road about 100 feet and turn right at a large sign for the Tower Trail. It rises gently, following the carriage road 1.6 miles to the stone tower. Climb the steps in the tower to its top, where you may find yourself standing in a strong breeze, looking out over the New Haven skyline and the long ridge of the Sleeping Giant stretching off to the east and west. Retrace your steps to return to the parking area.

**User groups:** Hikers and snowshoers. Dogs must be leashed. No wheelchair facilities. Bikes, horses, hunting, and skis are prohibited.

**Access, fees:** From April 1–November 1, a parking fee of $7 is charged for Connecticut vehicles, $10 for out-of-state vehicles, on weekends and holidays, while weekdays are free. The park closes at sunset.

**Maps:** A basic trail map is available at the state park and from the Connecticut State Parks Division (see address below). For topographic area maps, request Mount Carmel and Wallingford from USGS Map Sales, Federal Center, Box 25286, Denver, CO 80225, 888/ASK-USGS (888/275-8747), website: http://mapping.usgs.gov.

**Directions:** From Route 10 in Hamden, about 1.4 miles north of the junction of Routes 10 and 40, turn east onto Mount Carmel Avenue. Continue 0.2 mile to the state park entrance and parking on the left, across from Quinnipiac College.

**Contact:** Sleeping Giant State Park, 200 Mount Carmel Ave., Hamden, CT 06518, 203/789-7498. Connecticut State Parks Division, 79 Elm St., Hartford, CT 06106-5127, 860/424-3200, website: www.dep.state.ct.us/stateparks/index.htm. Connecticut Forest and Park Association Inc., 16 Meriden Rd., Rockfall, CT 06481-2961, 860/346-2372, website: www.ct-woodlands.org.

## 10 WEST ROCK RIDGE STATE PARK

**10 mi/6.5 hrs**

**in Hamden, Bethany, and Woodbridge**

This is an out-and-back hike along the West Rock Ridge, which offers views to the east and southeast of the New Haven area. You can walk any distance and turn back (which is why this hike receives a moderate difficulty rating); the first views of houses and other buildings in Hamden and the New Haven skyline in the distance are reached after 1.8 miles. There is very little elevation gain on this hike.

From the turnout, follow the blue blazes with red dots marking the Sanford Feeder Trail along various woods roads for 0.6 mile and then turn right (uphill) onto the blue-blazed Regicides Trail. Within 0.2 mile, the trail reaches and parallels paved Baldwin Road, which runs through West Rock Ridge State Park and is only open during the warmer months. The trail crosses the road 0.6 mile after first reaching it; continue 0.4 mile along the Regicides Trail to the first view. The trail reenters the woods and then crosses Baldwin Road again 0.1 mile beyond that first viewpoint. Over the next roughly 3.5 miles, the Regicides Trail passes several more outlooks. Return along the same route.

**User groups:** Hikers, snowshoers, and dogs. Dogs must be leashed. No wheelchair facilities. The trail is not suitable for bikes, horses, or skis. Hunting is prohibited.

**Access, fees:** Parking and access are free.

**Maps:** For topographic area maps, request New Haven and Mount Carmel from USGS Map Sales, Federal Center, Box 25286, Denver, CO 80225, 888/ASK-USGS (888/275-8747), website: http://mapping.usgs.gov.

**Directions:** From Route 10 in Hamden, about 1.5 miles north of the junction of Routes 10 and 40, turn west onto West Woods Road. Follow it 0.9 mile to its end; turn left onto Shepard Avenue and then immediately right again onto the continuation of West Woods Road. Proceed half a mile and bear right onto Choate; follow it to its end and turn left onto West Woods Road again. Follow it to the town line, where it becomes Brook Road. Just beyond the town line, drive straight through an intersection with a stop sign and continue another 0.4 mile. Park in a turnout on the left where the blue blazes with red dots marking the Sanford Feeder Trail enter the forest on an old woods road blocked by a chain. There may be no trail sign.

**Contact:** Connecticut Forest and Park Association Inc., 16 Meriden Rd., Rockfall, CT 06481-2961, 860/346-2372, website: www.ct-woodlands.org. West Rock Ridge State Park, c/o Sleeping Giant State Park, 200 Mount Carmel Ave., Hamden, CT 06518, 203/789-

7498. Connecticut State Parks Division, 79 Elm St., Hartford, CT 06106-5127, 860/424-3200, fax 860/424-4070, website: www.dep.state .ct.us/stateparks/index.htm.

## ⑪ BLUFF HEAD/ TOTOKET MOUNTAIN
**2.5 mi/1.5 hrs**
**in North Guilford**

After a brief, steep climb, the trail follows the edge of high cliffs all the way to the rocky outcropping known as Bluff Head, with an almost continuous, 180-degree vista of the forest and low hills in this rural corner of southern Connecticut, taking in the distant Long Island Sound and the tip of Long Island, as well as the Hartford skyline. From the parking area, follow the Mattabesett Trail's blue blazes to the left (south) for about 50 feet, where the trail turns right and ascends steeply. After about 0.2 mile, it levels out and follows a low ridge to an overlook at 0.4 mile. From here, a trail leaves to the left (west); you will return to it, but this hike continues north on the Mattabesett another 0.8 mile to Bluff Head, a high outcrop atop cliffs with wide and long views to the north, east, and south. Double back on the Mattabesett to the trail junction at the first overlook and turn right (west). Descend about 0.3 mile, turn left, and follow a woods road 0.2 mile back to your vehicle.

**User groups:** Hikers and snowshoers. No wheelchair facilities. Portions of this trail lie on private land, and use restrictions can change. Assume that bikes, dogs, and horses are not allowed unless a trail is specifically marked for them (although many landowners do not object to dogs). Most trails are open to cross-country skiing. Assume that hunting is allowed in season unless otherwise posted.

**Access, fees:** Parking and access are free.

**Maps:** For a topographic area map, request Durham from USGS Map Sales, Federal Center, Box 25286, Denver, CO 80225, 888/ASK-USGS (888/275-8747), website: http://mapping.usgs.gov.

**Directions:** From the junction of Routes 77

and 80 in Guilford, drive north on Route 77 for 4.3 miles and turn left into an unmarked dirt parking area.

**Contact:** Connecticut Forest and Park Association Inc., 16 Meriden Rd., Rockfall, CT 06481-2961, 860/346-2372, website: www.ct-woodlands.org.

## 12 WESTWOODS PRESERVE
**2 mi/1 hr**
**in Guilford**

With 1,000 acres, Westwoods is a popular local place for hiking, cross-country skiing, and mountain biking because of its trail network and the remote feeling it inspires just a few miles from busy I-95 and a short drive from New Haven. From the parking area, follow the obvious trail 0.1 mile and then turn left onto the white-blazed trail. You soon pass a side path leading left to large stone blocks; this detour rejoins the white trail within 0.1 mile. The white trail continues past marshes on the left and Lost Pond, a protected little body of water ringed by woods and bordering on a wildlife refuge, so expect to see lots of birds, such as egrets, ducks, and osprey. The trail turns back into the woods, passing numerous glacial erratics, including one boulder

split into halves, between which grows a stout cedar tree. At a trail junction at a nice overlook of Lost Lake, turn right onto the orange trail, following it back to the parking area.

**User groups:** Hikers, dogs, skiers, and snowshoers. Dogs must be leashed. No wheelchair facilities. Only a portion of this trail is suitable for bikes and horses. Hunting is allowed in season.

**Access, fees:** Parking and access are free.

**Maps:** A map board is posted at the trailhead, and maps of Westwoods Preserve are sold in several local stores. For a topographic area map, request Guilford from USGS Map Sales, Federal Center, Box 25286, Denver, CO 80225, 888/ASK-USGS (888/275-8747), website: http://mapping.usgs.gov.

**Directions:** Take I-95 to Exit 58 in Guilford. Drive south on Route 77 for half a mile and turn right onto U.S. 1 heading south. Continue 0.2 mile, turn left onto River Road, go another 0.6 mile, and turn right onto Water Street/Route 146. Follow it 0.8 mile, turn right onto Sam Hill Road, and park in the turnout immediately on the left.

**Contact:** Guilford Land Conservation Trust, P.O. Box 200, Guilford, CT 06437; 203-457-9253, website: www.guilfordlandtrust.org.

© MICHAEL LANZA

# Resource Guide

## Public Lands Agencies

### Acadia National Park
P.O. Box 177
Eagle Lake Rd.
Bar Harbor, ME 04609-0177
207/288-3338, fax 207/288-5507
website: www.nps.gov/acad
email: Acadia_Information@nps.gov

### Baxter State Park
64 Balsam Dr.
Millinocket, ME 04462-2190
207/723-5140
website: www.baxterstateparkauthority.com

### Blue Hills Reservation Headquarters
695 Hillside St.
Milton, MA 02186
617/698-1802
website: www.state.ma.us/mdc/blue.htm

### Cape Cod National Seashore
99 Marconi Station Site Rd.
Wellfleet, MA 02667
508/349-3785, fax 508/349-9052
website: www.nps.gov/caco/index.htm
email: CACO_Superintendent@nps.gov
*also:* Salt Pond Visitor Center
508/255-3421
*also:* Province Lands Visitor Center
508/487-1256

### Connecticut State Parks Division
79 Elm St.
Hartford, CT 06106-5127
860/424-3200, fax 860/424-4070
website: www.dep.state.ct.us/stateparks/
    index.htm

### Great Meadows National Wildlife Refuge
73 Weir Hill Rd.
Sudbury, MA 01776
978/443-4661
website: http://greatmeadows.fws.gov/

### Green Mountain National Forest Supervisor
231 North Main St.
Rutland, VT 05701
802/747-6700, fax 802/747-6766
website: www.fs.fed.us/r9/gmfl

### Maine Bureau of Parks and Lands
Department of Conservation
mailing address: 22 State House Station
Augusta, ME 04333-0022
207/287-2211, fax 207/287-2400
physical address: 286 Water St.
Key Bank Plaza, Augusta, ME
website: www.state.me.us/doc/parks.htm

### Massachusetts Division of State Parks and Recreation
251 Causeway St., Suite 600
Boston, MA 02114-2104
617/626-1250, fax 617/626-1449
website: www.state.ma.us/dem/forparks.htm
email: Mass.Parks@state.ma.us

### New Hampshire Division of Parks and Recreation
P.O. Box 1856
172 Pembroke Rd.
Concord, NH 03302
603/271-3556, fax 603/271-2629
camping reservations: 603/271-3628
website: www.nhstateparks.org
email: nhparks@dred.state.nh.us

## Parker River National Wildlife Refuge

6 Plum Island Turnpike
Newburyport, MA 01950
978/465-5753 or 800/877-8339 for the hearing impaired
website: http://parkerriver.fws.gov/

## Rhode Island Department of Environmental Management

235 Promenade St.
Providence, RI 02908-5767
401/222-6800
website: www.state.ri.us/dem
*note:* This department oversees the Division of Parks and Recreation and the Division of Forest Environment.

## Rhode Island Division of Forest Environment

1037 Hartford Pike
North Scituate, RI 02857
401/647-1439, fax 401/647-3590
website: www.state.ri.us/dem

## Rhode Island Division of Parks and Recreation

2321 Hartford Ave.
Johnston, RI 02919-1719
401/222-2632, fax 401/934-0610
website: www.riparks.com
email: riparks@earthlink.net

## Vermont Department of Forests

Parks and Recreation Commissioner's Office
103 South Main St.
Waterbury, VT 05671-0601
802/241-3655, fax 802/244-1481
website: www.state.vt.us/anr/fpr
email: parks@fpr.anr.state.vt.us

## White Mountain National Forest Supervisor

719 North Main St.
Laconia, NH 03246
603/528-8721 or TDD 603/528-8722
website: www.fs.fed.us/r9/white

# Map Sources

## DeLorme Publishing Company

800/642-0970
website: www.DeLorme.com

## New England Cartographics

413/549-4124 or toll-free 888/995-6277
website: www.necartographics.com
email: info@necartographics.com

## Rubel BikeMaps

P.O. Box 401035
Cambridge, MA 02140
website: www.bikemaps.com
email: info@bikemaps.com

## Trails Illustrated

800/962-1643
website: http://maps.nationalgeographic.com/trails

## United States Geological Survey

Information Services
Box 25286
Denver, CO 80225
888/ASK-USGS (888/275-8747),
fax 303/202-4693
website: http://mapping.usgs.gov

# Trail Clubs and Organizations

## Appalachian Mountain Club

5 Joy St.
Boston, MA 02108
617/523-0655
website: www.outdoors.org
email: information@outdoors.org

## Appalachian Mountain Club Pinkham Notch Visitor Center

P.O. Box 298
Gorham, NH 03581
603/466-2721
website: www.outdoors.org
email: information@outdoors.org

## Appalachian Trail Conference

799 Washington St.
P.O. Box 807
Harpers Ferry, WV 25425-0807
304/535-6331
website: www.appalachiantrail.org
email: info@appalachiantrail.org

## Ascutney Trails Association

George Smith, Jr.
P.O. Box 119
Hartland, VT 05048

## Cardigan Highlanders Club

Sanborn, Craig
P.O. Box 104
Enfield Center, NH 03749
603/632-5640

## Connecticut Forest and Park Association Inc.

16 Meriden Rd.
Rockfall, CT 06481-2961
860/346-2372
website: www.ctwoodlands.org
email: conn.forest.assoc@snet.net

## Friends of the Blue Hills

P.O. Box 416
Milton, MA 02186
781/828-1805
website: www.friendsofthebluehills.org

## The Friends of the Middlesex Fells Reservation

4 Woodland Rd.
Stoneham, MA 02180
781/662-2340
website: www.fells.org

## Friends of the Wapack

Box 115
West Peterborough, NH 03468
website: www.wapack.org

## Green Mountain Club Inc.

4711 Waterbury-Stowe Rd.
Waterbury Center, VT 05677
802/244-7037, fax 802/244-5867
website: www.greenmountainclub.org
email: gmc@greenmountainclub.org

## Guilford Land Conservation Trust

P.O. Box 200
Guilford, CT 06437
203/457-9253
website: www.guilfordlandtrust.org

## Maine Appalachian Trail Club

P.O. Box 283
Augusta, ME 04332-0283
website: www.matc.org

## Monadnock-Sunapee Greenway Trail Club (MSGTC)

P.O. Box 164
Marlow, NH 03456
website: www.msgtc.org

## Ragged Mountain Foundation

P.O. Box 948
Southington, CT 06489
website: www.raggedmtn.org

## Randolph Mountain Club

P.O. Box 279
Randolph, NH 03581
website: www.randolphmountainclub.org

## Squam Lakes Association

P.O. Box 204
Holderness, NH 03245
603/968-7336
website: www.squamlakes.org

## Wonalancet Out Door Club (WODC)

HCR 64 Box 248
Wonalancet, NH 03897
website: www.wodc.org

# Other Land Managers

## The Trustees of Reservations

Long Hill
572 Essex St.
Beverly, MA 01915-1530
978/921-1944
website: www.thetrustees.org
email: information@ttor.org

# Acknowledgments

I want to thank the many people who accompanied me on these trails, in particular my wife and hiking partner, Penny Beach. My parents, Henry and Joanne Lanza, deserve recognition—both for putting up with a son who has shown up at their door a few times since they first got rid of him, and for being good hiking partners. Of the friends who have shared trails with me, Mike Casino warrants special thanks for enduring innumerable miles in my company (and I still hope and pray he will again quit his job and have more free time for hiking). I also want to thank my editors and the rest of the very talented staff at Avalon Travel Publishing.

While I have personally walked every hike described in this book—some of them many times—updating a volume as comprehensive as this one cannot possibly be accomplished without the assistance of many people. To that end, I relied on friends, acquaintances, people active with hiking and conservation groups, and managers of public lands and private reserves to do some on-the-ground "scouting" of trails and send me current reports on the hikes in this book. Much deep appreciation goes out to: Joe Albee, Kathy Bagley, Todd Balf, Mike and Rick Baron, Ann and Rod Beach, Betsy Beach, Joe Bilancieri, Mark Bogacz, Denise Buck, Steve Buck, Peter Cole, Dan Corley, Ruth Corley, Brendan Corley, Jessica Corley, Mike Cunningham, Annette Ermini, Jim Ermini, Mark Fenton, Anna Garofalo, Marco Garofalo, Larry Gies, Judy Glinder, Kellen Glinder, Mike Hannigan, Betsy Harrison, Ed Hawkins, Joe Kuzneski, Brittany Lanza, Cassidy Lanza, Julie Lanza, Kaylee Lanza, Nicholas Lanza, Stephen Lanza, Marjorie LaPan, Carol Lavoie, Denis Lavoie, Peter Mahr, Diane Mailloux, Pete and Marilyn Mason, Eddie Maxwell, Nuala and Michael Mclaughlin, Bill Mistretta, Ken Morgan, Michele Morris, Kim Nilsen, Brion O'Connor, Ann Perkins, Ed Poyer, Gerry Prutsman, Keith Ratner, Christine Raymond, Lance Riek, Janet Scholl, Roger Scholl, Topher Sharp, Ann Sherwood, Bob Spoerl, Tim Symonds, Doug Thompson, Rod Venterea, Matt Walsh, Dick Whitehouse, and Barbara Wilkins.

There were also many helpful people at various organizations and public agencies, including: Acadia National Park; Appalachian Mountain Club; Appalachian Trail Conference; Ascutney Trails Association; The Audubon Society of Rhode Island; Baxter State Park; Beaver Brook Association; Bigelow Preserve; Block Island Chamber of Commerce; Camden Hills State Park; Cape Cod National Seashore; Cardigan Highlanders; Chatham Trails Association; Connecticut Forest and Park Association; Connecticut State Parks Division; DeLorme Publishing Company; Friends of Acadia; Friends of the Blue Hills; Friends of the Middlesex Fells; Friends of the Wapack; Green Mountain Club; Green Mountain National Forest; Maine Appalachian Trail Club; Maine Bureau of Parks and Lands; Massachusetts Audubon Society; Massachusetts Division of State Parks and Recreation; Metropolitan District Commission (Hartford, CT); Midstate Trail Committee; Monadnock-Sunapee Greenway Trail Club; Mount Greylock State Reservation; The Nature Conservancy; New England Cartographics; New Hampshire Division of Parks and Recreation; Randolph Mountain Club; Rhode Island's Division of Parks and Recreation and Division of Forest Environment; Rubel BikeMaps; Squam Lakes Association; Trails Illustrated; Trustees of Reservations; Vermont Department of Forests, Parks, and Recreation; White Mountain National Forest; Williams Outing Club; and Wonalancet Out Door Club.

# Index

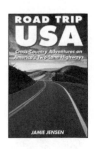

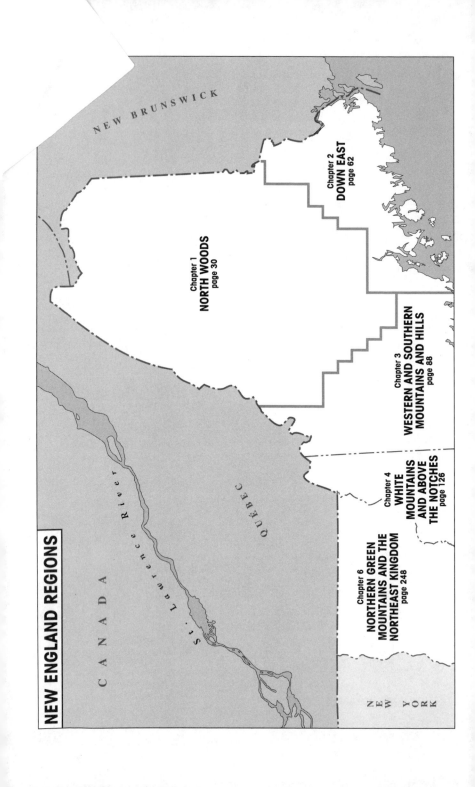

# NEW ENGLAND REGIONS

CANADA

NEW BRUNSWICK

QUEBEC

St. Lawrence River

N
E
W

Y
O
R
K

**Chapter 1**
**NORTH WOODS**
page 30

**Chapter 2**
**DOWN EAST**
page 62

**Chapter 3**
**WESTERN AND SOUTHERN**
**MOUNTAINS AND HILLS**
page 88

**Chapter 4**
**WHITE**
**MOUNTAINS**
**AND ABOVE**
**THE NOTCHES**
page 126

**Chapter 6**
**NORTHERN GREEN**
**MOUNTAINS AND THE**
**NORTHEAST KINGDOM**
page 248